Seventeenth-Century English Poetry

MODERN ESSAYS IN CRITICISM

Seventeenth-Century English Poetry

MODERN ESSAYS IN CRITICISM

REVISED EDITION

Edited by

WILLIAM R. KEAST

OXFORD UNIVERSITY PRESS

LONDON   OXFORD   NEW YORK

1971

OXFORD UNIVERSITY PRESS

London   Oxford   New York
Glasgow   Toronto   Melbourne   Wellington
Cape Town   Ibadan   Nairobi   Dar es Salaam   Lusaka   Addis Ababa
Delhi   Bombay   Calcutta   Madras   Karachi   Lahore   Dacca
Kuala Lumpur   Singapore   Hong Kong   Tokyo

Preface

During the half-century since the publication of H. J. C. Grierson's edition of the poems of John Donne, seventeenth-century English poetry has been studied with intense—one might almost say relentless —interest by a succession of critics, who have often used it as the basis for the statement or illustration of critical theory and as a touchstone of literary taste. From the hundreds of critical studies which the modern interest in seventeenth-century poetry has called forth, the present book gathers together twenty-seven essays. They range in time from Grierson's influential Introduction to his 1921 anthology of *Metaphysical Lyrics & Poems* and Eliot's perhaps even more influential essay on the metaphysicals (originally published as a review of Grierson's collection), to George Williamson's recent study of the background of Donne's "Extasie." The first five essays discuss seventeenth-century poetry generally; the others deal with particular poets and poems. There are no essays on Milton because he is to have a volume to himself in this series. The essays have been chosen not only because they say illuminating things about the poetry of the period but because they provide a fairly representative sample of the different critical procedures current in recent decades. It has seemed wise to concentrate on a limited number of poets and to provide several essays on each of the more important writers, in order to permit the student to compare critical assumptions, methods, and results.

Several colleagues and friends helped by suggesting essays and by commenting on my successive attempts to make a balanced selection from the rich body of critical literature on seventeenth-century poetry. I am grateful to them.

Ithaca, New York   William R. Keast
March 1962

v

Preface to the Revised Edition

In this edition I have retained seventeen essays from the first edition and have added a dozen new selections, most of them published since 1962. I hope that the new collection of twenty-nine essays, while retaining the most valuable features of the first edition and providing access to some of the seminal modern studies of seventeenth-century poetry, exemplifies more recent trends in criticism—especially in the work of younger critics—and reflects the growing interest in several poets previously neglected or under-rated in serious criticism.

I want to express my gratitude to the friends and colleagues who have suggested essays for this edition. I am especially grateful to Barbara Holler Hardy, my colleague in the Department of English at Wayne State University, who has helped throughout by reviewing the literature, recommending essays for inclusion, and offering thoughtful comments on the book's coverage and balance. My secretary, Annette Riley, has handled the preparation of the manuscript with her customary efficiency and skill.

Detroit, Michigan   WILLIAM R. KEAST
January 1971

Contents

H. J. C. GRIERSON   Metaphysical Poetry   3

T. S. ELIOT   The Metaphysical Poets   20

HELEN GARDNER   The Metaphysical Poets   32

EARL MINER   Wit: Definition and Dialectic   45

J. A. MAZZEO   A Critique of Some Modern Theories of Metaphysical Poetry   77

J. B. LEISHMAN   Donne and Seventeenth-Century Poetry   89

GEORGE WILLIAMSON   The Convention of *The Extasie*   106

LOUIS L. MARTZ   John Donne in Meditation: the *Anniversaries*   118

GEOFFREY WALTON   The Tone of Ben Jonson's Poetry   131

HUGH MACLEAN   Ben Jonson's Poems: Notes on the Ordered Society   174

WILLIAM V. SPANOS   The Real Toad in the Jonsonian Garden: Resonance in the Nondramatic Poetry   201

JOSEPH H. SUMMERS   The Poem as Hieroglyph   225

JEFFREY HART   Herbert's *The Collar* Re-read   248

ARNOLD STEIN   George Herbert: The Art of Plainness   257

G. A. E. PARFITT   The Poetry of Thomas Carew   279

H. M. RICHMOND   The Fate of Edmund Waller   291

L. A. BEAURLINE   "Why So Pale and Wan": An Essay in Critical Method   300

AUSTIN WARREN   Symbolism in Crashaw   312

BRUCE KING   Green Ice and a Breast of Proof   324

FRANK KERMODE   The Argument of Marvell's "Garden"   333

FRANK J. WARNKE   Play and Metamorphosis in Marvell's Poetry   348

HAROLD E. TOLIVER   Pastoral Form and Idea in Some Poems of Marvell   356

LEO SPITZER   Marvell's "Nymph Complaining for the Death of Her Faun": Sources versus Meaning   372

LOUIS L. MARTZ   Henry Vaughan: The Man Within   388

REUBEN A. BROWER   An Allusion to Europe: Dryden and Tradition   414

MARK VAN DOREN   John Dryden: The Lyric Poet   425

RUTH WALLERSTEIN   On the Death of Mrs. Killigrew: The Perfecting of a Genre   454

IAN JACK   Mock-Heroic: *MacFlecknoe*   464

VIVIAN DE S. PINTO   John Wilmot, Earl of Rochester, and the Right Veine of Satire   474

Seventeenth-Century English Poetry

MODERN ESSAYS IN CRITICISM

H. J. C. GRIERSON

✍

Metaphysical Poetry

I

Metaphysical Poetry, in the full sense of the term, is a poetry which, like that of the *Divina Commedia*, the *De Natura Rerum*, perhaps Goethe's *Faust*, has been inspired by a philosophical conception of the universe and <u>the rôle assigned to the human spirit in the great drama of existence.</u> These poems were written because a definite interpretation of the riddle, the atoms of Epicurus rushing through infinite empty space, the theology of the schoolmen as elaborated in the catechetical disquisitions of St. Thomas, Spinoza's vision of life *sub specie aeternitatis,* beyond good and evil, laid hold on the mind and the imagination of a great poet, unified and illumined his comprehension of life, intensified and heightened his personal consciousness of joy and sorrow, of hope and fear, by broadening their significance, revealing to him in the history of his own soul a brief abstract of the drama of human destiny. "Poetry is the first and last of all knowledge—it is as immortal as the heart of man." Its themes are the simplest experiences of the surface of life, sorrow and joy, love and battle, the peace of the country, the bustle and stir of towns, but equally the boldest conceptions, the profoundest intuitions, the subtlest and most complex classifications and "discourse of reason," if into these too the poet can "carry sensation," make of them passionate experiences communicable in vivid and moving imagery, in rich and varied harmonies.

It is no such great metaphysical poetry as that of Lucretius and

From *Metaphysical Lyrics & Poems of the Seventeenth Century* (Oxford, 1921), pp. xiii–xxxviii. Reprinted by permission of The Clarendon Press.

3

Dante that the present essay deals with, which this volume seeks to illustrate. Of the poets from whom it culls, Donne is familiar with the definitions and distinctions of Mediaeval Scholasticism; Cowley's bright and alert, if not profound mind, is attracted by the achievements of science and the systematic materialism of Hobbes. Donne, moreover, is metaphysical not only in virtue of his scholasticism, but by his deep reflective interest in the experiences of which his poetry is the expression, the new psychological curiosity with which he writes of love and religion. The divine poets who follow Donne have each the inherited metaphysic, if one may so call it, of the Church to which he is attached, Catholic or Anglican. But none of the poets has for his main theme a metaphysic like that of Epicurus or St. Thomas passionately apprehended and imaginatively expounded. Donne, the most thoughtful and imaginative of them all, is more aware of disintegration than of comprehensive harmony, of the clash between the older physics and metaphysics on the one hand and the new science of Copernicus and Galileo and Vesalius and Bacon on the other:

> The new philosophy calls all in doubt,
> The element of fire is quite put out;
> The sun is lost and the earth, and no man's wit
> Can well direct him where to look for it.
> And freely men confess that this world's spent,
> When in the planets and the firmament
> They seek so many new; they see that this
> Is crumbled out again to his atomies.

> Have not all souls thought
> For many ages that our body is wrought
> Of air and fire and other elements?
> And now they think of new ingredients;
> And one soul thinks one, and another way
> Another thinks, and 'tis an even lay.

The greatest English poet, indeed, of the century was, or believed himself to be, a philosophical or theological poet of the same order as Dante. *Paradise Lost* was written to be a justification of "the ways of God to men," resting on a theological system as definite and almost as carefully articulated in the *De Doctrina Christiana* as that which Dante had accepted from the *Summa* of Aquinas. And the poet embodied his argument in a dramatic poem as vividly and intensely conceived, as magnificently and harmoniously set forth, as the *Divina Commedia*. But in truth Milton was no philosopher. The subtleties of theological definition and inference eluded his rationalistic, practical, though idealistic, mind. He proved nothing. The definitely stated argument of the poem is an obvious begging of the question. What he did was to create, or give a new definiteness and sensible power to, a great myth which, through his poem, continued for a century or more to dominate the mind and imagination of pious protestants without many of them suspecting the heresies which lurked beneath the imposing and dazzling poem in which was retold the Bible story of the fall and redemption of man.

Metaphysical in this large way, Donne and his followers to Cowley are not, yet the word describes better what is the peculiar quality of their poetry than any other, e.g., fantastic, for poetry may be fantastic in so many different ways, witness Skelton and the Elizabethans, and Hood and Browning. It lays stress on the right things—the survival, one might say the reaccentuation, of the metaphysical strain, the *concetti metafisici ed ideali* as Testi calls them in contrast to the simpler imagery of classical poetry, of mediaeval Italian poetry; the more intellectual, less verbal, character of their wit compared with the conceits of the Elizabethans; the finer psychology of which their conceits are often the expression; their learned imagery; the argumentative, subtle evolution of their lyrics; above all the peculiar blend of passion and thought, feeling and ratiocination which is their greatest achievement. Passionate thinking is always apt to become metaphysical, probing and investigating the experience from which it takes its rise. All these qualities are in the poetry of Donne, and Donne is the great master of English poetry in the seventeenth century.

The Italian influence which Wyatt and Surrey brought into English poetry at the Renaissance gave it a more serious, a more thoughtful colour. They caught, especially Wyatt in some of the finest of his sonnets and songs, that spirit of "high seriousness" which Chaucer with all his admiration of Italian poetry had failed to apprehend. English mediaeval poetry is often gravely pious, haunted by the fear of death and the judgment, melancholy over the "Falls of Princes"; it is never serious and thoughtful in the introspective, reflective, dignified manner which it became in Wyatt and Sackville, and our "sage and serious" Spenser, and in the songs of the first group of Elizabethan courtly poets, Sidney and Raleigh and Dyer. One has but to recall "My lute, awake! perform the last," "Forget not yet the tried intent," "My mind to me a kingdom is," and to contrast them in mind with the songs which Henry VIII and Cornish were still composing and singing when Wyatt began to write, in order to realize what Italy and the Renaissance did to deepen the strain of English lyric poetry as that had flowed under French influence from the thirteenth to the sixteenth centuries. But French influence, the influence of Ronsard and his fellows, renewed itself in the seventies, and the great body of Elizabethan song is as gay and careless and impersonal as the earlier lyric had been, though richer in colour and more varied in rhythm. Then came Donne and Jonson (the schoolman and the classical scholar, one might say, emphasizing for the moment single aspects of their work), and new qualities of spirit and form were given to lyrical poetry, and not to lyrical poetry alone.

In dealing with poets who lived and wrote before the eighteenth century we are always confronted with the difficulty of recovering the personal, the biographical element, which, if sometimes disturbing and disconcerting, is yet essential to a complete understanding of their work. Men were not different from what they are now, and if there be hardly a lyric of Goethe's or Shelley's that does not owe something to the accidents of their lives, one may feel sure it was in varying degrees the same with poets three hundred years ago. Poems are not written by influences or movements or sources, but come from the living hearts of men. Fortunately, in the case of Donne, one of the most individual of poets, it is possible to some extent to reproduce the circumstances, the inner experiences from which his intensely personal poetry flowed.

He was in the first place a Catholic. Our history text-books make so little of the English Catholics that one is apt to forget they existed and were, for themselves at any rate, not a political problem, but real and suffering individuals. "I had my first breeding and conversation," says Donne, "with men of a suppressed and afflicted religion, accustomed to the despite of death and hungry of an imagined martyrdom." In these circumstances, we gather, he was carefully and religiously educated, and after some years at Oxford and Cambridge was taken or sent abroad, perhaps with a view to entering foreign service, more probably with a view to the priesthood, and visited Italy and Spain. And then, one conjectures, a reaction took place, the rebellion of a full-blooded, highly intellectual temperament against a superimposed bent. He entered the Inns of Court in 1592, at the age of nineteen, and flung himself into the life of a student and the life of a young man about town, Jack Donne, "not dissolute but very neat, a great visitor of ladies, a great frequenter of plays, a great writer of conceited verses." "Neither was it possible that a vulgar soul should dwell in such promising features." He joined the band of reckless and raffish young men who sailed with Essex to Cadiz and the Islands. He was taken into the service of Sir Thomas Egerton. Ambition began to vie with the love of pleasure, when a hasty marriage closed a promising career, and left him bound in shallows and in miseries, to spend years in the suitorship of the great, and to find at last, not altogether willingly, a haven in the Anglican priesthood, and reveal himself as the first great orator that Church produced.

The record of these early years is contained in Donne's satires—harsh, witty, lucid, full of a young man's scorn of fools and low callings, and a young thinker's consciousness of the problems of religion in an age of divided faiths, and of justice in a corrupt world—and in his Love Songs and Sonnets and Elegies. The satires were more generally known; the love poems the more influential in courtly and literary circles.

Donne's genius, temperament, and learning gave to his love poems certain qualities which immediately arrested attention and have given them ever since a power at once fascinating and disconcerting despite the faults of phrasing and harmony which, for a century after Dryden, obscured, and to some still outweigh, their poetic worth. The first of these is a depth and range of feeling unknown to the majority of Elizabethan sonneteers and song-writers. Over all the Elizabethan sonnets, in greater or less measure, hangs the suggestion of translation or imitation. Watson, Sidney, Daniel, Spenser, Drayton, Lodge, all of them, with rarer or more frequent touches of individuality, are pipers of Petrarch's woes, sighing in the strain of Ronsard or more often of Desportes. Shakespeare, indeed, in his great sequence, and Drayton in at any rate one sonnet, sounded a deeper note, revealed a fuller sense of the complexities and contradictions of passionate devotion. But Donne's treatment of love is entirely unconventional except when he chooses to dally half ironically with the convention of Petrarchian adoration. His songs are the expression in unconventional, witty language of all the moods of a lover that experience and imagination have taught him to understand—sensuality aerated by a brilliant wit; fascination and scornful anger inextricably blended:

> When by thy scorn, O murdress, I am dead
> And that thou think'st thee free
> From all solicitations from me,
> Then shall my ghost come to thy bed;

the passionate joy of mutual and contented love:

> All other things to their destruction draw,
>   Only our love hath no decay;

> This no to-morrow hath nor yesterday,
> Running it never runs from us away,
> But truly keeps his first, last, everlasting day;

the sorrow of parting which is the shadow of such joy; the gentler pathos of temporary separation in married life:

> Let not thy divining heart
> Forethink me any ill,
> Destiny may take thy part,
> And may thy fears fulfil;
> But think that we
> Are but turn'd aside to sleep;
> They who one another keep
> Alive ne'er parted be;

the mystical heights and the mystical depths of love:

> Study me then you who shall lovers be
> At the next world, that is, at the next Spring:
> For I am every dead thing
> In whom love wrought new Alchemy.

If Donne had expressed this wide range of intense feeling as perfectly as he has done at times poignantly and startlingly; if he had given to his poems the same impression of entire artistic sincerity that Shakespeare conveys in the greater of his sonnets and Drayton once achieved; if to his many other gifts had been added a deeper and more controlling sense of beauty, he would have been, as he nearly is, the greatest of love poets. But there is a second quality of his poetry which made it the fashion of an age, but has been inimical to its general acceptance ever since, and that is its metaphysical wit. " He affects the metaphysics," says Dryden, "not only in his satires but in his amorous verses where nature only should reign; and perplexes the minds of the fair sex with nice speculations of philosophy when he should engage their hearts and entertain them with the softness of love." "Amorous verses," "the fair sex," and "the softness of love" are the vulgarities of a less poetic and passionate age than Donne's, but metaphysics he does affect. But a metaphysical strand, *concetti metafisici ed ideali,* had run through the mediaeval love-poetry of which the Elizabethan sonnets are a descendant. It had attained its fullest development in the poems of Dante and his school, had been subordinated to rhetoric and subtleties of expression rather than thought in

Petrarch, and had lost itself in the pseudo-metaphysical extravagances of Tebaldeo, Cariteo, and Serafino. Donne was no conscious reviver of the metaphysics of Dante, but to the game of elaborating fantastic conceits and hyperboles which was the fashion throughout Europe, he brought not only a full-blooded temperament and acute mind, but a vast and growing store of the same scholastic learning, the same Catholic theology, as controlled Dante's thought, jostling already with the new learning of Copernicus and Paracelsus. The result is startling and disconcerting—the comparison of parted lovers to the legs of a pair of compasses, the deification of his mistress by the discovery that she is only to be defined by negatives or that she can read the thoughts of his heart, a thing "beyond an angel's art"; and a thousand other subtleties of quintessences and nothingness, the mixture of souls and the significance of numbers, to say nothing of the aerial bodies of angels, the phoenix and the mandrake's root, Alchemy and Astrology, legal contracts and *non obstantes,* "late schoolboys and sour prentices," "the king's real and his stamped face." But the effect aimed at and secured is not entirely fantastic and erudite. The motive inspiring Donne's images is in part the same as that which led Shakespeare from the picturesque, natural and mythological, images of *A Midsummer-Night's Dream* and *The Merchant of Venice* to the homely but startling phrases and metaphors of *Hamlet* and *Macbeth,* the "blanket of the dark," the

> fat weed
> That rots itself in ease on Lethe wharf,

"the rank sweat of an enseamed bed." It is the same desire for vivid and dramatic expression. The great master at a later period of dramatic as well as erudite pulpit oratory coins in his poems many a startling, jarring, arresting phrase:

> For God's sake hold your tongue and let me love:

> Who ever comes to shroud me do not harm
>   Nor question much
> That subtle wreath of hair, which crowns my arm:

> I taught my silks their rustling to forbear,
> Even my opprest shoes dumb and silent were.

> I long to talk with some old lover's ghost
> Who died before the God of love was born;

Twice or thrice had I loved thee
Before I knew thy face or name,
So in a voice, so in a shapeless flame,
Angels affect us oft and worshipped be;

And whilst our souls negotiate there
  We like sepulchral statues lay;
All day the same our postures were
And we said nothing all the day.

My face and brest of haircloth, and my head
With care's harsh, sudden hoariness o'er-spread.

These vivid, simple, realistic touches are too quickly merged in learned
and fantastic elaborations, and the final effect of every poem of Donne's
is a bizarre and blended one; but if the greatest poetry rises clear of
the bizarre, the fantastic, yet very great poetry may be bizarre if it
be the expression of a strangely blended temperament, an intense emotion, a vivid imagination.

What is true of Donne's imagery is true of the other disconcerting
element in his poetry, its harsh and rugged verse. It is an outcome of
the same double motive, the desire to startle and the desire to ap-
proximate poetic to direct, unconventional, colloquial speech. Poetry
is always a balance, sometimes a compromise, between what has to
be said and the prescribed pattern to which the saying of it is adjusted. In poetry such as Spenser's, the musical flow, the melody and
harmony of line and stanza, is dominant, and the meaning is adjusted
to it at the not infrequent cost of diffuseness—if a delightful diffuseness—and even some weakness of phrasing logically and rhetorically
considered. In Shakespeare's tragedies the thought and feeling tend
to break through the prescribed pattern till blank verse becomes almost rhythmical prose, the rapid overflow of the lines admitting hardly
the semblance of pause. This is the kind of effect Donne is always
aiming at, alike in his satires and lyrics, bending and cracking the
metrical pattern to the rhetoric of direct and vehement utterance. The
result is often, and to eighteenth-century ears attuned to the clear
and defined, if limited, harmony of Waller and Dryden and Pope was,
rugged and harsh. But here again, to those who have ears that care to
hear, the effect is not finally inharmonious. Donne's verse has a powerful and haunting harmony of its own. For Donne is not simply, no
poet could be, willing to force his accent, to strain and crack a prescribed pattern; he is striving to find a rhythm that will express the
passionate fullness of his mind, the fluxes and refluxes of his moods;

and the felicities of verse are as frequent and startling as those of phrasing. He is one of the first masters, perhaps *the* first, of the elaborate stanza or paragraph in which the discords of individual lines or phrases are resolved in the complex and rhetorically effective harmony of the whole group of lines:

> If yet I have not all thy love,
> Deare, I shall never have it all,
> I cannot breathe one other sigh, to move,
> Nor can entreat one other tear to fall,
> And all my treasure, which should purchase thee,
> Sighs, tears, and oaths, and letters I have spent.
> Yet no more can be due to me,
> Than at the bargain made was meant,
> If then thy gift of love was partial,
> That some to me, some should to others fall,
> Deare, I shall never have thee all.
>
> But I am none; nor will my sunne renew.
> You lovers for whose sake the lesser sunne
> At this time to the Goat is run
> To fetch new lust and give it you,
> Enjoy your summer all;
> Since she enjoys her long night's festival,
> Let me prepare towards her, and let me call
> This hour her Vigil and her Eve, since this
> Bŏth thĕ years | ănd thĕ days | deep mid|nĭght is.

The wrenching of accent which Jonson complained of is not entirely due to carelessness or indifference. It has often both a rhetorical and a harmonious justification. Donne plays with rhythmical effects as with conceits and words and often in much the same way. Mr. Fletcher Melton's interesting analysis of his verse has not, I think, established his main thesis, which like so many "research" scholars he over-emphasizes, that the whole mystery of Donne's art lies in his use of the same sound now in *arsis*, now in *thesis;* but his examples show that this is one of many devices by which Donne secures two effects, the troubling of the regular fall of the verse stresses by the intrusion of rhetorical stress on syllables which the metrical pattern leaves unstressed, and, secondly, an echoing and re-echoing of similar sounds parallel to his fondness for resemblances in thoughts and things apparently the most remote from one another. There is, that is to say, in

{ his verse the same blend as in his diction of the colloquial and the
bizarre. He writes as one who *will* say what he has to say without
regard to conventions of poetic diction or smooth verse, but what he
has to say is subtle and surprising, and so are the metrical effects with
which it is presented. There is nothing of unconscious or merely careless harshness in such an effect as this:

> Poor soul, in this thy flesh what dost thou know?
> Thou know'st thyself so little that thou knowst not
> How thou didst die, nor how thou wast begot.
> Thou neither know'st how thou at first camest in,
> Nor how thou took'st the poison of man's sin;
> Nor dost thou though thou know'st that thou art so
> By what way thou art made immortal know.

In Donne's pronunciation, as in southern English to-day, "thou," "how,"
"soul," "know," "though," and "so" were not far removed from each
other in sound and the reiterated notes ring through the lines like a
tolling bell. Mr. Melton has collected, and any careful reader may
discover for himself, many similar subtleties of poetical rhetoric; for
Donne is perhaps our first great master of poetic rhetoric, of poetry
used, as Dryden and Pope were to use it, for effects of oratory rather
than of song, and the advance which Dryden achieved was secured by
subordinating to oratory the more passionate and imaginative qualities
which troubled the balance and movement of Donne's packed but
imaginative rhetoric.

It was not indeed in lyrical verse that Dryden followed and developed Donne, but in his eulogistic, elegiac, satirical, and epistolary
verse. The progress of Dryden's eulogistic style is traceable from his
earliest metaphysical extravagances through lines such as those addressed to the Duchess of York, where Waller is his model, to the
verses on the death of Oldham in which a more natural and classical
strain has entirely superseded his earlier extravagances and elegancies.
In truth Donne's metaphysical eulogies and elegies and epistles are a
hard nut to crack for his most sympathetic admirers. And yet they have
undeniable qualities. The metaphysics are developed in a more serious,
a less paradoxical, strain than in some of the songs and elegies. In his
letters he is an excellent, if far from a perfect, talker in verse; and the
personality which they reveal is a singularly charming one, grave,
loyal, melancholy, witty. If some of the elegiac pieces are packed with
tasteless and extravagant hyperboles, the *Anniversaries* (especially the
second) remains, despite all its faults, one of the greatest poems on

death in the language, the fullest record in our literature of the disintegrating collision in a sensitive mind of the old tradition and the
new learning. Some of the invocational passages in *Of the Progresse
of the Soule* are among the finest examples of his subtle and passionate
thinking as well as of his most elaborate verse rhetoric.

But the most intense and personal of Donne's poems, after the love
songs and elegies, are his later religious sonnets and songs; and their
influence on subsequent poetry was even more obvious and potent.
They are as personal and as tormented as his earlier "love-song weeds,"
for his spiritual Aeneid was a troubled one. To date his conversion to
Anglicanism is not easy. In his satires there is a veiled Roman tone.
By 1602 he disclaims to Egerton "all love of a corrupt religion," but in
the autumn of the previous year he had been meditating a satire on
Queen Elizabeth as one of the world's great heretics. His was not
a conversion but a reconciliation, an acquiescence in the faith of his
country, the established religion of his legal sovereign, and the act
cost him some pangs. "A convert from Popery to Protestantism," said
Dr. Johnson, "gives up so much of what he has held as sacred as anything that he retains, there is so much laceration of mind in such a
conversion, that it can hardly be sincere and lasting." Something of
that laceration of mind is discernible in Donne's religious verse:

> Show me dear Christ thy spouse so bright and clear.

But the conflict between the old and the reformed faiths was not the
only, nor perhaps the principal trouble for Donne's enlightened mind
ready to recognize in all the Churches "virtual beams of one sun,"
"connatural pieces of one circle." A harder fight was that between the
secular, the "man of the world" temper of his mind and the claims of
a pious and ascetic calling. It was not the errors of his youth, as the
good Walton supposed, which constituted the great stumbling block,
though he never ignores these:

> O might those sighs and tears return again
> Into my breast and eyes, which I have spent,
> That I might in this holy discontent
> Mourn with some fruit, as I have mourned in vain.

It was rather the temperament of one who, at a time when a public
career was more open to unassisted talent, might have proved an
active and useful, if ambitious, civil servant, or professional man, at
war with the claims of a religious life which his upbringing had taught

him was incompatible with worldly ambition. George Herbert, a much more contented Anglican than Donne ever became, knew something of the same struggle before he bent his neck to the collar.

The two notes then of Donne's religious poems are the Catholic and the personal. He is the first of our Anglo-Catholic poets, and he is our first intensely personal religious poet, expressing always not the mind simply of the Christian as such, but the conflicts and longings of one troubled soul, one subtle and fantastic mind. For Donne's technique—his phrasing and conceits, the metaphysics of mediaeval Christianity, his packed verse with its bold, irregular fingering and echoing vowel sounds—remains what it had been from the outset. The echoing sounds in lines such as these cannot be quite casual:

> O might those *sighs* and tears return again
> Into my breast and *eyes,* which *I* have spent,
> That *I* might in this holy discontent
> Mourn with some fruit, as *I* have mourned in vain;
> In mine *Idolat'ry* what showers of rain
> *Mine eyes* did waste? What griefs *my* heart did rent?
> That sufferance was *my* sin; now *I* repent
> Cause *I* did suffer *I* must suffer pain.

In the remaining six lines the same sound never recurs.

A metaphysical, a philosophical poet, to the degree to which even his contemporary Fulke Greville might be called such, Donne was not. The thought in his poetry is not his primary concern but the feeling. No scheme of thought, no interpretation of life became for him a complete and illuminating experience. The central theme of his poetry is ever his own intense personal moods, as a lover, a friend, an analyst of his own experiences worldly and religious. His philosophy cannot unify these experiences. It represents the reaction of his restless and acute mind on the intense experience of the moment, a reading of it in the light now of one, now of another philosophical or theological dogma or thesis caught from his multifarious reading, developed with audacious paradox or more serious intention, as an expression, an illumination of that mood to himself and to his reader. Whether one choose to call him a metaphysical or a fantastic poet, the stress must be laid on the word 'poet'. Whether verse or prose be his medium, Donne is always a poet, a creature of feeling and imagination, seeking expression in vivid phrase and complex harmonies, whose acute and subtle intellect was the servant, if sometimes the unruly servant, of passion and imagination.

II

Donne's influence was felt in his own day by two strangely different classes of men, both attached by close ties to the Court. For the Court, the corrupt, ambitious, intriguing, dissolute but picturesque and dazzling court of the old pagan Elizabeth, the pedantic and drunken James, the dignified and melancholy and politically blinded Charles, was the centre round which all Donne's secular interests revolved. He can speak of it as bitterly and sardonically as Shakespeare in *Hamlet:*

> Here's no more newes, then vertue, I may as well
> Tell you Cales or St. Michael's tale for newes, as tell
> That vice doth here habitually dwell.
>
> . . . .
>
> But now 'tis incongruity to smile,
> Therefore I end; and bid farewell a while,
> *At Court,* though *From Court* were the better style.

He knows its corruptions as well as Milton and commends Lady Bedford as Milton might have commended Alice Egerton. All the same, to be shut out from the Court, in the city or the country, is to inhabit a desert, or sepulchre, for there:

> The Princes favour is defused o'er all,
> From which all Fortunes, Names, and Natures fall.
> And all is warmth and light and good desire.

It was among the younger generation of Courtiers that Donne found the warmest admirers of his paradoxical and sensual audacities as a love-poet, as it was the divines who looked to Laud and the Court for Anglican doctrine and discipline who revered his memory, enshrined by the pious Izaak Walton, as of a divine poet and preacher. The 'metaphysicals' were all on the King's side. Even Andrew Marvell was neither Puritan nor Republican. 'Men ought to have trusted God', was his final judgement on the Rebellion, 'they ought to have trusted the King with the whole matter'. They were on the side of the King, for they were on the side of the humanities; and the Puritan rebellion, whatever the indirect constitutional results, was in itself and at the moment a fanatical upheaval, successful because it also threw up the John Zizka of his age; its triumph was the triumph of Cromwell's sword:

> And for the last effect
> Still keep the sword erect.

> Besides the force it has to fright
> The spirits of the shady night,
>   The same arts that did gain
>   A power must it maintain.

To call these poets the "school of Donne" or "metaphysical" poets may easily mislead if one takes either phrase in too full a sense. It is not only that they show little of Donne's subtlety of mind or "hydroptic, immoderate thirst of human learning," but they want, what gives its interest to this subtle and fantastic misapplication of learning—the complexity of mood, the range of personal feeling which lends such fullness of life to Donne's strange and troubled poetry. His followers, amorous and courtly, or pious and ecclesiastical, move in a more rarefied atmosphere; their poetry is much more truly "abstract" than Donne's, the witty and fantastic elaboration of one or two common moods, of compliment, passion, devotion, penitence. It is very rarely that one can detect a deep personal note in the delightful love-songs with which the whole period abounds from Carew to Dryden. The collected work of none of them would give such an impression of a real history behind it, a history of many experiences and moods, as Donne's Songs and Sonnets and the Elegies, and, as one must still believe, the sonnets of Shakespeare record. Like the Elizabethan sonneteers they all dress and redress the same theme in much the same manner, though the manner is not quite the Elizabethan, nor the theme. Song has superseded the sonnet, and the passion of which they sing has lost most of the Petrarchian, chivalrous strain, and become in a very definite meaning of the words, "simple and sensuous." And if the religious poets are rather more individual and personal, the personal note is less intense, troubled and complex than in Donne's Divine Poems; the individual is more merged in the Christian, Catholic or Angelican.

Donne and Jonson are probably in the main responsible for the unconventional purity and naturalness of their diction, for these had both "shaken hands with" Spenserian archaism and strangeness, with the "rhetoric" of the sonneteers and poems like Venus and Adonis; and their style is untouched by any foreshadowing of Miltonic diction or the jargon of a later poetic vocabulary. The metaphysicals are the masters of the "neutral style," of a diction equally appropriate, according as it may be used, to prose and verse. If purity and naturalness of style is a grace, they deserved well of the English language, for few poets have used it with a more complete acceptance of the established tradition of diction and idiom. There are no poets till we come perhaps to Cowper, and he has not quite escaped from jargon, or Shelley, and his imagination operates in a more ethereal atmosphere, whose style is so entirely that of an English gentleman of the best type, natural, simple, occasionally careless, but never diverging into vulgar colloquialism, as after the Restoration, or into conventional, tawdry splendour, as in the century of Akenside and Erasmus Darwin. Set a poem by George Herbert beside Gray at his best, e.g.

> Sweet day so cool, so calm, so bright,
> The bridal of the earth and sky,
> The dew shall weep thy fall to-night,
> For thou must die; &c.

set that beside even a good verse from Gray, and one realizes the charm of simplicity, of perfect purity of diction:

> Still is the toiling hand of Care;
> The panting herds repose:
> Yet hark how through the peopled air
> The busy murmur glows!
> The insect-youth are on the wing,
> Eager to taste the honied spring,
> And float amid the liquid noon:
> Some lightly o'er the current skim,
> Some show their gaily-gilded trim
> Quick-glancing to the sun.

"The language of the age is never the language of poetry," Gray declares, and certainly some of our great poets have created for themselves a diction which was never current, but it is equally true that some of the best English poetry has been written in a style which differs from the best spoken language only as the language of feeling will naturally diverge from the language of our less exalted moods. It was in the seventeenth-century poets that Wordsworth found the best corrective to the jargon of the later eighteenth-century poetry, descriptive and reflective, which he admired in his youth and imitated in his early poems; for as Coleridge pointed out, the style of the "metaphysicals" "is the reverse of that which distinguishes too many of our most recent versifiers; the one conveying the most fantastic thoughts in the most correct language, the other in the most fantastic language conveying the most trivial thoughts."

But even the fantastic thoughts, the conceits of these courtly love poets and devout singers are not to be dismissed so lightly as a later, and still audible, criticism imagined. They played with thoughts, Sir Walter Scott complained, as the Elizabethans had played with words. But to play with thoughts it is necessary to think. "To write on their plan," says Dr. Johnson, "it was at least necessary to read and think. No man could be born a metaphysical poet, nor assume the dignity of a writer, by descriptions copied from descriptions, by imitations borrowed from imitations, by traditional imagery and hereditary similes, by readiness of rhyme and volubility of syllables." Consider a poem, *The Repulse*, by a comparatively minor poet, Thomas Stanley. That is not a mere conceit. It is a new and felicitous rendering of a real and thrilling experience, the discovery that you might have fared worse in love than not to be loved, you might have been loved and then abandoned. Carew's *Ask me no more* is a coruscation of hyperboles, but

> Now you have freely given me leave to love,
>   What will you do?

is a fresh and effective appeal to the heart of a woman. And this is what the metaphysicals are often doing in their unwearied play with conceits, delightfully naughty, extravagant, fantastic, frigid—they succeed in stumbling upon some conceit which reveals a fresh intuition into the heart, or states an old plea with new and prevailing force. And the divine poets express with the same blend of argument and imagination the deep and complex currents of religious feeling which were flowing in England throughout the century, institutional, theological, mystical, while in the metaphysical subtleties of conceit they found something that is more than conceit, symbols in which to express or adumbrate their apprehensions of the infinite.

The direct indebtedness of the courtly poets to Ben Jonson is probably, as Professor Gregory Smith has recently argued, small. But not only Herrick, metaphysical poets like Carew and Stanley and others owe much both of their turn of conceit and their care for form to Jonson's own models, the Latin lyrists, Anacreon, the Greek Anthology, neo-Latin or Humanist poetry so rich in neat and pretty conceits. Some of them, as Crashaw and Stanley, and not only these, were familiar with Italian and Spanish poetry, Marino and Garcilasso and their elegantly elaborated confections. But their great master is Donne. If he taught them many heresies, he instilled into them at any rate the pure doctrine of the need of passion for a lover and a poet. What the young courtiers and university wits admired and reproduced in different degrees and fashions were his sensual audacity and the peculiar type of evolution which his poems accentuated, the strain of passionate paradoxical reasoning which knits the first line to the last and is perhaps a more intimate characteristic than even the far-fetched, fantastic comparisons. This intellectual, argumentative evolution had been of course a feature of the sonnet which might fancifully be called, with its double quatrain and sestet, the poetical analogy of the syllogism. But the movement of the sonnet is slow and meditative, a single thought expanded and articulated through the triple division, and the longer, decasyllabic line is the appropriate medium:

> Then hate me when thou wilt; if ever, now;
> Now while the world is bent my deeds to cross,
> Join with the spite of Fortune, make me bow,
> And do not drop in for an after-loss;
> Ah, do not when my heart hath scaped this sorrow,
> Come in the rearward of a conquer'd woe,
> Give not a windy night a rainy morrow,
> To linger out a purpos'd overthrow.
> If thou wilt leave me, do not leave me last
> When other petty griefs have done their spite,
> But in the onset come; so shall I taste
> At first the very worst of Fortune's might;
> And other strains of woe which now seem woe,
> Compared with loss of thee will not seem so.

What Donne had done was to quicken this movement, to intensify the strain of passionate ratiocination, passionate, paradoxical argument, and to carry it over from the sonnet to the song with its shorter lines, more winged and soaring movement, although the deeper strain of feeling which Donne shares with Shakespeare, and with Drayton at his best, made him partial to the longer line, at least as an element in his stanzas, and to longer and more intricate stanzas. Lightening both the feeling and the thought, the courtly poets simplified the verse, attaining some of their most wonderful effects in the common ballad measure [4, 3] or the longer [4, 4] measure in couplets or alternate rhymes. But the form and content are intimately associated. It is the elaboration of the paradoxical argument, the weight which the rhetoric lays on those syllables which fall under the metrical stress, that gives to these verses, or seems to give, their peculiar *élan:*

> My love is of a birth as rare
> As 'tis for object strange and high;
> It was begotten by Despair
> Upon Impossibility.

The audacious hyperboles and paradoxical turns of thought give breath to and take wings from the soaring rhythm.

It is needless here to dwell at length on the several poets from whom I have selected examples of love-song and complimentary verses. Their range is not wide—love, compliment, elegy, occasionally devotion. Herrick had to leave the court to learn the delights of nature and country superstitions. Lord Herbert of Cherbury, philosopher and coxcomb, was just the person to dilate on the Platonic theme of soul and body in the realm of love on which Donne occasionally descanted in half ironical fashion, Habington with tedious thin-blooded serious-ness, Cleveland and others with naughty irreverence. But Lord Herbert's *Ode*, which has been, like most of his poems, very badly edited, seems to me the finest thing inspired by Donne's *Ecstasy* and more characteristic of the romantic taste of the court of Charles. But the poetic ornament of that Court is Thomas Carew. This young careless liver was a careful artist with a deeper vein of thought and feeling in his temperament than a first reading suggests. His masque reveals the influence of Bruno. In Carew's poems and Vandyke's pictures the artistic taste of Charles's court is vividly reflected, a dignified volup-tuousness, an exquisite elegance, if in some of the higher qualities of man and artist Carew is as inferior to Wyatt or Spenser as Vandyke is to Holbein. His *Ecstasy* is the most daring and poetically the hap-piest of the imitations of Donne's clever if outrageous elegies; Cart-wright's *Song of Dalliance* its nearest rival. His letter to Aurelian Townshend on the death of the King of Sweden breathes the very enchanted air of Charles's court while the storm was brewing as yet unsuspected. The text of Richard Lovelace's *Lucasta* (1649) is fre-quently corrupt, and the majority of the poems are careless and ex-travagant, but the few good things are the finest expression of honour and chivalry in all the Cavalier poetry of the century, the only poems which suggest what "Cavalier" came to mean when glorified by defeat. His *Grasshopper* has suffered a hard fate by textual corruption and from dismemberment in recent anthologies. Only the fantastic touch about "green ice" ranks it as "metaphysical," for it is in fact an experiment in the manner of the Horatian ode, not the heroic ode, but the lighter Epicurean, meditative strain of "Solvitur acris hiems" and

"Vides ut alta stet nive candidum," description yielding abruptly to reflection. A slightly better text or a little more care on the poet's part would have made it perfect. The gayest of the group is Sir John Suckling, the writer of what should be called *vers de société*, a more careless but more fanciful Prior. His beautiful *Ballad on a Wedding* is a little outside the scope of this volume. Thomas Stanley, classical scholar, philosopher, translator, seems to me one of the happiest of recent recoveries, elegant, graceful, felicitous, and if at times a little flat and colourless, not always flat like the Catholic puritan William Habington.

But the strongest personality of all is Andrew Marvell. Apart from Milton he is the most interesting personality between Donne and Dryden, and at his very best a finer poet than either. Most of his descriptive poems lie a little outside my beat, though I have claimed *The Garden* as metaphysical,

> Annihilating all that's made
> To a green thought in a green shade,

and I might have claimed *The Nymph and the Faun* had space permitted. But his few love poems and his few devotional pieces are perfect exponents of all the "metaphysical" qualities—passionate, paradoxical argument, touched with humour and learned imagery:

> As lines, so loves oblique, may well
>   Themselves in every angle greet:
> But ours so truly parallel,
>   Though infinite, can never meet;

and above all the sudden soar of passion in bold and felicitous image, in clangorous lines:

> But at my back I always hear
> Time's wingèd chariot hurrying near,
> And yonder all before us lie
> Deserts of vast eternity.
> Thy beauty shall no more be found;
> Nor in thy marble vault shall sound
> My echoing song: then worms shall try
> That long preserv'd virginity;
> And your quaint honour turn to dust;

And into ashes all my lust.
The grave's a fine and private place,
But none I think do there embrace.

These lines seem to me the very roof and crown of the metaphysical love lyric, at once fantastic and passionate. Donne is weightier, more complex, more suggestive of subtle and profound reaches of feeling, but he has not one single passage of the same length that combines all the distinctive qualities of the kind, in thought, in phrasing, in feeling, in music; and Rochester's most passionate lines are essentially simpler, less metaphysical.

When wearied with a world of woe,

might have been written by Burns with some differences. The best things of Donne and Marvell could only have been composed—except, as an imitative *tour de force*, like Watson's

Bid me no more to other eyes—

in the seventeenth century. But in that century there were so many poets who could sing, at least occasionally, in the same strain. Of all those whom Professor Saintsbury's ardent and catholic but discriminating taste has collected there is none who has not written too much indifferent verse, but none who has not written one or two songs showing the same fine blend of passion and paradox and music. The "metaphysicals" of the seventeenth century combined two things, both soon to pass away, the fantastic dialectics of mediaeval love poetry and the "simple, sensuous" strain which they caught from the classics—soul and body lightly yoked and glad to run and soar together in the winged chariot of Pegasus. Modern love poetry has too often sacrificed both to sentiment.

ᕝ

The Metaphysical Poets

By collecting these poems [1] from the work of a generation more often named than read, and more often read than profitably studied, Professor Grierson has rendered a service of some importance. Certainly the reader will meet with many poems already preserved in other anthologies, at the same time that he discovers poems such as those of Aurelian Townshend or Lord Herbert of Cherbury here included. But the function of such an anthology as this is neither that of Professor Saintsbury's admirable edition of Caroline poets nor that of the *Oxford Book of English Verse*. Mr. Grierson's book is in itself a piece of criticism and a provocation of criticism; and we think that he was right in including so many poems of Donne, elsewhere (though not in many editions) accessible, as documents in the case of "metaphysical poetry." The phrase has long done duty as a term of abuse or as the label of a quaint and pleasant taste. The question is to what extent the so-called metaphysicals formed a school (in our own time we should say a "movement"), and how far this so-called school or movement is a digression from the main current.

Not only is it extremely difficult to define metaphysical poetry, but difficult to decide what poets practise it and in which of their verses. The poetry of Donne (to whom Marvell and Bishop King are sometimes nearer than any of the other authors) is late Elizabethan, its feeling often very close to that of Chapman. The "courtly" poetry is derivative from Jonson, who borrowed liberally from the Latin; it expires in the next century with the sentiment and witticism of Prior. There is finally the devotional verse of Herbert, Vaughan, and Crashaw (echoed long after by Christina Rossetti and Francis Thompson); Crashaw, sometimes more profound and less sectarian than the others, has a quality which returns through the Elizabethan period to the early Italians. It is difficult to find any precise use of metaphor, simile, or other conceit, which is common to all the poets and at the same time important enough as an element of style to isolate these poets as a group. Donne, and often Cowley, employ a device which is sometimes considered characteristically "metaphysical"; the elaboration (contrasted with the condensation) of a figure of speech to the farthest stage to which ingenuity can carry it. Thus Cowley develops the commonplace comparison of the world to a chess-board through long stanzas (*To Destiny*), and Donne, with more grace, in *A Valediction,* the comparison of two lovers to a pair of compasses. But elsewhere we find, instead of the mere explication of the content of a comparison, a development by rapid association of thought which requires considerable agility on the part of the reader.

> On a round ball
> A workman that hath copies by, can lay
> An Europe, Afrique, and an Asia,
> And quickly make that, which was nothing, All,
> So doth each teare,
> Which thee doth weare,
> A globe, yea, world by that impression grow,
> Till thy tears mixt with mine doe overflow
> This world, by waters sent from thee, my heaven dissolved so.

Here we find at least two connexions which are not implicit in the first figure, but are forced upon it by the poet: from the geographer's globe to the tear, and the tear to the deluge. On the other hand, some of Donne's most successful and characteristic effects are secured by brief words and sudden contrasts:

> A bracelet of bright hair about the bone,

where the most powerful effect is produced by the sudden contrast of associations of "bright hair" and of "bone." This telescoping of images and multiplied associations is characteristic of the phrase of some of the dramatists of the period which Donne knew: not to mention Shakespeare, it is frequent in Middleton, Webster, and Tourneur, and is one of the sources of the vitality of their language.

Johnson, who employed the term "metaphysical poets," apparently having Donne, Cleveland, and Cowley chiefly in mind, remarks of them that "the most heterogeneous ideas are yoked by violence together." The force of this impeachment lies in the failure of the conjunction, the fact that often the ideas are yoked but not united; and if we are to judge of styles of poetry by their abuse, enough examples may be found in Cleveland to justify Johnson's condemnation. But a degree of heterogeneity of material compelled into unity by the operation of the poet's mind is omnipresent in poetry. We need not select for illustration such a line as:

Notre âme est un trois-mâts cherchant son Icarie;

we may find it in some of the best lines of Johnson himself (*The Vanity of Human Wishes*):

His fate was destined to a barren strand,
A petty fortress, and a dubious hand;
He left a name at which the world grew pale,
To point a moral, or adorn a tale.

where the effect is due to a contrast of ideas, different in degree but the same in principle, as that which Johnson mildly reprehended. And in one of the finest poems of the age (a poem which could not have been written in any other age), the *Exequy* of Bishop King, the extended comparison is used with perfect success: the idea and the simile become one, in the passage in which the Bishop illustrates his impatience to see his dead wife, under the figure of a journey:

Stay for me there; I will not faile
To meet thee in that hollow Vale.
And think not much of my delay;
I am already on the way,
And follow thee with all the speed
Desire can make, or sorrows breed.
Each minute is a short degree,
And ev'ry houre a step towards thee.
At night when I betake to rest,
Next morn I rise nearer my West

> Of life, almost by eight houres sail,
> Than when sleep breath'd his drowsy gale. . . .
> But heark! My Pulse, like a soft Drum
> Beats my approach, tells *Thee* I come;
> And slow howe'er my marches be,
> I shall at last sit down by *Thee*.

(In the last few lines there is that effect of terror which is several times attained by one of Bishop King's admirers, Edgar Poe.) Again, we may justly take these quatrains from Lord Herbert's Ode, stanzas which would, we think, be immediately pronounced to be of the metaphysical school:

> So when from hence we shall be gone,
>   And be no more, nor you, nor I,
>   As one another's mystery,
> Each shall be both, yet both but one.
>
> This said, in her up-lifted face,
>   Her eyes, which did that beauty crown,
>   Were like two starrs, that having faln down,
> Look up again to find their place:
>
> While such a moveless silent peace
>   Did seize on their becalmed sense,
>   One would have thought some influence
> Their ravished spirits did possess.

There is nothing in these lines (with the possible exception of the stars, a simile not at once grasped, but lovely and justified) which fits Johnson's general observations on the metaphysical poets in his essay on Cowley. A good deal resides in the richness of association which is at the same time borrowed from and given to the word "becalmed"; but the meaning is clear, the language simple and elegant. It is to be observed that the language of these poets is as a rule simple and pure; in the verse of George Herbert this simplicity is carried as far as it can go—a simplicity emulated without success by numerous modern poets. The *structure* of the sentences, on the other hand, is sometimes far from simple, but this is not a vice; it is a fidelity to thought and feeling. The effect, at its best, is far less artificial than that of an ode by Gray. And as this fidelity induces variety of thought and feeling, so it induces variety of music. We doubt whether, in the eighteenth century, could be found two poems in nominally the same metre, so dissimilar as Marvell's *Coy Mistress* and Crashaw's *Saint Teresa;* the one producing an effect of great speed by the use of short syllables, and the other an ecclesiastical solemnity by the use of long ones:

> Love, thou art absolute sole lord
> Of life and death.

If so shrewd and sensitive (though so limited) a critic as Johnson failed to define metaphysical poetry by its faults, it is worth while to inquire whether we may not have more success by adopting the opposite method: by assuming that the poets of the seventeenth century (up to the Revolution) were the direct and normal development of the precedent age; and, without prejudicing their case by the adjective "metaphysical," consider whether their virtue was not something permanently valuable, which subsequently disappeared, but ought not to have disappeared. Johnson has hit, perhaps by accident, on one of their peculiarities, when he observes that "their attempts were always analytic"; he would not agree that, after the dissociation, they put the material together again in a new unity.

It is certain that the dramatic verse of the later Elizabethan and early Jacobean poets expresses a degree of development of sensibility which is not found in any of the prose, good as it often is. If we except Marlowe, a man of prodigious intelligence, these dramatists were directly or indirectly (it is at least a tenable theory) affected by Montaigne. Even if we except also Jonson and Chapman, these two were notably erudite, and were notably men who incorporated their erudition into their sensibility: their mode of feeling was directly and freshly altered by their reading and thought. In Chapman especially there is a direct sensuous apprehension of thought, or a recreation of thought into feeling, which is exactly what we find in Donne:

> in this one thing, all the discipline
> Of manners and of manhood is contained;
> A man to join himself with th' Universe
> In his main sway, and make in all things fit
> One with that All, and go on, round as it;
> Not plucking from the whole his wretched part,
> And into straits, or into nought revert,
> Wishing the complete Universe might be
> Subject to such a rag of it as he;
> But to consider great Necessity.

We compare this with some modern passage:

> No, when the fight begins within himself,
> A man's worth something. God stoops o'er his head,
> Satan looks up between his feet—both tug—
> He's left, himself, i' the middle; the soul wakes
> And grows. Prolong that battle through his life!

It is perhaps somewhat less fair, though very tempting (as both poets are concerned with the perpetuation of love by offspring), to compare with the stanzas already quoted from Lord Herbert's Ode the following from Tennyson:

> One walked between his wife and child,
> With measured footfall firm and mild,
> And now and then he gravely smiled.
>> The prudent partner of his blood
>> Leaned on him, faithful, gentle, good,
>> Wearing the rose of womanhood.
> And in their double love secure,
> The little maiden walked demure,
> Pacing with downward eyelids pure.
>> These three made unity so sweet,
>> My frozen heart began to beat,
>> Remembering its ancient heat.

The difference is not a simple difference of degree between poets. It is something which had happened to the mind of England between the time of Donne or Lord Herbert of Cherbury and the time of Tennyson and Browning; it is the difference between the intellectual poet and the reflective poet. Tennyson and Browning are poets, and they think; but they do not feel their thought as immediately as the odour of a rose. A thought to Donne was an experience; it modified his sensibility. When a poet's mind is perfectly equipped for its work, it is constantly amalgamating disparate experience; the ordinary man's experience is chaotic, irregular, fragmentary. The latter falls in love, or reads Spinoza, and these two experiences have nothing to do with each other, or with the noise of the typewriter or the smell of cooking; in the mind of the poet these experiences are always forming new wholes.

We may express the difference by the following theory: The poets of the seventeenth century, the successors of the dramatists of the sixteenth, possessed a mechanism of sensibility which could devour any kind of experience. They are simple, artificial, difficult, or fantastic, as their predecessors were; no less nor more than Dante, Guido Cavalcanti, Guinizelli, or Cino. In the seventeenth century a dissociation of sensibility set in, from which we have never recovered; and this dissociation, as is natural, was aggravated by the influence of the two most powerful poets of the century, Milton and Dryden. Each of these men performed certain poetic functions so magnificently well that the magnitude of the effect concealed the absence of others. The language went on and in some respects improved; the best verse of Collins, Gray, Johnson, and even Goldsmith satisfies some of our fastidious demands better than that of Donne or Marvell or King. But while the language became more refined, the feeling became more crude. The feeling, the sensibility, expressed in the *Country Churchyard* (to say nothing of Tennyson and Browning) is cruder than that in the *Coy Mistress*.

The second effect of the influence of Milton and Dryden followed from the first, and was therefore slow in manifestation. The sentimental age began early in the eighteenth century, and continued. The poets revolted against the ratiocinative, the descriptive; they thought and felt by fits, unbalanced; they reflected. In one or two passages of Shelley's *Triumph of Life,* in the second *Hyperion,* there are traces of a struggle toward unification of sensibility. But Keats and Shelley died, and Tennyson and Browning ruminated.

After this brief exposition of a theory—too brief, perhaps, to carry conviction—we may ask, what would have been the fate of the "metaphysical" had the current of poetry descended in a direct line from them, as it descended in a direct line to them? They would not, certainly, be classified as metaphysical. The possible interests of a poet are unlimited; the more intelligent he is the better; the more intelligent he is the more likely that he will have interests: our only condition is that he turn them into poetry, and not merely meditate on them poetically. A philosophical theory which has entered into poetry is established, for its truth or falsity in one sense ceases to matter, and its truth in another sense is proved. The poets in question have, like other poets, various faults. But they were, at best, engaged in the task of trying to find the verbal equivalent for states of mind and feeling. And this means both that they are more mature, and that they wear better, than later poets of certainly not less literary ability.

It is not a permanent necessity that poets should be interested in philosophy, or in any other subject. We can only say that it appears likely that poets in our civilization, as it exists at present, must be *difficult.* Our civilization comprehends great variety and complexity, and this variety and complexity, playing upon a refined sensibility, must produce various and complex results. The poet must become more and more comprehensive, more allusive, more indirect, in order to force, to dislocate if necessary, language into his meaning. (A brilliant and extreme statement of this view, with which it is not requisite to associate oneself, is that of M. Jean Epstein, *La Poésie d'aujourd'hui*.) Hence we get something which looks very much like the conceit —we get, in fact, a method curiously similar to that of the "metaphysical poets," similar also in its use of obscure words and of simple phrasing.

> O géraniums diaphanes, guerroyeurs sortilèges,
> Sacrilèges monomanes!
> Emballages, dévergondages, douches! O pressoirs
> Des vendanges des grands soirs!
> Layettes aux abois,
> Thyrses au fond des bois!
> Transfusions, représailles,
> Relevailles, compresses et l'éternal potion,
> Angélus! n'en pouvoir plus
> De débâcles nuptiales! de débâcles nuptiales!

The same poet could write also simply:

> Elle est bien loin, elle pleure,
> Le grand vent se lamente aussi . . .

Jules Laforgue, and Tristan Corbière in many of his poems, are nearer to the "school of Donne" than any modern English poet. But poets more classical than they have the same essential quality of transmuting ideas into sensations, of transforming an observation into a state of mind.

> Pour l'enfant, amoureux de cartes et d'estampes,
> L'univers est égal à son vaste appétit.
> Ah, que le monde est grand à la carté des lampes!
> Aux yeux du souvenir que le monde est petit!

In French literature the great master of the seventeenth century— Racine—and the great master of the nineteenth—Baudelaire—are in some ways more like each other than they are like any one else. The greatest two masters of diction are also the greatest two psychologists, the most curious explorers of the soul. It is interesting to speculate whether it is not a misfortune that two of the greatest masters of diction in our language, Milton and Dryden, triumph with a dazzling disregard of the soul. If we continued to produce Miltons and Drydens it might not so much matter, but as things are it is a pity that English poetry has remained so incomplete. Those who object to the "artificiality" of Milton or Dryden sometimes tell us to "look into our hearts and write." But that is not looking deep enough; Racine or Donne looked into a good deal more than the heart. One must look into the cerebral cortex, the nervous system, and the digestive tracts.

May we not conclude, then, that Donne, Crashaw, Vaughan, Herbert and Lord Herbert, Marvell, King, Cowley at his best, are in the direct current of English poetry, and that their faults should be reprimanded by this standard rather than coddled by antiquarian affection? They have been enough praised in terms which are implicit limitations because they are "metaphysical" or "witty," "quaint" or "obscure," though at their best they have not these attributes more than other serious poets. On the other hand, we must not reject the criticism of Johnson (a dangerous person to disagree with) without having mastered it, without having assimilated the Johnsonian canons of taste. In reading the celebrated passage in his essay on Cowley we must remember that by wit he clearly means something more serious than we usually mean today; in his criticism of their versification we must remember in what a narrow discipline he was trained, but also how well trained; we must remember that Johnson tortures chiefly the chief offenders, Cowley and Cleveland. It would be a fruitful work, and one requiring a substantial book, to break up the classification of Johnson (for there has been none since) and exhibit these poets in all their difference of kind and of degree, from the massive music of Donne to the faint, pleasing tinkle of Aurelian Townshend—whose *Dialogue between a Pilgrim and Time* is one of the few regrettable omissions from the excellent anthology of Professor Grierson.

NOTE

[1] *Metaphysical Lyrics and Poems of the Seventeenth Century: Donne to Butler.* Selected and edited, with an Essay, by Herbert J. C. Grierson (Oxford: Clarendon Press).

HELEN GARDNER

↙

The Metaphysical Poets

The term "metaphysical poets" came into being long after the poets to whom we apply it were dead. Samuel Johnson, who coined it, did so with the consciousness that it was a piece of literary slang, that he was giving a kind of nickname. When he wrote in his *Life of Cowley* that "about the beginning of the seventeenth century appeared a race of writers that may be termed the metaphysical poets," his "may be termed" indicates that he did not consider that these poets had the right to be called "metaphysical" in the true sense. He was adapting a witty sally from Dryden who, writing in 1693, said of Donne:

> He affects the metaphysics, not only in his satires, but in his amorous verses, where nature only should reign; and perplexes the minds of the fair sex with nice speculations of philosophy, when he should engage their hearts, and entertain them with the softnesses of love. In this . . . Mr Cowley has copied him to a fault.

Between Dryden and Johnson comes Pope, who is reported by Spence to have remarked that "Cowley, as well as Davenant, borrowed his metaphysical style from Donne." But the only writer I know of before Dryden who spoke as if there were a "metaphysical school" is Drummond of Hawthornden (1585–1649) who, in an unfortunately undated letter, speaks of poets who make use of "Metaphysical *Ideas* and *Scholastical Quiddities*."

From *The Metaphysical Poets* (Oxford, 1961), pp. xix-xxxiv. Reprinted by permission of The Clarendon Press.

What we call metaphysical poetry was referred to by contemporaries as "strong lines," a term which calls attention to other elements in metaphysical poetry than its fondness for indulging in "nice speculations of philosophy" in unusual contexts. The term is used in connexion with prose as well as with verse—indeed the earliest use I know of is by a prose writer—and so invites us to look at metaphysical poetry in a wider context. Like the later term "metaphysical," the term "stronglined" is a term of disapprobation. It too is a kind of slang, a phrase which would seem to have been coined by those who disliked this way of writing. Thus Burton, in the preface to *The Anatomy of Melancholy* (1621), contrasts his own "loose free style" with "neat composition, strong lines, hyperboles, allegories," and later speaks disparagingly of the "affectation of big words, fustian phrases, jingling termes, strong lines, that like *Acastes* arrows caught fire as they flew"; and Quarles, in the preface to *Argalus and Parthenia* (1629), declares:

> I have not affected to set thy understanding on the Rack, by the tyranny of *strong lines*, which (as they fabulously report of *China* dishes) are made for the third *Generation* to make use of, and are the meere itch of wit; under the colour of which, many have ventured (trusting to the *Oedipean* conceit of their ingenious Reader) to write *non-sense*, and fellon-iously father the created expositions of other men; not unlike some painters, who first make the picture, then, from the opinions of better judgments, conclude whom it resembles.

These are complaints against an established manner in prose and verse. It is a manner which developed in the last decade of the sixteenth century with the cry everywhere for "More matter and less words." In prose, Cicero, the model for the sixteenth century, was dethroned in favor of the Silver Latin writers, Seneca and Tacitus. Recommending Sir Henry Savile's translation of Tacitus in 1591, Anthony Bacon commends Tacitus because he "hath written the most matter with the best conceit in the fewest words of any Historiographer," and adds "But he is hard. *Difficilia quæ pulchra;* the second reading will please thee more than the first, and the third than the second." The same conception that difficulty is a merit is applied to poetry in Chapman's preface to *Ovid's Banquet of the Sense* (1595), where he declares that poetry, unlike oratory, should not aim at clarity: "That Poetry should be as pervial as oratory and plainness her special ornament, were the plain way to barbarism." Poetry, like prose, should be close-packed and dense with meaning, something to be "chewed and digested," which will not give up its secrets on a first reading. In the 1590's also formal satire first appeared in English, and the satirists took as their model Persius, the most obscure of Roman satirists, and declared that satire should be "hard of conceit and harsh of style." The same period sees the vogue of the epigram and the great popularity of Martial.

What came to be called by its denigrators the "strong-lined" style had its origins in this general desire at the close of Elizabeth's reign for concise expression, achieved by an elliptical syntax, and accompanied by a staccato rhythm in prose and a certain deliberate roughness in versification in poetry. Along with this went admiration for difficulty in the thought. Difficulty is indeed the main demerit in this way of writing for those who dislike it, and the constant complaint of its critics is that it confuses the pleasures of poetry with the pleasures of puzzles. It is one of its merits for those who approve it. Jasper Mayne, in his elegy on Donne, put his finger on one of the delights of reading "strong-lined" verse when he said

Wee are thought wits, when 'tis understood.

It makes demands upon the reader and challenges him to make it out. It does not attempt to attract the lazy and its lovers have always a certain sense of being a privileged class, able to enjoy what is beyond the reach of vulgar wits. The great majority of the poets included in this book did not write to be read by all and sundry. Few of them published their poems. They were "Chamber poets," as Drayton, with the jealousy of the professional for the amateur, complains. Their poems passed from hand to hand in manuscript. This is a source of both weakness and strength. At times the writing has the smell of a coterie, the writer performing with a self-conscious eye on his clever readers. But at its best it has the ease and artistic sincerity which comes from being able to take for granted the understanding of the audience for whom one writes.

The first characteristic that I shall isolate in trying to discuss the admittedly vague and, it is often thought, unsatisfactory term "metaphysical poetry" is its concentration. The reader is held to an idea or a line of argument. He is not invited to pause upon a passage, "wander with it, and muse upon it, and reflect upon it, and bring home to it, and prophesy upon it, and dream upon it" as a "starting-post towards all the 'two-and-thirty Palaces.'" Keats's advice can be followed profitably with much poetry, particularly with Elizabethan and Romantic poetry; but metaphysical poetry demands that we pay attention and read on. For this reason I have resisted the temptation to print excerpts from longer poems. It is, of course, possible and pleasurable to linger over passages of striking beauty and originality, but, on the whole, I think that to do so is to miss the special pleasure that metaphysical poetry has to give. It does not aim at providing, to quote Keats again, "a little Region to wander in," where lovers of poetry "may pick and choose, and in which images are so numerous that many are forgotten and found new in a second Reading." A metaphysical poem tends to be brief, and is always closely woven. Marvell, under the metaphor of a garland, characterizes his own art finely in "The Coronet" when he speaks of a "curious frame" in which the flowers are "set with Skill and chosen out with Care." And Donne in a sermon, speaking of the Psalms as especially dear to him in that they were poems, stresses the same elements of deliberate art (curiosity), and economy of language, when he defines psalms as

Such form as is both curious, and requires diligence in the making, and then when it is made, can have nothing, no syllable taken from it, nor added to it.

Concentration and a sinewy strength of style is the mark of Ben Jonson as well as of Donne, and such adjectives as "strenuous" and "masculine" applied to him by his admirers point to a sense in which he too was in some degree a "strong-lined" man, and explain why so many younger writers were able to regard both him and Donne as equally their masters. Behind both, as behind much of the poetry of their followers, lies the classical epigram, and there is some truth in saying that a metaphysical poem is an expanded epigram. Almost all the poets in this collection exercised their skill in the writing of epigrams. Their efforts make on the whole very dreary reading; but the vogue of the epigram helped to form the taste for witty poetry. The desire for concentration and concision marks also the verse forms characteristic of seventeenth-century lyric. It appears in the fondness for a line of eight syllables rather than a line of ten, and in the use of stanzas employing lines of varying length into which the sense seems packed, or of stanzas built on very short lines. A stanza of Donne or Herbert is not, like rhyme royal or a Spenserian stanza, an ideal mould, as it were, into which the words have flowed. It is more like a limiting frame in which words and thought are compressed, a "box where sweets compacted lie." The metaphysical poets favoured either very simple verse forms, octosyllabic couplets or quatrains, or else stanzas created for the particular poem, in which length of line and rhyme scheme artfully enforced the sense. In a poem not included here, "The Triple Foole," Donne suggests, in passing, this conception of the function of rhyme and metre:

> I thought, if I could draw my paines,
> Through Rimes vexation, I should them allay,
> Griefe brought to numbers cannot be so fierce,
> For, he tames it, that fetters it in verse.

The second characteristic of metaphysical poetry, its most immediately striking feature, is its fondness for conceits, and here, of course, Jonson and Donne part company. A conceit is a comparison whose ingenuity is more striking than its justness, or, at least, is more immediately striking. All comparisons discover likeness in things unlike: a comparison becomes a conceit when we are made to concede likeness while being strongly conscious of unlikeness. A brief comparison can be a conceit if two things patently unlike, or which we should never think of together, are shown to be alike in a single point in such a way, or in such a context, that we feel their incongruity. Here a conceit is like a spark made by striking two stones together. After the flash the stones are just two stones. Metaphysical poetry abounds in such flashes, as when Cartwright in his New Year's poem, promising to be a new man, declares that he will not be new as the year is new when it begins again its former cycle, and then thinks of two images of motion without progression, the circulation of the blood and a mill:

> Motion as in a Mill
> Is busie standing still.

The wit of this depends on our being willing to suppress our memory of other features of mills, and particularly on our not allowing ourselves to think that mills are very usefully employed grinding corn while "standing still." Normally metaphor and simile allow and invite the mind to stray beyond the immediate point of resemblance, and in extended or epic simile, which is the diametrical opposite of the conceit, the poet himself expatiates freely, making the point of comparison a point of departure. In an extended conceit, on the other hand, the poet forces fresh points of likeness upon us. Here the conceit is a kind of "hammering out" by which a difficult join is made. I borrow the phrase from Shakespeare's poet-king Richard II, who occupies himself in prison composing a conceited poem:

> I have been studying how I may compare
> This prison where I live unto the world:
> And for because the world is populous,
> And here is not a creature but myself,
> I cannot do it; yet I'll hammer it out.
> My brain I'll prove the female to my soul . . .

Longer conceits set themselves to "prove" likeness. They may, as here, start from a comparison which the speaker owns is far from obvious and then proceeds to establish. Or they may start from one that is immediately acceptable generally and then make us accept further resemblances in detail after detail. Thus nobody, I imagine, would think Lady Macbeth is being particularly ingenious when she compares the troubled face of her husband to a book in which men may "read strange matters." She leaves our imaginations to give further content to this comparison of finding meaning in a book and meaning in a face and to the deliberately imprecise words "strange matters." But when Lady Capulet takes up the same comparison to urge Juliet to wed Count Paris she expands the comparison for us in detail after detail so that it becomes a conceit, and most people would add a very tasteless and ineffective one.

> Read o'er the volume of young Paris' face
> And find delight writ there with beauty's pen;
> Examine every married lineament,
> And see how one another lends content;
> And what obscur'd in this fair volume lies
> Find written in the margent of his eyes.
> This precious book of love, this unbound lover,
> To beautify him, only lacks a cover. . . .
> That book in many eyes doth share the glory
> That in gold clasps locks in the golden story:
> So shall you share all that he doth possess,
> By having him making yourself no less.

Elizabethan poetry, dramatic and lyric, abounds in conceits. They are used both as ornaments and as the basis of songs and sonnets. What differentiates the conceits of the metaphysicals is not the fact that they frequently employ curious learning in their comparisons. Many of the poets whom we call metaphysical, Herbert for instance, do not. It is the use which they make of the conceit and the rigorous nature of their conceits, springing from the use to which they are put, which is more important than their frequently learned content. A metaphysical conceit, unlike Richard II's comparison of his prison to the world, is not indulged in for its own sake. It is used, as Lady Capulet uses hers, to persuade, or it is used to define, or to prove a point. Ralegh's beautiful comparison of man's life to a play is a good example of a poem which seems to me to hover on the verge of becoming a metaphysical poem. Its concision and completeness and the ironic, colloquially made point at the end—"Onely we dye in earnest, that's no Jest"—bring it very near, but it remains in the region of the conceited epigram and does not cross the border. On the other hand, Lady Capulet's conceit fails to be metaphysical in another way. She does not force us to concede the justness of her initial comparison by developing it, she merely argues from various arbitrarily chosen points of comparison between a book and a bachelor. In a metaphysical poem the conceits are instruments of definition in an argument or instruments to persuade. The poem has something to say which the conceit explicates or something to urge which the conceit helps to forward. It can only do this if it is used with an appearance of logical rigour, the analogy being shown to hold by a process not unlike Euclid's superimposition of triangles. I have said that the first impression a conceit makes is of ingenuity rather than of justice: the metaphysical conceit aims at making us concede justness while admiring ingenuity. Thus, in one of the most famous of all metaphysical conceits, the comparison of the union in absence of two lovers with the relation between the two legs of a compass, Donne sustains the comparison through the whole process of drawing a circle, because he is attempting to give a "proof by analogy" of their union, by which he can finally persuade his mistress not to mourn. In another of his unfortunately rare asides on the art of poetry, Donne, again speaking of the Psalms, said:

> In all Metricall compositions . . . the force of the whole piece is for the most part left to the shutting up; the whole frame of the Poem is a beating out of a piece of gold, but the last clause is as the impression of the stamp, and that is it that makes it currant.

We might expand this by saying that the brilliant abrupt openings for which metaphysical poetry is famous, are like the lump of gold flung down on the table to be worked; the conceits are part of the beating out by which the metal is shaped to receive its final stamp, which is the point towards which the whole has moved.

Argument and persuasion, and the use of the conceit as their instrument, are the elements or body of a metaphysical poem. Its quintessence or soul is the vivid imagining of a moment of experience or of a situation out of which the need to argue, or persuade, or define arises. Metaphysical poetry is famous for its abrupt, personal openings in which a man speaks to his mistress, or addresses his God, or sets a scene, or calls us to mark this or see that. A great many of the poems in this collection are inspired by actual occasions either of personal, or, less often, public interest. The great majority postulate an occasion. We may not accept that Donne's "Good Friday" was actually "made as I was riding westward that day," as a heading in some manuscripts tells us, but we must accept as we read the poem that he is riding westward and thinking as he rides. Marvell calls us to look at little T.C. in her garden. The child of one of Marvell's friends, Theophila Cornewall, bore the same beautiful name as her elder sister who had died two days after her baptism, a name which has a foreboding ring since the proverb says that the "Darlings of the Gods" die young. This lovely poem would seem to have arisen from thoughts suggested by the name and family history of a friend's child. Whether Marvell actually caught sight of her in a garden we have no means of knowing. But he does not convey to us his sense of the transience of spring and the dangerous fragility of childhood through general reflections on human life. He calls us to watch with him a child "in a Prospect of Flowers." Equally, when his subject belongs to the ideal world of pastoral, not the world of daily life, his nymph is set before us complaining for her fawn while the little beast's life-blood is ebbing away. She tells of her betrayal in love as the tears are running down her cheeks in mourning for the creature who consoled her for that betrayal. Even poems of generalized reflection are given the flavour of spontaneous thought, as when Herbert opens his poem "Man" with "My God, I heard this day . . . ," and thus gives the poem the air of having sprung from the casual overhearing of a chance remark.

The manner of metaphysical poetry originates in developments in prose and verse in the 1590's. The greatest glory of that decade is that it saw the flowering of the drama. Metaphysical poetry is the poetry of the great age of our drama. Its master John Donne was, we are told, "a great frequenter of plays" in his youth. As an ambitious young man of social standing he would not have considered writing for the players, and his work is too personal, wilful, and idiosyncratic for us to imagine him doing so with any success. But his strong dramatic imagination of particular situations transforms the lyric and makes a metaphysical poem more than an epigram expanded by conceits.

I have begun this volume a little before Donne with poems which in some ways anticipate the metaphysical manner: Ralegh's fine passionate conceit of a pilgrimage, written when he was under sentence of death, some specimens of Fulke Greville's "close, mysterious and sentencious way of writing," Southwell's meditations, Shakespeare's strange celebration of married chastity in the most "strong-lined" of all poems, if "strong lines" are riddles, Alabaster's attempts at the concise expression of theological paradox, Wotton's laconic comment on the greatest scandal of the age. But the minute the reader reaches Donne, he will have the same sense of having arrived as when, in a collection of pre-Shakespearian plays, we hear the voice of Marlowe. Ralegh is too discursive, Greville too heavy and general, Southwell too dogged in his conceits and in his verse, one line padding at the same pace after another, Shakespeare too remote, and too symbolic, creating a static world where Love and Constancy are deified. The vehement, colloquial tone of the Satire "Of Religion" creates the sense of an actual historical situation in which urgent choices present themselves. In the three splendid Elegies a man is speaking to a woman at a moment when all the faculties are heightened, as in drama, by the thought of what impends. He is about to go to the wars—what will she say to him when he returns, perhaps mutilated? He has to travel and she wants to come with him as his page—he is horrified at the thought of such romantic folly and implores her to be his true mistress and "home of love." With the tide of passion rising in him, impatient for the moment when she will be his, he watches her undressing for bed. The sense of the moment gives Donne's wit its brilliance and verve, the aptness and incongruity of the comparisons being created by their contexts. Without this, as in some of his complimentary pieces, he labours to be witty and never becomes "airborne." The fading of this desire to make poems out of particular moments, made imaginatively present rather than remembered, and played over by wit rather than reflected upon, is apparent towards the end of this volume. The metaphysical style peters out, to be replaced by the descriptive and reflective poetry of the eighteenth century, a century which sees the rise of the novel and has virtually no drama.

The strong sense of actual and often very ordinary situations which the metaphysical poets convey makes me agree with Grierson in thinking that words such as "conceited" or "fantastic" do not sum up their quality at all. A reader may at times exclaim "Who would ever think such a thought in such a situation?" He will not exclaim "Who can imagine himself in such a situation?" Dryden praised Donne for expressing deep thoughts in common language. He is equally remarkable for having extraordinary thoughts in ordinary situations. The situations which recur in seventeenth-century lyric are the reverse of fantastic, and often the reverse of ideal or romantic situations. Thus, a very favourite topic is the pleasure of hearing a beautiful woman sing or play. This domestic subject is, of course, a favourite on the Continent, and not merely with the poets, but with the painters. Such poems usually go beyond compliment to create a sense of the occasion; as Waller, in praising Lady Isabella Rich, whom Dorothy Osborne described as "Lady Isabella that speaks and looks and plays and sings and all so prettily," expresses exactly the delight which we receive during an actual performance from artistry:

> Such moving sounds from such a careless touch,
> So unconcern'd her selfe, and we so much!

Again there are a great many poems which arise out of the common but unromantic situation of love between persons of very different ages. A mature man may rather ruefully complain to "a very young Lady"

> That time should mee so far remove
> From that which I was borne to love.

This Horatian theme of the charm of young girls to older men is given various twists. The situation is reversed when Cartwright persuades his Chloe not to mind being older than he is; and at the end of the period Rochester gives us a fresh variation on the theme that age and youth are not so incompatible as the romantics claim by writing a song for "A Young Lady to her Ancient Lover."

The most serious and impassioned love poetry of the century argues, or assumes as a base for argument, that love is a relation between two persons loving—"It cannot be love till I love her that loves me." The poems which Donne wrote on the experience of loving where love is returned, poems in which "Thou" and "I" are merged into "We," are his most original and profound contributions to the poetry of human love. It is not possible to find models for such poems as "The Good-Morrow," "The Anniversarie," "The Canonization," and, less perfect but still wonderful, "The Extasie." These poems have the right to the title metaphysical in its true sense, since they raise, even when they do not explicitly discuss, the great metaphysical question of the relation of the spirit and the senses. They raise it not as an abstract

problem, but in the effort to make the experience of the union of
human powers in love, and the union of two human beings in love,
apprehensible. We never lose our sense of a "little roome" which love
has made "an every where." In the lighter verses of Donne's followers
this theme that love is the union of two human beings, not the service
of a votarist to a goddess, is handled with a mixture of gallantry,
sensibility and good sense that has a peculiar charm:

> 'Tis not how witty, nor how free,
> Nor yet how beautifull she be,
> But how much kinde and true to me.

This is a very characteristic note. There are plenty of high and chivalrous fancies, and the Platonic ideal of love as the union of souls casts
its spell; but the tone of the bargain scene in *The Way of the World*
is anticipated in many lyrics in which the speaker sets forward the
terms on which he is willing to make the "world without end bargain"
of love. The question "What shall I do if she does not love me?" is
often handled and usually with a glance at the old chivalric answer.
Suckling's impudent "The devil take her" is flat blasphemy against
the religion of love. King's exquisite "Tell me no more how fair she
is" is chivalrous enough, as is Waller's "It is not that I love you less";
but earlier servants of love would not, I think, have shown so stoical
an acceptance of the fact that their love was hopeless, nor been so
sensible in resolving not to keep their wounds green by hearing the
lady's praises or by haunting her company. In one of his beautifully
tempered songs of love unreturned, Godolphin seriously considers
what creates the obligation to constancy. Parting for the wars, or
parting to go abroad, or the final parting of death, actual or anticipated, are also favourite subjects. They too inspire poems which are
metaphysical in both senses, as lovers ponder such questions as "Can
love subsist without the things that elemented it?" and "Shall we meet
in another world, and, if so, shall we know each other?"

The seventeenth century was, as Cowley said, "a warlike, various
and tragical age." A glance at the biographical notes will show how
many of the poets included in this book at one time or another "trailed
a pike" or "raised a troop of horse," or went on missions abroad, or
played a part in public affairs. They were for the most part men of
the world who knew its ways. Their wit, high-flown and extravagant
though it is, goes with a strong sense of the realities of daily life, the
common concerns of men and women. And in spite of Johnson's
accusation of pedantry, it has the flavour of the wit of conversation

between friends who urge each other on to further flights. Donne perhaps meant what he said when, in the stanza of "The Will" in which he restores gifts to those from whom he had received them, he leaves

> To Nature, all that I in Ryme have writ;
> And to my company my wit.

"I know the world and believe in God" wrote Fulke Greville, a Calvinist who was well acquainted with the winding stair of politics. Donne might have said the same, and Herbert has no need to tell us that he knows the ways of Learning, Honour, and Pleasure; it is apparent in all his poetry that he was not unworldly because of lack of knowledge of the world. The strength of the religious poetry of the metaphysical poets is that they bring to their praise and prayer and meditation so much experience that is not in itself religious. Here too the poems create for us particular situations out of which prayer or meditation arises: Donne riding westward, or stretched out upon his deathbed; Herbert praying all day long "but no hearing," or noting his own whitening hair, or finding, after a night of heaviness, joy in the morning; Vaughan walking to spend his hour, or sitting solitary at midnight thinking of departed friends. Even with Crashaw, where this sense of the poet's own situation is unimportant, how vividly he dramatizes, rather than narrates, the story of St. Teresa, and invokes the weeping Magdalen; and how vigorously he urges the hesitant Countess of Denbigh against delay.

Much stress has been laid recently upon the strongly traditional element in the conceits of metaphysical religious poetry. A good deal that seems to us remote, and idiosyncratic, the paradoxes and the twistings of Scripture to yield symbolic meanings, reaches back through the liturgy and through commentaries on Scripture to the Fathers and can be paralleled in medieval poetry. It is also true that the metaphysical manner of setting a subject, "hammering it out," and then "shutting it up" is closely allied to the method of religious meditation and that many metaphysical poems are poetical meditations. And yet, as strongly—or even more strongly—as in reading the secular poetry, the more we suggest common qualities and the more we set the poets in a tradition, the more strongly we are aware of their intensely individual treatment of common themes. How individually, for instance, Herbert treats the old theme of the stages of human life and the traditional lesson of the *Ars Moriendi* in "Mortification." Who else but Herbert would, with compassionate irony in place of the usual gloom of the moralist, show man as unconsciously amassing at each stage what he needs for his burial? And how tenderly and sympathetically he epitomizes each stage of our strange eventful pilgrimage, catching its very essence: the dreamless sleep of boyhood, the retraction of energies and interests in middle age, and the pathos of old age, unable to speak for rheum. The comparison of sleep to death, and of a bed to a grave, is stock enough. It is transformed by the further haunting image

> Successive nights, like rolling waves,
> Convey them quickly, who are bound for death.

The poem concludes with an old moral for its "shutting up"; but the moral is made new by the time we reach it, because Herbert has so expanded our understanding of our dying life. The metaphysical style heightens and liberates personality. It is essentially a style in which individuality is expressed. The best pupils in the school of Donne learned from their master how to speak their own minds in their own voices.

For this reason I have contented myself with describing some of the characteristics of metaphysical poetry and have not attempted to construct a definition of "a metaphysical poem." Such definitions do not seem to me very profitable, since none of these poets ever thought of himself as writing such a thing, and they usually lead their creators to finding fault with this or that poet for not conforming to the critic's definition. I am aware that I have included in this collection some poems whose presence under its title may be challenged. If I had the space I could defend them all on one ground or another, though my defence would of course have to take the form of "All these poems are metaphysical, but some are more metaphysical than others." I am more concerned that readers should find them beautiful and interesting than that they should approve or disapprove of them as conforming or not conforming to the idea of a metaphysical poem. All of them have a certain pungency in their thought, or in their turns of phrase, which makes them, whether profound or flippant, deserve the praise of being "fine and wittie."

🖎

Wit: Definition and Dialectic

Whose DEFINITION is a doubt
Twixt life & death, twixt in & out.
—Crashaw

If any feature of Metaphysical has seemed to be its prime characteristic, that has ben wit. To Carew, Donne had ruled, as no one else
might have, "*The universall Monarchy of Wit*" and to Dryden he was
"the greatest Wit, though not the best Poet of our Nation." [1] Dr. Johnson regarded wit as the chief feature distinguishing poets who might
be termed Metaphysical and advanced the subject considerably by
locating wit in a process of thought: "The most heterogeneous ideas
are yoked by violence together." [2] Although Johnson spoke of ideas and
did not restrict wit to images, it has since become common to think of
wit in terms of conceits, and Donne's "stiffe twin compasses" have become the archetype of all Metaphysical imagery and wit. Certainly
images are often yoked to ideas—Donne's use of public language and
imagery for private experience was remarked on in an earlier chapter
and may serve again for example. But Dr. Johnson meant ideas, that
Donne had thoughts and used them (whether with imagery or without) strikingly, often bizarrely or distastefully, but always conspicuously. Both the use of ideas and the strikingness or novelty of their
use were important meanings of "wit" in the century. Of the two, the

From "Wit: Definition and Dialectic," in Earl Miner, *The Metaphysical
Mode From Donne to Cowley* (copyright © 1969 by Princeton University
Press), pp. 118–58. Reprinted by permission of Princeton University Press.

>use of the intellect was the more dominant sense of the word. Dryden
was yet more particular. Donne, he said, "affects the Metaphysicks,
not only in his Satires, but in his Amorous Verses, where Nature only
shou'd reign; and perplexes the Minds of the Fair Sex with nice Speculations of Philosophy, when he shou'd ingage their hearts, and entertain
them with the softnesses of Love." [3] Dryden's usual critical sense de-
serts him at the end of this passage, leading him to think that a love
poem is less a poem than a real stage in wooing. But he is certainly
right in finding ideas in Donne's love poems as well as in his satires and
to suggest that they come from metaphysics and from science ("Philosophy"). Philosophical divinity and theoretical science *are* sources
of Donne's ideas and they *are* unusual in love poetry. But such ideas,
like their equivalents in the other Metaphysical poets, are also witty in
the freshness of their application and valuable for the way in which
they are set to work poetically.

   If we might summon up a sixteenth- or seventeenth-century schoolboy and ask him to identify the arts teaching how ideas are used and
put to work, he would not have spoken of philosophy and psychology
as we know them today, but of logic and rhetoric. Anyone who has
looked at the old logics and rhetorics that were memorized by, or
beaten into, a schoolboy three or four centuries ago is apt to regard
the lad with a sigh and heaviness of heart. Homozeuxis and homo-
zeugma are not calculated to touch modern hearts very deeply, and
the differences between Aristotle, Cicero, Quintilian, and Ramus in
matters rhetorical likewise do not seem matters of very pressing poetic
interest. What two central arts of the Renaissance and the seventeenth
century have less relevance to our familiar experience? What, we are
inclined to ask, do such "predicaments" as "substance," "accident," or
"quantity" have to do with *us?* Or with our understanding of Metaphysical poetry? On the other hand, if Donne's "Communitie" assumes
the form of (an exact complex disjunctive syllogism) the fact is a fact.
It is difficult to construct a modern parallel, since the comparable logic
today is so mathematical that it has little connection with poetry. But
what if all our poets had been taught at school and at the university to
memorize William Empson's *Seven Types of Ambiguity,* to analyze
writing in terms of each type along close lines by attention to the
"grammar" of Kenneth Burke and the "genres" of Northrop Frye, and
to compose constantly with the alternatives in mind? Then should
a critic three centuries hence be expected to know what all this is
about?

   The equivalent questions have been raised by some of our students
of Metaphysical poetry, and some very different answers have been

given, sometimes with a vigor approaching vehemence. Obviously, a
major difference of opinion is involved, not just of fact or of critical
method, but of how poetry should be, or how poetry in fact is, read. The
late Rosemund Tuve advocated one major position, arguing at length
and in thick detail, that both Elizabethan and Metaphysical imagery
(as she categorized the subject) grew from the same systems of logic
and rhetoric. In other words, the same poetic principles underlay the
work of a Spenser and a Donne; we must approach contemporaneous
writers with broadly the same expectations.[4] To this proposition of fact,
others, notably the very subtle and cogent William Empson, have responded with a proposition of literary effect—that Spenser and Donne
are palpably different in their poetic feel.[5]

Abstracting such central propositions from their entanglements in
other arguments, we must, I think, admit that both sides are right on
their own grounds and that they are talking at cross purposes. The
Tuves think of the mental training and disposition to certain forms of
expression in writers; the Empsons think of the very different effects of
differing poets on readers. The question is how we can use both
propositions to advance our understanding and appreciation of Metaphysical poetry, that entity quarreled over but lying, *Ding an sich,*✱
between the propositions of the Tuves and the Empsons. It must be
said at once that Spenser and Donne *are* different in poetic effect and,
indeed, in their drive toward what is important in human experience.
But I do not think that anyone has ever really doubted that. I think
it is also true, on the other hand, that most people who have read
poetry carefully over that century and a half running from Spenser to
Dryden would agree that it is distinguished by its learning, and that
to all the important poets ideas passionately mattered. As for Donne,
many of his best critics have recognized that there is in his poetry an
element variously characterized as scholastic or medieval, or represented in terms of philosophy, dialectic—or, indeed, as Dryden put it
three centuries ago, "Metaphysicks." But it will be remembered that
Dryden declared that Donne "affected" metaphysics, and it is true
that to Spenser, Milton, or Dryden the ideas themselves mattered more
in their poetry than they did in Donne's, whose poetry may be said
to *concern* ideas. To him, the ideas were outward signs of inward
states—or even, sometimes, sheer fun, as in the *Paradoxes and Problemes.* But as that work as well as the poems show, Donne calls upon
the resources of his whole education, upon the seven arts of *trivium*
and *quadrivium,* with certain religious and literary accessions as well.

The problem in approaching this large subject is that to study it
we would need to become schoolboys again. I shall return at the end

✱

of this chapter to historical questions in order to seek to explain how
such interests may have developed in Donne and to discriminate between those of his techniques that were put to work by subsequent
Metaphysical poets on the one hand, and similar but basically different
techniques employed by non-Metaphysical poets on the other. The
concerns that one needs to set before himself, it seems to me (or at
least what I find most workable), are certain poetic features of
Metaphysical wit that will serve, in spirit if not in letter, to embody
the propositions of the Tuves and the Empsons and the poems themselves. In other words, what we seek are features that stress the logical
and rhetorical nature of Metaphysical poetry emphasized by Rosemund
Tuve and others and that also enable us to explain the very distinct
effect that William Empson properly discerned Metaphysical poetry
to have. One such feature is certainly analogy. Argument or proof
from analogy is notoriously the most prone to error and the most
natural to the mind, especially if the mind is one composing poetry.
Donne's arguments from analogy are very thickly sown, and "The
Flea" may serve as one example among many. Another aspect of
his use of analogy is the employment of the simile. For some reason,
his very frequent use of this figure has never had the attention it deserves (probably because the simile, like allegory, has had a bad press
for some time), although Donne uses it for precisely its distinctive
feature, its directive force, a feature in which it excels other figures. It
should be evident that a directive figure (like the simile employed in
the opening stanza of "A Valediction forbidding mourning") has the
air of being more specific, of being logical, that is especially useful to
witty writers. Investigation would discriminate between numerous
kinds of similes, from casual, simple examples on to extended, complex
forms. We have learned in another connection that "composition by
similitude" is one possibility in the formal religious meditation drawn
upon by Donne for his divine poems. This feature is enormously important, if for no other reason than that figurative language is often so
crucial to poetry. But I find myself unable to pursue it in this book,
because I am unable to prove to my own satisfaction that these techniques outlasted Donne in Metaphysical poetry. In this, Donne and
Dryden resemble each other more than they are resembled by Herbert
and Marvell. My purpose is, therefore, to explore two logical-or-
rhetorical techniques, of a simple kind, for the use of criticism, even
as the poets had done for the uses of poetry. These techniques may be
called definition and dialectic.

Such a discussion can best begin with stress on one word of Dr.
Johnson's comment that in the wit of the Metaphysicals the most heter-

ogenous *ideas* are yoked together by violence (the yoking will subsequently take us to definition, and the "violence" or steady force of
thought to dialectic). I stress this because there is a peculiar idea
abroad that Metaphysical poetry is somehow quintessentially witty (in
a sense not true of other poets) for its imagery. But the distinction between air and angels in Donne's poem of that title is not primarily one
imagistic at all, but intellectual. To be sure, that distinction is more
the poetic basis than the poetic texture. But what of that poem,
"Breake of day," which is especially interesting for its use of a woman
as speaker?

> Must businesse thee from hence remove?
> Oh, that's the worst disease of love,
> The poore, the foule, the false, love can
> Admit, but not the busied man.
> He which hath businesse, and makes love, doth doe
> Such wrong, as when a maryed man doth wooe.   (13–18)

There is hardly an image in six lines, and the simile at the end is
without imagistic content. (No doubt one would have to consider a
pun on "businesse"—affairs and sexual intercourse.) And yet the ideas
sparkle as they move. So with Marvell:

> Therefore the Love which us doth bind,
> But Fate so enviously debarrs,
> Is the Conjunction of the Mind,
> And Opposition of the Stars.
> ("The Definition of Love," 29–32)

It may be that "bind" and "debarrs" are attenuated images, but it is
the use of "Conjunction" and "Opposition" that carries the wit. What
is necessary is, as these passages show, that the poem show that the
ideas are in use, that a mind is demonstrably at work—or at play.

A close look at either of these examples suggests that a fundamental
way in which the ideas work in Metaphysical poetry is through "definition," or "identification": the technique of saying of x that it means
thus-and-so, sometimes that it is identical to y, and often by "dialectic"
or argument that it means a, b, c, and therefore d. Business—"that's
the worst disease of love"; our love "Is the Conjunction of the Mind, /
And Opposition of the Stars." If our two souls "be two, they are two
so / As stiffe twin compasses are two." Or, as Herbert asks in "Jordan
(1)," "Is it no verse, except enchanted groves / And sudden arbours

shadow course-spunne lines?" The examples are chosen to illustrate various processes of definition, to suggest the continual effort in Metaphysical poetry to make logical propositions, to make images define abstractions or abstractions images, to bring ideas to mean what they had not earlier meant (and hence produce wit), or to pursue identities between unlike things (the operation of Fancy in faculty psychology, and hence to produce conceits). Whether with ideas alone, with images, or with the two mixed, definition is the commonest Metaphysical way of making single and dual ideas work.

To the examples given may be added others in a descending order of obviousness as to the fact that they are poetic versions of definitions. One of Donne's familiar Holy Sonnets begins, "I am a little world made cunningly," a definition of man that is used more often in his poetry than any other, though seldom as explicitly as here. In another he begins, "What if this present were the worlds last night?" The grammatical mode has shifted from declarative to interrogative, but the thrill comes from acceptance of the definition. So far the examples have employed the copula, but other less obvious means are common. "Busie old foole, unruly Sunne" is undeniably witty, precisely because it defines the sun as a busy old fool. Yet it should be observed here, since it is typical of Donne, that the logical process is not mere statement or apposition substituting for the copula. It it were apposition alone, the "unruly," which plays so large a part, would need to belong syntactically and logically with the preceding phrase: busy old unruly fool, you sun. There has been a kind of leakage from one term of the definition to the other. Rather than proceed now into such complex examples or to multiply examples from Donne, however, it will be more helpful to establish the use of simple definition in longer examples and in a limiting case, from another poet, in order to go on to the more complex extension of definition into working dialectic.

A thoroughgoing use of strict, brief definition will be found in Herbert's sonnet, "Prayer (1)," from which the opening and close may be quoted:

> Prayer the Churches banquet, Angels age,
>   Gods breath in man returning to his birth,
>   The soul in paraphrase, heart in pilgrimage,
> The Christian plummet sounding heav'n and earth; . . .
>
> The milkie way, the bird of Paradise,
>   Church-bels beyond the starres heard, the souls bloud,
>   The land of spices; something understood.

There is not, of course, a finite verb in the poem. The logic implied is that prayer is *a, b, c, d, . . . n*. The *n* is "something understood," one of those lovely simplicities of Herbert's complex mind and one which, in this case, is tantamount to saying what the absence of the verb has perhaps already implied: that in the end the full meaning of prayer cannot be defined. Definition is shown to be impossible only after its resources are fully exhausted. (Herbert's "H. Scriptures" and Vaughan's imitation with the same title are longer but less successful exercises in simple definition.) A partially similar technique of ransacking the resources of definition is to be found in Crashaw's much less successful, even ludicrous poem, "The Weeper":

> Hail, sister springs!
> Parents of sylver-footed rills!
>   Ever bubling things!
>   Thawing crystall! snowy hills,
> Still spending, neuer spent! I mean
> Thy fair eyes, sweet MAGDALENE!

>   O cheeks! Bedds of chast loves
> By your own showres seasonably dash't
> Eyes! nests of milky doves
> In your own wells decently washt,
> O wit of love! that thus could place
> Fountain & Garden in one face.   (1–6, 85–90)

No doubt we are tempted to respond in Herbert's terms, too little understood, and too much said. But the definition, the wit—exceeding the bounds of decorum—and in short the yoking together of heterogeneous ideas with violence is certainly there. The best source for a "limiting case" [6] to show the nature of definition in Metaphysical poetry is a poet whose verse is only partly in the Metaphysical line and whose most Metaphysical image is agreed upon. There may be argument whether Lovelace's "Grasse-hopper" is entirely a Metaphysical poem, but all have agreed that if there is anything in the poem answering to the name it is the well-known image, "Poore verdant foole! and now green Ice" (l. 17). A shift in the poem from summer to autumn and winter is of course involved, but the technique is the same kind of definition in apostrophe as in "Busie old foole, unruly Sunne."

Anyone with the works of the Metaphysical poets on his shelf or in his memory can quickly multiply examples of the purer or simpler forms of definition. What the limiting case of Lovelace demonstrates is therefore of more immediate utility. It shows that the <u>use of definition</u> <u>is more than characteristic</u>; it is also a means of discriminating what we feel to be Metaphysical from what we feel to be different. (Analogous practices in earlier poets will be discussed later.) It gives a specific formulation of what we more commonly speak of in terms of the characteristic wit or imagery of this poetry by telling us of their logical, <u>modal expression</u>.

The use of definition in longer passages often involves varieties of figurative language because, as has been shown, definition is often the basis of witty Metaphysical imagery. The kind of figure involved may be the simile, the most explicit and directive form of imagery, as is shown by a passage Dr. Johnson found objectionable in Donne's elegy, "The Comparison":

> As the sweet sweat of Roses in a Still,
> As that which from chaf'd muskats pores doth trill,
> As the Almighty Balme of th' early East,
> Such are the sweat drops of my Mistris Breast,
> And on her necke her skin such lustre sets,
> They seeme no sweat drops, but pearle carcanetts
>
> (1–6)

The lover goes on in a similar vein to contrast with his girl's sweet perspiration that "sweaty froth [which] thy Mistresse's brow defiles." The effort is to define the differing character of the two mistresses in terms of their attractive or repulsive sweat, with the similes carrying the role of definition, and a logical extension of definition into "dialectic," as we shall see in a moment. Underlying the similes is a further tacit identification in synecdoche of the mistresses' totalities with their differing perspirations. In a somewhat similar fashion, the most famous Metaphysical metaphor of all begins as a simile and advances to a metaphor for "two soules therefore, which are one":

> If they be two, they are two so
>   As stiffe twin compasses are two,
> Thy soule the fixt foot, makes no show
>   To move, but doth, if the'other doe. . . .   (25 ff.)

In these and the next eight lines of "A Valediction forbidding mourning" the imagistic vehicle of the metaphor is seized upon and worked out in logical extension. If we are like "stiffe twin compasses," then the identity must extend to feet, motion, and activity. What is tentatively directed by the simile is thereafter assumed a proven identity.

Other kinds of figures that may be involved are shown by Vaughan's best known poem, "The World":

> I Saw Eternity the other night
> Like a great *Ring* of pure and endless light,
>   All calm, as it was bright,
> And round beneath it, Time in hours, days, years
>   Driv'n by the spheres
> Like a vast shadow mov'd.   (1–6)

Again we have the directive figure, the simile, defining two abstractions, "Eternity" and "Time," as "light" and "shadow." The technique is more complicated of course, because the ring image is an emblem for eternity and the light image is a symbol, as the rest of the poem shows. Vaughan is quite capable of using the same symbol of light for eternity without definition: "They are all gone into the world of light!" And the result is a poem less strikingly Metaphysical.

The more emblematic poems of Donne and Herbert commonly set forth an image in the title and go on to define it in varying degrees of explicit connection, much after the manner of Herbert's "Prayer (1)" when most explicit, much more like the compass image in "A Valediction forbidding mourning" when less so. In poems like "The Blossome" and "The Primrose" Donne assumes the definition—that the heart is a blossom, for example—and proceeds to work out the implications of the unspecified definition. In "The Blossome" he begins, "Little think'st thou, poore flower," continuing to speak through the first stanza as if only with a blossom as subject but with enough conventional *sic vita* overtones to suggest that more is meant. The suggestions become very nearly explicit at the beginning of the second stanza, "Little think'st thou poore heart," with the rigorous rhetorical and even rhyme associations (cf. ll. 5 and 13, "bough . . . bow") to define implicitly the heart as the blossom. Thereafter Donne addresses the fated flower-heart, leaving the title to carry the force of the emblem. In "The Primrose," the emblematic image is worked out with greater detail and the use of definition is more thoroughgoing. Each assists in keeping the other in business, as the last stanza shows:

> Live Primrose then, and thrive
> With thy true number, five;

And women, whom this flower doth represent,
With this mysterious number be content;
Ten is the farthest number; if halfe ten
    Belonge unto each woman, then
    Each woman may take halfe us men,
Or if this will not serve their turne, Since all
Numbers are odde, or even, and they fall
First into this five, women may take us all.

From the identification of women in the flower emblem, Donne proceeds to the number of its petals and a complicated series of numerological definitions.

More truly and more frequently emblematic in his poetry, Herbert often works by positing in his title that which must be defined, more closely than does Donne, in the body of the poem. In a sense such shaped poems as "The Altar" and "Easter-wings" define the meanings of their titles partly by shape as well as by words, but the emblematic technique is more subtle and satisfying in such less formally emblematic works as "The Pulley" and "The Collar." Like the Jordan poems in their obscure way, "The Pulley" defines the image and idea of the title by working out a lyric narrative which in its totality defines the concept of the title, although without using (as Donne does) images which themselves explicitly define the title concept. God's creation of man, or such images as that of the glass of His blessings, or even the crucial concept of rest, have no overt defining connection whatsoever with the emblematic title:

    When God at first made man,
Having a glasse of blessings standing by;
Let us (said he) poure on him all we can:
Let the worlds riches, which dispersed lie,
    Contract into a span.

    So strength first made a way;
Then beautie flow'd, then wisdome, honour, pleasure:
When almost all was out, God made a stay,
Perceiving that alone of all his treasure
    Reste in the bottome lay.   (1–10)

It is the fourth stanza that shows how such varied ideas and images define the pulley emblem. God is speaking:

> Yet let him keep the rest,
> But keep them with repining restlessnesse:
> Let him be rich and wearie, that at least,
> If goodnesse leade him not, yet wearinesse
> May tosse him to my breast.   (16–20)

As is proper in an emblematic poem, only its totality defines the significance of the emblem, or "hieroglyph," which is in this case of course an image or concept expressed in the title rather than in a picture such as was favored by Francis Quarles. A somewhat comparable pulley emblem can be found in Quarles's *Emblemes*, Bk. I, emblem iv, but there is this difference in technique. Whereas Quarles anl other emblem writers usually "read" or define the significance of each detail in the picture, Herbert chooses to define a single concept— "The Pulley"—by talking of nothing that has to do with pulleys. In one sense his is a species of witty yoking exceeding Donne's conceits in "violence." Moreover, what is true of the single emblematic poem in *The Temple* is true of the whole collection. As Louis L. Martz has shown in *The Poetry of Meditation*, the separate poems of *The Temple* are so ordered as to be integrated into a sequence based upon worship: the separate poems constitute in part a definition of the title of the collection. "The Collar" is as it were midway between the technique of "The Pulley" or of *The Temple* as a whole and the technique of Donne's emblematic poems, in that while keeping the whole poem as the proper definition of the emblematic title, Herbert uses as well a number of images conveying, however ironically, the sense of restraint implied by the title. The images of "lines" (l. 4), of "cage" (l. 21), or "rope of sands" (l. 22), of "Good cable" (l. 24), and of "tie up" (l. 29) which the speaker rejects in his rebellion are not precisely like Donne's sub-images in being subordinate features of the defining image but rather parallel imagistic equivalents for the collar of the title. Herbert is more given to the emblematic, Donne to the dialectical.

Although the origins and specific poetic features of Metaphysical dialectic will be discussed subsequently, something by way of introductory description is necessary here. Dialectic is a form of logical argument. In the sixteenth and seventeenth centuries there was a strong tendency in Protestant countries to accept the conflation of logic and rhetoric into dialectic that had been advocated by Peter Ramus (i.e., Pierre de La Ramée). Since poetry is not a species of either philosophy or oratory but its own species, it necessarily used logic and rhetoric to its own purposes, that is, more rigorously and purely as poetry, less rigorously and purely as logic or rhetoric. But men trained in the tradition of Quintilian and Aquinas or excited by Ramist dialectic were well able to use these arts in a speech like Hamlet's "To be, or not to be" soliloquy or in Antony's praise of Caesar in *Julius Caesar*. What is remarkable about Metaphysical poetry is that it brought to lyric poetry a dialectic that had been known before only in the more extended forms and, lyric poetry being what it is, that it used the dialectic in ways at once psychological and epistemological. In Metaphysical poetry, dialectic means most characteristically a motion of ideas toward determined ends in such a way that an air of logic is maintained in order to persuade. It can be seen that poetic dialectic is likely to be a logical or rhetorical process drawing upon definitions, analogies, similitudes, arguments, and "proofs." When definitions (or other logical resources) are employed—not singly or even in isolated and therefore static parallels—but in sequence and therefore in kinetic fashion, then we have the dialectic of Metaphysical poetry. It is this motion, this dialectical ordering and liveliness in the whole, that distinguishes the *use* of Metaphysical definitions from Petrarchan. We can readily grasp the process by looking at Donne's poem, "The Flea," and by somewhat simplifying its definitions for the sake of clarity:

> Marke but this flea, and marke in this,
> How little that which thou deny'st me is;
> It suck'd me first, and now sucks thee,
> And in this flea, our two bloods mingled bee;
> Thou know'st that this cannot be said
> A sinne, nor shame, nor losse of maidenhead,
>   Yet this enjoyes before it wooe,
>   And pamper'd swells with one blood made of two,
>   And this, alas, is more than wee would doe.

(A. *Negative Definition*. The Flea's enjoyment before wooing proves that our enjoyment before wooing would not be: sin, shame, or loss of virginity.)

> Oh stay, three lives in one flea spare,
> Where wee almost, yea more than maryed are.
> This flea is you and I, and this
> Our mariage bed, and mariage temple is;
> Though parents grudge, and you, w'are met,
> And cloysterd in these living walls of Jet.
>   Though use make thee apt to kill mee,

> Let not to that, selfe murder added bee,
> And sacrilege, three sinnes in killing three.

(B. 1. *Positive Definition*. The Flea is: You, I, our marriage bed, and
marriage temple.
   2. *Definition Necessarily Following*. Given B. 1., to kill the Flea
   is to commit: suicide, murder, and sacrilege.)

> Cruell and sodaine, hast thou since
> Purpled thy naile, in blood of innocence?
> Wherein could this flea guilty bee,
> Except in that drop which it suckt from thee?
> Yet thou triumph'st, and saist that thou
> Find'st not thy selfe, nor mee the weaker now;
>   'Tis true, then learne how false, feares bee;
>   Just so much honor, when thou yeeld'st to mee,
>   Will wast, as this flea's death tooke life from thee.

(C. 1. *Concession of Faultiness of B. 2. to prove. A.* You disprove B. 2.
by killing the Flea, showing that to kill it is not to destroy ourselves, etc.
   2. Exactly. Therefore our enjoyment before wooing (A.) is no loss
of honor.)

Donne's dialectic is complicated and amusing in equal proportions.
But his is not the only version. Herbert's "Jordan (1)" offers another
version of the dialectical process. Its three stanzas are tissues of definitions, but those are so obvious as not to need specification. Unlike
Donne's, they have an appositive, static, repeated quality, and the
actual logical movement (as the summary arguments supply) is much
less paradoxical:

> Who sayes that fictions onely and false hair
> Become a verse? Is there in truth no beautie?
> Is all good structure in a winding stair?
> May no lines passe, except they do their dutie
>   Not to a true, but painted chair?

(A. *Interrogative Definition 1.* Is poetry something served only by
falsehood, deviousness, and pretense?)

Is it no verse, except enchanted groves
And sudden arbours shadow course-spunne lines?
Must purling streams refresh a lovers loves?
Must all be vail'd, while he that reades, divines,
    Catching the sense at two removes?

(B. *Interrogative Definition* 2. Is verse (a) only romantic gilding of trivial and ill-treated subjects; or is it (b) something obscure in obliqueness?)

Shepherds are honest people; let them sing:
Riddle who list, for me, and pull for Prime:
I envie no mans nightingale or spring;
Nor let them punish me with losse of rime,
    Who plainly say, *My God, My King.*

(C. 1. *Declared Definition.* Simple poets (like me) are honest.
2. *Concessive Definition.* I will allow fancy poets to be poets.
3. *Conclusive Definition.* But I am equally or more wholly a poet for speaking simple truth in simple ways.)

Such abstraction of the arguments of Donne's and Herbert's poems cannot substitute for the total poetic effect, but study of the dialectic suggests something of the skeleton, if not the fair flesh, of Metaphysical poetry. And an examination of the difference between Donne's degree of paradox and air of proof and Herbert's laying down of axioms suggests much of the difference between the two poets.

The dialectical usage of definition can be followed in poem after poem. A few less minutely pursued examples will serve to show some alternative versions of the technique. Donne's "Autumnall," on middle-aged beauty (often thought that of a patroness, Magdalene Herbert), follows a very sinuous, even tortuous, dialectical line, sometimes employing a definition as proof of a dialectical process involving subsidiary definitions. That is the nature of the case in the following passage, coming after praise of middle-aged, autumnal beauty:

But name not *Winter-faces*, whose skin's slacke;
    Lanke, as an unthrifts purse; but a soules sacke;
Whose *Eyes* seeke light within, for all here's shade;
    Whose mouthes are holes, rather worne out, then made;
Whose every tooth to'a severall place is gone,
    To vexe their soules at *Resurrection;*

> Name not these living *Deaths-heads* unto mee,
> For these, not *Ancient,* but *Antique be.* (37–44)

To the extent that wit involves the ingenious (as the Latin sense of
that word may be taken to suggest), it is commonly found in Donne
to be based on such logical hair-splitting, which is precisely a chop-
logic over definition and an arguing (that is, rhetoric) presented as
a reasoning process (that is, logic): a dialectic.

"Aire and Angels" provides a more serious example. Its dialectical
distinctions are inherent in the definitions proffered by the first stanza,
as a few lines show:

> Still when, to where thou wert, I came,
> Some lovely glorious nothing I did see,
> But since, my soule, whose child love is,
> Takes limmes of flesh, and else could nothing doe,
> More subtile then the parent is,
> Love must not be, but take a body too. (5–10)

Both the use of definition and the dialectical motion are evident, but
there is a larger dialectical process in the whole poem which becomes
clear in the definitions of the last eight lines:

> For, nor in nothing, nor in things
> Extreme, and scattring bright, can love inhere;
> Then as an Angell, face, and wings
> Of aire, not pure as it, yet pure doth weare,
> So thy love may be my loves spheare;
> Just such disparitie
> As is twixt Aire and Angells puritie,
> 'Twixt womens love, and mens will ever bee. (21–28)

Although there has been debate over the conclusion, the common interpretation that "womens love" is defined as the "lovely glorious nothing"
of "Aire" and of "mens" as the greater "Angells puritie" seems accurate.
An initial recondite distinction between two things highly similar but
different is employed to make the poem's slight but meaningful distinction between the loves of which the two sexes are capable. The
poem marches through subordinate definitions to the climactic definitions of its last three lines.

Since Crashaw was given as an example of Metaphysical addiction
to definition at its worst, it must in fairness be shown that he also

uses it at its moving best. In his hymn, "In the Holy Nativity of Our Lord God" (that very unusual though not unique thing, a Metaphysical pastoral), Tityrus and Thyrsis seek to set forth the nature of one of the mysteries of the Church, the Incarnation, stressing the Nativity, as is usual with Catholic poets. The two shepherds disagree about the fitting circumstances for the great mystery, Tityrus arguing that decorum calls for a contention among the world's powers to render the birth glorious. Thyrsis replies that such rivalry is wide of the mark, defining God's love as expressed in the Incarnation in various images and coming to a final climax identifying love as itself.

> Proud world, said I; cease your contest
> And let the MIGHTY BABE alone.
> The Phaenix builds the Phaenix' nest.
> Love's architecture is his own.   (44–47)

There are few more beautiful, more sublime lines in Metaphysical poetry than the last. Its logic is akin to that of Herbert's "Prayer (1)," which concludes, after all, that prayer is "something understood." Ultimately, human power must fail in its attempt to define mysteries and can only affirm that Love's architecture is—its own.

Marvell's "Definition of Love," which acknowledges the technique in its title, does not employ definition extensively in the simple sense of positing a meaning for love. Rather, like Donne in some poems, he chooses to develop a dialectical treatment of conceits and, like Herbert, he uses the whole poem as a means, although without an emblematic approach, to convey what the title promises. He begins by defining in terms of the rhetorical "places" of origin and ancestry:

> My Love is of a birth as rare
> As 'tis for object strange and high:
> It was begotten by despair
> Upon Impossibility.

He goes on (ll. 9–16) to speak of the fatedness of his love and to explain (ll. 17–28) that fatality in astronomical, cartographical, and geometrical conceits, gradually becoming more explicit in his use of definition:

> As Lines so Loves *oblique* may well
> Themselves in every Angle greet:

But ours so truly Paralel,
Though infinite can never meet.   (25–28)

The role of definition in the violent yoking together of the Meta-physical conceit emerges very clearly in those lines, and the last stanza gives us the formal definition promised by the title:

Therefore the Love which us doth bind,
But Fate so enviously debarrs,
Is the Conjunction of the Mind,
And Opposition of the Stars.

What requires emphasis is the fact that the element of logic and rhetoric—of wit—is something larger than the last stanza. It is found in details of conceits, and it is subsumed by the dialectical movement of the whole poem. Marvell's central aim is to define love, this love, as one by birth or origin fated to perfection and frustration. The origin, the wondrous perfection, and the frustration alike are sometimes con-veyed by defining images and sometimes by means not in themselves involving definition. To speak of Marvell's definition is, therefore, to speak of detail, of conclusion, and of a central conception worked out in dialectic. Both superficially and profoundly it rules the poem, and there is real significance in the fact that "The Definition of Love" has seemed to most readers Marvell's most Metaphysical poem because, for all its other important elements, it exemplifies in simple and com-plex ways the tendency to definition and dialectic in Metaphysical poetry from Donne forward.

The tendency expresses itself in various forms, revealing certain larger characteristics of this branch of seventeenth-century poetry. For one thing, the secular poems usually employ more startling definitions than do the religious. It is noteworthy that Dryden thought Donne affected the metaphysics too much in love poetry, and that Dr. John-son's examples of Metaphysical passages are exclusively taken from secular poems.[7] Occasionally among the best poets, and usually in Crashaw, one may find exceptions, but religious subjects normally restrained ingenuity. They imposed a kind of decorum upon those witty poets. This tendency is only a tendency, but it finds its characteristic expression in Herbert, as his quietly beautiful "Vertue" shows. In it there is a sequence of definitions—of a sweet day, a sweet rose, a sweet spring, and a sweet and virtuous soul. The dialectic involves a double process. On the one hand it argues that sweet days plus sweet roses

equal (as it were) sweet spring, though virtue must be added to make
a truly sweet soul. On the other hand it argues that the sweet day,
sweet rose, and sweet spring are mortal, but that the sweet (definition:
virtuous) soul lives chiefly when all else dies. The addition of virtue is,
as the title suggests, the crucial and unifying element for the two
arguments. Herbert's own sweetness or gentleness of manner is such
that the dialectical processes are more readily felt than described:

> Sweet day, so cool, so calm, so bright,
> The bridall of the earth and skie:
> The dew shall weep thy fall to night;
>   For thou must die.

> Sweet rose, whose hue angrie and brave
> Bids the rash gazer wipe his eye:
> Thy root is ever in its grave,
>   And thou must die.

> Sweet spring, full of sweet dayes and roses,
> A box where sweets compacted lie;
> My musick shows ye have your closes,
>   And all must die.

> Onely a sweet and vertuous soul,
> Like season'd timber, never gives;
> But though the whole world turn to coal,
>   Then chiefly lives.

To say that there was less ingenuity in the religious poetry is not to
say that there was little, and to say that because the process of definition in the religious poetry brought together less disparate things
is not to say that it therefore altogether lacked a violence in yoking
together. The identification of religious ardor with sexual ecstasy or
violence in Crashaw and Donne is ample reminder. Yet even such
identifications are mellowed by tradition, and it will usually be found
that the yokings in religious verse have the sanction of tradition in one
form or another.

If we take Donne at his most sublime, we can see this to be the
case: "What if this present were the worlds last night?" The logic is
that of hypothesis or question but the process is that of definition, and
a thrilling one to anyone with the slightest eschatological interest. Yet
the idea is itself familiar, and the beginning of a poem with such an

equation of times is part of the meditational procedure of "composition of place," as Louis L. Martz has shown.[8] Other seemingly extreme yokings possess the sanction of the emblematic tradition, as Herbert's "Pulley" and "Collar" show. The secular poems, chiefly on love, had a freer decorum permitting such witty excursions as Donne's "Flea" and, perhaps more importantly, allowing poets to introduce into private experiences a full panoply of learning and "universal" experience. Death, the constitution of the universe, eternity, and religious mysteries were but a few of these larger subjects absorbed into the personal and secular. Such definition of the limited private experience in terms, so to speak, of unlimited public universals is in fact a chief resource of Metaphysical poetry.

Another important feature of definition in Metaphysical poetry is, as has been observed, its tendency to become dialectic. That is probably what Dryden meant by saying that Donne affected the metaphysics and Dr. Johnson by his term "scholastick." Some modern critics, notably J. B. Leishman, have chosen "dialectic" partly because they think it more accurate than "Metaphysical" as a label for the "Donne tradition," and partly because the alternative term, rhetoric, has had a mixed critical reception in our day. More fundamentally, critics have traditionally recognized that logical process and intellection prior to feeling are characteristics of the poetry. (Critics of the past few decades are exceptional in thinking that the thought and feeling are simultaneous.) What makes this so seems to be the fact that the normative definition in Metaphysical poetry is witty—it is slightly askew, oblique; it is usually after but not in the manner of strict definition. With his usual penetration, and not infrequent prejudice, Dr. Johnson got at the matter in relation to metaphor: "The fault of Cowley, and perhaps of all the writers of the metaphysical race, is that of pursuing thoughts to their last ramifications. . . . Thus all the power of description is destroyed by a scrupulous enumeration; and the force of metaphors is lost when the mind by the mention of particulars is turned more upon the original than the second sense, more upon that from which the illustration is drawn than that to which it is applied."[9]

In modern terms, the Metaphysical poets were more interested in the vehicles than in the tenors of their metaphors. What is especially acute in the judgment is its perception that the two elements of metaphor are held at once apart and together, with a pursuit of "thoughts to their last ramifications" often emerging from the tension. Or, in the terms of ideas as well as metaphor, definition often becomes dialectic because of the poets' exploration of the gap between that which is defined and that which defines it, with most attention being given to the latter. Basically, the identification resides in a conceit which, as its seventeenth-century meaning implies, is not necessarily imagistic.[10] But it does define one element in terms of another which is different, often seemingly opposed. Sometimes the poet takes the defined elements in the conceit (whether imagistic or not) no further and simply passes on to another. But often a dialectical development follows, and it is convenient to distinguish two kinds of dialectic: extension and development. The extended definition is most familiar in the extended imagistic conceit, and that in Donne's compass image for parted lovers in "A Valediction forbidding mourning." Here, truly, the process is the pursuit Dr. Johnson recognized, to the last ramifications. Dialectical development, on the other hand, has the air of logical argument, of demonstration, of proof, either that the definition or other logical process is true or that some conclusion inevitably follows, or commonly both. Most of "Aire and Angels" functions to develop in "scholastick" terms the definitions of "womens love" with air and "mens" love with angels. Poems like *The Extasie*, "The Definition of Love," or "To his Coy Mistress" are far more complex in marshalling a highly involved dialectic with subordinate definitions towards a final proof. The ingenuity, or wit, is often prodigious, whether in the unextended definition, or the extended, or in the sustained dialectic, explaining why Dryden might term Donne "the greatest Wit, though not the best Poet of our Nation." The presence of such complexity is not open to dispute, however it be evaluated, so that its norms of working should claim our attention.

The norms can perhaps best be understood in terms of a further general observation on the characteristic processes of definition in Metaphysical poetry. In any event, it is convenient to distinguish between a procedure of assimilation of disparate elements in explicit or implicit definition—given the faculty psychology of the day, this is wit of fancy or imagination. There is also a discrimination of either similar or opposed elements—a wit of judgment or reason.[11] Assimilation, or "Fancy" wit, is an easily recognized procedure. The definition of lovers as saints in "The Canonization," of women's love with air or men's with angels in "Aire and Angels," or of many parallel images for "the merrie world" in Herbert's poem "The Quip" or in Vaughan's "The World" come at once to mind. But equally important in these very poems is a process of discrimination, of "Judgment" wit, since a definition must distinguish what something is not as well as what it is, and it often distinguishes between things apparently alike. Herbert and Vaughan distinguish the sinful world from sinless eternity or the resolved religious soul from created pleasure. The distinctions of "Aire and Angels" have already been sufficiently emphasized. "The Canonization" distinguishes between the love of the saints and the corrupt world of what Donne elsewhere calls (in a similar distinction) the laity, as also between the love of the saints in their golden age and that of lovers in inferior subsequent ages when invocation of those saints will be necessary. Marvell's "Definition of Love" and Donne's *Extasie* maintain a most difficult balance of assimilation and discrimination involving kinds of love or, in Donne's case, of bodies and souls, to the point of considerable disagreement among the poem's interpreters.

For wit, as for other central features of Metaphysical poetry, Donne is the Grand Master of the race. He is the most often witty, and the most often profoundly witty. His poems most often depend upon wit for their impact, and they employ it most complexly. If I may summarize in the terms of this chapter, it is he who most forcefully uses definition and dialectic, the wit of Fancy and the wit of Judgment. Various as he is, however, his varieties are not infinite, and he did not preempt all the possibilities, as Marvell alone shows. Moreover, certain patterns are discernible in the wit of all the Metaphysical poets. Most of the witty definitions are examples of Fancy wit, of finding resemblances in ideas or things which are dissimilar or even quite different. Most examples of dialectic, on the other hand, are those using Judgment wit. Commonly the two processes are combined, definition to provide the initial surprise and shock of wit, dialectic to provide the witty structure or development of the poem. In *The Comparison*, we are astonished to find a lover defining his mistress in terms of her sweat, however sweet, and his acquaintance's mistress in terms of her sweat, however rank and frothy. But the poem is worked out by discriminations of the Judgment (i.e., reason) in differentiating between things apparently like: two sweaty mistresses. Similarly in "Aire and Angels," if we accept the usual reading, women and their love are defined as air, men and their love as angels. But the dialectic discriminates between these two insubstantial substances. Donne uses this combination frequently, and it is one on which much of his best wit depends. Sometimes, however, he and the other poets will use wit of Judgment briefly, locally, and wit of Fancy for extension. Negative definitions, such as we have seen in "The Flea" or in "Jordon (1)" show how skillfully the discriminations of Judgment might contribute to basic distinctions of poetic wit. As a counterpart, the extended conceit is a sustained flight of Fancy wit in "pursuing thoughts to their last ramifications," as Dr. Johnson put it. Donne's compass image, Herbert's "Prayer (1)"—and, as the last chapter of this book will show, preeminently Herbert's longish poem, *The Flower*—sustain the central conceit to great lengths.

I am aware that this discussion has left, and no doubt too far behind, the logic and rhetoric learned by Donne and the other poets in their schools. Not Aristotle, nor Quintilian, nor Aquinas—not even Ramus—reduced the arts to such simplicities. In both the art of the closed fist of logic and that of the open hand of rhetoric there was so much more detailed concern and conceptualization. Figures and schemes, colors and figures, syllogisms and enthymemes played roles incomparably more complex and specific than those I have assigned to definition and dialectic. It is possible that close application of the famous dichotomies and hierarchies of Peter Ramus would gloss poems like "Aire and Angels" in minute detail. But, equally, I doubt the meaningfulness of such glossing to readers in this century. The important thing is rather to understand the principle: the poets used the arts of logic and rhetoric as poets had not used them before, to witty ends; but they also used them as the logicians and rhetoricians did not, namely as poets. As Dryden said of Donne, these poets "affect the Metaphysicks"; they seize the principles, sometimes the techniques, and usually the air of logic and rhetoric for their properly poetic ends. What is witty about such ends is, in Dr. Johnson's term, "violence," or surprise, brillance, and a rigor of thought unusual in lyric poetry. When Donne, for example, fancifully defines a as b, we are surprised and pleased. When he also fancifully defines c as d we are further astonished and pleased. And then, when a and c, and also b and d, turn out to be so like that the Judgment is required dialectically to distinguish and argue the differences in the terms of each pair, we are yet further astonished and pleased. That is the process and the effect of "Aire and Angels." Herbert's approach in "Prayer (1)" is different, but it too can be represented as it were algebraically. Prayer turns out to be defined as a and a^1 and a^2 and a^3 and a^4—and so on in a breathtaking sequence. I am not offering algebra (certainly not my algebra!) as a substitute for logic and rhetoric, much less for poetry. But I am certain that both the sudden and sometimes sustained identifications of what had seemed different and the brilliant discriminations or developments of what had seemed alike or simple provide the processes of Metaphysical poetry that may most readily explain to us today the nature of Metaphysical wit. Some poems possess little of these techniques, but they will also be found to possess little wit and are usually those which cause the most embarrassment to anyone seeking to define Metaphysical poetry. Donne's "Song"—"Sweetest love, I do not goe"—is an example. Of such a poem one can only say that it lacks some features we commonly associate with Metaphysical poetry, but that it retains others (e.g., the private mode, drama). The exceptions in Donne's case are partial, in another poet like Cowley so important as to lead us to say that the degree justifies our placing the poem in another line. The best Metaphysical poems, however, and those which therefore we like to think as characteristic of the race, vary in their wit without becoming less witty in their essences. Sometimes the approach is simple, as in Herbert's "Prayer (1)," and sometimes it is mixed and very complex, as in Donne's "A Valediction forbidding mourning." The example of Traherne is probably sufficient to show that if it was not necessary for a poem to be witty to be Metaphysical, it was necessary to be witty to be a great Metaphysical poet.

Such generalizations imply that definition and dialectic in their various forms are so important to Metaphysical poetry that they must have grown from real experience and from familiar ways of thought. The lack of real experience or any felt necessity to think in dialectical terms vitiates the Metaphysical poems of even such talented men as Cleveland and Cowley. Donne is another matter, and for him there is relatively abundant information early and late. A few sentences from "A Defence of Womens Inconstancy" in *Paradoxes and Problemes* will suffice to show that ingenious definition is as much a part of his prose thinking as his poetic:

> *Inconstancy* is a most commendable and cleanly quality . . .

> For as *Philosophy* teacheth us, that *Light things do always tend upwards,* and *heavy things decline downward;* Experience teacheth us otherwise, that the disposition of a *Light* Woman, is to fall down, the nature of women being contrary to all Art and Nature.

> To conclude therefore; this name of *Inconstancy,* which hath so much been poysoned with slanders, ought to be changed into *variety,* for the which the world is so delightfull, *and a Woman for that the most delightfull thing in the World.*[12]

The second quotation shows in addition that Donne imbibed the importance of definition, as well as many definitions themselves, from "Philosophy," as he and Dryden put it, from Dr. Johnson's "Scholastick" tradition, chiefly of Aristotle and accretions upon his method. As Donne himself says by way of justifying his numerous citations in that definition-riddled work, *Biathanatos*, "I did it the rather because scholastique and artificiall men use this way of instructing." [13] The definitions of ends, causes, and the rest, like the logical dialectic supporting them, were part of men's training in the old philosophy. And if at some moments the new philosophy seemed to call all in doubt for Donne, it was perhaps as much because of the alteration from familiar modes of thinking as because of a change in particulars of thought.

A related origin in Donne's background is the dialectic of logic and rhetoric, which had been clearly distinguished in antiquity and the middle ages but which were often confused in the Renaissance.[14] Certainly they tend to merge and even to become something other than themselves when they are made into a poetic argument or, as Leishman rightly put it, into dialectic. Once these necessary things are said, it remains true that Donne was aware that he had learned his ways of expression out of the books of the rhetoricians and logicians. In "An Essay on Valour" he says: "indeed it is cunning Rhetoricke to perswade the hearers that they are that already, which he would have them to be." [15] In its context the passage is itself "cunning Rhetoricke," and its witty awareness of definition is explicitly related to rhetoric. Donne had not been at Hart Hall and Lincoln's Inn to no purpose. If the expressive forms of logic and rhetoric, their rules and distinctions, seem sterile and overwrought today, they were absorbed as a system and made an integral part of the traditional ideas which their traditional modes expressed. In no area is this as true as in religion, and it is probably the logical and rhetorical procedures of theological writing that affected Donne most deeply. When Dr. Johnson spoke of the "scholastick" element in Donne, he was no doubt thinking generally of the Aristotelian methods of Aquinas and his followers, in which "Philosophy," dialectic, and doctrine are equally involved. The "Questions" of Aquinas and the "Problemes" of Donne are far apart in time and tone, but their methods are very like.

The problem of definition and of meaning, both in particular words and in modes, was of course peculiarly acute in the post-Reformation period. The Bible required interpretation, whether by Church, bishop, or inner light. Controversies over modes of meaning and over the definition of crucial words and phrases occupied the best minds of the day to a far greater extent than did the problems of science. To Donne, born a Catholic in a Protestant country of rival Establishment and reform factions, the crisis of conscience was in no small measure a question of defining religion aright, as a few quotations from *Satyre III* reveal:

Is not our Mistress[,] faire Religion . . .   (5)

Seeke true religion. O Where?   (43)
                    doubt wisely; in strange way
To stand inquiring right, is not to stray.   (77–78)

That thou mayest rightly'obey power, her bounds know;
Those past, her nature, 'and name is chang'd; to be
Then humble to her is idolatrie.   (100–102)

Defining religion aright itself involves definition, as the last two quotations make especially clear, because religion in its civil "power" must
be distinguished in its proper degree, beyond which submission to the
civil powers of religion is, as Donne defines it, "idolatrie." The tendencies raised by the general religious problem were enforced by the
religious genre most familiar to an Englishman: the sermon. Exposition of the text by definitions and paraphrase was not new, but it
became more crucial—as Donne's own sermons were to show—in an age
of conflicting religious systems and of crises of conscience in the
necessity of choice between them. If "Philosophy" and "Rhetoricke"
helped form the dialectical character of a good deal of Donne's poetry,
religion made it natural and inevitable.

In addition to these nonliterary sources of ways of thought and expression, earlier Renaissance poetry was greatly influential upon the
Metaphysical. Donne's poetry is often said to be anti-Petrarchan, which
is true enough, although it is commonly not realized how different his
anti-Petrarchan stance is from an un-Petrarchan, as the love poetry of,
say, Prior would show. The poetry that developed in England out of
the Petrarchanisms of Wyatt and Surrey is the trunk from which
Donne's fruitful and unusual branch grows. The similarity of the offshoot
to the parent is so marked that the task is not so much to show that
the two shared conceits, definitions, or conventions as to discriminate
between them.[16] Wyatt's familiar sonnet, "The lover compareth his
state to a ship in perilous storm tossed on the sea," is an extension of
parallel marine conceits for the lover's tortured state. The conceits are,
in fact, a series of definitions, with related psychological phenomena
being given definition by related marine phenomena—"And every oar
a thought in readiness," for example.

The resemblance between Petrarchan and Metaphysical poetry in
this respect is clear, but there are three important differences. To begin

with, definition is more characteristic of the later poets because it is more frequent and because it is a norm (as are also such other features as use of the private mode) in their kind of poetry. More importantly, Metaphysical definitions usually employ a dialectic relating and directing definitions and other logical features to a rhetorical end and a greater continued violence in their yoking of elements. This is true not so much because the yoked ideas of the Metaphysicals are more heterogeneous but because, as Dr. Johnson observed in his way, the Metaphysicals pursued the vehicle of the metaphor at the seeming expense of the tenor—what was defined commonly seemed to be lost sight of in the pleasure of defining:

> Call us what you will, wee'are made such by love;
>   Call her one, mee another flye,
> We'are Tapers too, and at our owne cost die,
>   And wee in us finde the'Eagle and the dove;
>   The Phoenix ridle hath more wit
>   By us, we two being one, are it.

In this famous and much analyzed passage (ll. 19–24) of "The Canonization," Donne comes close to the parallel development of conceit found in Wyatt and other earlier writers. It would be hard to say that his insects or birds are much more violently yoked to their ideas than Wyatt's marine images are to theirs. The significant difference is that the vehicles of Donne's images lead him on, both for their own sake and for a dialectic, and that in his usual way he begins with an imperative (sometimes an interrogative) version of definition and only ends with a declarative.

The third difference grows from the second.[17] Metaphysical definitions have more movement. Those of the Petrarchans appear to have been worked out in advance or to be static for such other reasons as that their conventional nature stirs little energy. The Metaphysical process possesses more movement because of the rapidity with which differing conceits are introduced, or because of the dialectical development of related images, or both. The earlier style lasted on, retaining its workability and beauty, as the last stanza of "Her Triumph" in Jonson's *Celebration of Charis* shows:

> Have you seene but a bright Lillie grow,
>   Before rude hands have touch'd it?
> Ha'you mark'd but the fall o'the snow

Before the soyle hath smutch'd it?
Ha'you felt the wooll o'the Bever?
Or Swans Downe ever?
Or have smelt o'the bud o'the Brier?
Or the Nard in the fire?
Or have tasted the bag of the Bee?
O so white! O so soft! O so sweet is she!

The movement towards the concluding definitions has something of the quality of Metaphysical dialectic, but the vigorous syntactic and verbal parallelisms of every other line are essentially static in effect. Moreover, as Dr. Johnson would have put it, the definitions stress the importance of the secondary sense more than the original (as in that "bag of the Bee"), emphasizing the tenor more than the vehicle, which is for the most part of a more acceptably "poetic" kind. Yet the area of Jonson's choice of imagery resembles Donne's in the passage quoted from "The Canonization." It is the handling that differs. The explanation of literary and other causes that might account for such differences in handling is very difficult to discern in the last decade of the sixteenth century, when there was such a remarkable swelling of poetic achievement in numerous styles and when the circulation of manuscripts or of tides of influence is most difficult to distinguish. About all that can be said is that in their differing ways Shakespeare and Sidney in their sonnets, like Ralegh, Fulke Greville, and Donne in other lyric forms, brought, at about the same time, a greater intellectuality into poetry and that Donne carried the development furthest in terms of wit and witty handling of imagery. Sidney, Fulke Greville, and Ralegh make use of greater intellectual reasoning than earlier poets, and without recourse to definitions that are at once clear and striking in their pursuit of the vehicles. They lack Donne's commitment to Dr. Johnson's secondary sense. Shakespeare must be distinguished on other grounds. He often uses definitions, most strikingly perhaps in Sonnet 129: "Th' expense of spirit in a waste of shame / Is lust in action. . . ." What differentiates such definitions from Donne's is simply what Dr. Johnson would term their naturalness and justice. The primary and secondary senses are at one with each other and the experience created. In the terms introduced earlier, his definitions assimilate, but their terms are elements very like, or made to seem very like; and within a given pattern of definition, as in Sonnet 129, the discrimination is intellectual and moral rather than radically witty. The fact that Shakespeare does not strike us as an essentially witty writer suggests in part that his use of definition, striking images, and a dialectic of ideas has a naturalness, a justice in the yoking that sets him off from the Metaphysical poets.

The balance, the sanity, and the justice of Shakespeare's use of words and ideas assist, however, in the major literary miracle of the language, and it will not do merely to compare the Metaphysical poets unfavorably to him. To do so would be merely to repeat T. S. Eliot's mistake in a new guise by attributing a dissociation of sensibility to Donne instead of to Milton and Dryden, as Eliot did, in a projection of his own post-eighteenth-century difficulties in ordering his world. It may well be true, as Dr. Johnson said, that the wit of the Metaphysical poets errs in some austere sense by overemphasis upon the primary sense of images, on the vehicle, rather than on the secondary sense, or tenor. By the same austere standard, poets from Dryden to Dr. Johnson himself increasingly err on the other side by emphasizing the secondary sense, the tenor, the tulipness rather than the streaks of the tulip. Each emphasis implies a conception of poetry, a type of intellectuality, and a special embodiment of feeling. In the best (which is not all) of Shakespeare and, I believe, in the best of such other authors as Chaucer and Dickens, a steadier balance is maintained. But the lack of balance of this kind is not in itself a sign of dissociation of sensibility or of an impairment of poetry. The wit of the Metaphysical poets may indeed explore, as Dr. Johnson had it, the primary sense of images to their last witty ramification. But it is an exploration to the end of understanding the secondary sense, of arriving at a view of life. Such themes will be touched on in the next chapter, but it may be said at once that the wit of a Donne is far from precluding feeling or a sense of wholeness of experience within his definition of his world.

The wit of Dryden sometimes (and the wit of Johnson nearly always) offers a counterpart to the wit of Donne by seeming to withhold the primary sense in favor of the secondary. *Absalom and Achitophel* steadily keeps the evaluative biblical story in view, but a man would be certifiably mad to think that it has no particular personal relevance to Dryden or to his time. Similarly, *The Vanity of Human Wishes* plays off the tenor, Johnson's age, and a suppressed vehicle or primary sense, Juvenal's Rome. Any careful reader of the two poems will see how far Dr. Johnson's somber, dignified, and Christian stoicism differs from the explosive, vehement anger of Juvenal. It is in some sense true, then, that such masters of their styles, such influential creators of visions of experience for their age as Donne and Dryden, are witty precisely for emphasis upon opposed literary features. But it is equally true that they are masters of their styles, and that their styles are significant, because the emphasis and the withholdings in each case are witty, not because what is suppressed is not there, but precisely because, being suppressed, it may be released with a more bounding energy.

The suppressive forces vary somewhat between Donne and Dryden and yet more between Donne and eighteenth-century poets. For Donne and the others of the Metaphysical race, that force is a wit embodying logical and rhetorical procedures in poetic adaptation. What is suppressed varies considerably, because the private world of the Metaphysicals differs so much from the public world of Dryden and of the Augustans. The wit is, after all, closely related to the worlds of experience created in their poetry, and Donne as well as Dryden outlined for two generations or more the worlds that they and their followers might explore. Their important followers are followers in the sense that they accept the essential terms of their wit and the means of conveying a view of life. And the followers are important in the sense that they modify the revealing wit and the revealed experience in ways undeniably their own. Cleveland is often so poor a Metaphysical poet precisely because his wit is unrevealing, because (in his Metaphysical poems) he has expressed chiefly language and images, and far less ideas or a view of life. No sensibility and no image in itself could make up for fact that his conception of life, in such poems, sometimes borders on the trivial.

There is sufficient evidence to show that Donne had his predecessors or, in any event, his contemporaries who were, like him, busy devising styles at variance from the received. In particular it may be recalled that Jonson and Donne have between them poems whose authorship has long been disputed. But to his contemporaries as well as to us, it was to Donne that might be attributed the role of fashioning an armory of techniques for private poetry that was to be useful for five or six decades and thereafter was to be employed at times by Dryden and even by Pope. The resemblances between Donne, Cowley, Jonson, and Dryden—in some of their poems—are ample reminder that concern with definition and dialectic has limits in assisting our understanding of the particular nature of Metaphysical poetry. But this concern, I hope, offers some advance over consideration of wit purely in terms of the imagistic conceit. The point is not that Metaphysical poetry is comprised of definition and dialectic any more than Tudor poetry consists of Petrarchanism or Restoration poetry of satire. All are merely features of some prominence among others. One may say with strict accuracy, however, that the poetry most commonly thought to be Metaphysical does use a dialectical process giving a motion to ideas, and in that motion resides the wit of the poetry. And it may be added, in both the historical and the descriptive senses, that it was Donne who gave definition to much of the poetry of the seventeenth century.

NOTES

[1] Carew, An Elegie upon . . . Dr. John Donne, l. 96. Dryden, epistle dedicatory to Eleonora, 3rd paragraph.

[2] Johnson, The Lives of the English Poets, ed. G. B. Hill, 3 vols. (London, 1905), I, 20.

[3] Dryden, Discourse Concerning Satire, The Poems of John Dryden, ed. James Kinsley, 4 vols. (Oxford, 1958), II, 604.

[4] Rosemund Tuve, Elizabethan and Metaphysical Imagery (Chicago, 1947). I have found two articles along similar lines very useful: Elizabeth Lewis Wiggins, "Logic in the Poetry of John Donne,," Studies in Philology, XLII (1945), 41–60; and Thomas O. Sloan, "The Rhetoric in the Poetry of John Donne," Studies in English Literature, III (1963), 31–44. The former is especially detailed and informative. It may be added that a recent book has, as it were, brought D. W. Robertson's Chaucerian views into Donne criticism; see John Donne: Conservative Revolutionary (Princeton, 1967), in which N. J. C. Andreasen argues that Elizabethan Christian morality must be taken to Donne's secular poems, so that there is a kind of comedy in which most of the lovers look idolatrous and foolish. My view is that criticism and literary history need a better balance between what can be discerned as views contemporary with the poet and as views relevant to the poem in terms of the experience of our own day.

[5] The most useful proponent of this view is William Empson: see "Donne and the Rhetorical Tradition," Kenyon Review, XI (1949), 571–87. One wishes that he had commented on the view of medieval Donne, as in John Hayward, ed., John Donne (London, 1929), p. xiii. Of yet another extreme view, Helen White commented in the right tone in The Metaphysical Poets (New York, 1936), p. 30: "So we find the strange vogue of John Donne as a 'modern,' an interpretation . . . that is likely to prove congenial enough at a time of confusion to last for some years more."

[6] I take the term from J. B. Leishman, The Monarch of Wit, 6th ed. (London, 1962). Since I have found Leishman the most congenial of Donne's critics, I must add that he preferred "dialectical" and that he doubted that "Metaphysical" had any utility.

[7] A good deal may still be gleaned from Dr. Johnson's Life of Cowley, as I hope to show a bit later in this chapter. I may say here that, as far as his examples go, Johnson's "Metaphysical race" consists of Cowley (twenty-seven passages in the section characterizing the "race"), Donne (sixteen), and Cleveland (two); that no divine poems are included; that Cowley's poems quoted are chiefly from The Mistress; and that Donne's are chiefly those that Grosart termed "verse-letters" and "funeral elegies," in which the Metaphysical styles do not show to best advantage.

[8] *The Poetry of Meditation* (New Haven, 1954), pp. 27 ff.

[9] *The Lives of the English Poets,* ed. G. B. Hill, 3 vols. (London, 1905), I, 45.

[10] For example, see the last line of Donne, "The triple Foole," "Who are a little wise, the best fooles bee." The twentieth-century bias for images has too often obscured the logical and rhetorical pleasures of writers as different as Donne, Dryden, and Pope. (See also Leishman, *The Monarch of Wit,* pp. 201–202.) There are few more thrilling lines in Donne than the unimagistic "Nothing else is" of "The Sunne Rising."

[11] My distinction between wit of Fancy and wit of Judgment is not, as far as I know, one made before the middle of the seventeenth century. In *Leviathan,* I, viii (1651), Hobbes remarks under the head of intellectual virtues and, in particular, wit, that "In a good poem, . . . both judgment and fancy are required." The year before, in his *Answer* to Davenant, Hobbes had remarked more specifically that "Judgment begets the strength and structure, and Fancy begets the ornaments of a poem" (*Critical Essays of the Seventeenth Century,* ed. J. E. Spingarn, 3 vols. [Bloomington, 1963], II, 59). In the account prefixed to *Annus Mirabilis* (1667), Dryden gives a more complex discussion of the relation of the faculties of the mind to literary composition.

[12] John Hayward, ed., *John Donne . . . Complete Poetry and Selected Prose,* 4th impression (London, 1946), pp. 336, and 337.

[13] Hayward, ed., pp. 424–25.

[14] See Wilbur Samuel Howell, *Logic and Rhetoric in England, 1500–1700* (Princeton, 1956), especially Chaps. IV and V. In spite of his frequent dichotomies and his striking use of "invention," Donne seems to me to exhibit not Ramist but traditional thought, modified no doubt by the contemporary confusion between logic and rhetoric occasioned by Ramus and by his own needs as a poet.

[15] Hayward, ed., p. 418.

[16] In what immediately follows, the discussion will again focus upon the way in which definition is basic to the conceit, whether that of Wyatt or of Donne. To some readers it may seem that definition is in a sense basic to all poetic metaphor and that it is therefore no surprise to find Donne and his followers using it. To this I would rejoin two things. First, that my use of the term implies verbal, syntactic, or dialectical processes of defining in the poem, not just in metaphor as an entity. Second, against the examples I give of definitions in poets before and after Donne may be placed the great bulk of familiar English poems. Anyone inspecting as a rude test the beginnings of *The Canterbury Tales, The Faerie Queene, Paradise Lost, The Rape of the Lock, The Prelude,* and other major works characteristic of other styles will find that what is common and characteristic in the Metaphysical poets is rare in the others. Of all important poets outside the Metaphysicals, Dryden probably approaches them more nearly in this, as indeed in certain other respects.

[17] I am aware of numerous other differences—as for example that between the social and private worlds of the two poetic lines—but these lie outside my purpose here. I should also add that I am aware of what has been claimed for Donne's continental sources by Mario Praz and others but that, without wishing to debate them, I simply wish to insist upon the importance of native development.

JOSEPH ANTHONY MAZZEO

🖋

A Critique of Some Modern Theories of
Metaphysical Poetry

Numerous theories of "metaphysical" poetry have been advanced ever since the appearance of Sir Herbert Grierson's great edition of Donne's poems in 1912 initiated the modern revaluation of the "metaphysical" poets. However, few of these theories seem to have approached the problem from the perspectives offered by sixteenth- and seventeenth-century literary critics themselves. One of the reasons for this oversight is the curious fact that there is no body of critical literature in English on the metaphysical movement written when that movement, under various names, such as "Concettismo," "Marinismo," and "Gongorismo," was flourishing throughout Europe. Another reason is that we seem to have forgotten that the word "conceit," "concetto," or "concepto" also meant metaphor as well as "conceit" in the sense in which Dr. Johnson used the word. This is especially surprising when we consider that many modern critics find the most striking characteristic of the metaphysical poet to be his desire to extend the range and variety of metaphorical expression.

Giordano Bruno, the first critic to attempt a conceptual formulation of "concettismo," as the "metaphysical" style was known in Italy, began his argument to *De gli eroici furori* with an attack on the Petrarchan theory of poetic inspiration. For the older notion of "amore" directed toward personal beauty, Bruno attempted to substitute the idea of "heroic love" directed toward the universe. This second kind

From *Modern Philology*, L (1952), pp. 88–96. Reprinted by permission of The University of Chicago Press.

of love he interprets as the gift which both the philosopher and the poet have for perceiving the unity of dissimilars or, in other terms, for making heterogeneous analogies. Thus, for Bruno, "metaphysical" poetry was essentially concerned with perceiving and expressing the universal correspondences in his universe.

This conception of the poet as one who discovers and expresses the universal analogies binding the universe together was later developed by the theorists of the conceit in the seventeenth century, the most familiar of whom are Baltasar Gracián in Spain and Emmanuele Tesauro in Italy, and was made the basis for a poetic of "concettismo" or, as I have called it elsewhere, "a poetic of correpondences." [1]

One of the cardinal tenets of the critics of the conceit is that the conceit itself is the expression of a correspondence which actually obtains between objects and that, since the universe is a network of universal correspondences or analogies which unite all the apparently heterogeneous elements of experience, the most heterogeneous metaphors are justifiable. Thus the theorists of the conceit justify the predilection of the "school of wit" for recondite and apparently strained analogies by maintaining that even the more violent couplings of dissimilars were simply expressions of the underlying unity of all things.

It is, of course, true that analogical thought is a fundamental property of the human mind in any age and that the notion of universal analogy has a long history which reaches back to Plato. The important point is that Bruno and the theorists of the conceit employed the principle as the basis of a poetic for the first time. The fact that they did so does not "explain" metaphysical poetry any more than Aristotle's *Poetics* "explains" Sophocles. This is not the function of a poetic or a theory of poetry. Rather, it formulates conceptually a concrete body of literature already in existence. As Hegel put it in his preface to *The Philosophy of Right*, "When philosophy paints its gray in gray, a shape of life has grown old . . . it cannot be rejuvenated but only understood. The owl of Minerva spreads its wings at twilight."

What a poetic can do, however, is make explicit the cultural presuppositions which may underlie a particular body of literature, a style, or a genre. That Bruno and the theorists of the conceit should have based their poetic on the principle of universal analogy meant that they wished to justify and formulate philosophically the actual practice of metaphysical poets in making recondite and heterogeneous analogies and in using mundane and "learned" images.

The principle of universal analogy as a poetic, or the poetic of correspondences, offers, in my opinion, a theory of metaphysical poetry which is simpler, in greater harmony with the evidence, and freer from internal contradictions than the major modern theories that have yet been formulated. It is in the light of this theory, contemporary to the metaphysical movement, that I propose to review the various modern theories.

One popular modern theory derives "metaphysical" poetry from the Petrarchan and troubadour traditions and describes it as a decadent and exaggerated version of these earlier traditions.[2] If this is so, we can hardly understand the deliberately "irregular" versification of many of the greatest "metaphysical" poets, such as Donne; the colloquial tone and the homely and technical imagery characteristic of "concettismo"; the fact that Bruno, a "concettista" himself and the probable founder of Neapolitan "concettismo," began his *De gli eroici furori* with an attack on the Petrarchan and troubadour conventions and offered a clear and determined substitute theory. He, at least, was certain that he was doing something else, and the poetic creations of the "metaphysicals" are sufficient evidence that he was. We can avoid this conclusion only if we insist on regarding the conceit as merely an odd or unusual image, in which case we can find it everywhere (and therefore nowhere) and even take its origin back to Martial. But it is clear that literary history cannot be made from superficial similarities and that the historian of taste must seek and determine the different cultural presuppositions that underlie the creations of minds as diverse as Bruno and Arnaut Daniel, without, at the same time, swallowing up the individual uniqueness and greatness of every great artist and work of art in the general historical categories we construct for them.

Another theory would attribute the "metaphysical" style to the influence of Ramistic logic, but it seems to me that this view raises more questions than it answers. Norman E. Nelson has made an acute criticism of the confusion between poetry, rhetoric, and logic that the defenders of the Ramistic theory are involved in.[3] It is at least questionable whether any system of inference or any empirical construction like rhetoric can have the kind of effect on a culture that Miss Tuve, the originator of this theory, describes. If her almost deterministic view of the influence of logic and rhetoric were true, she would still have to explain away the fact that Milton, who wrote a Ramist logic and defended Ramist theories, was surely no "metaphysical" poet. The connection between "concettismo" and Ramism, if one can be established, is not a causal relationship. Rather, they are both expressive, in different ways, of what we might call the "rhetoricizing" tendency of Renaissance humanism, the belief shared with Ramus by Valla and others that literature or rhetoric, rather than the old scholastic logic, revealed the true path which the mind must take in its quest for truth.[4] It would seem that the confusion of logic and poetry characteristic of our modern "Ramists" is a result of the current use of the term "logical image" to refer to the kind of expanded metaphor characteristic of much "metaphysical" poetry. It is, of course, clear that the "logic" of development of an expanded metaphor has often very little to do with the logic of a syllogism or system of inference and is, indeed, directed toward a different end.

Another group of scholars relates the "metaphysical" style to the baroque, but variously, sometimes completely identifying it with the baroque and sometimes distinguishing the two. Croce, for example, calls "concettismo" a baroque phenomenon but considers anything baroque a negative aspect of Renaissance history whose only excuse for existence was to purge Western civilization from medievalism. It is otherwise with Hatzfeld, who, distinguishing "concettismo" and baroque, gives the honors to the latter, of which the conceit and its uses are, at most, a degenerate parody.[5] It is difficult to discuss the views of this group, since the term "baroque" itself is, like "Renaissance" and "Romantic," so variable in reference. However, the notion has been applied with greatest success to the study of the visual arts, where it is at least referable to specific techniques. I do not propose to complicate further this already complex problem, but it would seem desirable to keep the characteristics of baroque painting, sculpture, and architecture firmly in mind when we extend this term to other cultural spheres and not allow ourselves to be misled by chronological simultaneity alone. The original fruitful use of the concept of the baroque with reference to the plastic arts suggests that Cassirer's category of "form" and the principle of universal analogy might well be kept separated and that true "concettismo" belongs to the latter, while the baroque, as Croce suggested, is best understood as the transformation of the Renaissance interest in "form" into a preoccupation with "ornament" and in a weakening of the distinctions between the arts.

Perhaps the most widespread theory of the "metaphysical" style is the emblem theory. This view, establishing a causal connection between the emblem movement or "emblem habit" and the conceit which is purportedly its result, is usually expressed in terms of a baroque theory of the "metaphysical" style. Mario Praz, the foremost representative of this group, bases his analysis on Croce's, without assuming the latter's negative attitude toward either the baroque or the "metaphysical" styles. However, his study of the actual creations of this literary movement leads him to a view of the conceit and the emblem which might be called the "game" theory, a position he assumes when he says of the conceit and emblem that they are of the nature of the charade or riddle—the by-products of an amusing, lighthearted (perhaps perverse?) verbal and pictorial game.[6] This is surely an astonishing description of a style in which some of the greatest religious poetry of all time was written, and it is, in effect, denied by the sensitivity of Praz's concrete criticism of John Donne and Richard Crashaw.

I believe that this conclusion is a consequence of Praz's insistence on the intimate relationship between emblem and conceit and between the mass of different styles, some of them quite perverse, which went under the name of "Marinismo," "Gongorismo," "Seicentismo," "Euphuism," etc. However, not only are the resemblances between Donne and Lyly superficial at best, but the easy application of some notion of strangeness or eccentricity in style will find resemblances where none exist and lead to false or useless descriptions of cultural phenomena. Praz seems closer to a working definition of the conceit when he says that it is to poetry what the illusory perspective is to art, although, in the light of both the theory and the practice of the "metaphysical" style, this insight is of somewhat limited utility and best describes a style like Crashaw's.

Praz makes much of the fact that the emblem was usually accompanied by an epigram, and, since he seems to hold that emblem and "metaphysical" poem are related to each other as cause and effect, he concludes that the epigram is the genre most characteristic of "concettismo." This conclusion, in turn, leads to his placing great emphasis on the diffusion of the *Greek Anthology* during the Renaissance as one of the important influences on the growth of the "metaphysical" movement.[7] However, while the *Greek Anthology* stimulated many imitators, it seems to have had little effect on the best of the poets of wit. The long and "conceited" works of Marino, Gongora, Donne, and others preclude accepting this view, at least in the form in which it is stated. Praz's stress on the epigram also leads him to emphasize brevity as the most desirable quality of a good conceit, a quality which presumably helped make it "sharp" or "pointed." Brevity in the conceit was commended by the theorists of the conceit themselves, but they also recognized what we would today call the "expanded metaphor," and they often seem to mean by "brevity" a quality opposed to the Ciceronian notion of *copia*. There is, of course, no reason why an epigram should not have conceits, but there is also no apparent reason to establish a determined relationship between "concettismo" and epigram and, via the epigram, between "concettismo" and the emblem. I shall take up the more fundamental inadequacies of the emblem theory in detail when I discuss the views of Austin Warren below, since he presents this theory in purer form than does Praz. In the latter's version the emblem plays an important role, but mediately, through the epigram, which had to be brief, playful, and puzzling and was analogous to illusory perspective in the arts. However, while this analysis is true of certain individual works, especially of some productions of the school of Marino, it is inadequate to the movement as a whole and gives no real clue to the *forma mentis* of a "concettista."

Indeed, this theory of the conceit was implicitly rejected by the seventeenth-century theorists of the conceit in whose works the emblem and *impresa*, as well as the epigram or "arte lapidaria," are treated as incidental topics involved in the analysis of conceit or metaphor. They were fully aware that any theory of the conceit had to be a theory of metaphor or analogy, not a theory of genres. Emmanuele Tesauro, for example, analyzed all genres, literary and artistic, as forms of "acutezze" or types of metaphorical expression by extending the categories of rhetoric to include all literary and figurative creations.[8] Thus Tesauro himself realized that the roots of "concettismo" lay deeper than any classification of genres and were rooted in the nature of expression itself. Not only the epigram but all genres, including the lyric itself, had become "metaphysical."

Austin Warren, as I observed above, shares some of Praz's conceptions about the emblem to an even greater degree. He says:

> The connection of the emblem with poetry was, from the start, close: indeed the term often transferred itself from the picture to the epigram which ordinarily accompanied it. . . . Thus the arts reinforced one another. The influence on poetry was not only to encourage the metaphorical habit but to impart to the metaphors a hardness, a palpability which, merely conceived, they were unlikely to possess. And yet the metaphors ordinarily analogized impalpabilities—states of the soul, concepts, abstractions. . . . Many emblems owe their undeniable grotesqueness to the visualization of metaphors, often scriptural, which were not intended so to be visualized.[9]

In this particular passage, I take it that Warren means by "hardness" a kind of precision and by "palpability" a strong visual or sensuous element in the image. In any case the "metaphysical" image purportedly acquired these properties from the "emblem habit," which helped to develop metaphorical habits of mind and, presumably, habits for making recondite metaphors instead of commonplace ones.

However, as I have already explained, the theorists of the conceit either do not deal with the emblem at all or treat it merely as one aspect of the general theory of wit, making no direct connection between emblem and conceit. Taking our cue from them once more, we might observe that the qualities of precision and the strong sensuous element to be found in much "metaphysical" poetry can be accounted for, to the degree that any poetic "accounts for" a living and creative poetic tradition, by their theory of wit (*ingegno, ingenio, esprit*) as the faculty which, like Bruno's *genio,* finds and expresses the universal analogies latent in the data of experience. The desire to draw correspondences between heterogeneous things and thereby reveal the unity of what appears fragmentary and the desire to develop these correspondences are bound to give to the resultant imagery some of those qualities Warren discerns in the poets of wit.

From a more general critical point of view, the "palpability" or "hardness" of an image is, after all, a function of what the poet wishes to say and can say. In its own way Dante's imagery is as "hard" and "palpable" as one could wish. What the poet can say and the way he can say it are in part given by his culture, in so far as the culture makes him a man of a particular place, time, and environment, and in large part by his imaginative power, which enables him to "inform" and universalize his cultural and personal experience. No poetic has yet explained the secret of his power, although a poetic which is true to the concrete works of art it attempts to describe theoretically can give us insight into the nature of the imagination by telling us what it did with what it worked with. Universal analogy and its later formulation as a poetic can thus tell us something about the Renaissance imagination and throw light on Donne, Marino, Crashaw, and others, in spite of their differences. In this light, it would seem to be an error to attribute a movement such as "concettismo" to some secondary cultural phenomenon such as the "emblem habit" or Ramist logic and try, by so doing, to obliterate the differences between poets by swallowing them up in an influence.

Warren's version of the emblem theory of "metaphysical" poetry is based on a general theory of imagery involving the nature of the analogues in a metaphor:

> All imagery is double in its reference, a composite of perception and conception. Of these ingredients, the proportions vary. The metaphorist can collate image with image, or image with concept, or concept with image, or concept with concept.[10]

After discussing the series of combinations according to which the "ingredients" of an image may be arranged, he continues:

> Then too, the metaphorists differ widely in the degree of visualization for which they project their images. The epic simile of Homer and of Spenser is fully pictorial; the intent, relative to the poet's architecture, is decorative. On the other hand, the "sunken" and the "radical" types of imagery—the conceits of Donne and the "symbols" of Hart Crane—expect scant visualization by the senses.[11]

This passage is especially important because the author is here distinguishing between those poets called "metaphysical" (he also seems to include the modern "neo-metaphysicals") and all others. However, in this passage Warren is not analyzing the school of wit and its imagery in terms of "palpability" or "hardness" purportedly derived from the emblem; indeed, he seems to be saying that the Donnean conceit is capable of "scant visualization." It would therefore lack the properties which the emblem supposedly gave to the conceit. In the passage previously cited, Warren closely connected the emblem to the conceit, while in this passage the conceit is completely severed from those properties which it was supposed to have derived from the emblem.

It is clear that we are involved in a contradiction. Unintentionally, Warren is pointing out one important thing about "metaphysical" poetry and about poetic imagery in general. The qualities of the "metaphysical" image seem to have nothing to do with whether or not it can be visualized or with the sensory content of the image itself, although it may be prominent. The qualities of the "metaphysical" image are a function of the *manner* in which the analogues are related, and it is this very point that the theorists of the conceit make when they insist that the wit is in the "form" of the conceit and not in the "matter."

A further reason for the inevitable inadequacy of the emblem theory is the historical fact that the emblem movement, initiated by the introduction of the *Hieroglyphica* of Horapollo to Renaissance Europe, is a cultural phenomenon distinct from the poetry of wit and has other cultural presuppositions. Although emblem and conceit were later found together, they are found together at a relatively late date and usually in minor authors like Quarles, who gave emblems already in existence a verse commentary.[12] Granted that a poet might find an emblem suggestive of some image or another, the vast bulk of the creations of the school of wit do not seem to be related to the emblem literature in any intrinsic way. The very grotesqueness of many of the emblems is testimony to the fact that the conceit preceded—and was therefore independent of—its graphic expression. If anything, it was the conceit which made the emblem grotesque rather than the emblem making the conceit "harder" and more "palpable." Emblems drawn to many of the conceits of Donne or Crashaw or to much of the so-called "decorative imagery" of Homer would all be equally grotesque.

Perhaps the basic unexamined assumption in this whole theory is that there is a radical distinction in kinds of imagery. The sharp cleavage between what are called "decorative" imagery and "functional" imagery needs to be closely examined. We might begin by asking in what sense the imagery of Homer can be said to be decorative. It is clear even from a cursory reading of the *Iliad* that many of Homer's analogues for the events of battle are drawn from the world of peaceful endeavor. One of the obvious functions of these analogues is to heighten the pitch of the battle scenes and to bring the "great" world of peace into relationship with the "little" world of war. In this sense the *Iliad* is as much about peace as about war; metaphor is the link between these two worlds, revealing the nature of war through analogy with the events and experiences of peace. It follows that the poet's "choice" of analogues depends upon what he wants to say, upon what elements in the world of men he wishes to bring into the world of his poem. This is at least one sense in which the microcosm-macrocosm analogy is still profoundly vital.

When Homer compares an attacking army to a huge wave breaking on a beach, he would, in the opinion of some, be making a fully pictorial metaphor. However, all the reader has to do is to try to think of the various ways in which an emblem might be constructed to represent this metaphor to see how grotesque the results could be. Two *separate* pictures could be drawn, and they could be quite photographic. But this would not result in the creation of an emblem, for the emblem would have to embody the whole metaphor at once in one representation. We must bear in mind that the metaphor is part identity and part difference. What Homer wants us to see is the way in which a wave under certain conditions is like an army under certain other conditions. By joining these two particular analogues, he selects those qualities of waves which can be transferred to armies. The pictorial quality is not in the whole metaphor or in the identity but in each analogue separately as a kind of sensuous residue remaining after the identity has been established, and as such it is part of the total effect of the image. Thus the pictorial quality remains precisely

that aspect of the image which cannot be transferred from one analogue to the other.

It follows from this analysis that, when we speak of "pictorial
imagery," we cannot mean that the metaphor can necessarily be absorbed into a pictorial representation or that, conversely, it was necessarily created by a graphic representation. Both historical evidence
and theoretical necessity, therefore, require abandoning the emblem
theory of "metaphysical" poetry. The emblem movement is more
closely related to the tendency in the baroque plastic arts toward
breaking down the barriers between the arts in the effort to create a
universal art which would somehow combine all of them. Its great
vogue was largely the work of the Jesuits, who found the emblem a
useful pedagogic device for propagating the faith.

The failure to see the way in which the emblem is related and the
extent to which it is not related to the conceit can lead to some further
misinterpretations. Praz, for example, derives the limbeck image as
used in the writings of the spiritual alchemists from the emblem tradition and believes that this image is a mere "conceit" or witticism.[13]
But it was part of the religious and symbolic vocabulary derived from
the symbols of empirical alchemy by application of the principle of
universal analogy whereby they were extended to apply to all levels
of existence. The limbeck was thus no mere suggestive and fanciful
image but the symbol of a process that was recapitulated in every
order of a universe seen *sub specie alchemiae*. The failure to realize
the nature of this image leads Praz to misunderstand the significance
of the work of Michael Maier, the alchemist who published an alchemical work containing both emblems and music to be sung to the
various stages of the alchemical process, as a very strange example
of baroque sensibility or "concettismo." [14] However, what Maier did
was to use the emblems for their pedagogic value, much as a chemistry textbook might have illustrations and equations. Music as a
necessary part of the alchemical process was a characteristic result of
the conviction that all things are universally related and affect each
other through correspondences.

Although, as Warren maintains, "both the emblem and the conceit
proceed from wit," they do not proceed from the same kind of wit, or
in the same way.[15] The relationship is not, above all, filial but, at
most, cousinly. Our own time is less "witty" than the time of Donne,
and universal analogy has passed out of existence as a common habit
of thought; the difficulty we have in penetrating this view of the world
from within and somehow understanding it as "natural" and not "perverse" is, perhaps, the most important reason of all for the confusion

about the nature of the poetry of wit. Many students of the movement have been aware that what may impress us as perverse, shocking, or recondite need not have had the same effect on contemporaries. This has sometimes been attributed to habitual usage and "taste." However, the "metaphysical" poets and their contemporaries possessed a view of the world founded on universal analogy and derived habits of thought which prepared them for finding and easily accepting the most heterogeneous analogies.[16]

NOTES

[1] Giordano Bruno, *Opere italiane*, ed. Giovanni Gentile, Vol. II (Bari, 1927). I refer the reader to two articles of mine: "A Seventeenth-Century Theory of Metaphysical Poetry," *RR*, XLII (1951), 245–55, and "Metaphysical Poetry and the Poetic of Correspondences," *JHI*, XIV (1953), 221–34.

[2] Helmut Hatzfeld, "A Clarification of the Baroque Problem in the Romance Literatures," *Comparative Literature*, I (1949), 115–16.

[3] This theory is advanced primarily by Rosemond Tuve, *Elizabethan and Metaphysical Imagery* (Chicago, 1946). Nelson's article on *Peter Ramus and the Confusion of Logic, Rhetoric and Poetry* is in the series "University of Michigan Contributions in Modern Philology," No. 2 (April, 1947).

[4] This view was characteristic of many humanists who were also nominalists and who therefore banished all previous metaphysical assumptions from logic. The new rhetoric-logic was to teach men how to follow in their voluntary thinking the same "natural" laws that were followed in involuntary thinking. Hence the numerous literary examples to be found in Ramist logics. However, although Ramus abandoned the old metaphysical assumptions, he reintroduced the old categories, arranging them by dichotomies in a purely arbitrary and empirical order.

[5] See René Wellek, "The Concept of Baroque in Literary Scholarship," *Journal of Aesthetics*, V (1946), 77–109, for a discussion of the concept of baroque and for a bibliography on the subject. The following treat the "metaphysical" movement or "concettismo" as a manifestation of the baroque: Benedetto Croce, *Storia della eta' barocca in Italia* (2d ed.; Bari, 1946); *Problemi di estetica* (4th ed.; Bari, 1949); *Saggi sulla letteratura italiana del seicento* (2d ed.; Bari, 1924); *Nuovi saggi sulla letteratura italiana del seicento* (Bari, 1931). Mario Praz, *Seicentismo e marinismo in Inghil-terra: John Donne—Richard Crashaw* (Florence, 1925). The studies of the two poets were reprinted separately in 1945. Also Praz, *Studies in Seventeenth-Century Imagery* (London, 1939, an Italian version of which last appeared as *Studi sul concettismo* (Florence, 1946). A companion volume to the English version of this book consisting of a bibliography of emblem books appeared in London in 1947 as Vol. II of the same title. Also see Marcellino Menéndez y Pelayo, *Historia de las ideas estéticas en España* (4th ed.; Madrid, 1928–33), Vol. II, Part II.

[6] Praz, *John Donne*, p. 7. Other works in support of the emblem theory are Rosemary Freeman, *English Emblem Books* (London, 1948); Austin Warren, *Richard Crashaw: A Study in Baroque Sensibility* (University, La., 1939); Ruth Wallerstein, *Studies in Seventeenth-Century Poetic* (Madison, 1950). Miss Wallerstein also agrees with Miss Tuve on the influence of Ramist logic.

[7] Praz, *Richard Crashaw*, pp. 114 ff. This desire to force "influences" leads Praz to find it strange that metaphysical poetry should have flourished in England, although the emblem did not have a very wide vogue there (cf. *Studi dul concettismo*, p. 202).

[8] Emmanuele Tesauro, *Il Cannochiale Aristotelico* (2d ed., 1663), chaps. xiv, xv. In these two chapters Tesauro sketched the outline of his generalized theory of wit. Cf. Croce, *Problemi di estetica,* pp. 313 ff.

[9] Warren, pp. 73-4.

[10] Ibid., p. 177.

[11] Ibid.

[12] Cf. *The Hieroglyphics of Horapollo*, trans. George Boas (New York, 1950). Mr. Boas' introduction is quite valuable. The standard work on the emblem movement is by Ludwig Volkmann, *Bilderschriften der Renaissance: Hieroglyphik und Emblematik in ihren Beziehungen und Fortwirkungen* (Leipzig, 1923). A typical late Renaissance edition of Horapollo is the work of Nicolao Caussino, *Symbolica Aegyptiorum sapientia,* together with a *Polyhistor symbolicus* (Paris, 1647). These two works, consisting of the text and translation of Horapollo, an anthology of classical remarks on symbols and hieroglyphics, and a hieroglyphic bestiary, constitute a kind of encyclopedia. The hieroglyphic-emblem movement seems to have been in part a continuation of the tradition of medieval exemplarism, especially zoölogical exemplarism. It is in this enriched form that the emblem movement reached Quarles: "Before the knowledge of letters, God was known by *Hieroglyphicks;* And, indeed, what are the Heaven, and Earth, nay every Creature, but *Hieroglyphicks* and *Emblems* of his glory" (see Francis Quarles, *Emblemes* [London, 1635], "To the Reader").

[13] Praz, *Studi sul concettismo,* pp. 49–50 n., 199–200.

[14] Michael Maier, *Atalanta fugiens* (Oppenheim, 1618). Also John Read, *Prelude to Chemistry* (New York, 1937), Chap. vi, which is on Maier. Some samples of his music in modern notation are appended to the work. For spiritual alchemy see H. Brémond, *Histoire littéraire du sentiment religieux en France* (Paris, 1925), Vol. VII, Part II, chap. v.; and Evelyn Underhill, *Mysticism* (16th ed.; New York, 1948), pp. 140 ff.

[15] Warren, p. 75.

[16] Ibid., p. 173.

J. B. LEISHMAN

丿

Donne and Seventeenth-Century Poetry

In the historical consideration of literature there are three dangers against which we should be continually on our guard: the danger that we may lose sight of the larger differences and distinctions through concentrating too much attention upon the subsidiary ones; the danger that we may pervert these subsidiary distinctions into antitheses; the danger that within these subsidiary distinctions we may insist too much upon identity and too little upon difference. In the present field of study we have, on the one hand, heard perhaps too much of a School of Jonson and a School of Donne, of the classical and the so-called metaphysical strains in seventeenth-century poetry, and not enough of those larger differences between the characteristic non-dramatic poetry of the Age of Elizabeth and that of the Jacobean and Caroline periods, differences in which both Jonson and Donne equally share; while, on the other hand, we have had, perhaps, too many generalizations about the so-called metaphysical poets and not enough insistence on the very important differences between them. It is, indeed, easier to perceive certain obvious differences between the poetry of Donne and Jonson than to perceive certain important resemblances, just as it is easier to perceive certain superficial resemblances between, say, Donne and Crashaw than to become aware of their fundamental differences. The ultimate purpose of such generalizations, classifications and distinctions is to increase awareness, to enable us, by analysis and comparison, to achieve a clearer recog-

From *The Monarch of Wit: An Analytical and Comparative Study of the Poetry of John Donne* (London, 1951; 3rd ed., 1957), pp. 9–26. Reprinted by permission of The Hutchinson Publishing Group.

89

nition, a more intense appreciation, of the peculiar virtue, the essential *thisness*, of whatever literature we may be studying; this, though, is a strenuous task, and most of us, I fear, tend unconsciously to manipulate these generalizations, classifications and distinctions, disregarding here, over-emphasizing there, until we have spread over everything a veil of custom and a film of familiarity which shall save us as much as possible from the insupportable fatigue of thought. Donne has been too often considered as a so-called metaphysical poet and too little as a seventeenth-century poet (many characteristic seventeenth-century poets began to write during the reign of Elizabeth); let us begin, then, by trying to reach some not too inadequate conception of the characteristics of seventeenth-century poetry in general and of the principal differences and varieties within that fundamental identity.

That such a conception is both real and necessary is proved by the fact that the poetry of those two very individual and very different poets, Ben Jonson and John Donne, who are commonly regarded as the founders of two different schools, has many important characteristics in common. They were—to begin with an important fact which has received too little attention—they were both, in a sense, coterie-poets, poets who made their initial impact not upon the common reader but upon comparatively small circles of intellectuals and literary amateurs. Apart from his contributions to the facetious commendations of Thomas Coryat in the latter's *Crudities* (1611) and to the elegies on Prince Henry in *Lachrymae Lachrymarum* (1613), the only poems Donne printed during his life-time were the two *Anniversaries* upon the religious death of Mistris Elizabeth Drury, in 1611 and 1612. The first collected edition of his poems was not published until 1633, two years after his death, and his great reputation as a poet during his life-time was gained entirely through the circulation of his poems in manuscript. Jonson, it is true, was a much more public poet than Donne: he wrote plays, which were not only acted, but published, under very careful supervision, by himself. Nevertheless, the great body of his non-dramatic verse was not published until after his death, and he too, though less exclusively and remotely than Donne, was the master, the *arbiter elegantiarum*, of a circle, of a coterie, of various young Templars and Courtiers who gathered round him in taverns, hung upon his words, begged copies of his verses, and were proud to be known as his sons.

When we speak, as we often do, of Jonson and Donne as the two great influences on the non-dramatic poetry of the first half of the seventeenth century, and when we think, as we often do, of that poetry

chiefly in its relation to either or both of them, we should not forget
that we are speaking and thinking only of that portion of seventeenth-
century poetry which we now chiefly read and remember, and that
much even of this poetry, easy, familiar, *harmlos* (to borrow a German
word) as it now seems to us, may well have seemed quite exception-
ally choice and sophisticated to its writers and first readers. There are
many seventeenth-century poems which may seem to us only very
superficially like Donne's, but which at the time may well have seemed
astonishingly *dernier cri* and quite beyond the reach of simple-minded
admirers of Forests of Arden and Bowers of Bliss. Both Jonson and
Donne were superior persons, and both seem to have been well aware
of their superiority, but Donne, though far more urbane, was a much
more superior person than Jonson, and, except superficially, much less
imitable. Contemporary allusions to his poetry are few and far between, and even quite advanced men seem to have remained ignorant
of it for an incredibly long time.[1] In the various miscellanies published
between 1640 and 1660, whose contents seem to have been derived
partly from printed texts and partly from manuscript commonplace
books, and which may be regarded as reflecting fairly accurately the
taste of the average cultivated gentleman of the time of Charles I, both
the number of Donne's poems included and any obvious traces of his
influence are remarkably small. The influence of Jonson, the epigrammatic rather than the moral Jonson, the Jonson of "Still to be neat, still
to be drest," "Come my Celia, let us prove," and "If I freely may discover," is far more striking. It is in the wittily, often impudently, argumentative love-poem, and in the indecently, sometimes obscenely,
witty "elegy," epigram, or paradox, that Donne's influence upon the
secular poetry of the seventeenth century is chiefly apparent.[2] Such
poems, though, are more frequent in the published works of particular
poets (Carew, Suckling, Lovelace, Cowley), and in certain manuscript
collections, than in the miscellanies, where the persistence both of the
hearty Elizabethan song and of the Elizabethan pastoral tradition is far
more noticeable. In the main, Donne's dialectic is simplified and his
wit coarsened by his imitators. One wonders what Donne thought of
them. (It must sometimes have been an embarrassment to him that, at
the time when he was preaching in St. Paul's, various obscene epigrams were being handed about and attributed to "Dr. Donne.")
Jonson, so often prickly and dogmatic, was probably a more indulgent
parent: when he declared that "my son Cartwright writes all like a
man," the modern reader finds it hard to know just what he meant,
and will perhaps reflect that, after all, it's a wise father who knows his
own children.

William Drummond of Hawthornden, a disciple of Spenser and of the Italians, has recorded that when Ben Jonson visited him in 1619 he told him that his poems "were all good . . . save that they smelled too much of the Schooles, and were not after the fancie of the tyme." Jonson, no doubt, was speaking for himself and for those who agreed with him, but it is really impossible to know just how many did agree with him, or to form even a rough estimate of the proportion of then readers of English poetry who shared this "fancie of the tyme." [3] In saying that the poetry of Jonson and of Donne was in a sense coterie poetry, I want to insist upon the fact that it is almost impossible to know just how far the coterie extended, whom it included, who, so to speak, were in the inner circle and who were merely on the fringe. Where fashion and mode are active the detection and disintrication of "influences" become formidably difficult. Milton admired Homer and Virgil and Ovid, Tasso and della Casa, not because anyone had told him to do so, but because he believed that was how great poetry should be written: one often feels, though, that many of his contemporaries admired Donne because to admire Donne was the done thing. Similarly, although to-day one constantly hears it said that contemporary English poets have been greatly influenced by Hopkins, by Mr. Eliot, and even by Rilke, it may well be that future generations will find the business of detecting these "influences" a most baffling task. Generalizations even about those seventeenth-century poets whose work is available in modern editions can at best be tentative. Not even the well-known poets will fit neatly into categories: even in them we encounter all manner of paradoxes and tergiversations. Cowley has related that it was the discovery of a volume of Spenser in his mother's parlour that made him irrecoverably a poet; when, however, he went out into the world he discovered that not Spenser but Donne was the man, and set himself to imitate Donne—"to a fault," as Dryden said, who himself confessed that Cowley had been the darling of his youth. When, though, one turns from the poets whose works are available in modern editions to the miscellanies and manuscript commonplace books of the age, the task of generalizing about seventeenth-century poetry, seventeenth-century taste, and seventeenth-century sensibility seems almost impossible. If I am now attempting to generalize myself, it is with an almost overwhelming conviction of the vanity of dogmatizing.

Each of these two very characteristic seventeenth-century poets, Jonson and Donne, was born during the reign of Elizabeth, and each had begun to establish his reputation during the last decade of the sixteenth century. Nevertheless, great as are the differences between them, the poetry of each has more in common with that of the other than it has with the poetry of Spenser, or of the Sonneteers, or with the lyrics in the song-books, or with such poems as *Venus and Adonis* and *The Rape of Lucrece*. On the one hand, neither Jonson nor Donne seems ever to have shared the ambition of Spenser and of several of Spenser's disciples to write a large-scale heroic or narrative poem. On the other hand, they both took the short poem more seriously than the typical Elizabethan poets did. Even if one leaves out of account the great mass of utterly undistinguished Elizabethan lyric, where the same rhymes, phrases, and properties appear over and over again with wearisome iteration, where nymphs and swains on the plains trip at leisure in a measure, view with pleasure Flora's treasure in meadows fresh and gay where fleecy lambs do play, weave in bowers crowns of flowers, or where fountains spring from mountains sigh and languish in their anguish—even if one forgets what the great majority of the poems (including Spenser's and Sidney's) in say, *Englands Helicon,* are really like—even if one confines oneself to the long-sifted contents of modern anthologies, one often feels that even the best Elizabethan poets just tossed off their delightful lyrics: partly, perhaps, because they were generally intended to be sung and therefore ought not to be too weighty or condensed. And one's general impression of the Elizabethan sonneteers is that they wrote too many sonnets and wrote them too easily. Jonson's foolish Matheo in *Every Man in His Humour* would, when melancholy, "write you your halfe score or your dozen of sonnets at a sitting." Both Jonson and Donne seem to have set a new fashion of writing short but very concentrated poems—Donne's always and Jonson's often intended to be handed round in manuscript and admired by connoisseurs. For it cannot be too strongly insisted that most of what we now chiefly remember of the non-dramatic poetry of the first half of the seventeenth century was poetry that for years had been circulating in manuscript before it finally found its way into print, while most of the non-dramatic poets who were publishing were either belated Elizabethans or pertinacious disciples of Spenser, and were regarded by the young intellectuals of the Court, the Inns of Court, and the Universities as old-fashioned and out of date. (One can go a good way towards "placing" the younger Milton among his contemporaries by saying that for him neither the *Faerie Queene* nor Ovid's *Metamorphoses* was out of date.) It is significant and almost symbolic that that grand old Elizabethan, Michael Drayton, who was born a year earlier than Shakespeare and who lived and wrote and published until 1631, should have twice rather bitterly and contemptuously protested against this new fashion for short poems circulated in manuscript. In 1612, in the Preface to the first part of his immense *Poly-olbion*, that "chorographical description of all the tracts, rivers, mountains, forests, and other parts of this renowned isle of Great Britain," he declared that

> in publishing this Essay of my Poeme, there is this great disaduantage against me; that it commeth out at this time, when Verses are wholly deduc't to Chambers, and nothing esteem'd in this lunatique Age, but what is kept in Cabinets, and must only passe by Transcription;

and in his *Epistle to Henry Reynolds, Esquire, of Poets and Poesie*, published in 1627, after reaching the end of his description of English poets from Chaucer to the two Beaumonts and William Browne, he added that he was not concerned with those poets who were too proud to publish and who chose to be known only through the circulation of their poems in manuscript.

Jonson, as I have admitted, was a less exclusive, a more public, poet than Donne, but he too wrote what he most valued for an audience fit though few. Spenser, one might almost say, wrote for all who cared for poetry at all; both Jonson and Donne wrote very emphatically for those who knew what was what. There is some analogy, though only a slight one, between the literary situation then and that which exists to-day; there was something, though only something, of the same gulf between "serious" and "popular" poetry. The position of Spenser had been in some ways similar to that of Tennyson; the position of Jonson and Donne was in some ways similar to that of Mr. Eliot. The Jacobean intellectuals, or some of them, reacted against the Elizabethans somewhat as the inter-war intellectuals did against the Victorians. This analogy, though, must not be pressed too far: [4] it is sufficient to insist that much of the most memorable non-dramatic poetry of the first half of the seventeenth century, a poetry very greatly influenced by the example of either Jonson or Donne or both, is a more exclusive and critical and intellectual kind of poetry than that which is typically Elizabethan. The phrase "strong-lined" is often used by seventeenth-century writers to describe the new qualities which they admired in the poetry both of Jonson and of Donne: something close-packed and strenuous, requiring some effort and connoisseurship to appreciate it, as distinguished from the easily appreciated, "the soft, melting and diffuse style of the Spenserians." [5] The facts, not merely that no one has ever thought of calling Jonson a metaphysical poet, but that his poetry shares many typical seventeenth-century characteristics with

Donne's, should suggest to us that it is worth while to try to consider Donne more as a typical seventeenth-century or "strong-lined" poet, and less as a so-called metaphysical one.

Jonson addressed two very encomiastic epigrams to Donne (xxiii and xcvi), as well as one (xciv) commending a manuscript of his Satires to the Countess of Bedford, and Donne, who never condescended to praise any other contemporary poet, contributed some very flattering Latin verses to the quarto edition of Jonson's *Volpone*. They had, indeed, much in common. Both, one might almost say, wrote as though Spenser had never lived: Spenser's national and patriotic strain, his Platonic idealism, his elaborate description, his amplification and ornamentation—all these find no place in their verse. They rejected too what one may call the Petrarchan tradition, the too often merely extravagant and conventional adoration of the sonneteers, and they rejected the elaborate and mainly frigid decoration of such poems as *Venus and Adonis* and *The Rape of Lucrece*. Both insisted on what Jonson called "language such as men do use," and would have disagreed with Gray and agreed with Wordsworth (in theory, though not always in practice) that there should be no essential difference between the diction of poetry and that of conversation. Both wrote much poetry that was satirical and realistic. Both—a very notable characteristic of the typical seventeenth-century as distinguished from the typical Elizabethan lyrist—stamped an image of themselves upon nearly all they wrote; for, while one of the chief characteristics of the Elizabethan lyric is a certain anonymousness, the song rather than the singer, seventeenth-century lyrists, as Professor Moorman has observed, lyrists otherwise so different as Crashaw, Vaughan, Suckling or Herrick, "whether their poetry be intense or not, stand revealed to us in what they write." Finally—to conclude this brief review of affinities—both Jonson and Donne wrote poems more sequacious, organic and untransposable than their predecessors, although with Donne this new sense of structure seems to have been stimulated by scholastic logic, with Jonson by the example of the classical lyric.

Seventeenth-century poetry, then, or much of seventeenth-century poetry, is colloquial in diction, undecorative and untraditional in imagery, dispensing with what Carew, in his elegy on Donne, called

> the goodly exil'd traine
> Of gods and goddesses, which in thy just raigne
> Were banish'd nobler Poems,

personal in tone and logical in structure. In these respects both Jonson and Donne are characteristic seventeenth-century poets. "But," some readers may be inclined to ask at this point, "what about Donne's metaphysics, what about his famous metaphysical wit?" In the pages that follow I shall hope to demonstrate, among other things, first, that Donne is certainly not a metaphysical poet in the wider sense of being a philosophic one; secondly, that although, in the narrower sense which Dryden had in mind when he declared that Donne "affected the metaphysics," he does indeed occasionally draw illustrations and analogies from the realms of philosophy, theology, and popular science, what, probably, most readers have in mind when they call him a metaphysical poet is an often syllogistic argumentation and argumentativeness which might, however, be more appropriately called scholastic or dialectical than metaphysical; thirdly, that in almost all Donne's best poetry there is a dramatic element, an element of personal drama, which is no less characteristic than the argumentative, scholastic or dialectical strain; and fourthly, closely connected with this element of drama, that there is in many of his poems a very strong element of sheer wit and paradox. Now if one regards Donne's poetry chiefly in this way, as what I have called the dialectical expression of personal drama, one will, I think perceive more clearly what are the really important resemblances and differences, on the one hand, between his poetry and that of other so-called metaphysical poets, and, on the other hand, between his poetry and that of Jonson and of poets who are commonly regarded as belonging to the School of Jonson. What, looked at in one way, seem differences in kind appear, when looked at in another way, to be rather differences in degree. The important thing, perhaps, is to decide which is the right way of looking, which is the viewpoint which will enable us to distinguish rightly between differences in degree and differences in kind, and to decide precisely at what point differences which at first seem merely differences in degree pass into differences in kind.

Consider, for example, the stylistic relationship between Herbert and Donne: the best poetry of both might equally well be described as the dialectical expression of personal drama. Herbert, like Donne, can make the purest poetry out of almost bare argument, and Herbert's expression of his relationship to God is no less dramatic than Donne's expression of various imaginary relationships with women and of his actual relationship with his wife; true though it be that Donne's dialectic is more ingenious than Herbert's and his analogies more various and, as it often seems to us, more far-fetched, and although in much of Donne's poetry there is an element of sheer invention, sheer wit and sheer paradox which we do not find in Herbert's. How much of the poetry of other so-called metaphysical poets may be appropriately described as the dialectical expression of personal drama? Certainly Marvell's *To his Coy Mistress* and *The Definition of Love*, although in most of Marvell's poetry the dialectical element is more apparent than the dramatic, and although the *Horatian Ode* is nearer to Jonson's kind of poetry than to Donne's. Crashaw's poetry is personal and often dramatic, but is it dialectical? Vaughan's poetry is personal, but less intimately so than Herbert's; dialectical, but less tightly and consistently so than Herbert's; occasionally, but not pervasively, dramatic, and with a strong element of vision and visual imagery that is found neither in Herbert's poetry nor in Donne's.

Now, on the other hand, between Donne's kind of poetry and Jonson's, which are the differences in degree and which are the differences in kind? Although the differences between Donne's kind of poetry and Jonson's are greater than those between Donne's kind of poetry and Herbert's, although very little, if any, of Jonson's poetry could be described as the dialectical expression of personal drama, and although the element of sheer wit is as absent from Jonson's poetry (though Jonson could admire it in Donne's) as it is from Herbert's, there still remain many differences which may perhaps be profitably regarded as differences within a fundamental identity, that, namely, of seventeenth-century poetry in general, differences in degree rather than in kind. Both Donne's language and Jonson's language is colloquial, "language such as men do use," but Donne's is more defiantly and resolutely colloquial. Jonson's poetry, in comparison with the typical Elizabethan lyric or with Spenser or with the sonneteers, is free from decoration, but Jonson does not exile the gods and goddesses so rigorously or reject the whole apparatus of classical mythology and allusion so utterly and consistently as Donne. Jonson's lyrics, in comparison with typical Elizabethan lyrics, are organic and untransposable, but they are seldom so rigorously logical, so capable of prose-analysis, as Donne's, Donne's dialectical method here introducing what almost amounts to a difference in kind. And although, in comparison with the anonymity of the typical Elizabethan lyric, Jonson's lyrics are personal and individual, they are so rather in the way in which Horace's Odes are so than in the way in which Donne's poems are. The style and tone are individual, but, as with Horace, never, or very seldom, eccentrically and unclassically individual, and the matter, as with Horace, is essentially public, "what oft was thought, though ne'er so well expressed."

Indeed, the idea or ideal of the kind of poetry that Jonson most wanted to write and was continually trying to write, a poetry memorably expressing that "high and noble matter" of which he spoke in his

Epistle *To Elizabeth Countesse of Rutland,* has been, I cannot but think, most perfectly realized in some of Horace's Odes. Were I limited to the choice of one ode which should represent as completely as possible both the manner and the matter of the graver Horace, I think I should choose the sixteenth of his Second Book, of which I here offer a translation "according to the Latin measure, as near as the language will permit":

Peace is what one, caught on the open sea, will
beg of heav'n above when the sombre storm clouds
hide the moon, and stars are no longer certain
guides for the sailor.

Peace the savage fighters of Thracia pray for,
peace, the Mede resplendent with broidered quiver,
peace, unbought, dear Grosphus, with proffered gold or
purple or jewels.

Ah, for neither treasure nor lictors bearing
rods before a Consul can check the spirit's
wretched civil strife or the cares that circle
costliest ceilings.

Well can fare on little, his humble table's
brightest piece of plate the ancestral salt-dish
one of whose light sleep not a fear or sordid
wish has deprived him.

Why, with such short span, do we so contend for
large possessions? Why do we seek for countries
warmed with other suns? Has an exile ever
quitted himself then?

Sickly Care can clamber aboard the brass-bound
galleys, keep abreast of the knightly riders,
swifter far than stags or the cloud-compelling
easterly breezes.

Let the soul, content with the present, scorn to
reck what lies beyond, and with smiles attemper
things that taste but sourly. From ev'ry aspect
nothing is perfect.

Early death removed the renowned Achilles,
age prolonged left little to cheer Tithonus;
me perhaps some blessing denied to you some
hour will have granted.

Flocks in hundreds bleat and Sicilian cattle
low around your folds, in the stables whinny
chariot-racing horses, and doubly-dyed in
African purple

glows the wool you're clad with; to me, with small
domain, the subtle spirit of Grecian Muses
came as Fate's mixed gift, and a soul aloof from
envious throngers.

It was, I say, towards poetry of this kind, individual indeed, but both in manner and in matter essentially public and classical, a poetry of statement and of weighty generalization, that Jonson was continually striving. I need not multiply examples: consider the concluding lines of *To the World: A farewell for a Gentle-woman, vertuous and noble:*

My tender, first, and simple yeeres
    Thou did'st abuse, and then betray;
Since stird'st vp iealousies and feares,
    When all the causes were away.
Then, in a soile hast planted me,
    Where breathe the basest of thy fooles;
Where enuious arts professed be,
    And pride, and ignorance the schooles,
Where nothing is examin'd, weigh'd,
    But, as 'tis rumor'd, so beleeu'd:
Where euery freedome is betray'd,
    And euery goodnesse tax'd, or grieu'd.
But, what we'are borne for, we must beare:
    Our fraile condition it is such,
That, what to all may happen here,
    If't chance to me, I must not grutch.
Else, I my state should much mistake,
    To harbour a diuided thought
From all my kinde: that, for my sake,
    There should a miracle be wrought.
No, I doe know, that I was borne

> To age, misfortune, sicknesse, griefe:
> But I will beare these, with that scorne,
>   As shall not need thy false reliefe.
> Nor for my peace will I goe farre,
>   As wandrers doe, that still doe rome,
> But make my strengths, such as they are,
>   Here in my bosome, and at home.

Or consider one of the most Horatian, I might almost say, one of the most Roman, things Jonson ever wrote, the verses *To Sir Robert Wroth*, penetrated with that characteristically Roman reverence for the traditional pursuits and festivals of the countryman which recurs so often, and with equal spontaneity, in the poems of Jonson's disciple Herrick. After describing, in magnificently animated and colourful verse, the varied activities of the estate and the hospitality of its owner, Jonson concludes with a passage which, in part at any rate, is no less Virgilian than Horatian, and which was probably inspired by some famous lines at the end of Virgil's second Georgic:

> Let others watch in guiltie armes, and stand
>   The furie of a rash command,
> Goe enter breaches, meet the cannons rage,
>   That they may sleepe with scarres in age.
> And shew their feathers shot, and cullors torne,
>   And brag, that they were therefore borne.
> Let this man sweat, and wrangle at the barre,
>   For euery price, in euery iarre,
> And change possessions, oftner with his breath,
>   Then either money, warre, or death:
> Let him, then hardest sires, more disinherit,
>   And each where boast it as his merit,
> To blow vp orphanes, widdowes, and their states;
>   And thinke his power doth equall *Fates*.
> Let that goe heape a masse of wretched wealth,
>   Purchas'd by rapine, worse then stealth,
> And brooding o're it sit, with broadest eyes,
>   Not doing good, scarce when he dyes.
> Let thousands more goe flatter vice, and winne,
>   By being organes to great sinne,
> Get place, and honor, and be glad to keepe
>   The secrets, that shall breake their sleepe:
> And, so they ride in purple, eate in plate,

Though poyson, thinke it a great fate.
But thou, my WROTH, if I can truth apply,
    Shalt neither that, nor this enuy:
Thy peace is made; and, when man's state is well,
    'Tis better, if he there can dwell.
God wisheth, none should wracke on a strange shelfe:
    To him, man's dearer then t'himselfe.
And, howsoeuer we may thinke things sweet,
    He alwayes giues what he knowes meet;
Which who can vse is happy: Such be thou.
    Thy morning's and thy euening's vow
Be thankes to him, and earnest prayer, to finde
    A body sound, with sounder minde;
To doe thy countrey seruice, thy selfe right;
    That neither want doe thee affright,
Nor death; but when thy latest sand is spent,
    Thou maist thinke life, a thing but lent.

It is in what may be called, in a wide sense, his moral poetry, that portion of his non-dramatic verse which is still far less widely known than it deserves to be, that Jonson is most fundamentally akin to Horace and, at the same time, most representative of one of the most characteristic strains in seventeenth-century and Augustan verse. From Wotton's

How happy is he born and taught
That serveth not another's will

to the youthful Pope's

Happy the man whose wish and care
A few paternal acres bound,
Content to breathe his native air
In his own ground

how much of the morality, one might almost say, how much of the religion, of English poets seems almost indistinguishable from that blend of Stoicism and Epicureanism which has been so perfectly expressed by Horace! How often we find it, the disintrication of the mean from its extremes, the exposure and rebuke of immoderate ambitions and desires and of every kind of too-muchness, the praise of moderate hospitality, of good talk and good wine, of the healthfulness of country life as distinguished from that of the city and the court, the celebration of antique virtue and simplicity—these, together with exhortations not to be too cast down by grief or ill-fortune, but to recognize and accept the conditions of human life.[6]

Although they both share in varying degrees those common characteristics of seventeenth-century poetry in general which I have tried to indicate, there is a very great difference, a difference not merely in degree but in kind, between Donne's exercises in sheer wit, Donne's dialectical expression of personal drama, and that essentially classical and public poetry towards which Jonson was always striving. Jonson's most memorable lines (often adapted from classical authors) are weighty and general:

> Men have beene great, but never good by chance.[7]
>
> Man may securely sinne, but safely never.[8]
>
> A good *Poet's* made, as well as borne.[9]
>
> 'Tis wisdom, and that high,
> For men to use their fortune reverently,
> Even in youth.[10]

Donne's most memorable lines are personal and dramatic:

> I wonder by my troth, what thou, and I
> Did, till we lov'd? [11]
>
> For Godsake hold your tongue, and let me love.[12]
>
> If yet I have not all thy love,
> Deare, I shall never have it all.[13]

Donne's style and manner are not only individual, but, in comparison with Horace's or Jonson's, eccentrically and unclassically individual. And as for the matter of his poetry, where he is being mainly witty and paradoxical, it is public only in the sense that we can imagine its being publicly recited and enjoyed in companies whose conceptions of wit, whose tastes, in comparison with Horace's or Pope's or Dr. Johnson's (for Ben Jonson, although his own practice was very different, could admire Donne's wit), were eccentric and unclassical. Where, on the other hand, Donne is being serious, or mainly serious, the matter of his poetry, in comparison with that of Ben Jonson or Horace, is essentially private, not "What oft was thought, though ne'er so well expressed," but something "seldom thought and seldom so expressed." A. N. Whitehead once defined religion as "What the individual does with his own solitariness": [14] nearly all Donne's serious poetry, his love-poetry no less than his religious poetry, and nearly all Herbert's poetry and Vaughan's, is in this sense essentially, not merely nominally, religious, is a record of what the poet has been doing with his solitariness. This solitariness, this privateness, this self-containedness, this, together with the often dialectical and dramatic expression of it, is, it seems to me, the most important difference between the serious poetry of Donne and the so-called Metaphysical School and that of Jonson and the Classical or Horatian School.

NOTES

[1] All hitherto known contemporary allusions to Donne's poetry have recently been collected (together with many discoveries of his own) by Mr. W. Milgate in a series of articles now appearing in *Notes and Queries* (27th May, 10th June, 8th July, 1950). Perhaps the most remarkable result of these investigations is their revelation of the extreme scarcity and comparative lateness of any definite allusions to Donne's lyrics. Round about 1606 or 1608 Francis Davison, editor of the *Poetical Rapsody* (1602), was compiling a list of "Manuscripts to gett," and he noted, among other things, "Satyres, Elegies, Epigrams etc. by John Don. q^{re}. some from Eleaz. Hodgson, and Ben: Johnson." Thus as late as 1606 or 1608 even so enthusiastic a poetry-lover as Francis Davison does not seem to have known (except, possibly, as an "etc.") that Donne had written lyrics. The first certainly dateable evidence that Donne's lyrics were in circulation is a setting of *The Expiration* in Alfonso Ferrabosco's *Book of Ayres,* 1609; the first reference to a (manuscript) "book" of "Jhone Dones lyriques" occurs in a list made by William Drummond of Hawthornden of books read by him during the year 1613. It was, as might be expected, for his Satires and Epigrams, those of his poems least unlike what many of his contemporaries were doing, and, to a lesser extent, for his Elegies (for which, it may be suggested, Marlowe's translation of Ovid's *Amores* had prepared the ground) that Donne was first admired. No surviving manuscript collection of his poetry bears an earlier date than 1620. Indeed, it was during the late 1620's and the 1630's that most of the surviving seventeenth-century manuscript commonplace books (private anthologies, one might call them), which in various ways owe so much to Donne, were put together. It would seem to have been during those years that the change of taste rather splenetically alluded to by Drayton in the Preface to the first part of his *Poly-olbion* (1612) became really widely diffused, at any rate among courtiers and university men, and that Ben Jonson was being in some sort its spokesman when, in 1619, he told Drummond that his poems were "not after the fancie of the tyme." It would seem to have been during these years that, among what one may call the literary amateurs, Donne's reputation and influence were at their height. Nevertheless, in discussing seventeenth-century poetic taste and the history of poetic reputations during that period, it seems necessary to make some distinction between what I have called literary amateurs and common readers. In a very important letter to the *Review of English*

Studies (January, 1946), occasioned by Dr. Percy Simpson's review of Professor G. E. Bentley's *Shakespeare and Jonson. Their Reputations in the Seventeenth Century Compared,* Dr. W. W. Greg suggested that, if the bibliographical evidence were placed beside that of literary allusion, the conclusion would seem to be that, while writers praised Jonson, readers read Shakespeare. In these matters it is very necessary to know, not merely who is speaking, but who he is speaking *for.* The great admirers of Donne were nearly all men who were accustomed to write a little poetry themselves, even if no more than an occasional eulogy or elegy.

2 His influence in a narrower and more specialized field, that of eulogy and funeral elegy (or, as he himself would have called it, "epicede"), was perhaps still more immediate and decisive. Poems of this kind, though, are more frequent in the manuscript commonplace books than in the miscellanies, except in such essentially academic miscellanies as *Parnassus Biceps.*

3 In an undated letter to the physician and celebrated Latin poet, Dr. Arthur Johnston, published in the folio edition of his *Works* (1711, p. 143), Drummond has expressed his own opinion of a certain "fancie of the tyme." Although (as we shall see later) he admired Donne as an "epigrammatist" and praised his Second Elegy, *The Anagram,* it is almost impossible not to suppose that Drummond is here alluding to Donne and to some of Donne's imitators. The letter begins abruptly with a Sidneian encomium on the antiquity and dignity of poetry, and then proceeds as follows: "In vain have some Men of late (Transformers of every Thing) consulted upon her Reformation, and endeavoured to abstract her to *Metaphysical* Idea's, and *Scholastical* Quiddities, denuding her of her own Habits, and those Ornaments with which she hath amused the World some Thousand Years. *Poesy* is not a Thing that is yet in the finding and search, or which may be otherwise found out, being already condescended upon by all Nations, and as it were established *jure Gentium,* amongst *Greeks, Romans, Italians, French, Spaniards.* Neither do I think that a good Piece of *Poesy,* which *Homer, Virgil, Ovid, Petrarch, Bartas, Ronsard, Boscan, Garcilasso* (if they were alive, and had that Language) could not understand, and reach the Sense of the Writer. Suppose these Men could find out some other new *Idea* like *Poesy,* it should be held as if Nature should bring forth some new *Animal,* neither Man, Horse, Lyon, Dog, but which had some Members of all, if they had been proportionably and by right *Symmetry* set together. What is not like the Ancients and conform to those Rules which hath been agreed unto by all Times, may (indeed) be something like unto *Poesy,* but it is no more *Poesy* than a Monster is a Man. Monsters breed Admiration at the First, but have ever some strange Loathsomness in them at last." Milton would probably have subscribed to every word of this.

4 The chief danger of such analogies is that they tend to make us forget what I may call the Elizabethan time-scale and the fact that scarcely anything of what now seems to us most memorable in Elizabethan poetry

and drama had been published or acted before the last decade of the sixteenth century. So far as we know, with the possible exception of Kyd's *Spanish Tragedy,* Marlowe's *Tamburlaine* (1587) was the first serious blank-verse drama to be acted on a public stage: some ten years later Shakespeare, who, like so many others, had begun by not very successfully attempting to imitate the "mighty line" and the "great and thundering speech," was already parodying them through the mouth of Ancient Pistol. When we speak of a "reaction" against Spenser or against the sonneteers we tend, perhaps, to convey the impression that Jonson and Donne had been brought up on the *Faerie Queene* and on sonnet-sequences, had been cloyed and surfeited with them, whereas in fact it was rather a case of dislike at first sight. The first three books of the *Faerie Queene* were not published until 1590, and the remaining three books not until 1596. The first Elizabethan sonnet-sequence, Thomas Watson's Ἑκατομπαθία, containing a hundred eighteen-line "sonnets," was published in 1582, but sonnet-sequences did not become the rage or the fashion until the publication of Sidney's *Astrophel and Stella* in 1591; then followed (to mention only the most famous) Daniel's *Delia* and Constable's *Diana* in 1592, Drayton's *Idea* in 1594, Spenser's *Amoretti* in 1595.

One may perhaps describe the situation with some approximation to truth by saying that the poetry of Spenser, of Jonson and of Donne and of their several disciples and imitators was all simultaneously competing for public favour, but that during the first half of the seventeenth century, among the more intellectual and sophisticated, the examples of Jonson and of Donne on the whole prevailed.

When we speak of nineteenth- or twentieth-century literary "movements" or "reactions," we are generally thinking in terms of generations; if we transfer these phrases to the Elizabethan literary scene we must learn to think in terms of a few years, or even, sometimes, of a few months.

[5] See an article by G. Williamson, "Strong Lines," in *English Studies,* 1936, 152 ff.

[6] There is, of course, another way of looking at the matter, which may be suggested by the following entry in the Diary of John Manningham, of the Middle Temple, under 12th February, 1602: "Ben Jonson the poet nowe lives upon one Townesend and scornes the world. (*Tho: Overbury.*)" ed. Bruce, Camden Society, p. 130.

[7] *An Epistle to Sir Edward Sacvile,* l. 124.

[8] *Epode,* "Not to know vice at all."

[9] *To the Memory of my beloved, the Author Mr. William Shakespeare.*

[10] *An Ode,* "High-spirited friend."

[11] *The good-morrow.*

[12] *The Canonization.*

[13] *Lovers infinitenesse.*

[14] *Religion in the Making,* 1927, p. 6.

↙

The Convention of *The Extasie*

Since Pierre Legouis challenged Grierson's interpretation of "The Extasie" and argued that it should be read as a poem of seduction, it has attracted more attention than any other poem by Donne. Merritt Y. Hughes, in reply, has tried to establish its Platonic lineage by means of Castiglione's *Courtier*.[1] But the problem raised by Legouis has a framework that has not been examined in subsequent discussion.

Long ago Morris W. Croll suggested this when he pointed to the original pattern for Fulke Greville's *Caelica* 75 in Sidney's Eighth Song of *Astrophel and Stella:*

> The two poems have in common the description of a May landscape, the walk of two lovers through "an enamel'd meade" (in Greville), in "a grove most rich of shade" (in Sidney), the long silence of both, with nice analysis of their emotions, finally a long casuistic dialogue on love, in which the ardor of the lover is restrained by the prudence of his mistress, or, in Greville's case, by her anger.[2]

For this pattern Janet G. Scott, in *Les Sonnets Elisabéthains*, found no precise antecedent, but a relation that lends support to Legouis:

> La chanson VIII a quelque ressemblance avec ces Chants de Mai ou "Reverdies" composés par les Trouvères et les Troubadours lorsqu'un souffle d'amour venait les troubler au

From *Seventeenth Century Contexts* (London: Faber & Faber; Chicago: The University of Chicago Press, 1960, 1961), pp. 63–77. Reprinted by permission of the publishers.

printemps. L'oeuvre de la Pléiade est remplie de similaires invitations à l'amour, mais le dialogue du poète anglais avec Stella introduit quelques différences non sans originalité.[3]

Yet what Croll calls the "casuistic dialogue on love" is a crucial difference in Sidney's invitation to love, and removes it equally from Marlowe's *Passionate Shepherd to his Love* or its successors.

In 1903 Croll outlined the "convention" begun by Sidney in a footnote to his comparison of the imitation by Fulke Greville:

> Poems following this convention are numerous in later poets. Compare Donne's *The Ecstacy,* Lord Herbert's *Ode on a Question moved whether Love should continue forever,* Wither's *Fair-Virtue, The Mistress of Phil'arete,* Sonnet 3. In Donne's poem by a characteristic subtlety the dialogue is reduced to a monologue spoken by the undistinguished soul of the two lovers. There may be an original in some foreign literature, or Sidney's Song may have suggested the rest. Sedley shows the abuse of the form in various poems and Cartwright protests against the Platonism which found expression in it in his *No Platonic Love.*

Various signs point to Sidney as the exemplar for the English poets, but his verse form undergoes some modification in the later poets. The popularization of Platonic theories, Miss Scott reminds us, was "due à des ouvrages comme les *Asolani* de Bembo, et le *Cortegiano* de Castiglione." Obviously Platonism is not the only love casuistry that finds expression in this convention. The variety of poets who employ this convention is in itself enough to challenge our interest, and more than enough to destroy some of our preconceptions. The probable chronological order of their poems is Sidney, Greville, Donne, Wither, and Lord Herbert. However, we shall examine their use of this convention not in chronological order but rather in that of complication: Sidney, Greville, Wither, Herbert, Donne. Various new elements or alterations of the old will enter into this complication.

Sidney's Song begins with a pastoral setting:

> In a Grove most rich of shade,
> Where Birds wanton musique made,
> *May,* then young, his pyed weedes showing,
> New perfum'd, with flowers fresh growing,
> *Astrophell* with *Stella* sweete,
> Did for mutuall comfort meete . . .

Theirs is an unhappy, forbidden love: "Him great harmes had taught much care,/ Her faire necke a foul yoake bare." Now they find solace for their grief in each other's company,

> While their eyes by Love directed,
> Enterchangeably reflected . . .
> But their tongues restrain'd from walking,
> Till their harts had ended talking.

Finally, "Love it selfe did silence breake," and Astrophell began a "blazon" of her beauties leading to a request, which is suggested by the lines, "*Stella,* in whose body is/Writ each Character of blisse." Fearing to put his request directly, he asks on his knees, "That not I, but since I love you,/Time and place for me may move you." Then all the elements of place and season conspire to preach love, "And if dumbe things be so wittie,/Shall a heavenly grace want pittie?" Finally his hands "Would have made tongues language plaine," but her hands "Gave repulse, all grace excelling." His argument has been based on the analogies of nature suggested by the pastoral setting.

Then Stella's argument begins, "While such wise she love denied,/As yet love she signified." Asking him to "Cease in these effects to prove" her love, she answers in terms of her situation, her "foule yoake." Thus she finds her only comfort in him, and swears her faith by the eyes he praised; in short, she gives all her love and faith, but not her body. For she is restrained by honour and would remain free of shame.

> There-with-all, away she went,
> Leaving him to passion rent:
> With what she had done and spoken,
> That there-with my Song is broken.

She can say "Tirant honour dooth thus use thee" because of the foul yoke which she wears, not because Stella herself would refuse him. Thus she does not argue in terms of the pastoral setting, but in terms of their social condition. These restraints lend vehemence to her vows.

In Greville's imitation of Sidney the brief setting is made more suggestive:

> In the time when herbs and flowers,
> Springing out of melting powers,
> Teach the earth that heate and raine
> Doe make *Cupid* live againe:
> Late when *Sol,* like great hearts, showes
> Largest as he lowest goes,
> *Caelica* with *Philocell*
> In fellowship together fell.

Her hair, however, is made suggestive of mourning, "Of hopes death which to her eyes,/Offers thoughts for sacrifice." The love of Philocell and the scorn of Caelica are then analysed as "Through enamel'd Meades they went,/Quiet she, he passion rent." Here the echo of Sidney leads into a reversal of roles in which Philocell protests his love when at length "His despaire taught feare thus speake":

> You, to whom all Passions pray,
> Like poore Flies that to the fire,
> Where they burne themselves, aspire . . .

These resemblances to Donne's "Canonization" begin a long appeal of the forlorn lover to the cruel mistress. Her cold answers show, says Greville, "How self-pitties have reflexion,/Backe into their owne infection." For she replies that her love is dead and advises him to "let Reason guide affection,/From despaire to new election." Now Philocell begs for pity, but implies doubt of Caelica; whereupon "His eyes great with child with teares/Spies in her eyes many feares." In fury she tells him to be gone, that men are full of contradictions, that he has imposed on her enough, and finally, "I will never rumour move,/At least for one I doe not love."

Then Greville takes up the defence of Philocell against Caelica:

> Shepheardesses, if it prove,
> *Philocell* she once did love,
> Can kind doubt of true affection
> Merit such a sharpe correction?

Thus Greville begins to elaborate the love casuistry as he spells out the argument, which involves Philocell's jealousy and Caelica's wrong. He argues that the nature of love excuses and explains its abuses, and that Philocell will remain faithful to his martyrdom. Greville concludes, "Here my silly Song is ended," but hastens to assure the nymphs that they can find faith in men if they will be constant.

In Greville the seductive element is almost lost in the extension and complication of the love casuistry. Sidney's descriptive praise of the lady is greatly reduced, and the pastoral setting finds no place in the love casuistry. While a more hopeless Petrarchan atmosphere is developed, the poem ends with a real problem in love casuistry and thus justifies the argumentative resolution. Sidney's Song was broken by an action which also completed its argument.

Wither's Sonnet 3 of *Fair Virtue* begins with the familiar setting:

> When Philomela with her strains
> The spring had welcomed in,
> And Flora to bestrow the plains

> With daisies did begin,
> My love and I, on whom suspicious eyes
>   Had set a thousand spies,
> To cozen Argus strove;
>   And seen of none
>   We got alone
> Into a shady grove.

Here "The earth, the air, and all things did conspire/To raise contentment higher"; so that if the lovers had "come to woo," nothing would
have been lacking. Hand in hand they walked, and talked "Of love
and passions past." Their "souls infus'd into each other were" and
shared each other's sorrow. But then their bodies begin to betray their
souls:

> Her dainty palm I gently prest,
>   And with her lips I play'd;
> My cheek upon her panting breast,
>   And on her neck I laid.
> And yet we had no sense of wanton lust . . .

Soon their passions overpower them:

> But kissing and embracing we
>   So long together lay,
> Her touches all inflamed me,
>   And I began to stray.
> My hands presum'd so far, they were too
>   bold . . .

As Wither makes this turn upon Sidney, his lover's virtue is "put to
flight," and his lady in tears begins to plead with him not to spot their
"true love," protesting "Whilst thee I thus refuse/In hotter flames I
fry." Her Platonic lament increases in vehemence:

> Are we the two that have so long
>   Each other's loves embraced?
> And never did affection wrong,
>   Nor think a thought unchaste?

Her argument now involves a line used by Sidney: "I should of all our
passions grow ashamed,/And blush when thou art named." But her
reasons are quite different, for those "who are to lust inclin'd,/Drive
love out of the mind." And she is no Stella:

No vulgar bliss I aimed at
When first I heard thee woo;
I'll never prize a man for that
Which every groom can do.

While she speaks he regains control of himself because in her

Those virtues shine
Whose rays divine
First gave desire a law.

Thus the blush of shame returns to him, for his "soul her light of reason had renew'd." Then he preaches to "wantons" contempt of the body, "Since every beast/In pleasure equals you." And because the conquest of evil brings "peace without compare." But lest the wantons still think his conquest slight, he puts it beyond the labours of Hercules and the chastity of Diana. Whether this persuaded the wantons of his higher love seems at best doubtful.

Wither has certainly made the Sidney convention a vehicle for a prurient Platonism. Nature conspires with the body, not the soul, but the argument turns against nature in the conclusion. When the rescued lover expresses the moral of Platonic love, he counts its dividends too much in the old currency to establish the new. Altogether the pastoral framework is at odds with the Platonism, and matters are not improved by mixing mythology into the realism of the poem.

Lord Herbert's "Ode upon a Question moved, whether Love should continue for ever?" has the most elaborate pastoral setting of all. Nature in flower waits for the sun, "the wish'd Bridegroom of the earth." Birds, wind, brook, lovers, all "An harmony of parts did bind." The lovers walked "towards a pleasant Grove" and reposed on the grass,

Long their fixt eyes to Heaven bent,
Unchanged, they did never move,
As if so great and pure a love
No Glass but it could represent.

Then Celinda raises the question of love's end at death, and does so in stanzas that are a temptation to quote, asking whether if love's fire is kindled with life, it will not go out with life. Since this also raises the problem of sense in love, Melander answers that their love is beyond but not above sense, and that they must reach toward the invisible through the visible.

Rephrasing her question, he answers that since their "virtuous habits" are born of the soul, they "Must with it evermore endure." In Herbert's *De Veritate* (ed. Carré, p. 123) this argument rests upon this proposition: "It is then reasonable to believe that the faculties with which we are born do not perish at death." If sin's guilt never dies, the joy of virtuous love is still more certain of survival. Otherwise Heaven's laws would be vain, "When to an everlasting Cause/They gave a perishing Effect." Where God admits the fair, he does not exclude love; nor does he exclude sense if bodies rise again:

> For if no use of sense remain
>   When bodies once this life forsake,
>   Or they could no delight partake,
> Why should they ever rise again?

The final postulate here alters the statement in *De Veritate* (p. 124): "When that which is corruptible in us is separated from what is incorruptible, which I hold to be the great unceasing work of nature, it is not the faculties which fall into decay, but the sense-organs." And if love is the end of knowledge here in imperfection, how much more perfect will it be in perfection. Then his argument takes its final turn: "Were not our souls immortal made,/Our equal loves can make them such." Although this suggests the end of Donne's "Good morrow," it turns toward propagation as a final answer to the question moved:

> So when one wing can make no way,
>   Two joyned can themselves dilate,
>   So can two persons propagate,
> When singly either would decay.

In this persuasive figure their relation to heaven is not forsaken as "Each shall be both, yet both but one." Indeed, her eyes "look up again to find their place":

> While such a moveless silent peace
>   Did seize on their becalmed sense,
>   One would have thought some influence
> Their ravish'd spirits did possess.

Thus Herbert exhibits no such dislocation of the Platonic mode as we find in Wither. But it is not quite so simple as saying that since their love is of the soul and the soul is immortal, therefore their love is immortal. For body is involved in this awareness, and so it becomes the last resort in persuasion and fulfilment, because God is best known and loved in his creatures.

Herbert's argument, however, needs to be understood not simply as Platonism but in terms of his *De Veritate*. It may be judged by this summary of his remarks on love (pp. 196–8): "Consequently, though our mind can become immersed in physical feelings while it concerns itself with the common good, yet I place love among the intellectual and spiritual faculties, because lust and similar cravings can be found in a plethoric body apart from love. . . . As for the objects of the intellectual and spiritual faculties, there are two kinds, namely, particular and general. In this respect they are also distinguished from the physical faculties, which seem only to have particular objects. The particular objects of the internal intellectual faculties are the divine attributes, while the common objects are physical objects. . . . Love was the first of the inner emotions. This faculty is above all sensitive to the divine beauty and goodness and afterwards to all the divine attributes. . . . The common object of this faculty is physical love. For this reason the feeling which relates to the perpetuation of the species, so long as it is not infected with unlawful lust or concupiscence, is humane and may spring from the faculty which seeks the general good."

While the final statement in this summary gives another dimension to the conclusion of his *Ode*, the relation between the physical and intellectual in love explains the form which his answer takes in arguing "that the faculties with which we are born do not perish at death." Once this has been said, however, one must return to the poetic cogency of the *Ode* which may be illuminated but cannot be replaced by the structure of *De Veritate*. The ambiguity of the conclusion to the *Ode* appears more clearly by virtue of our comparison, but we have to take care not to lose the meaning of the physical because of its intellectual implication, or else we will transform the primary impact of the poem and blunt the surprise of its ending. For the conclusion seems both to consummate their love and to compromise his answer. But even the beauty of stanzas like

> This said, in her up-lifted face,
> Her eyes which did that beauty crown,
> Were like two starrs, that having faln down,
> Look up again to find their place:

may owe something to the idea in Plato's *Timaeus* that souls, before their human birth, were in the stars. And Herbert's final turn gives a rarefied air to the conclusion of "The Extasie."

Donne, like Herbert, is interested less in the moral casuistry of love than in the philosophical questions provoked by it. Hence the debate in "The Extasie" may involve body and soul rather more than two lovers. Croll has said that "In *Astrophel and Stella* and the *Arcadia* the prevailing idea is the contrast between the abstract spiritual ideals which appeal to the soul alone and the concrete forms on which ordinary human desire is fixed." But he adds that the Platonic mode of thought is used by Sidney rather as a literary convention than as a serious philosophy. Obviously it is not a part of the convention of physical love introduced by Sidney's Eighth Song, which is more properly described as an invitation to love.

This convention may be restated for "The Extasie" as follows: description of the burgeoning of nature; description of lovers and their emotions; their absorption in the rapture of love; their relationship to some problem arising from this state of rapture; its investigation and solution; relation of the solution to their initial rapture.

The pastoral setting of "The Extasie" is reduced to the shortest and most carnally suggestive form yet found in this convention:

> Where, like a pillow on a bed,
>   A Pregnant banke swel'd up, to rest
> The violets reclining head,
>   Sat we two, one anothers best.

Hands and eyes as yet were "all the meanes to make us one,"

> And pictures in our eyes to get
> Was all our propagation.

In Sidney, it may be remembered, their eyes "Enterchangeably reflected." The last line sounds as if Donne were beginning where Herbert concluded, but it simply introduces the consummation of physical union toward which they seem bent. This consummation, however, remains uncertain because it must be decided by the souls, "which to advance their state" had left the bodies, their prisons. Now they "hung 'twixt her, and mee," preventing consummation until they have negotiated an agreement; meanwhile the bodies lie inanimate, like statues. Now this negotiation involves a discovery about the nature of their love, but it can be understood only by one refined enough by love to understand the language of the soul. Hence the character of the invoked witness and yet his inability to distinguish voices in a union of minds. For they discover that it was not sex but a mingling of souls that moved them to love. At this point it seems as if their original physical means to union have been completely invalidated. But a violet from the pastoral setting provides an analogy to show how transplanted souls also redouble in the abler soul of love.

> Wee then, who are this new soule, know,
>   Of what we are compos'd, and made,
> For, th' Atomies of which we grow,
>   Are soules, whom no change can invade.

And so their love acquires the superior powers that belong to the soul, and the negotiations would seem to have gone against the bodies, if it were not for the fact that the violet helped to elucidate the mystery of their love. Even so the shift to the voice of feeling takes us by surprise:

> But O alas, so long, so farre
>   Our bodies why doe wee forbeare?

We might suppose that isolated superiority is too much for them, or that some "defects of lonelinesse" are not controlled by their souls. But of course their ecstasy had a physical origin, and their negotiation requires some solution for the problem of the bodies.

In this argument the apology for body now begins. The bodies are not the souls, but their senses first brought the souls together. As sphere to intelligence, or as air to heaven, the body is the agent or medium of the soul. As blood ascends to spirits to unite body and soul, so even pure lovers' souls must descend to affections and faculties which sense may reach, or else the living soul is locked in a bodily prison, except in ecstasy.

> To' our bodies turne wee then, that so
>   Weake men on love reveal'd may looke;
> Loves mysteries in soules doe grow,
>   But yet the body is his booke.

Weak men require physical revelation, but initiates in love's mysteries, who do not, will see small change when their spiritual unity is manifested in the physical. Thus their original physical union may be consummated without spiritual adulteration, for the bodies are not "drosse to us, but allay." Thus the problem of the physical in love posed by the original situation has been solved by inclusion, not by rejection. Again the hypothetical listener—for the souls are still speaking—is called to witness the final turn of the argument.

Only the rejection of the physical would have saved "The Extasie" from any suggestion of an invitation to love, but even its inclusion probably did not assure its success for Dryden because it still "perplexes the minds of the fair sex with nice speculations of philosophy." And this philosophical turn is given form by Croll's observation: "In Donne's poem by a characteristic subtlety the dialogue is reduced to a monologue spoken by the undistinguished soul of the two lovers." And the reason for this form is that there is no contrariety between the lovers but only in the subject of their discourse. Hence the monologue is instrumental to the philosophy, and Donne uses the ecstasy for this mingling of souls to rise to the Platonic level. He does not, like Bembo in Castiglione's *Courtier*, make a kiss the cause of this mingling of souls, though "one alone so framed of them both ruleth (in a manner) two bodies" in his poem. But he did use the ecstasy as an expressive device in *Ignatius his Conclave:*

> I was in an *Extasie*, and
>> *My little wandring sportful Soule,*
>> *Ghest, and Companion of my body*
> had liberty to wander through all places . . .

Here of course it is a satiric device, not a Platonic device. In Donne's poem it becomes a means arising from the rapture of love by which to analyse that rapture in terms of the nature of man. In a subtler form this poem is a debate between the soul and body or an analysis of love in these terms without the sharp oppositions found in "A Valediction: of the booke" or "A Valediction: forbidding mourning."

Thus into a convention of physical love Donne introduces the Platonic convention as a means to investigate the nature of love. Up to a point the steps in both conventions coincide, but the conclusion denies and harmonizes the extremes of both. The physical convention is clear from the beginning; the Platonic is introduced by the ecstasy. The former includes the latter and is modified by it. The sensual, idyllic convention, united with the Platonic, issues in a mediate or combined position; but while posing the carnal versus spiritual contention, the poem never surrenders the primacy of the spiritual, nor ever rejects or condemns the carnal like Wither.

Donne's poetry runs the gamut of love described by Bembo on the basis of his analysis of man in Castiglione's *Courtier:*

> And because in our soule there be three manner waies to
> know, namely, by sense, reason, and understanding: of sense
> there ariseth appetite or longing, which is common to us with

brute beastes: of reason ariseth election or choice, which is proper to man: of understanding, by the which man may be partner with Angels, ariseth will.

Donne is more likely to base his analysis on the three souls mentioned in "A Valediction: of my name, in the window":

> Then, as all my soules bee,
> Emparadis'd in you, (in whom alone
> I understand, and grow and see,) . . .

Here the three souls are named by their major faculties in this order: rational, vegetable, animal or sensitive. But whichever scale is used, Donne treats the various kinds of love and lovers described by Bembo. On the sensual level it is bound by the limitations of the senses; on the Platonic level it is a relation of souls or mind, unaffected by the physical and its limitations of time and space. The problem of absence is usually solved on this level. But Donne is seldom a pure Platonist; he usually inhabits the region of "The Extasie," occasionally ascending higher on the scale or descending lower. He even has moments of scorn for "That loving wretch that sweares,/'Tis not the bodies marry, but the mindes," but it never reaches the mockery of Cartwright's "Tell me no more of minds embracing minds." Nevertheless, Bembo's discussion in the *Courtier* is the best introduction to Donne's treatment of love.

The study of this convention gives us a concrete lesson in the kind of literary continuity and change that took place between Elizabethan and Jacobean times. It also provides us with some insight into the relations between tradition and the individual talent in these poets. Of course the poems are not equally representative of their poets; but since the broad form is dictated by the convention, their own formal powers, both poetic and metrical, can be measured comparatively within a limited area. If such a comparison is thought to be altogether unfair, perhaps we could agree that this convention does not provide easy examples by which to illustrate the decline of poetry in Jacobean times. And possibly also that the usual course of such conventions is towards decline rather than the reverse. I do not think Donne and Herbert need to fear the verdict, and I find Greville worthy of more serious interest than either Sidney or Wither.

NOTES

[1] *Modern Language Review*, Vol. 27, No. 1.
[2] *The Works of Fulke Greville*, Philadelphia, 1903, p. 9.
[3] Paris, 1929, p. 47.

ʁ

John Donne in Meditation: the *Anniversaries*

Beare not therefore with her losses, for shee is won for ever, but with the momentary absence of your most happy sister: yea it can not iustly bee called an absence, many thoghts being daily in parlee with her, onely mens eyes and eares unwoorthy to enioy so sweet an obiect, have resigned their interest, and interested this treasure in their hearts, being the fittest shrines for so pure a Saint, whome, as none did know but did love, so none can nowe remember [but] with devotion. Men may behold hir with shame of their former life, seeing one of the weaker sexe honour her weaknesse wyth such a trayne of perfections. Ladies may admire her as a glorie to their degree, in whom honour was portraied in her full likenesse, grace having perfited Natures first draught with all the due colours of an absolute vertue: all women accept her as a patterne to immitate her gifts and her good partes.

> Robert Southwell, *The Triumphs over Death* (in memory of Margaret Sackville), 1595

I

From the early days of Donne's Satire 3, where meditation struggles to convert the methods of Roman satire, down to the late days of his

From *The Poetry of Meditation: A Study in English Religious Literature of the Seventeenth Century* (New Haven: Yale University Press; London: Oxford University Press, 1954), pp. 211–48. Reprinted, by permission of the publishers, with emendations from the 2nd edition (paperback, 1962).

"Hymne to God the Father," where he seems to transform the refrain of Wyatt's love-lament,[1] the distinctive note of Donne is always his ground-tone of religious quest, even when the overt mode of the poem is one of mockery. His search for the One underlies and explains his discontent with the fluctuations of transitory passion, as he makes clear in the *Second Anniversary*:

> But pause, my soule; And study, ere thou fall
> On accidentall joyes, th'essentiall.
> Still before Accessories doe abide
> A triall, must the principall be tride.
> And what essentiall joy can'st thou expect
> Here upon earth? what permanent effect
> Of transitory causes? Dost thou love
> Beauty? (And beauty worthy'st is to move)
> Poore cousened cousenor, *that* she, and *that* thou,
> Which did begin to love, are neither now;
> You are both fluid, chang'd since yesterday;
> Next day repaires, (but ill) last dayes decay.
> Nor are, (although the river keepe the name)
> Yesterdaies waters, and to daies the same.
> So flowes her face, and thine eyes, neither now
> That Saint, nor Pilgrime, which your loving vow
> Concern'd, remaines; but whil'st you thinke you bee
> Constant, you'are hourely in inconstancie. (383–400)

Consequently, in his "Songs and Sonets" the central power arises from the way in which, along with his insistence on the physical, he grips the thin Petrarchan affirmation of spiritual love, and builds it up on every side with theological proofs and profound religious images.

Thus readers have disagreed over whether "The Extasie" is a poem of seduction or a deep theological and philosophical exploration of the relationship between body and soul:[2] for it is all these things, simultaneously. The wit of the title depends upon the double reference to "sensuall Extasie" and mystical *extasis;* the whole poem develops from the physical desires implied in the curious "composition of place" with which the poem opens:

> Where, like a pillow on a bed,
> A Pregnant banke swel'd up . . . .

Those desires, then, after long intellectual analysis of human love, are finally reconciled with the spiritual in an exhortation that involves the theological concepts of incarnation and revelation:

> To'our bodies turne wee then, that so
>   Weake men on love reveal'd may looke;
> Loves mysteries in soules doe grow,
>   But yet the body is his booke.

Likewise, the somber tradition of meditation on death lies behind "The Funerall," with its half-mocking transformation of a symbol of physical lust into a religious "mystery":

> Who ever comes to shroud me, do not harme
>   Nor question much
> That subtile wreath of haire, which crowns my arme;
> The mystery, the signe you must not touch,
>   For 'tis my outward Soule,
> Viceroy to that, which then to heaven being gone,
>   Will leave this to controule,
> And keepe these limbes, her Provinces, from dissolution.

Or, more violently, in "Twicknam garden" the tears and sighs of the traditional lover are converted into agony by a bitter play upon religious images:

> But O, selfe traytor, I do bring
> The spider love, which transubstantiates all,
>   And can convert Manna to gall,
> And that this place may thoroughly be thought
> True Paradise, I have the serpent brought.

In his love-poems, then, the central wit consists in this: in taking up the religious motifs conventionally displayed in Petrarchan verse, and stressing them so heavily that any one of three results may be achieved. Sometimes the effect is one of witty blasphemy, as in "The Dreame," where he deifies his lady by attributing her arrival in his bedroom to her Godlike power of reading his mind. Sometimes, as in "The Extasie," the poem maintains a complex tone in which the playful and the solemn, the profane and the sacred, are held in a perilous poise:

> As 'twixt two equall Armies, Fate
> Suspends uncertaine victorie . . . .

And at other times human love is exalted to the religious level, notably in "A nocturnall upon S. Lucies day," where, in accordance with the ancient ecclesiastical usage of the term "nocturnal," or "nocturne,"

Donne presents a midnight service, a "Vigill," commemorating the death of his beloved—his saint. He recalls the passionate fluctuations of their worldly career, in terms that suggest a long period of frustrated spiritual devotion:

> Oft a flood
> Have wee two wept, and so
> Drownd the whole world, us two; oft did we grow
> To be two Chaosses, when we did show
> Care to ought else; and often absences
> Withdrew our soules, and made us carcasses.

But with her death his physical life has died, and he is "re-begot Of absence, darkenesse, death": in him love has "wrought new Alchimie" by expressing "A quintessence even from nothingnesse." His only life now lies in the spiritual realm where she now lives:

> You lovers, for whose sake, the lesser Sunne
> At this time to the Goat is runne
> To fetch new lust, and give it you,
> Enjoy your summer all;
> Since shee enjoyes her long nights festivall,
> Let mee prepare towards her, and let mee call
> This houre her Vigill, and her Eve, since this
> Both the yeares, and the dayes deep midnight is.

Surely Mr. Murray is right in arguing that this poem deals with Donne's love for his wife;[3] its conclusion seems to point the way toward the opening lines of Holy Sonnet 17:

> Since she whom I lov'd hath payd her last debt
> To Nature, and to hers, and my good is dead,
> And her Soule early into heaven ravished,
> Wholly on heavenly things my mind is sett.

It seems to me quite possible that Donne wrote the "Nocturnall" after his wife's death in 1617; though it might have been composed on some occasion of severe illness, such as one recorded in a letter by Donne (1606?), where he speaks of a certain "paper" written during a night of his wife's severe labor:

> It is (I cannot say the waightyest, but truly) the saddest
> lucubration and nights passage that ever I had. For it exer-

cised those hours, which, with extreme danger to her, whom
I should hardly have abstained from recompensing for her
company in this world, with accompanying her out of it,
encreased my poor family with a son. Though her anguish,
and my fears, and hopes, seem divers and wild distractions
from this small businesse of your papers, yet because they all
narrowed themselves, and met in *Via regia,* which is the
consideration of our selves, and God, I thought it time not
unfit for this despatch.[4]

In any case, the "Nocturnall" vividly illustrates the way in which
Donne's poetry, throughout his career, moves along a Great Divide
between the sacred and the profane, now facing one way, now another, but always remaining intensely aware of both sides. In his
love-poetry the religious aspects are frequently so strong that they
seem to overwhelm the fainter religious themes of Petrarchan poetry;
while in six of the "Holy Sonnets" (3, 13, 14, 17, 18, 19) the memories and images of profane love are deliberately used in love-sonnets
of sacred parody. One must observe, then, the greatest possible caution
in considering the relation between the "profane" and the "religious"
in Donne's work: individual poems will not fall easily into such categories; nor can the poems be safely dated by assumptions about the
more religious, and the less religious, periods of his life.

II

Donne may well have written some of his love-songs and some of
his "Holy Sonnets" during the same periods of his life: one of the most
dubious assumptions in modern studies of Donne has been the universal acceptance of Gosse's dating of all the "Holy Sonnets" in 1617
or after, simply because one of the sonnets refers to the death of
Donne's wife.[5] Grierson accepted this dating, and thereby gave it
currency, along with the view that Donne's religious poems "fall into
two groups": those written before his ordination, which are marked
by a more intellectual style, and those written after his ordination and
after the death of his wife, which are of a more passionate quality.
But such distinctions are at best hazardous with a personality so paradoxical as Donne's; moreover, as I have suggested in the case of "La
Corona," differences in style may also be explained by differences in
the meditative traditions which Donne is following in certain poems.
Grierson's examination of the manuscripts does not support the above
dating of the "Holy Sonnets." He points out, for example, that in the

Harleian manuscript they bear the heading: "Holy Sonnets: written 20 yeares since." After this general heading the manuscript then gives, under the special heading, "La Corona," the seven sonnets properly belonging to that sequence. "Thereafter follow," Grierson adds, "without any fresh heading, twelve of the sonnets belonging to the second group, generally entitled *Holy Sonnets*." Noting that the date 1629 is given to other poems in this manuscript, Grierson adds that this would bring us back to the year 1609, a dating which he is inclined to accept for "La Corona." But, as Grierson says, "the question is, did the copyist [of this manuscript] intend that the note should apply to all the sonnets he transcribed or only to the *La Corona* group?" Having already accepted Gosse's dating, he is forced to rule out the second group; yet the sonnet on Donne's wife is not among these twelve, and indeed the fact that only twelve of the sonnets occur here may suggest that the nineteen "Holy Sonnets" were not necessarily all written in the same period, as Gosse assumes. Grierson himself notes that he "cannot find a definite significance in any order," and that "each sonnet is a separate meditation"; this would seem to destroy the basis for Gosse's dating.[6]

Furthermore, it is a curious fact that Donne's "Elegie on Mistris Boulstred," who died on August 4, 1609,[7] seems unquestionably to represent a recantation of his famous sonnet:

> Death be not proud, though some have called thee
> Mighty and dreadfull, for, thou art not soe,
> For, those, whom thou think'st, thou dost overthrow,
> Die not, poore death, nor yet canst thou kill mee.

The opening lines of the elegy seem explicitly to answer this opening of the sonnet:

> Death I recant, and say, unsaid by mee
>   What ere hath slip'd, that might diminish thee.
> Spirituall treason, atheisme 'tis, to say,
>   That any can thy Summons disobey.

Lines 9–10 appear to reinterpret lines 7–8 of the sonnet:

> And soonest our best men with thee doe goe,
> Rest of their bones, and soules deliverie.

> Now hee will seeme to spare, and doth more wast,
>   Eating the best first, well preserv'd to last.

And indeed all the first half of the elegy (1–34) amounts to a denial of the sonnet's ending, "death, thou shalt die." We have the paren- thesis, "were Death dead" (15); and the exclamations, "O strong and long-liv'd death" (21), "How could I thinke thee nothing" (25), "O mighty bird of prey" (31). The conclusion seems inevitable that Holy Sonnet 10 must have been written before August 4, 1609. If this is so, could it not also be true of other "Holy Sonnets"?

The conjecture is supported by the evidence of Donne's painful letters from Mitcham, where he frequently speaks of his "medita- tion," [8] and by Grierson's dating of "La Corona" (1607–9), "The Annuntiation and Passion" (March 25, 1608), and "The Litanie" (1609–10). [9] Everything that we know of Donne indicates that, during the years from his marriage in 1601 down through the time of his ordination in 1615, he was engaging in the most fervent and painful self-analysis, directed toward the problem of his vocation. The crisis and culmination of these efforts, I believe, is represented in the two *Anniversaries*, both of which, surprisingly enough, may have been written in the year 1611. (See Appendix 2.) Thus they seem to come immediately before the first clear announcement by Donne, in his letter of c. 1612, that he has decided to enter the ministry: "having obeyed at last, after much debatement within me, the Inspirations (as I hope) of the Spirit of God, and resolved to make my Profession Divinitie . . . ." [10] The relationship of the *Anniversaries* to these "debatements" is reinforced by the very close verbal and thematic similarities, pointed out by Mrs. Simpson, between these poems and Donne's *Essayes in Divinity*: those "Several Disquisitions, Interwoven with Meditations and Prayers," which "were the voluntary sacrifices of severall hours, when he had many debates betwixt God and him- self, whether he were worthy, and competently learned to enter into Holy Orders." [11]

The *Anniversaries*, along with his other meditations of this period —including, perhaps, many of the "Holy Sonnets"—may be seen as part of the spiritual exercises which Donne was performing in the effort to determine his problem of "election": the term which St. Ignatius Loyola gave to that crucial portion of his *Exercises* of the Second Week (pp. 54–60), where the exercitant is faced with the problem of deciding upon a way of life, "as for example an office or benefice to be accepted or left." One of the problems here described by the *Exercises* is one that, according to Walton, troubled Donne when Morton in the year 1607 urged Donne to accept an office in the Church: "there are others that first desire to possess benefices and then to serve God in them. So these do not go straight to God, but wish God to come straight to their inordinate affections; thus they make of the end a means, and of the means an end; so that what they ought to take first they take last." [12] Among the Jesuit methods for "making a sound and good election" in such matters, it is interesting —with the "Holy Sonnets" in mind—to notice that meditations on the love of God, on death ("as if I were at the point of death"), and on the Day of Judgment are especially recommended, along with another method that may have some relation to the poem which Donne later wrote "To Mr Tilman after he had taken orders": "The second rule is to place before my eyes a man whom I have never seen or known, and to consider what I, desiring all perfection for him, would tell him to do and choose for the greater glory of God our Lord, and the greater perfection of his soul; and acting so, to keep the rule which I lay down for another." For these methods of "election" might be used to confirm a decision made, as well as to make the original decision. Finally, it is worth noting that among the various "methods of prayer" recommended in the *Spiritual Exercises*, there is one that is similar to the method followed by Donne in "The Litanie": it consists "in considering the signification of each word" in a public, liturgical prayer, and in dwelling "on the consideration of this word, so long as he finds meanings, comparisons, relish, and consolation in thoughts about this word." (p. 80)

The *Anniversaries*, then, were composed during a period when Donne appears to have been utilizing all the modes of meditation and self-analysis that he knew, in the effort to make the crucial decision of his life. It was a period when his weighing of the sacred and profane tendencies within himself must have reached a climax of intensity; and this, I believe, is why the two poems represent Donne's most elaborate examples of the art of sacred parody and his most extensive efforts in the art of poetical meditation.

Yet the *Anniversaries* are not usually treated as whole poems. For one thing, the biographical facts underlying these poems lead readers to approach them with suspicion, since they were written in memory of the daughter of Donne's generous patron, Sir Robert Drury—a girl who died in her fifteenth year, and whom Donne admits he never saw.[13] As a result, the elaborate eulogies of Elizabeth Drury are frequently dismissed as venal and insincere, while interest in the poems centers on those passages which reflect Donne's awareness of the "new philosophy," on explicitly religious portions, or on any portions which provide illustrative quotations for special studies of Donne and his period.

Such fragmentary appreciation of the poems has, I think, hampered an understanding of their full significance. For each poem is carefully designed as a whole, and the full meaning of each grows out of a deliberately articulated structure. Furthermore, a close reading of each poem shows that the two *Anniversaries* are significantly different in structure and in the handling of Petrarchan imagery, and are consequently different in value. The *First Anniversary*, despite its careful structure, is, it must be admitted, successful only in brilliant patches; but I think it can be shown that the *Second Anniversary*, despite some flaws, is as a whole one of the great religious poems of the seventeenth century.

III

Let us look at the structure of the *First Anniversary: An Anatomie of the World. Wherein, By occasion of the untimely death of Mistris Elizabeth Drury, the frailty and the decay of this whole World is represented*. The poem is divided into an Introduction, a Conclusion, and five distinct sections which form the body of the work. Each of these five sections is subdivided into three sections: first, a meditation on some aspect of "the frailty and the decay of this whole world"; second, a eulogy of Elizabeth Drury as the "Idea" of human perfection and the source of hope, now lost, for the world; third, a refrain introducing a moral:

> Shee, shee is dead; shee's dead: when thou knowest this,
> Thou knowest how poore a trifling thing man is.
> And learn'st thus much by our Anatomie . . . .

In each section the second line of this refrain is modified so as to summarize the theme of the whole section; in the following outline of the poem I use part of the second line of each refrain as the heading for each section:

Introduction, 1–90. The world is sick, "yea, dead, yea putrified," since she, its "intrinsique balme" and "preservative," its prime example of Virtue, is dead.
Section I, 91–190: "how poore a trifling thing man is."
1. Meditation, 91–170. Because of Original Sin man has decayed in length of life, in physical size, in mental capacity.
2. Eulogy, 171–82. The girl was perfect virtue; she purified herself and had a purifying power over all.
3. Refrain and Moral, 183–90. Our only hope is in religion.

Section II, 191–246: "how lame a cripple this world is."
  1. Meditation, 191–218. The "universall frame" has received injury from the sin of the Angels, and now in universe, in state, in family, " 'Tis all in peeces, all cohaerence gone."
  2. Eulogy, 219–36. Only this girl possessed the power which might have unified the world.
  3. Refrain and Moral, 237–46. Contemn and avoid this sick world.

Section III, 247–338: "how ugly a monster this world is."
  1. Meditation, 247–304. Proportion, the prime ingredient of beauty, no longer exists in the universe.
  2. Eulogy, 305–24. The girl was the "measure of all Symmetrie" and harmony.
  3. Refrain and Moral, 325–38. Human acts must be "done fitly and in proportion."

Section IV, 339–76: "how wan a Ghost this our world is."
  1. Meditation, 339–58. "Beauties other second Element, Colour, and lustre now, is as neere spent."
  2. Eulogy, 359–68. The girl had the perfection of color and gave color to the world.
  3. Refrain and Moral, 369–76. There is no pleasure in an ugly world; it is wicked to use false colors.

Section V, 377–434: "how drie a Cinder this world is."
  1. Meditation, 377–98. Physical "influence" of the heavens upon the earth has been weakened.
  2. Eulogy, 399–426. The girl's virtue has little effect on us now because of this weakened "correspondence" between heavens and earth; in fact the world's corruption weakened her effect while she lived.
  3. Refrain and Moral, 427–34. Nothing "Is worth our travaile, griefe, or perishing," except the joys of religious virtue.

Conclusion, 435–74.

It seems clear that the religious motifs in Petrarchan lament, found at their best in Petrarch's poems "To Laura in Death," have here combined with strictly religious meditation to produce a poem which derives its form, fundamentally, from the tradition of spiritual exercises. The Jesuit exercises, we recall, normally involve a series of five exercises daily for a period of about a month, each meditation being precisely divided into points, usually into three points.

At the same time it is important to recall the ways of celebrating
the Ideal Woman—the "Type, or an Idaea of an Accomplisht piety" [14]
—represented in the meditations of the rosary which have been discussed in Chapter 2. The divisions of the Dominican rosary fall into
three series of five meditations each, while, in Loarte's *Instructions,*
every meditation "is distinguished into three pointes." (f.6v.) Meditation on only five of these mysteries at a time was quite common: the
name "rosary," says Worthington, is "used sometimes largely, and
sometimes strictly"; "largely" it contains fifteen mysteries; "strictly"
it contains five, "as it is commonly ment, when one is appointed for
penance, or for pardon, or for other like cause to say a Rosarie."
(preface). Thus the number five becomes associated with the celebration of the Virgin: the five-petaled Rose becomes her flower.[15] This,
evidently, is what lies behind Donne's treatment of the five-petaled
flower in his poem, "The Primrose":

> Live Primrose then, and thrive
> With thy true number five;
> And women, whom this flower doth represent,
> With this mysterious number be content . . . .

With this symbolic number in mind, it is even more suggestive
to consider the Jesuit Puente's directions for using the rosary to
meditate upon the virtues of Mary. "The principall thing wherein
wee are to manifest our devotion, towards the Virgin," says Puente,
is "the imitation of her heroicall virtues, wherunto it will greatly ayd,
to meditate them in the recitall of the Rosarie, in every tenne Ave
Maries, one virtue." And in doing this, we are to follow a threefold
procedure: "fixing the eyes and intention upon three things."

1. Upon the heroicall acts which the Virgin exercised about
that virtue . . . admiring her sanctitie, reioycing therin,
glorifying God, who gave it unto her, and exulting for the
reward which he hath given for such a virtu. 2. To fixe mine
eyes upon the wante which I have of that virtu, and upon
the contrary faults and defects wherinto I fall, sorrowing for
them with great confusion and humiliation . . . . 3. To
make some stedfast purposes, with the greatest stabilitie that
I can, to imitate the B. Virgin in these acts of virtue, assigning to this effect some particular virtue, trusting in the favor
of this pious Mother, that shee will assist me to performe the
same. (2, 587)

Such a threefold division of meditation, within a larger fivefold structure, has a long tradition, as Wilmart has shown by his publication of the meditations of Stephen of Salley, an English Cistercian of the early thirteenth century.[16] Stephen gives fifteen meditations on the Joys of the Virgin, divided into three series of fives; the most interesting aspect of them here is the subdivision of each meditation into three parts: (1) *Meditatio*, on the mystery itself; (2) *Gaudium*, a summary of the "Joy"; (3) *Peticio*, prayer to the Virgin invoking her assistance in the achievement of Christian perfection—the whole meditation ending with the refrain of an Ave Maria.

Meditation on the Virgin might easily influence Petrarchan eulogy; in fact Petrarch himself suggests such an influence by concluding his sequence to Laura with a *canzone* to the Virgin Mary. His previous treatment of Laura is different only in degree, not in kind. Thus in a poem describing what Donne calls "the Idea of a Woman," some connotations of Mary would appear to be almost inevitable for a poet of Donne's background. At any rate, in Donne's Introduction to his *Anatomie*, along with Petrarchan hyperbole, we find Elizabeth Drury treated in terms which seem to adumbrate the practice of meditating on Mary: she is a "Queene" ascended to Heaven, attended by Saints; her Name has a mysterious power: [17]

> Her name defin'd thee [the world], gave thee forme, and frame,
> And thou forgett'st to celebrate thy name.

She is "A strong example gone, equall to law," she was "The Cyment which did faithfully compact, And glue all vertues." Nothing remains for us, in this dying world, but to arouse our souls to imitate her; such memory of her

> Creates a new world, and new creatures bee
> Produc'd: the matter and the stuffe of this,
> Her vertue, and the forme our practice is.

Yet we cannot sustain ourselves in this new "dignitie" without some defense against the assaults of the world upon us, and against that presumption which destroys the self-righteous:

> Yet, because outward stormes the strongest breake,
> And strength it selfe by confidence growes weake,
> This new world may be safer, being told
> The dangers and diseases of the old:

> For with due temper men doe then forgoe,
> Or covet things, when they their true worth know.

The twofold aim of religious meditation is suggested in the last two lines. Meditation on the sinfulness of the "old man" and on the corruption of the world will teach men to "forgoe" the things of this world; and, conversely, meditation on the Example of Virtue will lead men to "covet" the imitation of the perfect soul.

In this twofold purpose of meditation lies another aspect of spiritual exercises which deserves consideration: the practice of dividing meditations into two sequences according to the seven days of the week, with two kinds of meditation each day.[18] Thus, in general, the exercitant alternates meditation leading to contempt of the world and of self with consolatory and uplifting meditation on Christ. As Juan de Avila explains,

> They who are much exercised in the *knowledge* of themselves, (in respect that they are continually viewing their defects so neer at hand) are wont to fall into great sadnes, and disconfidence, and pusillanimity; for which reason, it is necessary that they do exercise themselves also in another *knowledge*, which giveth comfort, and strength, much more then the other gave discouragement . . . .
> It is therefore fit for thee, after the exercise of the *knowledge of thy selfe* to imploy thy mind, upon the *knowledge of Christ Iesus our Lord*.[19]

This widespread use of contrasting meditations is also given thorough development in an English work contemporary with the *Anniversaries*: Nicholas Breton's *Divine Considerations of the Soule* (1608). Breton gives two series of seven meditations, one on "the excellencie of God," the other on "the vilenesse of man," to be used in this manner:

> Looke then upon the greatnes of God and the smalnesse of man; the goodnes of God, and the vilenesse of man; the wisdome of God, and the folly of man; the love of God, and the hate of man; the grace of God, and the disgrace of man; the mercy of God, and the tyranny of man; and the glory of God, and the infamy of man: and fixing the eye of the heart upon the one and the other, how canst thou but to the glory of God, and shame of thy selfe . . . cry with the Prophet David, *Oh Lord what is man that thou doest visit him?* [20]

Donne's *Anatomie* seems clearly to fall into such a mold, with its alternation of contempt (Meditation) and glorification (Eulogy), Donne's Moral merely serves to draw a brief conclusion from this contrast.

These examples are, I hope, sufficient to suggest the various and flexible relationships that exist between Donne's *Anatomie* and the tradition of methodical meditation. In particular, his fivefold sequence and his alternation of contempt and praise within each section mark the poem as a spiritual exercise. But the ultimate question remains and has no doubt already been suggested by the above parallels: is it valid to write in such a tradition when the pattern of virtue is, literally taken, only a girl? Certainly the chief problem in evaluating the poem has been very shrewdly put in the blunt objection of Ben Jonson: "That Donne's Anniversary was profane and full of blasphemies; that he told Mr. Donne, if it had been written of the Virgin Mary it had been something; to which he answered that he described the Idea of a Woman and not as she was." [21]

IV

When does laudation of an Ideal Woman become thus objectionable in poetry with a strong religious note? It has not been generally considered so in Dante and Petrarch. Is it objectionable in Donne? An answer, so far as this poem is concerned, may be suggested by noting Petrarch's general treatment of Laura in Death. Petrarch has successfully combined eulogy with religious themes by keeping his sequence always focused on his central symbol of perfection: the *contemptus mundi*, the hyperbole of the world's destruction, the praise of Laura in Heaven, are all justified by maintaining Laura as the origin and end of the poems' emotions, and thus making her the First Cause of the sequence.

> The chosen angels, and the spirits blest,
> Celestial tenants, on that glorious day
> My Lady join'd them, throng'd in bright array
> Around her, with amaze and awe imprest.
> "What splendour, what new beauty stands confest
> Unto our sight?"—among themselves they say;
> "No soul, in this vile age, from sinful clay
> To our high realms has risen so fair a guest."
> Delighted to have changed her mortal state,
> She ranks amid the purest of her kind;

> And ever and anon she looks behind,
> To mark my progress and my coming wait;
> Now my whole thought, my wish to heaven I cast;
> 'Tis Laura's voice I hear, and hence she bids me haste.[22]

Donne's *Anatomie* has no such focus: it has instead a central incon-
sistency which defeats all Donne's efforts to bring its diverse materials
under control. For it is not correct to say, as Empson says, that "the
complete decay of the universe" is presented as having been caused
by the death of Elizabeth Drury. If this were so, the poem might
achieve unity through supporting a dominant symbol of virtue's power,
and one might be able to agree with Empson that the "only way to
make the poem sensible is to accept Elizabeth Drury as the Logos." [23]
But, after the Introduction has elaborately presented this hyperbole,
one discovers in the first Meditation that Elizabeth Drury has, basically, nothing to do with the sense of decay in the poem. The whole
first Meditation is strictly in the religious tradition; it meditates the
decline of man through sin from God's original creation:

> There is no health; Physitians say that wee,
> At best, enjoy but a neutralitie.
> And can there bee worse sicknesse, then to know
> That we are never well, nor can be so?
> Wee are borne ruinous . . . .
> For that first marriage was our funerall:
> One woman at one blow, then kill'd us all . . . .
>   (91–106)

The meditation opens with an echo of the general confession in the
Book of Common Prayer—"there is no health in us"—a theme developed by St. Bernard and countless others:

> Engendered in sin, we engender sinners; born debtors, we
> give birth to debtors; corrupted, to the corrupt . . . . We
> are crippled souls from the moment when we enter into this
> world, and as long as we live there, and we shall still be so
> when we leave it; from the sole of our foot to the crown of
> our head there is no health in us.[24]

Continuing with a descant on traditional conceptions of the decay
of man from his first grandeur,[25] the meditation comes to a full climactic close as (in St. Bernard's terminology) the indestructible

Image of God within man makes its traditional judgment of the
ruined Likeness:

> Thus man, this worlds Vice-Emperour, in whom
> All faculties, all graces are at home . . .
> This man, so great, that all that is, is his,
> Oh what a trifle, and poore thing he is! (161–70)

The first Meditation thus forms a unit in itself; it strikes one as having
no fundamental relation to the preceding account of the destruction
of the world by the girl's death.

Then, clumsily and evasively, the poem comes back to the girl
and to the Petrarchan hyperbole of the world's death:

> If man were any thing, he's. nothing now:
> Helpe, or at least some time to wast, allow
> T'his other wants, yet when he did depart
> With her whom we lament, hee lost his heart.
>
> (171–4)

The Eulogy is being tacked on; and soon the difficulty of including
this hyperbole in the poem becomes embarrassingly obvious:

> shee that could drive
> The poysonous tincture, and the staine of *Eve*,
> Out of her thoughts, and deeds; and purifie
> All, by a true religious Alchymie;
> Shee, shee is dead; shee's dead: when thou knowest this,
> Thou knowest how poore a trifling thing man is.
>
> (179–84)

But we have known it before, and not for these reasons; thus the section comes to a flat and forced conclusion. We pause, and begin the
second section almost as if the Eulogy and Moral had never intervened:

> Then, as mankinde, so is the worlds whole frame
> Quite out of Joynt, almost created lame:
> For, before God had made up all the rest,
> Corruption entred, and deprav'd the best:
> It seis'd the Angels, and then first of all
> The world did in her cradle take a fall . . . .
>
> (191–6)

This second Meditation includes the famous passage beginning "And new Philosophy calls all in doubt," where Donne sardonically turns the optimism of the scientists into proof of pessimism:

> And freely men confesse that this world's spent,
> When in the Planets, and the Firmament
> They seeke so many new; they see that this
> Is crumbled out againe to his Atomies. (209–12)

But this is not related to "the untimely death of Mistris Elizabeth Drury." The passage on the new philosophy is an integral part of a meditation on the effects of sin; the effects of the new philosophy represent the final stages in a long and universal sequence of decay.

The second Eulogy reveals an even further split in the poem. Instead of pursuing the explicitly religious imagery of the first Eulogy, Donne here attempts to secularize the compliments, at the same time using images traditionally associated with Mary:.[26]

> She whom wise nature had invented then
> When she observ'd that every sort of men
> Did in their voyage in this worlds Sea stray,
> And needed a new compasse for their way;
> She that was best, and first originall
> Of all faire copies, and the generall
> Steward to Fate; she whose rich eyes, and brest
> Guilt the West Indies, and perfum'd the East . . . .
> (223–30)

The traditional religious feelings which have thus far been growing in the poem are here balked, particularly by the references to "wise nature" and "Fate." The poem has broken apart, and the break is not mended by the blurred imagery one finds in the following Moral and in the transition to Section III (lines 237–50). Here Donne presents the imagery of "this worlds generall sicknesse" with an imprecise and damaging ambiguity. What is the "feaver," the "consuming wound"? Is it that conventional one described in the Introduction as the result of the girl's death? Or is it the infection of Original Sin? The vague and general imagery tries to include both elements, but it will not do. The last words of the transition—"ages darts"—tell us clearly that the third and fourth Meditations, on loss of proportion and color, deal with the results of sin, not with emotions related to the poem's alleged protagonist.

The remaining Eulogies and the Conclusion try desperately to maintain something of the introductory hyperbole, but it cannot be done. The poem does not justify the elaborate imagery with which Donne attempts to transmute the girl into a symbol of virtue's power. The imagery seems extravagant—even blasphemous—not because of what we know about the circumstances of the poem's composition, but because the imagery is not supported by the poem as a whole.

The very fact that the poem is rigidly divided into sections and subsections gives us another aspect of its failure. Nearly all the joints between sections and subsections are marked by strong pauses or by clumsy transitions; while the Morals are strained in an attempt to bring Meditation and Eulogy into some sort of unity. The parts will not fuse into an imaginative organism. One can omit all the rest of the poem and simply read through the Meditations consecutively; the sequence is consistent and, with a brief conclusion, would form a complete—and a rather good—poem.

We should not leave the *Anatomie* without noticing in some detail the richness with which Donne develops these strictly religious aspects of the work. Let us look for a moment at the third Meditation, as complex a passage as Donne ever wrote. It works by a fusion of two main ideas. Astronomical observations seem to prove that the universe is decaying as a result of sin, for it seems to have lost its spherical, circular nature, the sign of immutable perfection. At the same time the passage mocks the vanity and presumption of man in attempting to understand and control God's mysterious universe. The irony of such attempts is that they only reveal—in two ways—the corruption of all things. Nevertheless man persists in the intellectual, Abelardian effort to comprehend the unknowable or inessential, persists in the *curiositas* which St. Bernard denounced as the father of pride.

Donne begins (251 ff.):

> We thinke the heavens enjoy their Sphericall,
> Their round proportion embracing all.
> But yet their various and perplexed course,
> Observ'd in divers ages, doth enforce
> Men to finde out so many Eccentrique parts,
> Such divers downe-right lines, such overthwarts,
> As disproportion that pure forme:

"Perplexed" is the central word here. The course of the heavenly bodies is so involved, so tangled, that man cannot follow it and is "enforced" to discover, or to invent ("finde out"),[27] fantastically complicated scheme of the universe which serves to "disproportion that pure forme," but never surely hits the truth of things. We may also take "perplexed" in another sense: the heavenly bodies themselves seemed to be confused about their course.

> It teares
> The Firmament in eight and forty sheires,
> And in these Constellations then arise
> New starres, and old doe vanish from our eyes:
> As though heav'n suffered earthquakes, peace or war,
> When new Towers rise, and old demolish't are.

"It," grammatically, seems to refer to the heavens' "perplexed course." But in this context "It" may also refer by implication to the science of Astronomy which invented the forty-eight constellations; thus, when man's "knowledge" has settled things by violence ("teares"), erratic heaven refuses to conform. Nevertheless, presumptuous men

> have impal'd within a Zodiake
> The free-borne Sun, and keepe twelve Signes awake
> To watch his steps; the Goat and Crab controule,
> And fright him backe, who else to either Pole
> (Did not these Tropiques fetter him) might runne:

The Goat and Crab are ugly symbols of sensuality, and will the Sun obey such commanders? Apparently so; yet the Sun is full of guile that may deceive us:

> For his course is not round; nor can the Sunne
> Perfit a Circle, or maintaine his way
> One inch direct; but where he rose to-day
> He comes no more, but with a couzening line,
> Steales by that point, and so is Serpentine:
> And seeming weary with his reeling thus,
> He meanes to sleepe, being now falne nearer us.

The sun is degenerate, having fallen nearer to the sphere of corruption—serpentine in his winding and in his wiliness, and, like a drunken man, reeling toward a "lethargy" like that which has overtaken earth.

> So, of the Starres which boast that they doe runne
> In Circle still, none ends where he begun.

All their proportion's lame, it sinkes, it swels.
For of Meridians, and Parallels,
Man hath weav'd out a net, and this net throwne
Upon the Heavens, and now they are his owne.
Loth to goe up the hill, or labour thus
To goe to heaven, we make heaven come to us.
We spur, we reine the starres, and in their race
They're diversly content t'obey our pace.

Here the complex feelings of the Meditation reach a climax. All man's hubristic attempts have resulted only in a deceptive "mastery" of corruption. Man's claims to worldly power and knowledge mean only that he refuses to undergo the spiritual discipline necessary for his salvation.

The remainder of this third Meditation is not of such sustained power, and indeed goes to pieces in its last ten lines. A discussion of the earth's solidity interrupts the theme of proportion, and a shift to abstract morality at the close is too abrupt. The best of the poem is over.

V

The full title of Donne's *Second Anniversary* itself suggests the possibilities of a unity not achieved in the earlier poem: *Of the Progresse of the Soule. Wherein, By occasion of the Religious death of Mistris Elizabeth Drury, the incommodities of the Soule in this life, and her exaltation in the next, are contemplated.* Here, clearly, is an "occasion" to use Mistress Drury as a symbol naturally integrated with the traditional matter of religious meditation: a "Religious death" (not the "untimely death" of the *Anatomie's* title) is the ultimate aim in this life for all the devout. The poem's structure indicates that Donne is indeed moving throughout with the imaginative ease that marks the management of a truly unified conception.

The *Progresse* consists of an Introduction, only half as long as the Introduction to the preceding poem; a Conclusion, less than half as long; and seven sections which constitute the body of the work. These proportions, in a poem over fifty lines longer, indicate an important shift in emphasis. The Introduction and Conclusion to the *Anatomie,* with their emphasis on hyperbolic praise of the dead girl, make up a quarter of that poem; whereas these portions make up only about an eighth of the *Progresse.* Each section of the *Progresse* is subdivided in a manner reminiscent of the *Anatomie.* The first section contains (1) a Meditation on contempt of the world and one's self; (2) a

Eulogy of the girl as the pattern of Virtue; (3) a Moral, introduced
by lines which recall the refrain of the preceding poem:

> Shee, shee is gone; she is gone; when thou knowest this,
> What fragmentary rubbidge this world is
> Thou knowest, and that it is not worth a thought;
> He honors it too much that thinkes it nought.

But, as the following outline shows, the "refrain" does not appear
hereafter, and of the remaining sections, only the second concludes
with a distinct Moral; in the rest the moral is absorbed into the
Eulogy:

> Introduction, 1–44.
> Section I, 45–84.
>> 1. Meditation, 45–64.
>> 2. Eulogy, 65–80.
>> 3. Refrain and Moral, 81–4.
> Section II, 85–156.
>> 1. Meditation, 85–120.
>> 2. Eulogy, 121–46.
>> 3. Moral, 147–56.
> Section III, 157–250.
>> 1. Meditation, 157–219.
>> 2. Eulogy, 220–50.
> Section IV, 251–320.
>> 1. Meditation, 251–300.
>> 2. Eulogy, 301–20.
> Section V, 321–82.
>> 1. Meditation, 321–55.
>> 2. Eulogy, 356–82.
> Section VI, 383–470.
>> 1. Meditation, 383–446.
>> 2. Eulogy, 447–70.
> Section VII, 471–510.
>> 1. Meditation, 471–96.
>> 2. Eulogy, 497–510.
> Conclusion, 511–28.

This gradual modification of the strict mold which marked the sections of the *Anatomie* suggests a creative freedom that absorbs and
transcends formal divisions. The first striking indication that this is

true is found in the ease of the reader's movement from part to part. We are freed from the heavy pauses that marked the close of each section in the *Anatomie:* omission of the refrain and, above all, omission of the flat, prosy Morals, makes possible an easy transition from section to section; the only heavy pause occurs at the close of the long Moral in Section II. We are always aware that a new sequence is beginning: it is essential that we feel the form of the poem beneath us. But each new sequence, with the above exception, follows inevitably from the close of the preceding one, as at the close of the first section, where the words of the very brief Moral, "thought" and "thinkes," lead directly to the dominant command of the second Meditation: "Thinke then, my soule, that death is but a Groome . . . Thinke thee laid on thy death-bed . . . Thinke . . . Thinke . . ."; the traditional self-address of religious meditation.

The transition within each section from Meditation to Eulogy is even more fluent; we do not find here the sharp division of meaning which marked these two elements in the *Anatomie.* In the previous poem every Meditation was strictly a scourging of the world and of man, every Eulogy the picture of a lost hope. But in the *Progresse* every Meditation, together with this scourging, includes the hope of salvation which is imaged in the Eulogy, and in every Meditation except the first, this hope, this upward look, is stressed in the latter part of the Meditation, with the result that the reader is carried easily into the realm where the symbol of perfect virtue now lives.

In Sections III and V the distinction between Meditation and Eulogy is even further modified, for the Meditation itself falls into two contrasting parts. In Section III we have first (157–78) a meditation on the loathsomeness of the body, which "could, beyond escape or helpe," infect the soul with Original Sin. But Donne does not dwell long on this; he lifts his eyes from these "ordures" to meditate, in a passage twice as long (179–219), his soul's flight to heaven after death—a flight that leads directly to the Eulogy. Likewise, in Section V, after meditating the corrupt company kept on earth (321–38), Donne lifts his eyes to meditate (339–55) the soul's "conversation" with the inhabitants of Heaven—a theme which leads naturally into the Eulogy of Heaven's new inhabitant.

Fundamentally, the union of Meditation with Eulogy is due to a difference in Donne's treatment of the Eulogies in this poem. Here he has avoided a clash between eulogy and religious meditation by giving up, except in the brief Introduction and first Eulogy, the Petrarchan hyperbole which in parts of the *Anatomie* attributed the decay of the world to the girl's death. This hyperbole, together with the

single reminder of the refrain, appears to be brought in at the beginning of the *Progresse* to link this poem with its predecessor, in line
with Donne's original plan of writing a poem in the girl's memory
every year for an indefinite period. The labored Introduction to the
Progresse is certainly a blemish on the poem; yet it may be said that
the reminiscences of the *Anatomie* are functional: they suggest that
the negative "anatomizing" of the other poem may be taken as a
preparation for the positive spiritual progress to be imaged in the
second poem. At any rate, Donne does not use this hyperbole in the
six later Eulogies, nor in the brief Conclusion, of the second poem.
Instead, he consistently attempts to transmute the girl into a symbol
of virtue that may fitly represent the Image and Likeness of God in
man, recognition of which is, according to St. Bernard, the chief end
and aim of religious meditation.

Thus Juan de Ávila's *Audi Filia* begins its section on self-knowledge
with a chapter (57) summarizing the command to "know thyself"
which St. Bernard found in the famous verse of his beloved *Canticle:*
"Si ignoras te, O pulchra inter mulieres, egredere, et abi post greges
sodalium tuorum . . . ." [28] If the soul, the intended Bride, does not
know herself—that is, does not know whence she comes, where she
is, and whither she is going—she will live forever in the "Land of Unlikeness," that land of sin and disorder in which man forgets that he
was made in God's Image and Likeness, and thus lives in a state of
exile where the Image is defaced and the Likeness lost. As Gilson
explains, "Man is made to the image of God in his free-will, and he
will never lose it; he was made to the likeness of God in respect of
certain virtues, enabling him to choose well, and to do the good thing
chosen; now these he has lost" by sin. But the central fact is that the
Image—free will—is indestructible; and hence "to know ourselves is
essentially," in St. Bernard's view, "to recognize that we are defaced
images of God." [29] Take care, says St. Bernard, "now thou art sunk
into the slime of the abyss, not to forget that thou art the image of
God, and blush to have covered it over with an alien likeness. Remember thy nobility and take shame of such a defection. Forget not thy
beauty, to be the more confounded at thy hideous aspect." [30]

In accordance with the twofold aim of meditation implied in the
last sentence, Donne's *Second Anniversary* presents seven Meditations
which may be called, for the most part, a description of the "defaced
image," the Land of Unlikeness; while the seven Eulogies, for the
most part, create a symbol of the original Image and Likeness, the
lost beauty and nobility that must not be forgotten. That is not to say
that Donne gives up Petrarchan imagery; not at all—but this imagery

is now attuned to the religious aims of the poem. The Eulogies are
sometimes too ingenious; yet the excessive ingenuity remains a minor
flaw: it does not destroy the poem's unity.

The fifth Eulogy is a good example:

> Shee, who being to her selfe a State, injoy'd
> All royalties which any State employ'd;
> For shee made warres, and triumph'd; reason still
> Did not o'rthrow, but rectifie her will:
> And she made peace, for no peace is like this,
> That beauty, and chastity together kisse:
> She did high justice, for she crucified
> Every first motion of rebellious pride:
> And she gave pardons, and was liberall,
> For, onely her selfe except, she pardon'd all . . . .
>
> (359–68)

The hyperbole is here so tempered, so controlled, by interpretation in
terms of the virtue essential to a restored Likeness, that the more extravagant images which follow become acceptably symbolic of the
importance of such virtue in the world: it is the one thing needful:

> Shee coy'nd, in this, that her impressions gave
> To all our actions all the worth they have:
> She gave protections; the thoughts of her brest
> Satans rude Officers could ne'r arrest.
> As these prerogatives being met in one,
> Made her a soveraigne State; religion
> Made her a Church; and these two made her all.
>
> (369–75)

Thus throughout the *Progresse* Meditation and Eulogy combine to
present its central theme: the true end of man.

Let us look now at the whole movement of the poem; we can then
see that this central theme is clearly introduced at the beginning of
the first Meditation, carried to a climax in the fourth and fifth sections,
and resolved in the Eulogy of Section VI. There is no flagging of
power in this poem: it is a true progress. After the labored Introduction, Donne strikes at once into the heart of his theme:

> These Hymnes, thy issue, may encrease so long,
> As till Gods great *Venite* change the song. [end of Intro.]
> Thirst for that time, O my insatiate soule,

> And serve thy thirst, with Gods safe-sealing Bowle.
> Be thirstie still, and drinke still till thou goe
> To th' only Health, to be Hydroptique so. (43–8)

The "Bowle" is the Eucharist, a "seale of Grace," as Donne calls it in his sermons.[31] One thinks of the "Anima sitiens Deum" in St. Bernard—the Soul, the Bride, which thirsts for God, desiring a union of will between herself and God, that union which at last results in Perfect Likeness after death.[32] This imagery is then supported in Section II by the line, "And trust th' immaculate blood to wash thy score" (106); as well as by the lines of Section III (214–15) where Donne refers to death as the soul's "third birth," with the very significant parenthesis, "Creation gave her one, a second, grace." One needs to recall that at the close of the *Anatomie* Donne has said that he

> Will yearely celebrate thy second birth,
> That is, thy death; for though the soule of man
> Be got when man is made, 'tis borne but than
> When man doth die. (450–3)

The omission of Grace may be said to indicate the fundamental flaw of the *First Anniversary:* it lacks the firm religious center of the *Progresse.*

This promise of salvation is the positive aspect of the soul's progress; but, as Gilson says, "By this thirst for God we must further understand an absolute contempt for all that is not God." [33] This complementary negative aspect is consequently introduced immediately after the above lines on the Eucharist:

> Forget this rotten world; And unto thee
> Let thine owne times as an old storie bee.
> Be not concern'd: studie not why, nor when;
> Doe not so much as not beleeve a man. (49–52)

Donne is taking as his prime example of vanity that curiosity which forms the first downward step in St. Bernard's Twelve Degrees of Pride—curiosity, which occurs, St. Bernard tells us, "when a man allows his sight and other senses to stray after things which do not concern him."

> So since it [the soul] takes no heed to itself it is sent out of
> doors to feed the kids. And as these are the types of sin, I
> may quite correctly give the title of "kids" to the eyes and

the ears, since as death comes into the world through sin, so does sin enter the mind through these apertures. The curious man, therefore, busies himself with feeding them, though he takes no trouble to ascertain the state in which he has left himself. Yet if, O man, you look carefully into yourself, it is indeed a wonder that you can ever look at anything else.[34]

This theme of curiosity remains dormant until Section III of the poem, where it emerges gradually from Donne's magnificent view of his own soul's flight to Heaven after death. It is important to note that this is not, strictly speaking, "the flight of Elizabeth Drury's soul to Heaven," as most commentators describe it.[35] It is Donne's own soul which here is made a symbol of release, not only from physical bondage, but also from that mental bondage which is the deepest agony of the greatest souls:

> she stayes not in the ayre,
> To looke what Meteors there themselves prepare;
> She carries no desire to know, nor sense,
> Whether th' ayres middle region be intense;
> For th' Element of fire, she doth not know,
> Whether she past by such a place or no;
> She baits not at the Moone, nor cares to trie
> Whether in that new world, men live, and die.
> *Venus* retards her not, to 'enquire, how shee
> Can, (being one starre) *Hesper,* and *Vesper* bee.
>   (189–98)

In the last two lines Donne is renouncing one of his own witty *Paradoxes and Problems;* in the earlier part he is renouncing the astronomical curiosity which had drawn his scorn in the greatest passage of the *Anatomie.* Here, however, as Coffin has well shown (pp. 171, 185–92), there is a much stronger emphasis on problems such as "fire" and the moon which were being debated in Donne's own day. From all such vain controversies the soul is now freed and

> ere she can consider how she went,
> At once is at, and through the Firmament.
>   (205–6)

It is not until Section IV that this theme reaches its full, explicit development. Turning here from the heavens, Donne scourges the

search for physical understanding of earth and its creatures; yet, as
before, the very flagellation suggests an almost indomitable curiosity,
and shows a mind that has ranged through all the reaches of human
learning:

> Wee see in Authors, too stiffe to recant,
> A hundred controversies of an Ant;
> And yet one watches, starves, freeses, and sweats,
> To know but Catechismes and Alphabets
> Of unconcerning things, matters of fact—
>
> (281–85)

matters which do not concern the true end of man, as implied in the
following lines:

> When wilt thou shake off this Pedantery,
> Of being taught by sense, and Fantasie?
> Thou look'st through spectacles; small things seeme great
> Below; But up unto the watch-towre get,
> And see all things despoyl'd of fallacies: [36]
> Thou shalt not peepe through lattices of eyes,
> Nor heare through Labyrinths of eares, nor learne
> By circuit, or collections to discerne.
> In heaven thou straight know'st all, concerning it,
> And what concernes it not, shalt straight forget.
>
> (291–300)

All worldly philosophy is vain, for essential truth, says Donne, cannot
be learned through sense-impressions of external things, nor through
that "Fantasie" which transmits sense-impressions to the intellect.
Such philosophy is the way of pride; true knowledge comes only
through humility, as Donne, echoing St. Bernard, declares in a significant passage of his *Essayes*:

> It is then humility to study God, and a strange miraculous
> one; for it is an ascending humility, which the Divel, which
> emulates even Gods excellency in his goodnesse, and labours
> to be as ill, as he is good, hath corrupted in us by a pride, as
> much against reason; for he hath fill'd us with a descending
> pride, to forsake God, for the study and love of things worse
> then our selves.
>
> (pp. 3–4)

True knowledge lies within and leads to virtue, the fourth Eulogy explains:

> Shee who all libraries had throughly read
> At home in her owne thoughts, and practised
> So much good as would make as many more:
> Shee whose example they must all implore,
> Who would or doe, or thinke well . . .
> She who in th' art of knowing Heaven, was growne
> Here upon earth, to such perfection,
> That she hath, ever since to Heaven she came,
> (In a far fairer print,) but read the same. . . .
>
> (303–14)

Religious virtue creates, or rather *is,* the restored Likeness which, according to St. Bernard, makes possible some knowledge of God; with St. Bernard, as Gilson says, "the resemblance of subject and object is the indispensable condition of any knowledge of the one by the other." [37] This is made plain in the sixth Eulogy, which provides the resolution of the whole poem by obliterating all traces of Petrarchan compliment and giving explicitly in the terms of St. Bernard a definition of the soul's perfection on earth. The sixth Meditation leads the way into this Eulogy by an abstract definition of "essential joy":

> Double on heaven thy thoughts on earth emploid;
> All will not serve; Only who have enjoy'd
> The sight of God, in fulnesse, can thinke it;
> For it is both the object, and the wit.
> This is essentiall joy, where neither hee
> Can suffer diminution, nor wee. (439–44)

God is both the object of knowledge and the means of knowing; though this full knowledge and joy can never be achieved on earth, we can, the Eulogy explains, come closest to it by striving to restore the Divine Likeness, as did she,

> Who kept by diligent devotion,
> Gods Image, in such reparation,
> Within her heart, that what decay was growne,
> Was her first Parents fault, and not her owne:
> Who being solicited to any act,
> Still heard God pleading his safe precontract;

> Who by a faithfull confidence, was here
> Betroth'd to God, and now is married there . . .
> Who being here fil'd with grace, yet strove to bee,
> Both where more grace, and more capacitie
> At once is given . . . . (455–67)

Compare the words of St. Bernard, speaking of that conformity between the soul's will and God's which leads to mystic ecstasy:

> It is that conformity which makes, as it were, a marriage between the soul and the Word, when, being already like unto Him by its nature, it endeavours to show itself like unto Him by its will, and loves Him as it is loved by Him. And if this love is perfected, the soul is wedded to the Word. What can be more full of happiness and joy than this conformity? what more to be desired than this love? which makes thee, O soul, no longer content with human guidance, to draw near with confidence thyself to the Word, to attach thyself with constancy to Him, to address Him with confidence, and consult Him upon all subjects, to become as receptive in thy intelligence, as fearless in thy desires. This is the contract of a marriage truly spiritual and sacred. And to say this is to say too little; it is more than a contract, it is a communion, an identification with the Beloved, in which the perfect correspondence of will makes of two, one spirit.[38]

The "faithfull confidence" of Donne's poem is akin to the "confidence" (*fiducia*) of St. Bernard, an attribute of the soul which has passed beyond fear of divine punishment and stands on the threshold of mystic ecstasy.[39] This recognition of the end of man on earth and in Heaven is the fulfillment of the poem; the brief remainder is summary and epilogue.

In such a poem of religious devotion the sevenfold division of sections assumes a significance beyond that of the fivefold division of the *Anatomie.* Seven is the favorite number for dividing religious meditations: into those *semaines* and *septaines* that were characteristic of the "New Devotion" in the Low Countries;[40] or into the contrasting meditations for each day of the week that formed the basis of popular daily exercises throughout Europe. A glance at the summary of the latter exercises, as presented by Fray Luis (see above, Chap. 1, sec. 1), will show that Donne is following closely their general tenor and development: from thoughts of sin, death, and the miseries of this life, to thoughts of happy "conversation" with the blessed in Heaven, of "essentiall joy" and "accidentall joyes." [41] But the sevenfold division of this poem suggests more than a relation to the practice of methodical meditation. As Donne says in his *Essayes,* "*Seven* is ever used to express infinite." (p. 129) It is the mystic's traditional division of the soul's progress toward ecstasy and union with the Divine. St. Augustine thus divides the progress of the soul into seven stages,[42] and anyone familiar with mystical writings will realize how often the division has been used by later mystics, as in St. Teresa's *Interior Castle.* Thus Donne's *Progresse* uses both mystical structure and mystical imagery to express a goal: the Infinite, the One.

This does not mean that Donne's *Progresse* is, properly speaking, a mystical poem, even though he uses in his title the mystical term "contemplate," and in the poem cries, "Returne not, my Soule, from this extasie" (321). The next line after this—"And meditation of what thou shalt bee"—indicates that the ecstasy is metaphorical only. "Meditation" is always discursive, always works through the understanding; it is only the preparation for ascent to the truly mystical state now generally understood in the term "contemplation," which St. Bernard defines as "the soul's true unerring intuition," "the unhesitating apprehension of truth." [43] Donne's use of the word "contemplate" in the title of his *Progresse* may indicate a higher spiritual aim than the "represent" of the *Anatomie's* title, but his *Progresse* remains a spiritual exercise of the purgative, ascetic life. It represents an attempt to achieve the state of conversion best described by Donne himself in a prayer at the close of his *Essayes in Divinity:*

> Begin in us here in this life an angelicall purity, an angelicall chastity, an angelicall integrity to thy service, an Angelical acknowledgment that we alwaies stand in thy presence, and should direct al our actions to thy glory. Rebuke us not, O Lord, in thine anger, that we have not done so till now; but enable us now to begin that great work; and imprint in us an assurance that thou receivest us now graciously, as reconciled, though enemies; and fatherly, as children, though prodigals; and powerfully, as the God of our salvation, though our own consciences testifie against us.

NOTES

[1] See the epigraphs to Part 2; *Tottel's Miscellany,* ed. Rollins, 1, 62–3.

[2] See the controversy stirred up by Pierre Legouis' remarks in *Donne the Craftsman* (Paris, Henri Didier, 1928), pp. 61–9; cf. Merritt Hughes,

"The Lineage of 'The Extasie,' " *MLR*, 27 (1932), 1–5; Frank A. Doggett, "Donne's Platonism," *Sewanee Review*, 42 (1934), 274–92; George Reuben Potter, "Donne's *Extasie*, Contra Legouis," *PQ*, 15 (1936), 247–53. For a striking treatment of the contrast between "sensuall Extasie" and spiritual ecstasy, see St. François de Sales, *Love of God*, Bk. 7, Chap. 4.

3 W. A. Murray, "Donne and Paracelsus: An Essay in Interpretation," *RES*, 25 (1949), 115–23. One must, I think, discard Grierson's hesitant suggestion (*Poems of Donne*, 2, xxii, 10) that the poem may have been addressed to Lucy, Countess of Bedford; for the imagery of the "Saint Lucies night," which occurs also in the *Second Anniversary* (line 120), provides its own metaphorical occasion (St. Lucy's Day, Dec. 13, "being the shortest day," according to the old calendar). See the interesting discussion of this problem by J. B. Leishman, *The Monarch of Wit* (London, Hutchinson's University Library, 1951), pp. 170–73. Leishman tends to feel that the "Nocturnall" deals with Donne's wife, but finds it hard to believe that Donne wrote the poem "after the actual death of his wife in 1617, when he had been two years in orders." But if the poem is fundamentally religious, the difficulty seems to lessen.

4 Donne, *Letters*, pp. 126–7; cf. Edmund Gosse, *The Life and Letters of John Donne* (2 vols., London, Heinemann, 1899), *1*, 154. Gosse says the letter "seems to refer to the birth of Francis Donne, baptized at Mitcham on the 8th of January 1607."

5 Gosse, 2, 106. This assumption has now been effectively questioned by Miss Helen Gardner, in her recent edition of the *Divine Poems*. Her discussion of the dating of the "Holy Sonnets" (pp. xxxvii–l) seems to be absolutely convincing. She dates six of the sonnets between February and August, 1609, and most of the others shortly after; her printing of the sonnets in groups of twelve, four, and three is surely the right way to present them.

6 *Poems of Donne*, ed. Grierson, 2, 225–9, 231; and the textual notes for the sonnets, 1, 317–31. Miss Helen Gardner has called my attention to the fact that Grierson's description of the appearance of the "La Corona" sonnets in the Harleian manuscript is not quite accurate. He says (2, 227) that the general heading "is followed at once by 'Deign at my hands,' and then the title *La Corona* is given to the six sonnets which ensue." But all seven sonnets appear under this title, as I have since observed.

7 Idem, 2, 212. Miss Gardner (*Divine Poems*, pp. xlvii–xlviii) also discusses the significance of this recantation; she points out that E. K. Chambers, in his pioneer edition of Donne's poems (1896), had observed the relationship between this Elegy and Holy Sonnet 10 and suggested the priority of the sonnet.

8 See Gosse, 1, 174, 190, 195.

9 *Poems of Donne*, ed. Grierson, 2, 225–9, 238–9; Rhodes Dunlap (*Modern Language Notes*, 63 [1948], 258–9) has shown that the occasion of the second of these poems must be March 25, 1608, the first day of the year, old style. To all such evidence of Donne's meditation during this period

we should add the verse-letter to Rowland Woodward cited in Chap. 3 above, for Grierson (*Poems of Donne*, 2, 146–8) conjectures that this was written between 1602–8. Donne's advice here with regard to "Blowing our sparkes of vertue" reminds one of similar references to Donne's exercises in self-analysis that occur in a letter printed by Evelyn Simpson in *A Study of the Prose Works of John Donne* (2d ed., Oxford: Clarendon Press, 1948), pp. 313–14; the letter seems to date from sometime around 1600. For the importance of such introspection in Donne's middle years see George Reuben Potter, "John Donne's Discovery of Himself," *University of California Publications in English*, 4 (1934), 3–23.

[10] Gosse, 2, 20; Simpson, *Prose Works*, p. 29.

[11] John Donne, *Essayes in Divinity*, London, 1651: title-page and note "To the Reader." See the excellent edition of this work by Evelyn Simpson (Oxford: Clarendon Press, 1952), pp. xiii–xvii; and Simpson, *Prose Works*, pp. 207–11.

[12] Cf. Walton, *Lives*, p. 34: " 'And besides, whereas it is determined by the best of *Casuists, that Gods Glory should be the first end, and a maintenance the second motive to embrace that calling;* and though each man may propose to himself both together; yet the first may not be put last without a violation of Conscience, which he that searches the heart will judge. And truly my present condition is such, that if I ask my own Conscience, whether it be reconcileable to that rule, it is at this time so perplexed about it, that I can neither give my self nor you an answer.' " See Gosse, 1, 157–62.

[13] Donne, *Letters*, p. 219. For the interpretations of the *Anniversaries* recently advanced by Marjorie Nicolson and Marius Bewley, see my Appendix 2.

[14] Stafford, p. 219; see above, Chap. 2, sec. 5.

[15] See also the use of the number five in Ben Jonson's "Ghyrlond of the blessed Virgin Marie": "Here, are five letters in this blessed Name,/ Which, chang'd, a five-fold mysterie designe . . . ." (*Ben Jonson*, ed. C. H. Herford, Percy and Evelyn Simpson [11 vols., Oxford: Clarendon Press, 1925–52], 8, 412). The poem was first published in Stafford's *Femall Glory*.

[16] A. Wilmart, *Auteurs Spirituels et Textes Dévots du Moyen Age Latin* (Paris, 1932), pp. 317–60.

[17] For devotion to the Name of Mary see Puente, 1, 263–4.

[18] See above, Chap. 1, sec. 1.

[19] Juan de Ávila, *Audi Filia* ([St. Omer], 1620), pp. 336–8; the translation is attributed to Donne's friend, Sir Tobie Matthew.

[20] Nicholas Breton, *Works*, ed. A. B. Grosart (2 vols., Edinburgh, 1879), 2, 23.

[21] "Conversations with Drummond," *Ben Jonson*, ed. Herford and Simpson, 1, 133 (modernized).

[22] *Rime* 346 in the translation by John Nott: *The Sonnets, Triumphs and other poems of Petrarch*, trans. "various hands," London: G. Bell and

Sons, 1907 (there printed as Sonnet 75 of the sequence "To Laura in Death"). For Petrarch's use of the hyperbole of the world's destruction see *Rime* 268, 326, 338, 352; by Donne's time this had evidently become a convention of compliment, as in Donne's love-poem, "A Feaver," and in a sonnet by Sannazaro pointed out by Mario Praz: see *A Garland for John Donne,* ed. Theodore Spencer (Cambridge: Harvard University Press, 1931), pp. 66–9.

[23] William Empson, *English Pastoral Poetry* (New York: W. W. Norton, 1938), p. 84.

[24] St. Bernard, *Sermones de Diversis,* 42. 2; *Patrologiae cursus completus . . . Series [latina],* ed. Jacques Paul Migne (221 vols., Paris, 1844–65), *183,* 662. I quote the translation by Downes in Gilson's study of St. Bernard, p. 46 (see below, sec. 5, n. 2).

[25] See St. Cyprian, *Liber ad Demetrianum,* secs. 3, 4; *Patrologiae cursus completus, 4,* 564–7. One finds here the germ of many of Donne's comments on the world's decay throughout the *Anatomie.*

[26] Cf. Southwell's poem on the Virgin's Nativity: "Load-starre of all inclosed in worldly waves,/The car[d] and compasse that from ship-wracke saves." The imagery is based, of course, on the "Ave maris stella" and the interpretation of the name Mary as meaning "Star of the Sea": cf. Puente, *1, 263:* "Shee is the Starre of the sea, for that shee is the light, consolation, and guide of those, that sayle in the sea of this worlde, tossed with the greate waves, and tempestes of temptations . . . ." Cf. also Southwell's poem on the death of the Virgin, cited earlier, Chap. 2, sec. 6.

[27] See *OED,* "find," *v.,* 2, 15; 4, 20. Charles Monroe Coffin gives an interesting discussion of this whole Meditation in a different context: *John Donne and the New Philosophy* (New York: Columbia University Press, 1937), pp. 181–2.

[28] This quotation from the *Canticle* (1.7) is given in the version cited by St. Bernard in his *Sermones in Cantica Canticorum,* 34. 1; *Patrologiae cursus completus, 183,* 959; it differs from the modern Vulgate reading.

[29] Étienne Gilson, *The Mystical Theology of Saint Bernard,* trans. A. H. C. Downes (New York: Sheed and Ward, 1940), pp. 225 (n. 45), 70.

[30] St. Bernard, *Sermones de Diversis,* 12. 2; *Patrologiae cursus completus, 183,* 571. I quote the translation by Downes in Gilson's above study, p. 71.

[31] See Itrat Husain, *The Dogmatic and Mystical Theology of John Donne* (London: S.P.C.K., 1938), pp. 30–31.

[32] Gilson, *Saint Bernard,* pp. 111–12.

[33] Idem, p. 238, n. 161.

[34] St. Bernard, *The Twelve Degrees of Humility and Pride,* pp. 6, 55–6. See Gilson, *Saint Bernard,* Appendix I, on the importance of *curiositas* in St. Bernard's thought, where "kids" is shown to be another reference to the *Canticle,* 1.7: "Si ignoras te . . . ."

[35] Charles Monroe Coffin has made some helpful comments on this passage in a letter which he kindly allows me to quote: "in the imagined progress

of his own soul, he has implied the felicitous passage of hers . . . . There is, to me at least, a rather certain ambiguity in the situation, as I think there should be, and the momentary assimilation of the vision of his own progress into that which has 'exalted' E.D. into heaven seems appropriate and, I should say, inevitable."

36 Cf. Francisco de Osuna, p. 201: "Sion means 'a watchtower,' that is, the grace received by the heart during its recollection, whence much knowledge of God can be discerned."

37 Gilson, *Saint Bernard*, p. 148.

38 St. Bernard, *Sermons on the Song of Songs*, 83, 3; *Life and Works of Saint Bernard*, trans. Samuel J. Eales (London, 1889–96), 4, 508.

39 Gilson, *Saint Bernard*, pp. 24, 113, 138n.

40 See Debongnie, pp. 168, 170–71, 184–7, 209–11; and H. Watrigant, "La Méditation Méthodique et l'École des Frères de la Vie Commune," *Revue d' Ascétique et de Mystique, 3* (1922), 134–55. See also Puente, *1*, 43 f.

41 With the latter part of the *Second Anniversary* compare Loarte, *Exercise*, pp. 92–3:

Secondly, ponder what a comfort and sweete delight it shal-be, to be in that blessed societie of so many Angels, Saintes, Apostles, Martyrs, Confessors, Virgins, al of them being so bright and beautiful? what shal it be to see the sacred humanitie of Christ, and of his blessed mother? howe shal a man be ravished with the hearing of the sweet harmonie and melodious musicke that shal be there, and to enjoye so sweete a conversation everlastingly.

Thirdly consider howe yet besides these, ther shal be another glorye muche more excellent, and surpassinge all humane capacitie: which shal be, to see God face to face, wherin consisteth our essential beatitude. For that al other thinges, what soever may be imagined, be but accidental glorie: which being so exceeding great and incomparable, what shal the essential be?

42 See St. Augustine, *De Quantitate Animae*, with trans. by F. E. Tourscher (Philadelphia: Peter Reilly, 1933), Chaps. 33–5.

43 St. Bernard, *On Consideration*, trans. George Lewis (Oxford: Clarendon Press, 1908), p. 41.

GEOFFREY WALTON

The Tone of Ben Jonson's Poetry

It is well known that Pope imitated the opening couplet of Jonson's *Elegie on the Lady Jane Pawlet, Marchion: of Winton*:

> What gentle ghost, besprent with *April* deaw,
> Hayles me, so solemnly, to yonder Yewgh?

in his own opening couplet of the *Elegy to the Memory of an Unfortunate Lady*:

> What beck'ning ghost, along the moonlight shade
> Invites my steps, and points to yonder glade?

The similarity and the difference between the grand style of Pope and the slightly Spenserian language of Jonson on this occasion are obvious. I have chosen to begin with a reference to this piece of plagiarism, however, because these two poems may be taken to mark, in so far as there are any beginnings and ends in literature, the limits of my study, and because the debt draws pointed attention to the dignified and courteous tone of Jonson's poetry, especially in his occasional verses. Several lines of elegy, which often intersect and blend, run between Jonson's epitaphs and formal eulogies and Pope's poem, which seems to gather up into itself all the various threads, the earlier Metaphysical and philosophic meditation of Donne, the formality of Cowley on Crashaw, the tenderness of Cowley on Hervey, the satire of Dryden in

From *Metaphysical to Augustan: Studies in Tone and Sensibility in the Seventeenth Century* (London: Bowes & Bowes, 1955), pp. 23–44. Reprinted by permission of the publishers.

the ode on Anne Killigrew and the elegiac of Milton on the same Lady Jane.[1] Pope inherited a large measure of Metaphysical wit coming from Donne, but the predominant aspect of his genius, the Augustan decorum, can be traced back to Donne's contemporary, Jonson.

Although Jonson's greatness as a poet is generally recognized, very little has been written on his lyric and other non-dramatic poems. There is room for a detailed consideration of certain aspects of this work and for some redirection of attention towards poems hitherto neglected. Making a limited approach, I want to try to locate and define as clearly as possible his characteristic tone and civilized quality.

One often finds oneself trying, with a certain sense of frustration, to reconcile Professor C. H. Herford's morose rough diamond "with no native well-spring of verse music" and the kind of seventeenth-century Mallarmé implied by Mr. Ralph Walker.[2] The coarse side of Jonson must not be forgotten. He was rooted in the English life of tavern and workshop in his life and in his art, besides being the friend of Selden and Lord Aubigny. We have to take into account *The Voyage* as well as the *Hymn to Diana*, and remember the last line of *A Celebration of Charis*. Dr. Leavis places the odes to himself at the central point, as showing us both the independent, forthright working dramatist and the learned Horatian who brought out his plays annotated in folio.[3]

I disagree with Dr. Leavis about the odes. "The racy personal force" and the "weighty and assertive personal assurance" are indeed present. The poems are eminently successful in the sense that they communicate their content without hesitation or vagueness. One can accept and applaud the fiercely contemptuous satire on dullness and ill will, but the final effect, I think, embarrasses still, as it seems to have embarrassed the "Tribe" and as the author in person had earlier embarrassed Drummond of Hawthornden.[4] These odes are too personal and self-regarding. It is not the self-pity of a Shelley that is forced upon us, but self-assertion and unseemly pride:

> 'Twere simple fury still thyselfe to waste
> On such as have no taste. . . .

> 'Tis crowne enough to vertue still, her owne applause.

This is not redeemed by the finer aspiration of:

> Strike that disdaine-full heate
> Throughout, to their defeate,
> As curious fooles, and envious of thy straine,
> May, blushing, sweare no palsey's in thy braine.

Though Cartwright, Randolph and Cleveland approved, one can sympathize with that excellent literary critic, Thomas Carew, when he expostulates:

> 'Tis true (dear Ben) thy just chastizing hand
> Hath fixed upon the sotted Age a brand
> To their swolne pride, and empty scribbling due . . .
>   . . . but if thou bind,
> By Citie custome, or by *Gavell-kind*,
> In equall shares thy love on all thy race,
> We may distinguish of their sexe and place;
> Though one hand form them and though one brain strike
> Souls into all, they are not all alike.
> Why should the follies then of this dull age
> Draw from thy Pen such an immodest rage,
> As seems to blast thy (else immortall) Bayes,
> When thine owne hand proclaims thy ytch of praise?
> The wiser world doth greater Thee confesse
> Than all men else, than Thyself only lesse.

Along with his mastery of the irregular Donnean couplet, Carew shows here a fineness of feeling and a regard for his poetic father, a polish of tone and an integrity of character, which represent all that was best in the class and way of life from which he came. Carew feels that the great intellectual leader has been ungentlemanly in a very deep sense; that ideal demanded a measure of humility; it was something rooted in the traditional code and which became obliterated in the more superficial, if more formally polite, Augustan age. In an ode on the same theme, not published until the present century, Jonson expresses a proud but far more admirable attitude towards the public:

> Yet since the bright and wise
>   *Minerva* deignes
> Uppon this humbled earth to cast hir eyes,
>   Wee'l rip our ritchest veynes
> And once more strike the Eare of tyme with those fresh straynes:
>   As shall besides delight
>   And Cuninge of their grounde
> Give cause to some of wonder, some despight;
> But unto more despaire to imitate their sounde. . . .
>
>   Cast reverence if not feare
>   Throughout their generall brests

And by their taking let it once appeare
Who worthie come, who not, to be witts Pallace guests.

However, the point to be emphasized is that Jonson at his best has a superlatively civilized tone, and it was, in fact, in him that Carew found models for the expression of such a tone in poetry. In Jonson it springs, of course, mainly from his classical culture, that culture which Carew and his class shared in a way corresponding to Jonson's participation in the social activities which produced the manners and the tone of their world. The tone which issues in Jonson's poetry from this double source is best exemplified in the following ode:

> High-spirited friend,
> I send nor Balmes, nor Cor'sives to your wound,
> Your fate hath found
> A gentler, and more agile hand, to tend
> The Cure of that, which is but corporall,
> And doubtful Dayes, (which were nam'd *Criticall,*)
> Have made their fairest flight,
> And now are out of sight.
> Yet doth some wholesome Physick for the mind,
> Wrapt in this paper lie,
> Which in the taking if you misapply
> You are unkind.
>
> Your covetous hand,
> Happy in that faire honour it hath gain'd
> Must now be rayn'd.
> True valour doth her owne renowne command
> In one full Action; nor have you now more
> To doe, then to be husband of that store.
> Thinke but how deare you bought
> This same which you have caught,
> Such thoughts wil make you more in love with truth.
> 'Tis wisdom, and that high
> For men to use their fortune reverently,
> Even in youth.

This is no mere pindaric experiment. To whoever is addressed Jonson is giving extremely intimate personal advice, analysing a situation and a character instead of writing a conventional epithalamium, but his delicate movement and hesitating phrases, using the opportunities of the formal pattern, keep it free of all suggestion of patronage or importunity. There is great strength in the total effect of mature wisdom. Jonson is appealing to an ideal of human dignity and reasonable behaviour held in common with his reader which inspires frankness and at the same time sincere mutual respect. The ultimate basis is again the old idea of courtesy. This was a quality of the spirit which made it possible to consider serious moral matters in a social context without losing sight of their seriousness or doing anything in what would later be called "bad form." This ode by itself seems to me a refutation of Professor Herford's opinion that Jonson "for all his generous warmth lacked the finer graces of familiarity." It has both.

The wit of Jonson, like that of Donne, manifests itself in many ways. As an intellectual force it has a disciplinary and clarifying rather than a free-ranging and elaborating effect,[5] but the relationship between the two poets is shown in Jonson's admiration for Donne and in the common features of that group of elegies whose authorship has long been in dispute between them.[6] In discussing the more social aspect of Jonson's wit, the tone that he handed on to his "sons," usually in the form of an economy and polish of technique, I think that one can claim that these "finer graces" form one of Jonson's great qualities as a poet. "High-spirited friend . . ." and "Fair friend . . ." [7] that elegant, but closely reasoned and firmly phrased lyric, equally expressive of his distinctive classical urbanity, together give us the quintessence of Jonson's attitude towards his friends and fellow poets, his patrons and patronesses. It is not the formal decorum of a large polite world—such, in any case, did not yet exist—but one feels it to be, I think, the tone of small circles in which aristocratic and cultivated people knew each other intimately. One can back up these deductions by a short survey of Jonson's occasional and certain other verses and of imitations by his "sons." They have the kind of tone I have just noted, and they describe the life that contributed to produce that tone. Beside these poems much of the social verse, even of Pope, sounds brassy. One knows that life at Whitehall, particularly in the reign of James I, was often disorderly, not to say squalid, and that sports and pastimes on the best-ordered country estate were rough and cruel, but the refinement was also there, sometimes in the same people. In the poetry it is preserved for ever.

The epigram, *Inviting a Friend to Supper,* is admirable social verse, besides being a document of the Jonson world, an offering of scholarly conversation with simple but good food and wine—Virgil and Tacitus with canary. A long series of epigrams and complimentary verses sketch in the type of men with whom Jonson liked to associate and the qualities that for him made up a civilized life. *An Epistle, answering one that asked to be Sealed of the Tribe of BEN* is unfortunately little more than satire on smart London life and the masques of Inigo Jones. *An Epistle to a Friend, to persuade him to the Warres* with its finely realized opening:

> Wake, friend, from forth thy Lethargie: the Drum
> Beates brave and loude in Europe and bids come
> All that dare rowse . . .

is again mainly negative, a vigorous and racy denunciation of loose sexual morality and excessive drinking, but the ending sets up a heroic ideal of moral and physical valour, temperate, stoical and devout, the very reverse of the Renaissance braggart:

> Goe, quit 'hem all. And take along with thee
> Thy true friends wishes, *Colby*, which shall be
> That thine be just, and honest; that thy Deeds
> Not wound thy conscience, when thy body bleeds;
> That thou dost all things more for truth, then glory
> And never but for doing wrong be sory
> That by commanding first thyselfe, thou mak'st
> Thy person fit for any charge thou tak'st;
> That fortune never make thee to complaine,
> But what shee gives, thou dar'st give her againe;
> That whatsoever face thy fate puts on,
> Thou shrinke or start not, but be always one;
> That thou thinke nothing great, but what is good,
> And from that thought strive to be understood.
> So, 'live so dead, thou wilt preserve a fame
> Still pretious, with the odour of thy name.
> And last, blaspheme not, we did never heare
> Man thought the valianter, 'cause he durst sweare. . . .

The two poems to the brilliant young Earl of Newcastle, exalting his horsemanship and his fencing, show a kindred enthusiasm. As Professor Herford remarks, admiration for virility "gives eloquence to his verse." Vincent Corbet stands for graver and gentler virtues:

> His Mind was pure, and neatly kept,
> As were his Nourceries; and swept
> So of uncleannesse, or offence,
> That never came ill odour thence:
> And add his Actions unto these,
> They were as specious as his Trees.

'Tis true, he could not reprehend,
His very Manners taught to 'mend,
    They were so even, grave, and holy;
    No stubbornnesse so stiffe, nor folly
To licence ever was so light
As twice to trespasse in his sight,
    His looks would so correct it, when
    It chid the vice, yet not the Men.
Much from him I confesse I wonne,
And more, and more, I should have done,
    But that I understood him scant.
    Now I conceive him by my want. . . .

The poet's self-criticism emphasizes the respectfulness of his attitude
and deserves particular notice in this essay. In addressing Selden his
verse is less distinguished, but it must be quoted for the attitude to
himself shown in:

Though I confesse (as every Muse hath err'd,
And mine not least) . . .

and for the conception of scholarship and the literary life described:

Stand forth my Object, then, you that have beene
Ever at home: yet, have all Countries seene;
And like a Compasse keeping one foot still
Upon your Center, doe your circle fill
Of generall knowledge; watch'd men, manners too,
Heard what times past have said, seene what ours doe:
Which Grace shall I make love to first? your skill,
Or faith in things? or is't your wealth and will
T'instruct and teach? or your unweary'd paine
Of Gathering? Bountie'in pouring out againe?
What fables have you vext! what truth redeem'd!
Antiquities search'd! Opinions dis-esteem'd!
Impostures branded! and Authorities urg'd! . . .

In writing to Drayton, Jonson notes that they have not followed the
custom of exchanging verses and continues:

And, though I now begin, 'tis not to rub
Hanch against Hanch, or raise a rhyming *Club*
About the towne.

"Butter reviewers," said Mr. Nixon to the young Hugh Selwyn Mauberley.

This quotation rounds off my references to Jonson's verses on himself as a writer and his relation to the literary world. One does not take everything in seventeenth-century commendatory verses at its face value. Drayton was no Homer, but it is worth studying what Jonson says—and, more important, does not say—about the lesser figures whom he honours. The most interesting lines in the eulogy of Shakespeare are those calling upon the shades of the Greek tragedians. Jonson's critical acumen here breaks through all his own and the age's prejudices. Sir Henry Savile was somewhat above the Jonson circle and receives a formal epigram, but the ideals admired as embodied in him correspond to those of the epistle to Selden, literary skill joined to integrity of character [8]—a very solemn conception of the philosopher and the gentleman, to recall deliberately Addison's famous phrase:

> We need a man that knows the severall graces
>   Of historie, and how to apt their places;
> Where brevitie, where splendour, and where height,
>   Where sweetnesse is requir'd and where weight;
> We need a man, can speake of the intents,
>   The councells, actions, orders and events
> Of state, and censure them: we need his pen
>   Can write the things, the causes, and the men.
> But most we need his faith (and all have you)
>   That dares nor write things false, nor hide things true.

One sees in these poems the positive moral and intellectual values which are more usually merely implicit in the plays; young Wittipol in *The Devil is an Ass* emerges as a personality of some solidity and life, but the majestic Cicero is never an adequate dramatic foil to the political gangsters in *Catiline*. In the poems one can observe, described and felt in the texture of the poetry itself, the cultural ideals that gave Jonson his assurance and intellectual dignity and at the same time his feeling for civilized personal relationships. His tone only fails him when personal bitterness or excessive indignation causes him to lose his bearings and his sense of fellowship in the republic of letters.

Jonson was, however, conscious of a larger community than that meeting at the Devil Tavern with connections at the universities. Some of his finest verse celebrates this social scene and the characters who inhabited it and, in fact, led the nation. Courthope remarks that in this mode "Jonson is unequalled by any English poet, except perhaps

Pope at his best." [9] We know from the plays what he thought of the projectors and of other pioneers of nascent capitalism. He held older ideals of social justice and responsibility.[10] He saw the values he believed in embodied in certain noblemen and squires, and in statesmen and lawgivers such as Burleigh and Sir Edward Coke. The greatest document, and also the finest poem, in this connection is, of course, *To Penshurst:*

> Thou are not, PENSHURST, built for envious show,
>   Of touch, or marble; nor canst boast a row
> Of polish'd pillars, or a roofe of gold:
>   Thou hast no lantherne, whereof tales are told;
> Or stayre, or courts; but stand'st an ancient pile,
>   And these grudg'd at, art reverenc'd the while.

It is a medieval house—it happens to have been built about the year of Chaucer's birth. For Jonson a new genius presides over it from:

> That taller tree, which of a nut was set,
>   At his great birth, where all the *Muses* met.

It was now the seat of Sir Philip Sidney's brother, and Sidney appears several times in similar poems as the representative of civilization.[11] He brings the culture of *Il Cortegiano* to bear on the more active traditional idea of the gentleman expressed in, say, Langland's:

> Kings and knightes · sholde kepe it by resoun,
> Riden and rappe down · the reumes aboute,
> And taken transgressores · and tyen hem faste,
> Till treuthe had ytermyned · her trespas to ende,
> That is the profession appertly · that appendeth for knightes,
> And nought to fasten on Fryday · in fyvescore wynter,
> But holden with him and with her · that wolden al treuthe,
> And never leue hem for loue · ne for lacchyng of syluer.[12]

Penshurst is surrounded by all the beauty and wealth of nature, but it is much more than a house:

> And though thy walls be of the countrey stone,
>   They'are rear'd with no mans ruine, no mans grone,
> There's none, that dwell about them, wish them downe. . . .
> Where comes no guest, but is allow'd to eate,
>   Without his feare, and of thy lords own meate:

> Where the same beere, and bread, and self-same wine,
>   That is his Lordships, shall be also mine.
> And I not faine to sit (as some, this day,
>   At great mens tables) and yet dine away.

Jonson sees it is an active centre of a patriarchal community in which duties and responsibilities are as important as rights, and of a way of life in which all classes, including the poet—Jonson intimates that for him and for others such hospitality is becoming a thing of the past—yet live in close personal contact. *To Sir Robert Wroth* describes a very similar scene at Durance with rather more emphasis on the sporting life of the great estate—an aspect less likely to be forgotten:

> Or if thou list the night in watch to breake,
>   A-bed canst heare the loud stag speake,
> In spring, oft roused for thy masters sport,
>   Who, for it, makes thy house his court;
> Or with thy friends the heart of all the yeare
>   Divid'st, upon the lesser Deere:
> In Autumn, at the Patrich mak'st a flight,
>   And giv'st thy gladder guest the sight;
> And, in the winter, hunt'st the flying hare,
>   More for thy exercise, than fare;
> While all, that follow, their glad eares apply
>   To the full greatnesse of the cry:
> Or hawking at the river, or the bush,
>   Or shooting at the greedie thrush,
> Thou dost with some delight the day out-weare,
>   Although the coldest of the yeere!
> The whilst, the severall seasons . . .
> Thus PAN and SYLVANE having had their rites,
>   COMUS puts in, for new delights;
> And fills thy open hall with mirth and cheere,
>   As if in SATURNES raigne it were;
> APOLLO's harpe, and HERMES lyre resound,
>   Nor are the *Muses* strangers found.
> The rout of rurall folk come thronging in,
>   (Their rudenesse then is thought no sinne)
> Thy noblest spouse affords them welcome grace,
>   And the great *Heroes,* of her race,
> Sit mixt with loss of state, or reverence.
>   Freedom doth with degree dispense.

The Golden Age is thus naturalized in the hall of an English mansion in a real agricultural setting, and we end with an almost Homeric scene of feasting, in which bounty and humanity have temporarily overthrown the whole social hierarchy. Other contemporary moralists and commentators lamented that this old-fashioned "house-keeping" was dying out. In Selden's *Table Talk* the account of the *Hall* is significantly in the past tense:

> The Hall was the Place where the great Lord used to eat, (wherefore else were Halls made so big?), where he saw all his Servants and Tenants about him. He eat not in private, except in time of sickness: when he became a thing cooped up, all his greatness was spilled. Nay, the King himself used to eat in the Hall, and his Lords sat with him, and then he understood Men.

Inigo's Jones's Double Cube Room at Wilton, say, would not have lent itself to such a life. It may sound cheap to say that Jonson made the most of two worlds; he certainly wrote at a time when a highly cultivated society still kept in close contact with the community which supported it and still preserved traditions which encouraged it to maintain this kind of give and take, social, economic and cultural.

Nevertheless, despite changing architecture and changing habits of life, the ideal persisted. Jonson initiated an extremely interesting line of what, borrowing a modern analogy, one may call documentary poetry. It deserves a brief exploration. The most obvious imitations of his poems are Carew's *To Saxham* and *To my Friend G. N., from Wrest*. No one is going to claim that Carew shared his master's powers of social observation. The first poem is a light and fanciful thing; the other, less well known, which gives a detailed picture of the scene and of the social organization represented there, illustrates a number of points already made:

> Such pure and uncompounded beauties blesse
> This Mansion with a usefull comelinesse,
> Devoide of art, for here the Architect
> Did not with curious skill a Pile erect
> Of carved Marble, Touch or Porphyry,
> But built a house for hospitalitie. . . .
> The Lord and Lady of this place delight
> Rather to be in act, than seeme in sight.
> Instead of Statues to adorne their wall,

THE TONE OF BEN JONSON'S POETRY

They throng with living men their merry Hall,
Where, at large Tables fill'd with wholesome meates,
The servant, tenant, and kind neighbour eates.
Some of that ranke, spun of a finer thread,
Are with the Women, Steward, and Chaplaine fed
With daintier cates; Others of better note,
Whom wealth, parts, office, or the Heralds coate
Hath sever'd from the common, freely sit
At the Lords Table, whose spread sides admit
A large accesse of friends to fill those seates
Of his capacious circle. . . .
Nor crown'd with wheaten wreathes, doth *Ceres* stand
In stone, with a crook'd sickle in her hand;
Nor on a Marble Tun, his face besmear'd
With grapes, is curl'd uncizard *Bacchus* rear'd:
We offer not in Emblemes to the eyes,
But to the taste, those useful Deities,
We presse the juycie god and quaffe his blood,
And grind the Yeallow Goddesse into food.

The picture of the wine-press carries us away from the thoroughly
English scene; it shows the Cavalier taking his eye off the object in
order to classicize. But the mere fact that a man like Carew, derivative
as he clearly is, recognized the existence—and the value—of such a
scheme of things to the point of writing about it shows that the rather
artificial culture of Charles I's court with its extravagant masques and
its Italian pictures and Flemish painters had also not lost touch with
its roots. Vandyck perhaps overdoes the elegance and refinement in
his portrait of Carew and Killigrew, but when William Dobson paints
Endymion Porter he shows us a florid country squire with beautiful
laces and also dog and gun, leaning on a relief of muses and with a
classical bust of a poet in the background; it is a superb and highly
revealing work. Similarly Herrick in *The Hock-Cart* starts on the
shores of the Mediterranean and then hurries home:

Come Sons of Summer, by whose toile,
We are the Lords of Wine and Oile:
By whose tough labours, and rough hands,
We rip up first, then reap our lands.
Crown'd with the eares of corne, now come,
And, to the Pipe, sing Harvest home. . . .
Well, on, brave boyes, to your Lords Hearth,

Glitt'ring with fire; where, for your mirth,
Ye shall see first the large and cheefe
Foundation of your Feast, Fat Beefe. . . .
With sev'rall dishes standing by,
As here a Custard, there a Pie,
And here all tempting Frumentie.
And for to make the merry cheere,
If smirking Wine be wanting here,
There's that, which drowns all care, stout Beere;
Which freely drink to your Lords health,
Then to the Plough, (the Common-wealth). . . .

As a whole it is, with its colloquial language, a vivid picture of a
Devon harvest festival, and Herrick has suggested, in the reference
to the plough, the deeper meaning. Lovelace shows us that he was
something of a naturalist as well as a chivalrous Kentish squire in those
fanciful and moralized descriptions of insects and in *The Falcon* for
whom he laments:

Ah Victory, unhap'ly wonne!
Weeping and Red is set the Sun,
Whilst the whole Field floats in one tear,
And all the Air doth mourning wear:
Close-hooded all thy kindred come
To pay their Vows upon thy Tombe;
The *Hobby* and the *Musket* too,
Do march to take their last adieu.

The *Lanner* and the *Lanneret*,
Thy Colours bear as Banneret;
The *Goshawk* and her *Tercel*, rous'd
With Tears attend thee as new bows'd,
All these are in their dark array
Led by the various *Herald-Jay*.

But thy eternal name shall live
Whilst Quills from Ashes fame reprieve,
Whilst open stands Renown's wide dore,
And Wings are left on which to soar:
Doctor *Robbin*, the Prelate *Pye*,
And the poetick *Swan* shall dye,
Only to sing thy Elegie.

Whatever personal significance this may have had for Lovelace—it would seem to express a haunting regret for lost causes—its interest for us in the present context lies in his charming blend of the gentleman's knowledge of field sports and heraldry with poetic traditions—one thinks inevitably of the *Parlement of Foules*.[13] The idiom of these poems is, as Sir Herbert Grierson has put it, "that of an English gentleman of the best type, natural, simple, occasionally careless, but never diverging into vulgar colloquialism . . . or into conventional, tawdry splendour."[14] Several contributors to *Jonsonus Virbius* make plain the influence of Jonson in favour of "right and natural language." This is a stream of English poetry, the gentleman writing as a gentleman about his position and responsibilities, his interests and pleasures, which, if we omit Byron who is in any case often both vulgar and tawdry, now for better or worse dries up.

Early Stuart governments made several attempts to arrest the decay of the patriarchal household and the drift to London. Sir Richard Fanshawe wrote *An Ode, upon His Majesties Proclamation in the Year 1630. Commanding the Gentry to reside upon their Estates in the Countrey.* He sees what Jonson sees, and expresses the anxiety of those who realized how times were changing:

> Nor let the Gentry grudge to go
> Into those places whence they grew,
> But think them blest they may do so
>   Who would pursue.
>
> The smoky glory of the Town,
> That may go till his native Earth,
> And by the shining Fire sit down
>   Of his own hearth. . . .
>
> The Countrey too ev'n chops for rain:
> You that exhale it by your power,
> Let the fat drops fall down again
>   In a full shower. . . .

One thus sees embodied in verse of considerable distinction a picture of a social order, its natural setting and its occupations, and a sense of some of the dangers threatening it. The fact that it was written by men of very varying distinction of character and intelligence shows how widely the ideals expressed were held. That they were not always lived up to one may take for granted, though the enthusiasm of the verse seems to be more than merely literary. And as regards cultural standards there must have been, for a small number of houses like Penshurst, Wrest, Wilton, Great Tew or Bolsover, a very large number like that of Mr. Henry Hastings [15] or of far less individuality and long forgotten. The scheme of knightly prowess, literary and musical interests and public spirit set forth by Peacham in *The Compleat Gentleman* was not universally followed; he bitterly reproaches those who waste their substance in London, "appearing but as Cuckoes in the Spring, one time in the yeare to the Countrey and their tenants, leaving the care of keeping good houses at Christmas, to the honest Yeomen of the Countrey." [16] However, one finds in this verse evidence of a climate of social opinion and, more important, feelings and habits which, with all their imperfections, were civilized in the narrower artistic sense, and also in the wider sense of having a foundation of social justice. This world provided Jonson with his larger *milieu*, or rather *milieux*, for its being made up of small groups is an important feature; he had lived in the house of Lord Aubigny and was a visitor at several others. One does not find this scene in English poetry after the Restoration. Though English noblemen never became, as Fanshawe feared they might, mere court sycophants or men about town, manners in the widest sense changed in the era of the coffee-house. Life became more formally decorous. Pope, in the *Epistle to Boyle*, presents an ideal vision comparable to Jonson's:

> His Father's Acres who enjoys in peace,
> Or makes his Neighbours glad if he increase:
> Whose chearful Tenants bless their yearly toil,
> Yet to their Lord owe more than to the soil;
> Whose ample Lawns are not asham'd to feed
> The milky heifer and deserving steed;
> Whose rising Forests, not for pride or show,
> But future Buildings, future Navies grow:
> Let his plantations stretch from down to down,
> First shade a Country, and then raise a Town.

But fine as it is, and central to Pope's work, it does not imply so intimate and personal a relationship between the classes as the earlier poetry. The whole domestic layout had altered as ideas changed, and the lord was benevolent from the portico or the church steps rather than from the dais in the hall. Nevertheless one finds the spirit still alive in the age of "Squire Allworthy," of Coke of Norfolk and of Dr. Johnson's Club, and it was the tradition of culture that died first.

It need hardly be said that Jonson used an independent tone towards his patrons—except when he was in extreme financial straits. He had opinions about his rightful place at table in an age when all knew their own degrees and had their rightful places by birth or merit; "my Lord," he says that he said to the Earl of Salisbury, evidently a more remote patron than Sir William Sidney, "you promised I should dine with you, but I do not." [17] *An Epistle to Sir Edward Sacvile, now Earl of Dorset* treats, after Seneca, of the question of patronage and gratitude:

> You cannot doubt, but I, who freely know
> This Good from you, as freely will it owe;
> And though my fortune humble me, to take
> The smallest courtesies with thankes, I make
> Yet choyce from whom I take them; and would shame
> To have such doe me good, I durst not name:
> They are the Noblest benefits, and sinke
> Deepest in Man, of which when he doth thinke,
> The memorie delights him more, from whom
> Then what he hath receiv'd. Gifts stinke from some,
> They are so long a coming, and so hard;
> Where any Deed is forc't, the Grace is mard.

He goes on to analyse the characters of niggardly and ungracious patrons and those who sponge upon them. Jonson thought he knew who deserved his respect and why. In *Timber* he defines his conception of manners by implication, in the act of defining Courtesy in its euphemistic sense:

> *Nothing* is a courtesie, unlesse it be meant us; and that friendly, and lovingly. Wee owe no thankes to *Rivers,* that they carry our boats. . . . It is true, some man may receive a Courtesie, and not know it; but never any man received it from him, that knew it not. . . . No: The doing of *Courtesies* aright, is the mixing of the respects for his owne sake, and for mine. He that doth them meerly for his owne sake, is like one that feeds his Cattell to sell them: he hath his Horse well drest for *Smithfield.*

Good manners for Jonson were something that, while adorning the upper tiers of the social hierarchy, should yet permeate through it. He expected the same kind of consideration from a patron as he showed towards his "high-spirited friend," and he admired similar qualities in his friends in every sense.

The grace of Jonson's manner comes out in his addresses to noble ladies, especially the Countesses of Rutland, Montgomery, and Bedford, and Lady Mary Wroth. A consideration of them will form a conclusion to this study, for, though he flatters splendidly, he does not cringe. There were certain fixed viewpoints in Jonson's outlook.

He praises his patronesses partly for their beauty and their taste, partly for deeper qualities. He writes to Lady Mary Wroth with full Renaissance exuberance:

> Madame, had all antiquitie beene lost,
> All historie seal'd up, and fables crost;
> That we had left us, nor by time, nor place,
> Least mention of a *Nymph*, a *Muse*, a *Grace*,
> But even their names were to be made a-new,
> Who could not but create them all, from you?
> He, that but saw you weare the wheaten hat,
> Would call you more than CERES, if not that:
> And, drest in shepherds tyre, who would not say:
> You were the bright OENONE, FLORA, or *May?*
> If dancing, all would cry th' *Idalian* Queene,
> Were leading forth the *Graces* on the greene:
> And, armed for the chase, so bare her brow
> DIANA' alone, so hit, and hunted so.

Lady Montgomery is a new Susanna, and in Lady Bedford he bows before qualities of character which belong peculiarly to his own vision:

> This morning, timely rapt with holy fire,
> I thought to forme unto my zealous *Muse*,
> What kind of creature I could most desire,
> To honor, serve, and love; as *Poets* use.
> I meant to make her faire, and free, and wise,
> Of greatest bloud, and yet more good then great;
> I meant the day-starre should not brighter rise,
> Nor lend like influence from his lucent seat.
> I meant she should be curteous, facile, sweet,
> Hating that solemne vice of greatnesse, pride;
> I meant each softest vertue, there should meet,
> Fit in that softer bosome to reside.
> Onely a learned, and a manly soule
> I purpos'd her; that should, with even powers,
> The rock, the spindle, and the sheeres controule
> Of destinie, and spin her owne free houres.

> Such when I meant to faine, and wish'd to see,
> My *Muse* bad, *Bedford* write, and that was shee.

This beautifully polished epigram is a suitable vehicle for the presentation of a vision of aristocratic elegance, charm, virtue and intelligence—one notices the emphatic and subtle rhythm of the third quatrain—and the poet's admiration for them. One is reminded of the undirected, and possibly therefore more perfect, *Elegie:*

> Though Beautie be the Marke of Praise,
> And yours of whom I sing be such
> As not the World can praise too much,
> Yet is't your vertue now I raise,

where the sense of the rarity and fragility of such qualities is delicately realized in the cadence of:

> His falling Temples you have rear'd,
> The withered Garlands tane away;
> His Altars kept from the Decay,
> That envie wish'd, and Nature fear'd.

The dangers and difficulties besetting his ideals of the lady are magnificently argued out in "Not to know vice at all . . ." and *To the World. A farewell for a Gentle-woman, vertuous and noble:*

> No, I doe know, that I was borne
> To age, misfortune, sicknesse, griefe:
> But I will beare these, with that scorne,
> As shall not need thy false reliefe.

This is the simple but dignified Stoicism which conditions of the age made both necessary and desirable. Jonson admired it in others and possessed it himself. This moral strength and perception, along with his erudition and conscious art, discoursed on in *Timber,* and an ever-present sense of the whole gamut of living, combine with the tone of the Jacobean noble household, "curteous, facile, sweet," where in season "freedome doth with degree dispense," to support the brilliance of the famous lyrics. Like his gentlewoman he could say,

> Nor for my peace will I goe farre,
> As wandrers doe, that still doe rome,

> But make my strengths, such as they are,
>   Here in my bosome, and at home.

The end of it all is realized with unerring taste in such things as:

> Would'st thou heare, what man can say
>   In a little? Reader, stay.
> Under-neath this stone doth lye
>   As much beautie, as could dye:
> Which in life did harbour give
>   To more vertue, then doth live.
> If, at all, shee had a fault,
>   Leave it buryed in this vault.
> One name was ELIZABETH,
>   Th' other let it sleepe with death:
> Fitter, where it dyed, to tell,
>   Then that it liv'd at all. Farewell.

I am brought back to my starting-point, the *Elegie on the Lady Jane Pawlet,* through which the urbanity of Jonson links up directly with that of Pope. Jonson thought "couplets be the bravest sort of verses, especially when they are broken like hexameters," [18] and he has an important place in their development, but, as regards regularity, he broke them with a caesura in varied places, and the following lines from one of his livelier occasional poems are worth remembering:

> To hit in angles, and to clash with time:
>   As all defence, or offence, were a chime!
> I hate such measur'd, give me metall'd fire. . . .[19]

He liked a varied movement in poetry as well as fencing. The *Elegie,* like the other poems in couplets quoted, bears this out:

> I doe obey you, Beautie! for in death
>   You seeme a faire one! O that you had breath,
> To give your shade a name! Stay, stay, I feele
>   A horrour in mee! all my blood is steele!
> Stiffe! starke! My joynts 'gainst one another knock!
>   Whose Daughter? ha? Great *Savage* of the Rock? . . .
> Her Sweetnesse, Softnesse, her faire Courtesie,
>   Her wary guardes, her wise simplicitie,
> Were like a ring of Vertues, 'bout her set,

And pietie the Center, where all met.
A reverend State she had, an awful Eye,
    A dazling, yet inviting, Majestie:
What Nature, Fortune, Institution, Fact
    Could summe to a perfection, was her Act!
How did she leave the world? with what contempt?
    Just as she in it liv'd! and so exempt
From all affection! when they urg'd the Cure
    Of her disease, how did her soule assure
Her suffrings, as the body had beene away!
    And to the Torturers (her Doctors) say,
Stick on your Cupping-glasses, feare not, put
    Your hottest Causticks to, burne, lance, or cut:
'Tis but a body which you can torment,
    And I, into the world, all Soule, was sent!
Then comforted her Lord! and blest her Sonne!
    Chear'd her faire Sisters in her race to runne!
With gladnesse temper'd her sad Parents teares!
    Made her friends joyes to get above their feares!
And, in her last act, taught the Standers-by,
    With admiration, and applause to die!
Let angels sing her glories, who can call
    Her spirit home, to her originall! . . .

It combines a slightly naïve declamatory manner at the start with
Jonson's characteristic blend of urbanity, shrewd observation and simplicity in the description of the Marchioness's personality and an
anticipation of the more formal high decorum of the Augustans towards the end; but no Augustan would have written her words to the
doctors, overflowing as they are with "enthusiasm." Here in a lady at
the top of the social hierarchy one notes the hierarchy of virtues. They
correspond fairly to the qualities of men we have already seen portrayed. Together Jonson's lords and ladies form a brilliant, dignified,
benevolent and gracious society, "dazling, yet inviting." We can see
from the poems, and other evidence corroborates, that there was no
impassable gap between the world of the poet's vision and Jacobean
and Caroline England. *Eupheme* on the Lady Venetia Digby is usually
held up as an example of hyperbole; a passage in a quiet key on the
character of the Lady, whether true to life in this particular case or
not, shows, with a characteristic note of irony, a picture of deportment
which would be appropriate to any of the scenes or characters discussed:

All Nobilitie,
(But pride, that schisme of incivilitie)
She had, and it became her! she was fit
T'have knowne no envy, but by suffring it!
She had a mind as calme, as she was faire;
Not tost or troubled with light Lady-aire;
But, kept an even gate, as some streight tree
Mov'd by the wind, so comely moved she.
And by the awfull manage of her Eye
She swaid all bus'nesse in the Familie!

Jonson himself, as we have seen at the start, was sometimes guilty of "that schisme of incivilitie." He probably needed the stimulus of good company to bring out the full refinement of his literary culture. But it is brought out over and over again, and was, and is, a model of its kind. It is imposible finally to separate the qualities presented in the poems from the poet's attitude towards them; social manner and manners are infectious and the one seems to have evoked the other. We should need more biographical information than we possess to take the matter further but I do not think it is base to attribute to Jonson what might be called poetic "party manners."

One cannot sum up an achievement such as Jonson's in a word. I have only touched in passing on his trenchancy and seriousness as a satirist and his strength and delicacy as a lyric poet. I wanted to deal at some length with his tone and accent because, in considering the meaning of wit, I believe that, though it changed from an intellectual to a social spirit as the century wore on, nevertheless a social spirit of a clear and peculiarly noble kind was present in poetry from the start and that this spirit is exemplified particularly in Ben Jonson. His poetry, even more than his plays, links seventeenth-century culture and the polite civilization of the Augustans to the better features of the medieval social order and to the half-religious ideal of Courtesy.

NOTES

[1] Dr. F. R. Leavis has analysed Pope's poem in *Revaluation*, Chap. III.
[2] See *Ben Jonson*, ed. Herford and Simpson, Vol. II, p. 340; and R. Walker, "Ben Jonson's Lyric Poetry," *The Criterion*, Vol. XIII, 1934.
[3] *Revaluation*, Chap. I.
[4] *Conversations*, 19.
[5] See the discussion of wit in Chap. I.
[6] Praise outweighs blame in the *Conversations*, and, if one takes these remarks along with the two epigrams to the poet and that to Lady Bedford

"with Mr. Donne's Satires," the whole forms a brief but apposite critical estimate.

With regard to the disputed authorship of the four elegies, I think that Mrs. Simpson gives good reasons for what should be a final division of responsibility, allotting *The Expostulation* to Donne and the others to Jonson (*Jonson and Donne, R.E.S.,* Vol. XV).

[7] Professor Herford and Mr. and Mrs. Simpson give this poem to Godolphin (*Ben Jonson,* Vol. VIII, p. 265). If it is his, it not only shows his distinction as a poet, but also the remarkable homogeneity of tone within the "Tribe."

[8] Courthope notes that in dedicating to Savile a translation of Cicero, *De Oratore,* Lib. II, 62–3, Jonson reverses the order of qualities, making moral strength more important than literary skill (*History of English Poetry,* Vol. III, p. 181); it is typical of him.

[9] Ibid., p. 179.

[10] For the background of what follows I am much indebted to Professor Trevelyan's *England under the Stuarts,* Chaps. I–II, and Professor L. C. Knights's *Drama and Society in the Age of Ben Jonson,* Chaps. I–IV.

[11] Cf. *To Sir Edward Sacvile, To the Countess of Rutland* and *To Lady Mary Wroth.*

[12] *Piers Plowman,* B., Passus I, 94–101. I am indebted to Mr. Dawson's *The Vision of Piers Plowman* in *Medieval Religion* for this quotation. I quote Langland as a representative spokesman. I do not wish to suggest that seventeenth-century noblemen made a habit of reading him; Peacham refers to "that bitter *Satyre of Piers Plowman*" (*Compleat Gentleman,* ed. Gordon, p. 95), but he may mean one of the imitations, as he attributes it to Lydgate.

In the matter of culture Peacham lays down a scheme of literary, musical and artistic studies for the gentleman and suggests a suitable blend of pride and condescension in manners; similarly Lord Herbert ends his educational recommendations: "I could say much more . . . and particularly concerning the discreet civility which is to be observed in communication either with friends or strangers . . . many precepts conducing there unto may be had in *Guazzo de la Civile Conversation,* and *Galateus de Moribus*" (*Life,* ed. Lee, p. 42).

[13] As regards Chaucer's position in the early seventeenth century, it is, I think, worth recalling that, though Jonson strongly discourages the uses of "Chaucerisms," Peacham encourages his gentleman to "account him among the best of [his] English books in [his] library. . . . He saw in those times without his spectacles" (*The Compleat Gentleman,* ed. Gordon, p. 94).

[14] *Metaphysical Poetry,* p. xxxi.

[15] See *Characters of the Seventeenth Century,* ed. Nichol Smith, p. 44.

[16] Op. cit., p. 220.

[17] *Conversations,* 13.

[18] *Conversations,* 1.

[19] *An Epigram. To William Earle of Newcastle.*

↙

Ben Jonson's Poems:
Notes on the Ordered Society

"The reputation of Jonson," Mr. Eliot once remarked, "has been of the most deadly kind that can be compelled upon the memory of a great poet. To be universally accepted; to be damned by the praise that quenches all desire to read the book; to be afflicted by the imputation of virtues which excite the least pleasure; and to be read only by historians and antiquaries—this is the most perfect conspiracy of approval." [1] Perhaps the prospect is not quite so gloomy now: "Jonson criticism has at last commenced to grow green," Jonas Barish observes, and the articles he has recently collected indicate, over a variety of critical approaches, some avenues that may be profitably explored.[2] But it is striking that no essay in his collection bears directly on the lyric and occasional verse. If the lawn of Jonson criticism is newly green, brown patches are still perceptible.[3] That is not very surprising, of course, for *Timber* invites attention to the comedies:

> The *Poet* is the neerest Borderer upon the Orator, and expresseth all his vertues, though he be tyed more to numbers; is his equall in ornament, and above him in his strengths. And, (of the kind) the *Comicke* comes neerest: Because, in moving the minds of men, and stirring of affections (in which

From *Essays in English Literature from the Renaissance to the Victorian Age Presented to A.S.P. Woodhouse,* eds. Millar MacLure and F. Watt (Toronto: University of Toronto Press, 1964), pp. 43–68. Reprinted by permission of the author and publisher.

Oratory shewes, and especially approves her eminence) hee chiefly excells.[4]

Given this remark, and the elaborations that follow, to say nothing of the triumphant Jonsonian comedies themselves, later critics could hardly be expected to spare the poems more than an appreciative glance before passing to the main course of comedy. It has often been the fate of the poems to be praised chiefly (sometimes exclusively) for their formal virtues, while the best criticism of the comedies, more than ever since L. C. Knights's *Drama and Society in the Age of Jonson*, has kept steadily in view Jonson's comment that "the Study of [Poesy] (if wee will trust *Aristotle*) offers to mankinde a certaine rule, and Patterne of living well, and happily; disposing us to all Civill offices of Society." [5]

That is rather curious, too. The comedies, by their nature, present this "certaine rule, and Patterne" indirectly, appealing (as Knights says) to the "sardonic contemplation" of an audience characterized by "a lively sense of human limitations." [6] The epigrams, as a rule, repeat that method; but a significant number of the poems, particularly in *The Forrest*, deal explicitly and directly with "high and noble matter," with "the mysteries of manners, armes, and arts." Geoffrey Walton, following Leavis, remarks on Jonson's regular attention, in the poems, to "serious moral matters in a social context." [7] I suggest that, while the plays deal principally in the satiric recognition and description of the factors that contribute to social disorder, we find in the poems (with the *Discoveries* behind, as theory to practice), not an explicit and detailed outline of the social order Jonson admired, but rather "notes" on particular elements that ought to mark a society properly ordered, as well as suggestions for conduct in the midst of a disordered one. The negative strictures of the comedies, accordingly, are supplemented and completed by positive advices in the poetry and the *Discoveries*.

One must be careful not to claim too much: no integrated grand design for society emerges from the "lesser theatre" of these poems, so often committed to compliment. But the recurrence of three related themes is striking. In brief, the poems lay stress on the virtue of friendship between good men, who are receptive by nature to the free exchange of opinion and counsel, and on the strong resource such friendships constitute for the ordered society and the secure state. They reflect also Jonson's views on the relationship that ought ideally to obtain between prince and poet, in the interest of the people at large. Finally, they indicate the social attitudes and actions befitting a "ruling class" which thoroughly understands the nature of its responsibilities and desires to make them effective. It is relevant to observe here also that, when Jonson speaks to this third question, he is apt to select the verse-epistle as a vehicle peculiarly suited to the poet who outlines, for the benefit of those in high place, "holy lawes / Of nature, and societie." In this, as in much else, "there must be a Harmonie, and concent of parts." [8]

A dominant and recurring theme in the *Discoveries* is the humanistic insistence on man's power, in spite of his own nature and the vicissitudes of time, to maintain ethical standards, not in a spirit of reactionary opposition to change, but in large measure by adapting classical precepts to contemporary circumstance. "Rules," Jonson noted, "are ever of lesse force, and valew, then experiments"; men find truth by following "the *Ancients* . . . but as Guides, not Commanders." [9] Still, Jonson never pretended that this would be easy. He knew all about the shortcomings of human nature; when the character of mankind is in question, a note of disenchantment is often heard. "*Envy* is no new thing, nor was it borne onely in our times. The Ages past have brought it forth, and the comming Ages will. So long as there are men fit for it . . . it will never be wanting." "*Natures* that are hardned to *evill,* you shall sooner breake, then make straight; they are like poles that are crooked, and dry: there is no attempting them." Human nature "oft-times dies of a *Melancholy,* that it cannot be vitious enough." [10] It is clear too that Jonson recognized the threat of vice not merely to individuals but to the community much more.

> When too much desire, and greedinesse of vice, hath made the body unfit, or unprofitable; it is yet gladded with the sight, and spectacle of it in others: and for want of ability to be an Actor; is content to be a Witnesse. It enjoyes the pleasure of sinning, in beholding others sinne; as in Dicing, Drinking, Drabbing, &c.

Indeed, "A native, if hee be vitious, deserves to bee a stranger, and cast out of the Common-wealth, as an Alien." [11] It goes without saying that Jonson would never abandon the effort to improve matters by any available means. He gathers up, for instance, Quintilian's gentle suggestions about the best ways in education and in criticism.[12] But in the final analysis, he depends on a continuing supply of naturally "*Good men* . . . the Stars, the Planets of the Ages wherein they live, [who] illustrate the times." [13] The well-known observation, "Men are decay'd, and *studies:* Shee [Nature] is not," needs to be compared with less familiar passages in the poet's commonplace book: "They are ever good men, that must make good the times: if the men be naught, the times will be such." "A good life," for Jonson, "is a maine Argument." [14]

It is in the light of these attitudes that we should read those poems in which Jonson turns his attention to friendship. Geoffrey Walton touches on this matter but does not come closely to grips with it, beyond an approving glance at a few of the poems addressed to friends in various walks of life; and while it is true that in these pieces "one can observe . . . [Jonson's] feeling for civilized personal relationships," [15] there is more to be said. For Jonson, friendship is the bond enabling those good men who illustrate their times to group together and, by means of their collected virtue, cast out or resist vice. So they serve each other; but they help to safeguard the state as well.

These views are, of course, not original with Jonson, who might have been influenced by any of a number of authorities. But while it is not very feasible to suggest particular sources for his poetical comments on friendship (given their relatively orthodox detail, together with the wide range of his reading), it should at least be observed that Jonson, unlike Spenser, is not much interested in the conception of friendship "as a harmonizing and unifying principle of cosmic love operating in the realm of man to promote concord." [16] As usual with him, metaphysical theory takes second place to, or is eclipsed by, moral and social considerations. Friendship matters to Jonson because it is a moral virtue and because it contributes to social stability. His position recalls, in particular, that of Aristotle's dissertation on friendship (*Ethics*, VIII–IX), which contains some passages that must certainly have called out Jonson's approval, whether or not they directly influenced his poetry.[17] Having classified the three categories of friendship in terms of its object ("what is good, pleasurable, or useful"), Aristotle shows that friendships based on utility and pleasure must soon dissolve; he concludes that the only "perfect Friendship" subsists

> between those who are good and whose similarity consists in their goodness: for these men wish one another's good in similar ways; in so far as they are good (and good they are in themselves); and those are specially friends who wish good to their friends for their sakes, because they feel thus towards them on their own account and not as a mere matter of result; so the Friendship between these men continues to subsist so long as they are good; and goodness, we know, has in it a principle of permanence.[18]

"Some go so far as to hold that 'good man' and 'friend' are terms synonomous," he remarks in the same place, pointing out that "requital of Friendship is attended with moral choice which proceeds from a moral state." Relevant also is Aristotle's distinction between friendships moral and legal, and between elements within a "legal" friendship: "The Legal is upon specified conditions . . . the obligation is clear and admits of no dispute, the friendly element is the delay in requiring its discharge."

All this is reflected in Jonson's poems, which often repudiate, as in "An Epistle answering to one that asked to be Sealed of the Tribe of Ben" (9–15, 25–7), friendships based on utility or pleasure.

> Let those that meerely talke, and never thinke,
> That live in the wild Anarchie of Drinke,
> Subject to quarrell only; or else such
> As make it their proficiencie, how much
> They'ave glutted in, and letcher'd out that weeke,
> That never yet did friend, or friendship seeke
> But for a Sealing . . .
>
> .   .   .   .   .   .
>
> Let these men have their wayes, and take their times
> To vent their Libels, and to issue rimes,
> I have no portion in them. . . .[19]

Flattery, the extreme of that "friendship whose motive is utility," Jonson condemns in a thoughtful phrase: "To flatter my good Lord" is "To lose the formes, and dignities of men" (*Under-Wood* XV, 146–7). The view that "those are specially friends who wish good to their friends for their sakes, because they feel thus towards them on their own account and not as a mere matter of result," informs poems as various as "Inviting a friend to supper" or the ode to a "high-spirited friend" (*Und.* XXVI); notable too is the "Epistle to a friend" (*Und.* XXXVII),[20] where the quality of "friendship which no chance but love did chuse" is heightened by contrast (7–9) with that of

> Your Countrie-neighbours, that commit
> Their vice of loving for a Christmasse fit;
> Which is indeed but friendship of the spit. . . .[21]

These and other poems repeatedly emphasize certain qualities of

friendship: moderation, candour, generosity, mutual esteem. The opening lines of the "Epigram: To a Friend, and Sonne" (*Und.* LXIX),
perhaps to Lucius Cary, summarize those qualities with terse dignity:

> Sonne, and my Friend, I had not call'd you so
> To mee; or beene the same to you; if show,
> Profit, or Chance had made us: But I know
> What, by that name, wee each to other owe,
> Freedome, and Truth; with love from those begot:
> Wise-crafts, on which the flatterer ventures not.

That friendship is "attended with moral choice" is asserted by Jonson
less emphatically than one might expect. Still, membership in the
Tribe evidently involved selective distinction between suitable candi-
dates and those who sought friendship "but for a Sealing"; and the
poet seems to assume that his "high-spirited friend" cannot after all
"mis-apply" the "wholsome Physick for the mind" prescribed by
Jonson, but will in fact choose to accept the honest counsel of a friend.
Another kind of moral choice emerges in *Under-Wood* XXXVII
(25–30):

> It is an Act of tyrannie, not love,
> In practiz'd friendship wholly to reprove,
> As flatt'ry with friends humours still to move.
>
> From each of which I labour to be free,
> Yet if with eithers vice I teynted be,
> Forgive it, as my frailtie, and not me.

Friendship, in short, confers (or should confer) a capacity to recognize
and accept some frailities in human nature, and so to overlook minor
vices that may otherwise obscure or even destroy a relationship essentially virtuous: to resist vice, therefore, by a moral decision. One is
struck by Jonson's recurring use of the term "free": true friends may
fearlessly exchange ideas, give an opinion, advise, censure even. Men
come to know liberty through friendship; or again, to be a friend is to
free both oneself and one's friend. The term itself does not appear in
yet another "Epistle to a Friend" (*Und.* XVII), on the distinction
between legal and moral friendships, but the poem deals with the
right use of that freedom which only friends can know (1–6, 11–16):

> They are not, Sir, worst Owers, that doe pay
> Debts when they can: good men may breake their day,

> And yet the noble Nature never grudge;
> 'Tis then a crime, when the Usurer is Judge.
> And he is not in friendship. Nothing there
> Is done for gaine: If't be, 'tis not sincere. . . .
>
> . . . he that takes
> Simply my Band, his trust in me forsakes,
> And lookes unto the forfeit. If you be
> Now so much friend, as you would trust in me,
> Venter a longer time, and willingly:
> All is not barren land, doth fallow lie.

The associations of friendship with moral virtue, however, are no less important for Jonson than the role of friendship in its social context. Aristotle had said that "Friendship seems to be the bond of Social Communities," and also that, if some forms of "Communion"

> are thought to be formed for pleasure's sake, those, for instance, of bacchanals or club-fellows, which are with a view to Sacrifice or merely company . . . [yet] all these seem to be ranged under the great Social one, inasmuch as the aim of this is, not merely the expediency of the moment but, for life and at all times. . . . So then it appears that all the instances of Communion are parts of the great Social one: and corresponding Friendships will follow upon such Communions.[22]

In "An Epistle answering to one that asked to be Sealed of the Tribe of Ben" (*Und.* XLVII), Jonson draws his view of friendship between individuals together with a statement on the obligations of friends to the body politic. The poem suggests that Jonson regarded the Tribe, his own band of brothers, not at all as an association "formed for pleasure's sake . . . or merely company," but as a dependable nucleus of virtuous companions, secure in self-knowledge and the wit to eschew triviality, upon whom the state might rely in all honourable causes. No doubt, too, while he would endorse all friendly connections established between virtuous men, he was bound to pay particular respect to any such group including a majority of poets, whose art is that "*Philosophy,* which leades on, and guides us by the hand to Action. . . ."[23] The title, with its scriptural allusion, and the lines glancing at heaven's purposes decorously reinforce the note of high seriousness recurrently dominant in this poem. While the "Epistle" is not precisely balanced in its structure, it seems to be true that Jonson deals at first (1–30) with the distinguishing features of men unfit for friendship, and in conclusion (51–78) with the characteristics of true friends. The intervening passage, for the greater part a contemptuous catalogue of trivia dear to gossiping courtiers, contains also (37–42, at the poem's centre, as it happens) a concise and plain-spoken affirmation of the good citizen's obligation to act as a member of the larger community.

> I wish all well, and pray high heaven conspire
> My Princes safetie, and my Kings desire,
> But if, for honour, we must draw the Sword,
> And force back that, which will not be restor'd,
> I have a body, yet, that spirit drawes
> To live, or fall a Carkasse in the cause.

Fops chatter, men act. But the passage throws into high relief a more significant contrast. The wastrels described in the opening section of the poem may be "received for the Covey of Witts," but in fact no "ignorance is more then theirs." Their crass concerns mark them as slaves to passion. Knowing nothing of friendship, each cares for himself alone. Jonson's statement of personal principle that opens the concluding section (56–62) seems at first to assert merely another kind of self-centred aloofness. But the poet at once draws into his circle all men with whom "square, wel-tagde, and permanent" friendship is possible, men (that is) of Jonson's own stamp:

> . . . all so cleare, and led by reasons flame,
> As but to stumble in her sight were shame;
> These I will honour, love, embrace, and serve:
> And free it from all question to preserve.
> So short you read my Character, and theirs
> I would call mine. . . . (69–74)

Such men, devoted to principle not appetite, serve each other and the community; and on such men the state can rely when it is time to "draw the Sword." Through friendship, then, good men who understand the rights and duties of the freedom they enjoy, and who are prepared to act in defence of virtuous principles, form a reliable substratum upon which the state and society at large may depend for health and survival.[24]

To match what may be called this broad "horizontal" principle of friendship among men of active virtue, one means of preserving a desirable social order, Jonson was impressed also (as the *Discoveries* chiefly show) by the need for a "vertical" king-post of order: the healthy relationship of king and people. Details of mutual rights and duties, however, interested him less than the establishment of conditions that would be likely to ensure good government. Critics have often noticed that *dispositio*, arrangement, in plays or poems, receives Jonson's particular attention; the *Discoveries* everywhere reflect this concern.[25] In the state also, it is vital that administration be properly arranged, especially that the good prince shall be attended by good advisers; "for though the *Prince* himselfe be of most prompt inclination to all vertue: Yet the best *Pilots* have need of *Mariners*, beside Sayles, Anchor, and other Tackle," and "the good Counsellors to Princes are the best instruments of a good Age." "The best Counsellors," Jonson noted from Lipsius, "are books"; but the proposition implicit throughout the *Discoveries* is that, in fact, the best counsellor of all is the poet.[26]

Most of the Renaissance commonplaces about the relations of king and people are present in the *Discoveries*. "*The vulgar* . . . commonly ill-natur'd; and alwayes grudging against their *Governours*," are like a many-headed beast; the good prince "is the Pastor of the people . . . the *soule* of the Commonwealth; and ought to cherish it, as his owne body"; "*After God*, nothing is to be lov'd of man like the Prince." Jonson is orthodox on rebellion too: "Let no man therefore murmure at the Actions of the Prince, who is plac'd so farre above him. If hee offend, he hath his Discoverer. *God* hath a height beyond him." [27] For these views and others like them, there was plenty of authority in Seneca, Erasmus, Lipsius, and "the great *Doctor of State, Macchiavell*," on whom he draws directly for a mordant passage about advisers to the prince. Yet if he recognizes Machiavellian wisdom in some things, Jonson does not give way to cynicism. "The *Princes* Prudence" (as he notes from Farnese) may well be "his chiefe Art, and safety"; but it is "the mercifull *Prince* . . . safe in love, not in feare," whom Jonson admires. "A *good King* is a publike Servant," by no means "(as it is in the Fable) a crowned Lyon." He can agree that "*the strength* of Empire is in Religion. . . . Nothing more commends the *Soveraigne* to the Subject, then it," but then his own voice breaks in, "For hee that is religious, must be mercifull and just necessarily. . . . Justice is the vertue, that *Innocence* rejoyceth in." [28] The prudence that adjusts flexibily to change and circumstance, and yet serves virtue still, he thought an essential element of administration, that princely art. "*Wise*, is rather the attribute of a Prince, then *learned*, or *good*";

but the governor who is truly wise must in the nature of things be a good man too.[29]

Well enough; yet, "*Princes* are easie to be deceiv'd . . . what wisdome can escape it; where so many Court-*Arts* are studied?" One answer recalls that of Lipsius: "A *Prince* without Letters, is a Pilot without eyes." But a more effective response is to choose the right sort of counsellor: "Soveraignty needs counsell." Jonson knew from Vives what to look for:

> In being able to counsell others, a Man must be furnish'd with an universall store in himselfe, to the knowledge of all *Nature:* That is the matter, and seed-plot; There are the seats of all Argument, and Invention. But especially, you must be cunning in the nature of Man: There is the variety of things, which are as the *Elements,* and *Letters,* which his art and wisdome must ranke, and order to the present occasion. For wee see not all letters in single words; nor all places in particular discourses. . . . The two chiefe things that give a man reputation in counsell, are the opinion of his *Honesty;* and the opinion of his *Wisdome.* . . . *Wisedome* without *Honesty* is meere craft, and coosinage. And therefore the reputation of *Honesty* must first be gotten; which cannot be, but by living well.

And of all such persons, the poet is most clearly qualified:

> I could never thinke the study of *Wisdome* confin'd only to the Philosopher: or of *Piety* to the *Divine:* or of *State* to the *Politicke.* But that he which can faine a *Common-wealth* (which is the *Poet*) can governe it with *Counsels,* strengthen it with *Lawes,* correct it with *Judgements,* informe it with *Religion,* and *Morals;* is all these. Wee doe not require in him meere *Elocution;* or an excellent faculty in verse; but the exact knowledge of all vertues, and their Contraries; with ability to render the one lov'd, the other hated, by his proper embattaling them.[30]

The prince is the apex, so to speak, of society's pyramid, but he needs the special insight of the poet, who combines "goodnes of natural wit" with the capacity ("as by a divine Instinct") to utter "somewhat above a mortall mouth." When the prince attends to the counsel of his best adviser, the learned poet (who ought also to be his truest friend), he serves his people as ideal example, almost in the fashion Jonson noted from Euripides: "Where the *Prince* is good . . . *God is a Guest in a humane body.*" Philosopher-kings and poet-princes are rare: for the rest, "no man is so wise, but may easily erre, if hee will take no others counsell, but his owne." [31]

Jonson was ready and willing to advise the monarch: he said to Drummond, "so he might have favour to make one Sermon to the King, he careth not what yrafter sould befall him, for he would not flatter though he saw Death." [32] This was, perhaps, bravado, although the notes for a disquisition on kingship lay at hand in the *Discoveries,* and this poet, at least, enjoyed high favour, amounting almost to friendship, with James I. But Jonson was quite aware that the "free" exchange of advice and counsel natural to friends could scarcely be duplicated in these circumstances. He had read Vives on the problems of counselling kings, "especially in affaires of *State.*" And of course his own encounters with officialdom, notably in connection with *Sejanus* in 1603, when Northampton accused him "both of popperie & treason," must sufficiently have impressed even the poet who "never esteemed of a man for the name of a Lord." [33] In any event, although one could compose verse-epistles or odes to advise one's high-spirited friends, even, by judicious indirection, counsel a whole class of society, it was difficult to extend these methods to the monarch. A few pieces, however, are relevant to Jonson's prose observations on the conduct appropriate for the good prince; and these bear also on the poems to and about his patrons.

Most of the poems addressed by Jonson to royalty are "occasional" in a narrow sense; [34] one or two others repeat the commonplace that a poet ensures fame or notoriety for his subjects. "The lesse-*Poetique* boyes" may expect "a Snake"; but "in the *Genius* of a *Poets* Verse, The Kings fame lives" (*Und.* LXXVI, LXVIII). "The humble Petition of poore Ben: To . . . King Charles" (*Und.* LXXVI), however, primarily a request for more money, takes care to stress the rationale of the poet's position (3–7):

> . . . your royall *Father,*
> James *the blessed,* pleas'd the rather,
> Of his speciall grace to *Letters,*
> To make all the Muses debters,
> To his bountie. . . .

That Jonson claims his due "for goodnesse sake" is apt enough, since the best princes know that poetry is "neerest of kin to Vertue." Another "Epigram: To K. Charles . . . 1629" (*Und.* LXII) varies the same theme:

> Great Charles, among the holy gifts of grace
> Annexed to thy Person, and thy place,
> 'Tis not enough (thy pietie is such)
> To cure the call'd *Kings Evill* with thy touch;
> But thou wilt yet a Kinglier mastrie trie,
> To cure the *Poets Evill,* Povertie. . . .

This poem, too, concludes on a note of nearly explicit advice:

> What can the *Poet* wish his *King* may doe,
> But, that he cure the Peoples Evill too?

Jonson, however, does not as a rule presume to counsel the prince in these poems even thus indirectly. He prefers to draw attention to the fact (illustrated, fortunately, in both James and Charles) that the character and actions of a prince should be exemplary and therefore instructive, and to indicate some suggestive parallels between king and poet. An "Epigram: To . . . K. Charles" of 1629 (*Und.* LXIV) makes the first point, in somewhat fulsome tones:

> Indeed, when had great *Britaine* greater cause
> Then now, to love the Soveraigne, and the Lawes?
> When you that raigne, are her Example growne,
> And what are bounds to her, you make your owne?
> When your assiduous practise doth secure
> That Faith, which she professeth to be pure?
> When all your life's a president of dayes,
> And murmure cannot quarrell at your wayes? [35]

More striking are two of the *Epigrams.* "To King James" (IV) all but proclaims the monarch that ideal "poet-prince who needs no other counsel.

> How, best of Kings, do'st thou a scepter beare!
> How, best of *Poets,* do'st thou laurell weare!
> But two things, rare, the Fates had in their store,
> And gave thee both, to shew they could no more.
> For such a *Poet,* while thy dayes were greene,
> Thou wert, as chiefe of them are said t'have beene.

> And such a Prince thou art, wee daily see,
> As chiefe of those still promise they will bee.
> Whom should my *Muse* then flie to, but the best
> Of Kings for grace; of *Poets* for my test?

A second poem (XXXV) with the same title enlarges on the principle of rule.

> Who would not be thy subject, James, t'obay
> A Prince, that rules by'example, more than sway?
> Whose manners draw, more than thy powers constraine.
> And in this short time of thy happiest raigne,
> Hast purg'd thy realmes, as we have now no cause
> Left us of feare, but first our crimes, then lawes.
> Like aydes 'gainst treasons who hath found before?
> And than in them, how could we know god more?

The prince, then (who is the better ruler for a youthful poetic bent), governs, as the poet teaches, by persuasion and example; and at length, through the laws that reflect his wisdom, the subjects discover for themselves that here indeed, "God is a guest in a human body."

That these poems are few in number was to be expected: even if wisdom had not checked the impulse to counsel a king, Jonson was not the man to lavish his talents on this particular variety of panegyric. But an attractive alternative remained. One could, if one were reasonably decorous, address a ruling class instead. Those members of aristocratic families who extended their patronage and support to Jonson, especially those with whom the poet could consider himself to be on terms at least relatively informal, must in any event be honoured in the poet's verse. While he could not ordinarily expect to be as candid (or blunt) as with his own colleagues, he could claim with some justice to have attained something like friendship with a number of highly placed individuals. Relatively free, therefore, from the limitations imposed where princes were in question, yet still addressing or chiefly complimenting persons regularly concerned, in various spheres, with the maintenance of order in social and political life, Jonson could counsel while appearing chiefly to praise. For young Sir William Sidney, the poet might assume an oracular tone; with others, the note of approbation or reminder would often be more fitting. Particularly in *The Forrest*, but elsewhere too, he incorporates in gracefully complimentary verse those principles of social responsibility which the actions of a ruling class ought in his view to reflect. The poet, in short, transfers his advisory function (properly directed to a prince) to that class from which, as a rule, the monarch will draw his counsellors; and he can address some of them, at least, in a manner formal and "easy" at once.

Jonson's attitude to his patrons is conditioned primarily by three factors. He needed their support, of course, but that is in some ways the least important of the three: poems that openly request or acknowledge financial support appear only in the last years, when the poet's fortunes were palled. As a rule, Jonson chose to ignore the subject, or to make it the occasion for a lecture on the art of giving and receiving, as in the "Epistle to . . . Sacvile" (*Und*. XIII), which strikes a characteristic note.

> You . . . whose will not only, but desire
> To succour my necessities, tooke fire,
> Not at my prayers, but your sense; which laid
> The way to meet, what others would upbraid;
> And in the Act did so my blush prevent,
> As I did feele it done, as soone as meant:
> You cannot doubt, but I, who freely know
> This Good from you, as freely will it owe;
> And though my fortune humble me, to take
> The smallest courtesies with thankes, I make
> Yet choyce from whom I take them. . . . (7–17)

The lines reflect a cast of mind also apparent in Aubrey's allusion to "Mr. Benjamin Johnson (who ever scorned an unworthy patrone)." [36] No doubt unworthiness might consist in the refusal to honour a promise of support, as Epigram LXV ("To my Muse") may indicate. But the poem hints at deeper causes of scorn; and Epigram X ("To my lord Ignorant") is perhaps relevant:

> Thou call'st me *Poet*, as a terme of shame:
> But I have my revenge made, in thy name.

While the episode at Salisbury's table is familiar, there were others of the sort:

> Ben one day being at table with my Lady Rutland [Drummond writes], her husband comming in, accused her that she keept table to poets, of which she wrott a letter to him which

he answered   My Lord intercepted the letter, but never chal-
enged him.[37]

A patron may be "unworthy" on several counts, but his failure to acknowledge the poet's right to a privileged place in society is particularly reprehensible. Finally, Jonson expected the patron and his class
to exemplify virtuous conduct, and so to persuade a society and secure
a state. The *Epigrams* are dedicated to Pembroke, "Great Example of
Honor and Vertue"; and whatever Jonson thought of the man described
by Clarendon as "immoderately given up to women," Epigram CII
illustrates the poet's ideal.

> . . . thou, whose noblesse keeps one stature still,
> And one true posture, though besieg'd with ill
> Of what ambition, faction, pride can raise;
> Whose life, ev'n they, that envie it, must praise;
> That art so reverenc'd, as thy comming in,
> But in the view, doth interrupt their sinne;
> Thou must draw more: and they, that hope to see
> The common-wealth still safe, must studie thee.

More specifically (as the poems reveal), Jonson expected a patron to
pay more than lip-service to the ideal of fraternity; to illustrate in
thought and action the continuing virtue of ancient traditions; to
renew in each age, by the wise application of inherited talent, the
life and force of those traditions. When hard circumstance closed every
other avenue, there remained an obligation to exemplify (if need
be, "farre from the maze of custome, error, strife") the ideal of virtuous
life appropriate to one's station.

Jonson, accordingly, looked for a good deal more than financial
support from the highly placed persons who could sponsor him. And
he "counselled" his patrons, directly and indirectly, in a good many
genres, from the epigram to the ode. The verse-epistle in particular
he found well suited to his personality and his purposes. As Trimpi
shows,[38] the genre by Jonson's time combined regard for a continuing
stylistic tradition with an attitude toward the range of matter proper
to the verse-epistle considerably more liberal than that of classical
practice. Cicero's observations on the characteristics of the plain style
in oratory, and the view of Demetrius that, in genres suited to the
plain style (i.e., comedy, satire, epigram, epistle), "the diction
throughout [will be] current and familiar," particularly that the

epistle should "obey the laws of friendship, which demand that we should 'call a spade a spade,' as the proverb has it," contributed to a tradition of epistolary style endorsed by Lipsius, Vives, and John Hoskyns.[39] On the other hand, Demetrius' opinion that "there are epistolary topics, as well as an epistolary style," and that "in the case of the plain style, we can no doubt point to subject matter which is homely and appropriate to the style itself," had gradually given way to the view that the range of topics proper to the epistle may extend to "all public, private, and domestic concerns." [40]

A verse form at once traditional and evolving in this way suited Jonson very well. The manner of any one epistle will certainly vary with the occasion; one does not address a noble lord as one might ask a friend to dinner. Nor are we to expect advice directly given so much as the counsel implicit in the poet's approbation of the action and character he describes; for "it . . . behooves the giver of counsell to be circumspect." [41] Still, the humanist who allowed Aristotle his due while insisting on the right to "make further Discoveries of truth and fitnesse," and who thought rules less forceful than experiments, recognized the suitability of the verse-epistle for precepts turning on the principle, "Newnesse of Sense, Antiquitie of voyce!" [42] Again, it was an appropriate medium for the poet concerned to remind society and its leaders of the dangerous temptation to "rest / On what's deceast": rather (*Und.* XIII, 131-4),

> 'Tis by degrees that men arrive at glad
> Profit in ought; each day some little adde,
> In time 'twill be a heape; This is not true
> Alone in money, but in manners too.

And, of course, for one whose sense of injur'd merit lay always ready to hand, the relatively plain-spoken style of the verse-epistle might usefully reinforce expressions hinting at an equality of merit, or even at actual friendship, between poet and the highly placed person addressed.[43]

Evidently Jonson employs forms other than the verse-epistle proper to endorse or counsel the social actions of his patrons. It may be observed, however, that while XII and XIII in *The Forrest* are explicitly termed "epistles," III ("To Sir Robert Wroth") is surely one also. The "Ode: To Sir William Sydney" gives advice as directly as does the "Epistle to a Friend, to perswade him to the Warres" (*Und.* XV), or even the "Epistle to . . . Sacvile." And the *Epigrams* (among which appears "Inviting to a friend to supper") include several pieces not obviously representative of Jonson's taut standards for the epigram. Jonson was fond of mingling literary kinds, and in any event he had good classical precedents for the practice.[44] That various formal labels attached to these poems should not obscure the fact that they all reflect his conviction that the poet has a clear right, a duty even, to speak out to his patron in a manly fashion. Perhaps one may risk the suggestion that Jonson found the verse-epistle especially congenial and that something of its character and tone often echoes in poems not formally so described. If he employs the verse-epistle to remind a ruling group of the constant standard it must uphold and of the continual adjustment to circumstance this will require, and to insist besides on the essential fraternity of a healthy society, poems called "odes" or "epigrams" reflect those elements too.

"To Penshurst," formally both ode and "country-house poem," has been rather thoroughly examined by G. R. Hibbard (and others),[45] but since Jonson here explicitly considers the role of an aristocratic dynasty (in terms of one with which he felt particular sympathy), one or two points need emphasis. Penshurst, apt symbol of the Sidney line, instructively illustrates Jonson's social ideal in one aspect at least: the contrast with those more magnificent ancestral piles that betray pride and ambition points up Penshurst's vitality and their lack of it. But we are not regularly made aware of "the world outside" Penshurst in this poem, although opening and conclusion remind us of that world's existence: Jonson's emphasis falls deliberately on the positive ideal exemplified at Penshurst. That nature is everywhere compliant, even eager to serve man, effectively supplements the fraternal atmosphere prevailing in this household, where all classes are as welcome as the poet (45–50; 61–4):

> . . . though thy walls be of the countrey stone,
> They'are rear'd with no mans ruine, no mans grone,
> There's none, that dwell about them, wish them downe;
> But all come in, the farmer, and the clowne:
> And no one empty-handed, to salute
> Thy lord, and lady, though they have no sute. . . .
> [There] comes no guest, but is allow'd to eate,
> Without his feare, and of thy lords owne meate:
> Where the same beere, and bread, and self-same wine,
> That is his Lordships, shall be also mine.

And while the family that acknowledges its social responsibilities spreads genial influence on all sides, so too it prepares for its successors, those aristocratic patrons of the next age, by properly educating and directing offspring who (96–8) may

> every day,
> Reade, in their vertuous parents noble parts,
> The mysteries of manners, armes, and arts.[46]

If this is how a great family ought to act, Jonson remarks also on the conduct appropriate to individual members of that family. Of the various poems addressed to members of the clan, the "Ode: To Sir William Sydney, on his Birth-day" is of special interest; since the person addressed is at the point of transition from youth to manhood, his responsibilities to a noble line and to society at large are emphasized in conjunction. Jonson thought that "no perfect Discovery can bee made upon a flat or a levell"; also that "to many things a man should owe but a temporary beliefe, and a suspension of his owne Judgement, not an absolute resignation of himselfe, or a perpetuall captivity." [47] These principles underlie his advice to the young Sidney (27–50):

> . . . he doth lacke
>   Of going backe
>   Little, whose will
>   Doth urge him to runne wrong, or to stand still.
> Nor can a little of the common store,
>   Of nobles vertue, shew in you;
>   Your blood
>   So good
>   And great, must seeke for new,
> And studie more:
>   Not weary, rest
>   On what's deceast.
>   For they, that swell
>   With dust of ancestors, in graves but dwell.
> 'T will be exacted of your name, whose sonne,
>   Whose nephew, whose grand-child you are;
>   And men
>   Will, then,
>   Say you have follow'd farre,
> When well begunne:
>   Which must be now.
>   They teach you, how.
>   And he that stayes
>   To live until to morrow' hath lost two dayes.

These poems clearly reflect important elements in Jonson's "theory of social order": they are guide-lines for a ruling class that collectively and individually cares about its responsibilities. But they lack a dimension. The bright perfection of a Sidney-world obscures the sombre social backdrop that requires to be regulated by Sidneys and those like them. Leaders cannot forever prevent the incursions of vice, after all, by exemplifying virtue at a cool remove; they must often descend into the arena and actively wrestle with the enemy. Perhaps Jonson felt some reluctance, for reasons of decorum, to present Sidneys in postures other than serene: one recalls the "Epode" (*Forrest,* XI):

> Not to know vice at all, and keepe true state,
>   Is vertue, and not *Fate:*
> Next, to that vertue, is to know vice well,
>   And her blacke spight expell. (1–4)

In any case, other poems not addressed to members of the Sidney clan complement and amplify the views approved in "Penshurst" and counselled in the "Ode." And each presumes a context appropriate to the second couplet of the "Epode."

Epigram LXXVI ("On Lucy Countesse of Bedford") has often attracted the admiration of critics: "How to be" may be suggested as the theme of this poem, which wittily translates ideal into fact. Less often noticed, but more significant here, is Epigram XCIV ("To Lucy, Countesse of Bedford, with Mr. Donnes Satyres"), an equally polished piece, with the theme, "How to act."

> Lucy, you brightnesse of our spheare, who are
> Life of the *Muses* day, their morning-starre!
> If workes (not th'authors) their owne grace should looke,
> Whose poemes would not wish to be your booke?
> But these, desir'd by you, the makers ends
> Crowne with their owne. Rare poemes aske rare friends.
> Yet, *Satyres,* since the most of mankind bee
> Their un-avoided subject, fewest see:
> For none ere tooke that pleasure in sinnes sense,
> But, when they heard it tax'd, tooke more offence.
> They, then, that living where the matter is bred,
> Dare for these poemes, yet, both aske, and read,
> And like them too; must needfully, though few,
> Be of the best: and 'mongst these, best are you.

Lucy, you brightnesse of our spheare, who are
The *Muses* evening, as their morning-starre.

Here is a poem decorously circular in design, turning on the role
appropirate to patrons and exemplified by Lucy, who is not simply
"Life of the *Muses* day," but who has the wit to discern and distinguish: to be, in fact, one of those "rare friends" that "rare poems"
demand, patrons who, by extending favour to the poet, acknowledge
the quality of the poetry—one might say, pay court to it. Far from
assuming an attitude of aloofness and hauteur, his patroness, who
deliberately seeks out satirical poems for their "matter," is concerned
with the moral character of all levels of society, not merely her own.
As true aristocrat, the Countess of Bedford justifies her place in the
social order by gaining knowledge, through the mirror held up to
nature by the poet, of social conditions upon which she may then
(Jonson seems to imply) bring her beneficent influence to bear. But
even if she does not act in that way, her refusal to turn away from unpleasant or disturbing aspects of society, her insistence on a full view,
indicate the completeness of her own nature, one fit to be described
as evening and morning star both: a "full constant light," in fact,
perfectly exemplifying the recognition that ancient privilege never
exempts from present responsibility.

"To Sir Robert Wroth" (*The Forrest,* III) parallels "To Penshurst"
in its emphasis on the acquiescence of external nature in the pursuits
of man ("A serpent river leades / To some coole, courteous shade"),
and on the mingling in this household, when occasion arises, of all
classes (53–8):

> The rout of rurall folke come thronging in,
>   (Their rudenesse then is thought no sinne)
> Thy noblest spouse affords them welcome grace;
>   And the great *Heroes,* of her race,
> Sit mixt with losse of state, or reverence.
>   Freedome doth with degree dispense.

However, unlike the other, this poem continually reminls the reader of
threatening and vicious forces at court and in the world environing
Wroth's home; the "thousands" who (85–8)

> . . . goe flatter vice, and winne,
>   By being organes to great sinne,
> Get place, and honor, and be glad to keepe
>   The secrets, that shall breake their sleepe. . . .

The natural surroundings of Durrants provide, not a permanent haven, but merely a "securer rest," to which Wroth may intermittently retreat for spiritual refreshment and moral strength, before returning to the task Jonson considers appropriate to every leader: "To doe thy countrey service, thy selfe right." Further, while divine power and natural influences may direct Wroth and his highly placed fellows to peace of mind, and enable them to meet the temptations of city and court with equanimity, still (93–4)

> . . . when man's state is well,
> 'Tis better, if he there can dwell.

These tentative expressions point to the fact that the life even of the good man is one of continual and rigorous struggle, to shore up or regulate social order, and also, through self-examination, to guard against the "subtle traines" (as the "Epode" has it) by which "severall passions invade the minde, / And strike our reason blinde."

The "Epistle to . . . Sacvile" (*Und.* XIII), in which social vice and disorder are once again extensively detailed, with special attention to "hunters of false fame," adds a final note of counsel to the active leader. It is not enough merely to hold at bay the forces making for disorder in society and in oneself. The point of struggle is to secure virtue or to alter a vicious situation: to make something happen. At the very least, one may demonstrate in one's own person what others may also achieve (135–44). ("They are ever good men, that must make good the times").

> . . . we must more then move still, or goe on,
> We must accomplish; 'Tis the last Key-stone
> That makes the Arch. The rest that there were put
> Are nothing till that comes to bind and shut.
> Then stands it a triumphall marke! then Men
> Observe the strength, the height, the why, and when,
> It was erected; and still walking under
> Meet some new matter to looke up and wonder!
> Such Notes are vertuous men! they live as fast
> As they are high; are rooted and will last.

All these poems counsel or approve social actions befitting persons responsible for the maintenance and direction of social order. But what if society, hardened in bad moulds, too toughly resists the efforts of dedicated leaders to re-direct its course? For Jonson had read his

Seneca: "Wee will rather excuse [a vice], then be rid of it. That wee
cannot, is pretended; but that wee will not, is the true reason. . . . It
was impossible to reforme these natures; they were dry'd, and hardned
in their ill." [48] The "Epistle: To Katherine, Lady Aubigny" (*The
Forrest*, XIII) gives counsel for just such a situation. Not surprisingly,
Jonson advises his patroness to profit by the poet's example: fortitude
in adversity and confidence to endure in the midst of trial will both
be required. The poem opens with a warning:

> 'Tis growne almost a danger to speake true
> Of any good minde, now: There are so few.
> The bad, by number, are so fortified,
> As what th'have lost t'expect, they dare deride.
> So both the prais'd, and praisers suffer. . . .

But the poet, "at fewd / With sinne and vice, though with a throne
endew'd" does not recoil. "Though forsooke / Of *Fortune*," Jonson
proudly claims (15–20)

> [I] have not alter'd yet my looke,
> Or so my selfe abandon'd, as because
> Men are not just, or keepe no holy lawes
> Of nature, and societie, I should faint. . . .

The character of Lady Aubigny, "perfect, proper, pure and naturall"
(for so her "beauties of the mind" are shown in the poet's mirror),
enables her to take a stand analogous to that of the beleagured poet.
Even friendship may fail (53–58); but the individual's responsibility
to virtue remains constant (51–2):

> 'Tis onely that can time, and chance defeat:
> For he, that once is good, is ever great.

In an unregenerate world that "cannot see / Right, the right way," the
virtuous individual may continue to influence others merely by being
true to herself, as Jonson reminds Lady Aubigny (110–12),

> . . . since you are truly that rare wife,
> Other great wives may blush at: when they see
> What your try'd manners are, what theirs should bee.

But this, he knew, was rather to be wished than expected; and since even a poet might sing, in fierce adversity, "high, and aloofe," the key passage of the poem (59–63; 121–4) advocates the pursuit of virtue in a larger context. When the times defy moral redemption, and friends fall off,

> This makes, that wisely you decline your life,
> Farre from the maze of custome, error, strife,
> And keepe an even, and unalter'd gaite;
> Not looking by, or backe (like those, that waite
> Times, and occasions, to start forth, and seeme) . . .
>
> Live that one, still; and as long yeeres doe passe,
> *Madame*, be bold to use this truest glasse:
> Wherein, your forme, you still the same shall finde;
> Because nor it can change, nor such a minde.

Exemplary action, therefore, may now and again be matched by an exemplary endurance that conquers time and circumstance.

The "Epistle to Elizabeth Countesse of Rutland" (*The Forrest*, XII), to conclude, draws together a number of views already noted, now with special reference to the poet's central role. The epistle touches on the "credentials" of the poet-counsellor and on the conditions most favourable for the exercise of his gifts. As Hercules, Helen, gods and men owed their lives beyond life "onely [to] *Poets*, rapt with rage divine," so Jonson's poetry (89–91) will undertake

> . . . high, and noble matter, such as flies
> From braines entranc'd, and fill'd with extasies;
> Moodes, which the god-like Sydney oft did prove. . . .

In an age when

> . . . almightie gold . . .
> Solders crackt friendship; makes love last a day;
> Or perhaps lesse,

Sidney's daughter can be trusted to

> . . . let this drosse carry what price it will
> With noble ignorants, and let them still,
> Turne, upon scorned verse, their quarter-face:
> With you, I know, my offring will find grace.

For what a sinne 'gainst your great fathers spirit,
Were it to thinke, that you should not inherit
His love unto the *Muses,* when his skill
Almost you have, or may have, when you will?

But the poem intends more than this: by spelling out the nature of
that fame awaiting patrons fortunate enough to hold a place in Jonson's
verse, it establishes the claim of the poet to a seat among the highest
ranks of the social community. Jonson can promise "strange *poems,*
which, as yet, / Had not their forme touch'd by an English wit"; poems,
however, that also recall and confirm the powers of Orphic song.
Ancient truth will live again in modes newly suited to contemporary
conditions and taste. This poet can, of course, assure the worthy patron
of earthly fame, "like a rich, and golden *pyramede,* / Borne up by
statues." But Jonson's commitment is more explicit (86–7): to

. . . show, how, to the life, my soule presents
Your forme imprest there. . . .

The exemplary form of virtue embodied in the Countess of Rutland
while she lived will not merely be remembered through Jonson's
verse, but truly re-created in it; as "god-like Sidney" had given the
mark of the right poet to be his capacity so to create another nature.
"To flatter my good Lord," we recall, is "To lose the formes, and dignities of men." False friendship destroys life; but the poet, like a true
friend, preserves the "formes" of the men and women he addresses in
his poems. The true poet gives life, in fact, as kings can "create new
men" (*Ungathered Verse,* XVI). And only such poets, whose art "hath
a Stomacke to concoct, divide, and turne all into nourishment," [49] are
thoroughly qualified to counsel the princes and patrons whose art is
the ordering of society and the state. The structure of society severely
limits the extension of friendship proper, on the pattern of the Tribe;
that is a pity; but community of interest among good men may serve
instead. And Jonson's poems record his constant care for that harmonious ideal.

NOTES

[1] T. S. Eliot, "Ben Jonson," *Selected Essays, 1913–1932* (New York, 1932),
147.
[2] *Ben Jonson: A Collection of Critical Essays,* ed. J. A. Barish (Spectrum
Books, 1963), 10.
[3] R. M. Adams's admirable estimate, in *The Norton Anthology of English*

Literature, ed. M. H. Abrams *et al.* (New York, 1962), I, 750, may be cited to indicate the elements in Jonson's poetry most often stressed by his critics: ". . . Ben Jonson and his followers produced verse which had the special Latin quality of being 'lapidary.' At its best their poetry gave the impression of being written to be carved in marble. Restrained in feeling, deliberately limited in its subject matter, intellectually thin but meticulously clear and incisive in expression, the poems of Jonson are models of this style."

4 *Ben Jonson,* ed. C. H. Herford and P. Simpson (11 vols.; Oxford, 1925–52), VIII, 640. All references to Jonson's poetry and prose are made to this edition, hereafter cited as *H&S.* I have normalized i, j, u, v, and have reduced capitals to conform with modern usage.

5 *H&S,* VIII, 636. Critical works that attend to the "total achievement" of Jonson's poems include G. B. Johnston, *Ben Jonson: Poet* (New York, 1945); W. Trimpi. *Ben Jonson's Poems: A Study of the Plain Style* (Stanford, 1962), and the articles by G. R. Hibbard, Paul Cubeta, and Geoffrey Walton referred to in this essay (notes 7, 45). I am particularly indebted to the studies by Johnston and Trimpi and to Hibbard's article.

6 L. C. Knights, *Drama and Society in the Age of Jonson* (London, 1937), 208, 198.

7 Geoffrey Walton, "The Tone of Ben Jonson's Poetry," in *Seventeenth Century English Poetry,* ed. W. R. Keast, 2nd ed. (New York, 1971), 135.

8 *H&S,* VIII, 617.

9 *H&S,* VIII, 617, 567.

10 *H&S,* VIII, 571, 564, 608.

11 *H&S,* VIII, 608–9; see also 597, ll. 1083–90.

12 *H&S,* VIII, 614, 617–18.

13 *H&S,* VIII, 597.

14 *H&S,* VIII, 567, 571, 566.

15 Walton, 138.

16 C. G. Smith, *Spenser's Theory of Friendship* (Baltimore, 1935), 25.

17 The text referred to here is that edited by J. A. Smith: *The Ethics of Aristotle* (London, 1911).

18 This passage and those in the remainder of the paragraph are taken from *Ethics* (*ed. cit.*), 186–7, 183, 191, 205.

19 See also "An Epistle to a Friend, to perswade him to the Warres" (*Und.* XV), 11–18, in *H&S,* VIII, 162.

20 See also *Ungathered Verse* XLIX, in *H&S,* VIII, 421.

21 Compare *H&S,* VIII, 597 (*"Livery-friends,* friends of the dish, and of the *Spit,* that waite their turnes, as my Lord has his feasts, and guests"); and see also "An Epistle to Master Arth: Squib" (*Und.* XLV), 7–8, in *H&S,* VIII, 216.

22 *Ethics,* 182–3, 198.

23 *H&S,* VIII, 636.

24 This "Epistle" by Jonson should be compared with the following passage from Aristotle's *Ethics* (225): "The good man . . . must be specially

Self-loving, in a kind other than that which is reproached, and as far
superior to it as living in accordance with Reason is to living at the beck
and call of passion, and aiming at the truly noble to aiming at apparent
advantage. Now all approve and commend those who are eminently
earnest about honourable actions, and if all would vie with one another in
respect of the καλòν, and be intent upon doing what is most truly noble
and honourable, society at large would have all that is proper while each
individual in particular would have the greatest of goods, Virtue being
assumed to be such. . . . the good man does what he ought to do, because
all Intellect chooses what is best for itself and the good man puts himself
under the direction of Intellect.

Of the good man it is true likewise that he does many things for the
sake of his friends and his country, even to the extent of dying for them,
if need be. . . ."

[25] See, for example, *H&S*, VIII, 645 (Jonson's discussion of *"the magnitude,
and compasse of any Fable"*), and even 569–70 (on the *"tedious person"*).

[26] *H&S*, VIII, 601–2.

[27] *H&S*, VIII, 593, 602, 594, 600.

[28] *H&S*, VIII, 599, 594, 600–1.

[29] *H&S*, VIII, 594.

[30] *H&S*, VIII, 603, 601, 565–6, 595.

[31] *H&S*, VIII, 637, 600, 563.

[32] *H&S*, I, 141.

[33] *H&S*, VIII, 566; I, 141. A letter of 1605 requesting support from a sponsor
now unknown acknowledges that "there is no subject hath so safe an
Innocence, but may rejoyce to stand justified in sight of his Soveraignes
mercie. To which we must humblie submytt our selves, our lives and
fortunes" (*H&S*, I, 197).

[34] Epigram LI, "To King James, upon the happy false rumour of his death,"
many of the birthday poems in *The Under-Wood,* and the "Song of Welcome to King Charles" (*Ungathered Verse* XLIV), exemplify the range of
these pieces.

[35] "A Parallell of the Prince to the King" (*Poems Ascribed to Jonson,* II),
H&S, VIII, 429, rejected by Herford and Simpson as not Jonson's, never-
theless is reproduced in *Poems of Ben Jonson,* ed. G. B. Johnston (London,
1954), 301–2. On this hint, it is worth mentioning that the poem, likening
Charles to Achilles, includes the passage, "His all his time, but one
Patroclus findes, But this of ours a world of faithfull friends," and also,
"His had his Phoenix, ours no teacher needs, But the example of thy Life
and Deeds."

[36] John Aubrey, *Brief Lives,* ed. A. Powell (London, 1949), 371.

[37] *H&S*, I, 142.

[38] Trimpi, *Poems,* 60–75.

[39] *Ibid.,* 6–9.

[40] *Ibid.,* 68, 70.

[41] *H&S*, VIII, 566.

[42] "An Epistle to Master John Selden" (*Und.* XIV), 60: *H&S*, VIII, 160.

[43] In this connection, see J. A. Levine, "The Status of the Verse Epistle before Pope," *SP*, LIX (1962), 658–84, esp. 675–6.

[44] See Trimpi, *Poems*, 159–60.

[45] G. R. Hibbard, "The Country House Poem of the Seventeenth Century," *Journal of the Warburg and Courtauld Institute*, XIX (1956), 159 ff.; and see Paul Cubeta, "A Jonsonian Ideal: 'To Penshurst,'" *PQ* XLII (1963), 14–24.

[46] See also "An Epigram on . . . Burleigh" (*Und.* XXX), 13–19.

[47] *H&S*, VIII, 627–8.

[48] *H&S*, VIII, 580.

[49] *H&S*, VIII, 638.

WILLIAM V. SPANOS

ɬ

The Real Toad in the Jonsonian Garden: Resonance in the Nondramatic Poetry

I

"Ben Jonson's position, three hundred years after his death, is more than secure; it might almost be called impregnable. He is still the greatest unread English author." This is how Harry Levin character-ized the modern reputation of Shakespeare's less fortunate contempo-rary in 1939 in the well-known introduction to his anthology of Jonson's drama and poetry.[1] The reasons for this neglect are obviously com-plicated, but certainly the most important, aside from the biographical, lie in the apotheosis of Nature and aesthetic vitality and the con-comitant devaluation of classical, that is, consciously formal, art by nineteenth-century romantic poetic doctrine.[2] Since then the reaction against the romantic poetic activated by the New Criticism (as well as the publication of the monumental Oxford edition of the poet's works) has effected a revival of Ben Jonson's reputation as a dramatist. It can no longer be said that "his principal function has been to serve as a stalking-horse for Shakespeare." [3] Nevertheless, it is curious that the renewal of critical interest in his drama has not much affected Jonson's reputation as a poet. What Professor Levin said in 1939 about the status of his work as a whole still applies to his poetry or, as it is significantly referred to by most commentators, his "nondramatic verse." [4] Why Jonson's verse has not shared the recent fortunes of his drama is not easy to determine. Perhaps it is a matter of time lag, though my own feeling is that the romantic strain in the New Criticism has found Jonson's

From *Journal of English and Germanic Philology*, LXVIII (1969), pp. 1–23. Reprinted by permission of *Journal of English and Germanic Philology*.

classical mode lacking in spontaneous power.[5] Whatever the reason, the continuing neglect of Jonson as a poet is unfortunate, for the nondramatic verse is not only great but readable, not only superbly articulated but tuned for modern ears.

There have been a few recent efforts to resurrect Jonson's poetry from the grave in which the nineteenth-century contempt for artifice buried it. Of these, two of the most important—not only because they are intelligent and perceptive, but also because they are paradigmatic —are George Burke Johnston's *Ben Jonson: Poet* (1945) and the work of Ralph S. Walker, especially "Ben Jonson's Lyric Poetry" (1934).[6] In response to the nineteenth-century prejudice against Art as lifeless and mechanical, devoid of imaginative spontaneity and vitality, Johnston asserts that the traditional label "classical" is neither an adequate explanation nor definition of Ben Jonson's poetry. By revealing the significant role played by the native English tradition in the poetry, he demonstrates quite convincingly that it cannot be called "classical" if the term is meant to signify either the slavish use of the works of the ancients for subject matter or the imitation of their poetic forms.[7] Johnston thus frees the poetry from the long-standing onus of being merely imitative and opens it to re-examination from a fresh critical point of view. But in his effort to rescue the poet from a classification that has limited interest in the poetry, Johnston tends inadvertently to distort its essential character. By minimizing the formality in order to acknowledge the claims of the native tradition, he suggests a fruitful mode of approach to the poems. But despite his warning against classifying Jonson, he overemphasizes the native (which in his view seems to be synonymous with "vital") at the expense of the formality and thus implicitly identifies Jonson's poetry with the "romantic" strain of Elizabethan poetry.

Also aware of the nineteenth-century tendency to downgrade conscious art, R. S. Walker continues, nevertheless, to characterize Jonson's poetry (the lyrics) as "classical" in the sense of the artfully controlled expression of the normative, rather than the particular, in nature. But in order to redeem it from the charge of lifelessness, he defines the poet's classicism more specifically as a fusion of an ideal of beauty grounded in the perception of order and harmony in nature, with poetic craftsmanship:

> the inspiration of Jonson's poetry, as manifested in these "classical" lyrics, is not the abstract idea of this symmetry [in nature], so much as the idea realized in the ordered working of a finished creation. . . . Jonson's highest beauty is a beauty

of completion: "it might be" is beautiful only when it has become "it is." And because his ideal beauty is thus intimately linked with the creative act, where it finds adequate expression, it does so in a finished and conscious art.[8]

It is this consciously achieved fusion of ideal and craft, according to Walker, that renders Jonson's lyrical poetry both formal and vital. The insistence on the lyrics' classical form and tone against the tendency to romanticize Jonson is certainly justifiable. But in order to arrive at this rather special definition of the poet's classicism, Walker has to relegate all but a small handful of nondramatic poems to the status of unsuccessful experiments in the "decadent Elizabethan" manner.[9]

The contemporary effort to rehabilitate Jonson's poetry, then, has shed penetrating light on the poet's formal sources and methods and, in the process, has greatly minimized the dubious authority of the conventional judgment of the nineteenth century. Nevertheless, neither the approach exemplified by Johnston nor that by Walker has satisfactorily described the essential character of the poetry. On the one hand, there is the tendency to view it as essentially English and, in so doing, to emphasize the native or romantic strain at the expense of its obvious classical character and heritage, and, on the other, the tendency to define it as classical at the expense of its less obvious but equally real spontaneity and vitality which derive from the native poetic tradition. As a result, one cannot help feeling in reading this criticism that the positive judgment of these recent critics is, in the last analysis, putative. What it is *in the poetry* that justifies the attribution of greatness and readability to it remains obscure if not undiscovered.

The poetry of Ben Jonson contains both classical (in all three senses: use of subject matter, imitation of forms, and artfully controlled expression of the normative) and native elements, but if we are to speak intelligibly about its aesthetic effects, we must translate these terms into a language that is capable of aesthetic analysis. Both Walker and Johnston are right to minimize the usefulness of the meanings of "classical" that are associated with the discovery of sources of subject matter and generic forms. Unfortunately, Johnston's preoccupation with the search for native characteristics in Jonson's poetry precludes critical analysis of the aesthetic effect achieved by the mingling of native and classical elements. Walker's definition of the term "classical," on the other hand, is useful; for it is descriptive not of the subject matter and forms, but rather of the aesthetic character of poetry, and thus admits poems whose sources of subject matter and forms are various— the religious poetry, for example—into its sphere. But, surely, Jonson was attempting more than merely to bend the native element to the classical discipline. There are certainly more than a handful of good poems in the Jonsonian canon.

There is, it seems to me, no better definition of Jonson's classicism than that contained in the famous metaphor formulated by Marianne Moore (a modern poet whose classical verse resembles Jonson's in some significant respects) to suggest the nature of her aesthetic ideal. Poetry, she says, presents "imaginary gardens with real toads in them." The image may need no explanation, but for the sake of precision, it is necessary to paraphrase, even at the expense of its inexhaustible richness. The imaginary garden, in sharp if implicit contrast with the real toad, is a formally perfect artifact: a symmetrical unity, but an abstract and therefore lifeless one. The real toad, which is a deformity or, perhaps, an imperfection in the ordered pattern and yet an integral denizen of gardens, is what charges the garden world with a tension that gives it the impression of animation. The toad, therefore, is a symbol of the existence that breathes life into essence, that generates a transfiguring resonance within the very core of the idealized design. What strikes the reader of Jonson's poems is that a considerable number of them, particularly the lyrics (but also the plays), may be characterized in precisely these terms. A Jonsonian poem is indeed a highly wrought artifact—the verbal equivalent of the formal sixteenth-century English garden—the linguistic texture of which is activated by what on the surface *appears* to be an imperfection of one kind or other in it. It is, as it were, jarred into motion, thus rendering original what appears to be conventional, spontaneous what appears to be imitative, subtle what appears to be simple, and, above all, alive what appears to be inanimate. The Jonsonian poem, in the terms T. S. Eliot uses in *Four Quartets* to describe the garden which is history (and by analogy, a poem), is a stillness infused by motion, where "the pattern is new in every moment / And every moment is a new and shocking / Valuation of all we have been." [10] Indeed, Jonson's view of history as it is obviously implied in his view of the relationship between antiquity and the present, is significantly similar to Eliot's:

> Nothing is more ridiculous, then to make an Author a *Dictator*, as the schooles have done *Aristotle*. The dammage is infinite, knowledge receives by it. For to many things a man should owe but a temporary beliefe, and a suspension of his owne Judgement, not an absolute resignation of himselfe, or a perpetuall captivity. Let *Aristotle*, and others have their dues; but if wee can make farther Discoveries of truth and fitnesse

then they, why are we envied? . . . [We must] calmely study
the separation of opinions, find the errours have intervened,
awake Antiquity, call former times into question; but make no
parties with the present, nor follow any fierce undertakers,
mingle no matter of doubtfull credit, with the simplicity of
truth, but gently stirre the mould about the root of the Question. . . .[11]

It is this motion in stillness, which is generated by the stirring of the
mould about the root of the question—the classical tradition or anal-
ogously, the classical form—that constitutes the peculiar resonance of
Jonson's poetry.

II

Jonson's method of achieving the kind of resonance I have described
above consists ultimately of the deliberate inclusion at strategic junc-
tures of apparently incompatible elements of technique and/or subject
matter (in the lyric it is usually a single element) in an otherwise
perfectly conceived and executed creation, a creation that obeys all the
stylistic laws of propriety and decorum. Nevertheless, the method varies,
depending integrally, at its best, on the content and genre of particular
poems. Perhaps the variation most frequently employed by Jonson is
that of including realistic (usually native English) details in an
essentially Greek or Roman mythological atmosphere. The lyric "To
his Lady, then Mrs. Cary" provides a good example of this:

Retyr'd, with purpose your faire worth to praise,
     'Mongst *Hampton* shades, and PHOEBUS grove of bayes,
I pluck'd a branch; the jealous God did frowne,
     And bad me lay th'usurped laurell downe:
Said I wrong'd him, and (which was more) his love.
     I answered, DAPHNE now no paine can prove.
PHOEBUS replyed. Bold head, it is not shee:
     CARY my love is, DAPHNE but my tree.

                           (VIII, 80)

The source of the charm and the backward reverberating energy of
this "classical" poem lies in the sudden intrusion (which, however, has
been prepared for by the name "Hampton") of a human figure, Cary—
the omission of a first name or a title and Phoebus' rejection of Daphne
as unreal emphasize the English lady's immediate reality—into an unreal

and poetically distanced setting, in which even the poet conceives of himself as a mythological creature. The same method, employed with even greater success, is operative in the following stanza from "An Ode, To himselfe":

> Are all th'*Aonian* springs
>   Dri'd up? lyes *Thespia* wast?
> Doth *Clarius* Harp want strings,
> That not a Nymph now sings?
>   Or droop they as disgrac't,
> To see their Seats and Bowers by Chattring Pies defac't?
>
> (VI, 492)

Despite its classic clarity, simplicity, and grace, this conventional complaint of the poet who deplores the decline of high poetry could not possibly please as it does without the harsh contrast of "Chattring Pies" (and its equivalent in the metrics of the line) to charge its static and formalized landscape with tension.

In the poem "To Celia" (Poem VI in *The Forest*), it is not the setting so much as the form and theme that establish the classical atmosphere. Deriving its inspiration from Catullus (Carmen V), the poem begins with the conventional plea of an urbane and sophisticated lover for a secret kiss. In the following lines, which parallel Catullus, the number of kisses desired increases hyperbolically. But in the enumeration the imagery shifts ground and the tone of the whole poem is consequently modified:

> First give a hundred,
> Then a thousand, then another
> Hundred, then unto the tother
> Adde a thousand, and so more:
> Till you equall with the store,
> All the grasse that *Rumney* yeelds,
> Or the sands in *Chelsey* fields,
> Or the drops in silver *Thames*,
> Or the starres, that guild his streames
> In the silent sommer-nights,
> When youths ply their stolne delights.   (VIII, 103)

The ideal classical world has suddenly become seventeenth-century England; the Catullian lover, a Londoner; and his conventionally urbane tone, more sharply ironic and intimate. The gesture distanced by convention has become something like an immediate experience and, in the process, the artifact, a lively poem. As F. W. Bradbrook observes of this type of Jonsonian poem, "Such flexible and controlled transitions from an ideal classical world to the actualities of seventeenth-century London, with the accompanying sense of ironic contrast, distinguish Jonson from a poet such as Campion, and are a proof of his greatness." [12]

Closely related to the introduction of realistic details into a classical setting and atmosphere is the technique of introducing classical elements—particularly mythological figures—into an essentially realistic (although classically ordered) setting. This technique is clearly illustrated by Jonson's great ode celebrating the Sidney family, "To Penshurst," in which the natural bounty of a quite contemporary English country estate is shared by both mythological and real beings:

> Thy *Mount*, to which the *Dryads* doe resort,
> Where PAN, and BACCHUS their high feasts have made,
> Beneath the broad beech, and the chest-nut shade;
> That taller tree, which of a nut was set,
> At his great birth, where all the *Muses* met.
> There, in the writhed barke, are cut the names
> Of many a SYLVANE, taken with his flames.
> And thence, the ruddy *Satyres* oft provoke
> The lighter Faunes, to reach thy *Ladies oke*.
> Thy copp's too, nam'd of GAMAGE, thou hast there,
> That never failes to serve thee season'd deere,
> When thou would'st feast, or exercise thy friends.
> The lower land, that to the river bends,
> Thy sheepe, thy bullocks, kine, and calves doe feed:
> The middle grounds thy mares, and horses breed.
>
> (VIII, 93–94)

Whereas in the former case the pleasure has its source in the perception of the transformation (usually ironic) of the ideal into the real, in this it has its source in the transfiguration of the real into the ideal. Ultimately, the aesthetic pleasure derives from the resonance generated by the fusion of the opposites.[13]

It would seem that a variation of the technique employed in "To Penshurst" is that used in such poems as "An Execration upon Vulcan" and the mock heroic "Famous Voyage," in which Jonson radically nativizes mythological figures, usually deities, by placing them in a sordid modern setting, endowing them with Elizabethan psychological characteristics and making them patrons of contemporary low types or professions.[14] Actually, however, it is not. For the "realistic" excesses of such poems bring forth grotesques, which constitute a category quite different from and much narrower than that essentially classical one of which "To Penshurst" and "To Sir Robert Wroth" are representative, a category more appropriately analogous to that to which the gargoyles of medieval cathedral sculpture belong. The distinction is an important one; for though the similarity between the technique of "To Penshurst" and "An Execration upon Vulcan" reveals the creative thrust of Jonson's imagination, the difference helps define the class of poems that is central in the Jonsonian canon.

Although less frequently found in the poetry, the technique of introducing Christian details into a pagan setting is an authentic variation of the animating principle under consideraion. In "An Ode, or Song, by all the Muses," for example, where each muse sings a stanza in celebration of Queen Henrietta Maria's birthday, Thalia's call for music—

> Yet, let our Trumpets sound;
> And cleave both ayre and ground,
>   With beating of our Drums:
> Let every Lyre be strung,
> Harpe, Lute, Theorbo sprung.
>   With touch of daintie thum's!

is followed by Euterpe's ecstatic insistence that the music be pleasing enough to entrance even angels:

> That when the Quire is full,
> The Harmony may pull
>   The Angels from their Spheares:
> And each intelligence
> May wish it selfe a sense,
>   Whilst it the Dittie heares.   (VIII, 239)

These stanzas are clearly illustrative of the process by which are reconciled the incompatibles that in so many cases constitute the basic materials of Jonson's poetry. The language and rhythms of Thalia's speech suggest that the music is to be pagan in spirit. Then Euterpe demands that the harmony be entrancing enough to draw the angels down to earth and to evoke in them a desire not merely for a change of substance but also, what is more striking, a pagan sensibility. The device, therefore, in implying a paradoxically qualitative contrast between earthly music and the music of the spheres (the angels or angelic intelligences inhabiting the spheres enjoyed the heavenly harmony their motion made) and focusing the reader's attention on it, compels a special meaning on the word "sense," and thus not only integrates but also generates motion in a poem that at first glance appears to be an unreconcilable and static juxtaposition of disparate materials.[15]

The source of resonance in Jonson's poetry is not limited to the integration of native and classical material. It can often be traced to the infusion of a "personal" note into a subject that has otherwise been treated within the framework of an old literary tradition, thus activating surprise and rendering intimate what was distanced by formal and stylistic convention. This variant is illustrated by the beautiful and moving "Echo's Song" from *Cynthia's Revels:*

> Slow, slow, fresh fount, keepe time with my salt tears;
>   Yet slower, yet, O faintly gentle springs:
> List to the heavy part the music bears;
>   Woe weepes out her division, when shee sings.
>   Droupe hearbs, and flowres,
>   Fall griefe in showres;
>   Our beauties are not ours:
>   O, I could still,
> Like melting snow upon some craggie hill,
>   drop, drop, drop, drop,
> Since nature's pride is, now, a wither'd daffodill.   (IV, 50)

The poem is a highly stylized lament over the death of "nature's pride." The convention of the pathetic fallacy in the traditional pastoral elegy; in which the grieving shepherd summons nature to weep for the deceased, and the appropriately slow and regular movement of the verse, the simple, poetic diction, and the long, open vowel sounds all combine to produce the effect of ceremony. But the word "wither'd" in the last line modulates sharply into a different key. In comparison with the preceding diction it is a harsh word, both in sound (it is one of the few words whose stem vowel is clipped) and sense, a word that introduces an immediately emotional tone into the ritualistic distance of the whole. And the surprise—not enough, it should be noted, to unbalance the poem—reverberates retrospectively. Furthermore, the identification of the object of lament, "nature's pride," with a daffodil, the only particular in a poem that abounds in generic terms, serves to emphasize the intimately personal note struck by "wither'd." In presenting a lowly English flower in an ornate setting reminiscent of Theocritus, or Bion, Jonson combines the mingling of native and classical elements and the technique under immediate examination.

The variant is also illustrated by the epitaph "On My First Daughter," in which the matter is developed with characteristic classical simplicity and restraint of utterance until the final lines. In the first part of the poem the grieving father is consoled by his reflection that the infant has escaped this world unstained by its corruption and that her soul has been placed in the heavenly train of the Virgin Mary (whose name the child bears).

> Here lyes to each her parents ruth,
> Mary, the daughter of their youth:
> Yet, all heavens gifts, being heavens due,
> It makes the father, lesse, to rue.
> At sixe moneths end, shee parted hence
> With safetie of her innocence;
> Whose soule heavens Queene, (whose name shee beares)
> In comfort of her mothers teares,
> Hath plac'd amongst her virgin-traine. . . .   (viii, 33–34)

There is nothing intimate in this: it is a conventional Christian epitaph with a conventional Christian resolution which is further distanced by a carefully articulated form. But in the last lines, in which the poet's fancy returns to earth, a tonal shift occurs. After perceiving the child's soul in heaven "amongst Mary's virgin-traine," Jonson continues:

> Where, while that sever'd doth remaine,
> This grave partakes the fleshly birth
> Which cover lightly, gentle earth.

Being human, the poet cannot be sustained by his quite sincere belief in the immortality of his daughter's soul. For the child *he knew* lies in a freshly covered grave at his feet. The final line is a poignantly personal utterance that intentionally violates both the thought that precedes and the form in which it is embodied. The sudden shift of tone, underlined by the expression of the plea to the gentle earth in the form of a sentence fragment, throws the meaning of the preceding lines into a new and surprising light. They do not merely constitute a conventional epitaph after all. They represent, rather, an effort on the part of the poet to formalize and thus give distance to his grief. In other words, the tonal shift, which at first appears to be an imperfection, is actually the source of the emotional energy that spreads, like the rings of disturbed water, over the still, glasslike surface of the poem.[16]

Again in "A Hymne: On the Nativity of my Saviour," the formal beauty, classical in its simplicity, restraint, and symmetry (Jonson here employs the simplest and most frequently used of the medieval hymn forms: *a a b c c b*),[17] is disturbed in the fifth line of the third (penultimate) stanza by a single ironic word which careless reading might either overlook or interpret as a counter to complete a rhyme, "The Word was now made Flesh indeed . . ." (VIII, 130). Up to this point the hymn has celebrated the birth of Christ and the wisdom and beneficence of the Father, who foresaw the Crucifixion. But with this irony—the word "indeed" suggests the meaning "with a vengeance"— the formal tone suddenly becomes personal with the effect of shifting the focus from the distant and mysterious to the immediate and real, from divine wisdom and beneficence to human stupidity and cruelty. After this, the reader cannot allay the activated irony.

The most striking and effective variation of Jonson's strategy to achieve resonance is also the most difficult to describe, because the source of energy is so artfully, or, better perhaps, so integrally fused with the classical texture of the poem. It is, at the risk of oversimplification, the introduction into a strict rhetorical or image pattern of an ambiguity that, once recognized, transmutes and deepens the surface meaning of the poetry.

This variation occurs in "Hymne (to Cynthia)," in the last stanza of which the plea to the goddess to "Give unto the flying hart / Space to breathe, how short soever" (IV, 161) introduces by subtle insinuation the cruel daylight activity of the huntress goddess and her devotees and thus charges the lucid cameo-like imagery of night with a tension that is not at once apparent. It also occurs in the "Epitaph on Elizabeth, L. H." (VIII, 79), where the deliberate omission of the lady's surname and the focusing of attention on this omission compels speculation on the mystery which inevitably ends in the discovery that the lady *could be* Queen Elizabeth and in the consequent transformation of the surface meaning of the entire poem.[18] But it is in the fourth poem of *A Celebration of Charis* ("Her Triumph") that the variation is most effectively employed.

In the last stanza of "Her Triumph" Jonson enumerates by means of the ballad-like device of a series of rhetorical questions and exclamatory responses the simple, yet delicate beauties of Charis. In reading it, one is at first perplexed by the apparent omission of hearing from the otherwise full catalogue of the senses. In the first question,

> Have you seene but a bright Lillie grow,
> Before rude hands have touch'd it?

the sense referred to is obviously that of sight and the object is the lily before it has been discolored by human hands. In the second question,

> Have you mark'd but the fall o' the Snow,
> Before the soyle hath smutch'd it?

the sense referred to is *apparently* again that of sight, the object being the white snow before it has been discolored by the dirty earth. In the following three questions,

> Have you felt the wooll o' the Bever?
> Or Swans Downe ever?
> Or have smelt o' the bud o' the Brier?
> Or the Nard i' the fire?
> Or have tasted the bag o' the Bee?   (viii, 134–35)

the senses of touch, smell, and taste are referred to, respectively. At this point, however, it occurs to the reader that the sense of hearing has been omitted in the poet's enumeration. Inevitably, he returns to the two questions that apparently refer to the visual sense, and is compelled, both by the unnatural single omission and a closer reading, to conclude that the word "mark'd" in the second question is an ambiguity, referring not only to the visual but also to the auditory sense.

For the reader discovers that syntactically "seene" in the first question actually refers to the *growth* of the lily and "mark'd" in the second actually to the *fall* of the snow. This literal reading is important, for the stanza is not only about the purity of the lady but also about the purity of the singer. In the first question there is on this level a reference to the pure eye that can see what cannot be seen by a gross eye. And in the second there is a reference to the pure, the attuned, ear that can hear what the gross ear cannot. This interpretation of the lines is supported and their overtones are enriched by the association evoked (at least for the seventeenth-century reader) by the image of the poet who can hear the silent fall of the snow: the Platonic conception that only the spiritually pure can hear the music of the spheres. That this association is not farfetched is indicated by the parallel of the lily, a symbol of purity comparable in the seventeenth century to the symbol of the heavenly orchestra.

Because "smutch'd" means "smudged," it will be objected that the line "Before the soyle hath smutch'd it?" points to the color of snow and therefore forces a reading of "seen" for the word "mark'd." The texture of the first two questions and of the image itself, however, limits the validity of such an objection. In the first question the lily is seen as being contaminated by the willful action of human hands, and thus the image is logically and visually justified. If, however, "mark'd" in the second question is read as "seen," the visual image evoked is the rather surrealistic one of animated soil willfully throwing up earth to dirty the snow. On the other hand, if "mark'd" is read as "heard," the image called forth is logically and visually appropriate; for it is at the moment when the snow touches the ground that it is literally *silenced*. In other words, "smutched," although it carries the meaning "dirtied," can also be read as a metaphor for "silencing," a meaning that, when the conception of the music of the spheres is brought to bear on the reading, carries the sense of the contamination of spiritual music by the earth.

The recognition of the ambiguity of "mark'd" transforms the rhetorical pattern of the stanza into one that is intellectually and artistically more satisfying. On the surface the first exclamation in the response, "O so white!" refers to both the first and second questions and points to a single sense, that of sight; the second, "O so soft!" refers to the third question and points to a single sense, that of touch; and the third, "O so Sweet is she!" refers to the fourth and fifth questions and points to two senses, those of smell and taste. But when the ambiguity is taken into consideration, the first exclamation refers to the first question and points to a single sense, that of sight; the second refers to the second and third questions and points to two senses, those of hearing and touch; and the third refers to the last two questions and points to two senses, those of smell and taste. This reading, in short, in setting off the sense of sight, establishes it as the monarch of the hierarchy of senses, which in the seventeenth century it was.[19]

There are in Jonson's poetry other variations of the method of achieving animation, but these tend either to emphasize the poet's virtuosity (too often at the expense of the poetry) rather than generate the kind of resonance I have been trying to describe, or to give rise to a kind of vitality that places the poems more appropriately in a different, less central, category. Of the first type is the technique of developing a subject within a form that is by convention alien to it, as in "On Poet-Ape" (viii, 44), a strict English sonnet that scornfully satirizes the poetaster who imitates or plagiarizes the true poet's work.[20] Such also is the related technique of employing a literary convention or form to satirize the convention or form itself, as, for example, in "A Sonnet, To the Noble Lady, the Lady MARY WROTH" (viii, 182), an English sonnet that ridicules the sonnet form (not, however, without managing to praise the Lady's efforts in the genre),[21] or in "A Fit of Rime against Rime," in which a brilliant virtuoso performance in the use of rhymes is precisely the weapon Jonson uses to complain against the barbarism of "Rime, the rack of finest wits," imposed on the modern poet by the corruption of language:

> He that first invented thee,
> May his joynts tormented bee,
>   Cramp'd for ever;
> Still may Syllabes jarre with time,
> Still may reason warre with rime,
>   Resting never.
> May his Sense, when it would meet
> The cold tumor in his feet,
>   Grow unsounder.
> And his Title be long foole,
> That in rearing such a Schoole,
>   Was the founder.   (viii, 184)

Such also, finally, is the technique of distorting a conventional form, as in "On Lucy Countesse of Bedford" (viii, 52), the form of which is that of the English sonnet except that the poem contains four instead of three quatrains and a couplet.

Of the second type—that which generates a vitality that locates the poem in an entirely different category—is the method of emphasizing an extravagant and sustained conceit in an otherwise classically conceived form, as in the justly well-known "Epitaph on S[alomon] P[avy] A Child of W. E[lizabeths] Chappel" (viii, 77), and in "My Picture left in Scotland" (viii, 149–50).[22] In such poems the fresh impact derives not so much from the reconciling of incompatibles as from the sustained ingenuity of analysis by which the lines develop. They are, therefore, more appropriately classifiable under the category of metaphysical poetry. Nevertheless, it is clear that the thrust of the sensibility behind these techniques is essentially the same as that which lies behind the techniques considered above.

On the basis of this survey, then, it can be seen that many of Jonson's poems are indeed definable as "imaginary gardens with real toads in them." Though the application of the term "classical" to the poetry is valid, it is inaccurately descriptive if it does not include centrally in its meaning both the technique of integrating incompatible elements in an otherwise classically conceived and executed design and the effect that suggests animation, which I have called resonance. Our response to a Jonsonian poem is not essentially to its classical subject and form nor to the perfection of its craftsmanship, but rather to the reconciliation of incompatibles. It is not admiration for Jonson's knowledge of the classics nor for an artifact as cold and hard as a cameo that we experience. It is rather a poignant and concentrically expanding pleasure deriving from our discovery of "imperfection," of aliveness, in the ordered construct.[23] Clerimont, in Jonson's *Epicene,* is surely defining this ideal of artistic beauty and its concomitant effect when he sings:

> Give me a looke, give me a face,
> That makes simplicitie a grace;
> Robes loosely flowing, haire as free:
> Such sweet neglect more taketh me,
> Then all th'adulteries of art.
> They strike mine eyes, but not my heart.[24] (v, 167)

III

Thus far I have restricted the evidence in behalf of my argument about Jonson's poetics to his practice. The question that inevitably arises, especially since Jonson theorized about poetry, is whether or not he consciously emphasized the aesthetic principle I have attributed to him. It cannot be answered definitively, but enough evidence exists to support the possibility that he did. The discussion of the relationship between Jonson's ethics and his poetry that follows may at first seem tangential, but if the aesthetic principle of resonance is borne in mind, it will be seen that what appears to be a digression is in actuality very much a part of the argument and goes far to illuminate the essential perspective behind Jonson's art. For, I submit, the principle that animates and generates resonance in the Jonsonian poem is analogous to, indeed has its source in, the principle that animates and generates resonance in the Jonsonian man.[25]

In his collection of critical writings, *Timber: or, Discoveries,* Jonson reveals a strong attraction to the Renaissance critical doctrine *ut pictura poesis,* which holds, as Jonson puts it, that "Poetry [is] a speaking Picture, Picture a mute Poesie" (VIII, 609).[26] Although this doctrine was a commonplace in the sevententh century and therefore broadly conceived, it seems to have had a special significance for Jonson, the moralist. For the complimentary poems, which form the largest segment of his nondramatic output, are patently speaking portraits of great men. In these poems a third category is added to the picture-poetry equation: the great man himself. It is by no means accidental that the individuals being complimented in these poems are very often characterized by the equivalent metaphors of picture and poem or song (and occasionally of sculpture). Thus, for example, in "To William Earle of Pembroke" the subject's name "is an Epigramme, on all man-kind; / Against the bad, but of, and to the good" (VIII, 66); in "To Susan Countesse of Montgomery," the virtuous character drawn by Jonson is "A picture, which the world for years must know, / And like it too; if they look equally" (VIII, 67); in the magnificent ode to Sir Lucius Cary and Sir Henry Morison, the great life is defined throughout in the language of poetics:

> . . . for Life doth her great actions spell,
> By what was done and wrought
> In season, and so brought
> To light: her measures are, how well
> Each syllab'e answer'd, and was form'd, how faire;
> These make the lines of life, and that's her ayre. (VIII, 245)

Implicit in this addition of the character of great men to the equation is, of course, that Jonson's views about art and ethics have a common source and, therefore, that what he says about great men will apply equally to poetry. Indeed the integral relationship between language and ethics is a cardinal principle of Jonson's thought. Thus in *Timber* he writes, "*Language* most shewes a man: speake that I may see thee. It springs out of the most retired, and inmost parts of us, and is the Image of the Parent of it, the mind. No glasse renders a mans forme, or likenesse, so true as his speech. Nay, it is likened to a man; and as we consider feature, and composition in a man; so words in Language: in the greatnesse, aptnesse, sound, structure, and harmony of it" (VIII, 625). Elsewhere in *Timber* Jonson maintains, "Wheresoever, manners, and fashions are corrupted, Language is. It imitates the publicke riot. The excesse of Feasts, and apparell, are the note of a sick State; and the wantonnesse of language, of a sick mind" (VIII, 593).

Now it has often been observed that Jonson's ethics, like his poetry, are broadly classical in temper. In his contemporary verse the virtues that he invariably singles out for praise or holds up for emulation are reasonableness, constancy to traditional values, orderliness of habit, simplicity of manners, moderation, candor, and fortitude. Consequently he is merciless, as in "An Epistle to a Friend, to persuade him to the Warres," in his condemnation of excess of any kind:

> The whole world here leaven'd with madnesse swells;
> And being a thing, blowne out of nought, rebells
> Against his Maker; high alone with weeds,
> And impious ranknesse of all Sects and seeds:
> Not to be checkt, or frighted now with fate,
> But more licentious made, and desperate!
> Our Delicacies are growne capitall,
> And even our sports are dangers! what we call
> Friendship is now mask'd Hatred! Justice fled,
> And shamefastnesse together! All lawes dead,
> That kept man living! Pleasures only sought,
> Honour and honestie, as poore things thought
> As they are made! Pride, and stiffe Clownage mixt
> To make up Greatnesse! and mans whole good fix'd
> In bravery, or gluttony, or coyne,
> All which he makes the servants of the Groine,
> Thither it flowes. (VIII, 163)

Translated into the vocabulary of poetics, the virtues that Jonson commends become the defining qualities of classical art: simplicity, clarity, economy or brevity, order and wholeness, and those he condemns become the antitheses of these. In "An Epistle answering to one that asked to be Sealed of the Tribe of Ben," Jonson epitomizes (both in the content and in his style) the ethically ideal character precisely in these terms:

> . . . If I have any friendships sent,
>   Such as are square, well-tagde, and permanent,
> Not built with Canvasse, paper, and false lights,
>   As are Glorious Scenes, at the great sights;
> And that there be no fev'ry heats, nor colds,
>   Oylie Expansions, or shrunke durtie folds,
> But all so cleare, and led by reasons flame,

> As but to stumble in her sight were shame;
> These I will honour, love, embrace, and serve. . . .
>
> (VIII, 220)[27]

Yet, much as Jonson admired the classical discipline, he was aware, as the above passage indicates, that it lent itself to abuse by the time-server (the imitator), that it could be shaped into an elegant mask to hide moral corruption. Throughout the didactic verse and particularly in the satires he warns against or condemns elegant show and, conversely, insists, as in "To Sir Henry Nevil," that good manners must be animated from within:

> Who now calls on thee, NEVIL, is a *Muse,*
>   That serves nor fame, nor titles; but does chuse
> Where vertue makes them both, and that's in thee:
>   Where all is faire, beside thy pedigree.
> Thou art not one, seek'st miseries with hope,
>   Wrestlest with dignities, or fain'st a scope
> Of service to the publique, when the end
>   Is private gaine, which hath long guilt to friend.
> Thou rather striv'st the matter to possesse,
>   And elements of honor, then the dresse;
> To make thy lent life, good against the *Fates:*
>   And first to know thine owne state, then the States.
> To be the same in roote, thou art in height;
>   And that thy soule should give thy flesh her weight.
> Goe on, and doubt not, what posteritie,
>   Now I have sung thee thus, shall judge of thee.
> Thy deede, unto thy name, will prove new wombes,
>   Whil'st others toyle for titles to their tombes. (VIII, 70)[28]

The ethical principle of animation is usually in Jonson's poetry a Christian virtue, but more fundamentally and almost as often it is the recognition and humble, yet full, acceptance of what life has to offer. This principle and the ethical resonance it generates are, perhaps, nowhere better expressed by Jonson than in "To Penshurst," in which a magnificent panegyric of the ideal life culminates in the consciously symbolic distinction between the elegant house built for show and that built to be lived in:

> Now, PENSHURST, they that will proportion thee
>   With other edifices, when they see

Those proud, ambitious heaps, and nothing else,
May say, their lords have built, but thy lord dwells.
(VIII, 96)

It is, therefore, not unreasonable to conclude that this principle and
the moral vitality it generates are the ethical counterparts of the
aesthetic principle and its consequent resonance that constitute the
ultimate subject of Clerimont's song in *Epicene*, and, as I have suggested, govern so much of Jonson's poetry.

If Jonson's use of the principle of animation were deliberate, it is
likely that he would have had something specific to say about it in
his critical writings. Although there is no direct evidence in this area
of his work, the analogy between the inhabited house and the great
life-ideal poem that is discoverable in his poetry provides the basis for
an inference that further enforces the suggestion I am offering. As
R. S. Walker observes, what we have in *Timber* is not a grab bag of
critical scraps but rather a series of essays (finished and unfinished)
and notes that are classifiable into definite groups. One of these forms
a short unfinished *De Poetica* that "may have been intended as the
basis for a fuller written work or for a series of lectures of a formal
sort on the accepted theories of art." [29] In this unit Jonson begins his
discussion of the making of a poem by defining the magnitude and
compass of the epic or dramatic fable.[30] This is accomplished in four
sections in each of which the classical tenets he lays down are illustrated extensively by the analogy of the construction of a house.
Thus, for example, in the first section, where the fable is defined as
the imitation of one entire and perfect action whose parts are integral
with and proportionate to the whole, he illustrates:

> As for example; if a man would build a house, he would first
> appoint a place to build it in, which he would define within
> certaine bounds: So in the Constitution of a *Poeme*, the
> Action is aym'd at by the *Poet*, which answers Place in a
> building; and that Action hath his largenesse, compasse, and
> proportion. . . . So that by this definition wee conclude the
> fable, to be the *imitation* of one perfect, and intire Action; as
> one perfect, and intire place is requir'd to a building. By
> perfect, wee understand that, to which nothing is wanting; as
> Place to the building, that is rais'd, and Action to the fable,
> that is form'd. It is perfect, perhaps, not for a Court, or
> Kings Palace, which require a greater ground; but for the
> structure wee would raise. (VIII, 645)

The essay carries the reader up to a discussion of the one and entire action, the analogy developing accordingly until the house is a completed whole. In the middle of "The conclusion concerning the Whole, and the Parts" (VIII, 648), the essay breaks off. What we have, then, is the presentation of principles of composition the end of which is the creation of an externally symmetrical and ordered—a classical— artifact. On the basis of the recurrent and emphatic distinction between the emptiness of an elegant exterior and the full-bodied and vital organism—a distinction epitomized by the house built for show and the house that is lived in—it is indeed tempting to infer that had Jonson completed his *De Poetica* he would have extended the basic analogy until he had provided a source of resonance for both the house and the poem. The image of the authentic man in the classical house is not strictly analogous to the real toad in the classical garden. But it is similar enough to suggest how central to Jonson's sensibility was the impulse to activate motion in stillness, to generate resonance in the well-wrought formal construct.

NOTES

[1] Ben Jonson, *Selected Works*, ed. Harry Levin (New York, 1939), p. 1.

[2] A characteristic example of an early twentieth-century commentator who, despite admiration for her subject, inherits the Romantic judgment of Jonson is Esther C. Dunn. In *Ben Jonson's Art: Elizabethan Life and Literature as Reflected Therein* (London, 1925), she finds the nondramatic poetry of Samuel Daniel more attractive than that of Jonson because Daniel not only refuses to become "captive to the authority of antiquity," claiming that the English "are the children of nature as well as they [the Greeks and Romans]," but also because his work "is like Wordsworth before his time" (p. 87). See also C. H. Herford's and Percy Simpson's introduction to the poems, in *Ben Jonson, The Man and His Work*, II, ed. Herford and Simpson (Oxford, 1925), 337–413. For a late Victorian version of this attitude to Jonson's poetry, see Algernon Swinburne, *A Study of Ben Jonson* (London, 1889).

[3] Levin, "Introduction," p. 4.

[4] The measure of contemporary critical interest in the nondramatic verse is clearly revealed by the fact that in *Ben Jonson: A Collection of Critical Essays* (ed. Jonas Barish [Englewood Cliffs, N.J., 1963]) not one of the thirteen essays and only one of the entries in the "Selected Bibliography" deals specifically with the nondramatic verse. Of course, there has been much excellent critical discussion of Jonson's dramatic verse. But the failure to confront the nondramatic verse has tended to obscure the essential aesthetic characteristics of the former. As George Burke Johnston observes, Jonson "made it clear that even the author of his plays is

a poet and that they are poems" (*Ben Jonson: Poet* [New York, 1945], p. 2).

⁵ T. S. Eliot, for example, despite his high regard for Jonson's poetry, has said that it "is of the surface" ("Ben Jonson," *Essays on Elizabethan Drama* [New York, 1956], p. 66). For an excellent discussion of this question see John Hollander, "Introduction," *Ben Jonson,* The Laurel Poetry Series (New York, 1961), pp. 12 ff.

⁶ See n. 8, below. The best recent book on the nondramatic poetry, Wesley Trimpi's *Ben Jonson's Poems: A Study of the Plain Style* (Stanford, 1962), which explores the poetry in the light of Jonson's reaction against Petrarchanism and a Ciceronian high style in favor of an Attic plain style ("which was an attempt to revitalize language by replacing the emphasis firmly on intent rather than on expression," p. 95), is a notable contrast to the tenor of Professor Barish's anthology (see n. 4). Trimpi's study, however, is primarily historical and descriptive of the Jonsonian style and does not come to grips with the Jonsonian poem as a genre.

⁷ L. C. Knights also insists on the primary role of the native element in Jonson's poetry against the traditional view that the poet slavishly imitates the ancients. It is interesting to note, however, that Knights associates the native tradition with the medieval principle of order and of natural limitation rather than the vitality of Renaissance individualism and thus with a kind of classic rather than romantic aesthetic (*Drama and Society in the Age of Jonson* [London, 1937], p. 30).

⁸ Ralph S. Walker, "Ben Jonson's Lyric Poetry," *Criterion,* XIII (1934), 437–38. See also L. A. Beaurline's "The Selective Principle in Jonson's Shorter Poems" (*Criticism,* VIII [1966], 64–74), the thesis of which (that appropriateness governs the poetic act of selection) constitutes a more particularized (though not more authoritative) version of Walker's point.

⁹ "Ben Jonson's Lyric Poetry," p. 445. Walker cites not more than eleven successful lyrics.

¹⁰ T. S. Eliot, "East Coker," *Four Quartets, The Complete Poems and Plays, 1909–1950* (New York, 1952), p. 125. For a prose statement of this idea, see Eliot's definition of the historical sense in "Tradition and the Individual Talent," *Selected Essays* (New York, 1950), p. 4.

¹¹ Ben Jonson, *Discoveries, Ben Jonson,* ed. C. H. Herford and Percy Simpson, VIII (Oxford, 1947), 627. Jonson makes the same point in the following famous assertion: "I know *Nothing* can conduce more to letters, then to examine the writings of the *Ancients,* and not to rest in their sole Authority, or take all upon trust from them. . . . It is true they open'd the gates, and made the way, that went before us; but as Guides, not Commanders. . . ." (p. 567). Further references to this edition of Jonson's work in my text will be given with volume and page numbers within parentheses.

¹² "Ben Jonson's Poetry," *From Donne to Marvell,* ed. Boris Ford (London, 1956), p. 136.

¹³ The technique Jonson uses to generate resonance in "To Penshurst" is

employed with equal effectiveness in his epistle "To Sir Robert Wroth" (VIII, 96–100).

[14] George Johnston makes much of this type of poem in his effort to emphasize Jonson's contemporary sensibility.

[15] Both the technique and image are also employed in "The Musical Strife: In a Pastoral Dialogue." It is interesting to observe that Dryden uses the same image in "Song for St. Cecilia's Day." The difference between the "classicism" of Dryden's poem and that of Jonson's "An Ode, or Song" is the measure of the difference between the "classicism" generally attributed to Jonson and that which it is the purpose of this essay to define.

[16] See also "On My First Sonne" (VIII, 41), in which the personal note is struck in Jonson's bold equation of his "best piece of *poetrie*" with his son. The full pathos of this implicit pun on "maker" is realized by Jonson's consciousness of his audience's knowledge of the pride he felt about his poetry. For an excellent analysis of this poem, see L. A. Beaurline, "The Selective Principle in Jonson's Shorter Poems," pp. 66 ff.

[17] Johnston, *Ben Jonson: Poet*, p. 51.

[18] There is some factual evidence for this interpretation. As the editors indicate, the title in one of the manuscripts consulted (Rawlinson, 2) is "An Epitaph on Queene Elizabeth," and the poem is subscribed "B: Jonson." This is, however, only one of several extant titles, and thus suggests the possibility that the poet deliberately conceived the poem as an ambiguity. For an excellent variant reading of this lyric based on the possibilities generated by Jonson's deliberate withholding of the lady's identity, see Howard S. Babb, "The 'Epitaph on Elizabeth, L. H.' and Ben Jonson's Style," *JEGP*, LXII (1963), 738–44.

[19] It should be observed that in this poem as a whole Jonson is also employing the variation in which native matter is introduced into an essentially mythological atmosphere. The stanza to which I have referred above is fundamentally native, as the imagery and diction from rural English life clearly suggest, and thus cuts radically across the style of the rest of the poem, which throughout partakes of the characteristics of the first lines: "See the Chariot at hand here of Love, / Wherein my Lady rideth! / Each that drawes, is a Swan, or a Dove, / And well the Carre Love guideth" (VIII, 134). I am uncertain, however, as to whether or not the technique is successful in creating the kind of resonance I have been attempting to describe.

[20] See also "An Epigram, To the Household" (VIII, 241), an English sonnet the subject of which is both personal and sharply satirical.

[21] It might be worth while to point out here the peculiar mistake that John Hollander makes in his excellent introduction to his anthology *Ben Jonson* (The Laurel Poetry Series [New York, 1961], p. 22), when he refers to "A Sonnet, To the Noble Lady, the Lady Wroth" as Jonson's "sole sonnet." It is true that this is the only poem that Jonson refers to in his title as a sonnet, but even disregarding the several fourteen line poems such as "To My Booke" (VII, 27) "To William Camden" (p. 31), and "To Edward

Allen" (pp. 56–77), the rhyme schemes of which take the form of couplets, there are still at least two poems besides "To the Noble Lady" that are rather strictly English sonnets—namely, "On Poet-Ape" (pp. 44–45) and "To the Household" (p. 241).

22 See also "To the Right Honorable, the Lord high Treasurer of ENGLAND. An Epistle Mendicant" (VIII, 248).

23 It is my conviction that much can be learned about the dramatic form of Jonson's plays by examining them in the light of the aesthetic principle at work in his nondramatic poetry. Are not the notoriously harsh punishments meted out by the Avocator to Volpone and Mosca in *Volpone* and the unexpected alliance of the master of the house, Lovewit, and Face in *The Alchemist* the kind of incompatibles which jar the classical form into a motion that deepens the significance of these plays? At the end of *The Alchemist,* Lovewit curiously justifies his acceptance of the young widow (and her money) from Face by saying to the audience: "Therefore, gentleman, / And Kind Spectators, if I have out-stript'd / An old mans gravitie, or strict canon, thinke / What a yong wife, and a good braine may doe: / Stretch ages truth sometimes, and crack it too." In so doing, Lovewit unconsciously identifies himself with the other fools who thought they could magically transcend the limitations of nature, and thus undercuts the apparent theme that artistic virtuosity cancels out crime or sin. Furthermore, Face's justification for having "cleane / Got off" by implicitly equating his fraudulent methods of attaining "pelfe" with those of the audience ("yet I put my selfe / On you, that are my countrey"—v, 407) ironically convicts the audience, which had been casually drawn into admiration of the rogue's cleverness, of a greed for money or, in Jonson's view, for junk. This retrospective resonance is also mnemonic in character; it activates recollection of the animal imagery in the play, especially in the first act, and thus our consciousness of the underlying ferocity of their "tripartite" government by contract (v, 300).

24 Robert Herrick expresses the same artistic principle in his poem "Delight in Disorder" (although not with the conviction of Jonson). The parallel would seem to indicate that the aesthetic problem which formal perfection gives rise to was a topic of discussion among the members of the tribe of Ben in their lively conclaves at the Old Devil and the Apollo taverns.

25 The failure by Jonson's critics to perceive the significance of this crucial, if farfetched, analogy is another one of those cases that reveals dramatically the loss of the habit of analogy that the Western mind has suffered since the Cartesian *cogito* split subject and object in the seventeenth century. The most famous of these cases is, of course, that of Samuel Johnson's misunderstanding of the metaphysical conceit. See especially Marjorie Hope Nicolson, *The Breaking of the Circle: Studies in the Effect of the "New Science" upon Seventeenth-Century Poetry* (Evanston, 1950), and also S. L. Bethell, *The Cultural Revolution of the Seventeenth Century* (London, 1951). The failure to recognize the importance of the art-man analogy in Jonson has been partially rectified by Wesley Trimpi in *Ben*

Jonson's Poems, a large segment of which constitutes an analysis of the relationship between Jonson's ideal man and the plain style of his poetry. See especially pp. 115–90.

[26] For the history of this doctrine see W. Rensselaer Lee, "Ut pictura Poesis: The Humanistic Theory of Painting," *Art Bulletin,* xxii (1940), 197–269.

[27] See Wesley Trimpi's excellent discussion of "An Epistle to Master John Selden" in *Ben Jonson's Poems,* pp. 142–46.

[28] See also "To Sir Thomas Roe" (viii, 63), "On Some-thing That Walkes Some-where (p. 30), and "On Don Surly" (pp. 35–36). The artistic equivalent of time-serving, the particular abuse to which the classical ethical ideal lends itself, is, of course, imitation. See, for example, the similarity of theme and metaphor in "On Poet-Ape" (pp. 44–45) and "To Sir Henry Nevil" quoted above.

[29] "Introduction," *Ben Jonson's Timber or Discoveries* (Syracuse, 1953), p. 11.

[30] Although Jonson is talking about epic and dramatic poetry, the discussion is quite general and thus the broad aesthetic principles he posits are equally applicable to other genres of poetry.

ᘒ

The Poem as Hieroglyph

Too often Herbert is remembered as the man who possessed the fantastic idea that a poem should resemble its subject in typographical appearance, and who therefore invented the practice of writing poems in shapes such as wings and altars. Herbert, of course, no more invented the pattern poem than he invented "emblematic poetry" or the religious lyric: his originality lies in his achievement with traditional materials. "The Altar" and "Easter-wings," his two most famous pattern poems, are not exotic or frivolous oddities; they are the most obvious examples of Herbert's religious and poetic concern with what we may call the hieroglyph.

A hieroglyph is "a figure, device, or sign having some hidden meaning; a secret or enigmatical symbol; an emblem." [1] In the Renaissance "hieroglyph," "symbol," "device," and "figure" were often used interchangeably. Because of special meanings which have become associated with the other words, "hieroglyph" seems more useful than the others today, and even in the seventeenth century it was often considered the most inclusive term. [2] "Hieroglyphic," the older form of the noun, was derived from the Greek for "sacred carving," and the root usually retained something of its original religious connotation. Ralph Cudworth used it in its generally accepted meaning when he said in a sermon, "The Death of Christ . . . Hieroglyphically instructed us that we ought to take up our Cross likewise, and follow our crucified Lord and Saviour." [3] The hieroglyph presented its often manifold mean-

From *George Herbert, His Religion and Art* (London: Chatto & Windus, 1954; Cambridge: Harvard University Press), pp. 123–46. Reprinted by permission of the publishers.

ings in terms of symbolic relationships rather than through realistic representation. Francis Quarles's anatomy of the hieroglyphic significance of the rib is an extreme example of the general hieroglyphic state of mind:

> Since of a Rib first framed was a Wife,
> Let Ribs be Hi'rogliphicks of their life:
> Ribs coast the heart, and guard it round about,
> And like a trusty Watch keepe danger out;
> So tender Wiues should loyally impart
> Their watchfull care to fence their Spouses' heart:
> All members else from out their places roue
> But Ribs are firmely fixt, and seldom moue:
> Women (like Ribs) must keepe their wonted home,
> And not (like *Dinah* that was rauish't) rome:
> If Ribs be ouer-bent, or handled rough,
> They breake; If let alone, they bend enough:
> Women must (vnconstrain'd) be plyent still,
> And gently bending to their Husband's will.[4]

Quarles's poem suggests that wherever the poet found his hieroglyphs, their "meanings" tended to substantiate his own point of view. The central meanings for the serious religious poet were usually already established by the Bible and Christian tradition.

Aside from the metaphorical use of hieroglyphs common to almost all the poets of the time, the religious lyric poet could most obviously make his poem a meditation on one of the innumerable hieroglyphs in nature, art, or the Church, or he could use the hieroglyph as the central image in a meditation on some doctrine or experience. Quarles's poem and most of the poems written for the emblem books typify the first practice: the moral applications are drawn from the image point by point. Herbert never wrote a poem quite so crudely. "The Church-floore" is as close as he ever came, and that poem's departures from tradition are instructive. The first eighteen lines describe the hieroglyphic meanings of the "Church-floore":

> Mark you the floore? that square & speckled stone,
> Which looks so firm and strong,
> Is *Patience:*
>
> And th' other black and grave, wherewith each one
> Is checker'd all along,
> *Humilitie:*

The gentle rising, which on either hand
 Leads to the Quire above,
  Is *Confidence:*

But the sweet cement, which in one sure band
 Ties the whole frame, is *Love*
  And *Charitie.*

  Hither sometimes Sinne steals, and stains
  The marbles neat and curious veins:
 But all is cleansed when the marble weeps.
  Sometimes Death, puffing at the doore,
  Blows all the dust about the floore:
 But while he thinks to spoil the room, he sweeps.

An elaborate and promising hieroglyph is described, but in spite of
many hints its meaning is both abstract and ambiguous. We are told
that the elements which compose the floor are Patience, Humilitie,
Confidence, and Charitie, and that Sinne and Death attempt (and
fail) to deface it; but we are not told to what the floor is being compared. From the title of the poem the reader might assume that the
floor is a hieroglyph of the Church's foundation, which is based on
the theological virtues (Patience and Humilitie may be considered
as defining Faith in action), and against which the "gates of Hell"
(Sinne and Death) shall not prevail. Such an interpretation would
be thoroughly conventional, and the first eighteen lines might almost
serve as an unusually successful "explanation" of an emblem which
made that point. But Herbert's characteristic final couplet changes
that "explanation" and makes the poem:

  Blest be the *Architect*, whose art
  Could build so strong in a weak heart.

We discover with the last word of the poem that the principal referent
of the hieroglyph is not the institution of the Church but the human
heart. Patience, Humilitie, Confidence, and Charitie are the materials
with which God builds the structure of salvation within the heart.
God has built so that the "marble" heart will weep with repentance
and cleanse Sinne's stains. Death's intended triumph in blowing "all
the dust about the floore" only "sweeps" away the imperfections of
that flesh which is dust. Herbert nearly always presents the institutional as a hieroglyph of the personal rather than *vice versa*, and the

hieroglyph of "The Church-floore" has pictured primarily the marvellous art of God in decreeing the perseverance of the saints rather than
His art in the construction of the Church. Yet those two arts are
related; once raised, the image of the "Church-floore" as the foundation of Christ's Church is relevant. The final couplet is a dramatic
reminder to the meditator that "the most high dwelleth not in temples
made with hands" (Acts vii. 48), "that yee are the Temple of God,
and that the Spirit of God dwelleth in you" (I Cor. iii. 16). But in
relation to the subject of the meditation, the title of the poem, the
couplet is also a reminder that the structure which God has built
within the heart is truly the "floore" of both the Church Militant and
the Church Triumphant; that the conviction within the "weak heart"
that "Thou art the Christ, the sonne of the liuing God" is the "rocke"
upon which Christ built His Church.[5] The artful *"Architect"* has built
within the individual heart, equally indestructibly, the salvation of
the individual and the foundation of His Church. The structure, moreover, is one. Such a complex unfolding of meanings is far removed
from the practice of the emblematists, but it is characteristic of
Herbert.

In "The Bunch of Grapes" Herbert used the hieroglyph in the
second obvious fashion, as the central image in a meditation on a
personal experience. The title of the poem indicates the hieroglyph,
but the "cluster" is not mentioned until the end of the third stanza.
The subject of meditation is the problem of the absence of joy from
the Christian's life:

> Joy, I did lock thee up: but some bad man
>   Hath let thee out again:
> And now, me thinks, I am where I began
>   Sev'n yeares ago: óne vogue and vein,
>   One aire of thoughts usurps my brain.
> I did towards Canaan draw; but now I am
> Brought back to the Red sea, the sea of shame.

Joy, once possessed, has now escaped. Herbert prevents any misunderstanding of the traditional imagery of Canaan and the Red Sea by
explaining in the next stanza Paul's teaching that every event during
the wandering of the Children of Israel from Egypt to the Promised
Land was a type of the Christian's experiences in his journey between
the world of sin and heaven: [6] we may discover within the ancient
history the heavenly evaluations and solutions for our problems. With
the third stanza, Herbert enumerates some of the parallels:

Then have we too our guardian fires and clouds;
            Our Scripture-dew drops fast:
We have our sands and serpents, tents and shrowds;
            Alas! our murmurings come not last.
            But where's the cluster? where's the taste
Of mine inheritance? Lord, if I must borrow,
Let me as well take up their joy, as sorrow.

Joy may not be fully achieved until we reach the Promised Land, but the Christian should at least experience a foretaste of it, such a rich proof of its existence as was the cluster of Eshcol to the Children of Israel. But the introduction of Eshcol provides the answer. That "branch with one cluster of grapes," which was so large that "they bore it betweene two vpon a staffe," had represented a joy which the Israelites refused. To them the bunch of grapes substantiated the report that it was "a land that eateth vp the inhabitants thereof, and all the people that we saw in it, are men of a great stature. And there we saw the giants, the sonnes of Anak, which come of the giants: and we were in our owne sight as grashoppers, and so wee were in their sight" (Num. xiii. 32–33). From fear they turned to the rebellion which caused God to decree the wandering of forty years. Of all the adults who saw the grapes, only Caleb and Joshua entered the Promised Land. The image of the bunch of grapes suggests, then, not only the foretastes of Canaan and heaven, but also the immeasurable differences between those foretastes under the Covenant of Works and the Covenant of Grace:

But can he want the grape, who hath the wine?
            I have their fruit and more.
Blessed be God, who prosper'd Noahs vine,
            And made it bring forth grapes good store.
            But much more him I must adore,
Who of the Laws sowre juice sweet wine did make,
Ev'n God himself being pressed for my sake.

The bunch of grapes is a type of Christ and of the Christian's communion. "I have their fruit and more," for the grapes, of which the promise was conditional upon works, have been transformed into the wine of the New Covenant: "I" have both the foretaste and the assurance of its fulfilment. The prospering of "Noahs vine," like the cluster of Eshcol, was a sign of God's blessing. It was a partial fulfilment of "Bee fruitfull and multiply, and replenish the earth;" and of God's covenant with all flesh: "neither shall there any more be a flood to destroy the earth" (Gen. ix. 1, 11). Yet, as at Eshcol, God's blessings under the Law could become man's occasion for the renewal of sin and the curse: Noah's misuse of the vine resulted in the curse on Ham. The bunch of grapes has furnished the image of the poet's lost joy, the image of blessings refused or perverted, and also the image of the Christian's source of joy, ever present if he will cease his murmurings. The Holy Communion is a constant reminder of Christ's sacrifice which established the joyful Covenant of Grace; it is the instrument of present grace; and it foretells the joy of heavenly communion. The examination of the Christian's lack of joy has resolved rather than explained the original problem. The blessing and adoration of the final lines indicate that joy is no longer lost.

Herbert frequently used a hieroglyph to crystallize, explain, or resolve the central conflict in a poem. "Josephs coat," a strange sonnet with an unrhymed first line, concerns the mixture of joy and sorrow in the Christian life, and Joseph is not mentioned in the text. The conclusion, "I live to shew his power, who once did bring My *joyes* to *weep*, and now my *griefs* to *sing*," is an acknowledgment of God's power, but without the title it might be construed as an acknowledgment of a powerful and inexplicable Fate. The title, a reference to a traditional Christian type, gives Herbert's interpretation of the experience of contradictory joys and sorrows. Joseph's "coat of many colours" was the sign of his father's particular love.[7] It was also the immediate occasion for his brothers' jealousy and hatred and for his slavery and suffering; but the presentation of the coat was, finally, the initial incident in the long chain of causes which led to the preservation of the Children of Israel in Egypt. After all the suffering, the sign of Jacob's love ended in beatitude. The extraordinary mixture of joy and sorrow in the Christian's life is a particular sign of God's love. Joy has been made "to *weep*" to forestall that self-sufficience which leads to wilful pride, and "*griefs*" have been made "to *sing*" to preserve the soul and body from despair and death. God's "Cross-Providences" also lead to beatitude. For Herbert, "Joyes coat," with which anguish has been "ticed" was evidenced by his ability to "sing," to compose lyrics even when the subject was grief.

At first reading "Church-monuments" appears to belong to the group of poems which are explanations of a hieroglyph. For once the modern reader could surmise the title from the contents, for the poem is a considered meditation on "Church-monuments" in which all their hieroglyphic applications are drawn.

While that my soul repairs to her devotion,
Here I intombe my flesh, that it betimes
May take acquaintance of this heap of dust;
To which the blast of deaths incessant motion,
Fed with the exhalation of our crimes,
Drives all at last. Therefore I gladly trust

My bodie to this school, that it may learn
To spell his elements, and finde his birth
Written in dustie heraldrie and lines;
Which dissolution sure doth best discern,
Comparing dust with dust, and earth with earth.
These laugh at Jeat and Marble put for signes,

To sever the good fellowship of dust,
And spoil the meeting. What shall point out them,
When they shall bow, and kneel, and fall down flat
To kisse those heaps, which now they have in trust?
Deare flesh, while I do pray, learn here thy stemme
And true descent; that when thou shalt grow fat,

And wanton in thy cravings, thou mayst know,
That flesh is but the glasse, which holds the dust
That measures all our time; which also shall
Be crumbled into dust. Mark here below
How tame these ashes are, how free from lust,
That thou mayst fit thy self against thy fall.

The first stanza states the purpose of the meditation, that "my flesh
. . . betimes May take acquaintance of this heap of dust." Most obviously, the monuments form a hieroglyph worthy of the flesh's "acquaintance" because they contain the dust of formerly living flesh.
Yet, with the identification of "heap of dust" as that "To which the
blast of deaths incessant motion . . . Drives all at last," the meaning
expands to include the dissolution of all earthly things. Through con-
templating the monuments the "bodie" "may learn To spell his elements." The ambiguous "spell" (meaning both to "divine" the elements
and to "spell out" the inscriptions) introduces as part of the hieroglyph the inscriptions on the monuments. Their "dustie" physical state
(which makes them difficult to decipher) and their intended verbal
meaning cause them to serve as intermediate symbols relating the
flesh of man and the contents of the tomb. The "dustie heraldrie and
lines" factually tell the genealogies of the deceased and include some

conventional version of "for dust thou art, and vnto dust shalt thou return." ("Lines," associated with "birth" and "heraldrie," seems to signify genealogical "lines" as well as the lines of engraving.) The monuments are an ironic commentary on mortality; their states and messages mock at their composition of "Jeat and Marble"—too obviously fleshly attempts to deny the dissolution of the bodies which they contain. Can there be monuments to monuments? Can monuments hope for a memorial "When they shall bow, and kneel" as the body of the meditator is doing, or "fall down flat" in dissolution, as his body will do and as the bodies within the monuments have already done? The flesh can learn its "stemme And true descent" both in its origin in dust and in its decline into dust.

The figure of the hour-glass summarizes what "thou mayst know" from the contemplation of the monuments and further enriches the meaning:

> That flesh is but the glasse, which holds the dust
> That measures all our time; which also shall
> Be crumbled into dust.

It is one of Herbert's most successful condensations, and it is difficult only if we have failed to follow the careful preparation for its introduction. The hour-glass defines the flesh in terms of what has been learned from the monuments. The monuments, like the traditional *memento mori*, have told of more than physical death. It is "the exhalation of our crimes" which "feeds" "the blast of deaths incessant motion"; and the monuments, like the "grasse" of the Psalmist and Isaiah and the New Testament,[8] have served to exemplify the vain dust of the sin and the "goodlinesse" and "glory" of living flesh as well as that flesh's final dissolution. The function of proud flesh and proud monument is the same: to hold "the dust That measures all our time," whether it is the figurative dust of our vain goodliness and glory and sinful wills or the actual dust of our bodies. Dust is the true measure of "all our time" (not our eternity): the vanity and endurance of our lives and of our ashes provide the sole significances to the flesh and the monument. Finally, the flesh and the monuments, the containers, "shall Be crumbled into dust," both symbolic of and undifferentiable from the dust contained. The closing address directs the flesh's attention to the "ashes" rather than to the monuments:

> Mark here below
> How tame these ashes are, how free from lust,
> That thou mayst fit thy self against thy fall.

The flesh can escape neither its measuring content nor its final goal. The knowledge it has gained may, however, serve as bridle to "tame" its lust. The flesh may "fit" itself "against" its "fall" in that, in preparation for its known dissolution, it may oppose its "fall" into pride and lust.[9]

Such an analysis indicates the manner in which Herbert explained the complex meanings of the hieroglyph, but it does not explain "Church-monuments." The movement of the words and the lines, of the clauses and the sentences, conveys even without analysis a "meaning" which makes us recognize the inadequacy of any such prose summary. Yvor Winters has called "Church-monuments" "the greatest poem by George Herbert": "George Herbert's *Church Monuments,* perhaps the most polished and urbane poem of the Metaphysical School and one of the half dozen most profound, is written in an iambic pentameter line so carefully modulated, and with its rhymes so carefully concealed at different and unexpected points in the syntax, that the poem suggests something of the quiet plainness of excellent prose without losing the organization and variety of verse."[10] The effect which Winters praised is achieved largely through the extraordinary use of enjambment and the looseness of the syntax. Only three lines of the poem come to a full stop, and nine of the twenty-four lines are followed by no punctuation. Many of the semi-cadences indicated by the punctuation, moreover, prove illusory: the syntax demands no pause, and the commas serve as fairly arbitrary directions for a slight voice rest, obscuring rather than clarifying the simple "prose" meaning. Winters seems to praise "Church-monuments" for practices which are found in no other poem in *The Temple.* Herbert characteristically considered his stanzas as inviolable architectural units. Each usually contained a complete thought, representing one unit in the logic of the "argument," and the great majority of his stanzas end with full stops.[11] In the form in which it was printed in 1633 "Church-monuments" provides the only example of complete enjambment between stanzas in *The Temple,* and two of the three examples of stanzas in which the final points are commas.[12] When Herbert departs so dramatically from his usual consistent practice, it is advisable to look for the reason. It cannot be found, I believe, in an intent to suggest "something of the quiet plainness of excellent prose without losing the organization and variety of verse." These straggling sentences fulfil the criteria for excellence by neither Ciceronian nor Senecan nor Baconian standards of prose. They possess neither the admired periodicity, nor trenchant point, nor ordinary clarity. The series of clauses and participial phrases, each relating to a word in some preceding clause or phrase, threaten to dissolve the sentence structure. The repetitions of "that" and "which" give the effect of unplanned prose, a prose which seems to function more by association than by logic.

The poem is a meditation upon a *memento mori*, the hieroglyph of the monuments. One reason for the slowness of the movement and the "concealed" rhymes might be that the tone of the meditation was intended to correspond to the seriousness of its object. The most important clue, however, is in the manuscripts: in neither the Williams nor the Bodleian MSS. is the poem divided into stanzas at all. As F. E. Hutchinson remarked, "the editor of 1633 recognized that the rhyme-scheme implies a six-line stanza," [13] and subsequent editors followed the original edition and printed the poem in stanzas. But the manuscript arrangement was not the result of accident or carelessness. In the Williams MS., which Herbert corrected, the non-stanzaic form is emphasized by the indentation of line 17 to indicate a new paragraph.[14] The fact that Herbert established a six-line stanzaic rhyme scheme but did not create stanzas, either formally or typographically, is a minor but a convincing evidence that he intended the poem itself to *be* a *memento mori*, to function formally as a hieroglyph. The dissolution of the body and the monuments is paralleled by the dissolution of the sentences and the stanzas.

The movement and sound of the poem suggest the "falls" of the flesh and the monuments and the dust in the glass. The fall is not precipitous; it is as slow as the gradual fall of the monuments, as the crumbling of the glass, as the descent of the flesh from Adam into dust. Every cadence is a dying fall. Even the question of stanza 3 contains three commas and ends with the descriptive clause, "which now they have in trust," carrying no interrogation. Part of the effect is achieved by obvious "prose" means. "Dust" re-echoes seven times in the poem, and the crucial words and phrases describe or suggest the central subject: "intombe"; "blast of deaths incessant motion"; "dissolution"; "earth with earth"; "bow, and kneel, and fall down flat"; "descent"; "measures"; "crumbled"; [15] "ashes"; "fall." Herbert has also used every means to slow the movement of the neutral words. With the clusters of consonants, it is impossible to read the poem rapidly.[16] The related rhymes, with their internal echoes and repetitions, both give phonetic continuity to the poem and suggest the process of dissolution: "devotion" and "motion" are mocked by "exhalation" and "dissolution"; "betimes" and "crimes" modulate to "lines" and "signes" as do "learn" and "discern" to "birth" and "earth." "Trust" and "lust" are echoed incessantly by "dust," and, internally, by "blast," and "last." Continual internal repetition deprives the end-rhymes of any chime of finality: "blast-last," "earth with earth," "bow-now," "they-pray," "that-that," "which-which" disguise and almost dissolve the iambic pentameter line. Three of the six sentences in the poem take up five and a half lines each, but, straggling as they are, each is exhausted before it reaches what should be the end of the stanza. Although the sentences are hardly independent (the many pronominal forms create a complex of interdependent meanings), the expiration of each sentence marks a break which requires a new beginning: after the opening of the poem, each new sentence begins with a long syllable which usually causes a break in the iambic rhythm. The sentences sift down through the rhyme-scheme skeleton of the stanzas like the sand through the glass; and the glass itself has already begun to crumble.

"Church-monuments" differs in kind as well as degree from such poems as "The Church-floore" and "The Bunch of Grapes." The natural or religious hieroglyph was an eminently pleasant and profitable subject for a poem, and it could be used either as the object which the poem explained or as the image which explained the poem. Yet Herbert seems to have believed that it was more pleasant and profitable to make the poem itself a hieroglyph. To construct the poem so that its form imaged the subject was to reinforce the message for those who could "spell"; for the others it would not distract from the statement—and if they read and meditated long enough, surely they would discover the mirroring of the meanings within the form of the poem!

There were fewer readers who could not "spell" in Herbert's day than in ours. The attempt to make formal structure an integral part of the meaning of a poem assumed a general consciousness of traditional formal conventions. The disturbances of the rhyme schemes in "Grief" and "Home," for example, depend for their effects on the reader's firm expectation of a conventional pattern. Such an expectation could be assumed in readers accustomed to Renaissance English poetry, whether the poetry of the Court or the hymns of the Church or the doggerel of the broadsides. In his hieroglyphs Herbert never attempted to abandon rational control for an "identity" with a natural object: the poems always embody or assume a firm pattern of logic, rhyme, and rhythm. The formal organization of the subject was imitated by the formal organization of the poem.

The poems in which Herbert's "imitations" are obvious are those which are likely to draw the fire of strict advocates either of that art which conceals art or of that upwelling inspiration which is oblivious of form. But Herbert often intended the form of a poem to be obvious. The opening stanzas of "Deniall," for example, picture the disorder which results when the individual feels that God denies his requests:

> When my devotions could not pierce
> Thy silent eares;
> Then was my heart broken, as was my verse:
> My breast was full of fears
> And disorder:
>
> My bent thoughts, like a brittle bow,
> Did flie asunder:
> Each took his way; some would to pleasures go,
> Some to the warres and thunder
> Of alarms.

The final stanza, with its establishment of the normal pattern of cadence and rhyme, is the symbol of reconstructed order, of the manner in which men (and the poem) function when God grants the request:

> O cheer and tune my heartlesse breast,
> Deferre no time;
> That so thy favours granting my request,
> They and my minde may chime,
> And mend my ryme.

The stanza which had been the symbol of the flying asunder of a "brittle bow" has become a symbol for the achievement of order. The form of the final prayer indicates that its request has already been answered. The individual and the poem have moved from fear through open rebellion and "unstrung" discontent. "Deniall" is overcome through renewal of prayer: the ordered prayer provides the evidence.

Of Herbert's many other formal hieroglyphs ("Sinnes round," "A Wreath," "Trinitie Sunday," etc.) "Aaron" is one of the most effective.

> Holinesse on the head,
> Light and perfections on the breast,
> Harmonious bells below, raising the dead
> To·leade them unto life and rest:
> Thus are true Aarons drest.

> Profanenesse in my head,
>   Defects and darknesse in my breast,
> A noise of passions ringing me for dead
>   Unto a place where is no rest:
>   Poore priest thus am I drest.
>
>   Onely another head
> I have, another heart and breast,
> Another musick, making live not dead,
>   Without whom I could have no rest:
>   In him I am well drest.
>
>   Christ is my onely head,
> My alone onely heart and breast,
> My onely musick, striking me ev'n dead;
>   That to the old man I may rest,
>   And be in him new drest.
>
>   So holy in my head,
> Perfect and light in my deare breast,
> My doctrine tun'd by Christ, (who is not dead,
>   But lives in me while I do rest)
>   Come people; Aaron's drest.

Herbert may have chosen the five stanzas of five lines each partially because of the five letters in "Aaron"; if so, the technical problem may have been of importance to the poet, but it does not matter particularly to the reader. Nor does it seem that Herbert primarily intended that each stanza should "suggest metrically the swelling and dying sound of a bell": [17] the "bells" and the "musick" occur only in the third line of each stanza, and the rhymes are hardly bell-like. The central meaning of those identical rhymes and those subtly transformed stanzas [18] is clearly stated in the poem. The profaneness in man's head, the defects and darkness in his heart, the cacophonous passions which destroy him and lead him to a hell of "repining restlessnesse" [19] *can* be transformed through the imputed righteousness of Christ into the ideal symbolized by Aaron's ceremonial garments.[20] The "clay" [21] (like the stanzas) retains its outward form, but inwardly all is changed in the divine consumption of the self. As the "Priest for euer after the order of Melchisedec" "dresses" the new Aaron with the inward reality for which the first Aaron's garments were but the hieroglyphs, the poem moves with a ritualistic gravity from opposition to a climactic synthesis.

When we have understood Herbert's use of form in these poems, or, say, his extraordinarily formal picture of anarchy in "The Collar" and his divine numerology in "Trinitie Sunday" we may see the poems which derive from the Elizabethan acrostics and anagrams in a different light. Aside from the courtiers to whom any exercise in ingenuity was welcome, this type of poem had its serious religious adherents in the seventeenth century. If biblical exegesis demanded the solution of anagrams,[22] and if the good man was truly "willing to spiritualize everything," the composition of such poetry was a logical result. With due appreciation of the wit involved, the good man was likely to treat such poetry seriously. The seriousness depended on a religious subject and on the assumption that the poet would draw "true" meanings from his word-play. Herbert abided by the rules, and he never repeated the various forms. In *The Temple* there is one true anagram (labelled as such), one echo poem, one "hidden acrostic," one poem based on the double interpretation of initials, one based on a syllabic pun, and "Paradise," which can only be described as a "pruning poem." For his unique example of each type, Herbert usually chose that Christian subject which was most clearly illuminated by the device.

In some of these poems typography becomes a formal element. In "Paradise," for example, the second and third rhymes of each stanza are formed by "paring" off the first consonant of the preceding rhyme:

> I blesse thee, Lord, because I GROW
> Among thy trees, which in a   ROW
> To thee both fruit and order   OW.
>
> What open force, or hidden   CHARM
> Can blast my fruit, or bring me HARM
> While the inclosure is thine   ARM?

The device is artificial in the extreme, and it requires some wrenching of orthography. As an abstract form it is hardly satisfactory. But Herbert never used forms abstractly, and we are left in no doubt as to the reason for the form of this particular poem:

> Inclose me still for fear I   START.
> Be to me rather sharp and   TART,
> Then let me want thy hand & ART.
>
> When thou dost greater judgements SPARE,
> And with thy knife but prune and   PARE,
> Ev'n fruitfull trees more fruitfull   ARE.

> Such sharpnes shows the sweetest FREND:
> Such cuttings rather heal then   REND:
> And such beginnings touch their   END.

Except for the third stanza, the poem survives brilliantly the test of oral reading: its success does not depend upon the construction of the rhymes. Yet the "pruned" rhymes do compel the reader to "see" what the poem is saying concerning the positive function of suffering. The meaning is traditional, of course. The fate of the "unprofitable vineyard" was destruction rather than pruning. By changing the image from the vine to the English orchard, Herbert related the "pruning" more immediately to his readers' experience, but the point is the same: the surgical knife is necessary for the order which produces fruit. The final line of the poem is "naturally" ambiguous. For the religious man of the seventeenth century "end" nearly always implied purpose as well as finality. "And such beginnings touch their END" means that God's pruning causes the fruits of righteousness which are the end of man's creation. It also implies that the cutting away of the fruitless branches images the final "cutting away" of the body and the release of the soul at death.

In "The Altar" and "Easter-wings" Herbert extended the principle of the hieroglyph to a third level. If the natural or religious hieroglyph was valuable as content (used either as the object which the poem explained or as the image which crystallized the meaning of the poem), and if the poem could be constructed as a formal hieroglyph which mirrored the structural relationships between the natural hieroglyph, the poem, and the individual's life, it was but a further step to make the poem a visual hieroglyph, to create it in a shape which formed an immediately apparent image relevant both to content and structure.

Neither the conception of the pattern poem nor the two shapes which Herbert used were at all novel.[23] The Greek Anthology had included six pattern poems (including a pair of wings and two altars), and those patterns were widely imitated in the sixteenth century. Although Thomas Nashe, Gabriel Harvey, and Ben Jonson denounced such poems, the practice flourished.[24] After the appearance of The Temple patterns were published in profusion. Wither, Quarles,[25] Benlowes, Joseph Beaumont, Herrick, Christopher Harvey, and Traherne were among the practitioners. Both before and after 1633 the literary quality of most of these poems was notoriously low. The poets seemed usually to consider the shapes as a superficial or frivolous attraction for the reader. As the Renaissance poets and critics never tired of reiterating, pleasure *could* be made a bait for profit, but a superficial conception of the "bait" often resulted in very bad poems. Many of the patterns depended largely on wrenched typography, and it was a common practice to compose a poem in ordinary couplets, then chop the lines to fit the pattern.

Herbert's poems are another matter. From his knowledge of both the Greek originals and English practice,[26] Herbert chose the two patterns which could be most clearly related to the purposes of his Christian poetry. His patterns are visual hieroglyphs. The interpretation of them as naïve representations of "real" objects has resulted in the citation of "The Altar" as additional proof of Herbert's extreme Anglo-Catholicism. An examination of the poem in the light of its tradition and Herbert's formal practice shows it to be artistically complex and religiously "low."

> A broken A L T A R , Lord, thy servant reares,
> Made of a heart, and cemented with teares:
> Whose parts are as thy hand did frame;
> No workmans tool hath touch'd the same.
> A   H E A R T   alone
> Is such a stone,
> As   nothing but
> Thy pow'r doth cut.
> Wherefore each part
> Of my hard heart
> Meets in this frame,
> To praise thy Name:
> That, if I chance to hold my peace,
> These stones to praise thee may not cease.
> O let thy blessed [27] S A C R I F I C E be mine,
> And sanctifie this A L T A R to be thine.

When one reads "The Altar" it is well to remember that the word "altar" was not applied to the Communion Table in the Book of Common Prayer, and that the canons of Herbert's time directed that the Table should be made of wood rather than stone. Throughout his English writings Herbert always used "altar" and "sacrifice" according to the "orthodox" Protestant tradition of his time: "altar" is never applied to the Communion Table nor is the Holy Communion ever called a "sacrifice." [28] Yet Herbert and his contemporaries cherished the conception of the altar and the sacrifice. The Mosaic sacrifices were considered types of the one true Sacrifice, in which Christ had shed blood for the remission of sins once for all time. To man were left the "sacrifices" of praise, good works, and "communication" (Heb. xiii, 15–16). The Hebrew altar which was built of unhewn stones was a type of the heart of man, hewn not by man's efforts but by God alone. The engraving on those stones with which "all the words of this Law" were written "very plainely" (Deut. xxvii. 8) was a type of the "Epistle of Christ," the message of salvation engraved on the Christian heart (2 Cor. iii. 3). Herbert's conceptions that the broken and purged heart is the proper basis for the sacrifice of praise and that even stones may participate in and continue that praise were firmly biblical. In his psalm of repentance (Ps. li.) David had stated that the true sacrifices of God are "a broken and a contrite heart"; Christ had promised that "the stones" would cry out to testify to Him (Luke xix. 40); and Paul had stated that "Ye also as liuely stones, are built vp a spirituall house . . . to offer vp spirituall sacrifice" (I Pet. ii. 5).

There is hardly a phrase in "The Altar" which does not derive from a specific biblical passage. Yet the effect of the poem is simple and fresh. In an important sense this, the first poem within "The Church" (the central section of *The Temple*), *is* the altar upon which the following poems (Herbert's "sacrifice of praise") are offered, and it is an explanation of the reason for their composition. God has commanded a continual sacrifice of praise and thanksgiving made from the broken and contrite heart. The condition of mortality as well as the inconstancy of the human heart requires that such a sacrifice be one of those works which "doe follow them" even when they "rest from their labours." For the craftsman and poet, construction of a work of art resulted in that continual sacrifice and introduced the concept of the altar: the poem is a construction upon which others may offer their sacrifices; it is a "speaking" altar which continually offers up its own sacrifice of praise. The shape of Herbert's poem was intended to hieroglyph the relevance of the old altar to the new Christian altar within the heart. It was fittingly, therefore, a modification of the traditional shape of a classic altar rather than of what Herbert knew as the Communion Table.[29] F. E. Hutchinson's description of the changes in the printing of the poem furnishes a miniature history of progressive misinterpretation.[30] From 1634 to 1667 the shape was outlined merely to draw the reader's attention to its significance. The change in religious temper and vocabulary by 1674 was indicated by "an engraving of a full-length Christian altar under a classical canopy, with the poem set under the canopy": the assumption was that Herbert had attempted to image a "Christian altar." The final liturgical representation of the poem did not, however, occur until the nineteenth century: "In 1809 there is Gothic panelling and canopy-work behind a modest altar with fringed cloth, fair linen cloth, and the sacred vessels." Herbert's attempt to use the shape of a classical altar as a hieroglyph of his beliefs concerning the relationships between the heart, the work of art, and the praise of God failed to communicate its meaning to a number of generations. While not one of Herbert's greatest poems, "The Altar" within its context in *The Temple* is still an effective poem if we take the pains to understand it.

"Easter-wings" has been subject to fewer misinterpretations than "The Altar." In the last twenty years particularly it has generally been considered a good poem, although there has been little agreement as to the meaning and effectiveness of its pattern. It is the final poem in the group concerning Holy Week, and to read it within its sequence helps to explain some of the difficulties for the modern reader.

Lord, who createdst man in wealth and store,
Though foolishly he lost the same,
Decaying more and more,
Till he became
Most poore:
With thee
O let me rise
As larks, harmoniously,
And sing this day thy victories:
Then shall the fall further the flight in me.

My tender age in sorrow did beginne:
And still with sicknesses and shame
Thou didst so punish sinne,
That I became
Most thinne.
With thee
Let me combine
And feel this day thy victorie:
For, if I imp my wing on thine,
Affliction shall advance the flight in me.

The pattern is successful not merely because we "see" the wings, but because we see how they are made: the process of impoverishment and enrichment, of "thinning" and expansion which makes "flight" possible. By that perception and by the rhythmical falling and rising

which the shaped lines help to form, we are led to respond fully to
the active image and to the poem. The first stanza is a celebration
of the *felix culpa*. Man was created in "wealth and store," with the
capacity for sinlessness. Through Adam's sin Paradise was lost, yet
from one point of view the loss was not unhappy: "where sinne
abounded, grace did much more abound" (Rom. v. 20). If man "rises"
in celebration of Christ's victories, the fall will indeed further his flight
to God. The second stanza concerns the reduction of the individual
by God's punishment for sins. Again, if we "combine" with Christ
"And feel this day thy victorie," affliction can prove an advance to
flight, for it is through such affliction that souls are led to "waite vpon
the Lord" and "renew their strength," and the promise is specific:
"they shall mount vp with wings as Eagles, they shal runne and not
be weary, and they shall walke, and not faint" (Isa. xl. 31). The New
Testament had related the death and resurrection of the spirit and
the body to the germinal cycle of nature, and the favourite English
pun on "son-sun" seemed to acquire a supernatural sanction from
Malachi iv. 2: "But vnto you that feare my Name, shall the Sunne
of righteousnesse arise with healing in his wings." The "decaying" of
the first stanza of Herbert's poem implies the fruitful image of the
grain, and the conclusion of that stanza broadens to include the rise
of the "Sun," the "harmonious" ascent both of the flight and the
song of the larks.[31] The triumphant dichotomies are implied throughout the poem: sickness and health, decay and growth, poverty and
wealth, foolishness and wisdom, punishment and reward, defeat and
victory, the fall and rise of song and wings and spirit, sin and righteousness, burial and resurrection, death and life. These states are not
in polar opposition. The poem and its pattern constantly insist that
for man only through the fall is the flight possible; that the victory,
resurrection, whether in this life or the next, can come only through
the death of the old Adam.

The pattern poem is a dangerous form, and its successful practitioners before and after Herbert were few. The conception behind it,
however, is neither so naïve nor so dated as some critics have assumed:
writing with intentions differing greatly from Herbert's, E. E. Cummings and Dylan Thomas have created successful contemporary pattern poems.[32] For Herbert such poetry was a natural extension of his
concern with the hieroglyph. Most of the other poets of his time,
whether followers of Spenser, Jonson, or Donne, characteristically
used hieroglyphs as the basis for their imagery in either short or
extended passages. Herbert's distinction lies in his successful development of the conceptions that the entire poem could be organized

around a hieroglyph and that the poem itself could be constructed as a formal hieroglyph.

The hieroglyph represented to Herbert a fusion of the spiritual and material, of the rational and sensuous, in the essential terms of formal relationships. It may have been that his delight in the power and beauty of the hieroglyphic symbol helped to keep his poems from becoming only rational exercises or pious teachings. Yet reason and piety were central, for to Herbert the hieroglyph did not exist as a total mystery or as isolated beauty, but as a beauty and mystery which were decipherable and related to all creation. The message was precise and clear even if complex and subtle. A differing conception of the religious hieroglyph led Crashaw to ecstatic adoration and worship. For Herbert, however, celebration could never be divorced from examination. The hieroglyphs, whether of God's or of man's creation, were to be "read" rather than adored, and they sent the reader back to God. The chief tool for such reading was the logical use of man's reason.

It was, moreover, delightful as well as edifying for the poet to imitate God in the construction of hieroglyphs. As Sir Philip Sidney had remarked long before, the way in which God had worked in the creation of nature was not so mysterious as marvellous; man could observe and could imitate:

> Neither let it be deemed too saucy a comparison, to balance the highest point of man's wit with the efficacy of nature; but rather give right honour to the heavenly Maker of that maker, who having made man to his own likeness, set him beyond and over all the works of that second nature; which in nothing he showeth so much as in poetry; when, with the force of a divine breath, he bringeth things forth surpassing her doings, with no small arguments to the incredulous of that first accursed fall of Adam; since our erected wit maketh us know what perfection is, and yet our infected will keepeth us from reaching unto it.[33]

NOTES

[1] *NED*, Sb. 2.

[2] In his *Hieroglyphicorum Collectanea, ex Veteribus et Neotericis Descripta* ("In hoc postrema editione recognita & expurgata"; Lvgdvni, 1626), p. 7, Giovanni Pierio Valeriano summarized the general usage: "Ad hieroglyphica accedunt emblemata, symbola, insignia, quaemuis nomine differant, reipsa multi modis conuenir videntur."

[3] Quoted in *NED*, "Hieroglyphically," 2, from "Sermon I" (1642) in *A Discourse Concerning the True Notion of the Lord's Supper* (London, 1670), p. 210.

[4] "Meditatio tertia," *Hadassa: or The History of Queene Ester* (1621), *The Complete Works*, ed. A. B. Grosart (Edinburgh, 1880–81), II, 50.

[5] Matt. xvi. 16–18. I give the Protestant interpretation of the passage.

[6] I Cor. x. The marginal reading for "ensamples," v.11, is "Or, Types."

[7] George Ryley, "The Temple explained and improved," pp. 315–16, summarizes the biblical allusions: "Joseph's Coat was of *many colours;* very beautifull; and it was a token of his father's peculiar affection. *Gen.* 37.3. . . . This poem speaks the language of the prophet, Is. 61. 10, *I will greatly rejoice in the Lord, &c. for he hath cloathed me with the garments of salvation,* and of the Apostle, 2 Cor. 6. 10, *As sorrowfull, yet always rejoicing.*"

[8] Ps. cii. 11; Isa. xl. 6; I Pet. i. 24.

[9] "Against" and "fall" are used ambiguously. "Against" means both "in preparation for" and "in opposition to," and "fall" means both physical collapse and "fall" into sin. These ambiguities are characteristic of Herbert's use of the device. Neither is at all recondite: "against" in the sense of "in preparation for" often carried something of the meaning of "in opposition to," and "the fall" of man and angels had traditionally equated physical and moral movement.

[10] *Primitivism and Decadence: A Study of American Experimental Poetry* (New York, 1937), pp. 10, 123.

[11] On the rare occasions when a stanza ends with a colon or semicolon, modern usage would often require a period.

[12] The third example is stanza 5 of "The Bag." Here the comma after line 30, "And straight he turn'd, and to his brethren cry'd," is strong, since it precedes the two stanzas of direct quotation.

[13] *Works*, p. 499.

[14] *Works*, p. 65. In B the line begins a new page.

[15] The only significant change which Herbert made after the version in W was to introduce "crumbled" in line 22 for the less effective "broken."

[16] In the twenty-four lines the sound of *t* occurs 59 times; *th* and th, 36; *s* and z, 51; *sh*, 16; *n*, 35; *d*, 27.

[17] Grierson, *Metaphysical Lyrics*, pp. 231–2.

[18] Douglas Bush has remarked that in the first stanza describing the "type," the consonants *l, m,* and *r* predominate; in the second concerning the "natural man," *p, st, t, z,* and *s;* and in the final stanza the two patterns of consonants are united.

[19] "The Pulley."

[20] Hutchinson, *Works*, p. 538, summarizes the relevant passages from Exod. xxviii.

[21] Cf. "The Priesthood."

[22] See Kenneth B. Murdock's discussion and quotations in *Handkerchiefs from Paul* (Cambridge, Mass., 1927), pp. liv–lvi.

[23] In the discussion which follows I am indebted to Miss Margaret Church's "The Pattern Poem" (Doctoral thesis, Radcliffe College, 1944), the most useful discussion of the history and development of the European pattern poem which I have found. Miss Church's Appendix C., pp. 240–427, "includes copies of all the pattern poems discussed in the text with the exception of several *carmina quadrata* by P. Optatianus Porfirius and Hraban Maur."

[24] Church, p. 161, cites the comments of Nashe, "Have with you . . . ," *The Works*, ed. R. B. McKerrow (London, 1900), III, 67; Harvey, *Letter-Book*, ed. E. J. L. Scott (Westminster, 1884), pp. 100–101; and Jonson, *The Works*, ed. F. Cunningham (London, 1816), III, 320, 470, 488.

[25] Except for one "lozenge," "On God's Law," in the *Divine Fancies* of 1632, all of Quarles's patterns, like his emblems, were published after 1633. If there was any influence, it was Herbert who influenced Quarles.

[26] See Church, pp. 297 ff. English composers of altars before Herbert included Richard Willis (1573), Andrew Willet, and William Browne of Tavistock (in *The Shepherd's Pipe*, 1614). Willet's shapes were printed at the beginning of Sylvester's *Bartas His Devine Weekes & Workes* (1605–8). It seems safe to assume that Herbert, rhetorician, classicist, and poet by profession, knew the poems of the "Greek Anthology" as well as current practice. Arthur Woodnoth's letter to Nicholas Ferrar shortly before Herbert's death, *Ferrar Papers*, pp. 268–9, makes doubtful the hypothesis that Italian poetry directly influenced Herbert: "Sauonorola in Latine he hath of the Simplicity of Chr: Religion and is of great esteme wth him. He sayth he doth Vnderstand Italian a lyttle." Hutchinson notes, *Works*, pp. 564–5, that Herbert's translation of Luigi Cornaro's *Treatise of Temperance and Sobrietie* was based not on the original (Padua, 1558) but on Lessius's Latin version (Antwerp, 1613, 1614, 1623). A "lyttle" understanding of Italian would have sufficed for the translations in *Outlandish Proverbs*. Unlike Ferrar, Crashaw, and Milton, Herbert never went to Italy.

[27] Hutchinson, *Works*, p. 26, notes that in W the word "onely" has been corrected to "blessed." The change is a poetic improvement, but the original word substantiates my interpretation of the poem.

[28] Cf. the references cited by Cameron Mann, *A Concordance to the English Poems of George Herbert* (Boston and New York, 1927). For "sacrifice," see "The Church-porch," ll. 6, 275; "The Sacrifice" throughout and especially l. 19; "Mattens," l. 3; "Providence," l. 14; "Love unknown," l. 30. For "altar" see "Love (I)," l. 21 and the first of the "Sonnets to his Mother," l. 6. At first reading Chapter vi, "The Parson Praying," of *A Priest to the Temple* (*Works*, pp. 231–2) seems to provide an exception to Herbert's customary use of "altar." After a description of the parson's actions "when he is to read divine services," Herbert adds, "This he doth, first, as being truly touched and amazed with the Majesty of God, before whom he then presents himself; yet not as himself alone, but as presenting with himself the whole Congregation, whose sins he

then beares, and brings with his own to the heavenly altar to be bathed, and washed in the sacred Laver of Christs blood." Despite the familiar imagery, there is no reference here to the Eucharist. The "altar" and "the sacred Laver of Christs blood" are truly *in* heaven. Reading "divine services" to Herbert did not imply administering the Holy Communion. In Chapter xxii (p. 259), Herbert notes that the Country Parson celebrates the Communion "if not duly once a month, yet at least five or six times in the year. . . . And this hee doth, not onely for the benefit of the work, but also for the discharge of the Church-wardens, who being to present all that receive not thrice a year; if there be but three Communions, neither can all the people so order their affairs as to receive just at those times, nor the Church-Wardens so well take notice who receive thrice, and who not."

[29] Herbert may have sacrificed accuracy to symmetry as part of his image of "A *broken* altar." The altars of both Dosiados and Richard Willis followed the pattern of two short lines, longer for four, much shorter for eight, and longer for five at the base (see Church, p. 46). The first two short lines which Herbert omits represent the slab (sometimes identified as the altar proper) on which the sacrifice takes place. The opening phrase of Herbert's poem makes attractive the conjecture that his pattern is intended to convey both the perfect ordering of the ideal spiritual altar and the fact that this altar is not constructed for the ancient blood-sacrifice. Such a significance is, however, perhaps too recondite for Herbert to have intended his audience to grasp it. And against such an interpretation is the fact that "an Altare and Sacrifice to Disdaine" in *A Poetical Rhapsody* had been symmetrical (four long lines, twelve short, four long) without iconographical significance. See *A Poetical Rhapsody* (1602-1621), ed. H. F. Rollins (Cambridge, Mass., 1931), I, sig. 1₂ᵛ.

[30] *Works*, p. 484.

[31] See Bennett, *Four Metaphysical Poets*, p. 66.

[32] As Lloyd Frankenberg has pointed out, *Pleasure Dome: on reading modern poetry* (Boston, 1949), pp. 172–9, Cummings continually writes such poems; the fact that his patterns are based on individual and spontaneous gestures or situations or personalities rather than on symmetrical and abstract forms has disguised the fact from some readers. John L. Sweeney, *The Selected Writings of Dylan Thomas* (New York, 1946), p. xxi, has suggested that the pattern of Thomas's "Vision and Prayer" may have been inspired by "Easter-wings." As Theodore Spencer once remarked, the formal effects of James Joyce's *Ulysses* are directly related to the tradition of George Herbert's poetry.

[33] *The Defence of Poesy, The Miscellaneous Works*, ed. William Gray (Boston, 1860), pp. 69–70.

Herbert's The Collar Re-read

The Collar

I struck the board, and cry'd, No more.
I will abroad.
What? shall I ever sigh and pine?
My lines and life are free; free as the rode,
Loose as the winde, as large as store.
Shall I be still in suit?
Have I no harvest but a thorn
To let me bloud, and not restore
What I have lost with cordiall fruit?
Sure there was wine
Before my sighs did drie it: there was corn
Before my tears did drown it.
Is the yeare onely lost to me?
Have I no bayes to crown it?
No flowers, no garlands gay? all blasted?
All wasted?
Not so, my heart: but there is fruit,
And thou hast hands.
Recover all thy sigh-blown age
On double pleasures: leave thy cold dispute
Of what is fit, and not. Forsake thy cage,
Thy rope of sands,

From *Boston University Studies in English*, V (1961), pp. 65–73. Reprinted by permission of *Boston University Studies in English*.

Which pettie thoughts have made, and made to thee
    Good cable, to enforce and draw,
            And be thy law
While thou didst wink and wouldst not see,
            Away; take heed:
            I will abroad.
Call in thy deaths head there: tie up thy fears.
            He that forbears
        To suit and serve his need,
            Deserves his load.
But as I rav'd and grew more fierce and wilde
            At every word,
Me thoughts I heard one calling, *Child!*
        And I reply'd, *My Lord.*

According to the interpretations usually offered, *The Collar* describes
the struggle between discipline and pleasure, between the duties of a
clergyman and the satisfactions to be derived from the natural life,
or, as Joseph Summers puts it, the struggle between God's will and the
speaker's rebellious Heart.[1] But to leave the matter here is to miss,
I think, the full import of the poem. Properly read—read, that is, in
the context of Herbert's other poems, and with reference to the
tradition which informs his imagery with meaning—the poem gains
in complexity and power. It may be seen to represent in psychological
terms the events of the Christian moral drama—the Fall, the Atonement, and the Redemption. It is certainly true that the speaker, under
the influence of the Heart, rebels against discipline. But in reaching
for the "fruit," as did Adam, he simultaneously reaches for the supernatural fruit, the fruit of the Cross. Paradoxically, the "natural"
imagery of the poem, the fruit and wine and corn, in pursuit of which
the speaker rebels, is also the imagery traditionally associated with
the Eucharist. Therefore we may describe the moral events of the
poem in this way: just as the moral disorder entailed by the rebellion
of Adam and Eve was overcome by Christ's sacrifice, so the moral
disorder of the speaker's rebellion is to be finally overcome by the
sacrament of the Eucharist. Part of the brilliance of the poem lies
in the fact that it expresses rebellion and atonement in the same
vocabulary, and by so doing epitomizes its central idea: that rebellion
necessarily entails, because of God's justice and mercy, atonement.
    Joseph Summers has described very well the structure of the poem.
It is divided into four sections of argument. First the speaker, under
the influence of the Heart, complains; then the Will answers that

there is "fruit" if the Heart will seek it; next, the Heart repeats its complaint and its rebellious intention; and finally there is the resolution.[2] But if we look closely at the imagery the precise nature of the resolution becomes clear. We see, furthermore, that both Heart and Will are the unconscious instruments of God's will, and that His intention, latent from the start, gradually becomes manifest. Lines 6–12 contain the unmistakable references:

> Shall I be still in suit?
> Have I no harvest but a thorn
> To let me bloud, and not restore
> What I have lost with cordiall fruit?
> Sure there was wine
> Before my sighs did drie it: there was corn
> Before my tears did drown it.

"Suit" in line 6 suggests a petitioner. The speaker, as if in a court of law, seeks something which as yet is not forthcoming. The word also carries the sense of enforced attendance, the attitude of a courtier who has little to hope for. But as one analyzes the poem and becomes aware of its full implication, one realizes that the important word in this line is not "suit" but "still." The speaker is not a litigant in an earthly court, and he is not in suit before a secular prince: his suit is before a supernatural king, and is to be decided according to transcendent laws. He should, in other words, be *still*, although he does not know it; and at the end of the poem we are indeed aware of a kind of stillness: the speaker no longer needs all those words. In the next six lines we encounter a series of references which would have presented no difficulties to Herbert's contemporaries. The speaker's suit yields him a harvest only of thorn. I do not wish to insist upon a minor point, since the poem is clearly theological in its bearing, but I cannot suppose that the mixing of metaphors here, the legal and courtly suit entailing the unfortunate agricultural havest, is entirely without social meaning. But however this may be, we are told that the speaker's harvest yields only "a thorn" which makes him bleed. At the moment of his rebellion, the speaker understands his words in some such sense as this: my discipline is painful, in blocking the satisfaction of my desires it makes me bleed and sigh, and, to make matters worse, it brings no reward. However, the words he uses have an alternative signification. The thorn suggests the imperfections introduced into the world by the Fall, the damaging of the *rosa sine spina* of paradise. Such an association for "thorn" was commonplace. Bishop Bayly, for example, referred to "thornes, the first fruits of the curse," in his *Practice of Pietie* (1613), and Milton points out in *Paradise Lost* that Eden before the Fall boasted "Flow'rs of all hue, and without Thorn the Rose." Thus the thorn, which in its primary meaning in the poem signifies the discomforts the speaker experiences when his desires conflict with his discipline, also suggests the results of the Fall. Just as Adam, rebelling against the original "discipline" of Eden, introduced thorns into Eden, so the speaker, rebelling against *his* discipline, finds a thorn rather than fruit. But, and here is the third signification of "thorn," the thorn is not only the result of the sin of rebellion but also is associated with the means of its redemption. The speaker's harvest, the thorns which make him bleed, though at present bringing only pain, foreshadow the mode of his redemption: they are also the thorns of Christ's crown. To summarize: the speaker is linked in his rebellion with Adam, and like him he longs for "fruit"; his longing and rebellion lead to "thorns"; but, as in the case of Adam, the means of recovery is implicit in the act. The thorns are the thorns of Eden after the Fall, they are the thorns of the speaker's pain, and they are the thorns of Christ's crown, the symbol of *His* pain and therefore of the means of man's redemption.

The speaker is not aware of all this, however, at the moment the thoughts described in these lines occur. The full meaning of his rebellion, as defined by the *double entendres,* does not become clear to him until the end of the poem. In lines 8 and 9 he says merely that there is no relief for him, that his harvest is only of thorn. He is not aware, though we *are,* of the irony present in "only"—*only* Christ's crown. As far as the speaker is aware at this moment, he has no harvest which will "restore | What I have lost with cordiall fruit."

To Herbert's contemporaries the pun involved in "cordiall" would have been a routine matter: *cor, cordis.* "Cordiall' therefore alludes to that which comes from the heart, or blood. But what of "fruit"? "Cordiall fruit," the restorative fruit for which the speaker longs, is thus "bloody fruit." This would not have been a difficult allusion for a seventeenth-century reader to unravel. The Fall occurred when fruit was plucked from the forbidden tree. Because this theft introduced death into the world, the fruit Adam stole might plausibly be described as bloody. But Christ was the fruit which grew on a later tree. As Thomas Middleton put it, "The tree of Good and Evil brought forth an apple to cast us all away, and the Tree of Shame bare a fruit to save us all forever." Even a carol can count on an understanding of the conceit, and begins, "An earthly tree a heavenly fruit it bare." [3] Christ's body and blood thus constitute one meaning of the bloody fruit, or "cordiall fruit," of the poem. It is "cordiall fruit" in this sense that atones for man's rebellion, either the original rebellion of Adam or the rebellions which occur in every self much as they occur in the case of the speaker in *The Collar*.

The next three lines are fraught with implication, and, furthermore, elaborate upon the theme of the Eucharistic sacrifice.

> Sure there was wine
> Before my sighs did drie it: there was corn
> Before my tears did drown it.

Let us consider the possibilities present here. Wine and corn can represent natural food and drink, can represent the pleasures of eating which the speaker has denied himself because of his ascetic discipline. Considered in this way, they are the natural pleasures he longs for, objects of desire comparable to "fruit." But wine and corn (wheat) are also, of course, the elements of the Eucharist, wine and bread. At first the speaker seems to be saying that he desires the natural pleasures, the pleasures from which he has been cut off by discipline. But he is simultaneously saying that his tears and sighs are the manifestation of his need for the restorative, reordering powers of the sacrament. To put it another way: he *thinks* he desires natural pleasure, but the real object of his desire is supernatural, the cordial fruit of the Eucharist. Here, as in Dante, the true object of desire is not the earthly and the mutable, but the eternal. The implication is also present here that the speaker's tears and sighs have damaged the wine and corn. This may mean that the rigors of the speaker's discipline have denied him sensuous pleasure. But it can also mean that it is the speaker's emotional turmoil that has cut him off from an awareness of the restorative powers of the sacrament.

Now that we have identified the controlling imagery of the poem as Eucharistic, we can give certain details a fuller explication than they have yet received. According to Hutchinson, the "collar was in common use to express discipline, and 'to slip the collar' was often used figuratively. Preachers would use the word *collar* of the restraint imposed by conscience." [4] The speaker, it is clear, thinks of himself as a kind of prisoner, and like a prisoner he wishes to free himself from the restraints that have been imposed upon him. The "collar" of his discipline punishes him much as a criminal is punished by having to wear a real collar. The meaning of the comparison implicit in the title, between the speaker who is suffering amid tears and sighs and a criminal anxious to "slip the collar" of his punishment, was not unusual. For man, the descendant of Adam, was in fact guilty of a robbery, and was a "prisoner" because of it. As Herbert put it in *The Sacrifice*, where Christ Himself is the speaker, "Man stole the fruit, but I must climb the tree." The rebellion of the speaker in *The Collar* is a version of Adam's rebellion, or theft, and must be redressed in the same way.

It may be that the "board" in line 1 is Christ's table, the Communion table. The speaker, under the influence of the rebellious Heart, turns from the Communion table and entertains the possibility of gaining a kind of freedom through rebellion. He asserts argumentatively that in fact he *is* free, that in effect he has not fallen: "I will abroad . . . My lines and life are free; free as the rode, | Loose as the winde, as large as store." Entertaining the notion of his own guiltlessness, supposing that his life, "as large as store," need not be "restored," he proceeds to re-enact psychologically the events of the Fall. He has only to stretch forth his hand to pluck the fruit, he tells himself: "there is fruit, | and thou hast hands." The irony implicit here is that, reaching for one fruit, as Adam did, he will simultaneously reach for the other fruit, the cordial fruit which grew on the Cross. Rebellion sets in motion, unknown to the rebel, the process which leads to atonement, and at the very moment of his psychological rebellion the speaker sets forth implications which define the mode of his redemption. The series of questions beginning in line 13 admit of the answer "no" in two different senses.

> Is the yeare onely lost to me?
> Have I no bayes to crown it?
> No flowers, no garlands gay? all blasted?
> All wasted?

The rebellious Heart intends these to be rhetorical questions, expects the obvious answer that, no, the speaker has hands and may reach for the fruit. But the fruit here, as we have seen, is not only the fruit which is the object of rebellion but also is the fruit of the Cross, the "cordiall fruit" of the Eucharist. Therefore another answer suggests itself: no, the speaker has hands and may reach for the chalice. Thus, lines 17–18 can be read in two different ways. They can represent *agreement* with the Heart, the assent of the Will, now corrupted, to the Heart's rebellious argument. Or, they can suggest the truth at which the speaker eventually will arrive. The phrase "thou hast hands," therefore, signifies not only the hands which can rebelliously reach for the fruit, or the hands which *might* reach for the chalice, but the hands which *were* nailed to the Cross. Similarly, in view of the pun on "cordiall," the word "heart" in line 17 may also be identified with Christ. Christ is, in a sense, the speaker's "real" heart. These double meanings, themselves a kind of transubstantiation, the interpretation of two realms, anticipate the conclusion of the poem, in which the speaker and Christ are united analogically, both being "children" of God.

In addition, a third category of reference may be discerned here. The poem is also about the writing of poetry. The imagery of the questions just dealt with—bays, flowers, garlands—traditionally has been associated with poetry, as it is, for example, in *Lycidas* and in Carew's *An Elegy upon the Death of the Dean of Paul's, Dr. John Donne*. Herbert's use of such imagery here thus suggests a connection between loss of poetic power and the speaker's separation from the restorative powers of the Eucharist. The Eucharist, indeed, linking as it did two disparate realms, may be seen to have been the perfect symbol for the metaphysical conceit. Furthermore, if we do consider the flower imagery here to be associated with poetry, we may see that the rebellious Heart is longing for the *wrong* kind of poetry. In *Jordan*, we recall, Herbert rejected the pastoral mode, among others, as "false," and asserted that in plainly saying "My God, My King" he was expressing truth directly. In a similar way, the pastoral imagery employed by the rebellious Heart in *The Collar* is to be replaced by the "plain" truth of the last line.

The implication is also present in *The Collar* that the *form* of poetry is a kind of analogue of the order epitomized by the Eucharist. When the poet's "lines are free," that is, when his rhetoric escapes from poetic form, he has no bays and garlands, or poems, to crown the year. The rebellious Heart, ironically enough, does not see that even "false" poetry, pastoral poetry, requires the order of poetic form, does not see that rebellion against order is ultimately destructive even of inferior poetry. Helen White has pointed out that after these lines about garlands and bays the imagery becomes more vulgar as the emotion expressed grows "more fierce and wilde." [5] At the end of the poem, when the speaker's impulse toward rebellion has been overcome and he has recovered his sense of his relation to God, his lines begin to lose their "freedom," and poetic order returns along with moral and theological order.

In lines 19–34, the Heart goes on with its counsel of rebellion, oblivious to the implications we have found in lines 17–18. The Heart urges the poet-priest to seek "double pleasures," to regard the law (which, ironically, is operating silently in the very vocabulary of the poem) as a "rope of sands." "Leave thy cold dispute | Of what is fit, and not," the Heart urges. These lines are illuminated by Herbert's remark in *A Priest to the Temple* that "Contentiousnesse in a feast of Charity is more scandal than any posture." [6] Such "dispute" as, according to the Heart, the poet-priest has been engaged in is alien to the spirit of the sacrament. Perhaps, then, we can read these lines as suggesting that it has been "cold dispute" which has, at least in part, caused the poet-priest to lose his sense of the power of the Eucharist, a sense recovered by the "childlike" consciousness of the poem's conclusion (cf. "Unless you become like children . . . ," *Matthew* 18:3–4). At any rate, in lines 19–34 the Heart urges rebellion in peremptory terms. A chief result of the Fall, mortality, should not be feared: "Call in thy death's head there." But double meanings here, as previously, provide an undercurrent of ironic commentary on the Heart's speech. "He that forbears | To suit and serve his need, | Deserves his load" seems at first merely to justify rebellion. But looked at again, "suit" takes on the color of "Shall I be still in suit" (line 6), and the lines may be read as suggesting: "he that does not seek redemption deserves the burden of his sin."

Yet even as the speaker, under the influence of the rebellious Heart, raves and grows more wild, the ironies of the earlier lines are asserting themselves for his benefit. The line endings, we notice, reflect a gathering of order. Starting with line 27, earlier random endings are succeeded by a steady pattern of assonances (heed/abroad, fears/forbears, need/load, wilde/word, Child/Lord). And this re-assertion of pattern is heralded by the unsubtle *abba* rhyme of thee/draw/law/see, which brings to an abrupt end the chaotic rhyming of the first half of the poem. As Joseph Summers has summarized the function of form in this poem: "until the final four lines, the poem dramatizes expertly and convincingly the revolt of the heart, and its imitation of colloquial speech almost convinces us of the justice of the cause. But the disorder of the poem provides a constant implicit criticism, and with the final lines we recognize that *The Collar* is a narrative in the past tense: the message of the present concerns the necessity of order." [7]

We may now see what law obtains at the supernatural court in which the speaker, unawares, was "in suit." The re-establishment of order follows upon, is entailed by, rebellion. The speaker began by asserting the validity of rebellion. He then identified himself with Adam, imagined himself reaching for the fruit that brought about man's Fall. But the law remained in operation: the hands that reach for the fruit of rebellion reach also, unknown to the speaker when he is under the influence of the Heart, for Christ, reach for the chalice ("cordiall fruit," " corn," "wine") which, such is God's power, restores the speaker to his proper relationship to God. Line 34, indeed, admits of two interpretations. The speaker grows more fierce and wild "at every word"; but, also, "at every word" in the poem he now hears the voice of God: "Me thoughts I heard one calling, *Child!* | And I reply'd, *My Lord.*" The speaker's heart, previously united with Christ by means of *double entendre,* is now united with Him in a relationship which is part of the speaker's awareness: both Christ and His surrogate, the Priest who administers the Eucharist, are children of God. The moral hierarchy, epitomized in the hierarchy of father and son, and of Father and Son, has been restored.

NOTES

[1] Joseph Summers, *George Herbert: His Religion and Art* (London: Chatto & Windus, 1954), p. 90.

[2] Summers, p. 91.

[3] For these and other examples of Herbert's use of this kind of imagery, see Rosemond Tuve, *A Reading of George Herbert* (Chicago: Univ. of Chicago Press, 1952), pp. 81–87.

[4] *The Works of George Herbert,* ed. F. E. Hutchinson (Oxford: Clarendon Press, 1941), p. 531.

[5] Helen White, *The Metaphysical Poets* (New York: Macmillan, 1936), p. 183.

[6] *The Works of George Herbert,* p. 259.

[7] Summers, p. 92.

ARNOLD STEIN

🖎

George Herbert: The Art of Plainness

As a religious poet Herbert addresses God directly or writes with the intention of being overheard by Him. For traditional and for contemporary reasons, both religious and secular in origin, he aspires to an art of plainness that can achieve absolute sincerity. He is impatient with art but must practice patience. He distrusts rhetoric—as who does not? —but in order to speak sincerely he must master the rhetoric of sincerity.

Some of his more severe claims, assertions, and rejections lend themselves, a little too easily, to the purposes of critical definition. But we do not need to take him at his word in poems like the two sonnets which, according to Walton, were addressed to his mother, or in the pair of sonnets entitled "Love" (I and II). In these poems the contest between human and divine love is presented as if it were a moral scandal, to be treated only in terms of extreme contrasts and a single range of emotion. Everything is externalized, as if a safe imaginative distance were the only proper course. If plainness has anything to do with forthrightness and with the manner attributed to plain dealers, then we must acknowledge a kind of plainness in these poems, though they lack something in art. The case against their sincerity would have to point out that the attitude assumed by the author, and eloquently expressed, does not cost him very much. The desire to believe lends energy, vividness, sharpness, but not precision, depth, or fineness to the expression. When we speak of the rhetoric of sincerity, it is not with such poems in mind.

This is the shorter version of Chapter 1 of *George Herbert's Lyrics* (Baltimore: The Johns Hopkins Press, 1968). Reprinted by permission of The Johns Hopkins Press.

Let us turn to a poem which does not offer a stiff rejection but raises questions, and in a very mild and casual manner seems to present a radical solution. The poem is "A true Hymne," which begins:

> My joy, my life, my crown!
> My heart was meaning all the day,
> Somewhat it fain would say:
> And still it runneth mutt'ring up and down
> With onely this, *My joy, my life, my crown.*

Herbert then goes on to defend these words, which "may take part / Among the best in art" if they are "truly said." We may suspect that the naïvety is in part cultivated; it is plainly meant, however, and comes from a refinement of knowledge rather than a lack of knowledge. These words are symbols; they represent precious wisdom, the soul of living truth which the speaker may pronounce without possessing. It is hard to say them "truly"; the heart was "meaning" them all the day, but even the heart is uncertain—"Somewhat it fain would say," and it runs "mutt'ring up and down." The value of these words, whether in private thought or in art, depends on understanding what they mean and saying them truly.

Herbert ends the second stanza with a firm declaration:

> The finenesse which a hymne or psalme affords,
> Is, when the soul unto the lines accords.

This, though it has an admirable ring and expresses one clear concept of poetic sincerity, does not quite face the problems that have been raised. The accordance of the soul may assume that the heart has understood and that the words have been "truly said," but we are not told how these vital steps are taken, or even that they have been taken. Instead, we have been given a partial definition, which is then extended by a charming example of negative illustration—a whole stanza that shows how not to do it:

> He who craves all the minde,
> And all the soul, and strength, and time,
> If the words onely ryme,
> Justly complains, that somewhat is behinde
> To make his verse, or write a hymne in kinde.

The amused incoherence of the stanza parodies the ambitious poet who starts with high resolution and finds himself hung up, forcing rhyme, splicing syntax, and barely staggering through. After the brave opening, the only words that ring true are "Justly complains." Furthermore, the grounds have been shifted, and we have not followed up the problem of how the words are to be "truly said" or how that accordance of the soul is to be achieved.

The last stanza presents a solution that is indirectly relevant to the problems of literary expression but directly relevant to the heart seeking to address God:

> Whereas if th' heart be moved,
> Although the verse be somewhat scant,
> God doth supplie the want.
> As when th' heart sayes (sighing to be approved)
> O, could I love! and stops: God writeth, Loved.

We come to see that the writing of poetry has not been at the center of the poem after all. Instead, Herbert has used art as a metaphor to express an experience of religious life. In life, if not in art, the "somewhat scant" expression of the sincere heart may be amended and completed by God. When God writes "Loved," the desire to articulate and the desire to love are at once fulfilled. Their ends are achieved without the ordinary steps of a humanly conducted process. By authoritative acknowledgment virtual expression becomes actual.

If we look at the poem from one point of view, a miracle has taken place; but from another point of view we need recognize only an inspired compression—always possible in dialogue if the correspondent understands the intention, approves it, and fully reciprocates. We may observe, therefore, that Herbert is not simply invoking a miracle, for the ends of expression may often be realized without the full use of normal means. What we cannot do, however, is take the metaphorical analogy of writing poetry as if it were literal. Sincere feelings do not of themselves produce good poems. Herbert surely knew this as well as we do. But he must also have believed that whenever he felt a poem of his to be successful, God's hand had guided his in the composition; and if he felt a poem to be successful that feeling was the sure sense that the expression had realized its end, that God had blessed the end and given him the feeling by reflection. The humility of the man of God and the humility of the artist might both acknowledge that a fumbling, "muttering" intention had by some unexpected swiftness been clarified, and that the awkward wrongness of initial and intermediate stages had somehow been transformed into the triumphantly graceful and right. In retrospect, even the labor of composition—like some fictional by-product of the creative process—might seem to be compressed into a decisive instant of time. (Poets are notoriously inaccurate in reporting on these matters and prefer to believe that their perfect poems were "dictated": which is what we prefer to believe when the evidence to the contrary does not interfere.)

There are at least two ways, then, of looking at the issues raised by this poem. I have been emphasizing the "normal" conditions of the creative process because I am primarily interested in the poet Herbert; and because I am convinced that the religious lyric, though it must fulfill special conditions, must also, and does, answer all the questions we ask of other lyrics. From a literary standpoint the central metaphor of the poem can be interpreted as analogous to the ways in which inspiration figures in the writing of poems. Inspiration is of course the kind of concept that easily crosses a line between the secular and the sacred, and for Herbert so too does the act, or the metaphor, of writing poems. In this poem we are free to interpret the analogy, so long as we recognize that it is a metaphor and is not to be taken literally. But we must also recognize that, for Herbert, though the metaphor may apply to the writing of poetry it has been superseded, as it were, by the higher form of expression to which it refers. The wisdom descending from God crowns, not with understanding but with love, an apparently clumsy human effort to understand and express. We do not expect Herbert to be dissatisfied with the attainment of such an end simply because the means do not seem to justify it. But we do not therefore think Herbert believed that this was the way to write poems, and that the individual details of thought and expression might safely be ignored because they would leap intervening stages if only "th' heart be moved." Herbert knew better, both as poet and as man of God. That he hoped, humbly, for the easier path of inspiration—one does not need to be either poetic or religious to feel the attraction of that course.

But Herbert's metaphors are capable of moving in more than two directions. The central fiction of writing poetry, which may refer to the real writing of poetry and to something real in the experience of religious life, may have still a third reference. In presenting the fictional account Herbert is at the same time confessing his own unworthiness, his own desire, and intimating the authentic joy which he would feel if what he is describing should happen to him. In other words, the narrative is also a concealed prayer, composed by one of the modern masters of that difficult decorum and rhetoric by means of which one may properly address God and suggest to Him certain courses for human affairs.

And so the cultivated clumsiness of the poem, the shifting of grounds, the apparent naïvety, and what may have seemed to be a radical solution to the problems of writing poetry, when taken together are something else, or several things else. But if we are at all right about the poem it cannot be taken as a simple assertion about poetry; what seems to be assertion is ultimately part of a complex and tactful statement. Yet we cannot stop here, at the satisfying literary position. We must remember that, for Herbert, the metaphor of writing is in the poem superseded by the fulfillment of the end of expression—here a confirming act which writes and rhymes as poetry but means as metaphor. If he himself believes in the fiction of his poem, then he will find its conclusion a happier one than most of his poems provide, and toward the slower, labored uncertainties of most composition he will feel some understandable impatience.

At this point, if there were time, I should want to comment on the kind of plain style we find in "The Church-Porch," and to look at some poems in which Herbert accepts, or even flaunts, a division between truth and beauty. But these poems do not finally say anything distinctive or resonant. The gestures of sincerity by which art is used to expose art can at best make but limited points. A better and more characteristic performance is "The Forerunners." Whatever else he is saying in the poem, Herbert is also bidding a fictional farewell to poetry, to the "sweet phrases, lovely metaphors," which he has rescued from the poetic "brothels" in order to bring into the church, repentant and renewed: "My God must have my best, ev'n all I had." The excitement and affection of his address could serve as well for arrival as for departure: "Lovely enchanting language, sugar-cane,/ Honey of roses," he exclaims, as preface to imagining the unfortunate relapse as poetry returns to its old ways. He argues against what he knows will happen, and in doing so marks both a separateness of truth and beauty and the bridge of normal relations that leads to their unity:

> Let follie speak in her own native tongue.
> True beautie dwells on high: ours is a flame
>   But borrow'd thence to light us thither.
> Beautie and beauteous words should go together.

Here Platonic solution is emphasized, rather than Platonic division. The statement is handsome and, as well as we can judge from the context and from other poems, heartfelt—a major poetic belief, but not therefore the guiding inspiration of every lyrical utterance.

"Yet if you go," he adds, meaning, when you go, as the poet prepares
to settle down for a final accounting:

> Yet if you go, I passe not; take your way:
> For, *Thou art still my God,* is all that ye
> Perhaps with more embellishment can say.

And so a significant division appears, if not between truth and beauty,
at least between "true beauty" and what can be said in words. That
words are treated as no more than a conventionally detachable garment
of style may seem a little disappointing, but Herbert does at least say
"perhaps." Besides, in the context of the poem "Thou art still my God"
is an ultimate expression, one that can be and is developed in other
poems but cannot be here. Its meaning cannot be improved upon, and
the man preparing to give up everything will not need anything else.
The expression is complete, syntactically and otherwise, as the plain
saying of "My God, my King" and "My joy, my life, my crown" are
not. Nor does the poet's own attitude toward poetic language remotely
resemble the stiff certitude with which he elsewhere rejects the misguided efforts of misguided poets. He is not rejecting here but parting,
and with fine reluctance and such sweet sorrow.

In "The Forerunners" the act of writing poetry stands for the means,
made visible and audible, of communing with God; it is a human invention motivated by a borrowed flame "to light us thither," a means
of returning to the source of beauty. The house of the church, the
house of poetry, and the house of life, the "best room" of which is the
heart, are in the poem all reduced to an essential state. As the visible
church stands truly, beautifully, but imperfectly for the invisible church,
so do the "sweet phrases, lovely metaphors" express imperfectly the
"True beautie" on high. In its plainness the essential expression, "Thou
art still my God," will fulfill the end of expression, "And if I please
him, I write fine and wittie." The essentiality of the expression, when
one contemplates its meaning, by itself and in the context of the poem,
would seem to be better established than the poet's assurance of
writing "fine and wittie." That claim one may perhaps regard as a little
assertive, markedly different from the persuasive tact with which art
demonstrates the limitations of art in the argument of the poem.

The distinction is a fine one but it needs to be made. I mentioned
earlier that if Herbert felt a poem to be successful he would need to
believe that the expression had realized its end of pleasing God, and
that God had given him his feeling by reflection. But he does not
practice the art of silence or the art of discovering only the essential

expression, which he can then merely "mutter." He writes poems, even when their aim is to express, or transcend, the inadequacy of poetic expression. We may perhaps regard "Thou art still my God" as a symbolic plainness, an ideal to which his poetic art of plainness may aspire, but it is not itself an expression of that art.

I think we can put matters in the right perspective by drawing a distinction between the symbolic plainness of an ultimate expression and the plainness of a complete poetic action. The latter may (and in Herbert often does) move toward a clarification that resembles the symbolic plainness. But if the poetic action is complete its conclusion will be the result of a process of expression. Though the "true beauty" of "Thou art still my God" may be traced to the compressed inner meaning the expression holds for Herbert, nevertheless that statement does appear three times in the poem, and it works both with and against other statements. In "The Flower" Herbert makes another absolute statement: "Thy word is all, if we could spell." Some of his poems are advanced spelling lessons. If "The Forerunners" were, say, a poem like "Aaron," its process might have included some parsing of the implicit relations between "thou" and "my," or between "art" and "still."

Herbert is acutely aware, as poet and as Christian, of deception, evasiveness, and inadequacy within himself—and, for these, traditional attitudes toward language and art provided useful and established symbols. Besides, many of his more assertive poems take up positions that he does not intend to carry through uncritically. A paradox that furnishes much of his poetic material may help explain why the single attitude is often countered within its own poem and opposed by other poems. The "grosser world," toward the beauty and importance of which the poet feels conflicting emotions, is, in spite of his feelings, a fixed and orderly world regulated by the "word and art" of God. It is the "diviner world of grace" which suddenly alters, and of which God is every day "a new Creatour." [1]

What Herbert writes in "Superliminare" may be applied to all instances when he engages himself to "Copie out onely" this or that. He will admit

> Nothing but holy, pure, and cleare,
> Or that which groneth to be so.

That is a program which leaves room for and grants validity to the hopes of individual effort, without regard to cost and efficiency. Herbert's most important subject is the mystery of God's art with man, a subject he confronts with patience and imagination, both passionately involved and scrupulously detached. That God's art with man reveals God's nature he takes for granted, and he assumes that the mysteries which God has concealed in man encourage the study of things human as an authorized reflection of things divine.

We may put these observations together by saying that Herbert does not give us a single, consistent attitude toward expression, that his art of plainness does not bear a single stamp, and that his arguments with God are conducted with great freedom and inventiveness. Whenever as critics we take a single example as our model to copy, we become aware of statements on the other side and of stylistic demonstrations that force us to widen our definitions. From one point of view we may be satisfied to locate the essential Herbert in the ringing declarations of "H. Baptisme" (II): "Let me be soft and supple to thy will. . . . My soul bid nothing. . . . Childhood is health." But softness must be "tempered" and suppleness must exert itself in order to be what it is. We do not know enough when we know that the goal expressed so simply is a difficult one to achieve, and that the verbal summation stands for detailed, strenuous efforts by an individual conscious that millions of human beings have in effect said the same thing and have both failed and succeeded. Our general knowledge must also "descend to particulars," for exactness lies not in any general statement but in the clarified order which poetry may achieve when particular expressions work with and against each other. In Herbert's poetry the soul has other lessons to learn, not all of them compatible with what is here presented as the sum of wisdom. For the soul that bids nothing may hear nothing; nor is that spiritual state exempt from posing and artful presumption. Childhood is not health at all in "Mortification," but is only one of several stages in the art of dying. That art would seem to be more valuable than spiritual health itself; for the art of knowing possesses more fully whatever it desires and gains, and Herbert never deviates long from this old principle, which represents the uneasy, but enduring and fruitful, marriage of Athens and Jerusalem. Childhood generally symbolizes the will in his poems, but the education of the will is the patient task of intelligence, and Herbert, to his honor, seldom trusts for long any of the attractive substitutes for intelligence. Even that most famous conversion of "The Collar"—"Me thoughts I heard one calling, *Child! / And I reply'd, My Lord*"—rests on the demonstration of an argument that has ruined itself.

As for his plainness, which is not all of one kind, it is above all a rhetoric of sincerity, an art by which he may tell the truth to himself and God. The major devices are not traditional figures but psychological gestures and movements. The excesses of cheerful confidence and the defections of faith decked out as humility are given their full human voice, not as exotic monsters of thought and feeling, but as common faults "whose natures are most stealing, and beginnings uncertaine," faults which are most tenacious when they are not allowed to expose themselves by speaking in their "own native tongue." Belief in the divine desire for human desire grants the human feelings an essential dignity, even in error, and encourages a vigorous freedom of expression. That freedom comes under the general laws of art, and is enlarged, not restricted, by the necessities of religious tact and discipline—as it is enlarged by realizing the complex demands of poetic form.

I propose now to offer more than a token and less than a complete demonstration of his art of plainness by drawing upon three poems: "The Temper" (I), "The Pearl," and "Death."

"The Temper" (I) begins with a declaration:

> How should I praise thee, Lord! how should my rymes
> Gladly engrave thy love in steel,
> If what my soul doth feel sometimes,
> My soul might ever feel!

And ends with a declaration:

> Whether I flie with angels, fall with dust,
> Thy hands made both, and I am there:
> Thy power and love, my love and trust
> Make one place ev'ry where.

The "plain intention" of the poem is to transform its initial attitude into its concluding one. Our best approach, I think, is from the lines in "Love" (II) where God is asked:

> And kindle in our hearts such true desires,
> As may consume our lusts, and make thee way.

Most of "The Temper" is devoted to the consuming of false love, but the kindling of true desire coincides with the opening lines of the poem, which speak in the high hortatory voice of love convinced that it is sincere and deserves to have its way. The "how should" and the "if" mark the fiction that represents real desire and invokes the conventions of literary and religious praise. Although the power and sweep of the language obscure the personal motive, which is not in the conventions of praise an illegitimate one, Herbert's characteristic exercise of religious propriety never allows personal desire to speak for the whole man without some discriminating process of clarification. "Gladly engrave thy love in steel" rings beautifully, but pretends to forget that the only standard is God's approval of the offering. The poet's desire is not absurd, but he knows that its expression is, and he compensates in the second stanza by acting out his pretentiousness. If there are forty heavens, or more, when things are right with him he can "peere" over them all. At other times "I hardly reach a score." And sometimes there is a general minus, without arithmetic: "to hell I fall." The kindling and consuming are most intense in the next three stanzas, which clarify the issues and stand apart from the first and last two stanzas. In the middle three stanzas the excesses of pride and humility strive against each other in images of expansion and contraction, and in the movements up and down of actual and psychological space:

> O rack me not to such a vast extent;
>   Those distances belong to thee:
> The world's too little for thy tent,
>   A grave too big for me.

> Wilt thou meet arms with man, that thou dost stretch
>   A crumme of dust from heav'n to hell?
> Will great God measure with a wretch?
>   Shall he thy stature spell?

> O let me, when thy roof my soul hath hid,
>   O let me roost and nestle there:
> Then of a sinner thou art rid,
>   And I of hope and fear.

This ·last stanza (the fifth) is like the first in advancing personal desire while paying tribute to God. We may note that the eloquence of humility is no less moving, no less an expression of real desire, and no less wrong, than the eloquence of pride. By now the two extremes have exhausted each other, and some *tertium quid* must be called on to make peace. The sixth stanza explains the emblematic title, declares acceptance of the divine will, and advances the metaphor of music as a solution to the problem of praise:

> Yet take thy way; for sure thy way is best:
>   Stretch or contract me, thy poore debter:

> This is but tuning of my breast,
>   To make the musick better.

And so the stanza completes the action of consuming false love by translating the experiences of the poem into terms of acceptance which draw a moral. The metaphor of music discovers a retroactive purpose in the contradictions, a purpose which may also govern present and future action. But Herbert does not stop here, for the kindling and consuming have served "to make thee way," and the seventh stanza is the demonstration of what can happen when way has been made for God:

> Whether I flie with angels, fall with dust,
>   Thy hands made both, and I am there:
> Thy power and love, my love and trust
>   Make one place ev'ry where.

One may perhaps describe the metaphor of music as a rational discovery which orders in a quiet, reasonable way the passionate contradictions which have been expressed. But the final stanza establishes, without reference to music, a concord that is more comprehensive. In the language of religion the difference resembles that between intellectual acceptance and entire resignation. Herbert himself might well have thought that the old, restrictive terms were consumed in order to make way for the new, and that he was himself, in a minor, personal way, copying the process by which truth had once come to light—in Augustine's summary statement: "the New Testament reveals what was concealed in the Old." [2] In "The Quip" Herbert refuses the arguments of his opponents for he has a single answer ready penned; here the arguments come from his own soul and he must work through them to reach his answer. The simple perfection of that answer cannot be anticipated but comes suddenly, and after a slight pause.

Although the final stanza may be said to express and to demonstrate religious resignation, we may approach it from the traditions of rhetoric. First, we may draw on Aristotle's point that of the three "modes of persuasion furnished by the spoken word" the most important, by and large, is "the personal goodness revealed by the speaker"; in fact, "his character may almost be called the most effective means of persuasion he possesses." [3] Christian rhetoric accepts the point and advances it; where the unity of eloquence and wisdom occurs we may assume the effective presence of inspiration as a proof of character. The chief goal of eloquence is to move, and Christian high style could be thought of as assimilating all the characteristics of the plain style, deriving its elevation primarily from the personal fervor with which the saving truth was expressed.

The last stanza will not fit into a rhetorical category of style. It is adorned and elevated, but the dominant effect is that of plainness and simplicity. The graces of art are subtle though not inscrutable; and we could point to devices not in the handbooks of rhetoric (as Augustine is pleased to note of a passage from the Book of Amos),[4] and perhaps not even in the annals of microlinguistics. But we may spare that demonstration for now. The issues of the poem are resolved in a final expression that unites beauty and truth, eloquence and wisdom. There is no point of leverage for distinguishing between what is said, and the authoritative gift of being able to say it: inspiration is the proof of character. An expression as complete and as final in its way as "Thou art still my God" has emerged from a developing pattern of conflict; and although that expression can stand alone, it was created in the act of completing the poem, and it answers all the immediacies of conflict and form. It can stand alone but does not insist on its privilege, as a few ready-penned expressions make some show of doing. We may perhaps apply Herbert's metaphor of wisdom descending from above, the silk twist let down; though in "The Pearl" inspiration must precede and direct the poem in order to be present for the final confirmation. Or we may say that in "The Temper" when the poet stopped God wrote "loved" and spelled it out in a whole stanza.

Our next example is "The Pearl," a poem with a simpler argument and a basic plot—that of rejecting the ways of the world, the flesh, and the devil, each in a stanza. A final stanza explains why, clarifies the issues, confirms the character of the speaker, and in a simple statement organizes the procedures of the poem into their completed form. We find no acting out of inspiration at the end, but instead a quietly effective definition of the ways of love and understanding. In the penultimate stanza, for the sake of an ultimate plainness the poet unexpectedly elevates the plain style that has been serving him with perfect ease and variety.

The plot is basic and the formula for human temptation is the standard one, but Herbert's conception and performance are markedly fresh and individual. The temptation of the devil, as intellectual pride, he puts first. It is not a temptation at all but little more than an inventory, and not even an explicit rejection. By putting intellectual pride first but not treating it as pride, and by his casual manner and racy diction, he exhibits a surprising and witty indifference to the traditional power of that temptation. Indeed, if we do not recognize the historical issue, the first appearance of the refrain, "Yet I love thee," may seem a little forced and overemphatic. As the poem develops, and as we collect our bearings in motion, we are supposed to recognize that pride is not being located in the intellect alone but is distributed throughout all decisions involving a choice between the love of self and the love of God. In the second stanza the temptations of the world are rejected, without the dignity of a formal recognition but in the course of drawing up an inventory of the ways of honor. The casual raciness becomes intensified, and the tone advances to open mockery:

> I know the wayes of Honour, what maintains
> The quick returns of courtesie and wit:
> In vies of favours whether partie gains,
> When glorie swells the heart, and moldeth it
> To all expressions both of hand and eye,
> Which on the world a true-love-knot may tie,
> And bear the bundle, wheresoe're it goes:
> How many drammes of spirit there must be
> To sell my life unto my friends or foes:
>   Yet I love thee.

Then the third and climactic stanza presents the temptation of the flesh, the ways of pleasure. One does not expect to meet sensitively intelligent Christians who are confident that they are untempted by intellectual pride and the subtle allurements of the world; one expects even less to learn that so rare a person is frankly responsive to the appeals of pleasure:

> I know the wayes of Pleasure, the sweet strains,
> The lullings and the relishes of it;
> The propositions of hot bloud and brains;
> What mirth and musick mean; what love and wit
> Have done these twentie hundred yeares, and more:
> I know the projects of unbridled store:
> My stuffe is flesh, not brasse; my senses live,
> And grumble oft, that they have more in me
> Then he that curbs them, being but one to five:
>   Yet I love thee

These are not, to be sure, the common temptations of the flesh but reflect a refined, more philosophical, concept of pleasure—as if Herbert were revising Socrates' fable in the *Phaedrus* and attributing rebelliousness to the spirited horse of the psychic team. A twentieth-century reader might resent the antique novelty of assigning the products of culture to the ways of pleasure, but he might find some compensation in the formal emphasis on knowledge that echoes through the stanza: "mirth and musick *mean*," and the introductory expression, "I know," is used a second time only in this stanza. What is most distinctive, however, is the passionate immediacy, the full identification of the poet with the feelings expressed. The nonchalance of witty indifference abruptly disappears; and the stanza excludes, for the moment, those quantitative images of profit and loss which partly reflect the amused detachment and superiority of the speaker—the "stock and surplus," "quick returns," "gains," and "drammes of spirit." The controls of knowledge and love are not broken down, but they remain external and neither repress the feelings nor enter into their expression. As for the temptation itself, it is not considered in a formal way, but its presence and force are amply represented by the language of the speaker.

As a measure of Herbert's boldness and candor it is useful to quote an authoritative diagnosis of the symptoms and etiology of imaginative self-temptation. When, according to Augustine, the soul slackens in its powers of determination, the body will try to advance its own interests. Delighted by "corporeal forms and movements," the soul then "becomes entangled with their images which it has fixed in its memory, and is foully defiled by the fornications of the phantasy." When the soul places the end of its own good in the sensuous, it "snatches the deceptive images of corporeal things from within and combines them together by empty thought, so that nothing seems to it to be divine unless it be of such a kind as this." [5] Augustine's diagnosis, with its adaptation of Platonic and Stoic features, may describe the rebellious imagination as we see it, for instance, in "The Collar," and it may help identify an occasional lapse in Herbert's spiritual nerve, but it is remarkably irrelevant to the "corporeal forms and movements" of his third stanza. The feelings expressed there have dignity; they are immediate and real, without defilement and resulting self-hatred, and without confusions of the divine. In fact, only the ways of honor come directly under Augustine's analysis, for they are the artificial products of illusive symbolizing, the "deceptive images" patched together with "empty thought."

The first and second stanzas, we noted, resemble each other in their amused detachment. Their plain style is that of argument, which demonstrates indirectly, by witty analysis, that the major temptations do not tempt at all. The greater intensity of the second stanza by moving toward mockery increases the imaginative distance between the objects discussed and the speaker. The plain style of the last stanza will reverse that direction. It is argument, and intellectual, but not detached. Everything is drawn together, and toward the poet at the center of his experience. But the decisive change is initiated by the third stanza with its personal fervor and elevated style.

Let us compare in their relations these last two stanzas and the last two stanzas of "The Temper" (I). In that poem the penultimate stanza ("Yet take thy way; for sure thy way is best") presents an intellectual acceptance which is rather dry and detached but provides the necessary bridge to the comprehensive solution of the last stanza, which is highly charged with feeling but registers as an inspired clarification. In "The Pearl" the general procedure is the same but the parts are reversed. The conflict does not take shape until the penultimate stanza, where the climax also occurs; that stanza brings about the shift in direction from analytical distance to synthetic immediacy, as the necessary bridge to the comprehensive solution of the last stanza. In "The Pearl" it is the penultimate stanza which is elevated in style and charged with feeling. But its expression is, though intense and candid, consciously limited by the external controls of the context; it cannot speak for the whole man in the poem. Though eloquent and moving, the voice of the stanza cannot possibly bring eloquence and wisdom into the unison of a single speech. The last stanza names inspired wisdom as a presence which has governed the whole action of the poem, but which does not, as in "The Temper" (I), make a personal appearance. The clarification of love and understanding is quietly intellectual, not passionate, and includes the humble disclaimer that whatever has been accomplished by the poem was merely by following instructions:

> Yet through these labyrinths, not my groveling wit,
> But thy silk twist let down from heav'n to me,
> Did both conduct and teach me, how by it
> To climbe to thee.

In this poem there is no pause inviting God to write the last stanza; an affirming act of the intellect builds on a moment of passion, rather than the reverse. But the proof of character lies in the integration and in the poet's being at one with what he says. There has been no spectacular inspiration, but everything has been drawn together, and the silk twist which has led him through the labyrinths has brought him to the expressive center of what he concludes.

Our final example is the poem "Death," which acknowledges no conflict. The fictional pretext is a slight and transparent one: the difference between the way we used to look at death and the way we look at it now. The plot is not likely to surprise, and since there is no formal conflict the poet's own feelings do not directly participate in the action. Coming to the poem after "The Temper" (I) and "The Pearl," one is at first perhaps more conscious of the differences, but the similarities are more significant.

As in many poems that are relatively straightforward and simple in statement, Herbert invents fine devices on which the materials turn, move, and develop—as if they were proceeding by means of the more visible structures of argument, dramatic conflict, or narrative plot. Each stanza of "Death" is a kind of self-contained scene, into which the last line brings an unexpected effect. The reader is not likely to be aware that an argument is also being produced, until he encounters the open "Therefore" at the beginning of the sixth and last stanza. There are three parts of the argument, arranged in a formal diminution of 3:2:1. The first three stanzas give us the old wrong views of death, the next two corrected present views, and the conclusion is drawn in a single stanza. Let us begin with the first three:

> Death, thou wast once an uncouth hideous thing,
> Nothing but bones,
> The sad effect of sadder grones:
> Thy mouth was open, but thou couldst not sing.
>
> For we consider'd thee as at some six
> Or ten yeares hence,
> After the losse of life and sense,
> Flesh being turn'd to dust, and bones to sticks.
>
> We lookt on this side of thee, shooting short;
> Where we did finde
> The shells of fledge souls left behinde,
> Dry dust, which sheds no tears, but may extort.

The mementos of death are handled with remarkable verve and gaiety. Of "The Temper" (I) we could say that the intention of the poem was to transform its initial declaration into its concluding one. Here we have attitudes rather than declarations; and that strange, bluff greeting to death, though startling, original, and arbitrary, does not register at once as a "wrong" attitude asking for correction. Nevertheless, the tone is the exaggerated one of an extreme which the development of the poem will transform. If we borrow an observation from our study of "The Pearl," we may describe the speaker's opening attitude as detached and superior, as if enjoying his analytical distance from the object of his attention. In the fifth stanza the tone will be countered by an opposite extreme of immediacy and identification. Then the argument, expression, and tone of the last stanza will transform the extremes of psychic distance and immediacy into a final attitude.

The second and third stanzas drop the concentrated focus on skull, bones, and grinning jaws, and drop the harsh, summary definition of life as a music of groans, and death as the arrested image of that music. The reason now given for that hideousness is not concentrated and shocking but leisurely and general, as befits an intellectual speculation prefaced by "For we consider'd." The error in human understanding is caused by our faulty sense of time. We think in spans of six or ten years from now and judge death by its appearances then. The detachment is quietly intellectual but does not therefore eliminate some tension of divided attitude. The reader will not find that the studied casualness of rhythm, tone, and detail prevents him from considering any thought of his own death, "some six / Or ten years hence." Furthermore, the ironic turn in the last line of each stanza reintroduces the opportunity for personal concern and relation: "Flesh being turn'd to dust, and bones to sticks. . . . Dry dust, which sheds no tears, but may extort." And that beautiful euphemism for skeletal remains, "The shells of fledge souls left behinde," is a little too successful; we admire the imaginative act and in so doing are reminded of the natural state of the material thus translated.

In addition to these psychological movements which endue a sense of developing conflict, we may note the presence of significant atttiudes toward time. The first stanza greets death as it was, not once upon a time but "once," as it was in time past. But the imaginative time of that stanza is the feeling-present, which the shock of the image produces, in spite of the summary intellectualizing of the cause in the immediate past and the assertion that all of this visible effect is not what it seems to be but is what it was "once." The assertion is left dangling as a challenge that is to be made good, but not in the formal time of the second and third stanzas, which does not go all the way back to the "once." The feeling-present returns, though less emphatically, in the suggestions of personal death and in the reference to the dust "which sheds no tears, but may extort." Still more elusively, the sense of future time enters these stanzas. There is an ambiguity in

the "six / Or ten years hence"—depending on whether we were considering the case of stanza one, or were considering some case, perhaps
our own, from a point in the past identical with our consideration and
extending six to ten years into the future. But since the point in the
past is not located firmly, the sense of future time is at best weak.
Similarly, the flesh and bones "being turn'd" to dust and sticks presents
us with a free composition of past, present, and future; any single
dimension of time can dominate in that formula, depending on the
formal perspective. Finally, the "fledge souls" do evoke the future in a
definite but small way; the transaction itself points ahead, and the
habits of metaphorical thought on this familiar subject move naturally
from the place "left behinde" to the far future.

Everything we have considered thus far will reappear, with changes,
in the next step of the argument, which begins in the fourth stanza:

> But since our Saviours death did put some bloud
>   Into thy face;
>   Thou art grown fair and full of grace,
> Much in request, much sought for as a good.

The verve and gaiety continue, but now the mementos of death are
looked at from the perspective of life after death. Out of the conventions of that perspective Herbert draws details that emphasize
the imaginative nature of his presentation. The hideousness of
the skull in the first stanza was the product of its appearance, our
perspective, and the grotesque associations brought to bear. In the
fourth stanza the perspective and associations are changed; a show
of appearance is made, but the literal, physical terms are dominated by
their symbolic and metaphorical meanings. The language is matter-
of-fact, "But since our Saviours death did put some bloud / Into thy
face," and more comforting than "Thy mouth was open, but thou
couldst not sing"; but both statements are self-consciously imaginative,
two opposing ways of looking at death, each an exaggeration based
upon a different view of the truth. The stanza continues to emphasize
its imaginative play as it moves further from the possibility of literal
presentation. Both the face which is now "fair and full of grace" and
the beholder's eye are altered, and the newness of the relationship is
underlined by the pleasantry of "grace." The last line of the stanza
draws back a little, with a kind of wry humor far gentler than the
irony in each of the preceding last lines. Death is "Much in request"—
as if by a change in fashion. That death is "much sought for as a good"
moves the significance further from its physical base and advances

the dignity of its attractiveness by the deliberate introduction of language that has philosophical associations.

The "But since" which opens the fourth stanza is the sign both of argument and of time. Though the dominant time-sense is present it is derived from the Savior's act in the past and lightly suggests the future in "sought for as a good." The sense of the present, however, is not *felt* as in the first stanza but serves mostly as a kind of intellectual transition to the strong present of the fifth stanza. Finally, to touch again on the point of imaginative distance: the fourth stanza maintains a distinctive kind of detachment, because of its intellectualized emphasis on the metaphorical and the witty.

The fifth stanza completes the corrected view of death, bringing the poem to a sudden climax:

> For we do now behold thee gay and glad,
>> As at dooms-day;
>> When souls shall wear their new aray,
> And all thy bones with beautie shall be clad.

Each of the first three stanzas presents a thesis abruptly at the beginning and then makes additional points to tighten and complicate the scene. In the fourth and fifth stanzas the thought requires the whole four lines for its development, and in the fifth stanza rises to a declarative climax in the last line, reversing the established ironic twist of the first three stanzas and the mildly humorous withdrawal of the fourth. More important, all of the motions of detachment, all of the varieties of analytical distance in the poem are reversed in the sudden rush of imaginative immediacy.

The developing attitudes toward time are also brought to a climax, but the details are more involved and cannot be seen without analysis. Let me summarize briefly. In the first three stanzas the formal time was past, the finished past of "once" in the first stanza and a less definite, recent past in the second and third stanzas. But in the first a sense of the feeling-present dominates; in the second and third present and future both enter, but elusively. In the fourth stanza a similar blend occurs, though the formal time is present. But when we come to the fifth stanza, suddenly there is no sense of the past. The present dominates but draws its intensity from a prophetic vision of the future. That future comes into the poem strongly and positively at this one point, and fully answers the finished past of stanza one. Since that future is imagined as intensely present, the effect is a formal reply to the feeling-present of stanza one.

These answers composed of the oppositions of time and the oppositions of psychic direction are not conclusive. A quiet "Therefore" converts their striking emphasis into mere transition, as if the real answer has been waiting for the commotion to subside:

> Therefore we can go die as sleep, and trust
> Half that we have
> Unto an honest faithfull grave;
> Making our pillows either down, or dust.

Now the time is wholly present: it is the unique product of imagined past and future, but emerging also from the varying stresses on the present which have been drawn like a thread through the labyrinth to this open place. As for either analytical detachment from death or imaginative identification—the final attitude rejects the terms of the contradiction, but draws an essential indifference from detachment and an essential acceptance from identification. The human present of the last stanza copies the calm of eternity, into which no agitations of past or future intrude. Death is not an alien object exciting mixed emotions, nor a lover to be sought and embraced. The imagination of the poem has made death familiar and neutral; it can have no place even in dreams when it has been made subject to a common, everyday idiom which says, "we can go die."

The activity of the mind is less prominent than in the conclusion of "The Pearl," but as in that poem an affirming act of the intellect quietly builds on a moment of passion, and the mind that dismisses itself has demonstrated the power and clarity of its self-possession. There is no pause, as in "The Temper" (I), inviting God to write the last stanza. The spectacular inspiration comes in the prophetic vision of doomsday, which is followed by the rarest kind of personal clarity, casual and laconic, as if inspiration were part of the everyday order and could be taken for granted. The final state of simplicity is not one of reduced but of alert, refined consciousness. One sign is the attitude toward the body, which is no less than "Half that we have." And even more remarkable than calling the grave "honest" and "faithfull" is doing so with the air of not saying anything unusual. As in "The Pearl," the excited elevation of style in the penultimate stanza is followed by an authoritative descent to the plain style. In "Death" it is an assimilative plain style, confidently challenging comparison with the height of the preceding stanza. The power of that plain style lies in the passion excluded, in the resistance mastered, and in the deliberate grace of saying difficult things with ease. The grandeur and force of the high style are achieved while talking in an off-hand, humble manner in the common imagery of going to bed. An enlightened rhetorician would observe that this plain style does not austerely reject ornament, which may persuade but must first provide esthetic pleasure. He would add, I am sure, that these graces of style are so natural and fine as to seem in the very grain. The last line, "Making our pillows either down, or dust," awakens a delicate echo of the earlier ironies, as a farewell touch of recognition. And the order of "die as sleep" is beautifully reversed and balanced by "down, or dust."

I shall end by introducing another viewpoint for a moment. In reading Donne Coleridge described the delight of "tracing the leading thought thro'out the whole," by means of which "you merge yourself in the author, you *become He*." [6] Herbert he declares to be "a true poet, but a poet *sui generis*, the merits of whose poems will never be felt without a sympathy with the mind and character of the man." A true poet who requires a conscious act of sympathy would seem to have a different and lesser merit than the poet who compels you to "*become He*." Coleridge justly admires Herbert's diction, "than which nothing can be more pure, manly, and unaffected." But some of the thoughts are "quaint," and he does not try to follow a leading thought throughout. Identifying oneself with the author would seem to be a modern extension of the most important mode of rhetorical persuasion, "the personal goodness revealed by the speaker" in ancient rhetoric, or the inspired unity of wisdom and eloquence in Christian rhetoric. The merits of identifying oneself with the poet are debatable. But we can draw two firm points from Coleridge's remarks. First, it is clear that Herbert is a master who draws a leading thought through authentic obstacles which both test and refine the ultimate expression of that thought. Secondly, the rhetorical proof of character lies in the poet's convincing demonstrations that *he* becomes what he says, that the flow and shape of his words lead to a unity of eloquence and wisdom, and that he is at the expressive center of what he concludes.

It is tempting to end here, adding only that there are many true poets but few masters of this art of plainness. But it may be well to back up and remember that Herbert's art of plainness is an art and not a summary feature. If we have touched on the essential quality, good; but we can no more do without a full apparatus for understanding his art than he could write poems by plainly saying "Thou art still my God."

NOTES

[1] "The Temper" (II).

[2] *City of God*, V, xviii.

[3] *Rhetoric*, I, ii (1356ª).

[4] *The Christian Doctrine*, IV, vii (15–20).

[5] *The Trinity*, XII, 9 (14)–10 (15), trans. Stephen McKenna (The Catholic University of America Press, 1963).

[6] These passages are collected in *Coleridge on the Seventeenth Century*, ed. R. F. Brinkley (Duke University Press, 1955), pp. 523, 534.

G. A. E. PARFITT

𝒦

The Poetry of Thomas Carew

I

No-one seems really sure what to do with Carew, partly perhaps because no fully adequate account of English poetry in the first half of the seventeenth century has been written. In *Revaluation*, Dr. Leavis suggested an approach which makes Carew an important link between Jonson and Marvell, thus giving his work a greater prominence than it usually has, but Leavis's remarks have not been followed up and so the traditional view of Carew, linking him vaguely with "the Cavalier poets," is still dominant.

One reason why this traditional view matters is that, insofar as it follows Jonson, Cavalier poetry shows a narrowing of range of reference and interest, becoming courtly in a sense which suggests a decisive split between "court" and "country" and a consequent concentration upon relatively few areas of emotional experience and, more specifically, upon narrowly circumscribed facets of society. One result is cynical knowingness and surface sophistication; another is that reactions to experience become conventional and simplified. Leavis, in linking Carew with Jonson and Marvell, is implying that Carew, like these greater poets, has a width of reference and variety of response which distinguishes him from Suckling, Lovelace, or even Herrick. This essay is an attempt to demonstrate that implication, to show that Carew can react to a wide range of experiential stimuli; and has some-

From *Renaissance and Modern Studies*, X–XII (1966–68), pp. 56–67. Reprinted by permission of the author.

thing of that varied awareness of what is involved in being human which is one of the marks of major poetry.

Although Carew is primarily thought of as a love poet, his work is perhaps best approached by some consideration of his writing in other *genres*. "Obsequies to the Lady Anne Hay" is an elegy on a distant cousin of the poet's and these are its opening lines:

> I heard the Virgins sigh, I saw the sleeke
> And polisht Courtier, channell his fresh cheeke
> With reall teares; the new-betrothed Maid
> Smild not that day; the graver Senate layd
> Their business by; of all the Courtly throng,
> Griefe seald the heart, and silence bound the tongue.

The poet, obviously, is praising the dead woman by asserting that her death had a national impact; a theme which could easily seem empty hyperbole. But we will dismiss these lines as such only if we allow stock resistance to public elegy to block our awareness of their real poetic activity. For Carew is seldom obviously original; he works instead by revitalising a conventional *genre* or attitude. Here, for example, "I heard" and "I saw" in the first line give, through the repetition, an effect of factual statement as well as a sense of verisimilitude. Then there is the precision of the adjectives describing the courtier: "sleeke" and "polisht" suggest superficiality and an artifice hostile to true emotion, while "fresh" checks this implication, without destroying it, and yet adds the complementary idea of inexperience of deep feeling. So when Carew says that this courtier's tears were "reall" the impact comes from the surprise: "sleeke" and "polisht" courtiers should weep tears of feigned feeling. Anne Hay's worth was such as to break the smooth surface and touch the man beneath the rôle. Finally, we should note how the solemn subordinate sense-units build up to the balanced and assured abstractions of "Griefe seald the heart, and silence bound the tongue," where the strongly active verbs give the personifications force and point.

In this passage, working within a conventional *genre*, Carew's verse is fully alive: he is using language precisely to re-enliven the human situation which lies behind all conventions but which repetition so easily deadens. The concluding lines of "To my worthy friend Master Geo. Sands"—written within the convention of the verse-compliment— show Carew again re-animating the tradition. The poet has been comparing his love poetry with Sands' religious verse:

Perhaps my restlesse soule, tyr'de with persuit
Of mortall beauty, seeking without fruit
Contentment there, which hath not, when enjoy'd
Quencht all her thirst, nor satisfi'd, though cloy'd;
Weary of her vaine search below, Above
In the first Faire may find th' immortal Love.
Prompted by thy example then, no more
In moulds of clay will I my God adore;
But teare those Idols from my heart, and write
What his blest sprit, not fond love shall indite;
Then, I no more shall court the verdant Bay,
But the dry leavelesse Trunke on Golgotha;
And rather strive to gaine from thence one Thorne,
Then all the flourishing wreaths by Laureats worne.

Carew is here aware of the conflict between divine and secular love, a conflict generally recognized and always implicit in love poetry of the Christian era but seldom used to real effect. Usually—one thinks of Donne and Vaughan—poets who explicitly bring the two together reject sexual love outright, but, although Carew aims at such rejection, its glibness is avoided, for his "Perhaps" suggests uncertainty and self-awareness, while the statement that "mortall beauty . . . . hath not, when enjoy'd / Quencht all her thirst, nor satisfi'd, though cloy'd" contains an awareness of both the value and limitations of human love. Similarly, while the imagery of the last four lines sets the "dry leavelesse Trunke on Golgotha" and the "Thorne" against "the verdant Bay" and "the flourishing wreaths" mainly to stress the paradox that Christ's humiliation and death is more fruitful for the Christian than the glory of earthly achievement, the images do at the same time give weight to the richness of secular experience.

Carew, then, can demonstrate in his verse both an exact sense of language and an alert, sensitive mind. These qualities, with the independence which springs from them, enable him to use conventional *genres* without being inertly conventional himself. The independence of Carew's mind can be very clearly seen in the poem "To Ben Jonson Vpon occasion of his Ode of defiance annext to his play of the new Inne." As is well known "The New Inn" was hissed from the stage when, in 1629, it was first produced, and when Jonson published it in 1631 it was accompanied by a powerful 60-line attack on popular taste, a poem magnificently vituperative but narrow in tone and outlook. Carew's poem is part of the considerable literary and sub-literary activity caused by Jonson's attack, and its beginning is perhaps what we should expect from a friend of Jonson:

> Tis true (deare Ben) Thy just chastizing hand
> Hath fixt upon the settled age a brand
> To their sworne pride, and empty scribbling due,
> It can nor judge, nor write . . . .

But Carew was no sycophant, and he goes on

> and yet 'tis true
> Thy commique Muse from the exalted line
> Toucht by thy Alchymist, doth since decline . . . .

The rest of the poem is a judicious mixture of praise and advice, making clear that Carew both knew where Jonson's greatness lay and what dangers were inherent in the sarcastic rage of the attack on the playgoers. Like the better-known elegy on Donne, "To Ben Jonson" is primarily an achievement of critical intelligence, but it is also one of honesty. Both features suggest an intelligence which, when we turn to the love poems, should make us hesitate before we dismiss them as elegantly conventional.

But before we look at the love poems we should briefly take account of Carew's country-house poems, "To Saxham" and "To my Friend G.N. from Wrest." The *genre* owes its establishment in England mainly to Jonson and Carew's two poems show clearly the influence of "To Penshurst." At Saxham the disadvantages of winter are overcome, because, addressing the house,

> thou within thy gate,
> Art of thy selfe so delicate;
> So full of native sweets, that blesse
> Thy roof with inward happinesse;
> As neither from, nor to thy store
> Winter takes ought, or Spring addes more.

Like "To Penshurst" Carew's poem is about generosity, openness and hospitality, being relevant to, and gaining weight from, the environment of contemporary legislation and concern about the gentry's social function. At Saxham nature delights in supplying food, guests are welcomed ungrudgingly and the welcome does not depend on wealth or rank. The qualities celebrated and enacted relate to society in a way which makes "To Saxham" relevant and responsible to an extent beyond anything in Suckling or Lovelace. Nevertheless, one can see a narrowing of range in Carew's poem, in the way that hyperbole is dangerously near to over-balancing into absurdity:

> The scalie herd, more pleasure tooke,
> Bath'd in thy dish, then in the brooke,

and, the final couplet,

> And as for Thieves, thy bounties such,
> They cannot steale, thou giv'st so much.

Carew's limitations can be measured by comparing this ending with the conclusion of "To Penshurst": Jonson's rich sense of the family as an humane unit working for the wider good and his more general feeling for its civilizing influence are both lacking. But Carew remains aware of this kind of influence and his control of moral overtone is found in the detail of his lines (in "delicate" and "inward" in the lines already quoted) and in the effective use of paradox here:

> Thou hast no Porter at the doore
> T'examine, or keep back the poore;
> Nor locks, nor bolts; Thy gates have bin
> Made only to let Strangers in.

Neither "To Saxham" nor "To my friend G.N. . . . ." is a great poem, although there is greatness in the opening part of the latter, but both indicate Carew's concern with a full and satisfying life, reaching towards Jonson rather than reminding us of Suckling's posturing or Herrick's elegance.

II

The seriousness and range of matter which characterize the poems discussed so far both link Carew with Jonson, in a way which suggests that, as Leavis hints, it is more fruitful to approach Carew by way of Jonson than to lump him with the Cavaliers, a term as vague and deceptive as most of its kind. The discussion of Carew's work outside love-poetry should also help to make us alert to the revitalization of conventions which is almost always going on in the love poems.

It is, for example, going on in the couplet lyric called "The Spring," which has received little attention from critics. Its theme—that the poet's mistress is at odds with Nature in being unresponsive to the poet-lover—is common enough, used by, for example, Weelkes in his madrigal "Now every tree renews his Summer green," by Drummond in the sonnet "With flaming hornes the Bull . . . ," and by Petrarch in "Zefiro torno . . . . ." Carew, however, makes more effective use of the theme than any of these men, comes closest, that is, to realizing its potential.

At first we may be bothered by our post-romantic difficulty in really accepting that here, as in most pre-romantic verse, natural description is not primarily used objectively, that the poem is not concerned with nature itself so much as with natural description as a way of making a point against a human being. If we take a quietly humorous detail of description such as "wakes in hollow tree the drowzie Cuckow" as the norm we may be puzzled by the artificiality of the opening lines or of such a couplet as:

> Now doe a quire of chirping Minstrels bring
> In tryumph to the world, the youthful Spring.

But if we suppress preconceptions we become gradually aware that formalizing Nature serves a purpose, to isolate the mistress against the whole force of Nature. More precisely, Nature is formalized in the sense that it is described in human terms, because the poem's success necessitates a relationship being established between Nature and Mistress such as to make poetically valid conclusions drawn from the analogy between them. "Robes" (l. 2), "tender" (l. 6), "drowzie" (l. 8) all have human connotations, while the language used to describe winter ("Candies," "ycie," "silver," "Chrystall") establishes a kind of beauty which—and these connotations become relevant later—includes a sense of inhumanity and, perhaps, superficiality. This frozen Nature is aspiring to the condition of Art of an almost Byzantine kind: its immediate appropriateness is in the contrast made with the description of Spring which follows, where we find this sequence of key words: "warms . . . . . thawes . . . . . benummed . . . . . tender . . . . . sacred birth . . . . . dead . . . . . wakes . . . . . drowzie" (ll. 5–8). Something fluid and alive is replacing Winter's icy beauty.

The description of life replacing death in Spring reaches its climax at lines 11 and 12; immediately an exception is stated:

> Now all things smile; only my Love doth lowre:
> Nor hath the scalding Noon-day Sunne the power,

> To melt that marble yce, which still doth hold
> Her heart congeald, and makes her pittie cold.

"Now" sums up the progress of all things to life in Spring and "smile" has strong human connotations: for both reasons the reversal of the movement in "only my Love doth lowre" is—even if expected—a shock. By implication the woman's behaviour is inhuman, unnatural, as we realize that she is being associated with the winter of the opening lines, an association stressed by the overlap of vocabulary. But Carew has suggested that winter is dead and unnatural, and that its natural movement is towards spring; now, speaking of the woman, he takes the full effect of associating her with winter, for the verb "hold" implies that woman's heart is not naturally hard, while "pittie" is said to be part of her make-up, even if it is "cold." The suggestion is that the natural and the human is being denied expression by this woman.

Instead of ending here, having demonstrated the isolation of his mistress from natural rhythms, Carew turns to further illustration. Structurally, this enacts the woman's unnatural isolation, stressing her exception to the norm by surrounding her with it. Further, the pastoral episode of Amyntas and Chloris acts as an explicit statement that the woman is by human standards unnatural. Carew concludes with a summary:

> all things keepe
> Time with the season, only shee doth carry
> June in her eyes, in her heart January.

The statement mimes in syntax the gap between appearance and reality.

Competent, exact use of language, clarity and neatness of structure, accuracy of detail are the basic virtues of successful poetry, and "The Spring" has these. But I have analysed it closely to show that Carew's lyrics repay close reading: the detail of his writing activates his work, giving a conventional theme here new energy and life. The relationship claimed between woman and the seasons is artificial, but it functions significantly in allowing Carew to emphasize the woman's unnaturalness by indicating it as the sole exception to a natural rhythm. The patterning of language contrasting the frozen with the fluid, the dead with the alive, works to revitalize the worn idea of the cold-hearted mistress, and in so doing re-emphasizes a connection between life and "literary love" such as the poets of the Elizabethan sonnet tradition had tended to blur. We may also note that insofar as court-centred poetry of the early seventeenth century draws on a more limited range of experience than does that of Donne and Jonson, Carew is at least partially an exception; for if his attitude to Nature is basically formal and "courtly" (such terms as "silver" and "Chrystall" imply the art-language of a social élite) he is, nevertheless, using rather than simply applying this attitude and is still able to introduce the ox and a number of closely-observed details ("benummed," "drowzie").

It is this ability to work within and to re-animate convention that gives originality to much of Carew's love-poetry. Sometimes, in a sense, this originality is itself conventional, as in poems like "To my inconstant Mistris" and "Ingratefull Beauty Threatned" where the poet-lover becomes aggressively demanding rather than humbly submissive. Here the attitude reminds us of Donne, but antedates him, and the emphasis it receives in Carew reminds us of his concern to anchor love in the range of normal human behaviour. The process—often one of restating a convention's relation to life—can be seen clearly in "A Divine Mistris," which starts with the routine claim that the mistress is perfect in beauty and of divine origin:

> my faire love
> Who fram'd by hands farre more divine;
> For she hath every beauteous line . . . . .

This is followed at once by the qualification:

> Yet I had been farre happier
> Had Nature that made me, made her;

and the poem concludes bluntly:

> Shee hath too much divinity for mee,
> You Gods teach her some more humanitie.

In what is scarcely a complex poem Carew simultaneously feels and renders the traditional urge to write hyperbolically about his mistress while yet introducing a more complex poet-persona than usual. The stress on the earth-bound limitations of the poet's nature is in part the conventional pose of the poet's inferiority, and as such a compliment to the mistress, but Carew also reminds us that the attitude his persona adopts has validity, hyperbole is being held in check by a kind of realism. So "humanitie" does more than make the obvious contrast with "divinity"; it also reminds us that idealisation of the mistress can dehumanise a situation. Although this poem lacks the precise "placing" through vocabulary which "The Spring" has, the presentation of the lady as perfect beauty carries an element of criticism in "humanitie" and the direct commonsense of the poet's attitude. Carew is not, as Donne often is, rejecting the conventional machinery, but, more like Jonson, is restating its relationship with life.

In some cases, as in "A Divine Mistris," the process is one of emphasizing the human basis implied by conventional attitudes to love; but often it is more a question of animation, less by adapting or augmenting a convention than by precision of diction. "Vpon a Ribband" is a trivial poem, opening with these lines:

> This silken wreath, which Circles in mine arme,
> Is but an Emblem of that mystique charme,
> Wherewith the magique of your beauties binds
> My captive soule, and round about it winds
> Fetters of lasting love; This hath entwin'd
> My Flesh alone, That hath empalde my mind:
> Time may weare out These soft weak bands; but These
> Strong chaines of brasse, Fate shall not discompose

This development of a single syntactical unit is controlled and clear, its articulation shaped by the marked antitheses. Variety and liveliness of sense-units re-animate the conventional "Fetters of lasting love," while the antitheses bring out strongly the contrasts in the argument. Words in their placing, like "entwin'd," "empalde," and "discompose," enforce attention on what exactly is being said. Constantly this re-establishment of some traditional idea as living currency happens, as in these magnificent lines from "A beautiful Mistris,"

> If thou but show thy face againe,
> When darknesse doth at midnight raigne,
> The darkness Flyes, and light is hurl'd
> Round about the silent world.

But one important aspect of Carew's love poetry has not yet been mentioned, the erotic element. This links Carew with Cavaliers like Suckling, Lovelace and Randolph rather than with Jonson or with Donne's main emphases. It is a striking, if seldom noticed, fact that while overt eroticism is largely absent from personal love poetry in the sixteenth century, it emerges strongly in the early decades of the seventeenth. The possible reasons for this cannot be discussed here, but the main one may be that as Puritanism gained strength it drove a wedge between the religious and less religious, isolating the latter by its extremism and pushing them to react with another type of extremism. Certainly in the erotic poetry of Cleveland, Cartwright, Lovelace and Suckling there is a hectic, overwrought quality, suggestive of immaturity and moral uncertainty. Both the exclusion of, and undue emphasis on, the physical in love-poetry is immature in the sense of being insufficient to give a full sense of love; and if the Cavaliers reduce love to a set of physical contacts a lot of Elizabethan poetry suffers from thin-blooded pseudo-spirituality. Between 1500 and 1650 few non-dramatic poets face up to the problem of sexuality in a Christian society. Donne sometimes, usually obliquely, manages to do so and Marvell in "To His Coy Mistress" bombards the dilemma with an intense awareness of Time's inexorability. But in some senses Carew comes closer than either to bringing into contact an awareness of the delights of sex and a sense that this can scarcely be expressed within the traditional framework of Christian thought.

If this is so the linking of Carew with the Cavaliers because his verse has an overt erotic element must be superficial, hiding more than it reveals. When Professor Kermode describes Carew's most successful erotic poem, "A Rapture," as one of "the libertine versions of sensual innocence" (together with pieces by Randolph and Lovelace) he reveals an inadequate awareness of the poem and, for him, an unusual deadness in relation to tone. Carew's use of direct eroticism is confined to relatively few poems but these are not isolated from the main body of his work, because the human "realism" which anchors so many of his lyrics, preventing both inert conventionality and any over-spiritual stress, involves an implicit awareness of the importance of sex and an unwillingness to pretend that love is either just a game or just a matter of the union of souls. This does not necessarily mean that when Carew writes directly of sex he will manifest the reconciliation of physical and spiritual demands which we can call mature: "The Second Rapture," with its nymphet theme and deadness of sympathy, is as unpleasant as anything in Suckling or Lovelace. Nor, when Carew writes erotically, is he necessarily taking direct account of the religio-erotic tension which is constantly implicit in love-poetry of the Christian era. "An Eddy," for example, is a success principally because of the richly erotic suggestion projected on to the image of the river, a success of strategy and of beauty rather than of moral awareness. But in "To A.L. Perswasions to Love" there is an attempt to take account of this tension by stressing that the poet's "perswasion" of the lady involves fidelity and a kind of love which can survive the decay of beauty:

. . . . . wisely chuse one to your Friend,
Whose love may, when your beauties end,
Remaine still firme . . . . .   (ll. 49–51)

Cull out amongst the multitude
Of lovers, that seeke to intrude
Into your favour, one that may
Love for an age, not for a day . . . . .   (ll. 55–58)

In this poem Carew stresses the importance of sex and is also aware that other values bear upon sexual relationships. The poem's value is that it takes account of more factors of human existence than persuasion poems commonly do, although it stops short of direct confrontation between opposing ideals. This is the area in which "A Rapture" is important. The poem is long and complex, too much so to discuss here, but it comes nearer perhaps than any other poem written between 1500 and 1650 to evoking a full sense of the erotic while accepting and giving expression to the conflict between this and accepted Christian moral standards. The normal Elizabethan tactic, when expressing overt eroticism, is to condemn what is being expressed or to use some kind of pre-Christian setting; the usual Cavalier device is to ignore the Christian code, to pretend that poet and mistress are somehow exempt from it, or to emit a smoke-screen of pseudo-argument. Carew, however, not only acknowledges a conflict betwen Christianity and the erotic but suggests that such a clash is inevitable, while his embodiment of the erotic has such force and beauty that it makes the erotic-moral opposition a real factor in the poem, makes the poem a disturbing phenomenon, puzzling and extending our experience as poetry should do.

III

I have claimed for Carew a sensitivity to language and have argued that this presupposes and reveals an alert and enquiring mind. Neither quality makes Carew a major poet, for both are surely pre-requisites of any real success as a poet at all. Nor does either quality necessarily distinguish Carew and the Cavaliers, for both qualities appear in the best of Suckling and Lovelace, and more consistently in Herrick. The distinction is more a matter of scope, sympathy and complexity.

Because Donne's influence on seventeenth-century poetry has been more fully discussed than Jonson's and because the latter's influence is usually dealt with in relation to his own love lyrics, the fundamental nature of Carew's affinity with Jonson has been obscured. Yet Carew's fondness for the couplet, his range of material, and his ability to work effectively within conventional frameworks all remind us of Jonson. Although Carew can and does make use at times of fairly complex stanza forms (as indeed Jonson also does) his normal manner is simple in a way which resembles Jonson's formal simplicity and reminds us of the latter's stress on matter above manner. The similarity is most clearly seen, perhaps, in the country-house poems, but throughout his work Carew returns constantly to a human base: his criticism of his mistress is of failures of humanity; his concern with sex arises from an awareness of the body-soul paradox which, in "A Rapture" especially, he will not sublimate or suppress; his concern over Jonson's attack on the public is about the dangers it has for Jonson's own personality; and his involvement over Anne Hay is, in part, a desire to demonstrate human virtue breaking through the armour of artifice. Carew lacks Jonson's firm moral base and seldom follows him in developing a moral attitude satirically, but he has the same basic humanity, which allows moral distinctions to be drawn and gives his writing a sense of involvement with the real world. Broadly speaking, the cynicism of Suckling, the coarseness of Cleveland's sensibility, Herrick's restricted prettiness, and Lovelace's odd dissociation (he shows at times a sense of ideals, stated but seldom embodied in his verse) are all lacking in Carew. The negatives become positives because Carew's linguistic awareness reveals when examined that for Carew the conventions and pretensions of art must constantly be related to human life, and that life for Carew is something fuller—more complex, less abstract and simplified—than it is for, say, Suckling. Insofar as Carew draws upon Jonson and Donne he does simplify, as lesser poets following greater commonly do, reducing Jonson's range of concern and his moral firmness, smoothing Donne's intense verbal attacks on experience, his ability to make words think: But this is only a degree of simplification, involving Carew neither in the sacrifice of his individuality nor in that abandonment of an adequate range of experience which thins so much Cavalier verse. By pretending that Carew is in any serious sense Cavalier we reduce the homogeneity of the term, stress peripheral rather than central aspects of Carew's work, and ultimately distort the picture of early seventeenth-century poetry.

↙

The Fate of Edmund Waller

When Waller died in 1687, his tomb at Beaconsfield was dignified by an epitaph from the Historiographer Royal. It is in the usual fulsome, empty style which dissipates trust by overemphasis, but surprisingly its claim that Waller endeared English literature to the muses is approved by Waller's most distinguished literary contemporaries. In Dryden's preface to Walsh's *Dialogue Concerning Women* (1691), for example, we read, "Unless he had written none of us could write"; and in his preface to *The Second Part of Mr. Waller's Poems* (1690) Atterbury boldly declared, thinking primarily of Waller, "I question whether in Charles the Second's Reign *English* did not come to its full perfection; and whether it has not had its *Augustan Age.*"

Modern critics have, however, responded to this rather too liberal praise with equally immoderate censure. Mr. J. B. Emperor's study of "The Catullian Influence in English Lyric Poetry" (University of Missouri Studies, 1928) alludes to the poet as "the frigid and time-serving Waller, who rhymed insipidly under both Jameses, both Charleses, and the Protector." The same critic continues, "Perhaps none of the men considered in these studies had less of the truly poetic and lyric than he; in him the Augustan age definitely begins and begins indifferently.

From *South Atlantic Quarterly*, LX (1961), pp. 230–38. © Duke University Press. Reprinted by permission of H. M. Richmond and Duke University Press.

He is a thoroughly bad poet. His love verse is cold, artificial, and absurd." Such severity seems hardly more discriminating than the earlier elaborate praise, but it is nevertheless shared by the best modern authorities. "No poetical reputation of the seventeenth century has been so completely and irreparably eclipsed as that of Edmund Waller," writes Douglas Bush in his history of seventeenth-century literature. "Whereas Cowley and Cleveland can still give pleasure, Waller's name calls up scarcely more than two lyrics of attenuated cavalier grace, "'On a Girdle', and 'Go Lovely Rose', and a dim memory of much complimental verse. . . . For us he remains a fluent trifler, the rhymer of a court gazette."

The sharpness of the conflict between the views of the seventeenth century and of our own suggests that Waller would present an unusually interesting figure on which to focus a study of developing critical opinion. The motives which apparently govern his decline into disrepute are unexpected and revealing, both of Waller's age and of ours. Clearly the bitterness of J. B. Emperor, and also of Edmund Gosse, in his *Seventeenth Century Studies* (to whom Waller was "the easy turn coat" who wrote "smooth, emasculated lyrics"), stems ultimately not from critical analysis of the poet's works so much as from a transferred judgment on Waller's apparently regrettable life. There can be no doubt that Waller's career does tempt the censorious minded, and it is bizarre enough to demand close examination and review in the light of our experience since the time when Gosse and Emperor wrote. Only so can a dispassionate estimate of his work be accomplished.

Waller's life invites censure because of its unhappy central episode —his regrettable collapse of character under threat of execution in 1643. During the early stages of the clash between parliament and king, Waller had behaved with a wisdom and integrity which marked him out as a politician of exceptional promise. Stockdale, an early editor (1772), writes in his preface without much exaggeration that: "Waller at this time acquired a very great political reputation. He vindicated the rights of the people, but he likewise supported the dignity and authority of the crown; he had chosen that just and virtuous medium, to which it is so difficult to adhere in times of tumult, fanaticism and rebellion." He was welcomed by both parliament and the king as one of the commissioners sent to treat with Charles after Edgehill.

Nevertheless, seven months later Waller was under arrest for treason to parliament and was condemned to death soon after by a court martial. Pathetically, Waller's search for a peaceful compromise had involved him, accidentally, in a plot not merely to publicize the king's case, as Waller thought, but to further a revolt led by a royalist hothead, Sir Nicholas Crispe. Parliament refused, on discovering the plot, to disentangle these relationships, and Waller was condemned for intentions alien to his character and purpose. However, while some of his associates were hanged, Waller successfully deferred his death by desperate subterfuges—feigned madness, mass bribery, and informing on casual associates—until feeling against him declined and his sentence was reduced to fine and exile. After he spent a few penurious years abroad, Cromwell, to whom he was distantly related, allowed him to return.

This return, chiefly due to the threat of starvation if he remained abroad, is one source of censure, a rather superficial one under the circumstances. The earlier betrayals of confidence are the other grounds on which he is chiefly attacked. In the modern world, conditioned by works like *Darkness at Noon* and *1984*, we may be less harsh, if still critical of Waller's conduct under threat of unmerited death. "Time-serving" scarcely serves to describe a man who surely felt with Marvell that "the cause was too good to have been fought for."

This brief account may serve to set a little more in perspective the outraged censure of many of his critics who clearly share the views of Plato and Milton—that good poetry can only be written by conventionally good men. There is, however, another obstacle to Waller's return to popular esteem—ignorance. The latest edition of his poems, a "pocket" one, first appeared in 1893; and in the last twenty-five years *PMLA* lists only three slight references to Waller. Since the turn of the century only Mr. F. W. Bateson's "A Word for Waller" in his *English Poetry* (1950) makes a brief attempt at examining Waller sympathetically. On the other hand, the standard evaluation of him is stabilized because every history of English literature stereotypes him as reference point for the dawn of Augustanism. Bell's edition (1861) illustrates this interest-killing appreciation by noting, "His principal merit is that of having been the first who uniformly observed the obligations of a strict metrical system." This editor's fullest praise is: "There are very few of his lines that do not read smoothly, and but one in which a syllabic defect can be detected." Few histories improve on this approach—with inevitable consequences on the interest of potential readers.

There is one more complex reason for Waller's lack of reputation—the historical myth of the "unified sensibility" which Mr. Eliot fostered in his two essays "The Metaphysical Poets" and "Andrew Marvell." Eliot seeks to demonstrate a deep and valuable tension between thought and feeling in such poets as Donne which later poets like Waller and Milton are held to lack. However, critics like Mr. Leonard Unger, in his essay "Fusion and Experience" (in *The Man in the Name,* 1956), have asked "Where in Donne's poetry is there a 'felt thought,' or a 'thought feeling'?" and denied that the concept of such fusions is relevant to any Stuart poetry, Donne's included. Probably what we have in Donne is the blend of intellectual ingenuity with strong verbal emphasis used in the context of various stock emotional situations— partings, betrayals, attempted seduction. We value this verbal vigor and the intellectual virtuosity which Donne uses to create the scene— but neither of these resources has actually been forfeited by Waller as is usually claimed. Each quality has merely been developed to suit the social needs of a later, more urbane age. Waller's sense of conversational flow is as sure as Donne's, but more discreet, and his intellectual liveliness is at least equal to that of the author of "The Flea."

Perhaps the easiest illustration of Waller's capacity as a wit to transform a social situation by applying his quickness and felicity of mind to it is to relate two conspicuous examples from court life which Johnson notes in his life of Waller. The first occurred when Waller "upon sight of the Duchess of Newcastle's verses on the *Death of a Stag,* declared he would give all his own compositions to have written them; and being charged with the exorbitance of such adulation, answered that 'nothing was too much to be given that a lady might be saved from the disgrace of such a vile performance.'" Here we see the devastating cynicism and mocking slyness which Donne also exploits in a poem like "Woman's Constancy." Again, when Charles reproached him on the superiority of his *Panegyric* to Cromwell over his *Congratulation* to the King, Waller answered, "Poets, Sir, succeed better in fiction than in truth." Could Donne have found a more ingenious excuse? If these qualities of liveliness are transferred to his poetry, as I think they are, then surely Waller has a claim to our respect and is not wholly unworthy of the great predecessor to whom he is usually so unfavorably compared.

Let us examine some of these resources in his verse itself, avoiding those poems normally praised. For example, his poem about inconstancy, "Chloris! farewell," has never been noticed by either critics or editors:

> Chloris! farewell. I now must go;
> For if with thee I longer stay,
> Thy eyes prevail upon me so,
> I shall prove blind, and lose my way.
>
> Fame of thy beauty, and thy youth,
> Among the rest, me hither brought;

Finding this fame fall short of truth,
Made me stay longer than I thought.

For I'm engaged by word and oath,
A servant to another's will;
Yet, for thy love, I'd forfeit both,
Could I be sure to keep it still.

But what assurance can I take,
When thou, foreknowing this abuse,
For some more worthy lover's sake,
Mayst leave me with so just excuse?

For thou mayst say, 'twas not thy fault
That thou didst thus inconstant prove;
Being by my example taught
To break thy oath, to mend thy love.

The poem concludes with Waller's rueful departure. These stanzas illustrate fairly Waller's virtues as a poet. The style is bare and natural, the situation precisely visualized, and the outcome both ingenious and salutary. The most effective part of the poem is the poet's insight into social and psychological patterns. The shock which tragically overtakes Beatrice in Middleton's *Changeling* when she discovers that murder leads to self-victimization has in Waller's poem been transposed to the level of more normal relationships. The shock effect remains in the unexpected reversal of the predictable outcome, based on what can only be called moral insight.

Ingenuity thus here acquires both literary and social value in a way comparable but superior to Waller's epigram about the Duchess of Newcastle's poem. In Waller's verse we find then at very least the penetration of "metaphysical" wit and ingenuity into the finest texture of social relationships; and it is in this deft investigation of even conversational manners that the foundations of eighteenth-century sophistication were laid. It is not surprising that Waller's verse was so fashionable in that century, nor that, in less sophisticated modern society, he is disregarded.

Waller's resources are by no means so limited as modern critics pretend. In a stiffer, more Horatian style, Waller can be compared with Jonson or Herrick as we see in his poem "To a Lady in Retirement":

Sees not my love how time resumes
The glory which he lent these flowers?

> Though none should taste of their perfumes,
> Yet must they live but some few hours;
> Time what we forbear devours!
>
> Had Helen, or the Egyptian Queen,
> Been ne'er so thrifty of their graces,
> Those beauties must at length have been
> The spoil of age, which finds out faces
> In the most retired places.
>
> Should some malignant planet bring
> A barren drought, or ceaseless shower,
> Upon the autumn or the spring,
> And spare us neither fruit nor flower;
> Winter would not stay an hour.
>
> Could the resolve of love's neglect
> Preserve you from the violation
> Of coming years, then more respect
> Were due to so divine a fashion,
> Nor would I indulge my passion.

This is not the feeble writing which we are led to expect from Waller. The poem is firmly organized, and sophisticated. The subdued mockery of the couplet:

> The spoil of age, which finds out faces
> In the most retired places.

agreeably offsets the aureate allusions introduced discreetly into the text of the poem. It is not improper to note a hint in Waller's conclusion for the last lines of Marvell's first stanza of "To his Coy Mistress" since Waller's poems first appeared in 1645, some years before Marvell's best verse was probably written. That Marvell knew these poems and valued them is shown by the well-known and unmistakable debt owed by "The Bermudas" to Waller's "The Battle of the Summer Islands" (see Margoliouth's edition of Marvell).

In fact Waller's poem about "Dorothea" ("At Penshurst") also probably provided a popular model for that series of "promenade poems" praising ladies which includes "Appleton House," and of which this Waller poem is probably the first English example. It is no mean achievement to have set a precedent for Marvell's praise of the young

Maria—and Cleveland's "Upon Phillis Walking in a Morning" as well. (Many lesser poets such as Hammond, Heath, and Hooke also conform to Waller's pattern.)

Waller is also by no means a trivial poet because he chooses to write lightly. The savage vehemence and aggressive ingenuity of Donne are by no means the only mood and method for effective comment on human nature. "Of Silvia" displays a lithe sinuosity of analysis coupled with an irony as inconspicuous as the poem's intention is razor-like:

> Our sighs are heard; just Heaven declares
> The sense it has of lover's cares;
> She that so far the rest outshined,
> Silvia the fair, while she was kind,
> As if her frowns impaired her brow,
> Seems only not unhandsome now.
> So when the sky makes us endure
> A storm, itself becomes obscure.
>
> Hence 'tis that I conceal my flame,
> Hiding from Flavia's self her name,
> Lest she, provoking Heaven, should prove
> How it rewards neglected love.
> Better a thousand such as I,
> Their grief untold should pine and die,
> Than her bright morning, overcast
> With sullen clouds, should be defaced.

Ostensibly this is the familiar lover's complaint, but the discriminations on which the progression of the poem depends are of unusually subtle character. The dogma of the moral nature of beauty, in the Platonic style, is invoked with polished ease—that which is ungracious is shown to be not fair. How lightly the effective censure of fickleness is achieved can be seen in the phrase "seems not unhandsome now." The subjective and sentimental nature of the lover's sense of his lady's beauty is suavely stressed—but gallantly and moderately. "Not unhandsome" is a more original because a more poised mode of rejection than, say, one of Horace's blistering curses on Barine. However, the climactic irony lies in the mock gallantry of the second stanza. Lovers should not avow their loves, says Waller, because the regrettable lack of graciousness shown by a woman knowing of a lover's infatuation is bound to disgust him!

If this caustic yet urbane little poem is set against Donne's song,

"Go and catch a falling star," which makes a somewhat comparable attack on female nature, it will be seen that Donne's poem is memorable for its stylistic virtuosity, while Waller's is distinguished for its poised evaluation of social and moral tensions. Donne's poem is simply an assertion, though vivid and memorable; Waller's is an elegant algebraic demonstration. This is the quality which it shares with the first poem which we discussed; and it is that sharp sense of the significance of politely conversational exchanges which distinguishes all Waller's best verse.

This natural yet sensitive tone was certainly also his greatest social asset, restoring him to favor with the court even after his Cromwellian connection. And equally it was his political stock in trade, perfectly adapted to parliamentary eloquence. It was Waller's particular tragedy that in the middle of his life he found himself involved in events of a confusion and violence for which his unique talents were altogether unsuited. However, his contemporaries could distinguish these talents and admire them while admitting his public failures as a man.

We are less wise, and yet ironically even the one or two poems of Waller still conventionally admired, are good because of exactly those virtues which I have sought to display in his neglected verse and personality. Take his deservedly famous song:

> Go, lovely Rose!
> Tell her that wastes her time and me,
> That now she knows,
> When I resemble her to thee,
> How sweet and fair she seems to be.
>
> Tell her that's young,
> And shuns to have her graces spied,
> That hadst thou sprung
> In deserts, where no men abide,
> Thou must have uncommended died.
>
> Small is the worth
> Of beauty from the light retired;
> Bid her come forth,
> Suffer herself to be desired,
> And not blush so to be admired.
>
> Then die! that she
> The common fate of all things rare
> May read in thee;

> How small a part of time they share
> That are so wondrous sweet and fair!

It is ironic that Waller's best-known poem should so obviously lack that marked originality of intention which we noted in some of his other verse, for clearly this poem conforms in aim explicitly to Martial's famous admonition ("I felix rosa . . ."). However, this conventional frame allows us to see exactly where Waller's true originality lies. Compare the poem with Jonson's "To Celia" (in *Volpone*), Herrick's "Gather Ye Rosebuds," or Marvell's "To his Coy Mistress" and it will be seen that though all these pleas for love are impressive and picturesque, none is so economical and so devoid of the "poetic." The sentiment is expressed here with the minimum of effort—neither tone nor imagery is other than the actual situation permits. Perhaps for the first time in English the full force of poetic sensibility has focused on a social situation without distortion or heightening, and yet retained the magnetism of true art. The imagery is not exotic but drawn from immediate experience—the extraordinary tact of "Suffer herself to be desired" shows a sense of the pride of modesty which colors the poem as vividly as sensuous details. The swift conjunction of the second line, "Tell her that wastes her time and me," shows that mastery of reserved yet pointed expression which distinguishes Waller. But most of all the spoken flow of the whole shows something definitive in English. No poem can be read without false intonation more infallibly than this one. The control is not only metrically impeccable, it is, socially speaking, masterly. Henry James could hardly seek more. Such a fascinating conversationalist as Waller here shows himself to be deserves to be more talked about himself.

L. A. BEAURLINE

✑

"Why So Pale and Wan":
An Essay in Critical Method

I

Sir John Suckling's song "Why So Pale and Wan Fond Lover" is one of the most famous lyrics in English. It is seldom left out of an anthology and has received attention from every generation of musicians, who seem to find it especially attractive for musical setting.[1] But to the critic it is a challenge—obviously a fine poem; yet what can a critic say about it? Beyond an appraisal such as "How clever!" what language do we have to describe the poem's excellence? We are embarrassed by its simplicity; if we cannot show its complexity or illuminate its obscurities we feel the poem is inconsequential. Among academic critics especially, such a tendency exists because of the need to have "something to talk about" to a class of students. But surely that attitude is dangerously misleading for literary criticism, because it equates artistic excellence with difficulty, as if a poem were good in direct proportion to the number and height of the barriers between the reader and the sense of the poem, or between the poet's aim and his execution. Reading a poem is not like running an obstacle course; a daring athlete admires the most difficult and ingenious plan. The influence of the standard of complexity in literary criticism partly accounts for the reputation of metaphysical poetry today and for some of the neglect of Ben Jonson, Herrick, Suckling, Waller, and Rochester.

From *Texas Studies in Literature and Language*, IV (1962–63), pp. 553–63. Reprinted by permission of the University of Texas Press.

A moment's thought about the principle of difficulty teaches us its obvious weaknesses as a general critical standard, for a simple poem may very well be more difficult to write than a complex poem. Furthermore, a difficult or obscure mode of composition can easily mask shoddy craftsmanship, muddled thought, and imprecise feeling. Who is to say exactly where confusion ceases and complexity begins in such poems as "The Waste Land," "Ode to a Nightingale," and "A Song to David"? At best, the standard of difficulty is fruitful for the criticism of Donne, Blake, and Eliot, who themselves seem to have valued obscurity. But it is ill suited to lyrists whose aim was at all costs to avoid "darkness" and "strong" writing.

Nevertheless the critic has an uneasy feeling that he will be left without anything to say if he cannot invoke the principles of irony, tension, and complexity. We have no language to discuss simplicity.

This paper's aim is to show that there is at hand a language which can help us with poems like "Why so pale and wan," if we will only use it. We want clear and versatile tools of analysis, and we can find them in two places: in the critical discussions of contemporaries of the poet, and in the traditional terms of rhetorical and dramatic criticism. In other words, when we talk about seventeenth-century wit, we should not go to Eliot for a definition, but to Jonson, Cowley, and Dryden. And when we want to describe a poem's structure, we should not clutch at terms that tend to distract us from the obvious construction. Terms such as tension, irony, and symbol, reduce the poem to considerations of the words alone; terms such as myth, imagination, and intuition direct us to contemplate some archetype above or beneath the poem. The poem is left behind or is at least put in a secondary position.

I shall discuss "Why so pale and wan" under four headings: situation, character, thought (which includes emotion and argument), and language, in order to show that the perfection of the whole lies in its powerful depiction of each element of the whole poem.[2] With precision and economy Suckling has fashioned a language to fit the thought and the thought to fit the character of the speaker in a situation. By brilliantly fulfilling a seventeenth-century standard of wit in language and thought, "Why so pale and wan" displays unusual artistry that is appreciated in any age.

The use of both universal and historical critical terms assumes that no basic contradiction exists between historical scholarship and criticism, if the scholarship is relevant and the criticism is comprehensive; that the most important object of study in literature is the work and not the audience or the author; that ideas, taste, and traditions of an author's contemporaries should be used as a check on anachronistic interpretations and as a means of exhibiting more sharply certain values implicit in a work; but that ultimately a work has to appeal to men of later times by its inherent power and artifice, calculated to please any reasonably literate and sensitive reader. Historical knowledge, therefore, is a supplement and sharpener of critical tools. It is beyond the scope of this paper to examine the above assumptions, for the aim here is heuristic, to demonstrate the value of a method for the study of a simple lyric. This paper does not attempt to solve all problems in evaluating lyrics, but merely tries to point the way for further investigation. It is a demonstration of a method. Nor am I trying to make a simple poem seem difficult, but to explain in detail the reasons why a poem has pleased readers and musicians for over three hundred years, to explain the obvious but inarticulate values. By precisely stating what everyone knows, we can rediscover the basic poetic values.

II

"Why so pale and wan" is obviously more a comic than a serious poem, a representation of a sophisticated and slightly cynical man giving advice to a less sophisticated friend, as if the poem were a short speech in a play, although the speech is complete in itself and not dependent upon other speeches. The argument falls into two parts: first, gentle questions tease the foolish lover, but when they do not elicit the correct response, the speaker turns to blunter statements. The thought in the poem was "ne'er so well express'd," each word is so exactly right. This much is clear. The real problem for a critic is the emotional force. If this is a dramatic lyric how can we accurately describe the emotional power of the whole?

Perhaps our response is something like detached amusement. This feeling is, no doubt, similar to our reaction to a clever device used by Face in *The Alchemist,* by Horner in *The Country Wife,* or by any other comic rogue who succeeds by means of superior intellect, experience, or sophistication. We might feel a certain delight in the easy cynicism which does no obvious harm. The poem may supply a release from conventional attitudes toward love. None of these descriptions, however, is adequate to define the precise tone of this kind of poem. The usual terms of rhetoric or poetics do not help, and modern psychology is even less helpful, for today psychologists do not try to differentiate precise emotions. They aim, instead, to gather specific feelings together under some large classes such as guilt, love, self-respect, and adjustment. Our critical (or psychological) vocabulary is simply

not finely enough developed to describe the qualities of emotion, and
without greater precision in understanding the effect, we cannot carefully observe the artistic choices which determine it.

Historical scholarship comes to our aid here, for there is evidence of
what Suckling and his near contemporaries thought about sophisticated
love poems such as "Why so pale and wan." We know that Suckling
generally disapproved of the "ancient wits" who wrote earlier in the
seventeenth century. Although he once complimented Sir William
Davenant for being the incarnation of the great lord of wit, Donne, his
usual view of metaphysical poetry was unfavorable: in "A Sessions of
the Poets" he chided Sidney Godolphin for writing in "strong lines,"
and reprimanded Thomas Carew for being too "hard bound," a lau-
reate's muse should be easy and free. In a forgotten essay "Concerning
Petty Poetry" by Lord Dudley North (1581–1666), published in 1645
but written considerably earlier in the century,[3] are some strictures on
metaphysical poetry which Suckling knew and apparently approved.
In the same book as the essay, A Forest of Varieties, North printed a
letter to Suckling where he thanked the poet for requesting a copy
of the essay, and North says that Suckling "honored" the piece with his
"pretended conversion." The essay objects to fashions of the time:
poems which torment the reader's brains, "in their high and obscure
flight"; like "ill ranging Spaniels they spring figures, and [are] ravished
by their extravagant fancies." A poet's labor should end at the first birth
of his poems, and so should the reader's labor end at the first reading,
the poems being so "plain and easy." Lord North is opposed to those who
think "nothing good that is easie, not any thing becomming passion
that is not exprest with an hyperbole above reason." He likes love
poetry that approximates conversation, "possessing a free puritie of
unadulterated wit. And as we often see that those women that have
bestowed on themselves the most Art and costly dressing, nay, many
times that have the best proportion, are not yet the most winning:
So in Verses there is to bee exprest a naturall spirit and moving ayre
(or accent) more alluring and charming the affection." He agrees with
Horace that verses should have a "round, current, cleare and gracefull
delivery."

> To conclude, lines of a farre fecht and labour'd fancy with
> allusions and curiosity, and in similes of little more fruit or
> consequence, then to ravish the Reader into the writers fine
> Chamæleon colours, and feed him with aire, I approve not so
> much, as heighth and force of spirit . . . wit needs not rack
> it self where matter flowes; embroideries become not a rich

stuffe; and art is best exprest where it least appears. A strong
wing is to be preferred before a painted, and good sense and
matter elegantly delivered before extravagancy of fancy and
conceit.

From these brief selections we can conclude that Lord North and
probably Suckling rejected the fashionable techniques of metaphysical
poetry on the one hand and the conscious artistry of, say, Ben Jonson
on the other hand. They aimed for easy, cultivated, but conversational
poems—verses that would not perplex a superficial reader, but please
him with their elegance and concealed art. These observations, however, are still not precise enough ideas on which to base a critical analysis. We must turn to the best critic of the seventeenth century, John
Dryden, for a further clue. North's essay, along with Suckling's occasional remarks, provides a general attitude toward lyric verse: Dryden,
with the help of Quintilian, defines the term that best describes the
poem.

Dryden especially singled out Suckling as the poet who brought the
conversation of a gentleman into verse, who was easy and free; [4] and
at one point Dryden criticizes Ben Jonson for not being as urbane as
the poets who wrote in a courtly and gentlemanly style. He explains
this conversational tone as having a quality of wit associated with the
terms "*urbana, venusta, salsa, faceta* and the rest which Quintilian
reckons up as the ornaments of wit." [5] Following this lead into Quintilian, we find an elaborate discussion of the nature of urbanity. In the
Institutes of Oratory, the most influential classical rhetoric, he says that
urbanity means a talent for courtly writing and genteel conversation.
He distinguishes it from rusticity, and describes it as a kind of politeness in words and accents and usage, having the taste of the town and
even a tincture of erudition, derived from association with well-edu-
cated men.[6] In a large sense, urbanity is a kind of wit in which
everything "that is incongruous, coarse, unpolished and exotic whether
in thought, language, voice or gesture" has been removed, an "elegance
of taste peculiar to the capital city." Then Quintilian lists certain sub-
categories of urbanity: saltiness, agreeableness, jesting, raillery, and
elegant facetiousness. The last term, *elegant facetiousness*, is the one
which will be most useful to an examination of "Why so pale and wan."
Quintilian says, "I do not regard the epithet *facetus* as applicable solely
to that which raises a laugh. If that were so Horace would never have
said that nature granted Virgil the gift of being *facetus* in song. I
think that the term is rather applied to a certain propriety and polished
elegance . . . a graceful wit." [7] Other evidence from seventeenth-

century dictionaries and usage confirms that Suckling's contemporaries thought of facetiousness as a kind of elegant playfulness.[8]

My contention is that the term *elegant facetiousness* best illuminates this poem, for it fits the peculiar tone of the song, the air of the speaker, the quality of the language, and the color of our emotional reaction. Although facetiousness is not an emotion itself, the charm or amusement that we feel arises from the facetiousness of the speaker in the poem. The sophisticated speaker with whom we are sympathetic arouses a highly cultivated mirth in the listener, a charmed amusement at his elegant facetiousness. A close look at the poem will reveal its facetiousness in each part.

> Why so pale and wan fond Lover?
>   Prithee why so pale?
> Will, when looking well can't move her,
>   Looking ill prevaile?
>   Prithee why so pale?
>
> Why so dull and mute young Sinner?
>   Prithee why so mute?
> Will, when speaking well can't win her,
>   Saying nothing doo't?
>   Prithee why so mute?
>
> Quit, quit, for shame, this will not move,
>   This cannot take her;
> If of herselfe shee will not Love,
>   Nothing can make her,
>   The Devill take her.   *Aglaura* 1638

The speaker, presumably a gallant, experienced in the ways of love, is advising a foolish young man how to behave toward his beloved. If the younger man aspires to be like the speaker, he ought to accept the advice. Thus far the young sinner (or another fond lover) has not been able to win a lady by the brilliance of his repartee or the attractiveness of his manner. He is not behaving properly, for he is pale, dull, and mute—the conventional signs of an unrequited lover. He is unrealistic, too obviously passionate, and too clearly worried about his passion.

However, the rhetorical situation is not all that simple. Quite likely the speaker also intends to have his words overheard by women, just as the Petrarchian complaint, for instance Wyatt's "My lute awake! perfourme the last Labor," was calculated to be heard by the cruel mistress. Donne's "The Funeral" is explicitly directed to whoever comes to shroud the speaker's corpse, but clearly it is meant to be read by the lady; line 24 betrays his intention where the speaker drops his pretense and talks straight to *you,* the lady. "The Canonization," "The Sun Rising," and "The Relique" maintain the pretended audience to the end, as Suckling's poem does. Modern poems use the same device occasionally, as Housman, in "To an Athlete Dying Young" addresses the dead man, but his ideas are expected to have an effect on the living mourners. In this way Housman achieves a detachment and restraint that he could not so easily have found otherwise. And Suckling's speaker gains a certain impish advantage if his words are supposed to deflect toward all coy mistresses. He is, in effect, threatening that men will withdraw their attentions if ladies do not behave realistically; beyond a certain point the coy mistress is not worth any more effort.

Historical evidence verifies this theory of a "double audience" for the poem because the song is sung in Act IV of Suckling's play, *Aglaura,* by a gallant named Orsames, a young "antiplatonic" lord, a cynical libertine, who scoffs at the "new religion in love." He does not sing the song to a fond lover; rather he sings it to the platonic ladies, Semanthe and Orithie. While they await the arrival of the queen, they ask Orsames to sing. He at first refuses because his voice is hoarse from walking out at night in his shirt serenading his mistress. After he sings, he says that this was a bit of advice given to a friend fallen into a consumption, and Orithie says that she could have guessed it was the product of Orsames' brain even if she had not been told. To be sure, most Elizabethan plays use songs strictly for ornament, but in this play Suckling explicitly connects the song with the dialogue; the rhetorical situation, therefore, presupposes the presence of the ladies.

What I have called a "double audience" in the poem is different, nevertheless, from a dramatic monologue such as "My Last Duchess" where *x* speaks to *y* but *x*'s words are intended to be heard by a public audience; we judge the speaker's statements differently than does his immediate audience, *y,* as in Suckling's poem; yet the full meaning is directed to a much less restricted group of readers. Browning intends to have his poem read by an undifferentiated audience; Suckling intends his song to be overheard by the platonic ladies. Thus Orsames' song is not only advice to a fond lover but a pose of the gallant and a threat to any coy mistress—if she does not return a man's love, if she does not react as a flesh-and-blood human being, she will be left behind. She will be the rejected one and the gallant will find a woman who will satisfy him.

The doubleness of the rhetorical situation is one of the reasons why this poem is so charming and playful. It gives us, the general readers or third audience, a special detachment, and it probably contributes to the conventional character of the speaker. The whole of the reader's relation to the poem is like a window-peeper watching an eavesdropper hearing a conversation.

But the argument reveals a great deal more of the character of the gallant, because he conceals an implied premise behind the explicit premises of the first two stanzas. The last step in the argument clarifies this larger assumption, and the reader suddenly sees its full implications in the last line: love is not a serious business; it is a game, a sport. Notions of romantic love, or, in the court of Charles I, notions of spiritual or platonic love—that men and women should contemplate each others' souls but not feel any need to descend to vulgar, physical pleasure, that women should hold out forever, and that men should suffer agonies of denial and rejection—these notions are questioned by the speaker. He is not fooled by a fashionable ploy of women. The assumption about romantic love, then, is skeptical and opportunistic. It is a libertine assumption.

In order to counteract the ladies' false view, the experienced man first uses a subtle approach, concealing his basic premise. With just a tinge of mockery and an air of superiority, he plays with the attitudes and behavior of his friend. The method is to point out contradictions between the fond lover's purpose and his actions. A rough paraphrase is as follows: "You say that you want to win her. You or others before you made an attractive first appearance and she would have nothing to do with you. Now do you imagine that she will like you better when you have lost your good appearance and begin to mope? You or others tried to speak as persuasively as you could and she rejected you. Then do you expect your tedious silence to impress her?" Thus far the reader's attention is on the fond lover, and the only inferences to be drawn concern the right way to win a maiden—by looking well and speaking well, not by behaving after the fashion of a suffering lover, complaining about the cruelty of his mistress. The powers of looking well and speaking well are "always the noblest and most reliable equipment of a gentleman," especially in the game of love.[9]

These ideas are barely hinted at and we are over-reading the poem if we insist that they are explicitly stated. The method of argument requires that the speaker coyly conceal his real attitude in the first two stanzas. But in the third stanza he changes his strategy. Subtlety and coyness have not worked on the friend (just as they do not work on a woman), so he turns to the direct technique. Nothing is concealed; all is straightforward and blunt. And we are allowed to see the playful cynicism of the speaker. None of the illusions about virtue and soul-mates will satisfy him, for women are good for one thing; and the game of love is like any other game: the winner is the man with superior prowess and wit, who knows enough not to waste his energies where there is no chance of ultimate triumph. If a woman takes it into her head to be in love, she will love of her own accord. If she gets a notion that she is not going to submit, nothing can make her. This implies an absolute skepticism about the objectivity of feelings. Our emotional responses bear little relation to the object of our feelings. Love is a whimsical thing.[10]

Although less important structurally, the language of the song works in a powerful way. For in the language the speaker embodies the most vivid depiction of urbanity and elegant facetiousness. By his language he demonstrates the conversation of a gentleman. It is especially important to observe that the signs of "poetic" writing are almost wholly absent. The sentences are in the natural order of speech: they fall as "in the negligence of prose." The vocabulary is limited to ordinary cultivated speech: no "liquifaction" or "sublunary," no phoenix, nymphs, or Cytherea. Of course, there are the usual rhetorical figures of repetition and balance, and questions, but the "poetic" images that we expect from Renaissance writers are conspicuously omitted—no simile, metaphor, hyperbole, allegory, heaping figure, catachresis, and so forth. Nevertheless, the language is handled artfully, so as to create the impression of remarkable ease within an extremely limited pattern of clauses, phrases, and rhythm. The grammar, vocabulary, and rhetoric conspire to create an air of playful carelessness. The game, at first, is to set up a rigid scheme of rhetorical questions, in trochaic meter, punctuated by amusing rhymes: *love her, move her; sinner, win her,* ending with the most facetious of all, *doo't* and *mute.* The fun of the second stanza lies in the way it faithfully imitates the pattern of the first, while escaping mere redundancy. Almost every phrase and every word in the second stanza are the same parts of speech and serve the same grammatical functions as their counterparts in the first. Filling out the stanza has become a game. This feature is probably one of the reasons why the song is attractive to musicians, because both stanzas will fit the musical accent and phrasing identically.

The language expresses the speaker's thought with the utmost economy and concision. A comparison of several lines with a variant version will show the efficiency and grace of the original. Lines 3–4 and 8–9 which appear in the *Academy of Complements,* 1646 (p. 200) are:

If looking well, it will not move her,
Can looking ill prevail?

If speaking well, it cannot win her
Can saying nothing do't?

The language also reveals the strategy of the speaker, for in the first two stanzas he is careful to be gentle. He merely questions and does not force an open admission in a plain statement, and he chooses the colloquial, deferential request, "Prithee," four times in ten lines. The word has just the right feigned delicacy for this part of the argument. Then at the turn, he switches from questions to bold, short commands, from trochaic meter to a spondee followed by iambs, from deferential requests to a common oath (but not so common as to be vulgar). The phrasing is similar to the pattern of the first two stanzas, but every detail deviates as far as possible from the established form. Even the double rhyme, *take her, make her,* occurs in the second, fourth, and fifth rather than the first and third lines. These sharp deviations contribute to the brilliant surprise of the last stanza, and our expectation of another repetition such as "Prithee why so pale," along with the trick of the rhymes, especially focuses attention on the last line. Instead of repetition the listeners get surprise and a common oath. The closing lines made for an eighteenth-century setting of the song, show how all the piquancy, the saltiness (to use Quintilian's phrase) can be taken out. It is insipid.

Quit for Shame this will not gain her,
This will never, never do;
If thy whining can't attain her;
Then no more no more persue.
Fly from her, as she flys from you.
Clio and Euterpe [1759], I, 86.

At that point where force is needed, Suckling's original has force. When speaking well will not "take" (i.e. charm) a lover or a friend, a man must change and speak bluntly. The gallant not only recommends "speaking well," but his own words are a model of how to speak well and a demonstration of when to be blunt. Both his words and his actions show the value of ease, brevity, urbanity, agreeableness, elegant facetiousness, and all the other ornaments of wit.

There are other ways of discussing this poem, but I have tried to be as comprehensive as possible by bringing together a number of critical terms: unity, vividness, surprise, expectation, detachment, economy, force, imitative form, ease, subtlety, appropriateness, and other terms from the analysis of plays. I conceived the poem as a dramatic lyric whose central quality is facetiousness, defined historically. But the other terms have had more universal application. The poem is successful because it has pleased readers for over three hundred years, many readers who did not know the seventeenth-century concept of wit. However, if we do know the older meaning of wit, we are better able to describe the special charm that Suckling's poem possesses.

NOTES

[1] The earliest setting was by William Lawes, in NYPL MS Drexel 4041, pp. 10–12 (Willa M. Evans, *Henry Lawes*, New York, 1941, pp. 145–146) An anonymous manuscript setting is in the Bodleian copy of Playford's *Select Musical Ayres*, 1653. Subsequent settings were by Lewis Ramondon (1705), and Thomas Arne (*c*. 1745), and at least seven others in the last hundred and fifty years. The lyrics alone appeared over fourteen times in seventeenth-century manuscripts and books.

[2] See Elder Olson, "An Outline of Poetic Theory," *Critiques and Essays in Criticism, 1920–1948,* ed. Robert Wooster Stallman (New York, 1949), reprinted in *Critics and Criticism,* ed. R. S. Crane (Chicago, 1952).

[3] The entire Essay has been reprinted in *The Huntington Library Quarterly,* XXV (1962), 299–313.

[4] *Essays,* ed. Ker (Oxford, 1900), I, 7, and 34–35.

[5] *Ibid.,* I, 139.

[6] *Inst.* VI. 3. 17–21; VI. 3. 45; VI. 3. 103–107 (Loeb Library).

[7] *Ibid.,* VI. 3. 19–20, my adaptation of the Loeb translation. The first English translator, W. Guthrie (1756), renders *facetum* as "arch" and comments: "The word . . . is extremely difficult to translate into English by any one word. It implies a delicate archness of wit that steals upon the mind of the hearer, without altering one feature in the speaker."

[8] Randle Cotgrave, *A Dictionarie of the French and English Tongues,* (1632) says, "*Facetie:* Witty mirth, a merry conceit, a pretty encounter in speech." Richard Flecknoe, in *A Short Discourse of the English Stage,* characterizes Fletcher's wit as having "nothing of the superfice, or dross of words, as clenches, quibbles, gingles, and such like trifles have: it is that, in pleasant and facetious discourse, as eloquence in grave and serious," (J. E. Spingarn, ed., *Critical Essays of the Seventeenth Century* [Oxford, 1908], II, 94). For its association with grace see passages in the *O.E.D.* under *facetious* and *facetiousness.*

[9] Kathleen Lynch says this characterizes all of Suckling's work (*The Social Mode of Restoration Comedy* [New York, 1926], p. 72.)

[10] This is one of Suckling's favorite themes. Love is an appetite that needs

satisfying, and the lover is an epicure who enjoys all the preliminaries just so long as they lead to the big feast (*Aglaura*, I, v, 52–100); a soldier in a siege must hope to take the fort, or else he will not fight ("Tis now since I sate down before," *Fragmenta Aurea*, 1646, B8). Concerning the subjectivity of feelings, the best example is in "Of thee (kind boy) I ask no red and white" where the speaker argues that fancy creates beauty; if a man takes a fancy to black and blue in a lady's complexion, fancy makes it beautiful:

> Tis not the meat, but 'tis the appetite
> makes eating a delight,
> and if I like one dish
> More than another, that a Pheasant is.
> *Fragmenta*, A8^v.

AUSTIN WARREN

ⵣ

Symbolism in Crashaw

The poet's birthright, his imagery, is that part of him which is least controllable by effort and discipline. His sensuous aridity or fertility; the relative predominance of eye over ear or of both over the nostrils; his sensitivity to tint and shade or his bold reduction to line drawing or charcoal sketch; the precision of his observation or his subjective diminutions and hyperboles; the domains from which he elicits his tropes—whether moor and mountain, or cathedral and drawing room, from natural history or unnatural: these aesthetic characters reveal his breed. Doubtless the poet as self-critic can prune the luxuriance of the imagery, make austere sacrifice of those clusters growing in contiguity too close; but the kind of grapes he rears owes dependence to soil and climate. So far, that is, as imagery is not pastiche and imitation, it lays bare the temperamental self and can change its character only as, and so far as, the poet is susceptible of personal conversion.

In his life alone does Nature live. Even among the romantic poets, one notes their unconscious selection from what they have experienced. The spirit of Childe Harold finds representative embodiment in the vast and horrendous, in altitude and solitude—the ocean, the mountain, the storm; Shelley, the aerial, in the cloud, the skylark, the west wind; Wordsworth in the quietly pastoral, the landscape domesticated by man or indwelt and tempered by the World Spirit.

From *Richard Crashaw: A Study in Baroque Sensibility* (Louisiana State University Press, 1939; reissued by The University of Michigan Press, and by Faber & Faber, 1957), pp. 176–93. Reprinted by permission of the publishers.

All imagery is double in its reference, a composite of perception and conception. Of these ingredients, the proportions vary. The metaphorist can collate image with image, or image with concept, or concept with image, or concept with concept. He can compare love to a rose, or a rose to love, or a pine grove to a cathedral, or religious ecstasy to intoxication. Then, too, the metaphorists differ widely in the degree of visualization for which they project their images. The epic simile of Homer and of Spenser is fully pictorial; the intent, relative to the poet's architecture, is decorative. On the other hand, the "sunken" and the "radical" types of imagery [1]—the conceits of Donne and the "symbols" of Hart Crane—expect scant realization by the senses.

Symbolism may be defined as imagery understood to imply a conceptual meaning: such definition is latitudinarian enough to admit the poetry of Mallarmé as well as the ceremonial of the Church. The concept may be a mere overtone, a darkly descried vista, or it may be a category susceptible of prose statement. Some symbolisms are private, founded upon the poet's childhood associations of thing and sentiment; without biographical aid, the reader is likely to find them mere imagism or a congeries of oddly juxtaposed perceptions. Others —like the Christian emblems of dove, lamb, shepherd, cross—are communal. Others must be well-nigh universal, even to men topographically untraveled: the plain, the mountain, the valley, the ocean, the storm, darkness and light, are broadly human.

Parable and allegory may be defined as symbolic narratives in which a conceptual sequence runs parallel to—or, rather, is incarnate in—an imaginative sequence; they are, too, the most explicit forms. Christ parabolically identifies himself with the Good Shepherd; the Word, with the seed; the fig tree, with the unproductive life. Spenser and Bunyan label their persons and places: the Giant Despair, Fidessa, Orgolio, Mr. Worldly Wiseman, Faithful; the Bower of Bliss, the House of Holiness, Doubting Castle, the Delectable Mountains.

The proportion of strength between the image and the concept ranges widely. In eighteenth-century personification, the picture frequently evaporated till but a capital remained; in Mallarmé, the imagery only is presented, though, by its lack of naturalistic congruence, its disjunction, it disturbs the consciousness till the latter evokes some coherent psychological pattern for which all the images are relevant.

Crashaw, sensuous of temperament, wrote a poetry mellifluously musical, lavishly imagistic. At first acquaintance it seems the song of the nightingale hovering over her skill, "bathing in streams of liquid melody"; later, it seems the passage work, the cadenzas, the glissandi of an endowed and much-schooled virtuoso. Yet his life shows him to have been an ascetic, denying his senses all save their homage to God. In turning to religion and religious poetry, he "changed his object not his passion," as St. Augustine said of the Magdalen: [2] the images of his secular poetry recur in his sacred. He loves his God as he might have loved his "supposed mistress."

Not a preacher or prophet, Crashaw had no "message" to announce. He had suffered and exulted, and exulted in suffering; but his experiences did not tempt him to philosophy or other prose formulation. His was to be a poetry in which the rhythms and images would tell their own tale.

To his symbolism he supplied no chart of prose equivalents. Yet no reader has long studied his poems without feeling that their imagery is more than pageant; that, rather, it is a vocabulary of recurrent motifs.[3]

Nor is this symbolism really undecipherable. In the main it follows traditional Christian lines, drawing on the Bible, ecclesiastical lore, and the books of such mystics as St. Bernard and St. Teresa. Even when it is "private"—as, in some measure, every poet's will be—it yields to persistent and correlating study. Not widely ranging, Crashaw's images reappear in similar contexts, one event elucidating another. No casual reader of his poems, for example, but has been arrested by the recurrence of "nest," usually in rhyming union with "breast"; and, surely, no constant reader has long doubted its psychological import, its equivalence to shelter, refuge, succor.

It need not be maintained—it is, indeed, incredible—that Crashaw constructed a systematic symbolism. It is unlikely, even, that he knew why certain images possessed, for him, particular potence. Obviously much concerned with his technique, given to revision, a lover of the arts, he seems, as a man, ingenuous, free from self-consciousness, imaginatively uncensored.

In his steady movement from secular poetry to an exclusive preoccupation with sacred, from Latin to the vernacular, he relinquished —deliberately, it would seem—the Renaissance decoration of classical mythology. As a schoolboy he had written hymns to Venus, poems on Pygmalion, Arion, Apollo and Daphne, Aeneas and Anchises; and in his Latin epigrams, and in "Music's Duel," there occur classical embellishments. From the English sacred poems, however, such apparatus is conspicuously absent. Giles Fletcher, of his English predecessors closest to him in temper and idiom, had compared the ascending Christ to Ganymede, snatched up from earth to attend upon Jupiter; but no such bold correlation of pagan and Christian finds place in

Crashaw's poetry. Donne and Herbert, also erudites, had made a similar surrender of their classicism; [4] and to Herbert's example in particular he may have been indebted.

Otherwise, Crashaw makes no attempt to differentiate his sacred from his secular imagery; many characteristic figures and metaphors, "delights of the Muses," are reënlisted in the service of Urania. For example, the familiar paradox of the Incarnation, whereby Jesus is at once the son and the father of the Blessed Virgin, is anticipated in the apostrophe to Aeneas carrying Anchises: "Felix! *parentis* qui *pater* diceris esse tui!" [5] The persistent motif of the mystical poems first appears in "Wishes":

> A well tam'd heart
> For whose more noble smart
> Love may bee long chusing a Dart.

Unlike Herbert, Crashaw rarely recollects homely images of market place and fireside; and allusions to the polities and economies of the Stuart world come but seldom. Christ, dying, is called "his own legacy." With the Blessed Virgin, Crashaw, who, too, has set "so deep a share" in Christ's wounds, would draw some "dividend." To these financial metaphors, one may add what at first view seems Herbertian —the angels with their bottles, and the breakfast of the brisk cherub.[6] Yet, though "breakfast" Herbert would surely not have disdained, such intimacy with the habits of cherubs is peculiarly alien to the Anglican spirit of *The Temple*. It is Mary's tears which, having wept upwards, become, at the top of the milky river, the cream upon which the infant angel is fed, adding "sweetnesse to his sweetest lips"; and this context, by its extravagant lusciousness, reduces the blunt word to but a passing grotesquerie.

Some feeling for Nature, especially the dawn and flowers, the young Crashaw undoubtedly had; but even the early poems evince no botanical niceness, no precision of scrutiny. The first of the Herrys poems develops a single metaphor, that of a tree whose blossoms, ravished by a mad wind, never deliver their promised fruit; but unlike Herbert's "orange tree," this is a tree of no specific genus.[7] Crashaw's habitual blossoms are the conventional lily and rose.

These flowers, which appear briefly, in his earliest poems, as outward and visible creatures, do not disappear from his later verse; but they soon turn into a ceremonial and symbolical pair, a liturgical formula, expressive of white and red, tears and blood, purity and love. Already in the panegyric on the Duke of York, lines which begin with a delicate naturalism, end with a reduction to liturgical red and white, in a prefigurement of Crashaw's final style.

> So have I seene (to dresse their Mistresse *May*)
> Two silken sister flowers consult, and lay
> Their bashfull cheekes together, newly they
> Peep't from their buds, shew'd like the Gardens eyes
> Scarce wakt: like was the Crimson of their joyes,
> Like were the Pearles they wept. . . .[8]

In the "Bulla," or "Bubble," the flowers have become antithetic colors in shifting transmutations.[9]

If Crashaw's *flora* soon turn symbols, his *fauna* have never owed genuine allegiance to the world of Nature. The worm; the wolf, the lamb; the fly, the bee; the dove, the eagle, the "self-wounding pelican," and the phoenix: all derive their traits and their significance from bestiary or Christian tradition, not from observation; and their symbolism is palpable. In their baseness men are "all idolizing worms"; in their earthly transience and fickleness and vanity, foolish wanton flies. The bee, a paragon of industry, is still more a creator, preserver, or purveyor of mystic sweetness. The Holy Name of Jesus is adored by angels that throng

> Like diligent Bees, And swarm about it.
>   O they are wise;
> And know what *Sweetes* are suck't from out it.
>   It is the Hive,
>   By which they thrive,
> Where all their Hoard of Hony lyes.

The dove and lamb, of frequent appearance, betoken innocence and purity; they are also meet for votive offering. Sometimes the doves emblemize elect souls, whose eyes should be "Those of turtles, chaste, and true"; sometimes, the Holy Ghost. The *Agnus Dei,* the white lamb slain before the foundation of the world, was Crashaw's favorite symbol for Christ and for him, among all symbols, one of the most affecting.

"By all the Eagle in thee, all the dove": so Crashaw invokes the chaste Teresa, the mystic whose wings carried her high, whose spiritual vision was unflinching and acute.

> Sharpe-sighted as the Eagles eye, that can
> Out-stare the broad-beam'd Dayes Meridian.

Meditating her books, the responsive reader finds his heart "hatcht" into a nest "Of little Eagles, and young loves." [10]

To the phoenix, Crashaw devoted a Latin poem, a "Genethliacon et Epicedion," in which the paradox of a fecund death shows its expected fascination for him. The fragrant, unique, and deathless bird reappears in the Latin epigrams, and in the English poems, both secular and sacred. It occurs twice in the sequence of Herrys elegies; it is belabored at length in the panegyric to Henrietta Maria, "Upon her Numerous Progenie," where it becomes a symbol of supreme worth. In the sacred poems, it assumes its traditional Christian office as sign of the God-man, virgin-born, only-begotten, and immortal.

With most artists, the pleasures of sight are pre-eminent; with Crashaw, in spite of his interest in pictures and emblems, the fuller-bodied and less sharply defined senses would appear to have afforded richer, more characteristic delight.

His colors are elementary, chiefly conventional, readily symbolic. In his religious poetry, but three occur: red (or purple = *purpureus*), with its traditional relation, through fire and the "Flaming Heart" to love; black; and white. Black is, for him, the sign not of mourning or penitence but of sin and, still more, of finiteness, of mortality: "Dust thou art, and to dust thou shalt return." In his translation of Catullus, men are "dark Sons of Sorrow." Augmented, the phrase reappears in "The Name of Jesus" as "dark Sons of Dust and Sorrow." Elsewhere in the religious poems, man is "Disdainful dust and ashes" or "Darke, dusty Man."

White, perhaps as the synthesis of all colors, perhaps as the symbol of luminous purity, is the most exalting adjective in Crashaw's vocabulary. It occurs in his secular verse, especially in his panegyrics upon the royal family. But it is more frequent in his *carmina sacra*, used customarily of the Blessed Virgin or Christ, and most strikingly of Christ as the Lamb.

> Vain loves, avaunt! bold hands forbear!
> The Lamb hath dipp't his white foot here.[11]

The absence from the religious poetry of green, the color of nature, and blue—in the tradition of Christian art, the color of truth and of the Blessed Virgin—is conspicuous; so is the absence of chiaroscuro. By other means, he produces a sensuous luxuriance; but, in respect to the palette, he turns, like the Gospels, to bold antithesis of black and white.

For evidence that Crashaw was a lover of music, one need not ap-

peal to "Music's Duel." "On the Name of Jesus," among his four or
five masterpieces, calls to celebration all sweet sounds of instrument—

> Be they such
> As sigh with supple wind
> Or answer Artfull Touch. . . .

These flutes, lutes, and harps are the "Soul's most certain wings,"
Heaven on Earth; indeed, in a moment of quasi-Platonic identification
of reality with highest value he equates "All things that Are" with all
that are musical. Assuredly, Crashaw intended his own poetry to be—
what by virtue of his mastery of vowel and consonant sequences and
alliteration it habitually is—sweet to the ear, Lydian. But, for him, it is
also true, human music was an initiation into an archetypal music, the
harmonious concert of the spheres "which dull mortality more feels
than hears." The ears are "tumultous shops of noise" compared with
those inner sensibilities which, properly disciplined, may hear, as from
afar, the inexpressive nuptial hymn.[12]

Crashaw's favorite adjectives, "sweet" and "delicious," mingle fragrance and taste. His holy odors are chiefly traditional—those of
flowers and of spices. "Let my prayer be set forth in Thy sight as the
incense," said the Psalmist; but the simile finds its analogy in the
ascent of both. The fragrance of spices pervades that manual of the
mystics, the *Song of Songs*. To the Infant Jesus, the magi brought
frankincense and myrrh. The Magdalen dies as "perfumes expire."
The Holy Name is invoked as a "cloud of condensed sweets," bidden
to break upon us in balmy and "sense-filling" showers. In his ode on
Prayer, the most mystical of his poems, Crashaw bids the lover of
God, the virgin soul, to seize the Bridegroom

> All fresh and fragrant as he rises
> Dropping with a baulmy Showr
> A delicious dew of spices. . . .

Sometimes Crashaw's gustatory delights, like those of the

> sweet-lipp'd Angell-Imps, that swill their throats
> In creame of Morning *Helicon* . . .[13]

remain innocently physical. But customarily the pleasure of the palate,
too, becomes symbolic, as it is when the Psalmist bids us "taste . . .

how good the Lord is." The angels who swarm about the Holy Name are wise because they "know what Sweetes are suck't from out of it." This palatal imagery might be expected to culminate in apostrophes to the Blessed Sacrament; but not so. For Protestants, the Holy Communion is a symbolic as well as commemorative eating and drinking; to Crashaw, who believed in Transubstantiation, the miraculous feast seemed rather the denial of the senses than their symbolic employment. His expansive paraphrases of St. Thomas' Eucharistic hymns are notably sparse in sensuous imagery. It is not the Blood of Christ on the altar but the redeeming blood on the cross which prompts him to spiritual inebriation.

Crashaw's liquids are water (tears, penitence); milk (maternal succor, nutrition); blood (martyrdom on the part of the shedder, transference of vitality to the recipient); wine (religious inebriation, ecstasy). Fluid, they are constantly mixing in ways paradoxical or miraculous. In one of his earliest poems, a metrical version of Psalm 137, blood turns into water. In one of the latest, "Sancta Maria," "Her eyes bleed Teares, his wounds weep Blood." From the side of Christ, crucified, flowed an "amorous flood of Water wedding Blood." The angels, preparing for a feast, come with crystal phials to draw from the eyes of the Magdalen "their master's Water: their own Wine." Milk and blood may mingle, as when maternal love induces self-sacrifice; water turns to wine when tears of penitence become the happy token of acceptance and union; wine is transubstantiated into blood in the Sacrament; blood becomes wine when, "drunk of the dear wounds," the apprehender of Christ's redeeming sacrifice loses control of his faculties in an intoxication of gratitude and love.

The last of the senses is at once the most sensuous and the least localized. To it belong the thermal sensations of heat and chill. Fire, the cause of heat, is, by traditional use, the symbol of love; its opposites are ordinarily lovelessness and—what is the same—death. The "flaming Heart" of Christ or of the Blessed Virgin is the heart afire with love. St. Teresa's ardor renders her insensitive to love's antonym and opposite, the chill of the grave. Crashaw is likely to unite the opposites. Since she is both Virgin and Mother, Mary's kisses may either heat or cool. Lying between her chaste breasts, the Infant Jesus sleeps in snow, yet warmly.[14]

The supremities of touch, for Crashaw's imagination, are experienced in the mystical "wound of love," in martyrdom, and in nuptial union. In the former states, torment and pleasure mix: the pains are delicious; the joys, intolerable. In his mystical poems, Crashaw makes free use of figures drawn from courtship and marriage. Christ is the "Noble

Bridegroom, the Spouse of Virgins." Worthy souls are those who bestow upon His hand their "heaped up, consecrated Kisses," who store up for Him their "wise embraces." The soul has its flirtations, its "amorous languishments," its "dear and divine annihilations." St. Teresa, love's victim, is sealed as Christ's bride by the "full Kingdom of that final Kiss"; and her mystic marriage has made her the mother of many disciples, many "virgin-births."

In the spirit of St. Ignatius' *Exercitia Spiritualia*, Crashaw performs an "Application of the Senses" upon all the sacred themes of his meditation. God transcends our images as He transcends our reason; but, argues the Counter-Reformation, transcension does not imply abrogation. Puritanism opposes the senses and the imagination to truth and holiness; for Catholicism, the former may be ministering angels. "How daring it is to picture the incorporeal," wrote Nilus Scholasticus in the *Greek Anthology;* "but yet the image leads us up to spiritual recollection of celestial beings." [15] Not *iconoclasts*, some censors would grant that visual imagery, emanating from the "highest" of the senses, may point from the seen to the unseen; there they would halt. Crashaw, like one persistent school of mystics, would boldly appropriate the whole range of sensuous experience as symbolic of the inner life.

Studied case by case, Crashaw's striking imagery will yield its symbolic intent. But its most characteristic feature emerges only when image is collated with image. Poetic symbolism may constantly devise new alliances of sense and concept; indeed, the poet Emerson objected to Swedenborg's "Correspondences" on the precise ground of their fixed and systematic character. With Crashaw, though rigidity is never reached, his metaphors yet form a series of loosely defined analogies and antitheses and cross references, a system of motifs symbolically expressive of themes and emotions persistently his.

Associated images recur like ceremonial formulas. In the secular poems, the lily and the rose have appeared, singly and together. The association continues into the religious poems, but the metaphorical character of the flowers has become explicit. In the epigram on the Holy Innocents, the mother's milk and the children's blood turn, for Crashaw's pious fancy, into lilies and roses. A characteristic later juxtaposition, in the "Hymn for the Circumcision," gives the metamorphosis: "this modest Maiden Lilly, our sinnes have sham'd into a Rose."

A similar ritual coupling is that of the pearl and the ruby. Sometimes these symbols appear singly, sometimes together. In the same "Hymn for the Circumcision" Crashaw sees Christ's drops of blood as rubies. The tears of the Magdalen are Sorrow's "richest Pearles." They are united in the eighteenth stanza of "Wishes." Still united, they reappear in the religious poetry: When men weep over the bloody wounds of Christ,

> The debt is paid in *Ruby*-teares,
> Which thou in Pearles did'st lend.[16]

Another frequent union—and this not of contrasts but of contradictories—couples fire and water, an oxymoron of images. Already, in an early poem, the sun is represented as paying back to the sea in tears what, as fire, it borrowed. When the Magdalen washes Christ's feet with tears, wiping them with her hair,

> Her eyes flood lickes his feets faire staine,
> Her haires flame lickes up that againe.
> This flame thus quench't hath brighter beames:
> This flood thus stained fairer streames.[17]

The Blessed Virgin is the "noblest nest Both of love's fires and floods." The tears of contrition or of sorrow, so far from extinguishing the fire of love, make it burn more ardently.

But one cannot thus far have surveyed Crashaw's imagery without perceiving how the whole forms a vaguely defined but persistently felt series of inter-relations. There are things red—fire, blood, rubies, roses, wine—and things white—tears, lilies, pearls, diamonds: symbols of love and passion; symbols of contrition, purity, innocence.

On its sensuous surface, his imagination sparkles with constant metamorphosis: tears turn into soft and fluid things like milk, cream, wine, dew; into hard things like stars, pearls, and diamonds. Beneath, the same experiences engage poet and poem.

All things flow. Crashaw's imagery runs in streams; the streams run together; image turns into image. His metaphors are sometimes so rapidly juxtaposed as to mix—they occur, that is, in a succession so swift as to prevent the reader from focusing separately upon each. The effect is often that of phantasmagoria. For Crashaw, the world of the senses was evidently enticing; yet it was a world of appearances only —shifting, restless appearances. By temperament and conviction, he was a believer in the miraculous; and his aesthetic method may be interpreted as a genuine equivalent of his belief, as its translation into a rhetoric of metamorphosis. If, in the Gospels, water changes to wine and wine to blood, Crashaw was but imaginatively extending this principle when he turned tears into pearls, pearls into lilies, lilies into pure Innocents.

Style must incarnate spirit. Oxymoron, paradox, and hyperbole are figures necessary to the articulation of the Catholic faith. Crashaw's *concetti*, by their infidelity to nature, claim allegiance to the supernatural; his baroque imagery, engaging the senses, intimates a world which transcends them.

NOTES

[1] These terms come from H. W. Wells' admirable analysis of *Poetic Imagery*.

[2] "I believe without any levity of conceipt, that hearts wrought into a tendernesse by the lighter flame of nature, are like mettals already running, easilier cast into Devotion then others of a hard and lesse impressive temper, for Saint *Austin* said, *The holy Magdalen changed her object only, not her passion . . .*" (Walter Montagu, *Miscellanea Spiritualia . . . , 32*).

[3] Cf. intimations in Osmond, *Mystical Poets*, 118, and Watkin, *The English Way*, 287.

Discussing "Conceits," Kathleen Lea wrote: "In his frequent use of the word 'nest' I do not believe that the image of a bird's nest presented itself to him. . . . For Crashaw we have an even longer list of words, such as 'womb,' 'tomb,' 'grave,' 'day,' 'death,' and 'fount,' which he used as it were ritualistically and in a colourless sense of his own. While it is proof of his greatness that he had this peculiar idiom of speech, it is also significant of his weakness that this idiom must be re-learned and explained." (*Modern Language Review*, XX [1925], 405.) This was a penetrating insight into the nature of Crashaw's poetic method; and it is the central merit of Miss Wallerstein's *Crashaw* that in some brilliant pages (especially 126-8) it develops and extends this thesis.

[4] Cf. Warren, "George Herbert," *American Review*, VII, 258 ff.

[5] "Fortunate man, you who may be said to be the father of your parent" (Martin, 222-3).

[6] Ibid., 286 (stanza 9); cf. "Charitas Nimia," ibid., 280, and ibid., 309 ("The Weeper," stanza 5).

[7] Ibid., 167; Herbert, "Employment."

[8] Ibid., 178.

[9] Ibid., 218
> Flagrant sobria lilia.
> Vicinis adeo rosis
> Vicinae invigilant nives,
> Ut sint et nivae rosae
> Ut sint et rosae nives. . . .

[10] On the lore of the eagle, cf. Phipson, *Animal-Lore*, 232-3.

[11] Cf. "Hymn to St. Teresa":
> Thou with the LAMB, thy Lord, shalt goe;
> And whereso'ere he setts his white
> Stepps, walk with HIM those wayes of light . . .

and the "To the Queen's Majesty":
> A Golden harvest of crown'd heads, that meet
> And crowd for kisses from the LAMB'S white feet.

[12] In my discussion of sensuous correspondences I am indebted to Miss M. A. Ewer's important *Survey of Mystical Symbolism.*

[13] "Music's Duel."

[14] "A Hymne of the Nativity" (Martin, 107):
> With many a rarely-temper'd kisse,
> That breathes at once both Maid and Mother,
> Warmes in the one, cooles in the other.

[15] *Greek Anthology,* Bk. I, epigram 33. Cf. also epigram 34 (from Agathias Scholasticus): "Greatly daring was the wax that formed the image of the invisible Prince of the Angels, incorporeal in the essence of his form. But yet . . . a man looking at the image directs his mind to a higher contemplation. No longer has he a confused veneration, but imprinting the image in himself, he fears him as if he were present. The eyes stir up the depths of the spirit, and Art can convey by colours the prayers of the soul."

[16] "On the Wounds of our Crucified Lord" (Martin, 99).

[17] English epigram (Martin, 97).

BRUCE KING

Green Ice and a Breast of Proof

One purpose of rhetoric is to lie. Poetic affirmations should be regarded with suspicion, especially if the poet is not religious or mystical. Consider *To Althea, From Prison*. Every school child knows the poem, and knows that it represents the gay, confident, debonair Cavalier spirit. But does it? Isn't our concept of the Cavalier spirit partly Restoration propaganda and partly a nineteenth-century romanticization derived from Scott? For that matter is Lovelace's tone really so confident? "Stone walls doe not a Prison make, / Nor I'ron bars a Cage." This might sound like a confident affirmation to someone with an ear for Victorian music; by Caroline standards it sounds a little strained. *Althea* is not about chivalry or public virtues, it is about states of mind ("And in my soule am free"). Its idealism might be considered as a strategy for denying the effect of physical surroundings upon the mind. The poem's affirmation is really a turning inward, a process that is common to many of Lovelace's poems. *The Vintage to the Dungeon* might be a blueprint for the strategy of *Althea:*

I

Sing out pent Soules, sing cheerfully!
Care Shackles you in Liberty,
Mirth frees you in Captivity:
Would you double fetters adde?
Else why so sadde?

From *College English,* XXVI (1965), pp. 511–15. Reprinted by permission of the National Council of Teachers of English.

Chorus

Besides your pinion'd armes you'l finde
Griefe too can manakell the minde.

II

Live then Pris'ners uncontrol'd;
Drinke oth' strong, the Rich, the Old,
Till wine too hath your Wits in hold;
   Then if still your Jollitie,
    And Throats are free;

Chorus

Tryumph in your Bonds and Paines,
And daunce to th' Musick of your Chaines.

The Vintage is not a simple drinking song; as in *Althea* the theme is deceptive. It says sing, affirm, drink, do anything to fight off the effects of imprisonment upon the mind.

   Lovelace's power derives not from a simple chivalric code but from a complex awareness that his ideals offer protection against reality. The best poems acknowledge the actual world, while trying out idealistic postures in reply. The ideals offered in *Althea, The Grasse-hopper,* and *To Lucasta, Going to the Warres* might be described as defensive masks. The lesser poems are more completely disillusioned and do not offer any protection, or do so crudely. In *To Lucasta from Prison, An Epode* Lovelace lists his grievances against life. Here, and also in *Mock Song,* the awkward wit is more painful than relieving. Tensions accumulate and are not discouraged. How, Lovelace asks, can peace love him, if it despises the earth. "War is lov'd so ev'ry where." Parliament is "beheaded," property is insecure; and ever since Parliament began borrowing money on it "Publick Faith" has become a mockery: "For she that couzens all, must me." A religious reform might be desirable,

       But not a Reformation so,
        As to reforme were to ore'throw;
       Likes Watches by unskilfull men
        Disjoynted, and set ill againe.

Here is Lovelace's image of his time:

> And now an universall mist
> Of Error is spread or'e each breast,
> With such a fury edg'd, as is
> Not found in th's inwards of th' Abysse.

With the world out of joint Lovelace's defense against total demoralization is a purposefully blind trust in monarchy and honor. He appears
to have been aware that while ideals are without power in the world,
they may be psychologically necessary. The snail is one of his favorite
images: "Wise Emblem of our Politick World, / Sage Snayl, within
thine own self curl'd." The snail's self-containment is an example of how
to keep one's values during times of evil and disorder:

> But banisht, I admire his fate
> Since neither Ostracisme of State,
> Nor a perpetual exile,
> Can force this Virtue change his Soyl;
> And wheresoever he doth go,
> He wanders with his Country too.
>
> (*Another*)

Lovelace's poems often record a feeling of exile.

When reality makes demands upon people, vague public values are
often used to cover resulting conflicts. The famous song *To Lucasta,
Going to the Warres* mocks while affirming soldierly values. The surprising wit of its middle stanza represents a discharge of psychic
tension. The rhetoric of courtship provides pivotal words ("chase,"
"imbrace," "mistresse") upon which to introduce, and then by mockery
to master, the pressures of reality:

> True, a new Mistress now I chase,
> The first Foe in the Field;
> And with a stronger Faith imbrace
> A Sword, a Horse, a Shield.

Lovelace's confidence is a not very consistently worn mask, the purpose
of which is to ward off reality. Honor represents a tension of will, the
snail's ability to remain true to itself in exile; but demoralization lies
behind the affirmations, waiting for a relaxation of will, a moment of
slackness.

While his values may seem quixotic and arbitrarily imposed upon disintegrating forms of society, without such a blind affirmation of honor Lovelace's sentiments become crude. In a *Saraband* ("Nay, prethee Dear") there is a coarsening of touch:

> See all the World how't staggers,
>   More ugly drunk then we,
> As if far gone in daggers,
> And blood it seem'd to be.

The carefree Cavalier attitude suddenly appears as a desperate reaction to brutal reality. The withdrawal and the turning to drink become gross sensuality:

> Now, is there such a Trifle
>   As Honour, the fools Gyant?
> What is there left to rifle,
>   When Wine makes all parts plyant?
>
> Let others Glory follow,
> In their false riches wallow,
> And with their grief be merry;
> Leave me but Love and Sherry.

If the subject of *Saraband* bears obvious similarities to other Cavalier libertine poems, the tone is coarser and more aggressive. Carew's libertinism has a strategic value in the battle of the sexes,[1] but Lovelace's libertinism lacks balance and suggests a total disillusionment with experience. It has none of the allure of libertinism that Milton warns against in *Comus*. It is a libertinism that results rather from hatred of life than love of the senses.

The pressure of reality must have been very great upon Lovelace. It comes into his poems unexpectedly, often breaking their mood, but creating the necessary tension that raises his best work above that of most Caroline lyricists. It is not surprising that many poems in the posthumous edition of 1659 are distrustful, violent, even paranoiac in reaction to society. The natural world becomes filled with emblems of a distasteful reality. "A Fly caught in a Cobweb" is described as "Small type of great ones, that do hum, / Within this whole World's narrow Room." The snail becomes a "Wise Emblem of our Politick World." The Ant represents the new order ("For thy example is

become our Law"), which is seen as uselessly striving against devour-
ing fate. The law of the animal world is also the law of man. Because
life is insecure, deferment of pleasure is pointless:

> Thue we unthrifty thrive within Earths Tomb,
> For some more rav'nous and ambitious Jaw:
> The *Grain* in th' *Ants*, the *Ants* in the *Pies* womb,
> The *Pie* in th' *Hawks*, the *Hawks* ith' *Eagles* maw:
> So scattering to hord 'gainst a long Day,
> Thinking to save all, we cast all away.   (*The Ant*)

This is a truth about Lovelace which is often missed: he is not untouched by the sceptical or cynical; indeed, his more affirmative poems
are examples of a disillusioned mind trying to hang on to something,
anything, in a world where it can find no resting place, no secure
perch. Nor is the cynicism merely political. The disillusioned streak in
Lovelace's poetry is not a matter of party or commitment. The distrust
is deeper, and it affects the antennae of his sensibility, changing the
way he feels the world. References to imprisonment and images of
dungeons are common to his poetry, often occurring in such unexpected
places as the opening lines of *The Triumphs of Philamore and Amoret*,
and of *Night*, an otherwise innocent poem ("Night! loathed Jaylor of
the lock'd up Sun").

Miss Wedgwood suggests that after the death of Charles I the
Cavalier poets lost their spirit of gallantry and that disintegration set in.
She speaks of a rotting away of the cause.[2] Lovelace's *Advice* to his
brother illustrates a deeper insecurity, however, than merely having
been vanquished. The insecurity is spiritual and physical as well as
political. There is a generalized distrust of the world. The poem begins
with Lovelace warning his brother to avoid sea voyages; all activity
leads to disaster:

> . . . dream, dream still,
> Lull'd in *Dione's* cradle, dream, untill
> Horrour awake your sense, and you now find
> Your self a bubled pastime for the Wind,
> And in loose *Thetis* blankets torn and tost;
> *Frank* to undo thy self why art at cost.

If the sea is dangerous, land is no better; inactivity also leads to
disaster. The image for this insecurity is metaphysical in the best sense;

it finds a correspondence betwen a particular idea and the nature of the world:

> Nor be too confident, fix'd on the shore,
> For even that too borrows from the store
> Of her rich Neighbour, since, now wisest know,
> (And this to *Galileo's* judgment ow)
> The palsie Earth it self is every jot
> As frail, inconstant, waveing as that blot
> We lay upon the Deep; . . .

The poem is an uneven, confused, but surprising performance. Its scepticism is intense. All things on earth will be "Turn'd to that Antick confus'd state they were." There is no way out of such a condition. The "golden mean" has "wrongs entail'd upon't." Stoic indifference should be a means to neutralize pain: "A breast of proof defies all Shocks of Fate, / Fears in the best, hopes in the worser state!" but the poem's conclusion suggests Lovelace's inability to anaesthetize the turmoil of reality:

> Draw all your Sails in quickly, though no storm
> Threaten your ruine with a sad alarm;
> For tell me how they differ, tell me pray,
> A cloudly tempest, and a too fair day.

This is distrust of optimism with a vengeance.

If we were to compare Lovelace's *Advice* to his brother with Dryden's poem to his *Honor'd Kinsman*, we would see two radically different reactions by Royalists to revolution. Whereas Dryden speaks of retirement as a means of achieving happiness "Unvex'd with anxious cares, and void of strife," Lovelace advocates a desperate withdrawal from reality. Whereas Dryden's poem is a prescription for happiness and future reward, Lovelace's poem is meant to neutralize hope. Dryden's aim is to praise a constructive, decent style of life, Lovelace's is to avoid harm. But, amazingly, Lovelace's poem is *meant* to be optimistic. Its tone is occasionally even jaunty, and it contains several passages to the effect that life cannot always be so bad as it is now; but no sooner does Lovelace say this than he warns against hope. Even the fairest day may lead to ruin. The poet's theme of cautionary balance is strongly in conflict with his insecure and fearful attitude.

With *Going to the Warres* and *Althea, The Grasse-hopper* is central to any interpretation of Lovelace. But it is a poem in which the poet's attitude and the conventions of his theme need to be separated. *The Grasse-hopper* belongs to the mid-seventeenth-century tradition of poetry of solitude and retirement: a tradition usually associated with disappointed Royalists, but which might well include Marvell and others who, though perhaps not Royalists, found rural retreat a comfort, whether in fact or symbolically, from the confusions of the Civil War and the resulting chaos. I think Professor D. C. Allen is right when he writes of the grasshopper as Cavalier and poet.[3] Lovelace's mind does seem to channel political pressures into traditional images; *The Ant, The Grasse-hopper's* companion piece, is an image of husbandry and puritanism: "thy example is become our Law." Singing insects are poets of whom the Ant is an enemy:

> And thou almighty foe, lay by thy sting,
> Whilst thy unpay'd Musicians, Crickets, sing.

The Grasse-hopper is not, however, limited to despair at the Royalist defeat. Rather than political events it is nature as revealed in images of time and seasons that is the destroyer of man's happiness. The moral is almost medieval. The material world is subject to change and decay; all things are mutable. Earthly joys are insecure.

I do not think that Lovelace is using traditional images of mutability to express a change in the political climate. The images are metaphors of something fundamental rather than topical. They express a similar insecurity before the temporal world to that expressed in Lovelace's *Advice* to his brother. Lovelace does not complain. He has already adopted a psychological attitude to defend himself against reality. Man is a fool not to have expected the worst:

> But ah the Sickle! Golden Eares are Cropt;
>   *Ceres* and *Bacchus* bid good night;
> Sharpe frosty fingers all your Flowr's have topt,
>   And what sithes spar'd, Winds shave off quite.
> Poore verdant foole! and now green Ice! thy Joys
>   Large and as lasting, as thy Peirch of Grasse,
> Bid us lay in 'gainst Winter, Raine, and poize
>   Their flouds, with an o'reflowing glasse.

These images are recalled at the end of the poem where the unpleasantness of the actual world, as represented by the political situation and the winter season, will be ignored and replaced by a subjective reality.

The conclusion of *The Grasse-hopper* involves a strategy for dealing with reality. The poem has long since stopped being about insects. But what is the central subject of the poem and what is Lovelace's solution to the problem it raises? If the poem has primarily been about defeated Royalists then its conclusion affirms the primacy of personal relationships during a period of public confusion. The structure of the poem, however, argues against such an interpretation. After the two movements describing the joys and fate of the grasshopper we are seemingly offered drink and friendship as consolations for life. However, to see conviviality as Lovelace's reply to reality would be to miss the point. It would replace one set of external props with another, and would make nonsense of the poem's final stanza:

> Thus richer then untempted Kings are we,
> That asking nothing, nothing need:
> Though Lord of all what Seas imbrace; yet he
> That wants himselfe, is poore indeed.

The prominence given to friendship in the final stanzas is deceptive. Lovelace, like Marvell and other mid-seventeenth-century poets, tends to give more prominence to examples and less to development of theme than we usually expect. It is almost the style of the period, and it is sometimes confusing. Perhaps that is why Geoffrey Walton claims "*The Grasshopper* is an invitation to conviviality of which the insect is supposed to set an example;" [4] if Professor Walton were right, the fate of the insect would be sufficient argument against accepting the invitation. While the grasshopper is normally a symbol of lightheartedness, it is used here as an example of the false joys of the external world and therefore of the vanity of human wishes. The poem's theme is neither politics nor conviviality, but attitudes of mind; its final defense against reality is rather stoical fortitude and lack of desire than friendship. To be "untempted" by any hope is to ask nothing and is one way to cope with a mutable world. The attitudes that Lovelace creates are striking, but they are, finally, defenses against demoralization.

NOTES

[1] I have discussed this in "The Strategy of Carew's Wit," *A Review of English Literature,* 5 (1964), 42–51.

[2] C. V. Wedgwood, *Poetry and Politics Under the Stuarts* (Cambridge, 1960), p. 108.

[3] D. C. Allen, "Richard Lovelace: 'The Grasse-Hopper,'" *Image and Meaning: Metaphoric Traditions in Renaissance Poetry* (Baltimore, 1960), pp. 80–92.

[4] Geoffrey Walton, "The Cavalier Poets," *A Guide to English Literature: From Donne to Marvell*, ed. Boris Ford (Harmondsworth: Penguin, 1956), pp. 170–71.

FRANK KERMODE

乄

The Argument of Marvell's "Garden"

I

"The Garden" is an *étude d'exécution transcendante* which has been interpreted by so many virtuosi in the past few years that a stiff-fingered academic rendering is unlikely to be very entertaining. However, since it appears that the brilliant executants have been making rather too many mistakes, there may be some value in going slowly over the whole piece.

It may be useful to point out in advance that these mistakes are of three kinds. The first is historical, as when Mr. Milton Klonsky, writing in the *Sewanee Review* (LVIII, 16–35), seizes on a passage in Plotinus as the sole key to the poem. He is wrong, not because there is no connection at all between Plotinus and Marvell's lyric, but because he has misunderstood the relationship and consequently exaggerated its importance. He fails to observe that Marvell, like other poets of the period, uses philosophical concepts, including those of Neo-Platonism, in a special way, with reference not to the body of formal doctrine in which those concepts are originally announced, but to genres of poetry which habitually and conventionally make use of them. The process is familiar enough; for example, the nature of the relationship between pastoral poetry and philosophic material such as the debates on Action and Contemplation, Art and Nature, is tolerably well understood. It is not customary to find the only key to the works of Guarini or Fletcher in some Greek philosopher; but these poets have

From *Essays in Criticism*, II (1952), pp. 225–41. Reprinted by permission of the publishers.

not, like Donne and Marvell, been distorted by the solemn enthusiasm of modern exegetes. In a sense all philosophical propositions in Marvell are what Professor Richards used to call "pseudo-statements," and his is a "physical" rather than a "platonic" poetry. However, rather than risk myself in these deep waters, I shall support myself on a raft of Mr. Wellek's construction: "The work of art . . . appears as an object *sui generis* . . . a system of norms of ideal concepts which are inter-subjective. . . ." Above all, it is possible "to proceed to a classification of works of art according to the norms they employ" and thus "we may finally arrive at theories of genres." [1] The point is that we must not treat these "norms" as propositions, for if we do we shall fall into the toils of Mr. Klonsky. Miss Ruth Wallerstein, who has worked so hard and so sanely to liberate seventeenth-century poetry from modern error, is none the less guilty of Mr. Klonsky's fault, in her *Studies in Seventeenth Century Poetic* (1950). Not only the indolent cry out against the suggestion that "The Garden" needs to be explicated in terms of Hugo of St. Victor and Bonaventura. Doubtless there is, for the historian of ideas, a real connection between the poem and the Victorine and Neo-Platonic systems of symbolic thought; for there is a connection between Plato and "Trees." However interesting this may be, it has nothing to do with what most of us call criticism. If we read "The Garden" as historians of poetry, and not as historians of ideas, we shall resist all such temptation to treat the "norms" as ideas, even if it proceeds from Diotima herself, to whom Professor Richards succumbed in a recent lecture on the poem.

The second kind of mistake is one which, particularly when it as-sumes its more subtle shape, we are all liable to yield to, though it appears to be seductive even in its usual grossness. Sufficient, how-ever, to say that "The Garden" must not be read as autobiography. "What was Marvell's state of mind as he wandered in Fairfax's York-shire garden?" is a very bad question to ask, but it is obviously one which comes readily to the minds of learned and subtle interpreters; both Marvell and Donne have suffered greatly from this form of mis-applied scholarship, and it is comforting to reflect that the date of "The Garden," is quite unknown, so that it cannot be positively stated to be the direct record of some personal experience at Nun Appleton. It could conceivably have been written much later. The pseudo-bio-graphical critic is wasteful and deceptive; he diverts attention from the genre just as certainly as Mr. Klonsky does when he presents a picture of the poet torturing himself with Chinese boxes of Forms, or Mr. Empson when he invites us to reflect upon the Buddhist enlighten-ment (*Some Versions of Pastoral*, pp. 119–20).

The third kind of critical failure is clearly, in this case, the most important, for the others would not have occurred had there not been this cardinal error. It is the failure to appreciate the genre (the system of "norms" shared by other poems) to which "The Garden" belongs. Despite the labours of Miss Bradbrook, Miss Lloyd Thomas,[2] and Miss Wallerstein, poets like Théophile, Saint-Amant, Randolph, Lovelace, Fane and Stanley have simply not been put to proper use in the criticism of Marvell. This is the central difficulty, and the one which this paper is intended to diminish. The first necessity is to distinguish between the genre and the history of the ideas to which the genre is related.

II

"We cannot erre in following Nature": thus Montaigne, "very rawly and simply," with this addition: "I have not (as *Socrates*) by the power and vertue of reason, corrected my natural complexions, nor by Art hindered mine inclination." [3] This is a useful guide to that aspect of "naturalism" in the thought of the late Renaissance which here concerns us. The like consideration governs all the speculations of the older Montaigne; Nature is to be distinguished from Custom; the natural inclinations are good, and sensual gratifications are not the dangerous suggestions that other and more orthodox psychologies hold them to be. Sense and instinct seek and find their own temperance without the interference of reason. It is good to satisfy a natural appetite, and it is also, of course, innocent. Thus men behaved, says Montaigne, in the Golden World, and thus they still behave in the Indies.

The question how far Montaigne believed in his own "primitivism" seems to me a difficult one, but it scarcely concerns us at the moment. It is legitimate to use him as spokesman for naturalism; and before we leave him it will be prudent to glance at some of his references to Plato, in order to have at hand some record of the naturalist reaction to the Platonic theory of love. In short, as the foregoing quotation implies, Platonic love is rejected. No longer "an appetite of generation by the mediation of beauty," love is in fact "nothing else but an insatiate thirst of enjoying a greedily desired subject" (III, 105). "My Page makes love, and understands it feelingly; Read *Leon Hebraeus* or *Ficinus* unto him; you speake of him, of his thoughts and of his actions, yet undersands he nothing what you meane . . ." (III, 102). Much more sympathetic are "the ample and lively descriptions in *Plato*, of the loves practised in his dayes" (III, 82). If one is not over-careful—if, for instance, one fails to discriminate between the orations

of Socrates and those who precede him, one may without much difficulty extract from the *Symposium* itself very different theories of love
from those developed by Ficino or Milton. In Marvell's own youth
antithetical versions of Platonism flourished contemporaneously at
Cambridge and at Whitehall.

So far we have concerned ourselves, very briefly, with the informal
naturalism of Montaigne, and hinted at a naturalistic version of Plato.
What of the poetry which concerns itself with similar issues? One
thinks at once of Tasso, and specifically of that chorus in his *Aminta*,
O bella età de l'oro, which was so often imitated and debated in the
poetry of the age. In the happy Golden Age lovers concerned themselves with their own love and innocence, and not with honour, that
tyrant bred of custom and opinion, that enemy of nature. In the garden of the unfallen just, whatever pleases is lawful. The paradise of
these fortunate innocents is abundant in its appeal to the senses; law
and appetite are the same, and no resolved soul interferes with the
banquet of sense offered by created pleasure. Thus an ancient pastoral
tradition accommodates new poetic motives, and poetry, though affirming nothing, strengthens its association with the freer thought of its
time. The formal opposition to Tasso's statement is properly made in
poetry which belongs to the same genre; and it may be found in the
Chorus in Act IV of Guarini's *Il Pastor Fido*. Parallel debates could go
on in the great world, and in the little world of poetry; the debate
about naturalism was a serious one, since it involved theological cen-
sures. The poetical debate is of a different quality. The proper answer
to Tasso is Guarini's. A genre of poetry developed which assumed the
right to describe the sensuality of a natural Eden, and a specialized
kind concentrated on sexual gratifications as innocent, and the subject
of unreasonable interference from Honour. The proper reply is, again,
in terms of the "norms" of the genre, and there is evidence that the
very poets who stated the extreme naturalist case were quite capable
of refuting it. One might call the "norms" of the refutation an anti-
genre. "The Garden" is a poem of the anti-genre of the naturalist
paradise.

Marvell therefore rejects the naturalist account of love, and with
it that Platonism which was associated with the delights of the senses.
The poets of the Renaissance were profitably aware of the possible
antitheses in Platonic theories of love, just as they were aware of
Plato's argument against their status as vessels of the truth.[4] Spenser
makes comfortable bedfellows of two Platonisms in his *Hymns;* the
two Aphrodites easily change into each other in poem and emblem.
Nothing is more characteristic of Renaissance poetry than the syn-

thesis of spiritual and erotic in poetic genre and image. It was encouraged by centuries of comment on the *Canticum Canticorum* and the eclecticism of mystics as well as by the doctrinaire efforts of Bruno to spiritualize the erotic Petrarchan conceits. Much more evidence could be brought, if it were necessary, to establish the existence of genre and anti-genre in Platonic love-poetry. They not only co-exist, but suggest each other. Marvell could pass with ease from the libertine garden to the garden of the Platonic *solitaire*, soliciting the primary *furor* of spiritual ascent. (The ease of such transitions was partly responsible for the development of another genre—that of the palinode.)

"The Garden" stands in relation to the poetry of the gardens of sense as the *Hymn of Heavenly Beauty* stands in relation to the *Hymn of Beauty*. It is poetry written in the language of, or using the "norms" of, a genre in a formal refutation of the genre. In fact, this was a method Marvell habitually used, sometimes almost with an affectation of pedantry, as I have elsewhere shown of "The Mower Against Gardens." [5]

III

The garden is a rich emblem, and this is not the place to explore it in any detail; indeed I shall say nothing of the symbolic gardens of the Middle Ages which were still alive in the consciousness of the seventeenth century. The gardens to which Marvell most directly alludes in his poem are the Garden of Eden, the Earthly Paradise, and that garden to which both Stoic and Epicurean, as well as Platonist, retire for solace or meditation. The first two are in many respects one and the same; the third is the garden of Montaigne, of Lipsius, and of Cowley. I shall not refer to the *Hortus conclusus*, though at one point in my explication of Marvell's poem I allude to a Catholic emblem-writer. Doubtless the notion of Nature as God's book affects the poetic tradition; it certainly occurs in poems about solitude at this period. But I think it is misleading to dwell on the history of the idea.

Of the complexity of the Earthly Paradise, with all its associated images and ideas, it is not necessary to say much: it is of course a staple of pastoral poetry and drama, and the quality of Marvell's allusions to it will emerge in my explication. But a word is needed about the garden of the solitary thinker, which Marvell uses in his argument against the libertine garden of innocent sexuality.

It is to be remembered that we are not dealing with the innocence of Tasso's Golden Age, where there is a perfect concord between appetite and reason, or with the garden of innocent love that Spenser sketches in *Faerie Queene,* IV, x, where "thousand payres of louers walkt, Praysing their god, and yeelding him great thankes," and "did sport Their spotlesse pleasures, and sweet loues content." The libertines use the argument of the innocence of sense to exalt sensuality and to propose the abolition of the tyrant Honour, meaning merely female chastity. This is the situation of the *Jouissance* poetry which was fashionable in France, and of which Saint-Amant's well-known example, excellently translated by Stanley, is typical. It is equally the situation of Randolph's "Upon Love Fondly Refused" and his "Pastoral Courtship," Carew's "Rapture" and Lovelace's "Love Made in the first Age." In Randolph's Paradise there is no serpent—"Nothing that wears a sting, but I" [6]—and in Lovelace's

> No Serpent kiss poyson'd the Tast
> Each touch was naturally Chast,
> And their mere Sense a Miracle.[7]

And so it is throughout the libertine versions of sensual innocence. The garden, the place of unfallen innocence, is identified with a naturalist glorification of sensuality. The garden which is formally opposed to this one by Marvell is the garden where sense is controlled by reason and the intellect can contemplate not beauty but heavenly beauty.

It was Montaigne, this time in his Stoic role, who gave wide currency to the pleasures of *solitary* seclusion. The relevant ideas and attitudes were developed into a poetic genre. Many poets certainly known to Marvell practised this genre, among them Fane and Fairfax and the French poets, notably Saint-Amant, whose *Solitude* demonstrates how easily he moved in this, the antithesis of the *Jouissance* mode. This famous poem was translated by Fairfax and by Katharine Phillips. This is the poetry of the meditative garden, whether the meditation be pseudo-Dionysian, or Ciceronian, or merely pleasantly Epicurean, like Cowley's. There is, of course, a play of the senses in which woman has no necessary part, though the equation of all appetite with the sexual appetite in the libertines tends to ignore it; this unamorous sensuality is firmly castigated by Lipsius in his treatment of gardens. If the garden is treated merely as a resort of pleasure, for the "inward tickling and delight of the senses" it becomes "a verie sepulchre of slothfulnes." The true end of the garden is "quietnes, withdrawing from the world, meditation," the subjection of the distressed mind to right reason.[8] The true ecstasy is in being rapt by intellect, not by sex.

Retirement; the study of right reason; the denial of the sovereignty of sense; the proper use of created nature: these are the themes of Marvell's poem laboriously and misleadingly translated into prose. As poetry the work can only be studied in relation to its genre, though that genre may be related to ethical debates. To the naturalist *Jouissance* Marvell opposes the meditative *Solitude*. The fact that both these opposed conceptions are treated in the work of one poet, Saint-Amant, and a little less explicitly in Théophile and Randolph also, should warn against the mistaking of seriousness for directness of reference to ethical propositions. "The Garden" uses and revalues the "norms" of the genre: it is not a contribution to philosophy, and not the direct account of a contemplative act.

IV

Henry Hawkins, the author of the emblem-book *Partheneia Sacra*, adopts a plan which enables him, in treating the emblematic qualities of a garden, to direct the attention of the pious reader away from the delights of the sense offered by the plants to a consideration of their higher significance. As in Marvell, sensual pleasure has to give way to meditation.[9] We now proceed to the explication of Marvell's poem, with a glance at Hawkins's wise disclaimer: "I will not take upon me to tel al; for so of a Garden of flowers, should I make a Labyrinth of discourse, and should never be able to get forth" (p. 8).

The poem begins by establishing that of all the possible gardens it is dealing with that of retirement, with the garden of the contemplative man who shuns action. The retired life is preferred to the active life in a witty simplification: if the two ways of life are appraised in terms of the vegetable solace they provide it will be seen that the retired life is quantitatively superior. The joke is in the substitution of the emblem of victory for its substance. If you then appraise action in terms of plants you get single plants, whereas retirement offers you the solace of not one but *all* plants. This is a typical "metaphysical" use of the figure called by Pluttenham the Disabler. The first stanza, then, is a witty dispraise of the active life, though it has nothing to distinguish it sharply from other kinds of garden-poetry such as libertine or Epicurean—except possibly the hint of a secondary meaning "celibate" in the word *single* and a parallel sexual pun on *close*,[10] which go very well with the leading idea that woman has no place in this garden.

The Innocence of the second stanza cannot itself divide the poem from other garden-poems; for Innocence of a sort is a feature of the libertine paradise, as well as of the Epicurean garden of Cowley and indeed most gardens.

> Your sacred Plants, if here below,
> Only among the Plants will grow—

lines which are certainly a much more complicated statement than that of *Hortus*—seem to have stimulated Mr. Klonsky to astonishing feats. But the idea is not as difficult as all that. Compare "Upon Appleton House"—

> For he did, with his utmost Skill,
> *Ambition* weed, but *Conscience* till,
> *Conscience,* that Heaven-nursed Plant,
> Which most our Earthly Gardens want. (XLV)

Your sacred plants, he says, addressing Quiet and Innocence, are unlike the palm, the oak and the bays in that if you find them anywhere on earth it will be among the plants of the garden. The others you can find "in busie Companies." The joke here is to give Quiet and her sister plant emblems like those of the active life, and to clash the emblematic and the vegetable plants together. The inference is that Innocence may be found only in the green shade (*concolor Umbra* occurs at this point in the Latin version). Society (with its ordinary connotations of "polish" and "company") is in fact all but rude (unpolished) by comparison with Solitude, which at first appears to be lacking in the virtues Society possesses, but which possesses them, if the truth were known, in greater measure (the Ciceronian-Stoic "never less alone than when alone" became so trite that Cowley, in his essay "Of Solitude," apologized for referring to it).

We are now ready for a clearer rejection of libertine innocence. Female beauty is reduced to its emblematic colours, red and white (a commonplace, but incidentally one found in the libertine poets) and unfavourably compared with the green of the garden as a dispenser of sensual delight. This is to reject Saint-Amant's "crime innocent, à quoi la Nature consent." [11] A foolish failure to understand the superiority of green causes lovers to insult trees (themselves the worthier objects of love) by carving on them the names of women. (This happens in Saint-Amant's *Jouissance.*) Since it is the green garden, and not women that the poet chooses to regard as amorous, it would be farcically logical for him to carve on the trees their own names. The garden is not to have women or their names or their love in it. It is natural (green) and amorous (green—a "norm" of the poem) in quite a different way from the libertine garden.

Love enters this garden, but only when the pursuit of the white and red is done, and we are without appetite. (Love is here indiscriminately the pursued and the pursuer. Weary with the race and exertion (*heat*) it "makes a retreat" in the garden; hard-pressed by pursuers it carries out a military retreat.) The place of retreat has therefore Love, but not women: they are metamorphosed into trees. The gods, who might be expected to know, have been misunderstood; they pursued women not as women but as potential trees, for the green and not for the red and white. Marvell, in this witty version of the metamorphoses, continues to "disable" the idea of sexual love. Here one needs quite firmly to delimit the reference, because it is confusing to think of *laurel* and *reed* as having symbolic significations. It is interesting that this comic metamorphosis (which has affinities with the fashionable mock-heroic) was practised for their own ends by the libertine poets; for example, in Saint-Amant's "La Metamorphose de Lyrian et de Sylvie," in Stanley's Marinesque "Apollo and Daphne," in Carew's "Rapture," where Lucrece and other types of chastity become sensualists in the libertine paradise, and very notably in Lovelace. Thus, in "Against the Love of Great Ones":

> *Ixion* willingly doth feele
> The Gyre of his eternal wheele,
> Nor would he now exchange his paine
> For Cloudes and Goddesses againe. (*Poems,* p. 75)

The sensuous appeal of this garden is, then, not sexual, as it is in the libertines. It has, none the less, all the enchantment of the Earthly Paradise, and all its innocence: this is the topic of the fifth stanza. The trees and plants press their fruit upon him, and their gifts are in strong contrast to those of the libertine garden,

> Love then unstinted, Love did sip,
> And Cherries pluck'd fresh from the Lip,
>   On Cheeks and Roses free he fed;
> Lasses like *Autumne* Plums did drop,
> And Lads, indifferently did crop
>   A Flower, and a Maiden-head. (*Poems,* p. 146)

The fruits of green, not of red and white, are offered in primeval abundance, as they are in the Fortunate Islands or in any paradise.

Everything is by nature lush and fertile; the difference between this and a paradise containing a woman is that here a Fall is of light consequence, and without tragic significance. ("Insnar'd with *flowers, I* fall on grass.") In the same way, Marvell had in "Upon Appleton House" (LXXVII) bound himself with the entanglements not of wanton limbs, in the libertine manner of Carew, Randolph and Stanley, but of woodbine, briar and bramble. The same imagery is still in use for amorous purposes in the poetry of Leigh.

In this garden both man and nature are unfallen; it is therefore, for all its richness, not a trap for virtue but a paradise of perfect innocence. Even the fall is innocent; the sensuous allurements of the trees are harmless, and there is no need to "fence The Batteries of alluring Sense." It is evident that Empson and King were quite right to find here a direct allusion to the Fall.

Modern commentators all agree that the sixth stanza, central to the poem, is a witty Platonism, and of course this is so. The danger is that the Platonism can be made to appear doctrinal and even recherché, when in fact it is reasonably modest, and directly related to genre treatments of love in gardens. There is, however, a famous ambiguity in the first two lines: how are we to take "from pleasure less"? It can mean simply (1) reduced by pleasure, or (2) that the mind retires because it experiences less pleasure than the senses, or (3) that it retires from the lesser pleasure to the greater. The first of these might be related to the doctrine of the creation in *Paradise Lost,* VII, 168f.— "I am who fill Infinitude, nor vacuous the space. Though I uncircumscrib'd myself retire, And put not forth my goodness. . . ." This would be consistent with the analogy later drawn between the human and the divine minds. But the second is more likely to be the dominant meaning, with a proper distinction between mind and sense which is obviously relevant to the theme. ("None can chain a mind Whom this sweet Chordage cannot bind"). The third meaning is easily associated with this interpretation. The mind withdraws from the sensual gratification offered in order to enjoy a happiness of the imagination. In terms of the genre, it rejects the *Jouissance* for the *Solitude*—indeed, Saint-Amant, in a poem which prefers the contemplative garden, writes of it thus:

> Tantost, faisant agir mes sens
> Sur des sujets *de moindre estofe,*
> De marche en autre je descens
> Dans les termes du philosophe;
> Nature n'a point de secret

Que d'un soin libre, mais discret,
Ma curiosité ne sonde;
Et, dans ma recherche profonde,
Je loge en moy tout l'univers.
Là, songeant au flus et reflus,
Je m'abisme dans cette idée;
Son mouvement me rend perclus,
Et mon âme en est obsedée. (I, 32; my Italics)

To put it another way, one prefers a different kind of ecstasy from that of the libertine, described by the same poet in his *Jouissance,* which Stanley translated. Saint-Amant represents his solitary as acquiring from nature knowledge of the forms, and the next two lines of Marvell's stanza seem to do likewise. The metaphor is not unfamiliar— "Some have affirm'd that what on earth we find The sea can parallel for shape and kind"—and the idea is that the forms exist in the mind of man as they do in the mind of God. By virtue of the imagination the mind can create worlds and seas too which have nothing to do with the world which is reported by the senses. This is the passage which seems to have caused such trouble to commentators, who look to learned originals like Plotinus and Ficino for the explanation: but in fact the Platonism here is dilute and current.

It is commonplace of Renaissance poetic that God is a poet, and that the poet has the honour of this comparison only because of the creative force of fancy or imagination. Nor is the power exclusive to poets. The mind, which "all effects into their causes brings," [12] can through the imagination alone devise new and rare things: as Puttenham says, "the phantasticall part of man (if it be not disordered) is a representer of the best, most comely and bewtifull images or apparences of thinges to the soule and according to their very truth" (p. 19). Puttenham shuns "disordered phantasies . . . monstruous imaginations or conceits" as being alien to the truth of imagination, but it is conceivable that Marvell, in his suggestion of the mind's ability to create, refers to a more modern psychology and poetic, with its roots in the Renaissance, but with a new emphasis. Thus Cowley in his Pindaric "The Muse" says that the coach of poetry can go anywhere:

And all's an *open Road* to *thee.*
Whatever *God* did say,
Is all thy plain and smooth, uninterrupted *Way.*
Nay, ev'n beyond his *Works* thy *Voyages* are known,
Thou hast a thousand *Worlds* too of thine *own.*

> Thou speak'st, great *Queen*, in the same *Stile* as *he*,
> And *a new World* leaps forth, when *thou* say'st, *Let it be*.

And in a note he obligingly explains this:

> The meaning is, that *Poetry* treats not only of all Things
> that are, or can be, but makes *Creatures* of her own, as *Cen-
> taurs, Satyrs, Fairies,* &c., makes *Persons* and *Actions* of her
> own . . . makes *Beasts, Trees, Waters,* and other irrational
> and insensible Things to act above the Possibility of their
> Natures as to *understand* and *speak;* nay makes what *Gods*
> it pleases too without *Idolatry,* and varies all these into in-
> numerable *Systems,* or *Worlds* of Invention.

These other worlds are thoughts in the mind of man as the world is a
thought in the mind of God. Empson is probably right in his guess
that *streight* means "packed together" as well as "at once." The whole
idea is illuminated by a passage of extraordinary interest in Leigh
(who was imbued with that passion for optics which later became
common among poets) in which the reduced images of the eye are
contrasted with the illimitable visions of the mind. The mind contains
everything undiminished by the deficiencies of sense.[13] The mental
activity which Marvell is describing is clear; it is the working of the
imagination, which, psychologically, follows sense and precedes intellection, and is therefore the means of rejecting the voluptuous suggestions of sense; and which "performs its function when the sensible
object is rejected or even removed." [14] The mind's newly created
worlds are, in the strict sense, phantasms, and without substance: and
since they have the same mental status as the created world, it is fair
to say that "all that's made" is being annihilated, reduced to a thought.

But a green thought? This is a great bogey; but surely the thought
is green because the solitude is green, which means that it is also the
antithesis of voluptuousness? Here the normative signification of green
in the poem is in accord with what is after all a common enough notion
—green for innocence, Thus, in "Aramantha" Lovelace asks:

> Can trees be green, and to the Ay'r
> Thus prostitute their flowing Hayr? (*Poems,* p. 112)

But I cannot think the green has any more extensive symbolic intention. Green is still opposed to red and white; all this is possible only
when women are absent and the senses innocently engaged.

The stanza thus alludes to the favourable conditions which enable the mind to apply itself to contemplation. The process is wittily described, and the psychology requires no explanation in terms of any doctrinaire Platonism, whether pseudo-Dionysian, Plotinian, or Florentine.

The seventh stanza is also subject to much ingenious comment. The poet allows his mind to contemplate the ideas, and his soul begins a Platonic ascent. Here there are obvious parallels in the English mystics, in Plotinus, in medieval and Florentine Platonism; but we must see this stanza as we see the rest of the poem, in relation to the genre. Failing to do this we shall be involved in an endless strife between rival symbolisms, as we are if we try to find an external significance for *green*. As it is, there is no need to be over-curious about the fountain; its obvious symbolic quality may have an interesting history, but it is primarily an easily accessible emblem of purity As for the use of the bird as an emblem of the soul, that is an image popularized by Castiglione,[15] and used by Spenser of the early stages of the ascent:

> Beginning then below, with th'easie vew
> Of this base world, subject to fleshly eye,
> From thence to mount aloft by order dew,
> To contemplation of th'immortall sky,
> Of that soare faulcon so I learne to fly,
> That flags awhile her fluttering wings beneath,
> Till she her selfe for stronger flight can breath.
> (*Hymne of Heavenly Beauty*, pp. 22–8)

Spenser has just passed from the consideration of woman's love and beauty to the heavenly love and beauty. The bird which prepares its wings for flight is evidently a symbol with as settled a meaning as the dew, which Marvell also shared with many other poets.

The hungry soul, deceived with false beauties, may have "after vain deceiptfull shadowes sought"—but at last it looks "up to that soveraine light, From whose pure beams al perfect beauty springs" (*H.H.B.*, 291, 295). Marvell's bird "Waves in its Plumes the various Light." Once more we might spring to Ebreo or Plotinus or even Haydocke, but we shall do better to note how this same image is used in literature more closely related to Marvell.

> Les oyseaux, d'un joyeux ramage,
> En chantant semblent adorer
> La lumière qui vient dorer
> Leur cabinet et leur plumage—

thus Théophile, in his Ode, "Le Matin." [16] In *Partheneia Sacra* Hawkins uses the dove as other poets use the dew or the rainbow—

> Being of what coulour soever, her neck being opposed to the Sun wil diversify into a thousand coulours, more various then the Iris it-self, or that Bird of *Juno* in al her pride; as scarlet, cerulean, flame-coulour, and yealding a flash like the Carbuncle, with vermilion, ash-coulour, and manie others besides. . . . (p. 202)

Marvell's use of the Platonic light-symbolism is therefore not technical, as it might be in Chapman, but generalized, as in Quarles or Vaughan, and affected by imagery associated with the garden genres. We are thus reminded that the point about the ascent towards the pure source of light is not that it can be achieved, but that it can be a product of *Solitude* rather than of *Jouissance* and that it is an alternative to libertine behaviour in gardens. It is the ecstasy not of beauty but of heavenly beauty.

The eighth stanza at last makes this theme explicit. This is a special solitude, which can only exist in the absence of women, the agents of the most powerful voluptuous temptation. This has been implied throughout, but it is now wittily stated in the first clear reference to Eden. The notion that Adam would have been happy without a mate is not, of course, novel; St. Ambrose believed it. Here it is another way of putting the case that woman offers the wrong beauty, the wrong love, the red and white instead of the green. Eve deprived Adam of solitude, and gave him instead an inferior joy. Indeed she was his punishment for being mortal (rather than pure Intelligence?). Her absence would be equivalent to the gift of a paradise (since her presence means the loss of the only one there is). This is easy enough, and a good example of how naturally we read references to the more familiar conceptions of theology and philosophy as part of the play of wit within the limited range of a genre.

In the last stanza the temperate quiet of the garden is once more asserted, by way of conclusion. (The Earthly Paradise is always in the temperate zone.) The time, for us as for the bee (a pun on "thyme") is sweet and rewarding; hours of innocence are told by a dial of pure herbs and flowers. The sun is "milder" because in this zodiac of flowers fragrance is substituted for heat; Miss Bradbrook and Miss Lloyd Thomas have some good observations here. The time computed is likewise spent in fragrant rather than hot pursuits. This is the *Solitude*, not the *Jouissance;* the garden of the *solitaire* whose soul rises towards divine beauty, not that of the voluptuary who voluntarily surrenders to the delights of the senses.

This ends the attempt to read "The Garden" as a poem of a definite historical kind and to explore its delicate allusions to a genre of which the "norms" are within limits ascertainable. Although it is very improbable that such an attempt can avoid errors of both sophistication and simplification, one may reasonably claim for it that in substituting poetry for metaphysics it does no violence to the richness and subtlety of its subject.

NOTES

[1] "The Mode of Existence of a Literary Work of Art," *Critiques and Essays in Criticism, 1920–1948,* ed. R. W. Stallman, 1949, pp. 210–23.

[2] M. C. Bradbrook, "Marvell and the Poetry of Rural Solitude," *RES,* XVII (1941), 37–46; M. C. Bradbrook and M. G. Lloyd Thomas, *Andrew Marvell* (Cambridge, 1940).

[3] Montaigne, *Essayes,* trans. by John Florio, Everyman Edition, III, 316.

[4] See F. A. Yates, *The French Academies of the Sixteenth Century,* 1947, pp. 128 ff. From Plato (*Symposium* 202A, *Republic* 477, et seq.) through the Pléiade to Sidney there ran the argument that poets were not competent to make philosophical statements; they affirm nothing.

[5] *Notes and Queries,* March 29th, 1952, pp. 136–8.

[6] *Poems,* ed. G. Thorn-Drury, 1929, p. 110.

[7] *Poems,* ed. C. H. Wilkinson, 1930, p. 147.

[8] *De Constantia, Of Constancie,* trans. by Sir J. Stradling, ed. R. Kirk and C. M. Hall, 1939, pp. 132 ff.

[9] *Partheneia Sacra,* ed. Iain Fletcher, 1950 (reprint of 1633), p. 2.

[10] Proposed by A. H. King, *English Studies,* XX (1938), 118–21.

[11] *Œuvres Complètes,* ed. Ch.-L. Livet, 1855, I, 119.

[12] Sir John Davies, *Nosce Teipsum* ("The Intellectual Powers of the Soul," stanza 5).

[13] *Poems,* ed. Hugh Macdonald, 1947, pp. 36 ff.

[14] Gianfrancesco Pico della Mirandola, *De Imaginatione,* ed. and trans. H. Caplan, 1930, p. 29.

[15] *The Book of the Courtier,* translated by Thomas Hoby, Everyman Edition, p. 338.

[16] *Œuvres Complètes,* ed. M. Alleaume, 1856, I, 174–5.

FRANK J. WARNKE

✍

Play and Metamorphosis in Marvell's Poetry

Marvell's well-known complexity as a lyric poet derives largely from his juxtaposition of opposed kinds of experience. In "Upon Appleton House," a poem of ingenious intellectual compliment turns into a profound celebration of the metamorphoses of Nature; in "The Garden" the experiences of the body, mind, and soul are reproduced but not coordinated with each other; in "To His Coy Mistress" an attitude of rueful humor underlies but does not undercut a desperate passion. In each of these famous cases the poet's tone—which might be described as combining levity and transport in more or less equal proportions—is his chief vehicle for conveying his sense of the contradictions of experience. This tone of serious playfulness is found elsewhere in Marvell too—notably in "The Gallery," "The Picture of Little T. C. in a Prospect of Flowers," and "A Dialogue between the Soul and Body." I should like to concentrate primarily on these three poems in the hope of demonstrating that the poet's playfulness has significant connections with the elements of myth and metamorphosis which occur in his poetry, and that a consideration of these connections may possibly lead to a new guiding principle for approaching this most elusive of poets.

"The Gallery," which takes its form as a series of tableaux of the speaker's mistress in the various aspects she assumes in his mind, strikes us at once with its extreme variations of tone, which range from the ludicrous to the seductive, from the playful to the transcendent.

From *Studies in English Literature 1500–1900*, V (1965), pp. 23–30. Reprinted by permission of *Studies in English Literature*.

Some of the pictures are very funny, as when she appears as ". . . an Inhumane Murtheress;/Examining upon our hearts/Thy fertile Shop of cruel Arts" or as ". . . an Enchantress . . . Vexing thy restless Lover's Ghost," one who "by a Light obscure dost rave/Over his Entrails, in the Cave;/Divining thence, with horrid Care,/How long thou shalt continue fair." [1] The humor springs not only from the grotesque parody of Petrarchan convention but also from the monstrous, almost farcical exaggeration of that parody. And yet it is impossible to dismiss the poem as simple parody. The tableaux which alternate with those already quoted make such a procedure impossible. In the first of them the girl appears as Aurora:

> But, on the other side, th' art drawn
> Like to *Aurora* in the Dawn;
> When in the East she slumb'ring lyes,
> And stretches out her silky Thighs;
> While all the morning Quire does sing,
> And *Manna* falls, and Roses spring;
> And, at thy Feet, the wooing Doves
> Sit perfecting their harmless Loves.

In the second she is Venus:

> But, against that, thou sit'st a float
> Like *Venus* in her pearly Boat.
> The *Halcyons,* calming all that's nigh,
> Betwixt the Air and Water fly.
> Or, if some rowling Wave appears,
> A Mass of Ambergris it bears.
> Nor blows more wind than what may well
> Convoy the Perfume to the Smell.

In each instance Marvell's appeal is to the myth-oriented sensibility of the Renaissance, and in neither does his evocation appear to be modified by satire or irony; on the contrary, in both stanzas the transformation of the mistress is achieved in full mythic terms: that is, the mythological similes are justified by the identification of the mistress with aspects of Nature, specifically the sky and the sea, rather than being simply applied as conventional compliment or ornament. It is surprising that the poem as a whole is not shattered by the extreme tension which spans it, a tension between poles of parodistic hyperbole and quasi-ritualistic incantation. Somehow the poem maintains its unity, convincing us both that there is a sense in which the poet seriously in-tends his comic exaggerations and that there is a sense in which he is amused by his lyric-evocations. (The same thing, I think, is true in "The Unfortunate Lover," in which burlesque overstatement does not destroy the effect of passionate intensity which runs through the entire poem.) To return to "The Gallery," perhaps the final stanza will provide a clue as to the spirit in which we should take the whole complex structure of riddling tonal suggestions:

> But, of these Pictures and the rest,
> That at the Entrance likes me best:
> Where the same Posture, and the Look
> Remains, with which I first was took.
> A tender Shepherdess, whose Hair
> Hangs loosely playing in the Air,
> Transplanting Flow'rs from the green Hill,
> To crown her Head, and Bosome fill.

The diverse metamorphoses of which the beloved is capable have their origin in her role as Shepherdess. This aspect, in which the speaker first beheld her, is as it were the source of her various masquerades, and her characteristic activity under this aspect is a significant one— "Transplanting Flow'rs from the green Hill,/To crown her Head, and Bosome fill"—associating herself, perhaps even identifying herself, with the green world of Nature. At this point one might think of the green world as it is evoked in "The Garden" and "Upon Appleton House"— "that unfathomable Grass" which is simultaneously an emblem of hope, rejuvenation, and rebirth, a stage-setting susceptible of innumerable changes and metamorphoses, and a sea in which individual identity is swallowed up only to re-emerge transformed. The versatile Clora of "The Gallery" is all things to her lover—murderess, Aurora, enchantress, and Venus—because she is a shepherdess and hence directly in touch with the metamorphic principle of Nature. She is also, as the poem does not let us forget, a cultivated lady capable of being amused by her lover's ingenuity.

The last observation implies a warning. Ought one to seek any sort of intellectual consistency in a poem as frankly playful as "The Gallery"? It seems to me that it is precisely the poem's playfulness which supplies its consistency and its artistic unity—if we remember that the concept of *play* incorporates meanings not only of *jest, levity, game,* and *make-believe,* but also of *contest* and *drama.* As play, "The Gallery" is an amusing poem, but in exactly the same capacity it is a serious attempt to participate in the realities of Nature and Love. For the play-spirit, in its riddling evocation of the contradictions of experience, aims, however paradoxically, at participating in reality; the mere act of play-ing at an identity, making believe that one is other than oneself, consti-tutes a breakthrough into an area not circumscribed by the limitations of individuality—even as such an act, since one is not really deceived, simultaneously serves to assert one's individuality. The act of play is, even in its more primitive manifestations, a kind of meta-physical ac-tivity. In *Homo Ludens,* his provocative study of the play element in culture,[2] Johan Huizinga maintains that play is the central element in all civilization, and that the play-attitude, hovering somewhere beyond both belief and disbelief, is the defining feature of myth and ritual. Play, in its guise as riddle or conundrum, mirrors forth "the eternal conflict of opposites which is the root-principle of existence." [3] The quotation seems a very apt description of what happens in a Marvell poem, even one as seemingly uncomplicated as "The Gallery." It surely explains why Clora assumes so many disguises, why she operates as a mythic figure, and why, somehow, she amuses her devoted lover.

"The Picture of Little T. C. in a Prospect of Flowers" is another poem in which the play-element is conspicuous: the familiar parody of Petrarchanism appears in stanzas 2 and 3, intensified immensely by the playful consideration that in this case the *dolce guerrera,* the "virtuous Enemy of Man" whose elevated chastity will drive men to despair, is a little girl. The effect is comparable to that achieved near the end of "Upon Appleton House," when little Maria Fairfax makes her appear-ance and is promptly likened to the world-soul. In both cases the poet's attitude is complicated: he doesn't mean his outrageous compliments in any single sense, and yet there is a sense in which both compliments are justified—Maria, as a representative of the virtuous Fairfax family and as an agent of the fertility principle celebrated throughout the poem, is, in a way, accurately described by the following stanza:

> 'Tis *She* that to these Gardens gave
> That wondrous Beauty which they have;
> *She* streightness on the Woods bestows;
> To *Her* the Meadow sweetness owes;
> Nothing could make the River be
> So Chrystal-pure but only *She;*
> *She* yet more Pure, Sweet, Streight, and Fair,
> Then Gardens, Woods, Meads, Rivers are.
>   ("Upon Appleton House," stanza LXXXVII)

Similarly, T. C. is a bud who will become a blossom, a girl who will become a woman, through the natural metamorphoses of the green world of which she is both an aspect and an interpreter.

Despite her youth—or perhaps because of it—T. C. stands in a more complicated relationship to Nature than does Clora at the end of "The Gallery." Like Clora, she is associated with the green world of transformation and rebirth, but she is identified not only with the female principle of generation but also with the general human principle of intellect or spirit. Her activity in the first stanza is like that of Adam in the Garden of Eden—she names the flowers and, in so doing, bestows on the entities of Nature the higher reality which comes only through being perceived by mind:

> In the green Grass she loves to lie,
> And there with her fair Aspect tames
> The Wilder flow'rs, and gives them names:
> But only with the Roses playes;
> And them does tell
> What Colour best becomes them, and what Smell.

Marvell is fully aware of the ironies involved in making a child stand for human intellect, and stanza 4 indicates that he is aware of yet deeper ironies, those implicit in the pretensions of mind itself in its supremely arrogant confrontation of external Nature:

> Mean time, whilst every verdant thing
> It self does at thy Beauty charm,
> Reform the errours of the Spring;
> Make that the Tulpis may have share
> Of sweetness, seeing they are fair;
> And Roses of their thorns disarm:
> But most procure
> That Violets may a longer Age endure.

Both as the shaping impulse of human intellect and as the potential champion of chastity, T. C. is equated with Spirit, and yet her posture in stanza 1, like that of Clora, associates her intimately with Nature. It is his remarkably balanced sense of the relative claims of these centrally opposed conceptions (the *Geist* and *Natur* of Thomas Mann) which leads Marvell to the subtle warning which closes the poem:

> But O young beauty of the Woods,
> Whom Nature courts with fruits and flow'rs,
> Gather the Flow'rs, but spare the Buds;
> Lest *Flora* angry at thy crime,
> To kill her Infants in their prime,
> Do quickly make th' Example Yours;
>   And, ere we see,
> Nip in the blossome all our hopes and Thee.

Man is never wholly either Nature or Spirit, as the drawn battle in Marvell's "Dialogue between the Soul and Body" reminds us, and the poet's warning to the little girl is based on his sense of the metaphysical complexity of experience. But to speak too somberly of "warning" and "balance" is to injure fatally the delicate tone of the poem, for it is concerned not with making allegorical statements about experience but with participating in the reality of experience through the magic ritual of play—which, by pretending that a little girl is alternately a devastating love object and the mind of man itself, imitates the transforming alchemy of that Nature which is the frame of subject and poem alike.

I have mentioned the "Dialogue between the Soul and Body" as an exemplification of Marvell's awareness of the balanced claims of the traditional components of man. It is also, in its agonistic structure, characteristic of the play-ritual which Huizinga posits as central to the mythic confrontation of reality. The immediately striking trait of the initial arguments of both Soul and Body is their self-defeating quality; neither can conceive of its desired liberty in terms other than those provided by its opponent. Soul begins the debate with the following complaint:

> O who shall, from this Dungeon, raise
> A Soul inslav'd so many wayes?
> With bolts of Bones, that fetter'd stands
> In Feet; and manacled in Hands.
> Here blinded with an Eye; and there
> Deaf with the drumming of an Ear.
> A Soul hung up, as 'twere, in Chains
> Of Nerves, and Arteries, and Veins.
> Tortur'd, besides each other part,
> In a vain Head, and double Heart.

And Body replies in lines which puzzlingly imply its own death as the only possible condition of liberty. Soul's final protestation, that only

non-material existence can satisfy it, is traditional enough, but the lines
with which Body closes the poem are startling in their suggestions:

> What but a Soul could have the wit
> To build me up for Sin so fit?
> So Architects do square and hew,
> Green Trees that in the Forest grew.

What emerges from the debate is a kind of balanced scheme: an ideal
world of pure Spirit toward which Soul is impelled, and an ideal world
of pure, undifferentiated Nature (the "green world" of so many of
Marvell's poems) toward which Body longs. Each constitutes an ideal
order in itself, but man can find his rest in neither. He remains, to borrow again from Thomas Mann, the *Herr der Gegensätze,* the "Lord
of the Counterpositions."

Neither Body nor Soul can possibly win the eternal debate, and
Marvell's tone scrupulously avoids even hinting at a judgment between
them. Ultimately, the agon in which they are engaged is both necessary
and inconclusive, as the abstract reduction of the irreconcilable contradictions in the center of which man takes his being, the contradictions
which give Clora her multiple aspects and which make little T. C.
simultaneously a part of Nature, an expression of pure Spirit, a goddess
of chastity, and a little girl lying in the grass. The play-attitude enables
the poet to engage fully, without commitment, in the dance of contradictions which makes up experience.

The unspoken assumptions underlying my reading of these poems are
for the most part conventional enough, those of modern criticism in
general. They include the beliefs that a poem is unparaphraseable, that
the author's conscious aim, even if ascertainable, does not exhaust the
poem's area of meaning, and that a poem ought to be regarded as an
esthetic construction rather than as a discursive statement. But Marvell's poetry, it seems to me, requires that we apply these assumptions
with special rigor. For, although it is unusually intellectual poetry in
both its rhetoric and its typical structure, it is poetry which is never
reducible to statement, scarcely, indeed, reducible to meaning in the
accepted sense of the word. For literary critics—in general quite properly concerned with the unearthing of meanings—such poetry can be
troublesome. One of the strengths of Empson's brilliant analysis of "The
Garden" is the critic's awareness that he is dealing with implications
rather than statements, but, if one agrees with his contention that "The
chief point of the poem is to contrast and reconcile conscious and unconscious states, intuitive and intellectual modes of apprehension," [4] it

is advisable to bear in mind that the reconciliation can only take place as play and in the sphere of play, as a performance rather than as a demonstration.

Many otherwise impressive analyses of Marvell's work are weakened, I think, by a failure to allow for the full force of the play-element. Don Cameron Allen's erudite and useful study of "Upon Appleton House," [5] for example, errs, I think, in abstracting from that complicated poem too forceful and serious a meaning. The perfect balance between the claims of engagement and those of withdrawal as presented in the poem makes it impossible for me to agree that its aim is simply to urge Fairfax's return to public life, and the playful tone of the entire mowing scene leads me to find in it not the "bitter pastoralism" of a serious allegory of the Civil War but rather the innocuous and ideal pastoralism of a played equivalent of that war—violence metamorphosed into a life-giving ritual of fertility. What I am suggesting is that Marvell, even when he most distinctly seems to be conveying meanings to us, is really playing with us, indulging in *trompe-l'intellect* effects as the Baroque plastic artist indulges in *trompe-l'oeil* effects, and that a consistent awareness of his playfulness is essential to a full response to his art. At the heart of Marvell's achievement we find always the sportive elements of game, contest, and make-believe—the constituents of a play attitude which enables the poet to turn metaphor into metamorphosis, to create a world with the materials of his own sophisticated version of the mythic imagination.

NOTES

[1] All quotations from Marvell are from Andrew Marvell, *Poems and Letters*, ed. H. M. Margoliouth, 2 v. (Oxford, 2nd. ed., 1952).

[2] J. Huizinga, *Homo Ludens*, Beacon Press ed. of Eng. translation (Boston, 1955).

[3] Huizinga, p. 116.

[4] W. Empson, *Some Versions of Pastoral* (London, 1935), p. 119.

[5] D. C. Allen, in *Image and Meaning: Metaphoric Traditions in Renaissance Poetry* (Baltimore, 1960), pp. 115–153.

HAROLD E. TOLIVER

Pastoral Form and Idea in Some Poems of Marvell

Because pastoral often involves an opposition between an idealized concept of nature and actual existence, and a conflict between the search
for simplicity and a complex, pressing society, it is not surprising that
Marvell found it a hospitable medium. Overwhelmed by the existent,
the pastoral poet frequently retreats from the "red and white" world
into the "green" world. In poems of "pastoral success" (as I shall call
them—without, of course, implying a value judgment), he often con-
solidates gains, becomes reoriented toward the world, and finally re-
enters society. The general pattern varies from poet to poet and from
poem to poem, but is remarkably persistent. "The Garden," of all
Marvell's poems, perhaps most obviously falls into the general pattern.
Though the poet does not emerge from the *hortus conclusus* where fair
Quiet and Innocence dwell, he nevertheless endorses the processes of
time which have threatened to destroy the contemplative life: "How
could such sweet and wholsome Hours/Be reckon'd but with herbs and
flow'rs!" "Upon Appleton House," too, works within the same general
framework. The poet leaves the contemplative sanctuary of the grove
having gained a new capacity to deal with the active world. The order
and harmony of the forest is suffused through both art and the moral
life: the scorching sun in the warlike meadow is metamorphosed into
the *"tuned* Fires" of the birds and only the "equal Flames" of the stock
doves "burn." Hence, after leaving the protective shades, Marvell finds

From *Texas Studies in Literature and Language*, V (1963–64), pp. 83–97.
Reprinted by permission of the University of Texas Press.

the world to be no longer "a rude heap together hurl'd," a "putrid Earth," but a cosmos "vitrifi'd" by a "flame" tried in heaven. The forest-sanctuary is in a sense an instrument of immanence brought into action by the symbols the poet finds there, symbols which enable art to re-order, "tune," and "straighten" nature.

In Christian pastoralists such as Spenser and Milton, nature in the broad sense of the word, including human nature, presents stronger barriers to reconciling what is and what ought to be—to expect flowers to atone for death is simply to "dally with false surmise." If ideal being is to be conceived, Milton discovers, the poet must seek not an Eden of natural innocence—Adam lost that beyond recovery—but a pastoral of transcendent dimensions in which one hears "the unexpressive nuptiall Song" in "other groves, and other streams." Even in "The Garden," of course, the processes of distillation, metamorphosis, and annihilation are necessary in order to control the real world and to rise to creative "green thought in green shade."

This pattern of retreat, discovery of creative capacity, and resurgent control of nature we discover in much pastoral poetry: distraction, motion, and diversity are frozen, and in a quiet moment of meditation or song the "shepherd" relocates himself. In so doing he may re-examine the function of poetry itself, that is to say, relate self-creation to artistic creation. The soul in "The Garden," singing and waving in its plumes the various lights, combines the creative power of the mind and the vegetative functions of the body reveling in melons and curious peaches. It reflects physical nature but transforms, "*idea*lizes" it. When the antagonism between the self and what exists, or between art and nature, is found to be resolvable like this, the effect is usually one of release—the prophetic poet goes off to "fresh woods and pastures new" or simply enjoys in a spontaneous way the "fruits and flow'rs."

In contrast to this discovery of elemental "being," antipastoral poems, or poems of "pastoral failure," to give them a convenient name, describe an inability to stay inside the protected world where "letting things be" is possible: Keats's nightingale is "buried deep/ In the next valley-glades" leaving him in a state of bewilderment, alone in the unsatisfactory company of his "sole self." Juliana causes the Mower to get lost in the forest, never to find his "home"; a corrupted idea of art destroys the natural "garden" and turns the Mower into a destructive agent, a "Mower against Gardens"; or "wanton Troopers" destroy the garden shelter of the nymph. In all of these, awakening to the "real" world signifies an incompatibility between essence and existence. In addition, the difficulty of the artist to shape his environment into poetic symbol may be involved. If the link with nature is broken, hopes of achieving order and meaning fail, or in the special jargon of the pastoral, the "greenness of the Grass" is destroyed, as Juliana destroys the Mower, the keeper of the meadow: "She/ What I do to the grass, does to my Thoughts and me." Rather than achieving rapport with nature, the Mower acknowledges the descent of chaos: "And Flow'rs, and Grass, and I and all/ Will in one common Ruine fall," just as Spenser's Colin falls in ruin as lover, religious reformer, and artist in the December Eclogue. And so in "A Dialogue between Thyrsis and Dorinda," Elysium lies only in "yonder Skie" where all shepherds are equal. In this world, shepherds are "sick, and fain would dye" and so the artist's instruments are of no avail. (In heaven where "thine Ears/ May feast with Musick of the Spheres" without the mediation of artists, they have no practical use.)

The "successful" pastoral as a form, then, fuses the real and the ideal without destroying either: if Adonis is dead and bleeding, "the blood and tears become flowers upon the ground," as Bion's "Lament for Adonis" says; "of the blood comes the rose, and of the tears the windflower." But poems of pastoral failure, while keeping that fusion before us as an ideal to be sought, move toward dissolution and disharmony. We are perhaps more at home with the latter side of pastoral, the destruction of the ideal by the real. When Yeats projects the modern world against the old comfortable myths, for example, it invariably fails to measure up to them, but wins anyway:

> Locke sank into a swoon;
> The Garden died;
> God took the spinning-jenny
> Out of his side.

The companion of the modern Adam, his Jenny, is a mere machine; the providential garden has become a deistic mechanism, a "clock-watcher" universe. Hence the "Song of the Happy Shepherd" is not a happy song:

> The woods of Arcady are dead,
> And over is their antique joy;
> Of old is the world on dreaming fed;
> Grey truth is now her painted toy.

And, as Eliot indicates in "Burnt Norton," the pastoral ideal serves primarily as a reminder of what might have been:

> Footfalls echo in the memory
> Down the passage which we did not take
> Towards the door we never opened
> Into the rose-garden.

Modern pastoral, generally speaking, has but "one foot in Eden," in Edwin Muir's phrase, or perhaps none at all, as is discovered by the man with the double axe in Frost's "New Hampshire," who

> went alone against a grove of trees;
> But his heart failing him, he dropped the axe
> And ran for shelter quoting Matthew Arnold:
> "Nature is cruel, man is sick of blood; . . ."
> He had a special terror of the flux
> That showed itself in dendrophobia.

Marvell in some ways predicts this "terror of the flux." Unlike Frost's New York alec in "the new school of the pseudo-phallic," he finds in nature imagery and symbols for some of his richest and most compressed poetry, and he does not, of course, lose composure. But on the other hand neither does he suffer from the dendro-eudaemonia of a later period which holds that "One impulse from a vernal wood/ May teach you more of man,/ Of moral evil and of good,/ Than all the sages can." Rather, poems of pastoral success and pastoral failure exist side by side and explore the same problem from slightly different points of view. "The Coronet," "Bermudas," "Clorinda and Damon," and the mower poems will serve to illustrate some of the major variations.

In "The Coronet" involvement in nature is found to be costly in terms of personal sacrifice, but the kind of pastoral which looks for atonement in the beauty and innocence of nature is rejected only to find a valid use for another kind. If the coronet is spoiled as a crown for the head of "the king of Glory," it may still crown His feet—in fact, the very act of writing the pastoral poem, symbolized by the gathering and weaving of the flowers, shows the natural man to be compatible with the religious man. The poetic garland, violently shattered at Christ's feet, becomes the "spoils" of victory as well as the spoiled wreath:

> When for the Thorns with which I long, too long,
> With many a piercing wound,
> My Saviours head have crown'd,
> I seek with Garlands to redress that Wrong:
> Through every Garden, every Mead,

I gather flow'rs (my fruits are only flow'rs)
    Dismantling all the fragrant Towers
That once adorn'd my Shepherdesses head.
And now when I have summ'd up all my store,
    Thinking (so I my self deceive)
    So rich a Chaplet thence to weave
As never yet the king of Glory wore:
    Alas I find the Serpent old
    That, twining in his speckled breast,
    About the flow'rs disguis'd does fold,
    With wreaths of Fame and Interest.
Ah, foolish Man, that would'st debase with them,
And mortal Glory, Heavens Diadem!
But thou who only could'st the Serpent tame,
Either his slipp'ry knots at once untie,
And disintangle all his winding Snare:
Or shatter too with him my curious frame:
And let these wither, so that he may die,
Though set with Skill and chosen out with Care.
That they, while Thou on both their Spoils dost tread,
May crown thy Feet, that could not crown thy Head.

The final lines in which Satan is shattered along with the "curious frame" may refer obliquely to the prophecy of Genesis 3:15: "I will put enmity between thee and the woman and between thy seed and her seed; it shall bruise thy head and thou shalt bruise his heal." [1] St. Gregory had found the mystery of the Incarnation symbolized by Christ's feet, by which divinity touched earth; [2] and so the coronet of flowers, like the flowers in Vaughan's "St. Mary Magdalen," finds its place at that point where the supernatural meets and subdues the natural:

    Why art thou humbled thus, and low
    As earth, thy lovely head dost bow?
    Dear *Soul!* thou knew'st, flowers here on earth
    At their Lords foot-stool have their birth;
    Therefore thy wither'd self in haste
    Beneath his blest feet thou didst cast,
    That at the root of this green tree
    Thy great decays restor'd might be.

The flowers which the meads and gardens yield are thus not entirely useless; if they cannot be salvaged in any other way, they may at least serve a sacrificial function. The impulse to create something of value out of nature is neither pure nor impure, the coronet neither complete gain nor complete loss. But only when the act of gathering and weaving the flowers, "set with Skill and chosen out with Care," is made does one arrive at self-recognition and an awareness of the gulf that separates nature and grace. The pastoral daydream is shattered by fame and interest, but the result is the discovery of a valid function for the pastoral artist, not a total failure to integrate existence and essence.

In a like manner, in "Clorinda and Damon" Marvell discovers in a version of the "book of nature" a further means of justifying pastoral poetry, a means equally dependent upon the incarnation, but conceding more immediate value to human artistry. Damon at first finds sensuous objects to be merely temptations, a banquet of pleasure like that rejected by the Resolved Soul; but the poem eventually centers upon the possibility of finding in the fountain's liquid bell and the flowers something which can match the beauty of the song of Pan (Christ). Only by comparison to that song do natural things appear to Damon to be spoiled by sensuality, the cave of love to be a cave of iniquity. The "sun" from which the pastoral retreat offers protection reminds Damon of "Heaven's Eye" (*Sol justitiae*) which sees every place and exposes the sheltered darkness to an unmerciful scrutiny. Nor is the pagan fountain baptismal, a place where the soul might bathe and "slake its Drought." [3] But reading nature in the way the divine *allegoria* of the Canticles was read offers a solution to these problems by suggesting an epistemological function in the very husk of things. Without shaping the poem into an allegory, Marvell suggests that nature may in fact possess such an intelligibility. The opening lines suggest that the process of reading clearly and purely the signs on the grassy "Scutcheon" were lost when the flock went astray, when, in shepherd dialogue, there was a loss of integrity in Adam's golden world: "*C. Damon* com drive thy flocks this way./ *D.* No: 'tis too late they went astray." And this fall from innocence makes pagan nature dangerous; it has taught Damon to expect death in Arcadia:

> *C.* I have a grassy Scutcheon spy'd,
>   Where *Flora* blazons all her pride.
>   The Grass I aim to feast thy Sheep:
>   The Flow'rs I for thy Temples keep.
> *D.* Grass withers; and the Flow'rs too fade.

The flowers Clorinda offers him for his temples are thus undermined by the fall, and their beauty, though possessed of splendor as Clorinda sees them, is found to be too transient to satisfy the Christian shepherd. The limitations inherent in these signs on nature's "Scutcheon" are overcome, however, in the song of Pan:

> C.   What did great *Pan* say?
> D.   Words that transcend poor Shepherds skill,
>   But He ere since my Songes does fill:
>   And his Name swells my slender Oate.

The "Name" or Word is that incarnate truth which supersedes the imperfect and crude signs on Flora's "Scutcheon." But an enlightened shepherd like Damon, with this name swelling his pipe, may utilize these "signs" in his song, which is thus composed of harmonic parts and of precisely those images from nature just rejected:

> *Chorus*
> Of *Pan* the flowry Pastures sing,
> Caves eccho, and the Fountains ring.
> Sing then while he doth us inspire;
> For all the World is our *Pan's* Quire.

Nature's various forms as divine *vestigia*, then, are allowed a function; though they "swell" the shepherd's pagan "Oate," they do not make it altogether a different instrument. After comprehending the meaning of "great Pan's" song, Damon finds the world becoming "our *Pan's* Quire" by means of its echoing capacity. Man and his counterparts in the macrocosm reflect the pattern of Pan each in his own way, and a Miltonic hierarchy reclaims all forms of life from lowest to highest: Damon is for Pan, Clorinda for Pan through Damon ("Sweet must *Pan* sound in *Damons* Note"), and the rest of creation for Pan through their combined song.

Marvell returns to the concept of nature as a divine hieroglyph on several occasions, most explicitly in "Bermudas." In the idyllic climate of the Bermudas Marvell, like others before him, saw a hint of prelapsarian Eden, an embodiment of what history redeemed by the hand of providence could be at any time, and the promise of the future Eden. The remote past and the future are united in this natural shrine; its message is a "gospel" transmitted to the listening winds by the pilgrims in their small boat on the dividing edge between their old, unstable world and this "far kinder" one. The "watry maze" leads back to a place now "long unknown" which the pilgrims find rising above the storms of their journey:

> What should we do but sing his Praise
> That led us through the watry Maze,
> Unto an Isle so long unknown,
> And yet far kinder than our own?
> Where he the huge Sea-Monsters wracks,
> That lift the Deep upon their Backs.
> He lands us on a grassy Stage;
> Safe from the Storms, and Prelat's rage.
> He gave us this eternal Spring,
> Which here enamells every thing.

By wracking sea monsters, pruning nature, and regulating time, providential art resolves the tension between tameness and wildness. Even while things change and grow, spring is "eternal" and everything is "enameled" (that is, both "made stable" and of "surpassing adornment"). The islands are a "grassy Stage" combining in one compressed form the fullest potentials of art and nature. Fowl visit daily in harmony with cosmic purposes, while Providence itself

> . . . hangs in shades the Orange bright,
> Like golden Lamps in a green Night.

Fruit hangs in shades for beauty and guidance, set like divine light brilliantly against a threatening and somewhat intangible background of "green Night." From their side of the line, rowing simply "along" in their small boat and singing, the pilgrims give thanks for this presence of grace in nature. For God

> in these Rocks for us did frame
> A Temple, where to sound his Name.

The song from their Protestant English craft may not pierce directly to Spanish and Catholic "Mexique Bay," but if they sing loudly enough it may perhaps get there rebounded from "Heavens Vault." Meanwhile, the temporal task of rowing the small boat is perfectly synchronized with, and regulated by, their religious "Chime." The song is "An holy and a chearful Note" because of that divine-human congruity which gets their boat to its goal; its holiness is "natural," its naturalness "holy"; essence and existence, art and nature, are perfectly and harmoniously fused.

The mower poems, which as a group have not received the close scrutiny they deserve, are concerned with the loss of that congruity, a loss doubly unfortunate because neither nature nor grace is within grasp alone. Man's fall occasions nature's corruption and so the integrity of the self and the integrity of garden and meadow are lost together. Love, along with death the "shepherd's" inescapable enemy, causes the Mower to turn the instrument of his trade against himself, stop his song, and bring chaos to the meadow. In the Mower's "accident," the fall is re-enacted, bringing death once again to Arcadia: [4]

> Only for him no Cure is found
> Whom Julianas Eyes do wound.
> Tis death alone that this must do:
> For Death thou art a Mower too.

Thus death the mower replaces the orderly keeper of nature and the Mower who has mowed himself awaits it as his "cure."

It is impossible to say whether or not the mower poems were meant to be taken as a series, but in the original folio order (retained by Margoliouth) the progress in the Mower's dilemma up to this point of self-destruction is unmistakable and, I think, meaningful when considered in relation to the general pastoral pattern we have examined. The Mower's loss of identity and his alienation from nature should be measured against the ideal harmony of mind and landscape and of nature and art which is native to pastoral idea and form. In the first poem, the Mower is sharply critical of society's sins but has no perception of his own fallibility. His attitude leads to a clear-cut opposition between art and nature—he is simply nature's mower against society's gardens. As John D. Rosenberg writes, he surprises by the fine excess of his vituperation, being a single but strong voice calling from the wilderness to a false civilization.[5] But to him, of course, no real wilderness exists, only a "wild and fragrant Innocence" on the one hand and total corruption on the other. Any imposition of form upon nature makes the living air a "dead and standing pool." But if his voice is angry, it is also subtly modified; he is an articulate and lyrical Diogenes striking out against the arts of horticulture, which stand for all sophistication and artful complexity:

> Luxurious Man, to bring his Vice in use,
>   Did after him the World seduce:
> And from the fields the Flow'rs and Plants allure,
>   Where Nature was most plain and pure.

Having already fallen, man tries to get "use" out of vice; playing Satan to nature, he forces voluptuousness upon it and causes it to become fragmented like himself: "The Pink grew then as double as his Mind; /The nutriment did change the kind." Man's "natural" condition is to think green thought in green shade; his greatest sin is tampering with the natural hierarchy until nature becomes a conglomeration of "forbidden mixtures," a false *hortus conclusus* locked against innocence. And in this poisonous pool of air, the ordinary pastoral situation in which the controlled, artistically shaped green world reduces motion and flux to the benefit of the shepherd is totally inverted. Though little T. C. tells the untamed flowers what smell becomes them, the Mower can only lament such presumption:

> With strange perfumes he did the Roses taint.
> And Flow'rs themselves were taught to paint.
> The Tulip, white, did for complexion seek;
> And learn'd to interline its cheek.

The difficulty with the Mower's position is that the normal machinery for effecting a compromise between nature and art is destroyed. Harmony must therefore be based upon absolute innocence in which one can safely "lose" oneself. Because he believes any degree of civilization to be suffocating, the Mower becomes uncritically involved in what he believes to be unfallen "meadows" and "sweet Fields." Whatever the polish of formal garden statues, real "Fauns and Faryes" live only in the meadow, and they far transcend artistic reproductions: "Howso'ere the Figures do excel,/The *Gods* themselves with us do dwell." And this too, of course, is a denial of the solution that often occurs in traditional pastoral in which the creative art of the shepherd imposes human order upon a potentially chaotic nature. For the Mower, "Fauns and Faryes" simply exist; they do not "till" the meadows, which have no need of cultivation. Though Candide might sensibly warn, "cela est bien dit, mais il·faut cultiver le jardin," he surrenders completely to the pagan dream.

The extent to which Marvell endorses this position is somewhat enigmatic. The plural voicing of the conclusion, the obvious moral fervor, and the tone of personal conviction lead Mr. Rosenberg to believe that the Mower and Marvell speak more or less together (p. 161), a justifiable conclusion but one which requires isolating the poem from the rest of the series. If the Mower's point of view has Marvell's sympathy, it is a momentary and limited sympathy overstated in order to give force·to the satire of "Luxurious Man." Succeeding poems show that a state of innocence, however desirable it may be, cannot endure in the face of human weakness and that nature is not always "plain and pure." In "Damon the Mower," having been "stung" with love of Juliana, the Mower discovers that a number of correspondences exist between his fair enemy, his own fallen state, and nature. Fair eyes and fair day, scorching sun and "am'rous care," sharp "Sythe" and "Sorrow," withered hopes and grass, all of these reveal a new level to the man-nature identity:

I

Heark how the Mower *Damon* Sung,
With love of *Juliana* stung!
While ev'ry thing did seem to paint
The Scene more fit for his complaint.
Like her fair Eyes the day was fair;
But scorching like his am'rous Care.
Sharp like his Sythe his Sorrow was,
And wither'd like his Hopes the Grass.

The "pathetic fallacy" shows the correspondences between man and nature to be indeed real but not in the way the Mower had assumed. Under the influence of Juliana, nature turns quickly into a wasteland, and the Mower's identification with it on the assumption of both its innocence and his own becomes more and more a disheartening entanglement. Meadows formerly filled with Fauns are now seared with heat:

II

Oh what unusual Heats are here,
Which thus our Sun-burn'd Meadows sear!
The Grass-hopper its pipe gives ore;
And hamstring'd Frogs can dance no more.
But in the brook the green Frog wades;
And Grass-hoppers seek out the shades.
Only the Snake, that kept within,
Now glitters in its second Skin.

The same scorching sun quite often causes shepherds to retreat to the noonshade, but the Mower, taken by surprise and too suddenly conscious of realistic animal and astronomical facts, finds no solace there.

The grasshoppers quit singing and the limping movement of hamstrung frogs replaces the innocent dance of the Fauns.

The Mower's alliance with innocence not only fails to protect him but also fails, apparently, to impress the fair shepherdess, who is indifferent to the breed of snakes "Disarmed of its teeth and sting" and to "Oak leaves tipt with hony due" which he brings her as signs of his good intentions. Likewise, his country achievements, related with such naive braggadocio, leave her unmoved:

VI

I am the Mower *Damon*, known
Through all the Meadows I have mown.
On me the Morn her dew distills
Before her darling Daffadils.
And, if at Noon my toil me heat,
The Sun himself licks off my Sweat.
While, going home, the Ev'ning sweet
In cowslip-water bathes my feet.

I think, however, that Damon's rusticity and crudeness should not weaken our response to his discovery of himself; he has a natural poetry which gradually takes on dimensions lacking in his earlier expressions of innocence. His crudeness offers an ironic means for Marvell to show that rusticity is not the same as simplicity. But he is no less attractive for his tattered clothes; though his sense of economics and his competitive pride are no more refined than his botany and zoology, they are equally ingratiating:

This Sithe of mine discovers wide
More ground then all his Sheep do hide.
With this the golden fleece I shear
Of all these Closes ev'ry Year.

His harvest, which is no less than the "fleece" of nature, is comparable to the golden fleece of the mythic sheep and the heroic quest. He is totally absorbed in his task, just as he is mirrored in his scythe, "as in a crescent Moon the Sun"—an especially fortunate simile because he gives the mirror whatever "light" it has. If he were indeed "fragrant," more dear to the morning than the daffadils are and encircled always by the ring of "deathless Fairyes"; if he were in fact the artful keeper of the meadows, his scythe would not turn against him. But the quasi-ritualistic dance of the Mower and his scythe now belongs to the past (despite the present tense):

> The deathless Fairyes take me oft
> To lead them in their Danses soft;
> And, when I tune my self to sing,
> About me they contract their Ring.

The unfortunate part of the Mower's condition, then, is not his country crudeness but his growing alienation from true simplicity. The disruption which Juliana brings distracts his mind from its singleness and true nourishment. Song and dance are given over and the protective circle is broken, as innocence ceases to be an immediate reality and becomes, like the distant reminiscence of Arcadia in much late Victorian and Georgian pastoral, an intangible property of memory. "How happy might I still have mow'd," the Mower laments, "Had not Love here his Thistles sow'd!"

> But now I all the day complain,
> Joyning my Labour to my Pain;
> And with my Sythe cut down the Grass,
> Yet still my grief is where it was:
> But, when the Iron blunter grows,
> Sighing I whet my Sythe and Woes.

Undoubtedly the Mower's *anagnorisis* is limited, but it is impressive in particularly Marvellian ways. The very clumsiness and the half-conscious adroitness with which he characterizes himself are dramatically functional: this is the psychological state of one who began in innocence, fell into confusion, and does not as yet know quite what to do with himself. Like the drunken dizziness of Milton's Adam after eating the apple, the ineffectual swinging of the scythe, the "joyning" of simple labor to complex "Pain," is the first staggering movement of the dance of death. Woes are whetted with the scythe, grief grows where the grass falls, and eventually the "fall" itself comes:

> The edged Stele by careless chance
> Did into his own Ankle glance;
> And there among the Grass fell down,
> By his own Sythe, the Mower mown.

So sharp a satire could easily have destroyed the balance between comic absurdity and pastoral simplicity, but the Mower's awkwardness only prepares for a final, and I think generally sympathetic, irony in the recognition of death as mower, an irony leading beyond the Mower's limited vision. (The poem begins and ends with the poet's own voicing.) The Mower looks to death as a cure for his love-wound, against which the crude folk-cures, the "Shepherds-purse, and Clowns-all-heal," will be of no use; but a more complete identity of the two "mowers" is implied. Damon and Death work side by side in the once innocent meadow and are a single image; the unqualified quest for innocence leads to a quest for death, to the Mower mowing himself.

If we discover the ambiguity of nature in going from "The Mower against Gardens" to "Damon the Mower," in "The Mower to the Glo-Worms" nature nevertheless still serves as a reminder of, and guide to, innocence. The Mower, however, has increasing difficulty in identifying with it. The poem falls somewhere between the "idyllic" and the "waste-land" versions of pastoral. The Mower is outside a paradise irretrievably lost and yet the myth of a perfect "garden" is in some ways as real as the fact of disillusionment: that which impairs the wholeness of the mind (its feeling of being "home") is an intimate part of the mind's experience, but so is its concept of an ideal and unfallen nature.

I

Ye living Lamps, by whose dear light
The Nightingale does sit so late,
And studying all the Summer-night,
Her matchless Songs does meditate;

II

Ye Country Comets, that portend
No War, nor Princes funeral,
Shining unto no higher end
Then to presage the Grasses fall;

III

Ye Glo-worms, whose officious Flame
To wandring Mowers shows the way,
That in the Night have lost their aim,
And after foolish Fires do stray:

IV

Your courteous Lights in vain you wast,
Since *Juliana* here is come,
For She my Mind hath so displac'd
That I shall never find my home.

The Mower's intimate address to the "living Lamps" reveals his sense of alienation: he is lost, needs light, and the light therefore becomes "dear" light. The existence of an ideal world of mutual cooperation and moral order is taken for granted, but the Mower see it from an ambiguous and confused position. He exists in two worlds, an innocent one of harmless comets which he now sees only as an outsider, and a world of experience where comets predict the fall of princes, in which he is now caught. Having addressed the glow-worms as lamps and comets, in the third apostrophe he grows more directly personal; the glow-worms, guides through the dark wood where "the straight way is lost," seem the more necessary in getting moral bearings as they serve more in vain.

Finally, "The Mower's Song," a song of experience in which innocence is all but destroyed, deals with another side of "displacement." Mowing the grass becomes a hostile act turning the disrupted meadow itself into a "selva selvaggia" where the mind, once "the true survey/ Of all these Medows fresh and gay," finds nothing but hatred and enmity. Mower and nature in "one common ruine" will fall; grass will no longer serve as a companion but as "heraldry" for the Mower's tomb. Juliana thus succeeds in dividing the Mower both from the green meadow (which continues to grow luxuriantly despite his own "blight") and from his own thoughts; he turns against himself with the very doubleness of mind he has cursed in "The Mower against Gardens":

III

Unthankful Medows, could you so
A fellowship so true forego,
And in your gawdy May-games meet,
While I lay trodden under feet?
When *Juliana* came, and She
What I do to the Grass, does to my Thoughts and Me.

The Mower's dilemma is serious and humorous at the same time. (Perhaps no pastoralist since Theocritus has so skillfully maintained an ambiguous attitude toward a simple and yet dignified rustic.) But as the puritanical temperament grows more prominent, the irony with which Marvell handles the Mower cuts deeper:

IV

But what you in Compassion ought,
Shall now by my Revenge be wrought:
. . . .

V

And thus, ye Meadows, which have been
Companions of my thoughts more green,
Shall now the Heraldry become
With which I shall adorn my Tomb.

It is appropriate that the adornment on the tomb be dead grass, a sign both of thoughts once "more green" which Juliana—herself a mower like death—has now mown, and of the flesh. After his song is finished, arranging the heraldic grass will be the Mower's last act of order: the "successful" shepherd's mastery of nature through art, mastery especially of love and death, is thus fully inverted. The Mower's reason for laying waste the meadow is succinctly put and has a simple appeal; it is limited in self-awareness and yet pathetically accurate in expressing the ease with which the world of innocence has broken up: "For Juliana comes, and She/ What I do to the Grass, does to my Thoughts and Me."

NOTES

1 Quoted by Walafrid Strabo, *Glossa Ordinaria*, in *Patrologie Latine*, J. P. Migne, gen. ed. (Paris, 1844–), CXIII, 95; cf. John Diodati, *Pious Annotations* (London, 1648), p. 4; Henry Vane, *The Retired Mans Meditations* (London, 1655), p. 402.

2 "Potest quoque per pedes ipsum mysterium in carnationis eius intelligi, quo divinitas terrum tetigit, quia carnem sumpsit," *Homiliarum in Evangelia*, Lib. II, Migne, *PL*, LXXVI, 1242.

3 Cf. John D. Rosenberg's excellent analysis of the poem, "Marvell and the Christian Idiom," *Boston University Studies in English*, IV (1960), 152–161.

4 See Erwin Panofsky's essay on this theme in the Renaissance and later, "*Et in Arcadia ego:* On the Conception of Transience in Poussin and Watteau" in *Philosophy and History*, R. Klibansky and H. J. Paton, eds. (Oxford, 1936), pp. 223–254; also in *Meaning in the Visual Arts*, pp. 295–320.

5 "Marvell and the Christian Idiom," pp. 159–160.

LEO SPITZER

Marvell's "Nymph Complaining for the Death of Her Faun": Sources versus Meaning

In the considerable literature in which attempts have been recently made to define the meaning of Marvell's poem there may be distinguished three schools of thought: one that takes literally the love of the nymph for her fawn (Legouis in his book on Marvell published thirty years ago; T. S. Eliot in his essay on Marvell; LeComte [1]); a second that proposes an allegorical explanation (the fawn is Christ [Bradbrook and Thomas] or the stricken Anglican church [Douglas Bush, E. H. Emerson]); a third that attempts to reconcile these two views by admitting "religious overtones" without claiming that the "ground bass" is religious (Karina Williamson and, it seems to me, Legouis in his latest utterance: "la perte de son faon par une jeune âme *religieuse*"; italics mine).

In this discussion critics have analyzed mainly the vocabulary and the imagery of the poem according to its historic or stylistic provenance, with the blind faith that the origin of the images or motifs must decide implicitly the meaning of the poem. If LeComte is able to prove the pagan origin of expressions such as "nymph," "Diana's shrine," or of the central motif of the grief for a pet that has been killed (in Ovid, Virgil,[2] etc.), he believes that no religious meaning is implied in the poem. If, on the contrary, Miss Williamson has located the origin of the motifs "fawn" or "feeding among lilies" in the Song of

From *Modern Language Quarterly*, XIX (1958), pp. 231–43. Reprinted by permission of the publishers and Anna Granville Hatcher.

Songs,[3] she is convinced that the meaning of the poem includes religious overtones.

It has been for a long time my conviction that what I would call "imagistic positivism" (the exaggerated reliance of contemporary critics on imagery to the detriment of other elements of poetry) is likely to preclude the understanding of a poem such as Marvell's in which structure, thought, psychology, must play parts at least equal to imagery. In the case of our poem, it strikes me as strange that none of the critics has analyzed this from beginning to end as a structured whole whose parts correspond to the phases of the psychological development of the Nymph. This is the more indicated since T. S. Eliot has remarked that "the suggestiveness of the poem" is "the aura around a bright clear center" (Marvell takes a "slight affair, the feeling of a girl for her pet," [4] and gives it a connection with that "inexhaustible and terrible nebula of emotion which surrounds all our exact and practical passions"), which remark is echoed by Miss Williamson: "The experience manifested in the poem is felt to belong to the total of human experience."

But none of these critics tells us what exactly and actually the "nebula of emotion" or the "total experience" of the Nymph who has lost her fawn is, although that nebula of total experience seems to me clearly, if discreetly, indicated in the poem. Whenever the critics think that a "slight affair" is treated with enormous seriousness of tone, either the poem cannot be good (but all critics are agreed as to the excellence of our poem), or there must be a flaw in their understanding. In a good poem form cannot go its own way, apart from content. Obviously, then, the poem is not about a "slight affair"—how could it possibly be if the end of the Nymph is that of Niobe? [5]

The protagonist of our poem is, indeed, not the fawn, but the Nymph, who dies together with the fawn, and it is quite incomprehensible why the critics have shown no curiosity as to the reason why a young girl whose pet has died should herself have chosen death. To explain this reason, my analysis will consist in simply repeating elements expressed in the poem as well as in pointing out some elements that are only slightly, but clearly, suggested in it. The delicate art of the poet has so willed it that, in the inner monologue of the Nymph that is the poem, the description of her pet reflects on her own character in indirect characterization, the increasing idealization of the fawn allowing inferences about the maiden who so idealizes it. It is the task of the commentator—a commentator who should be less a "professional" of literary criticism than a simple reader who asks relevant human questions [6]—to bring out clearly the deep tragedy of the Nymph. We are, indeed, given an indirect description of her feelings while the animal is dying (lines 1–92), after its death (93–110), and before the death of the Nymph, when she is planning the consecration by a monument to her own as well as to the fawn's memory (111–22).

The poem starts with the address of the Nymph to the fatally wounded fawn in which she reveals her, as it were, modern attitude of revulsion against the wanton slaying of a harmless animal. That this is a passage significant for the history of ideas (or feelings) has been duly noted by Legouis who devotes one and one-half pages to the rise and growth of this feeling as expressed in English literature. But I would point out two other, more personal, attitudes of the Nymph that are expressed in the first verse paragraph (1–24), both indicative of a feeling that her life has come to an end with the death of the fawn: that of evangelical forgiveness for the murderers of the pet—she does not "wish them ill," but prays for them, weeping (6–12)—and that of readiness to offer her own life as a sacrifice to the God of revenge (17–24). That this is indeed the meaning of these lines may perhaps be contested. Legouis translates (italics mine):

> Quand bien même ils laveraient leurs mains criminelles
> *dans ce sang chaud qui se sépare*
> *de ton cœur et dont la vue perce le mien,*
> ils ne pourraient se purifier: leur souillure
> est empreinte sur eux d'une pourpre trop éclatante.
> Il n'y a pas au monde *un autre animal*
> semblable qu'ils puissent offrir pour racheter leur péché.

But if "this warm life-blood" were that of the fawn "which doth part / From thine" (understood as "thy heart," with "heart" taken from the following "wound me to the heart"), this anticipative ellipsis would seem rather difficult. More important, however, how should we understand that the criminals who killed the fawn would think, in order to become guiltless, of washing their bloody hands in the blood of their victim (would Lady Macbeth wash off her guilt in King Duncan's blood)? And how would the lines 23–24 which obviously allude to a sacrificial offering (a *deodand*) connect with the preceding lines, especially if "such another" meant an animal, as Legouis has it: in the preceding lines there was to be found only an allusion to criminals who wish to wash off their guilt.

Thus I am led to believe that in "this warm life-blood" the pronoun *this* represents the first person ("my") and means the warm blood of the Nymph who would wish to redeem (a new Iphigenia, as LeComte has seen) the spilt blood of the fawn, though to no avail for its murderers whose "stain" is irremovable.[7] With this explanation the lines "There is not such another in / The World to offer for their Sin" connect excellently with the thought of the preceding passage: "no other *being* (including me) could atone for that unique fawn." What strikes us here is that at the moment of the fawn's death the Nymph is already considering her own death, a death of expiation which she, however, seems to reject at this time because of her unworthiness. Thus this first part of the poem must be interpreted not only in the light of the history of ideas, but as a story of an extraordinary human being, the Nymph.

What this story has been we learn from the second paragraph (lines 25–36): it is the story of her love for Sylvio who betrayed her. We notice that between Sylvio and the troopers there exists a certain analogy (the vocatives *inconstant Sylvio—ungentle men*, underline this parallelism): both acted wantonly, cruelly, regardless of the "smart" of the girl; both killed, the one her young loving heart, the others the young object of her later love. Sylvio's frivolity appears in the words with which he accompanies his gifts, the fawn and the silver chain: "look how your Huntsman here / Hath taught a Faun to hunt his *Dear*"—words that made a deep impression on her at the time, but which gained an even stronger significance after Sylvio's breach of faith, as is indicated by the elaborate manner in which she reports these words:

> One morning (I remember well)
> . . . nay and I know
> What he said then; I'me sure I do.
> Said He. . . .

These simple words and this simple syntax carry a sense of convincingness and sincerity. What is more, the repetitious phrasing seems to imply that the maiden, even now, must make an effort not to wince at the hurting quality which those words still contain. She realizes, of course, in retrospect, that Sylvio spoke as a "huntsman" who saw the fawn in the light of his huntsmanship (as an animal trained to "hunt his *Dear*," to pursue her, frolic around her) and that she herself was for Sylvio the huntsman nothing but a quarry or a plaything.

Thus in his words, she now realizes, fate had spoken. What should we think of the puns in this passage (*dear–deer, heart–hart*)? They seem practically superfluous, but they are probably intended to characterize the ambiguous atmosphere of "huntsman's frivolity" which is proper to Sylvio's adventures.[8] The sober significance of lines 25–36 is that the early experience of the Nymph who suffered from her lover's faithlessness must be seen together with the love which will develop between her and the fawn: the one conditions the other. There is also an indication of a parallelism in the Nymph's and the animal's fate: both fall prey to wanton, cruel men. Although the Nymph's feelings for Sylvio are worded in a simple, untragic manner ("smart" is the only word that allows us to measure her grief), we may assume that a deep wound has existed in her since the time of Sylvio's betrayal.

There apparently followed upon the adventure with Sylvio, as the third paragraph suggests (37–46), a respite from grief, respite from deep feeling, in which the playful animal helped the Nymph to forget. The fawn meant to her first relaxation, a "content" in "idleness": the sportive nimbleness of the fawn invited her to the "game" of racing, of "hunting." But with the lines "it seem'd to bless / Its self in me" a new note is sounded. The happiness enjoyed by the animal in her company, within her atmosphere, could not be depicted more graphically than by the surprising reflexive use of the English verb "to bless" that I may translate by the Italian *bearsi* (which has a relation to *beato, beatitudine,* similar to that of *to bless oneself* to *bliss*). The fawn "called itself blessed," "found its delight, happiness, bliss in her."

Strangely enough, Miss Williamson has failed to list this extraordinary use of the verb "to bless" among the expressions with "religious overtones." It is first attested in 1611 in the biblical passage (Jeremiah 4:2): *the nations shall bless themselves in him* [sc. God]. The pivotal line "it seem'd to bless / Its self in me" with its solemn (as if religious) ring marks the first sign of true love [9] that came to the Nymph and asked from her the response of love. The wording of the next lines, again very simple and truly convincing, "How could I less / Than love it? / O I cannot be / Unkind," sounds apologetic: the Nymph herself feels the momentum of the totally unexpected, sudden inner development. The Nymph who had experienced inconstancy and frivolity in love has now received a new revelation, that of pure, unsolicited, gratuitously, unselfishly offered, abiding love that developed imperceptibly, gradually, out of gaiety and playfulness (the even flow of the lines in question mirrors this development).

But, as the next paragraph (47–54) shows, the Nymph, even at the moment of the fawn's death, is still not quite prepared to believe that the revelation of true love that was imparted to her was final: "Had it liv'd long" might the fawn not have developed into another

Sylvio? (We infer from the lingering comparison and from the lingering doubt even at this moment how deeply wounded by her first
experience the Nymph still is.) But no, she is now assured that the
fawn's love "was far more than the love of false and cruel men"
("cruel" being a word used by her now when she is able to compare
Sylvio and the fawn).

The next three paragraphs (55–92), the last of which ends with
the line "Had it liv'd long" that gives the answer to the question
voiced there, are inspired by an ever-growing sureness about the
significance of her love. In these paragraphs Sylvio is finally forgotten,
yet some of the Nymph's statements suggest to the reader the contrast
between then and now:

> It is a wond'rous thing, how fleet
> 'Twas on those little silver feet.
> With what a pretty skipping grace,
> It oft would challenge me the Race:
> And when 't had left me far away,
> 'Twould stay, and run again, and stay.
> For it was nimbler much than Hindes;
> And trod, as on the four Winds.

We may contrast the fawn's "silver feet" with the "silver chain" given
by Sylvio: now there is no need for a chain, since the fawn, more
faithful than Sylvio, though it leaves the maiden temporarily, always
returns to her, leaves her playfully to return faithfully.

The commentators who point out that lines 67–69 may be inspired
by Pliny and the expression "trod, as on the four Winds" by the
Psalmist, have missed the main point: the contrast between the nimbleness given to the animal by nature and its unfailing conscientious
returnings to its mistress (note the repeated *stay* in Marvell's wording and the repeated *fuga* in Pliny: with the latter, the stag runs—
stays—runs; with the former it stays—runs—stays). When we read
lines such as "It oft would challenge me the Race," we realize—and
perhaps the Nymph realized it too at that point of her "Complaint"
—that the fickle hunter's definition of the fawn has unexpectedly
come true, only in another sense than was meant by him: the fawn
has been trained to "hunt Sylvio's *Dear*," to hunt her "constantly."

The reader will note the lavish use of metaphysical wit in these
paragraphs which are intended to extol the fawn's virtues and its
beauty, qualities that become more and more of a supernatural kind as
they transcend the Nymph's own virtues and beauty. The description

proceeds by comparison (or identification) of these virtues and beauties with those of other objects and beings in which they are traditionally embodied in undefiled purity. The fawn was nourished with milk and sugar by the fingers of the maiden—it became more white and sweet than this food (it acquires, in addition, sweet fragrance [10]) and its feet more soft and white than her (or any lady's) hand; it lies in a bed of lilies and feeds on roses (so that its mouth will seem to bleed)—had it lived longer, it could have become "Lillies without, Roses within."

This sequence of images which climaxes in this last "witty" identification may have its origin in the Song of Songs, but its function here is the metamorphosis of the animal into a paragon of virtues that are not found combined even in a human being: the coolness of virginal chastity and the flame of ardent love (the rose being the symbol of the latter—witness the fawn's rose-kiss that seems to come from a bleeding heart). Wit, which here, as always with Marvell, has a functional role, suggests the possibility of a miracle: the possibility of moral or spiritual qualities becoming sensuously perceptible as though they were objects in outward nature in a $\varkappa\alpha\lambda o\varkappa\dot\alpha\gamma\alpha\vartheta\dot\iota\alpha$ of their own. A miracle is after all nothing but the substantiation of the supernatural.[11]

Here I may permit myself a digression about metaphysical wit in general. In T. S. Eliot's statements on this subject (espoused by Miss Williamson) one feels a certain embarrassment, as though he, who appreciates so highly seventeenth-century wit, had not reached a description quite satisfactory to himself, when, after having set wit (but not entirely) apart from "erudition" and "cynicism," he writes the final sentence: "It involves, probably [!], a recognition, implicit in the expression of every experience, of the other experiences which are possible" (and this is basically the same idea as that, quoted above, on the "slight affair," supposedly treated in our poem, to which the poet would have added that "inexhaustible and terrible nebula of emotion" that surrounds all our "exact and practical passions").

But such a description of wit seems to me far too general: would the metaphysical poet add any other experience to the one he is treating? [12] Marvell envisages a metamorphosis of the fawn into lilies and roses, a very precise change related to its way of living, not some vague connection with, or nebula of, "other experiences." His metamorphosis seems to me based on a public belief in miracles whereby a supernatural development may not only become physically perceptible in beautiful forms, but may live a physical life of its own according to a precise pattern of psychological analogy. The fawn who lies in a bed of lilies and feeds on roses (that is, is pure as the lily and embodies, like the rose, the flame of love) may become lilies and roses because organic beings may, in a sort of mythological metabolism, become what they eat.

This is, of course, a miracle of the poet's making, but one that goes back historically [13] to medieval religious beliefs, according to which the spirituality of saints and martyrs acted in similar analogy on the physical world. Metaphysical wit has here simply laicized, and preserved in poetry, the substantiation of the supernatural current in hagiographic legend. To give but one example, borrowed from Curtius' *European Literature and the Latin Middle Ages* (appendix on "comic spirit in hagiography"): St. Lawrence, when grilled over the flames, is reported by St. Ambrose to have said to his torturers: *assum est, versa et manduca* "my body is cooked, turn it to the other side and eat it"—the underlying idea being that the saint's supernatural fortitude was able to triumph over physical pain to the point that he could accept, in its most extreme form, the transformation of his flesh into meat to which, then, all the normal culinary procedures (the mechanics of cooking) and pleasures (the eating—which here becomes anthropophagy) may be applied, while his mind remains miraculously intact (able to formulate the physical miracle).

The comic spirit in hagiography is probably at the bottom of metaphysical wit. Just as, according to Bergson, all comic effect is a result of mechanization of the organic, in the process of living flesh becoming meat we are faced with a mechanization of a spiritual force—whose comic effect is, of course, different from other comic writing, surrounded as it is, at least for the believer, with awe. Some of this quasi-religious comic spirit or awesome wit (poetry being, as is so often the case, the reënactment in secularized form of ancestral beliefs) is also present in Marvell's suggestion that the animal lying among lilies and feeding on roses may become all lilies and roses. Here the poetic miracle has inherited from the truly religious miracle its paradoxical logic, its psycho-physical analogy, and the mechanization of the spiritual (there is no "cynicism" involved in such a transfer).

The extension of the orinigally religious wit to secular subject matter [14] may have been encouraged by certain genres of pagan poetry that were revived in modern poetry, for instance, by the Ovidian metamorphosis: for the change of the fawn into lilies and roses is nothing but an Ovidian imagination. With Ovid such a metamorphosis would fancifully explain, according to a mythical, that is prescientific, science of analogy, the birth of an object or being in nature by means of a legendary event that once befell a human being (the cypress was originally the youth Cyparissus, the laurel was originally the nymph Daphne), the underlying idea being one of pantheism which "sees a nymph behind every tree." Certain analogies obtain between the form of the object in nature and the human situation that gave birth to it. With Ovid the change of forms is from the human to the non-human, the latter being anthropomorphosized. When the Christian spirit moves the medieval and the Renaissance poets, their metamorphosis will emphasize the superhuman that is present in the physical: we will remember the medieval tradition (not lost in the Renaissance) of *Ovide moralisé* which will give to the pagan metamorphosis Christian religious or moral overtones (cf. the *Roman de la Dame à la Lycorne* mentioned below in note 15).

Thus Marvell's wit in our poem is located at the point of confluence of two powerful literary currents, Ovidian and Christian—no wonder that modern classifications of our poem, now as pagan, now as Christian, do violence to one-half of its inspiration since it participates in both currents. We shall find, in harmony with that Protean quality, inherited from Ovid, of poetry of wit, or its "omnivorousness," as Father Ong calls its ability "to attract into its orbit experiences on most various levels provided that they are brought together with a higher meaning"—we shall find in our poem several other examples of wit, of psycho-physical analogy and change of forms particularly in the scenes of the death and the afterlife of the fawn.

The death of the fawn (93–100) is surrounded by an atmosphere of beauty and virtue combined in a miracle. It is the death of a "saint" who, in spite of his "calm," is accessible to human emotions to the point of shedding tears, tears of farewell to love (as it appears from the comparison with the tears of the "brotherless *Heliades*"). And the tears will become beautiful substances: wit will compare them, in their fragrance and visual beauty, with "gumme," "frankincense," and "amber" (the last of which, suggested by Ovid's metamorphosis of the sisters of Phaëthon, has probably given the impulse to the series of analogies).[15] It is the acme of metaphysical wit that the liquid substances into which the tears of the fawn have been changed can themselves be presented anthropomorphically: "So weeps the wounded Balsome." In the world of poetic identification of opposites the road between human being and thing may be traveled in both directions. The final identification of the flowing tears with solid amber suggested to the poet a further "substantification" of the tears of the animal, their congealing into "two crystals" (each representing one eye of the fawn), a jewel, as it were, a thing of beauty that will forever preserve the essence of the transient moment of the fawn's death, a pagan relic to be offered in a golden vial (which should also contain the Nymph's tears, that are less "crystallized" and "overflow" its brim) to Diana's shrine. It is only at this moment and by this gesture that our realization that the destiny of the fawn and of its mistress is one and the same becomes final. Both being too sublime for this world of wantonness and cruelty, both victims of their own purity, they belong together forever like their tears that will be preserved in the shrine of chastity.

In the whole description of her relationship with the living animal the Nymph has kept herself in the background, minimizing the depth of her feeling and indeed comparing herself disadvantageously with the animal (she "blushed" at its whiteness). Even in death the white fawn will transcend her: for while her own final destiny is not mentioned, she is assured that he will dwell in Elysium with the other white animals that embody purity. The animal that has "stayed" with her (faithfully) is asked not "to run too fast" toward Elysium (109) —a graceful conceit: even in death the deer will preserve its natural fleetness. And even in the monument to be erected after her death the figure of the fawn will be of "alabaster" that never can be "as white as thee," but whiter than the "marble" that will perpetuate her own figure. While the relationship between mistress and animal will be expressed by the position of the fawn's image at her feet (just as on medieval tombstones traditionally faithful dogs lie at the feet of their masters), the mistress will remain forever the human mourner rather than the traditional owner. The Nymph will become a Niobe,[16] endowed, if not with the boastfulness, with the disconsolate feelings of that "unhappy" mother. Her evolution which began with simple delight and enjoyment of a graceful young being, after having reached the depth of true love, ends in the grief of a bereaved mother. Her tears (that overflow all boundaries) will petrify into the statue that weeps, that is "engraved" by her tears: the two aspects of grief, the feeling of numbness and of dissolution, are brought together in the image of the stone-that-weeps.[17]

This tragic story could be called in modern (Freudian) terms one of frustration overcome by sublimation [18]—and as such it would verge on comedy, replacement of love for a person by love for an animal (the stock situation in which old spinsters are involved) coming dangerously close to the grim caricature of Flaubert's *Un cœur simple*. But Marvell has placed this story of disillusionment within a baroque setting of sad beauty,[19] a metamorphosis of ancient tradition being overlaid by the feeling for the transiency of things earthly. The *lacrimae rerum* are made to crystallize into things of beauty that commemorate tragedy (the statue, the crystals in the golden vial), just as in another, typically baroque and conceptual, poem of Marvell's, disillusionment becomes beauty, tears become jewels:

> What in the world most fair appears,
> Yea, even Laughter, turns to tears;
> And all the Jewels which we prize
> Melt in these pendants of the Eyes.

We understand now the particular tone of our "Complaint" in which the protagonist tells her story in an "inner monologue" of rather simple, direct words which contrast with the sophisticated examples of metaphysical wit.[20] This stylistic contrast reflects the inner contrast between sadness and beauty: the sadness of disillusionment is reflected convincingly by the simple speech, not unknown to Marvell, while the miraculous metamorphosis into sensuous beauty finds its expression in the mirages of wit.[21]

NOTES

[1] The bibliography of this discussion may be found in the two articles by LeComte and Miss Williamson in *MP*, L (1952) and LI (1954), to which there must be added the article by E. H. Emerson and Legouis's rejoinder in *Études Anglaises*, VIII (1955), 107–12.

Needless to say, I share the outspokenly "French" horror of Legouis ("un esprit français . . . n'arrive pas à se débarrasser d'un excès de logique quand il étudie la poésie anglaise") when faced with the lack of logic implied by the assumption of allegorical explanations that explain only parts of the literary work—a procedure, now current in America, obviously based on the gratuitous belief that an allegorical explanation is in itself of higher quality than a non-allegorical one (whereas the true touchstone of any explanation is whether or not it actually "explains" convincingly and completely), a belief that in turn may represent an excessive reaction of overcompensation for traditional American qualities which have come to be felt in certain quarters as too pedestrian: good sense, matter-of-factness, realism. As for Marvell, the various ambiguities which Emerson, enthusiastically followed by some American critics, found in our poet can generally be discarded, after a close analysis, in favor of one explanation that alone fits the context. In other words, Marvell, like Góngora for whom Dámaso Alonso has found the key of understanding, is "difficult, but clear." Those poets ask from the reader the effort to make his way through the maze of ambiguities toward the unique true explanation. The critic who stops at pointing out several possible meanings has stopped halfway on the road that Marvell expected him to travel. To superimpose contemporary anarchy of meanings on Marvell's poetry is a blatant anachronism.

[2] But why does he not mention also the ancient and Renaissance tradition of epitaphs for pets (Catullus, Martial, Navagero, Du Bellay, Ronsard, etc.)?

[3] It may be noted, however, that the comparison in the Song of Songs of the beloved with a roe or hart is not identical with Marvell's presentation of a deer as a lover: in the first case a human being is represented with the freshness, unpurposiveness, and mystery of nature; in the second, an animal in nature with the potentialities of feeling of human beings. Surely the first is a more sensuous, the second a more spiritual approach—and the second is the procedure of our metaphysical poet who is following, as we shall see later, a medieval tradition.

[4] How does this assertion fit another, to be found later on in the article on Marvell, emphasizing the "precise taste" of Marvell's which finds for him the proper degree of seriousness for every subject which he treats?

[5] The presence of this ancient motif has been mentioned only in passing by LeComte. Indeed, at the end of his article, when he comes to formulate pointedly the role of Marvell's Nymph, he says that if she should be given a name, it should be "Silvia rather than Pietà"—he should rather have contrasted with the Pietà the ancient equivalent of a mourning mother.

[6] We have indeed come to the point where the quiet de-humanized professional of literary criticism considers it his duty to deal with "imagery" and similar specialized, technical, or philological questions, to the exclusion of the human element which is at the bottom of all poetry and consequently should inform philology, the humanistic science.

[7] "This warm life-blood, which doth part / From thine" must then mean "which now departs [must depart] from thy life-blood"; "and wound me to the Heart" belongs rather together with "Though they should wash their guilty hands" (if they should wash . . . and wound me . . . , that is, kill me).

[8] The puns may be considered within the framework of the other examples of metaphysical wit to be found in our poem and also within the framework of other puns to be found in the poetry of Marvell and Marvell's contemporaries. But, believing as I do that any stylistic device is an empty form which may be filled by most divers contents, I should prefer to treat each manifestation of wit, puns, etc., *in situ,* in the precise situation in which it appears. It is the juncture of a particular *significandum* and *significatum* that gives precise meaning to any stylistic device (as well as to any linguistic utterance). Consequently, I feel entitled to treat the puns of the passage just mentioned separately from the other examples of wit which we shall find in our poem.

[9] It must be noted that in the episode which, according to LeComte, constitutes the model of our poem, Virgil's *Aeneid* VII, 475 (Sylvio's stag wounded by Ascanius; cf. also the story of Cyparissus in Ovid's *Metamorphoses* X, 106, which is an imitation of the Virgilian passage), we

find as the only active person the mistress who tames her stag and takes loving care of him ("soror omni Silvia cura / mollibus intexens ornabat cornua sertis / pectebatque ferum puroque in fonte lavabat"; cf. in Ovid: "tu [Cyparissus] pabula cervum / ad nova, tu liquidi ducebas fontis ad undam, / tu nodo texebas varios per cornua flores . . ."). With Marvell it is the fawn who has the active part: it is he, already trained by Sylvio, who by his loving behavior makes his mistress love him. And, of course, there can be no question in Virgil or Ovid of the animal becoming superior to its mistress.

[10] For Miss Williamson this is an echo of the Song of Songs: "his lips like sweet lilies, dropping sweet myrrh . . . his mouth is most sweet." But I find in the epitaph of the French Renaissance poet Du Bellay on the dog Peloton (in *Divers jeux rustiques*) the lines:

> Peloton ne mangeoit pas
> de la chair à son repas:
> ses viandes plus prisees,
> c'estoient miettes brisees,
> que celui qui le paissait
> de ses doights ammollissait:
> *aussi sa bouche estoit pleine*
> *toujours d'une douce haleine.*

[11] On the contrary "poetic miracles" performed by a Marino have, it seems to me, no supernatural connotations: with him the transformation is from one sensuous object to another, more perfect in its sensuous beauty. To choose an example, parallel to Marvell, in which a comparison between animal and human body is involved:

> Mentre Lidia premea
> dentro rustica coppa
> a la lanuta la feconda poppa,
> i' stava a rimirar doppio candore,
> di natura e d'amore;
> nè distinguer sapea
> il bianco umor da le sue mani intatte,
> ch'altro non discernea che latte in latte.

Thanks to the alchemy of *amore*, the white hand of the beloved becomes milk (milk that encompasses milk)—an entirely sensuous miracle.

[12] Probably Eliot's description was prompted by the lines of Cowley on wit which he quotes:

> In a true piece of Wit all things must be
> Yet all things there agree . . .

> Or as the primitive forms of all
> (If we compare great things with small)
> Which, without discord or confusion, lie
> In that strange mirror of the Deity.

It seems to me that Father Ong was better inspired when, quoting the same lines of Cowley, he considered as a secondary result of a poetry that moves on higher and lower planes at the same time, what he calls the "omnivorousness" which enables wit poetry "to devour all sorts of experience in one gulp," "to digest all experience, raw if necessary, and make something of it."

[13] This historical succession has been proved by Father W. J. Ong, S.J., in his classical article, "Wit and Mystery: A Revaluation in Medieval Latin Hymnody" (*Speculum,* XXII [1947], 310 ff.), who attests wit (including puns, paradoxes, etc.) in the hymns of Prudentius, Thomas Aquinas, Adam of St. Victor, used as a device to express certain paradoxical mysteries inherent in the Christian dogma (for example, the Tri-une Godhead). One facet of the same procedure is what I am treating here: wit expressing miracles, the miracle being different from the mystery in that the former constitutes a temporary interruption of the so-called laws of nature while the religious mystery is above those laws or underlying them.

The historical fact, stated by Eliot, that poetry of wit is absent from eighteenth- and nineteenth-century poetry may be explained in the same manner as the disappearance of allegory in those same centuries. At that time belief in the concrete reality of abstract qualities of perfection had become lost while previous centuries had retained from earlier medieval thought the capacity of thinking, at least poetically, of shapes into which perfection is able to materialize. In allegorical poetry abstractions assume a body; in poetry of wit abstract qualities concretize themselves in objects. With a renascence in the twentieth century of abstract thought, as a reaction against the overcrowding material world; poetry of wit has been reinstated.

[14] What is called in English "metaphysical wit" is called in French *préciosité,* although the realization of this identity has not yet found its way into orthodox French literary history. The usual definition given for *précieux* passages: "une métaphore poussée jusqu'au bout" (*il en rougit, le traître,* said of a dagger; *brûlé de plus de feux que je n'en allumai,* said of a lover) would seem to suggest a futile automatic game, while in reality the "metaphor pushed to its extreme" originates in France as elsewhere in religious poetry (La Cépède, D'Aubigné, etc.) and has, even in its better known secular variety, inherited something of that "miraculous psycho-physical parallelism" that is characteristic of the belief in the efficacy of spiritual forces. In that poetic world there exists a blushing of shame that may become indistinguishable from blood, a love whose flame is more consuming than actual fires multiplied.

[15] The coupling of Christian with pagan elements, which I mentioned above

as characteristic of our poem, is reflected by the outspoken reference to a metamorphosis of Ovid (the Heliades) following immediately after the expression "holy frankincense" which points to Christian church service.

The lack of nuances in the poetic sensibility of those critics who decide for an "either-or" in our poem may be explained in part by their unfamiliarity with medieval lay poetry that combines the worldly and the unworldly to a degree unbelievable for us moderns; for instance, in the fourteenth-century French *Roman de la Dame à la Lycorne et du Chevalier au Lyon,* we find the story of the love of a noble lady, who is a paragon of virtue and grace, for a courageous and virtuous knight. This story is replete with romantic adventures à la Chrétien de Troyes of one of whose heroes the knight riding on a lion is reminiscent—while the *dame à la lycorne* rides the unicorn which equals her in virtue (ed. Gennrich, lines 183 ff.):

> . . . par ce qu'est [la dame] de tout bien affinee
> *Jhesu Christ* volt, que li fust destinee
> *Une merveille,* que chi vus conterai:
> C'est d'une bieste, que *Diex* donna l'otrai,
> Et tel franchise e si tres grant purté
> Il li donna, qu'ele avoit en vilté
> Tous vilains visces . . .
> Pource donna a la dame tel don
> *Li Diex d'Amours,* que tous temps avoit non:
> "La dame blanche qui la Lycorne garde,"
> Qui onc nul temps de mal faire ne tarde.

Here then, in a medieval secular, if moralizing, love story, it is Christ and Amor who give to the perfect lady the animal that, in bestiaries and tapestries alike, was thought to embody Christ. The evidently present "religious overtones" do not guarantee the presence of a religious poem.

[16] Niobe was killed by the arrows of the two children of Leto whom she had offended, Apollo and Diana—we may surmise that it was Diana who killed Marvell's Nymph out of pity for her fate.

[17] We witness here the paradoxical coupling of two opposite attitudes as before when "cold virginity" and "ardent love" were found combined in the fawn. Already in Ovid, *Metamorphoses* VI, 303 ff., we find:

> Deriguitque malis . . .
> . . . intra quoque viscera saxum est:
> Flet tamen . . .
> . . . et lacrimis etiam nunc marmora manant.

But the "witty" idea of the statue being "sculptured" by the Nymph's tears belongs, of course, to Marvell.

[18] In Gottfried of Strassburg's medieval romance *Tristan und Isold* we have

perhaps a story reminiscent of that of Marvell, though leading to a quite different conclusion. With Gottfried, the absent Tristram, thinking faithfully of Isold and reflecting how he could relieve her loneliness, sends her the graceful dog, Petitcreü, a dog possessed of miraculous qualities, about whose neck is hung on a chain a bell with a tone so sweet that all who hear it forget their grief. But Isold, unwilling to forget her grief while Tristram is unable to forget his own, finally decides to tear the marvelous bell from the chain of the dog—which thereby loses immediately its miraculous power. By parallel wording the poet emphasizes the exemplary behavior of these two faithful lovers who refuse consolation: Tristram "who has given up his joy and his life to grief . . ."—Isold "the faithful, constant one who has given up her life to longing and to Tristram."

[19] Another baroque combination of sadness and beauty consists in presentation of the beauty of the world as undermined by transiency (the motif of *sic transit gloria mundi*).

[20] To that rather modern technique belong those temporal elements in the spoken complaint that mark the passing of time ("The wanton Troopers . . . *Have shot* my Faun"; "Oh help! o help! *I see* it faint"; "Now my Sweet Faun *is vanish'd*; "for *I Will* but *bespeak* thy Grave"). It may very well be that the second passage just quoted reflects the *auxilium vocat* of Silvia in the *Aeneid*, but Marvell has fitted it into the, as it were, temporal economy of the "Complaint."

[21] After having handed in this article to the *MLQ*, I read a study of our poem by D. C. Allen, published in *ELH*, XXIII (June, 1956). I am pleased to note that he considers the fawn a *surrogatus amoris*, but he fails to follow through in detail the development of the motif in the poem and rather concentrates on the history of the *topoi* that went into its composition (without mentioning, however, the—for me essential—parallel of Niobe).

LOUIS MARTZ

𝒦

Henry Vaughan: The Man Within

1. Modes of Communion

In the year 1649 Richard Crashaw died in exile at Loreto, a little more than six months after his master King Charles died on the scaffold at Whitehall. An era had ended for English political and religious institutions, and also for English religious poetry. With Crashaw's death the power of liturgical and eucharistic symbols died away in English poetry of the seventeenth century: the symbols earlier celebrated by Southwell, Alabaster, Donne, and Herbert. These poets had their doctrinal differences, and I do not wish to minimize those differences; but they had something more in common: a devotion to the mysteries of the Passion and to a liturgy that served to celebrate those mysteries. All five of these poets entered into holy orders; all five would have agreed with George Herbert's vision of "The Agonie":

> Who knows not Love, let him assay
> And taste that juice, which on the crosse a pike
> Did set again abroach; then let him say
> If ever he did taste the like.
> Love is that liquour sweet and most divine,
> Which my God feels as bloud; but I, as wine.

From *PMLA*, LXXVIII, 1963, pp. 40–49. Copyright 1963 by the Modern Language Association. Reprinted by permission of the publisher. This essay also appeared in *The Paradise Within: Studies in Vaughan, Traherne, and Milton.* Copyright © 1964 by Yale University Press.

In 1650 Andrew Marvell wrote his famous "Horatian Ode" in honor of the man who

> Could by industrious Valour climbe
> To ruine the great Work of Time,
> And cast the Kingdome old
> Into another Mold.

And in the same year appeared the first edition of Henry Vaughan's *Silex Scintillans,* a volume that, along with Milton's miscellaneous *Poems* of 1645, marks the emergence of the layman as a central force in religious poetry of the period. Vaughan's volume, though written by a staunch Royalist and Anglican, nevertheless stands as a sign of a profound mutation in human affairs. Without neglecting the highly individual qualities of Vaughan's vision, I should like here to consider his volume of 1650 as the symbol of a vital transformation in the religious outlook of the age.

It is important to look closely at *Silex Scintillans,* 1650. For Vaughan's enlarged volume of 1655, with its second part and its greatly expanded opening matter, presents a modified outlook, a less consistent fabric, and a weaker body of poetry, despite the fact that seven or eight of Vaughan's finest poems did not appear until the 1655 edition. The common charges against Vaughan's poetry—that his poems often begin with a flash of power, but then dwindle off into tedious rumination, that he works by fits and starts, that he cannot sustain a whole poem —these charges find their chief support in Book II of *Silex,* which reveals many signs of a failing inspiration. There is a greater reliance on the ordinary topics of piety, especially in the many labored poems based on Biblical texts; there is a marked decline in the frequency of Herbertian echoes, and a corresponding rise in the use of conventional couplet-rhetoric, after the manner of the Sons of Ben Jonson: a school to which Vaughan showed his allegiance in his undistinguished volume of secular poems in 1646. At the same time the crabbed and contentious Preface of 1655 strikes a tone quite out of line with the dominant mode of the poems in the 1650 volume, here bound up as the first "book" of what has now become a religious miscellany.[1] But the volume of 1650 is a whole, like Herbert's *Temple;* and indeed there are many signs that the volume was deliberately designed as a sequel, a counterpart, and a tribute to Herbert's book.

Vaughan's subtitle is exactly the same as Herbert's: "Sacred Poems and Private Ejaculations"; but the main title represents a vast difference, enforced, in the 1650 volume alone, by the engraved title page presenting the emblem of the Flashing Flint—the stony heart weeping, bleeding and flaming from the hand of God that strikes direct from the clouds, steel against flint. Furthermore, a careful look at this flinty heart will reveal something that I never noticed until my friend Evelyn Hutchinson, examining this title page with his scientific eye, asked, "Do you see a human face peering forth from within the heart?" It is certainly so: a man within can be clearly seen through an opening in the heart's wall.[2] And facing this we have, again in the 1650 volume only, an intimate confession in the form of a Latin poem, explaining the emblem. Perhaps a literal version of this cryptic Latin will show how essential this poem and this emblem are for an understanding of the 1650 volume as a whole:

The Author's Emblem (concerning himself)

You have often touched me, I confess, without a wound, and your *Voice*, without a voice, has often sought to counsel me; your diviner breath has encompassed me with its calm motion, and in vain has cautioned me with its sacred murmur. I was deaf and dumb: a *Flint:* You (how great care you take of your own!) try to revive another way, you change the Remedy; and now angered you say that *Love* has no power, and you prepare to conquer force with *Force*, you come closer, you break through the *Rocky* barrier of my heart, and it is made *Flesh* that was before a *Stone*. Behold me torn asunder! and at last the *Fragments* burning toward your skies, and the cheeks streaming with tears out of the *Adamant*. Thus once upon a time you made the *Rocks* flow and the *Crags* gush, oh ever provident of your people! How marvellous toward me is your hand! In *Dying*, I have been born again; and in the midst of my *shattered means* I am now richer.[3]

Authoris (de se) Emblema.

Tentâsti, fateon, sine vulnere sœpius, & me
  Consultum voluit Vox, *sine voce, frequens;*
Ambivit placido divinior aura meatu,
  Et frustrà sancto murmure præmonuit.
Surdus eram, mutusq; Silex: *Tu, (quanta tuorum*
  Cura tribi est!) aliâ das renovare viâ,
Permutas Curam: Jamq, irritatus Amorem
  Posse negas, & vim, Vi, *superare paras,*
Accedis propior, molemq;, & Saxea *rumpis*

> *Pectora, fitq;* Caro, *quod fuit ante* Lapis.
> *En lacerum! Cœlosq; tuos ardentia tandem*
>   Fragmenta, *& liquidas ex* Adamante *genas.*
> *Sic olim undantes* Petras, Scopulosq; *vomentes*
>   *Curâsti, O populi providus usq; tui!*
> *Quam miranda tibi manus est!* Moriendo, *revixi;*
>   *Et* fractas *jam sum* ditior *inter* opes.

At once, after this story of a sudden, violent illumination, comes the short and simple poem headed, like the opening poem of Herbert's *Temple,* "The Dedication,"; [4] it contains a number of verbal echoes of Herbert, and the whole manner of the poem represents a perfect distillation of Herbert's intimate mode of colloquy:

> Some drops of thy all-quickning bloud
> Fell on my heart, these made it bud
> And put forth thus, though, Lord, before
> The ground was curs'd, and void of store.

These three elements, then: engraved title page, Latin confession, and Herbertian Dedication form the utterly adequate preface to *Silex Scintillans,* 1650. They introduce a volume that will have two dominating themes: first, the record and results of the experience of sudden illumination; and second, a tribute to the poetry of George Herbert, which, it seems, played an important part in cultivating Vaughan's peculiar experience. Thus, toward the middle of Vaughan's volume, after hundreds of unmistakable echoes of Herbert in title, phrasing, theme, and stanza-form,[5] Vaughan at last openly acknowledges his debt by accepting the invitation of Herbert's poem "Obedience," where Herbert offers his poetry as a written deed conveying himself to God, with this conclusion:

> He that will passe his land,
>   As I have mine, may set his hand
> And heart unto this Deed, when he hath read;
>   And make the purchase spread
> To both our goods, if he to it will stand.
>
> How happie were my part,
>   If some kinde man would thrust his heart

> Into these lines; till in heav'ns Court of Rolls
> They were by winged souls
> Entred for both, farre above their desert!

Vaughan, in "The Match," answers in Herbert's own mode of familiar address: [6]

> Dear friend! whose holy, ever-living lines
> Have done much good
> To many, and have checkt my blood,
> My fierce, wild blood that still heaves, and inclines,
> But is still tam'd
> By those bright fires which thee inflam'd;
> Here I joyn hands, and thrust my stubborn heart
> Into thy *Deed* . . .

As we look back, this joining of hands and hearts between Vaughan and Herbert is almost equally evident in the opening poem of the volume proper: "Regeneration." Here the allegorical mode of the painful quest, the imagery of struggling upward toward a "pinacle" where disappointment lies, the sudden cry mysteriously heard upon this hill, and even some aspects of the stanza-form—all these things show a poem that begins by playing variations on Herbert's poem "The Pilgrimage," which leads the speaker through "the wilde of Passion" toward the hill suggesting Calvary:

> When I had gain'd the brow and top,
> A lake of brackish waters on the ground
> Was all I found.

> With that abash'd and struck with many a sting
> Of swarming fears,
> I fell, and cry'd, Alas my King!
> Can both the way and end be tears?
> Yet taking heart I rose, and then perceiv'd
> I was deceiv'd:

> My hill was further: so I flung away,
> Yet heard a crie
> Just as I went, *None goes that way*
> *And lives*: If that be all, said I,

> After so foul a journey death is fair,
> And but a chair.

But Vaughan's pilgrimage has quite a different theme: in the fourth stanza the Herbertian echoes fade out, as Vaughan's pilgrim is called away into an interior region of the soul, here imaged with the combination of natural and Biblical landscape that often marks Vaughan at his best:

> With that, some cryed, *Away;* straight I
>   Obey'd, and led
> Full East, a faire, fresh field could spy
>   Some call'd it, *Jacobs Bed;*
> A Virgin-soile, which no
>   Rude feet ere trod,
> Where (since he stept there,) only go
>   Prophets, and friends of God.

The allusion to Jacob's vision and journey toward the East (Genesis 28:10–22; 29:1) is only the first of many such allusions by Vaughan to the "early days" of the Old Testament; here the scene begins an allegorical account of the mysterious workings of grace; the pilgrim enters into a state of interior illumination, where he is prepared to apprehend the presence of God and to hear the voice of the Lord. In the remaining six stanzas the setting mysteriously changes to another landscape, a springtime scene, where a grove contains a garden with a fountain; the state of grace is imaged by combining the natural imagery of spring with subtle echoes of the most famous of all spring-songs: the Song of Solomon. The key to these stanzas is given by Vaughan himself in a verse from the Canticle appended to the poem: "Arise O North, and come thou Southwind, and blow upon my garden, that the spices thereof may flow out." It is the Garden of the Soul: one of the great central symbols in the Christian literature of meditation and contemplation. For Vaughan's poem here we need to recall especially the four verses of the Canticle (4:12–15) that immediately precede Vaughan's citation:

> A garden inclosed is my sister, my spouse; a spring shut up, a fountain sealed.
> Thy plants are an orchard of pomegranates, with pleasant fruits; camphire, with spikenard,

Spikenard and saffron; calamus and cinnamon, with all trees of frankincense; myrrh and aloes, with all chief spices:
A fountain of gardens, a well of living waters, and streams from Lebanon.

So in Vaughan's spiritual landscape "The aire was all in spice," while

> Only a little Fountain lent
> Some use for Eares,
> And on the dumbe shades language spent
> The Musick of her teares;
> I drew her neere, and found
> The Cisterne full
> Of divers stones, some bright, and round
> Others ill-shap'd, and dull.
>
> The first (pray marke,) as quick as light
> Danc'd through the floud,
> But, th'last more heavy then the night
> Nail'd to the Center stood;

Vaughan is developing his favorite image-cluster of light and darkness through symbols that suggest one of his favorite Biblical passages: the third chapter of St. John's gospel, where Nicodemus hears the words of Jesus by night:

Except a man be born of water and of the Spirit, he cannot enter into the kingdom of God.
That which is born of the flesh is flesh; and that which is born of the Spirit is spirit.

So in Vaughan's allegory, the spiritual part of man is here reborn, made bright and "quick" as light; while the fleshly part remains dull and heavy, nailed to the earth. Much the same significance is found in the following scene, where in a bank of flowers, representing his own interior state, the speaker finds

> Some fast asleepe, others broad-eyed
> And taking in the Ray . . .

And finally, all the images and themes of this poem coalesce with a three-fold allusion to the "winds" of grace: the "rushing mighty wind" of Pentecost (Acts 2:2), the winds that are prayed for in Vaughan's quotation from the Canticle, and the wind described in the words of Jesus to Nicodemus: "The wind bloweth where it listeth, and thou hearest the sound thereof, but canst not tell whence it cometh, and whither it goeth: so is every one that is born of the Spirit." And so the poem concludes:

> Here musing long, I heard
> A rushing wind
> Which still increas'd, but whence it stirr'd
> No where I could not find;
>
> I turn'd me round, and to each shade
> Dispatch'd an Eye,
> To see, if any leafe had made
> Least motion, or Reply,
> But while I listning sought
> My mind to ease
> By knowing, where 'twas, or where not,
> It whisper'd; *Where I please.*
>
> Lord, then said I, *On me one breath,*
> *And let me dye before my death!*

So the poem,[7] like dozens of others by Vaughan, begins with echoes of George Herbert, whose simplicity of language and intimacy of tone pervade the whole poem and the whole volume of 1650; but, like all of Vaughan's better poems, "Regeneration" moves away from Herbert to convey its own unique experience through its own rich combination of materials, in which we may discern three dominant fields of reference: the Bible, external Nature, and the interior motions of the Self. There is in "Regeneration" not a single reference that could be called eucharistic. Yet Herbert opens the central body of his poems with an emblematic Altar, typographically displayed upon the page, and he follows this with the long eucharistic meditation entitled "The Sacrifice," where he develops the meaning of the Passion through a variation on the ancient Reproaches of Christ, spoken from the Cross as part of the Good Friday service. Nothing could speak more eloquently of the vast difference between these two poets.

In accordance with his central symbols, at the outset of his *Temple* Herbert gives seventy-seven stanzas of epigrammatic advice on how to lead a good life, under the title, "The Church-porch"; these stanzas form a preparation for the mental communion that constitutes the heart of Herbert's central body of poetry, "The Church," as he makes plain by these lines on the threshold:

> Thou, whom the former precepts have
> Sprinkled and taught, how to behave
> Thy self in church; approach, and taste
> The churches mysticall repast.

Now Henry Vaughan also has a group of stanzas in this epigrammatic form, under the title "Rules and Lessons"; they come exactly in the center of the 1650 volume, as though the advice there given formed the center of the volume's devotional life. But Vaughan's advice bears no relation to any ecclesiastical symbolism: it is as though the earthly church had vanished, and man were left to work alone with God.[8] Vaughan's rules and lessons for the devout life lay down, in twenty-four stanzas, certain ways of individual communion with God in every hour of the day, from early morning, through the worldly work of midday, and on through night, until the next day's awakening: one couplet gives the essence of the rules:

> A sweet *self-privacy* in a right soul
> Out-runs the Earth, and lines the utmost pole.

Man's duty is to cultivate the inner self, using as aids the two "books" that we have seen in "Regeneration": the Book of Nature, and the Book of Scripture, as Vaughan suggests in his advice for morning devotions:

> Walk with thy fellow-creatures: note the *hush*
> And *whispers* amongst them. There's not a *Spring,*
> Or *Leafe* but hath his *Morning-hymn;* Each *Bush*
> And *Oak* doth know *I AM;* canst thou not sing?
> O leave thy Cares, and follies! go this way
> And though art sure to prosper all the day.
>
> Serve God before the world; let him not go
> Until thou hast a blessing, then resigne
> The whole unto him; and remember who
> Prevail'd by *wrestling* ere the *Sun* did *shine.*
> Poure *Oyle* upon the *stones,* weep for thy sin,
> Then journey on, and have an eie to heav'n.

Note the rich and curious complex of the Biblical and the natural: the allusion to the bush from which Moses heard the voice of God; the extended reference to the time when Jacob wrestled with the mysterious stranger "until the breaking of the day," when he won the stranger's blessing and knew at last that he had "seen God face to face" (Genesis 32:24–30); and the shorter allusion to the familiar scene of Jacob's vision, after which "Jacob rose up early in the morning, and took the stone that he had put for his pillows, and set it up for a pillar, and poured oil upon the top of it" (Genesis 28:18).

The Bible, Nature, and the Self thus come together in a living harmony, as in Vaughan's "Religion" (a poem that, typically, seems to take its rise from Herbert's poem "Decay"):

> My God, when I walke in those groves,
> And leaves thy spirit doth still fan,
> I see in each shade that there growes
> An Angell talking with a man.
>
> Under a *Juniper,* some house,
> Or the coole *Mirtles* canopie,
> Others beneath an *Oakes* greene boughs,
> Or at some *fountaines* bubling Eye;
>
> Here *Jacob* dreames, and wrestles; there
> *Elias* by a Raven is fed,
> Another time by th' Angell, where
> He brings him water with his bread;
>
> In *Abr'hams* Tent the winged guests
> (O how familiar then was heaven!)
> Eate, drinke, discourse, sit downe, and rest
> Untill the Coole, and shady *Even* . . .

One must read several stanzas before it becomes clear that the "leaves" here are essentially the leaves of the Bible,[9] where the self can learn to live intimately with God; but at the same time the vivid apprehension of natural life here may suggest that nature itself is still inspired by the divine presence.

The fact that Vaughan so often, in his best poems, seeks out these individual ways of communion with God does not mean that he chooses to neglect or ignore traditional devotions to the Eucharist. On the contrary, he is acutely aware of the importance of the eucharistic allusions in Herbert's *Temple*, for he makes frequent efforts to follow Herbert's central mode of mental communion. But he does not often succeed, as we may see in four sizable poems in the 1650 volume that are devoted to eucharistic celebration. His poem "The Passion" is an extended effort to meditate upon the traditional themes, but the poem is wooden, labored, and forced in its effect. One may perhaps trace a cause of this failure to the fact that Vaughan does not visualize the Passion "as if he were present," in the ancient tradition of such meditations; instead, he puts the whole occasion in the past. He does not memorialize the Passion as a present reality. In another poem, "Dressing," he performs a preparation for "Thy mysticall *Communion*," but the poem is so worried by contemporary doctrinal quarrels that it ends with a bitter attack on Puritan views, and not with any devotional presence. Another poem, entitled "The Holy Communion," begins by echoing the first two lines of George Herbert's eucharistic poem, "The Banquet": "Welcome sweet, and sacred feast; welcome life!" but Vaughan's poem immediately veers away from the feast to ponder the action of grace within the self, and the operation of God's creative power over the entire universe.

Vaughan's one and only success in this kind of poetic celebration comes significantly in his poem "The Sap," where he approaches the Eucharist indirectly, through a tale told to himself by his inmost self:

> Come sapless Blossom, creep not stil on Earth
>   Forgetting thy first birth;
> 'Tis not from dust, or if so, why dost thou
>   Thus cal and thirst for dew?
> It tends not thither, if it doth, why then
>   This growth and stretch for heav'n? . . .
> Who plac'd thee here, did something then Infuse
>   Which now can tel thee news.
> There is beyond the Stars an hil of myrrh
>   From which some drops fal here,
> On it the Prince of *Salem* sits, who deals
>   To thee thy secret meals . . .
> Yet liv'd he here sometimes, and bore for thee
>   A world of miserie . . .
> But going hence, and knowing wel what woes
>   Might his friends discompose,
> To shew what strange love he had to our good
>   He gave his sacred bloud

> By wil our sap, and Cordial; now in this
>   Lies such a heav'n of bliss,
> That, who but truly tasts it, no decay
>   Can touch him any way . . .

The whole poem, as several readers have pointed out,[10] bears some resemblance to Herbert's poem "Peace," but the contrasts are more
significant. In Herbert's poem the seeker after peace comes upon a
"rev'rend good old man" who tells him the story of "a Prince of old"
who "At Salem dwelt"—alluding to Christ under the figure of Mel-
chizedek, who "brought forth bread and wine" (Genesis 14:18;
Hebrews 7). Herbert's poem presents an allegory of the apostolic
succession: the "good old man" offers the bread of life derived from
the "twelve stalks of wheat" that sprang out of Christ's grave:

> Take of this grain, which in my garden grows,
>   And grows for you,
>   Make bread of it: and that repose
>   And peace, which ev'ry where
> With so much earnestnesse you do pursue,
>   Is onely there.

But Vaughan does not end his poem with such an echo of the ecclesiastical ritual; instead he closes with what appears to be yet another
tribute to the poems of George Herbert, as he seems to echo here at
least four of Herbert's eucharistic poems.[11]

>   Then humbly take
>   This balm for souls that ake,
>   And one who drank it thus, assures that you
>   Shal find a Joy so true,
>   Such perfect Ease, and such a lively sense
>   Of grace against all sins,
>   That you'l Confess the Comfort such, as even
>   Brings to, and comes from Heaven.

But this comfort remains, in Vaughan's poetry, a promise and a hope:
his central channels of communion lie elsewhere, channels with a long
and venerable history.[12]

2. The Augustinian Quest

Perhaps the discussion of Vaughan's characteristic triad, the Bible,
Nature, and the Self, has already suggested the three "books" culti-

vated by the medieval Augustinians, and especially by St. Bonaventure: the Book of Scripture, the Book of Nature, and the Book of the Soul.[13] The three books are essentially, one: the revelation given in the Bible shows man how to read, first nature, and then his own soul. That is to say, in Augustinian terms: man, enlightened by Biblical revelation, can grasp the Vestiges, the "traces," of God in external nature; and from this knowledge he can then turn inward to find the Image of God within himself.[14] It is an Image defaced by sin, but with its essential powers restored by the sacrifice of Christ. Man is not simply fallen: he is fallen and redeemed. It is man's responsibility, with the omnipresent help of grace, to clear and renew this Image, until it may become a true Similitude. But the renewal can never be wholly accomplished in this life: thus, as in "Regeneration," the poems that relate Vaughan's journey of the mind toward God end with a cry for help, a prayer for some momentary glimpse of perfection, as in his "Vanity of Spirit," where he performs a journey like that in Bonaventure's *Itinerarium*,[15] first searching through all Nature, and then finding at last within himself

> A peece of much antiquity,
>   With Hyerogliphicks quite dismembred,
>   And broken letters scarce remembred.
> I tooke them up, and (much Joy'd,) went about
> T' unite those peeces, hoping to find out
>   The mystery; but this neer done,
>   That little light I had was gone:
>   It griev'd me much. At last, said I,
>   *Since in these veyls my Ecclips'd Eye*
>   *May not approach thee, (for at night*
>   *Who can have commerce with the light?)*
>   *I'le disapparell, and to buy*
>   *But one half glaunce, most gladly dye.*

In this effort to piece together broken letters scarce remembered, by the aid of an interior light, Vaughan displays the essential action of that kind of meditation which may be termed Augustinian. Its finest explanation is still the one most easily available: it lies in the great climactic section of Augustine's *Confessions,* the chapters of the tenth book (6–27) where he marvels at and meditates upon the power of Memory. If we read and reread these chapters, we may come to feel them acting more and more as a commentary upon the poems of *Silex*

Scintillans, 1650; and we may come to understand more clearly the ways in which Vaughan's finest poetry draws its strength from the great central tradition of Platonic Christianity.

The process of Augustinian meditation begins, as Vaughan's volume of 1650 begins, with an effort to apprehend the meaning of an experience of sudden illumination: *percussisti cor meum verbo tuo, et amavi te*—"Thou hast strucken my heart with thy word, and therupon I loved thee. . . . What now do I love, whenas I love thee?"

> not the beauty of any *corporall thing*, not the order of times; not the brightnesse of the *light*, which to behold, is so gladsome to our eyes: not the pleasant *melodies* of songs of all kinds; not the fragrant smell of flowers, and oyntments, and spices: not *Manna* and honey, nor any *fayre limbs* that are so acceptable to fleshly embracements.
>
> I love none of these things, whenas I love my God: and yet I love a certaine kinde of *light*, and a kind of *voyce*, and a kinde of *fragrancy*, and a kinde of *meat*, and a kind of *embracement*. Whenas I love my God; who is both the *light*, and the voyce, and the sweet *smell*, and the *meate*, and the *embracement* of my inner man: where that *light* shineth unto my soule, which no place can receive; that *voyce* soundeth, which time deprives me not of; and that fragrancy *smelleth*, which no wind scatters . . .
>
> This is it which I love, when as I love my God.[16]

Here is the spiritual landscape of the redeemed soul, described by Vaughan in his "Regeneration," glimpsed throughout his volume in the many fresh images from nature that he uses to relate the experience, and summed up once again near the close of the volume, in the poem "Mount of Olives." This title represents a traditional symbol of the soul's retirement to prayer and meditation, here to recall, like Augustine, a moment which gave his life its meaning:

> When first I saw true beauty, and thy Joys
> Active as light, and calm without all noise
> Shin'd on my soul, I felt through all my powr's
> Such a rich air of sweets, as Evening showrs
> Fand by a gentle gale Convey and breath
> On some parch'd bank, crown'd with a flowrie wreath;
> Odors, and Myrrh, and balm in one rich floud

O'r-ran my heart, and spirited my bloud . . .
I am so warm'd now by this glance on me,
That, midst all storms I feel a Ray of thee;
So have I known some beauteous *Paisage* rise
In suddain flowres and arbours to my Eies,
And in the depth and dead of winter bring
To my Cold thoughts a lively sense of spring.

With the memory of such an experience within him, the Augustinian seeker turns to question external nature, as in the *Confessions:*

> I askt the *Earth,* and that answered me, *I am not it;* and whatsoever are in it, made the same confession. I asked the *Sea* and the *deepes,* and the *creeping things,* and they answered me, *We are not thy God, seeke above us.* . . . I asked the heavens, the Sunne and Moone, and Starres, Nor (say they) are wee the *God* whom thou seekest.   [10.6]

All creatures give for Augustine the same answer: "they cryed out with a loud voyce, *He made us*" (10.6). It is the questioning of nature that runs throughout Vaughan's poetry, where "Each *tree, herb, flowre* / Are shadows of his *wisedome,* and his Pow'r." [17] Thus in "The Tempest" Vaughan prays that man "would hear / The world read to him!" and declares:

> all the vast expence
> In the Creation shed, and slav'd to sence
> Makes up but lectures for his eie, and ear.

(lectures in the old medieval sense, readings of the book, with commentary and elucidation:)

> Sure, mighty love foreseeing the discent
>   Of this poor Creature, by a gracious art
>   Hid in these low things snares to gain his heart,
> And layd surprizes in each Element.

> All things here shew him heaven; *Waters* that fall
>   Chide, and fly up; *Mists* of corruptest fome
>   Quit their first beds & mount: trees, herbs, flowres, all
> Strive upwards stil, and point him the way home.

And the way home lies through an interior ascent, climbing upward and inward through the deepest regions of the human soul:

> I beg'd here long, and gron'd to know
> Who gave the Clouds so brave a bow,
>   Who bent the spheres, and circled in
>   Corruption with this glorious Ring,
>   What is his name, and how I might
>   Descry some part of his great light.
> I summon'd nature: peirc'd through all her store,
> Broke up some seales, which none had touch'd before,
>   Her wombe, her bosome, and her head
>   Where all her secrets lay a bed
>   I rifled quite, and having past
>   Through all the Creatures, came at last
>   To search my selfe, where I did find
>   Traces, and sounds of a strange kind.
>   ("Vanity of Spirit")

So Augustine turns to search within himself and comes "into these fields and spacious palaces of my *Memory,* where the treasures of innumerable *formes* brought into it from these things that have beene perceived by the *sences,* be hoarded up."

> And yet doe not the things themselves enter the *Memory;* onely the *Images* of the things perceived by the *Sences,* are ready there at hand, when ever the *Thoughts* will recall them. . . .
>   For there have I in a readinesse, the heaven, the earth, the sea, and what-ever I can thinke upon in them. . . . There also meete I with my *selfe,* I recall my *selfe,* what, where, or when I have done a thing; and how I was affected when I did it. There be all what ever I remember, eyther upon mine owne experience, or others credit. Out of the same store doe I my selfe compare these and these likelyhoods of things; eyther of such as I have made experience of, or of such as I have barely beleeved upon experience of some things that bee passed: and by these doe I compare actions to *come,* their *events* and *hopes:* and upon all these againe doe I meditate, as if they were now present. . . .
>   Great is this force of *memory,* exessive great, O my *God:* a large and an infinite roomthynes [*penetrale:* inner room],

who can plummet the bottome of it? yet is this a *faculty* of
mine, and belongs unto my nature: nor can I my self comprehend all that I am.   [10.8]

Yet things even more wonderful lie beyond, as he probes ever and
ever more deeply into the recesses of the memory. "Here also bee all
these precepts of those *liberall Sciences* as yet unforgotten; coucht as
it were further off in a more inward place" (10.9). These things could
not have been conveyed within by the senses; how was it then that he
came to accept these precepts as true?

     unlesse because they were already in my memory; though so
     farre off yet, and crowded so farre backeward as it were into
     certaine secret caves, that had they not beene drawne out by
     the advice of some other person, I had never perchance beene
     able so much as to have thought of them?   [10.10]

Here the hint of the presence of something like innate ideas [18] in the
deep caves of the soul leads directly to a long account of what might
be called the dramatic action of Augustinian meditation. It is an action
significantly different from the method of meditation later set forth by
Ignatius Loyola and his followers; for that later method shows the
effects of medieval scholasticism, with its powerful emphasis upon the
analytic understanding, and upon the Thomist principle that human
knowledge is derived from sensory experience. Ignatian meditation is
thus a precise, tightly articulated method, moving from the images that
comprise the composition of place into the threefold sequence of the
powers of the soul, memory, understanding, and will, and from there
into the affections and resolutions of the aroused will. But in Augustinian meditation there is no such precise method; there is, rather, an
intuitive groping back into regions of the soul that lie beyond sensory
memories. The three powers of the soul [19] are all used, but with an
effect of simultaneous action, for with Augustine the aroused will is
using the understanding to explore the memory, with the aim of apprehending more clearly and loving more fervently the ultimate source of
the will's arousal.

     Wherfore we find, that to learne these things whose *Images*
we *sucke* not *in* by our Sences, but perceive *within* by themselves, without Images, as they are; is nothing else, but by
meditating to *gather together*, and by diligent *marking*, to

take notice of those same *notions* which the *memory* did before contayne more scatteringly and confusedly . . . [10.11]

But these things are evasive and elusive; unless we engage in a continual act of re-collection, "they become so drowned againe, and so give
us the slip, as it were, backe into such remote and privy lodgings, that
I must be put againe unto new paines of meditation, for recovery of
them to their former perfection . . . they must be *rallied* and drawne
together againe, that they may bee knowne; that is to say, they must
as it were be *collected* and *gathered together* from their dispersions:
whence the word *cogitation* is derived" (10.11).

The seventeenth-century translator has been frequently rendering
the word *cogitare* by the word *meditate,* thus providing his own account of Augustinian meditation: to draw together these things scat-
tered in the memory. It would seem that poetry composed under the
impulse of this kind of meditation would differ considerably in its
structure from any poetry written under the impulse of the Ignatian
mode of meditation—such as Donne's Holy Sonnets. The poetry of
Augustinian meditation would perhaps tend to display an order akin
to that which Pascal saw in the writings of Augustine: "Cet ordre
consiste principalement à la digression sur chaque point qu 'on rapporte
à la fin, pour la montrer toujours." [20] That *Pensée* may at least suggest
the poetry of Vaughan, where the order often consists chiefly in what
appear to be digressions, but are really exploratory sallies or *excursus*
in the manner indicated by the following passage of the *Confessions:*

> Great is this power of Memory; a thing, O my God, to bee
> amazed at, a very profound and infinite multiplicity: and this
> thing is the minde, and this thing am I. . . . Behold, in those
> innumerable fields, and dennes, and caves of my memory,
> innumerably full of innumerable kinds of things, brought in,
> first, eyther by the *Images,* as all *bodies* are: secondly, or by
> the *presence* of the *things* themselves, as the *Arts* are: thirdly,
> or by certaine *notions* or *impressions,* as the *Affections* of
> the mind are . . . Thorow all these doe I runne and tumble
> [*discurro et volito*]; myning into them on this side, and on
> that side, so farre as ever I am able, but can finde no bottome.
> So great is the force of memory, so great is the force of this
> life of man, even whilest hee is mortall.   [10.17]

Thus in many of Vaughan's best poems, as in "Regeneration," the
characteristic movement is a "mining" of associations, a roving search

over a certain field of imagery, a sinking inward upon the mind's resources, until all the evocative ramifications of the memory have been explored; and then the poem ends rather abruptly, with a cry for divine help, or some generalizing moral conclusion. The movement is seen at its best in "Corruption," where the mind lingers over the memories of the "early days" of Genesis:

> Sure, It was so. Man in those early days
>   Was not all stone, and Earth,
> He shin'd a little, and by those weak Rays
>   Had some glimpse of his birth.
> He saw Heaven o'r his head, and knew from whence
>   He came (condemned,) hither,
> And, as first Love draws strongest, so from hence
>   His mind sure progress'd thither.

Under the impulse of this love, Vaughan's mind progresses backward to recover the memory of Paradise:

> He sigh'd for *Eden,* and would often say
>   *Ah! what bright days were those?*
> Nor was Heav'n cold unto him; for each day
>   The vally, or the Mountain
> Afforded visits, and still *Paradise* lay
>   In some green shade, or fountain.
> Angels lay *Leiger* here; Each Bush, and Cel,
>   Each Oke, and high-way knew them,
> Walk but the fields, or sit down at some *wel,*
>   And he was sure to view them.

Deep within all such associations lies that essential memory toward which Augustine's digressive and "tumbling" meditations have been subtly and inevitably leading: the memory of a "happy life," a "blessed life," *beata vita.*

> Is not an happy life the thing which all desire; and is there any man that some way or other desires it not? But where gate they the knowledge of it, that they are so desirous of it? where did they ever see it, that they are now so enamored of it? Truely we have it, but which way, I know not . . .
> How they come to know it, I cannot tell: and therefore have they it by, I know not, what secret notice; concerning

which, in much doubt I am, whether it bee in the memory or no: which if it bee, then should wee sometimes have beene blessed heretofore. [*quia, si ibi est, iam beati fuimus aliquando; utrum singillatim omnes, an in illo homine, qui primus peccavit . . . non quaero nunc; sed quaero, utrum in memoria sit beata vita.*]

But whether every man should have beene so happy as severally considered in himself, or as in the loynes of that man who first sinned . . . I now inquire not: but this I demaund, whether this blessed life bee in the memory, or no? [10.20]

It must be so, he concludes, for it is known to people in different languages, under different names: "And this could not bee, unlesse the thing it selfe expressed by this name, were still reserved in their memory." But what, precisely, is this thing?

> there is a ioy which is not granted unto the ungodly; but unto those onely which love thee for thine owne sake; whose joy thy selfe art. And this is the blessed life, *to reioyce unto thee, concerning thee, and for thy sake:* this is the happy life, and there is no other. [10.22]

> *a happy life is a ioying in the truth:* For this is a ioying in thee, who art the truth, O God my light, the health of my countenance, and my God. This is the blessed life that all desire . . . Where therefore gaynd they the knowledge of this happy life, but even there, where they learned the truth also? . . . which yet they would not love, were there not some notice of it remayning in their memory. . . . For there is a dimme glimmering of light yet un-put-out, in men: let them walke, let them walke, that the darknesse overtake them not. [10.23]

It is the central image of *Silex Scintillans:* [21] the flash, the spark, the glance, the beam, the ray, the glimmering of light that comes from the memory of an ancient birthright of blessedness—*utrum singillatim omnes, an in illo homine, qui primus peccavit:* whether it be a memory of each man's individual life, or whether it be a memory of Adam's original happy life—that memory remains, yet un-put-out in men. The image is notable in the poem "Silence, and stealth of dayes," where this Augustinian motif is used in recalling the memory of a loved one who has died (evidently Vaughan's brother):

As he that in some Caves thick damp
          Lockt from the light,
Fixeth a solitary lamp,
          To brave the night
And walking from his Sun, when past
          That glim'ring Ray
Cuts through the heavy mists in haste
          Back to his day,
So o'r fled minutes I retreat
          Unto that hour
Which shew'd thee last, but did defeat
          Thy light, and pow'r,
I search, and rack my soul to see
          Those beams again . . .

The "Sun" here is the "solitary lamp" within the cave of the speaker's soul: the memory of his loved one is the light within that serves as an interior sun. Sometimes, carried toward the things of the outer world, the speaker tends to walk away from that "glim'ring Ray," but, re- membering that he has forgotten, he walks, he walks, in Augustine's way, back toward the memory of light. The beams of this loved one's soul, he comes to realize, now shine in heaven, and he cannot track them there; yet something bright remains within, as he concludes:

Yet I have one *Pearle* by whose light
          All things I see,
And in the heart of Earth, and night
          Find Heaven, and thee.

It is the indestructible Image of God, apprehending the presence of God in the memory: "Sure I am, that in it thou dwellest: even for this reason, that I have preserved the memory of thee, since the time that I first learnt thee: and for that I finde thee in my memory, whensoever I call thee to remembrance" (*Confessions*, 10.25).

So the memory of that inner presence runs throughout Vaughan's volume of 1650, as Vaughan struggles backward on his ancient journey of return toward the memory of blessedness. Sometimes the journey backward takes the form of "The Retreate" toward the days of the individual's childhood:

Happy those early dayes! when I
Shin'd in my Angell-infancy.

Before I understood this place
Appointed for my second race,
Or taught my soul to fancy ought
But a white, Celestiall thought,
When yet I had not walkt above
A mile, or two, from my first love,
And looking back (at that short space,)
Could see a glimpse of his bright-face;
When on some *gilded Cloud*, or *flowre*
My gazing soul would dwell an houre,
And in those weaker glories spy
Some shadows of eternity . . .
   O how I long to travell back
And tread again that ancient track!
That I might once more reach that plaine,
Where first I left my glorious traine,
From whence th' Inlightned spirit sees
That shady City of Palme trees;
But (ah!) my soul with too much stay
Is drunk, and staggers in the way.
Some men a forward motion love,
But I by backward steps would move,
And when this dust falls to the urn
In that state I came return.

The poem presents the essence of the *Phaedo*, as qualified and developed by Christian Platonism. Indeed, the *Phaedo* gives the closing image of the drunken man, in an important passage that suggests the kernel of this poem:

> And were we not saying long ago [asks Socrates] that the soul when using the body as an instrument of perception, that is to say, when using the sense of sight or hearing or some other sense . . . were we not saying that the soul too is then dragged by the body into the region of the changeable, and wanders and is confused; the world spins round her, and she is like a drunkard, when she touches change? . . .
>
> But when returning into herself she reflects, then she passes into the other world, the region of purity, and eternity, and immortality, and unchangeableness, which are her kindred . . .[22]

In Vaughan, as in Augustine's *Confessions*, there is of course only the most guarded and glancing use of the Platonic doctrine of reminiscence: any hint of the soul's pre-existence is used by Vaughan as a metaphor of innocence; and the whole poem is toward the close clearly transmuted into orthodox Christianity. The poet superimposes upon the Platonic suggestions the concept of the "Inlightned spirit" which catches a vision of the promised land, as did Moses when he "went up from the plains of Moab unto the mountain of Nebo . . . And the Lord shewed him all the land of Gilead . . . and all the land of Judah, unto the utmost sea, And the south, and the plain of the valley of Jericho, the city of palm trees . . ." (Deuteronomy 34: 1–3).

So the "early days" of the individual's childhood become one with the "early days" of the human race, as related in the Old Testament; and both together form powerful symbols of the memory of a happy life that lives, however glimmeringly, within the soul that has, through regeneration, come into yet a third state of childhood: the state of the "children of God" set forth in the eighth chapter of Romans.

Such is the paradise within, compounded of the Bible, of Nature, and of the Self, which lies at the heart of Vaughan's *Silex Scintillans*, 1650: a vision that results from the constant effort to remember the beauty of the sudden illumination described in his opening Latin confession. That Latin poem and its emblem of the Flashing Flint, with its image of the man within, are once more brought to mind by the well-known passage that concludes Augustine's sequence of meditations on the force of memory:

> Too late beganne I to love thee, O thou beauty both so ancient and so fresh, yea too too late came I to love thee. For behold, thou wert *within* mee, and I *out* of my selfe, where I made search for thee; deformed I, wooing these beautifull pieces of thy workmanship. . . . Thou *calledst*, and criedst unto mee, yea thou even brakest open my *deafenesse*. Thou discoveredst thy beames, and *shynedst* out unto mee, and didst chase away my blindnesse. Thou didst most *fragrantly blow* upon me, and I drew in my *breath* and panted after thee. I *tasted* thee, and now doe *hunger* and *thirst after thee*. Thou didst *touch* mee, and I even burne against to enioy thy peace.   [10.27]

NOTES

1 The unsold sheets of the 1650 volume, with two canceled leaves, were bound up with new materials and a new title page to form the 1655

edition of *Silex Scintillans;* the engraved title page of 1650 and the Latin poem facing the engraving were omitted in 1655: see *The Works of Henry Vaughan,* ed. L. C. Martin (2d ed. Oxford, Clarendon Press, 1957), p. xxiv.

2 The profiles of at least two human faces may also be seen along the outer edges of the heart; the whole heart, then, is animate: the stone has been made flesh, as Vaughan says in his Latin poem facing the emblem.

3 I am indebted to the Rev. Marcus Haworth for suggesting some of the phrases in this translation.

4 In 1655 this fourteen-line poem becomes the first part of a poem in 46 lines, with the elaborate dedicatory heading: "To my most merciful, my most loving, and dearly loved Redeemer, the ever blessed, the onely Holy and Just One, Jesus Christ, The Con of the living God, And the sacred Virgin Mary." The added lines of 1655 are plodding couplets of conventional piety.

5 Most of the important echoes have been listed in the notes to Martin's second edition of Vaughan's *Works.* The echoes have been perceptively discussed by E. C. Pettet, *Of Paradise and Light: A Study of Vaughan's Silex Scintillans* (Cambridge University Press, 1960), ch. 3. See also the helpful article by Mary Ellen Rickey, "Vaughan, *The Temple,* and Poetic Form," *Studies in Philology,* 59 (1962), 162–70.

6 The allusion was pointed out by Elizabeth Holmes, *Henry Vaughan and the Hermetic Philosophy* (Oxford, Blackwell, 1932), pp. 12–13.

7 This brief account of "Regeneration" deals only with those aspects important to the present study; for more detailed interpretations, differing in some respects from my own, see the illuminating studies of this poem by R. A. Durr, *On the Mystical Poetry of Henry Vaughan* (Cambridge, Mass., Harvard University Press, 1962), pp. 82–99; by Ross Garner, *Henry Vaughan: Experience and the Tradition* (University of Chicago Press, 1959), pp. 47–62; and by Pettet, pp. 104–17.

8 By 1650 Vaughan's earthly Church of England had in fact vanished: Vaughan's twin-brother Thomas, the parish priest of Vaughan's own local church, was evicted from his post in 1650, and the post remained vacant for nearly eight years. See F. E. Hutchinson, *Henry Vaughan: A Life and Interpretation* (Oxford, Clarendon Press, 1947), pp. 109–13.

9 For the trees of the second stanza see 1 Kings 19:4–8 (Elijah under the juniper tree); Zechariah 1:8–11 ("the man that stood among the myrtle trees"); Judges 6:11 ("And there came an angel of the Lord, and sat under an oak which was in Ophrah").

10 See *Works of Vaughan,* ed. Martin, 2d ed., p. 744.

11 See Herbert, "The H. Communion," two poems under one title; the first deals with the action of grace against sins; the second celebrates the "ease" with which the soul now communicates with heaven: "Thou hast restor'd us to this ease / By this thy heav'nly bloud." See also "The Invitation," esp. st. 4, dealing with "joy"; and "The Banquet," celebrating the "sweet

and sacred cheer" of the Communion, and its power of raising the soul to "the skie."

[12] The literary consequences of modifications in eucharistic doctrine form the subject of Malcolm Ross's controversial study, *Poetry and Dogma: The Transfiguration of Eucharistic Symbols in Seventeenth Century English Poetry* (New Brunswick, N.J., Rutgers University Press, 1954). Ross's work deserves attention for the light it throws upon the central issues; but many readers will disagree with his conclusions.

[13] See G. H. Tavard, *Transiency and Permanence: The Nature of Theology According to St. Bonaventure* (Franciscan Institute, St. Bonaventure, N.Y., 1954), chs. 2–4.

[14] See Gilson, *Philosophy of Saint Augustine,* pp. 210–24.

[15] See *The Paradise Within,* pp. 55–57.

[16] *Confessions,* 10.6. Quotations from this work in English are in this section taken from the translation by William Watts (London, 1631); the contemporary version here seems especially helpful in bringing out affinities with Vaughan. In other portions of this book, where literal accuracy in the translation seems indispensable, I have used the corrected version of Watts's translation in the Loeb Library edition of the *Confessions,* from which the Latin quotations have been taken.

[17] See "Rules and Lessons," lines 85–96.

[18] For Augustine's view of "innatism," as distinguished from the Platonic view, see the judicious discussion by Gilson, *Philosophy of Saint Augustine,* pp. 75–76.

[19] Memory, understanding, and will are not discussed as "the powers of the soul" in the *Confessions,* although something close to this triad is implied in one chapter of the final book (13.11), where Augustine discusses the triad: *esse, nosse, velle.* The full development of Augustine's exploration of the interior trinity of powers, the Image of the Trinity in man, is found in his *De Trinitate,* completed about twenty years after the *Confessions.* See the discussion of Traherne, *The Paradise Within,* pp. 81–83.

[20] *Pensées,* ed. Léon Brunschvicg (5th edn., Paris, Hachette, 1909), no. 283.

> *L'ordre. Contre l'objection que l' Écriture n'a pas d'ordre.*—Le coeur a son ordre; l'esprit a le sien, qui est par principe et démonstration, le coeur en a un autre. On ne prouve pas qu'on doit être aimé, en exposant d'ordre les causes de l'amour: cela serait ridicule.
>
> Jésus-Christ, saint Paul ont l'ordre de la charité, non de l'esprit; car ils voulaient échauffer, non instruire. Saint Augustin de même. Cet ordre consiste principalement à la digression sur chaque point qu'on rapporte à la fin, pour la montrer toujours.

This analogy was suggested by the citation of this *Pensée* in an essay by Jacques Maritain, "St. Augustine and St. Thomas Aquinas," in *A Monu-*

ment to Saint Augustine (London, Sheed and Ward, 1930). See also Gilson, *Philosophy of Saint Augustine,* pp. 235–37, where Gilson discusses the implications of this *Pensée* and concludes: "Digression is Augustinism's natural method. The natural order of an Augustinian doctrine is to branch out around one center, and this is precisely the order of charity."

[21] For a group of suggestive passages in which Augustine refers to his intuition of God under the symbolism of a flash of light, see John Burnaby, *Amor Dei: A Study of the Religion of St. Augustine* (London, Hodder and Stoughton, 1938), p. 33.

[22] *The Dialogues of Plato,* trans. B. Jowett (3d ed. 5 vols. Oxford University Press, 1892), 2, 222.

ⵣ

An Allusion to Europe: Dryden and Tradition [1]

It is perhaps easier to bury Dryden than to praise him: so much depends on the tradition we choose to place him in and on the standards by which we measure poetic success. If we follow Dr. Johnson and set Dryden in the succession of Waller and Denham, we arrive at a pious tribute to the "reformer of our numbers." If we follow Dr. Leavis and trace "the line of wit," we bring out Dryden's undeniable limitations as compared with Donne or Marvell. (Dr. Leavis's strategy was justified in relation to his aims and results: he has made us aware that "serious wit" did not end with the Metaphysicals.) But if we are to make a positive estimate of Dryden's achievement, we should include in his ancestry English poets of the earlier and later Renaissance and their ancient predecessors, and we need to maintain a keen sense of what Dryden accomplished for his contemporaries. So viewed, Dryden marks the re-affirmation of "Europe" in English poetry and culture after an experiment in insularity and at a time of artificial essays in continental "Classicism."

Again, it would be easy to arrive at a rather tepid estimate of Dryden's career—true enough, but hardly of much concern to readers with a live interest in either history or poetry. Dryden's re-affirmation matters—aesthetically and historically—because it is a poet's affirmation, realized in the shaping of new modes of expression and in the writing of poetry which is imaginatively various and unified. His direct

From *ELH: A Journal of English Literary History*, XIX (1952), pp. 38–48. Reprinted by permission of the publishers.

critical propaganda for French and Latin literary standards counts for relatively little in the continuing life of the Renaissance tradition. A more adaptable Arnold, like Pope

> He won his way by yielding to the tide.

By "indirection," by creating his unique satirical mode, Dryden reaffirmed important European values, while engaging the most lively concerns of his readers. It is to this poetic feat that I want to draw attention.

Dryden's accomplishment is more remarkable in view of the situation in which he wrote. Charles had been "restored," and with him an audience that was alien to the most vigorous of the surviving older poets. Milton withdrew; Cowley retired without producing much of the "wit" he prescribed. Marvell dived as a Metaphysical and came up as a satirist; but as a poet he belonged to another world. Although Dryden talked sentimentally of "retiring," he was unequivocally the "first" man of this

> Laughing, quaffing, and unthinking time.

His success lay in his ability to draw on a wide range of English and European literary traditions while "speaking home" to this audience of Court and City. A glance at his development as a dramatist will suggest how he attained a style which had this two-fold effectiveness.

In the period between *Astraea Redux* and *Absalom and Achitophel*, while Dryden was mightily pleasing his auditors in the theatre, he struck out two more or less distinct styles which were blended in the successes of his maturity: one, the "heroic"; and the other, the style of public address which he somewhat scornfully regarded as Horatian. Whatever we call them, both styles bear traces of their mixed European and English origin. In the process of making his outrageous experiments in drama, the Heroic Plays, Dryden invented a style that gave an impression of ancient epic grandeur; at times, in narratives of quite incredible exploits, the impression became almost convincing, thanks to the skill with which Dryden combined Virgilian allusions with rather obvious echoes of Virgilian rhythm.

In the last and best of these plays, *Aureng-Zebe*, we first hear distinctly what Professor Van Doren calls Dryden's "grouping" of couplets, an enlargement of rhythm which comes when he had been reading Shakespeare, and, more significantly, soon after his re-working of *Paradise Lost*. Milton's example, along with Sylvester's and Cowley's, helped fix the Old Testament-ecclesiastical strain in Dryden's mature heroic style, as it finally emerged in *Absalom and Achitophel*. In tone the style is unmistakably a "translation out of the original tongues."

While Dryden was cultivating a manner that had almost no appropriateness to his auditors—except by a law of literary contraries—he was learning to speak to them with directness and ease in his prologues and epilogues. Here he acquired his mastery of more varied tones; and here "the great reform" of language and rhythm was most happily realized. The language is "such words as men did use" (in an age less polished than our own); and the molding of speech idiom to the patterns of the couplet is admirable. After the tepid velleities of Waller—the "crooner" of the couplet—Dryden's prologues mark a partial recovery of the toughness and "juice" of Jonsonian English. But though they are highly original, they are linked via Jonson with an earlier tradition. The prologue, as used by Jonson to give instruction in literary taste, is a theatrical form of the Roman epistle. Dryden's later blend of the prologue-satirical style with the heroic is anticipated in the insolent debates of the plays and in the prologues themselves. Given a very slight excuse, Dryden will sound off with an ancient literary parallel, or a debased parody of one. Part of the game of amusing his listeners consisted in deliberately talking over their heads.

The "huddled notions" of Dryden's satiric mode lay in readiness when the Monmouth "conspiracy" offered the occasion his genius had been waiting for. He could now compose heroic narrative and dialogue while talking to his familiar audience. What is remarkable is that in scoring a journalistic and political success he produced poetry of a high order. Here is a representative passage, the commemoration of Titus Oates, the Presbyterian "weaver's issue" who testified that the Jesuits were plotting to murder Charles II.

> Yet, *Corah,* thou shalt from Oblivion pass;
> Erect thy self thou Monumental Brass:
> High as the Serpent of thy Metal made,
> While Nations stand secure beneath thy shade.
> What though his Birth were base, yet Comets rise
> From Earthy Vapours, e'r they shine in Skies.
> Prodigious Actions may as well be done

By Weaver's issue as by Prince's son.
This Arch-Attestor for the Publick Good
By that one Deed enobles all his Bloud.
Who ever ask'd the Witnesses high race
Whose Oath with Martyrdom did *Stephen* grace?
Ours was a *Levite,* and as times went then,
His tribe were God-almighties Gentlemen.
Sunk were his Eyes, his Voice was harsh and loud,
Sure signs he neither Cholerick was, nor Proud:
His long Chin prov'd his Wit; his Saint-like Grace
A Church Vermilion, and a *Moses's* Face.
His Memory, miraculously great,
Coud Plots, exceeding mans belief, repeat;
Which, therefore cannot be accounted Lies,
For humane Wit coud never such devise.
Some future Truths are mingled in his Book;
But where the Witness fail'd, the Prophet spoke:
Some things like Visionary flights appear:
The Spirit caught him up, the Lord knows where:
And gave him his *Rabinical* degree,
Unknown to Foreign University.

To see the imaginative unity of these lines is to see the blending of Dryden's earlier styles and to feel the active pressure of older literary traditions. As in most satirical verse, the lines are held together in part by the broad illogic of irony: Dryden makes a series of triumphant assertions every one of them the opposite of the truth from the Court point of view. But it is Dryden's "intonation" that sets his mark on the lines and gives them life and singleness of effect. His note is clearly heard in "arch-attestor," with its upper level of churchly associations, and in "prodigious," which nicely combines Latin solemnity with the literal Latin meaning of "monstrous." Dryden has anticipated the high level of this commemoration by suggesting that it belongs to a Homeric catalogue; he then addresses Oates in a line so nobly reminiscent of Virgil that it is hardly recognizable as parody:

Yet, *Corah,* thou shalt from Oblivion pass . . .

The occasionally Latin flavor of the diction is also vaguely suggestive of Virgilian epic, while at many points the language is more or less

Biblical, ranging from near-quotation to expressions with religious or churchly associations. Working within a fairly narrow range of allusion Dryden maintains a declamatory tone that is both Biblical-ecclesiastical and Roman-heroic. But the "venom" of the address depends on the contrast of another tone which is unmistakably the voice of the prologues, insolently vulgar and knowingly unliterary:

> Ours was a *Levite,* and as times went then,
> His tribe were God-almighties Gentlemen.

The blend of manners is most subtle in the lines of greatest imaginative variety:

> Yet, *Corah,* thou shalt from Oblivion pass;
> Erect thy self thou Monumental Brass:
> High as the Serpent of thy Metal made,
> While Nations stand secure beneath thy shade.

The focus of the ironies is also the focus of opposing styles and of the widest range of literary and religious associations, the ironies arising mainly from the double references of "monumental" and "brass." Taking "monumental" on its high Latinate side, in a Virgilian address, we feel that this beneficent hero is "monumental" in greatness. Or we may read the whole line as a preposterous parody of Horace's

> Exegi monumentum aere perennius. . . .

But Biblical and ecclesiastical connotations of "brass" and "monuments" suggest that our hero is worthy of a "monumental brass" in an English church, the rude command implying that this monument, contrary to decent custom and the laws of gravity will rise of its own power. Finally, "brass" in its vulgar sense reminds us that such effrontery is otherwise "monumental."

In these lines Dryden's satirical mode appears at its characteristic best. There are the black-and-white oppositions of irony with rhetorical and metrical emphasis striking in unison. There is the smack of life and vulgarity in a word from "Jonsonian" London, the word which imparts the ironic intention and gives force to Dryden's thrust. But the irony is most concentrated in a word of classical origin which is rich in literary and historical connotations and which suggests the Roman oratorical tone.

These features appear in close combination in many of the best lines in Dryden's satirical verse:

> A fiery Soul, which working out its way,
> Fretted the Pigmy Body to decay:
> And o'r informed the Tenement of Clay.

(The reminiscences of Aristotle and Plato, Bishop Fuller and Carew have often been pointed out.) Or

> Besides, his goodly Fabrick fills the eye
> And seems design'd for thoughtless Majesty:
> Thoughtless as Monarch Oakes that shade the plain,
> And, spread in solemn state, supinely reign.
> *Heywood* and *Shirley* were but Types of thee,
> Thou last great Prophet of Tautology:

or

> But gentle *Simkin* just reception finds
> Amidst this Monument of vanisht minds;

or

> Thou leaps't o'r all eternall truths in thy
>   *Pindarique* way!

Finally, a delicious blend of neo-Platonic fancy and shrewd analysis in these lines on the Church of England:

> If as our dreaming Platonists report,
> There could be spirits of a middle sort,
> Too black for heav'n, and yet too white for hell,
> Who just dropt half way down, nor lower fell;
> So pois'd, so gently she descends from high,
> It seems a soft dismission from the skie.

From these examples and from our analysis, it is clear that "allusive irony" is a more adequate term than "mock-heroic" for Dryden's satirical mode, whether in *Absalom and Achitophel* and *Mac Flecknoe* or in passages of incidental satire in his argumentative verse. His mode is allusive in a wide variety of ways: in close imitation or parody of other writers, in less exact references to language, styles, and conventions of other literatures—Classical, Biblical, and French—in drawing on the large materials of philosophy and theology, in playing on popular parallels between contemporary religious and political situations and those of ancient history, sacred and secular. Through this mode Dryden makes his "affirmation of Europe."

A solemn claim and a preposterous one, if we think of the mode as devices for heightening style. The difference between allusive irony and the heroic trimmings added to the *Annus Mirabilis* lies in the imaginative union of tones and levels of meaning that I have been describing: "thou Monumental Brass"! The vulgar thrust is inseparable from the reference to high literary styles and to heroic behavior and ecclesiastical splendor.

That the union of styles was more than an academic trick is further shown by the success of the poem with contemporary readers. As compared with Restoration plays or lampoons and gazettes, *Absalom and Achitophel* spoke to more of the interests of the reading public in 1681, and, as Beljame observed, to *more* of the public. Although the Classical heroic was especially flattering to the aristocrats' view of themselves, Latin culture was the common possession of educated men, whatever their political and religious allegiances might be. Dryden, Milton, and Marvell have at least this in common. The Old Testament flavor, satirically amusing to the Court, was richly meaningful and insidiously attractive to Nonconformists. And the colloquial idiom brought the high talk down to the level where Court and City lived. By responding so naturally to the double claims of both his audience and his development as a poet, Dryden "made himself heard" and created a fresh form of art in English poetry.

By this fact alone, he affirmed an important European value to his audience: that poetic craft matters. Dryden's admiration for what Boileau had done for French satire is a sign of his belief that he had performed a similar service for English satire. Boileau would have recognized as art of a high order the poise and finish of Dryden's mode:

> At his right hand our young *Ascanius* sate,
> *Rome's* other hope and Pillar of the State.
> His Brows thick fogs, instead of glories, grace,
> And lambent dullness plaid around his face.

The poise is evident in the balance between crude burlesque in "thick fogs" and the subtle gravity of "lambent dullness"; the finish is felt in the melodious and resilient verse. But the smoothness is not merely fashionable: it functions poetically in the strategy of civilized irony. The reader is momentarily beguiled into taking the lines as an exquisite compliment. Dryden had a right to claim that like Boileau he was bringing into modern satire a Virgilian refinement of "raillery." In the fine Latin wit of *"lambent* dullness" or "spread in solemn state, *supinely* reign," Dryden is "alluding" to a culture and the fineness of response which it fostered.

It is no great compliment to describe Dryden's achievement as a triumph of neo-classicism, if we mean by neo-classicism mechanical use of conventions borrowed from Boileau or Rapin. Dryden's achievement is not one of "meeting requirements"; the conventions "at work," as in the lines just quoted, are expressive of larger aesthetic and cultural values. In writing verse which combined the normality and vigor of good talk with a musical pattern that was the apt accompaniment of ironic wit and in using language which was equally alive in its reference to immediate interests and to literary tradition, Dryden expressed a community in attitude and standards of art with European poets and critics. Some of these attitudes and standards—the detachment, the refinement of ironic censure, the insistence on design and precise mastery of language—were particularly salutary for readers too well pleased with *Hudibras* and for writers who mistook ease for art. But Dryden did not sacrifice the vigor of Butler to "correctness." The Augustan reform, as initiated by Dryden, unlike that of Addison, kept close contact with a masculine audience. Dryden's allusive mode shows a positive strength in neo-classicism which the odious term and its theories completely conceal.

Let us consider more particularly how this mode worked, how and why epic allusions offered Dryden a way of expressing important values. In ironic contexts, the more or less close imitations of epic introduced a standard of manners and actions by which the exploits of politicians and poetasters might be measured. Fomenters of Popish plots and rash rebellions and slipshod writers were exposed to ancient and Biblical ideals of prince and prophet, and their operations were socially and intellectually "placed." In contexts less purely ironic, as in parts of the Shaftesbury and Monmouth "characters," the allusions to Classical and Biblical heroic had another effect. The magnificence imparted by the Miltonic flavor was not merely literary. For Shaftesbury had great abilities as a judge and diplomat; Monmouth had noble looks and manners, and Dryden himself confessed a "respect" for "his heroic virtues." By granting their loftiness some degree of pride the satirist, too, attained a largeness of temper: "Preposterous plottings, but rather splendid persons!" Nevertheless, as Dr. Johnson observed, there are limits in heroic allegory: "Charlès could not run continually parallel with David." But though the David-Aeneas incarnation cannot be taken seriously, the tone adopted in addressing Charles and attributed to him and his courtiers, did have a certain validity. The parallel between state manners and Roman aristocratic manners was justified, even in Restoration England. In public discourse, the English aristocracy, like the Roman, had a hereditary right to high oratory. And heroic poetry had been by a long tradition an aristocratic possession.

The grand yet lively eloquence that characterizes and satirizes Shaftesbury and Buckingham is thus quite different from the inflated and dully insistent rant of the heroic plays, for Dryden had found the one kind of situation in which a Restoration poet might adopt the heroic style. As spokesman for aristocracy, Established Church, and monarchy, he could rightly assume the Roman dignity of Renaissance epic. As the critic of the King's enemies, he could parody his own heroic style and so express still another true relationship between contemporary events and the heroic ideal. The discovery of relationships which were true for Dryden both as poet and citizen made it possible for him to use his accumulated literary skills with a new freedom. His satirical poetry exhibits a fluidity and force and a concentrated range of reference which his earlier verse had rarely shown.

Why may we reasonably describe this success as "European"? Not simply because Dryden's satiric mode was widely and often precisely allusive to European writers and styles and to English writers who were most consciously European in their styles and critical standards. Nor simply because he satisfied a continental standard of literary craft, although this is significant. But rather because he brought the larger light of European literature and a European past into verse of local public debate. He invited his readers, including Nonconformists, to take a less parochial attitude toward the persons and events of contemporary history. We have only to compare *Absalom and Achitophel* or *The Medal* with Marvell's satires to appreciate the imaginative value of linking these smaller and greater worlds. The Marvell of the *Ode* on Cromwell had brought to political history a similar largeness of scene and a poise of values much finer than Dryden's. But breadth of vision and sureness of rhythm are missing in *Last Instructions to a Painter*, although the poem has some of the obvious earmarks of epic satire. The spectacle is rather painful: the earlier Marvell could not address this world without sacrificing many of his virtues as a poet. Dryden could; with losses, too, if his poetry is measured by the standard of the Cromwellian *Ode;* but he managed to translate to his audience something of the larger historic vision, the noble manner, and the justness of style of the Renaissance tradition in which the younger Marvell wrote. He was a vigorous civilizer among the sons of Belial.

Dryden did something else for his generation that Marvell and Milton, much less Cowley, could not do: he reaffirmed the public role of the poet, the Graeco-Roman conception of the poet as the voice of a society. It is true that Dryden succeeded only too well in fixing the public tone as the Augustan norm; but the voice we hear is not solely that of the party or class or church. Thanks to Dryden the tone of Augustan poetry is less parochial than it might have been: it is resonant with echoes of other literary worlds, of larger manners and events. Minor Augustan poetry is dead for modern readers not because it was too "general," but because it was too local.

In praising Dryden for reaffirming the European tradition in his satirical mode, it is well to recall the conditions of our praise. The eighteenth century is littered with epics, odes, and philosophical poems that are traditional in the academic sense; the "forms" and the "diction" are too often reminiscent of the best writers of Greece and Rome. Dr. Johnson's remark on Gray's *Odes* is the appropriate comment on such products: "They are forced plants raised in a hot-bed; and they are poor plants; they are but cucumbers after all." Dryden's achievement matters because the verse through which he draws on the European tradition satisfies us as other poetry does by offering concentrated and surprising richness of relationship: we feel that language is being "worked" for all it is worth. (The allusive mode is for Dryden what the symbolic metaphor was for the Metaphysicals.) But Dryden's use of tradition satisfies also a condition of another sort. In the act of writing poetry that was far from provincial in implication, Dryden engaged the most active political and intellectual interests of his immediate audience. The particular issues are of little concern for us at present; but we can recognize their importance in the late seventeenth century, and see that the general issues involved are of a sort that is central in any conceivable society. There are local successes in literature that are instructive to later generations: Dryden's is one of them.

NOTE

[1] This paper was one of a series on English writers and tradition that was read at the 1950 meeting of the Modern Language Association in New York. The analysis of *Absalom and Achitophel*, lines 632–659, is taken with some changes from the author's book, *The Fields of Light*, copyright by the Oxford University Press, Inc., 1951, and is reprinted here with the publisher's permission.

↙

John Dryden: The Lyric Poet

Dryden owes his excellence as a lyric poet to his abounding metrical energy. The impetuous mind and the scrupulous ear which Wordsworth admired nourished a singing voice that always was powerful and sometimes was mellow or sweet. The songs, the operas, and the odes of Dryden are remarkable first of all for their musical excitement.

The seventeenth century was an age of song. Composers like John Dowland, Thomas Campion, William and Henry Lawes, Nicholas Laniere, John Wilson, Charles Coleman, William Webb, John Gamble, and the Purcells, together with publishers like John and Henry Playford, to mingle great with small, maintained a long and beautiful tradition of "ayres"; miscellanies and "drolleries," with their fondness for tavern tunes, urged on a swelling stream of popular melody; while poets, from Ben Jonson to Tom D'Urfey, never left off trifling with measured catches high or low. But there were changes from generation to generation. The poets of the Restoration sang in a different key from that of the Jacobeans; and it was generally believed that there had been a falling off.

"Soft words, with nothing in them, make a song,"

wrote Waller to Creech. It was charged that France had corrupted English song with her Damons and Strephons, her "Chlorisses and

From *John Dryden: A Study of His Poetry* (New York: Holt, 1946; reissued by The University of Indiana Press, 1960), pp. 174–206. Copyright 1946 by Mark Van Doren and reprinted by permission of Nannine Joseph, agent for Mark Van Doren.

Phyllisses," and that the dances with which she was supposed to have vulgarized the drama and the opera had introduced notes of triviality and irresponsibility into all lyric poetry. Dryden for one was fond of dances, and ran them into his plays whenever there was an excuse. In *Marriage à la Mode* Melantha and Palamede quote two pieces from Molière's ballet in *Le Bourgeois Gentilhomme*. Voiture's airy nothings also had their day in England. The second song in Dryden's *Sir Martin Mar-All*, beginning,

> Blind love, to this hour,
> Had never, like me, a slave under his power.
> Then blest be the dart
> That he threw at my heart,
> For nothing can prove
> A joy so great as to be wounded with love,

was adapted from Voiture:

> L'Amour sous sa loy
> N'a jamais eu d'amant plus heureux que moy;
> Benit soit son flambeau,
> Son carquois, son bandeau,
> Je suis amoreux,
> Et le ciel ne voit point d'amant plus heureux.

But the most serious charge against France was brought against her music.

Music had an important place in the education of gentlemen and poets throughout the Europe of the sixteenth and seventeenth centuries. A larger proportion of trained minds than before or since claimed intimate acquaintance with musical technique. The studies of philosophers as well as poets included ecclesiastical and secular song, the uses made of it being various, of course. Hobbes, says Aubrey, "had alwayes bookes of prick-song lyeing on his Table:—e.g. of H. Lawes &c. *Songs*—which at night, when he was abed, and the dores made fast, & was sure nobody heard him, he sang aloud, (not that he had a very good voice) but to cleare his pipes: he did beleeve it did his Lunges good, and conduced much to prolong his life." Poets drew much of their best knowledge and inspiration from musicians, so that any alteration in musical modes was certain to affect the styles of verse.

The seventeenth century in England was a century of secularization, first under Italian and then under French influences. In former times, when music had been bound to the service of the church, clear-cut rhythms had been avoided as recalling too much the motions of the body in the dance, and composers of madrigals had been confined to the learned contrivances of counterpoint. John Dowland, the Oxford and Cambridge lutanist, Thomas Campion, magical both as poet and as composer, and Henry Lawes, the friend of all good versifiers, three seventeenth-century native geniuses who were also disciples of Italy, introduced in succession new and individual song rhythms which were so compelling that by the time of the Restoration there had come into being an excellent body of sweet and simple secular airs with just enough strains of the older, more intricate harmonies lingering in them to remind of the golden age. Even in church and chamber music there had been a tendency to substitute songs for madrigals and dance-tunes for choral measures.

The Restoration saw complete and rapid changes. Charles II, who insisted on easy rhythms at his devotions to which he could beat time with his hand, sent his choir-boys to France to school, and encouraged his musicians to replace the lute and the viol with the guitar and the violin. The violin or fiddle, which John Playford called "a cheerful and sprightly instrument," was as old as the Anglo-Saxons, but it had been used before only for dancing, not in the church or the chamber. It was the rhythm of the dance that now pervaded theater and chapel and all the world of lyric poetry. There was hearty objection to the new mode. Playford began the preface to his *Musick's Delight on the Cithera* (1666) with the remark: "It is observed that of late years all solemn and grave musick is much laid aside, being esteemed too heavy and dull for the light heels and brains of this nimble and wanton age." The preface to the sixth edition of the same author's *Skill of Musick* in 1672 continued the complaint: "Musick in this age . . . is in low esteem with the generality of people. Our late and solemn Musick, both Vocal and Instrumental, is now justled out of Esteem by the new Corants and Jigs of Foreigners, to the Grief of all sober and judicious understanders of that formerly solid and good Musick." John Norris of Bemerton, in the preface to his *Poems* (1678), declared that music like poetry had degenerated "from grave, majestic, solemn strains . . . where beauty and strength go hand in hand. 'Tis now for the most part dwindled down to light, frothy stuff." Henry Purcell objected on the whole with greater effect than the others against what he called "the levity and balladry of our neighbours"; for his attack upon French opera in favor of Italian opera was in the end entirely successful. Yet even Purcell was well aware that French music had "somewhat more of gayety and Fashion" than any other, and he was not so insensible to current demands as to compose songs for the stage that were lacking in vivacity.

Dryden, who had secured the services of a French musician, Grabut, for his opera *Albion and Albanius* in 1685, was considered in 1690 a convert to "the English school" when in the dedication of *Amphitryon* he wrote of "Mr. Purcell, in whose person we have at length found an Englishman, equal with the best abroad. At least my opinion of him has been such, since his happy and judicious performances in the late opera (*The Prophetess*), and the experience I have had of him in the setting my three songs for this 'Amphitryon.'" Before Purcell died in 1695 he had not only written the accompaniment for an opera of Dryden's, *King Arthur*, but set to music the songs from *Cleomenes*, *The Indian Emperor*, an adaptation of *The Indian Queen*, *Aureng-Zebe*, *Oedipus*, *The Spanish Friar*, *Tyrannic Love*, and *The Tempest*; so that Dryden had the full advantage of an association with this powerful composer who, as Motteux put it in the first number of his *Gentleman's Journal* in 1692, joined "to the delicacy and beauty of the Italian way, the graces and gayety of the French."

It is debatable whether the musical personalities of Purcell and other contemporary composers were in general a good or a bad influence on Restoration lyric style. It is at least thinkable that as the new rhythms asserted themselves more powerfully the writers who supplied words for songs were somehow the losers in independence and originality. There was complaint at the end of the century that jingling music from France had won the field and was domineering over poetry. Charles Gildon in his *Laws of Poetry* (1721) pointed to a degeneration in song, attributing it to "the slavish care or complaisance of the writers, to make their words to the goust of the composer, or musician: being obliged often to sacrifice their sense to certain sounding words, and feminine rhymes, and the like; because they seem most adapted to furnish the composer with such cadences which most easily slide into their modern way of composition." Others besides Gildon felt with justice that genius was being ironed out of lyric verse; song was becoming sing-song. Relations between poets and composers were now the reverse of what they had been in the time of Henry Lawes. Lawes had been content to subordinate his music to the words; for him the poetry was the thing. If it seemed difficult at first glance to adapt a given passage to music, the difficulty was after all the composer's, and the blame for infelicities must accrue to him. "Our English seems a little clogged with consonants," he wrote in the preface to the first book of *Ayres and Dialogues* (1653), "but that's much the composer's fault, who, by judicious setting, and right tuning the words, may make it smooth enough." Milton was acknowledging the generous, pliant technique of his friend in the sonnet of 1646:

> Harry, whose tuneful and well-measured song
> First taught our English music how to span
> Words with just note and accent, not to scan
> With Midas' ears, committing short and long;
> Thy worth and skill exempts thee from the throng,
> With praise enough for Envy to look wan;
> To after age thou shalt be writ the man
> That with smooth air could humour best our tongue.

It was the delicacy and justness of Lawes that won him the affection of the most gifted lyrists of the mid-century; it will always be remembered of him that he loved poetry too well to profane the intricate tendernesses of songs like Herrick's to the daffodils.

Whatever conditions imposed themselves upon English song in the Restoration, Dryden for his own part was inclined to welcome swift, simple, straight-on rhythms, and he was destined to become master of the lyric field solely by virtue of his speed. His range of vowels was narrow; his voice was seldom round or deep, limiting itself rather monotonously to soprano sounds. Nor was the scope of his sympathies wide; a number of contemporaries sang more human songs. Rochester's drinking-pieces, like that which begins,

> Vulcan, contrive me such a cup
> As Nestor used of old,

Sedley's love-lines,

> Not, Celia, that I juster am,
> Or better than the rest,

And Dorset's playful flatteries,

> To all you ladies now at land,
> We men at sea indite,

are likely to touch nerves which Dryden leaves quiet. Congreve's
diamond-bright cynicism and Prior's ultimate social grace exist in
worlds far removed from his own. It was sheer lyrical gusto and
momentum that carried Dryden forward, that drew to him the attention of the Playfords as they published their new collections, that
made the editor of the *Westminster Drolleries* of 1671 and 1672
hasten to include his six best songs to date in those "choice" volumes.

Dryden's first song had something of the older Caroline manner
in that its stanzas were tangled and reflective. It was sung in *The
Indian Emperor,* and began:

> Ah fading joy, how quickly art thou past!
>   Yet we thy ruin haste.
> As if the cares of human life were few,
>   We seek out new:
> And follow fate that does too fast pursue.

Dryden passed swiftly from this to a more modern, more breathless
world of song, a world where he fell at once, in *An Evening's Love,*
into the dactylic swing that was to win him his way into the irrepress-
ible *Drolleries:*

> After the pangs of a desperate lover,
>   When day and night I have sighed all in vain,
> Ah what pleasure it is to discover,
>   In her eyes pity, who causes my pain.

Another song in *An Evening's Love* ran more lightly yet; it was marked
by the anapestic lilt which on the whole is Dryden's happiest discovery:

> Calm was the even, and clear was the sky,
>   And the new-budding flowers did spring,
> When all alone went Amyntas and I
>   To hear the sweet nightingale sing.
> I sate, and he laid him down by me,
>   But scarcely his breath he could draw;
> For when with a fear, he began to draw near,
>   He was dashed with "A ha ha ha ha!"

This lilt is heard in Dryden as many as fifteen times, being at its best in *Marriage à la Mode:*

> Why should a foolish marriage vow,
>   Which long ago was made,
> Oblige us to each other now,
>   When passion is decayed?
> We loved, and we loved, as long as we could,
>   Till our love was loved out in us both;
> But our marriage is dead, when the pleasure is fled;
>   'Twas pleasure first made it an oath.
>
> If I have pleasures for a friend,
>   And farther love in store,
> What wrong has he whose joys did end,
>   And who could give no more?
> 'Tis a madness that he should be jealous of me,
>   Or that I should bar him of another;
> For all we can gain is to give ourselves pain,
>   When neither can hinder the other;

in *Amphitryon,* where Dryden for once is very much like Prior:

> Fair Iris I love, and hourly I die,
> But not for a lip nor a languishing eye:
> She's fickle and false, and there we agree,
> For I am as false and as fickle as she.
> We neither believe what either can say;
> And, neither believing, we neither betray.
>
> 'Tis civil to swear, and say things of course;
> We mean not the taking for better or worse.
> When present, we love; when absent, agree;
> I think not of Iris, nor Iris of me.
> The legend of love no couple can find,
> So easy to part, or so equally joined;

and in *The Lady's Song,* a piece of Jacobite propaganda which represents Dryden's long, loping jingle in its most gracious and mellow aspects:

A choir of bright beauties in spring did appear,
To choose a May-lady to govern the year;
All nymphs were in white, and the shepherds in green;
The garland was given, and Phyllis was queen;
But Phyllis refused it, and sighing did say:
"I'll not wear a garland while Pan is away."

While Pan and fair Syrinx are fled from our shore,
The Graces are banished, and Love is no more;
The soft god of pleasure, that warmed our desires,
Has broken his bow, and extinguished his fires;
And vows that himself and his mother will mourn,
Till Pan and fair Syrinx in triumph return.

Forbear your addresses, and court us no more,
For we will perform what the deity swore;
But if you dare think of deserving our charms,
Away with your sheephooks, and take to your arms:
Then laurels and myrtles your brows shall adorn,
When Pan, and his son, and fair Syrinx return.

The Lady's Song calls to mind two iambic pieces of a graver sort. The song from *The Maiden Queen* is subdued to a plane of elegy which Dryden seldom visited:

I feed a flame within, which so torments me,
That it both pains my heart, and yet contents me;
'Tis such a pleasing smart, and I so love it,
That I had rather die than once remove it.

Yet he for whom I grieve shall never know it;
My tongue does not betray, nor my eyes show it:
Not a sigh, nor a tear, my pain discloses,
But they fall silently, like dew on roses.

This to prevent my love from being cruel,
My heart's the sacrifice, as 'tis the fuel;
And while I suffer this, to give him quiet,
My faith rewards my love, tho' he deny it.

On his eyes will I gaze, and there delight me;
Where I conceal my love, no frown can fright me;

To be more happy, I dare not aspire;
Nor can I fall more low, mounting no higher.

The "Zambra Dance" from the first part of *The Conquest of Granada*
begins with two stately stanzas that shed a soft Pindaric splendor:

Beneath a myrtle shade,
Which love for none but happy lovers made,
I slept; and straight my love before me brought
Phyllis, the object of my waking thought.
Undressed she came my flames to meet,
While love strewed flowers beneath her feet;
Flowers which, so pressed by her, became more sweet.

From the bright vision's head
A careless veil of lawn was loosely spread:
From her white temples fell her shaded hair,
Like cloudy sunshine, not too brown nor fair;
Her hands, her lips, did love inspire;
Her every grace my heart did fire;
But most her eyes, which languished with desire.

Dryden has used the iambic measure only slightly more often than the
anapestic, but he has used it more variously. The two poems just
quoted are far removed from the Cavalier conciseness of these lines
in *An Evening's Love:*

You charmed me not with that fair face,
    Tho' it was all divine:
To be another's is the grace
    That makes me wish you mine;

or from the lively languor of these in *The Spanish Friar:*

Farewell, ungrateful traitor!
    Farewell, my perjured swain!
Let never injured creature
    Believe a man again.

The pleasure of possessing
Surpasses all expressing,

But 'tis too short a blessing,
    And love too long a pain;

or from a pretty, rocking conceit like this in the *Song to a Fair Young
Lady Going Out of Town in the Spring:*

Ask not the cause, why sullen Spring
    So long delays her flowers to bear;
Why warbling birds forget to sing,
    And winter storms invert the year.
Chloris is gone, and fate provides
To make it Spring where she resides.

The trochaic pieces, such as that in *Tyrannic Love,*

Ah how sweet it is to love!
Ah how gay is young desire!

and that in *King Arthur,* sung in honor of Britannia,

Fairest isle, all isles excelling,
    Seat of pleasures and of loves;
Venus here will choose her dwelling,
    And forsake her Cyprian groves,

attack the ear with characteristic spirit.

The songs of Dryden never go deeper than the painted fires of
conventional Petrarchan love, but in a few cases they go wider. The
"Sea-Fight" from *Amboyna,* the incantation of Tiresias in the third act
of *Oedipus,* the Song of Triumph of the Britons and the Harvest Song
from *King Arthur* are robust departures in theme from the pains and
desires of Alexis and Damon. The incantation from *Oedipus* brings
substantial relief, promising cool retreats:

Choose the darkest part o' the grove,
Such as ghosts at noon-day love.
Dig a trench, and dig it nigh
Where the bones of Laius lie.

The one hymn known to be Dryden's, the translation of *Veni,
Creator Spiritus* which appeared under his name in the third *Miscel-*

lany of 1693, is in a certain sense a rounder and deeper utterance than any of the songs. The vowels are more varied and the melody has a more solid core to it; the bass of a cathedral organ rumbles under the rhythms. Scott on poor authority printed two other hymns as Dryden's, the *Te Deum* and what he called the *Hymn for St. John's Eve;* but it has been convincingly denied that, with the exception of *Veni, Creator Spiritus,* any of the hundred and twelve hymns which made up the Catholic *Primer* of 1706 had been translated from the Latin by the great convert between 1685 and 1700.[1] Dryden was a born writer of hymns, though the hymns he wrote were never, save in this one case, labeled as such. Praise with him was as instinctive as satire; he delighted as much in glorious openings and upgathered invocations as in contemptuous "characters." The King's prayer in *Annus Mirabilis,* Achitophel's first words to Absalom, the beginning of the *Lucretius,* the beginning of the *Georgics,* and the prayers in *Palamon and Arcite* are his most godlike pleas. "Landor once said to me," wrote Henry Crabb Robinson in his *Diary* for January 6, 1842, "Nothing was ever written in hymn equal to the beginning of Dryden's *Religio Laici,*—the first eleven lines."

> Dim as the borrowed beams of moon and stars
> To lonely, weary, wandering travellers,
> Is Reason to the soul; and, as on high
> Those rolling fires discover but the sky,
> Not light us here, so Reason's glimmering ray
> Was lent, not to assure our doubtful way,
> But guide us upward to a better day.
> And as those nightly tapers disappear
> When day's bright lord ascends our hemisphere;
> So pale grows Reason at Religion's sight;
> So dies, and so dissolves in supernatural light.

Dryden's operas, as poetry, are unfortunate. Here for once, partly from apathy towards a form of writing which the prologues and epilogues show did not command his respect, partly from a sense of obligation or dependence, he capitulated to the composer; thinking to produce new musical effects with his pen, he succeeded in bringing forth what was neither poetry nor music. The result in each of two cases, at least, was what St. Evremond defined any opera to be, "an odd medley of poetry and music wherein the poet and the musician, equally confined one by the other, take a world of pain to compose a wretched performance." *The State of Innocence,* which was never performed but which was first published as "an opera" probably in 1677, is not one of the two cases. It is an independent poem of some originality and splendor. *Albion and Albanius* (1685), however, and its sequel *King Arthur* (1691) deserve a fair share of St. Evremond's disdain. Dryden has taken the trouble in connection with them to describe his labors as a poet-musician. In the preface to *Albion and Albanius* he says he has been at pains to "make words so smooth, and numbers so harmonious, that they shall almost set themselves." In writing an opera a poet must have so sensitive an ear "that the discord of sounds in words shall as much offend him as a seventh in music would a good composer." "The chief secret is the choice of words"; the words are "to be varied according to the nature of the subject." The "songish part" and the chorus call for "harmonious sweetness," with "softness and variety of numbers," but the recitative demands "a more masculine beauty." The superiority of Italian over French or English as a musical language is heavily stressed; and it is plain that throughout the opera Dryden has aimed at an Italian "softness" through the use of feminine rhymes and dissyllabic coinages similar to those which were to mark the *Virgil.* The work as a whole is inane, and often it is doggerel; it is at best a welter of jingling trimeters and tetrameters, tail-rhyme stanzas, heroic couplets, and tawdry Pindaric passages. One song by the Nereids in Act III begins better than it ends:

> From the low palace of old father Ocean,
> Come we in pity your cares to deplore;
> Sea-racing dolphins are trained for our motion,
> Moony tides swelling to roll us ashore.
>
> Every nymph of the flood, her tresses rending,
> Throws off her armlet of pearl in the main;
> Neptune in anguish his charge unattending,
> Vessels are foundering, and vows are in vain.

King Arthur is in blank verse, with many departures into song and dance. The dedication praises Purcell and admits that the verse has in certain cases been allowed to suffer for the composer's sake. "My art on this occasion," says Dryden, "ought to be subservient to his." "A judicious audience will easily distinguish betwixt the songs wherein I have complied with him, and those in which I have followed the rules of poetry, in the sound and cadence of the words." The "freezing scene" in the third act does neither the poet nor the composer any credit; the effect of shivering, even if legitimate, is not exactly happy. The best songs are those in which, as Dryden says, he has "followed the rules of poetry": those like "Fairest isle, all isles excelling," the "Harvest Home," and the song of the nymphs before Arthur:

> In vain are our graces,
>   In vain are our eyes,
>   If love you despise;
> When age furrows faces,
>   'Tis time to be wise.
> Then use the short blessing,
> That flies in possessing:
>   No joys are above
>   The pleasures of love.

The short *Secular Masque* which Dryden wrote for a revival of Fletcher's *Pilgrim* in 1700 is the least objectionable of the pieces which he designed to accompany stage music. The masque celebrates the opening of the new century. Janus, Chronos, and Momus hold a sprightly review of the century just past and come to the conclusion that the times have been bad. Diana, representing the court of James I, is the first to pass in review, singing as she goes a hunting song which long remained popular:

> With horns and with hounds I waken the day,
> And hie to my woodland walks away;
> I tuck up my robe, and am buskined soon,
> And tie to my forehead a wexing moon.
> I course the fleet stag, unkennel the fox,
> And chase the wild goats o'er summits of rocks;
> With shouting and hooting we pierce thro' the sky,
> And Echo turns hunter, and doubles the cry.

The three gods agree with her of the silver bow that

> Then our age was in its prime,
> Free from rage, and free from crime;
> A very merry, dancing, drinking,
> Laughing, quaffing, and unthinking time.

Mars next thunders in and recalls the wars of Charles I. But Momus
is a pacifist:

> Thy sword within the scabbard keep,
>   And let mankind agree;
> Better the world were fast asleep,
>   Than kept awake by thee.
> The fools are only thinner,
>   With all our cost and care;
> But neither side a winner,
>   For things are as they were.

Venus now appears to celebrate the softer conquests of Charles II and
James II. But she also is found wanting, and so Dryden's poem ends
with a sweeping dismissal of three Stuart generations:

> All, all of a piece throughout;
> Thy chase had a beast in view;
> Thy wars brought nothing about;
> Thy lovers were all untrue.
> 'Tis well an old age is out,
> And time to begin a new.

The force which drove Dryden forward through the somewhat
foreign waters of song plunged him into a native ocean in the ode.
His greatest lyrics are odes. He was constitutionally adapted to a form
of exalted utterance which progressed by the alternate accumulation
and discharge of metrical energy. The study of his utterances in this
kind begins not with his first formal ode, but with the first appearance
of swells in the stream of his heroic verse. That first appearance, as has
been suggested before, is in the heroic plays, where the thump and
rattle of the couplets is relieved from time to time by towering
speeches like that of Almanzor to Lyndaraxa. *The State of Innocence*
is virtually one protracted ode. Partly in consequence of a new and
close acquaintance with Milton's blank verse, partly as the fruit of his
experience among rhythms, Dryden here has swollen his stream and
learned to compose with a powerful, steady pulse. Milton's paragraph-
ing, whether or not it has been an important inspiration, is after all
Dryden's greatest example in this instance, though Milton's metrical
progression is little like that of his junior. Milton relies chiefly upon
enjambement to give roll to his verse; as can best be seen for the
present purpose in the *Vacation Exercise* of 1628, which is in heroic

couplets. The bond of the couplets is broken only once, and then by drawing the sense variously from one line into another. The poet is addressing his native language:

> Yet I had rather, if I were to choose,
> Thy service in some graver subject use,
> Such as may make thee search thy coffers round,
> Before thou clothe my fancy in fit sound.
> Such where the deep transported mind may soar
> Above the wheeling poles, and at Heaven's door
> Look in, and see each blissful Deity
> How he before the thunderous throne doth lie,
> Listening to what unshorn Apollo sings
> To the touch of golden wires, while Hebe brings
> Immortal nectar to her kingly sire;
> Then, passing through the spheres of watchful fire,
> And misty regions of wide air next under,
> And hills of snow and lofts of piléd thunder,
> May tell at length how green-eyed Neptune raves,
> In heaven's defiance mustering all his waves;
> Then sing of secret things that came to pass
> When beldam Nature in her cradle was;
> And last of Kings and Queens and Heroes old,
> Such as the wise Demodocus once told
> In solemn songs at King Alcinous' feast,
> While sad Ulysses' soul and all the rest
> Are held, with his melodious harmony
> In willing chains and sweet captivity.

Dryden relies less on *enjambement,* though occasionally he relies on that too, than on sheer rhythmical enthusiasm, an enthusiasm that expresses itself first through a series of rapidly advancing couplets and last in a flourish of triplets or Alexandrines. One example has been given from *The State of Innocence.* Another is the speech of Lucifer at the end of the first scene:

> On this foundation I erect my throne;
> Through brazen gates, vast chaos, and old night,
> I'll force my way, and upwards steer my flight;
> Discover this new world, and newer Man;
> Make him my footstep to mount heaven again:
> Then in the clemency of upward air,

> We'll scour our spots, and the dire thunder scar,
> With all the remnants of the unlucky war,
> And once again grow bright, and once again grow fair.

Eve's account of Paradise in the third act is more elaborately heaped:

>   Above our shady bowers
> The creeping jessamin thrusts her fragrant flowers;
> The myrtle, orange, and the blushing rose,
> With bending heaps so nigh their blooms disclose,
> Each seems to swell the flavor which the other blows;
> By these the peach, the guava and the pine,
> And, creeping 'twixt them all, the mantling vine
> Does round their trunks her purple clusters twine.

The State of Innocence was only a beginning. Dryden's proclivity towards the ode grew stronger each year. His addresses, his invocations, his hymns were only odes imbedded in heroic verse. Even a prologue might end with a lyrical rush, as for instance that "To the Duchess on Her Return from Scotland" (1682):

> Distempered Zeal, Sedition, cankered Hate,
> No more shall vex the Church, and tear the State:
> No more shall Faction civil discords move,
> Or only discords of too tender love;
> Discord like that of Music's various parts;
> Discord that makes the harmony of hearts;
> Discord that only this dispute shall bring,
> Who best shall love the Duke and serve the King.

It is perhaps a question whether the poem on Oldham is an elegy or an ode. The "epiphonema" of the *Eleonora* is surely an ode of a kind; and the *Virgil* is one long Pindaric narrative.

Dryden's habit of dilating his heroic verse with Alexandrines not only grew upon him so that he indulged in flourishes when flourishes were not required, but it became contagious. Poetasters like John Hughes who lacked the impetus of Dryden learned his tricks and abused his liberties. There was something tawdry, in fact, about all but the very best of even Dryden's enthusiastic rhythms. It seemed necessary at least to Edward Bysshe in 1702, when he was compiling some "Rules for making English Verse" for his *Art of English Poetry,* to warn against license and to place restrictions on the use of long lines, allowing them only in the following cases:

1. "When they conclude an episode in an Heroic poem."
2. "When they conclude a triplet and full sense together."
3. "When they conclude the stanzas of Lyrick or Pindaric odes; Examples of which are frequently seen in Dryden and others."

Regardless of form, there always have been two distinct modes of utterance in the ode, two prevailing tempers. The Horatian temper is Attic, choice, perhaps didactic, and is stimulated by observation of human nature. The Pindaric temper is impassioned and superlative, and is inspired by the spectacle of human glory. In English poetry the Horatians have been Ben Jonson, Thomas Randolph, Marvell, Collins, Akenside, Cowper, Landor, and Wordsworth in the *Ode to Duty;* the Pindars have been Spenser, Milton, Cowley, Dryden, Gray, Wordsworth in the *Intimations,* Coleridge, Byron, Shelley, Keats, Tennyson, and Swinburne. Cowley is included among Pindaric writers of odes more by courtesy than from desert, for he was mortally deficient in afflatus; his importance is that of a preceptor and experimentalist, not that of a creator. His *Pindaric Odes* of 1656, with the preface and the explanatory notes that accompanied them, constituted a kind of charter for a whole century of English *vers librists* who sought in the name of Pindar to become grand and free. A parallel movement in France involved a gradual departure from the rigors of Malherbe and enlisted such men as Corneille, La Fontaine, Molière, and Racine; Boileau making himself the spokesman in 1693 when in his *Discours sur l'Ode* he defended Pindar against the current charges of extravagance and declared for the principle of enthusiasm in lyric poetry. Cowley considered that he was restoring one of the "lost inventions of antiquity," restoring, that is, what he believed was Pindar's art of infinitely varying his meter to correspond to the involutions of his theme. It was his notion that Pindar had been lawless in his splendor, or at the most only a law to himself; that he had proceeded without a method, now swelling, now subsiding according as his verse was moved to embrace great things or small. Cowley's *Praise of Pindar* began:

> Pindar is imitable by none,
>   The Phoenix Pindar is a vast species alone;
> Whoe'er but Daedalus with waxen wings could fly
>   And neither sink too low, nor soar too high?

> What could he who followed claim,
> But of vain boldness the unhappy fame,
>   And by his fall a sea to name?
> Pindar's unnavigable song
> Like a swoln flood from some steep mountain pours along;
> The ocean meets with such a voice
> From his enlarged mouth, as drowns the ocean's noise.
>
>
>   So Pindar does new words and figures roll
> Down his impetuous dithyrambic tide,
>   Which in no channel deigns to abide,
>   Which neither banks nor dykes control;
>   Whether the immortal gods he sings
>   In a no less immortal strain,
> Or the great acts of God-descended kings,
> Who in his numbers still survive and reign;
>   Each rich embroidered line
>   Which their triumphant brows around
>   By his sacred hand is bound,
>   Does all their starry diadems outshine.

Cowley had an interesting theory that the Hebrew poets were sharers with Pindar of the great secret. In his preface he remarked: "The Psalms of David (which I believe to have been in their original, to the Hebrews of his time . . . the most exalted pieces of poesy) are a great example of what I have said." And one of his *Pindaric Odes* was a version of Isaiah xxxiv. "The manner of the Prophets' writing," he observed in a note, "especially of Isaiah, seems to me very like that of Pindar; they pass from one thing to another with almost Invisible connections, and are full of words and expressions of the highest and boldest flights of Poetry." Gildon followed Cowley in his *Laws of Poetry* (1721) when he cited among the great odes of the world the psalm that begins: "By the waters of Babylon we sat down and wept, when we remembered thee, O Sion."

Congreve wrote a *Discourse on the Pindarique Ode* in 1706 to prove that Cowley had violated the first law of Pindar when he discarded shape; he explained the rigid strophic structure of the Greek ode and deplored the "rumbling and grating" papers of verses with which Cowley's loose example had loaded the England of the past half century. He was not the first to make this point; Edward Phillips in the preface to his *Theatrum Poetarum* (1675) had observed that

English Pindaric writers seemed ignorant of the strophe, antistrophe, and epode, and that their work seemed rather on the order of the choruses of Aeschylus; while Ben Jonson had left in his ode on Cary and Morison a perfect specimen of Pindar's form. But Congreve was the first conspicuous critic of Cowleian *vers libre*, and it was not until after him that Akenside and Gray and Gilbert West demonstrated on an extensive scale what could be done with strophe and antistrophe in a Northern tongue. Yet the difference between Cowley and Gray was far more than the difference between lawless verse and strophic verse. Cowley's crime had been not so much against Pindar as against poetry: he had written and taught others to write what metrically was non-sense. The alternation of long with short lines in itself does not of necessity make for grandeur; often, as Scott suggests, the effect of a Restoration ode was no different rhythmically from that of the inscription on a tombstone. Cowley was out of his depth in the company of Pindar; he was constituted for wit, for "the familiar and the festive," as Dr. Johnson said, but not for magnificence. The passage which has been quoted from the *Praise of Pindar* is not equaled by him elsewhere; most of the time he is writing like this, at the conclusion of *The Muse:*

> And sure we may
> The same too of the present say,
> If past and future times do thee obey.
> Thou stop'st this current, and does make
> This running river settle like a lake;
> Thy certain hand holds fast this slippery snake;
> The fruit which does so quickly waste,
> Man scarce can see it, much less taste,
> Thou comfitest in sweets to make it last.
> This shining piece of ice,
> Which melts so soon away
> With the sun's ray,
> Thy verse does solidate and crystallize,
> Till it a lasting mirror be!
> Nay, thy immortal rhyme
> Makes this one short point of time
> To fill up half the orb of round eternity.

The trouble here is simply that there are no "numbers"; the stanza is not organic; there are no involutions which the ear follows with the

kind of suspense with which it follows, for instance, an intricate passage in good music. Cowley has thought to forestall such an objection
in the general preface to his folio of 1656. "The numbers are various
and irregular," he says, "and sometimes (especially some of the long
ones) seem harsh and uncouth, if the just measures and cadences be
not observed in the pronunciation. So that almost all their sweetness
and numerosity (which is to be found, if I mistake not, in the roughest,
if rightly repeated) lies in a manner wholly at the mercy of the
reader." But the most merciful and best of readers must fail to make
certain of the odes of Cowley sound like poetry. Cowley had not a
dependable ear.

It was Dryden's "excellent ear" which saved the Pindaric ode for
Gray. Dryden diagnosed the ills of contemporary Pindarism with lofty
precision in the preface to *Sylvae* in 1685. "Somewhat of the purity
of English, somewhat of more equal thoughts, somewhat of sweetness
in the numbers, in one word, somewhat of a finer turn and more lyrical
verse is yet wanting. . . . In imitating [Pindar] our numbers should,
for the most part, be lyrical . . . the ear must preside, and direct the
judgement to the choice of numbers: without the nicety of this, the
harmony of Pindaric verse can never be complete; the cadency of one
line must be a rule to that of the next; and the sound of the former
must slide gently into that which follows, without leaping from one
extreme into another. It must be done like the shadowings of a picture,
which fall by degrees into a darker colour." This is by far his most
significant statement on the ode: it is not only an accurate analysis of
the errors of others; it is an intimation of his own ideal, and incidentally it embodied a forecast of his best accomplishment. For his peculiar contribution was none other than the shading and the "finer
turn" of which he speaks here. He let his ear preside; he let his
cadences rule and determine one another in the interests of an integral
harmony. He placed his words where they would neither jar nor
remain inert, but flow. His best Pindaric passages are streams of words
delicately and musically disposed.

The earliest instance of all, the "Zambra Dance" [2] from *The Conquest of Granada,* is fine but slight. The first ambitious effort is the
translation of the twenty-ninth ode of the third book of Horace in
Sylvae. "One ode," explains Dryden in the preface, "which infinitely
pleased me in the reading, I have attempted to translate in Pindaric
verse. . . . I have taken some pains to make it my master-piece in
English: for which reason I took this kind of verse, which allows more
latitude than any other." The combination of Horatian felicity with

Pindaric latitude is the happier for Dryden's excellent understanding
of the bearings of each. Creech's *Horace*, published the previous year
with a dedication to Dryden, had shown, as certain pieces from
Horace in the first *Miscellany* (1684) had shown, what might be done
in the way of running the Stoic odes into elaborate stanzaic molds;
but Creech was most of the time perilously near prose. His version of
the present poem, not particularly spirited but solid and just, may
have suggested further possibilities to Dryden, who indeed did appropriate his predecessor's best phrases. As for the language of Horace,
says Dryden, "there is nothing so delicately turned in all the Roman
language. There appears in every part of his diction . . . a kind of
noble and bold purity. . . . There is a secret happiness which attends
his choice, which in Petronius is called *curiosa felicitas*." As for his
own versification, which of course is anarchy compared with Horace,
he hopes that it will help to convey the Roman's "briskness, his jollity,
and his good humour." The result is as nice as anything in Dryden.
The ear has presided, and the shading is almost without flaw. Only
five lines disappoint; four of these are Alexandrines (lines 33, 38, 59,
64) and one is a fourteener (line 39). Dryden has not learned as yet
in this least rigid of all forms to dispose his long lines so well that
none of them will halt the movement and kill the stanza; in the present
instance it is significant that all of the five dead lines are attempts at
reproducing effects of Nature. The first, second, third, fourth, sixth,
eighth, ninth, and tenth stanzas are unexceptionable. The poem begins
with a passage of remarkable carrying power; something somewhere
seems to be beating excellent time:

> Descended of an ancient line,
>   That long the Tuscan scepter swayed,
> Make haste to meet the generous wine,
>   Whose piercing is for thee delayed:
> The rosy wreath is ready made,
>   And artful hands prepare
> The fragrant Syrian oil, that shall perfume thy hair.

The eighth stanza is in a way the most distinct and final writing that
Dryden did:

> Happy the man, and happy he alone,
>   He, who can call today his own;
>   He who, secure within, can say:

"Tomorrow, do thy worst, for I have lived today.
   Be fair, or foul, or rain, or shine,
The joys I have possessed, in spite of fate, are mine.
   Not Heav'n itself upon the past has power;
But what has been has been, and I have had my hour."

This is brisk yet liquid. The current of the stream widens and accelerates swiftly, but there is no leaping or foaming. The "cadency" of each line noiselessly transmits energy to the next. Alliteration helps to preserve an equable flow, while varied vowels heighten the murmur. And the monosyllables now have their revenge; for fifty-nine words of the sixty-eight are monosyllables.

The next Pindaric ode of Dryden's, the *Threnodia Augustalis*, is rambling and arbitrary in its rhythms; there is little or no momentum. A few passages, however, shine in isolation. At the news that Charles had rallied and might live, says Dryden,

Men met each other with erected look,
The steps were higher that they took,
Friends to congratulate their friends made haste,
And long-inveterate foes saluted as they passed.

There is a pride of pace in these lines that suits the sense. When Charles was restored from France, continues Dryden,

The officious Muses came along,
A gay harmonious choir, like angels ever young;
(The Muse that mourns him now his happy triumph sung.)
Even they could thrive in his auspicious reign;
   And such a plenteous crop they bore
Of purest and well-winnowed grain
   As Britain never knew before.
Though little was their hire, and light their gain,
Yet somewhat to their share he threw;
Fed from his hand, they sung and flew,
Like birds of Paradise, that lived on morning dew.

The ode *To the Pious Memory of the Accomplished Young Lady, Mrs. Anne Killigrew*, written in the same year with the *Horace* and the *Threnodia*, while it is sadly uneven is yet the most triumphant of the three. For although its second, third, fifth, sixth, seventh, eighth, and

ninth stanzas are equal at the most only to Cowley and are indeed a
good deal like him, the first, fourth, and tenth are emancipated and
impetuous. The first stanza, which Dr. Johnson considered the highest
point in English lyric poetry, rolls its majestic length without discord
or hitch; its music is the profoundest and longest-sustained in Dryden,
and its grammar is regal. The fourth stanza hurls itself with violent
alliteration down the steep channel which it describes:

> O gracious God! how far have we
> Profaned thy heavenly gift of poesy!
> Made prostitute and profligate the Muse,
> Debased to each obscene and impious use,
> Whose harmony was first ordained above
> For tongues of angels and for hymns of love!
> O wretched we! why were we hurried down
> This lubric and adulterate age,
> (Nay, added fat pollutions of our own,)
> To increase the steaming ordures of the stage?
> What can we say to excuse our second fall?
> Let this thy vestal, Heaven, atone for all.
> Her Arethusian stream remains unsoiled,
> Unmixed with foreign filth, and undefiled;
> Her wit was more than man, her innocence a child!

The last stanza is a musical and grammatical triumph like the first,
but one of a lesser magnitude. The triplet in the middle of it is something of an obstruction, and three near-conceits give the effect of a
melody scraped thin. The *Ode on the Death of Mr. Henry Purcell*
(1696) also suffers from conceits, being nowhere remarkable save
perhaps in the first stanza, which aims at prettiness:

> Mark how the lark and linnet sing;
> With rival notes
> They strain their warbling throats
> To welcome in the spring.
> But in the close of night,
> When Philomel begins her heavenly lay,
> They cease their mutual spite,
> Drink in her music with delight,
> And listening and silent, and silent and listening,
> and listening and silent obey.

It seems now to have been almost inevitable that there should grow up at the end of the seventeenth century a custom of celebrating St. Cecilia's Day with poems set to music; so close were poets and musicians together, and so worshipful of music in that age were men as different from one another as Milton, Cowley, Waller, Marvell, and Dryden. During half a century before 1683, when the first Feast was celebrated, Orpheus and Amphion had been among the mythological personages most affectionately cultivated in English verse; and a whole splendid language had been constructed for the praise of the powers of harmony. Dryden's *Song for St. Cecilia's Day* in 1687 and his *Alexander's Feast* in 1697 were the most distinguished performances of the century, each making fashionable a new and sensational method. There was something sensational and monstrous, it must be admitted, about the whole series of music odes from Fishburn, Tate, Fletcher, and Oldham before Dryden to Bonnell Thornton in the eighteenth century, whose burlesque ode called into service of sound and fury such implements as salt-boxes, marrow-bones, and hurdy-gurdies. There was very little excellent poetry on the whole laid at the feet of St. Cecilia, and there was a deal of cheap program-music offered to her ears, even by Purcell and Handel. But the music had always a saving vigor; sixty voices and twenty-five instruments, including violins, trumpets, drums, hautboys, flutes, and bassoons, could make amends of a kind for the paltriest verse. Dryden's odes, if artificial and sensational, were the last thing from paltry; they are among the most amazing *tours de force* in English poetry.

The *Song* of 1687 established a new kind of imitative harmony in which verse became for practical purposes an orchestra, the poet drawing upon his vowels and his phrases as a conductor draws upon his players. Dryden had toyed with somewhat similar devices before. The song from *The Indian Emperor* had ended with the noise, he thought, of gently falling water:

> Hark, hark, the waters fall, fall, fall
> And with a murmuring sound
> Dash, dash upon the ground,
>   To gentle slumbers call.

Oldham in his Cecilia Ode of 1684 had employed some such scheme as Dryden was soon to make famous. And of course it had been almost a century since Spenser had performed his miracles of sound with verse. But Dryden now was the first to declare a wholly orchestral purpose and to rely upon a purely instrumental technique. The first stanza is a rapid overture which by a deft, tumbling kind of repetition summons and subdues to the poet's hand all the wide powers of harmony. The second stanza slips through liquid cadences and dissolves among the sweet sounds of a harp:

What passion cannot Music raise and quell!
When Jubal struck the corded shell,
His listening brethren stood around,
And, wondering, on their faces fell
To worship that celestial sound.
Less than a god they thought there could not dwell
Within the hollow of that shell
That spoke so sweetly and so well.
What passion cannot Music raise and quell!

A suggestion for this may have come from Marvell's *Music's Empire:*

Jubal first made the wilder notes agree
And Jubal tunèd Music's Jubilee;
He called the echoes from their sullen cell,
And built the organ's city, where they dwell;

although Marvell has only hinted of the possibilities that lie in the figure of Jubal and in the "-ell" rhymes; while Dryden has extracted the utmost, whether of drama or of sound, from both. The third, fourth, and fifth stanzas secure by obvious but admirable means the effects of trumpets, drums, flutes, and violins. From the sixth there ascend the softly rushing notes of the organ. The "Grand Chorus" which closes the poem is cosmically pitched:

As from the power of sacred lays
The spheres began to move
And sung the great Creator's praise
To all the blest above;
So, when the last and dreadful hour
This crumbling pageant shall devour,
The Trumpet shall be heard on high,
The dead shall live, the living die,
And Music shall untune the sky.

Dryden, as has been said, seems always to have been moved by the idea of universal dissolution. The Hebrew notion of the Day of Judgment had reached him through the Bible and Joshua Sylvester. The Lucretian theory of disintegration had fascinated him when he was at the university if not before. He must have long been acquainted with Lucan's rehearsal of the final crumbling in the first book of the *Pharsalia*. His concern was with the physics rather than the metaphysics of a disappearing world. Milton's *Solemn Musick* and *Comus* spoke of a mortal mold which original sin had cursed with discord but which on the last day would melt into the great harmony of the invisible spheres. Dryden is not theological; his finale is the blare of a trumpet, and his last glimpse is of painted scenery crashing down on a darkened stage. His ode on Anne Killegrew and his *Song* of 1687 end hugely and picturesquely, like Cowley's ode on *The Resurrection*, where Dryden had read:

> Till all gentle Notes be drowned
> *In the last Trumpet's dreadful sound*
> That to the spheres themselves shall silence bring,
> *Untune* the universal string. . . .
> Then shall the scattered atoms crowding come
> Back to their ancient Home.

On the third of September, 1697, Dryden informed his sons at Rome: "I am writing a song for St. Cecilia's Feast, who, you know, is the patroness of music. This is troublesome, and no way beneficial; but I could not deny the stewards of the feast, who came in a body to me to desire that kindness." There is a tradition that he became agitated during the composition of this song, which was to be the *Alexander's Feast*, and that Henry St. John, afterwards Lord Bolingbroke, found him one morning in a great tremble over it. It is likely that he worked coolly enough at all times; yet he may well have exulted when the idea for this most famous of his lyrics first took shape in his mind. The idea of casting a music ode into narrative or dramatic form was itself a new and happy one. The materials for the story of Alexander probably came harder and were only gradually pieced together in Dryden's imagination. It had been a commonplace among classical, post-classical, and Renaissance writers that ancient Greek music, especially "the lost symphonies," had strangely affected the spirits of men; Pythagoras had cured distempers and passions by the application of appropriate harmonies. Longinus had written (xxxiv): "Do not we observe that the sound of wind-instruments moves the souls of those that hear them, throws them into an ecstasy, and hurries them sometimes into a kind of fury?" Athenaeus had cited Clitarchus as authority for the statement that Thais was the cause of the burning of the palace in Persepolis. Suidas, quoted by John Playford in his *Skill of Musick,* had related that Timotheus moved Alexander to arms. "But the story of Ericus musician," added Playford, "passes all, who had given forth, that by his musick he could drive men into what affections he listed; being required by Bonus King of Denmark to put his skill in practice, he with his harp or polycord lyra expressed such effectual melody and harmony in the variety of changes in several keyes, and in such excellent Fugg's and sprightly ayres, that his auditors began first to be moved with some strange passions, but ending his excellent voluntary with some choice fancy upon this Phrygian mood, the king's passions were altered, and excited to that height, that he fell upon his most trusty friends which were near him, and slew some of them with his fist for lack of another weapon; which our musician perceiving, ended with the sober Dorick; the King came to himself, and much lamented what he had done." Burton, after Cardan the mathematician, had said in *The Anatomy of Melancholy* that "Timotheus the musician compelled Alexander to skip up and down and leave his dinner." Cowley's thirty-second note to the first book of the *Davideis,* a veritable discourse on the powers of harmony, had contained the remark: "Timotheus by Musick enflamed and appeased Alexander to what degrees he pleased." Tom D'Urfey's ode for St. Cecilia's Day in 1691 had run merrily on through change after change of tempo, somewhat in the manner which Dryden was to employ:

> And first the trumpet's part
> Inflames the hero's heart; . . .
> And now he thinks he's in the field,
> And now he makes the foe to yield, . . .
> The battle done, all loud alarms do cease,
> Hark, how the charming flutes conclude the peace . . .
> Excesses of pleasure now crowd on apace.
> The ravishing trebles delight every ear,
> And mirth in a scene of true joy does appear. . . .
> Now beauty's power inflames my breast again,
> I sigh and languish with a pleasing pain.
> > The notes so soft, so sweet the air,
> > The soul of love must sure be there,
> That mine in rapture charms, and drives away despair.

In Motteux's *Gentleman's Journal* for January, 1691–2, was written: "That admirable musician, who could raise a noble fury in Alexander, and lay it as easily, and make him put on the Hero, or the Lover, when he pleased, is too great an Instance of the power of Music to be forgotten." And only three months before Dryden was writing to his sons at Rome, Jeremy Collier, who is seldom thought to have been a benefactor of Restoration poets, had published in the second part of his *Essays upon Several Moral Subjects* an essay *Of Musick* wherein it was told how "Timotheus, a Grecian, was so great a Master, that he could make a man storm and swagger like a Tempest, and then, by altering the Notes, and the Time, he would take him down again, and sweeten his humour in a trice. One time, when Alexander was at Dinner, this Man played him a Phrygian Air: the Prince immediately rises, snatches up his Lance, and puts himself into a Posture of Fighting. And the Retreat was no sooner sounded by the Change of Harmony, but his Arms were Grounded, and his Fire extinct; and he sate down as orderly as if he had come from one of Aristotle's Lectures." Such were the scraps that lay at Dryden's disposal in September of 1697.

"I am glad to hear from all hands," he wrote to Tonson in December, "that my Ode is esteemed the best of all my poetry, by all the town: I thought so myself when I writ it; but being old I mistrusted my own judgment." It is a question whether *Absalom and Achitophel* and the *Oldham* are not better poetry than *Alexander's Feast*, which perhaps is only immortal ragtime. Some of the cadences are disappointing; lines 128, 139, 140, and 145 puzzle and lower the voice of the reader. Yet few poems of equal length anywhere have been brought to a finish on so consistently proud a level and in such bounding spirits. Here is brilliant panorama; here are responsive, ringing rhythms; here is good-nature on the grand scale.

And thrice he routed all his foes, and thrice he slew the slain.

The enormous vitality of this ode not only has insured its own long life; for a century it inspired ambitious imitators and nameless parodists. John Wilkes in 1774 [3] and the Prince of Wales in 1795 [4] found themselves hoisted in mockery to the highest throne that pamphleteers could conceive, the imperial throne of Philip's warlike son.

NOTES

1. *Hymns Attributed to John Dryden.* Edited with an Introduction and Notes by George Rapall Noyes and George Reuben Potter. (Berkeley, California: University of California Press, 1937.)
2. See page 394.
3. W——s's Feast, or Dryden Travesti: A Mock Pindaric Inscribed to His Most Incorruptible Highness Prince Patriotism. (London, 1774.)
4. Marriage Ode Royal After the Manner of Dryden. (1795.)

RUTH WALLERSTEIN

✒

On the Death of Mrs. Killigrew: The Perfecting of a Genre

It is often said of Dryden, especially if we are speaking of those poems to which we are least sympathetic, that his frigidity is due to the conception of rhetoric which thought of an art of expression essentially divorced from substance. Or more recently, that to Hobbes's divorce of fancy from judgment may be attributed Dryden's false lights. And the use of the word *colors* in the famous and ubiquitous comparison is adduced as evidence of his view. But in Dryden's day the use of such a word is no clue to meaning. For the seventeenth century in its criticism still very largely followed the mediaeval pattern of thought in one important respect. It did not start its definitions afresh but accepted the terms of definition handed on by tradition, and altered them by criticism and redefinition from within. Accordingly, in writers of that age, it is particularly important to understand every individual term in the whole context of its use, rather than the reverse. Only so can we grasp both one basic point of view which determines the primary meaning of each term and at the same time that complex of meanings which in the Renaissance adheres around each term and which allows different contexts to attract meanings to different facets as a result of the endeavor to fuse many systems of analysis. But it is not my purpose here to define what the term *color* or any other term

From *Studies in Philology*, XLIV (1947), pp. 519-28. Reprinted by permission of the publishers.

connoted to Dryden. Rather, I wish to ask what we can learn of his method and aims not from his criticism but by a necessary parallel method, by a close consideration of two related poems, his earliest, the elegy on Hastings, and one from his ripest maturity, his ode "To the Memory of Mrs. Killigrew." Taken together, these poems show us Dryden's evolution out of the dying metaphysical age into full neo-classicism without, however, any dimming of his sense of the English tradition. They also show, I think, throughout his art the continuity of an ideal of a poem which we may surmise to have taken shape in his schooldays under Busby's eye.

The music of his elegy on Hastings is so toneless to our ears, its imagery falls with such dusty dryness upon our imaginations, what is worse, the bones of its theology and of its social sentiment rattle so deadly in our thought, that we have been content to dismiss it with the term "metaphysical," using that term in a more than usually ill-defined sense. Yet it is an astounding achievement in structure for a boy of eighteen, highly revealing of Dryden's training. And if we consider it in its context, it is a valuable harbinger of the ode which succeeded it nearly forty years later. I propose to sketch the character of this elegy very briefly, with due apology for the dogmatism such brevity seems to give my comment, and then against this background to show how the ode on Mrs. Killigrew evolved.[1]

In his "Elegy upon the Death of the Lord Hastings," Dryden sought to integrate three types of elegy, pruning them to the compass of his own feeling, all three being part of the living tradition just before him or contemporary with him. *Lacrymae Musarum,* the volume in which the poem appeared, falls in its pagination into two parts. There were, first, a number of elegies by mature poets and poetasters, among them Sir John Denham, Robert Herrick, Andrew Marvell, the latter just coming into print, but ten years Dryden's senior. Second, several sets of verses by older hands which had presumably come in late to the printer and with them a group of laments by Hastings' schoolfellows. Of these last the others are very brief exercises, of the sort Busby would commonly have exacted from his students; Dryden's is a full scope endeavor in the elegy as then practised by England's leading poets.

Internal evidence makes it probable that the boys had seen the elegies by maturer hands before they composed their own; Dryden touches most of the themes sounded in them and hardly any theme not among them. But besides these immediate models, he had the larger background of elegies which had formed one of the most significant and characteristic types of seventeenth century poetry, such as the numerous poems on the death of Prince Henry in 1612,[2] and those of the *Lycidas* volume. Among these elegies, two forms dominated, pastoral allegory and what we may call the theological or devotional elegy.

Of the latter Donne had created the form and set the themes. But while his own elegy on Prince Henry is in the strictest religious sense a meditation or devotion, cast in the form of a thesis and its resolution, the elegies which followed him were often merely theological reflections, lacking both the metaphysical scope and the prayer form of his "Elegie upon the Death of Prince Henry" and of his "Anniversaries." Yet the form he had created was a powerful and a flexible one. And Denham's elegy on Hastings is the genuine heir of Donne's, though its religious emotion is turned outward upon the state and the martyred king, its verse regularized, and its ordonnance and imagery classicized. Marvell's is classicized in another direction, retaining the contemplative view and the emblem imagery, but arresting itself in a classical appeal to Fate.

Besides the organic forms defined in these two types of poem there still flourished the tradition of poetry-writing which taught the writer how to constitute a poem by aggregation of a selection of motives from a common store of themes suitable to one's subject. This method, which doubtless owed much to the tradition of invention as applied to poetry from the Middle Ages on down, had been clarified or given direction by the study of Quintilian. But it was still inorganic. Scholars have abundantly illustrated the process in relation to the pastoral.[3] Chapman's poem on Prince Henry well illustrates it in the non-pastoral elegy. For the seventeenth century, this method had been restated, and its motives and its devices of style classified by the Jesuit rhetorician Pontanus.[4] Though Scaliger is Pontanus's professed Bible, the work is distinctly what we should call a rhetoric and not a poetic. In tone and teaching it is thoroughly rational. Among the motives which Pontanus most strongly recommends in the funerary elegy is a description or *prosopopoeia* of the death of the subject, a precept abundantly heeded by the elegists on Hastings, who ring the changes on the smallpox, as eleven years earlier had been done on the watery death of Edward King. In style the Jesuit teaching fosters a witty ingenuity which should be carefully distinguished from the ampler symbolic and metaphysical vein of Donne and the religious poets of the seventeenth century in general except where the two touch in such a poet as Crashaw.

Now, how does Dryden combine the three? Like all the other contributors to the volume, Dryden turns his back upon the pastoral allegorical elegy which had begun in England with Spenser and which
Milton had perfected only eleven years before. But though he discarded the allegory and the naturalism of "Lycidas" he kept the
rational classical parts of its design. These steps clearly constitute its
form: a lament for the particular death; a questioning of the nature
of life; an expression of grief, including a lament for the state of the
world; a consolation. Within this structure, he combines the theological elegy in the tradition of Donne with inventions taken from rhetoric
of the Jesuit kind, they supplying the substance of the classical parts.
To Donne belong the discussion of Hastings' character and his significance and the lament for the state of the world; to Pontanus the
Death, the most universally used of the inventions and of course frequent in a less rigid form also in the pastoral; the comparison to the
great dead; and the social reflection which Dryden draws on both for
the lament of the mourners and for the consolation. Of Dryden's schoolboy treatment of these grand themes, I shall take time to say only a
word on his handling of faith. It is characteristic of the changing age.
The tide of seventeenth-century religious emotion which lifts the wave
of Donne's prayer

Look to me faith! and look to my faith God!

has fallen. That man's knowledge and virtue are the marks in him of
the image of God in which he is created has ceased to be the spur to
the most daring contemplative and epistemologic speculation and has
become the timid staple of current rational theology. Dryden asserts
this truth objectively, as he heard it in sermon and treatise, with a
naïvely fresh and honest application of it to his schoolmate. After the
theological speculation, we should have expected a consolation in the
beatific vision, where instead we find a promise that Hastings will live
in the memory of his beloved. But Denham and Marvell have the same
classical orientation.

A close study of seventeenth-century poetry shows that particular
types of imagery or expression, not mere *degrees* of elaboration, were
often held to belong by decorum to particular types of subject matter.
The Donnian theme is expressed in accord with this seventeenth-century decorum in an emblematic image. The sickness, by the same
decorum, in the type of witty ingenuity which Jesuit elegy and epigram had spread across Europe for such themes.

Perhaps the most notable aspect of the poem, if we look to the future of Dryden's poetry, is its fine ordonnance. Jesuit rhetoric contains no structural principle. Dryden's opening question and fine peroration rising in and returning to a single theme replace Donne's thesis and resolution, classical rhetoric replacing mediaeval dialectic. They draw his disparate materials together into a single perspective, the chief light falling on that aspect of Hastings' death which was probably most significant to his fellows, his snatching away just as he was leaving his childhood and entering into the full responsibilities of his place and name.

> Must noble Hastings immaturely die,
> The honor of his ancient family,
> Beauty and learning thus together meet,
> To bring a *winding* for a *wedding* sheet?
>
>   . . . his best
> Monument is his spouse's marble breast.

Between this callow poem on Hastings and Dryden's ode "To the Memory of Mrs. Anne Killigrew" thirty-seven years had elapsed, but the two are bound together by their relation to a tradition, and by Dryden's unremitting endeavor to realize and redefine structural forms in terms of the new attitudes he molded to expression in them. Meanwhile, he had been studying Milton and Donne, among others, unsparingly. The study of Donne may be related to Dryden's conversion and to the fact that he was at this time giving serious attention to religious thought and to Catholic themes of devotion. Donne offered Dryden the sole great models in English of solemn verse of compliment in the religious field; and not only great models, but models Catholic in theme and spirit. Between the two poems had come also the major part of Cowley's work, and in particular the establishment by Cowley of the Pindaric ode as the form for high occasional poetry. The salient points of an ode upon which Cowley had seized had been its enthusiastic attack upon great concepts and intellectual events, the bold play of figures and ideas, and the large and varied metrical structure. He believed in embellishing high poetry; and he gathers about his central theme a play not only of witty figures but of scholastic concepts such as Donne had loved to bring to bear on his experience; but to Cowley they are now obsolete as thought and exist only as the material of sheer intellectual play, useful for poetic amplification.[5] Such was the embellishment suited to his extremely secular, rationalistic, and Epicurean temper; and the undisciplined energy of his meter perhaps does not come amiss to it.

Very different is Dryden's conception of the Pindaric ode as a genre, though he acknowledges Cowley as his authoritative predecessor in the form. Dryden sought to find its most universal forms both of thought and of structure, and he regarded the "embellishment" as a branching out of these. He has left on record his criticism of Cowley's Pindaric measures, namely that Cowley failed to study the organic relation of his varied line lengths to each other.[6] It is clear from his own odes that he did not believe that Cowley had adequately studied the structure of the ode any more than its meter. Such a form he himself seeks to perfect in his ode on Mrs. Killigrew.

In his poem he unites once more the tradition of the Greek and Latin elegy with the tradition of Donne, more particularly the Donne of the "Anniversaries," combining them within the form of a Pindaric ode. The classical lament supplies the main invention, Donne the philosophical meditation on man's fate. He does not, of course, return to the pastoral allegory. Both the descriptions and the personification of nature would have been alien to his taste as to that of his age, and alien to the Pindaric ode. More significantly, that conception of the relation between natural man and man as the creature of grace which enabled Milton to pass so triumphantly from the pagan grief of man and nature to Christian vision is a distinctive attitude of Renaissance Christian humanism, of Platonic humanism, outside the range of Dryden's thought. But the more immediate human grief for human loss which is another treatment of death in central classical poetry had from the time of Jonson taken its appointed place in that sense of order and of the bounds which define order that is the very heart of classicism in Dryden's age. In Dryden's ode, if we compare it with the elegy on Hastings, we find the theme deepened by a closer study of "Lycidas," and, seemingly, of the Sicilian odes themselves. Perhaps also Cartwright offered some suggestions.[7] To this classical theme we are first awakened by echoes of Milton and of the Greeks, echoes as deliberately suggested to our ear as Virgil's of Homer or Milton's of both.

> Whether adopted to some neighboring star,
> Thou rollst above us in thy wandering race, . . .
> Cease thy celestial song a little space . . .
>
> But thus Orinda died . . .

If we look at the structure of the ode with "Lycidas" in mind we see clearly these following parts: The statement of the theme of death, here an address to the dead; the praise of the dead; a lament for the times (stanza IV); the admission of the ineluctable claims of fate, closing with a reference to an earlier poetess; the lament of the mourners (stanza VIII); the consolation. But in actual development Dryden's poem has nothing of Milton's sense of the mystery of death and decay; rather Dryden evokes that other classical humanist theme of the Renaissance, only partially submerged by the great impulses of the religious revival and of Platonism, the theme of a great society and of art as the ornament of that society. This difference between Dryden and Milton renders easier and more decorous Dryden's transformation of the pattern of the elegy into the form of the Pindaric ode. On a close consideration of the transformation Dryden's critical and social temper stands forth clearly. The Pindaric was a poem celebrating some great idea. And for this Cowley had used it. In Cowley's Pindarics, however, there is little movement aside from the development of this idea itself, no great lyric structure. Dryden imitated the structural parts of Pindar's odes more closely, adapting the parts of the elegy with amazing neatness to that form. The elegiac praise of the dead transforms itself into what is in the *epinicea* the praise of the victor. The lament for the times opens out in stanzas V, VI, VII into the celebration of the idea —in this poem a critical definition of the new principles of painting of which Mrs. Killigrew was one of the first practitioners.

Thus in general Dryden follows the invention of the classical elegy. The theme of contemplation, however, is drawn from Donne and from the theological elegy.

The poem opens with a vision of Mrs. Killigrew among the blessed, in which there is an echo of Milton, but which is also probably reminiscent of the ascent of the soul of Elizabeth Drury. It closes with a Last Judgment and with a Renaissance and classical coda on fame. Cowley had written a Pindaric on the Judgment, but Dryden is closer to Donne in his development of the theme than is Cowley. And yet despite the resemblance to Donne the two scenes might be taken as typical of the difference between the ages of Donne and of Dryden.

> At the round earth's imagin'd corners, blow
> Your trumpets Angells, and arise, arise
> From death, you numberlesse infinities
> Of soules, and to your scattered bodies goe, . .

But let them sleepe, Lord, and mee mourne a space,
For, if above all these, my sinnes abounde, . . .

When in mid-air the golden trump shall sound
   To raise the nations underground;
      When in the valley of Jehosephat
The judging God shall close the book of fate,
   And there the last assizes keep
   For those who wake and those who sleep;
   When rattling bones together fly
   From the four corners of the sky:
When sinews o'er the skeletons are spread,
Those clothed with flesh, and life inspires the dead;
The sacred poets first shall hear the sound . . .

Donne evokes in the first eight lines of his Judgment sonnet the experience of every single soul surprised by the trumpets blowing at the
round earth's imagined corners. In Dryden, the whole outline of the
Judgment scene is blocked in, but the description is impersonal, general, not carrying us inward to one individual soul facing itself, but
diffusing outward to social comment and so by an easy step to a defense of poesy.

For Donne and for Milton, in different ways, the world is symbolic.
For Dryden it is, despite his conversion, the essential imaginative
reality. This is the fact which underlies or gives meaning to Dryden's
imagery and to any theory of elocution that helped to shape it. The
ode might well have been a reflective poem. But the poet has chosen
to deal with the general idea of death, and accordingly to throw his
thoughts into the form of the Pindaric. He must, therefore, develop
the poem in the high style especially suited to the Pindaric ode, a style
which will harmonize all the parts, and which by its imagery will
startle and command our passion suitably to the greatness of the
theme. The stanzas dealing with the thought are sustained by the
elaborate statement of that thought and do not need additional color.
It is different with stanzas I, III, and IX, expressing the lament. Since
the lament is a ritual, these are the stanzas which in Dryden's view, as
we may surmise, needed most amplification to sustain their passion and
to elevate it to the level of the thought of death. Dryden, therefore,
replaces the natural description which he has discarded by imagery
drawn from elementary science and cosmic lore. These are just such
amplifications as he had used many years before in his formal praise

of Cromwell. Only the palms of Cromwell are become the palms of
heaven. The image of the clustering bees had appeared in Beaumont's
elegy on King James, a fact which reminds us of the deliberately traditional character of these adornments. Moreover, the play of ideas
shown in amplification constituted the special character of the Pindaric. The ideas which Dryden brings into play are, unlike those of
Cowley, of genuine interest to him and integrally related to his theme.
He believed, at least at the end of his life, in judicial astrology; and
the discussion of the origin of the soul had still a recognized place in
orthodox treatises on the immortality of the soul. But still they are the
outpourings of a discursive thought, not the substance of a concentrated intuition that draws thought and feeling inward towards a center.

The music of Dryden's ode, like its invention and its imagery, is
true to neo-classical principles of formal design. Its beauty is inherent
in the pure metrical pattern of the ode itself, objectively conceived, in
the varied cadences of the lines within the stanza. It is conceived and
managed with perfect artifice. To my ear, despite its fine numerous-
ness, it never, like his lines on Oldham, takes emotion from its theme.

The ode on Mrs. Killigrew is at once illustrative of the grandeur of
Dryden's analysis and reconstitution of the great formal genres of literature, and of the thin spiritual air he often had to breathe in his
perennial struggle between the fading mediaeval world and the rising
world of science and social enlightenment, in the midst of the disillu-
sion of the first Stuart courts. Sometimes he failed to find a soul to
inform what he designed, leaving it as yet only a bodily essence. But
he maintained in England the tradition of high poetry. And it was by
no trivial ideal of expression but by a profound sense of the forms of
great poems that, even where he could not succeed himself he had left
so much ready to the imaginations of those who followed.

NOTES

[1] I hope shortly to publish a detailed analysis of the elegies against the
background of which I am here considering Dryden's poems.

[2] For the complete list the reader may refer to Mr. E. C. Wilson's volume,
published since I made this study, *Prince Henry in English Literature*
(Ithaca, 1946).

[3] See, for instance: Merritt Y. Hughes, "Spenser and the Greek Pastoral
Triad," *Studies in Philology,* XXX (1923), 184–215; T. P. Harrison, Jr.,
"Spenser and the Earlier Pastoral Elegy," *University of Texas Studies in*

English, XIII (1933), 36–53; Don Cameron Allen, ed., *Meres on Poetry* (Cambridge, 1938).

4 Jacobi Pontani De Societate Jesu, *Poeticarum Institutionum Libri III.* I am familiar with *Editio Secunda Emendatior* (Ingoldstatii, MDXCVIII). Pontanus in the digest of Buechler was certainly widely current, and it is to be presumed that the full book was well known. Dryden certainly used Pontanus's edition of Virgil, which might well have contributed more than has been made account of to his conception of the emotions and of the heroic treatment of character.

5 See Cowley's notes to his Pindarics. Cowley's figures in the odes had of course been defended against the charge of fustian and praised for the beauty of their singular strength by Dryden in his *Apology for Heroic Poetry and Poetic License* in 1677.

6 Preface to the *Sylvae; Essays,* ed. Ker, I, 267–8.

7 As is suggested to me by Mr. Gwynne Blakemore Evans, who is shortly to bring out an edition of Cartwright.

IAN JACK

𝒦

Mock-Heroic: *MacFlecknoe*

Il n'y a rien . . . de plus ridicule que de raconter une histoire comique et absurde en termes graves et sérieux.

Boileau [1]

I

"More libels have been written against me," Dryden remarked in the
Discourse concerning the Original and Progress of Satire, "than almost
any man now living. . . . But let the world witness for me, that . . .
I have seldom answered any scurrilous lampoon, when it was in my
power to have exposed my enemies: and, being naturally vindicative,
have suffered in silence, and possessed my soul in quiet." [2] If we accept Johnson's definition of a lampoon as "a personal satire; abuse;
censure written not to reform but to vex," we must admit that the
fundamental impulse behind *MacFlecknoe* is that of the lampooner.
It is so evidently inspired by no wish to reform Shadwell, or to reform
anyone, that it sets a problem for the moral apologist for satire. Dryden
felt this difficulty when he came to write his own essay on satire, and
was forced to conclude that a lampoon is "a dangerous sort of weapon,
and for the most part unlawful. We have no moral right on the reputation of other men. 'Tis taking from them what we cannot restore to
them." [3]

From *Augustan Satire: Intention and Idiom in English Poetry, 1660–1750*
(Oxford, 1952; 1957), pp. 43–52. Reprinted by permission of The Clarendon Press.

The immediate occasion of *MacFlecknoe* is uncertain. No doubt Dryden felt that he had been "notoriously abused"—which he allows as a partial exculpation for writing a lampoon. All that is definitely known is that during the year 1678 something acted as a match to the heaped-up straw of Dryden's contempt for Shadwell and set him writing the only poem in his work which is wholly devoted to satirizing a private enemy. It is noteworthy that Dryden confines himself to Shadwell's literary character; in spite of the misleading sub-title, *A Satyr upon the True-Blew-Protestant Poet, T. S.*,[4] nothing is said of Shadwell's religious or political opinions; nor is his moral character seriously attacked. Dryden confines himself to portraying him as a literary dunce. The words "wit," "sense," "art," "nature," "nonsense," "tautology," and "dulness," which had been the current coin of Dryden's prolonged critical warfare with Shadwell, sound through the poem like a fanfare.

In its original impulse, then, *MacFlecknoe* may be considered as a lampoon. Dryden also described it as a Varronian satire, a category for which its primary qualification seems to be that it is based on a story of the poet's own invention. But the most helpful classification of the poem, as well as the most familiar, is that of the mock-heroic. Faced with the task of making Shadwell ridiculous, Dryden chose as his method the ironical politeness of the mock-epic.

MacFlecknoe is highly original. There are several English poems, of which the *Nun's Priest's Tale* is the least unlikely, which may have given Dryden a hint. But there is no earlier poem in the language which is at all comparable with it as a whole. The manner of the greatest satirist of the previous age, already cheapened by a host of imitators, was unacceptable to Dryden. When he remarks that Boileau "had read the burlesque poetry of Scarron, with some kind of indignation, as witty as it was," [5] the parallel with his own attitude to Butler is unmistakable. Dryden aspired to write "manly satire" and felt that the style of *Hudibras* "turns earnest too much to jest, and gives us a boyish kind of pleasure." [6] Believing satire "undoubtedly a species" of heroic poetry,[7] he had to look elsewhere for a model which would teach him how to give weight to his censure. He found what he wanted in *Le Lutrin*. "This, I think . . . to be the most beautiful, and most noble kind of satire," he was later to sum up. "Here is the majesty of the heroic, finely mixed with the venom of the other; and raising the delight which otherwise would be flat and vulgar, by the sublimity of the expression." [8]

II

Fully to appreciate the use of a mock-heroic idiom for highly un-complimentary purposes it is necessary to be familiar with the pane-gyrical use of the heroic style. Fortunately the approach to *MacFleck-noe* is rendered easy by the fact that many passages of *Absalom and Achitophel* exemplify the use of the heroic style for panegyric which is here parodied. Any misconception of the modern reader's that a mock-heroic poem is designed to ridicule the heroic genre, or that it will be written in a bombastic, ranting style, is removed by a glance at *MacFlecknoe*. Dryden does not, like Pope's Blackmore,

> Rend with tremendous Sound [our] ears asunder,
> With Gun, Drum, Trumpet, Blunderbuss & Thunder.[9]

On the contrary a reader who did not know both poems well would be at a loss to say which of the following passages belonged to the heroic poem, which to the mock-heroic:

> (a) This aged Prince now flourishing in Peace,
>   And blest with issue of a large increase,
>   Worn out with business, did at length debate
>   To settle the Succession of the State.

> (b) With secret Joy, indulgent *David* view'd
>   His Youthful Image in his Son renew'd;
>   To all his wishes Nothing he deni'd
>   And made the Charming *Annabel* his Bride.[10]

The style of many passages in *MacFlecknoe* is identical with the polished heroic idiom of *Absalom and Achitophel*. The joke that makes it "a poem exquisitely satirical" [11] consists in using this style, which was soon to prove a perfect medium for a poem about the King and weighty matters of State, to describe Shadwell and his insignificant affairs. Nor is Shadwell so insignificant before Dryden gets to work: it is the elevated style that makes him so. A small man is not in himself a ridiculous object: he becomes ridiculous when he is dressed up in a suit of armour designed for a hero. The discrepancy between the im-portant matters that the style is continually suggesting and the ques-tion of Flecknoe's successor is so marked that a shock of laughter ensues.

The purpose of such a poem must be made clear, as wittily as possible, right from the start. Here Dryden succeeds perfectly, striking the full mock-heroic note with a grave *sententia:*

> All humane things are subject to decay,
> And, when Fate summons, Monarchs must obey.

These lines might form the opening of a panegyrical funeral elegy on a royal personage; but the direction of the *prosecutio* which follows indicates the mock-heroic intention beyond all doubt:

> This *Fleckno* found.[12]

Right from the start, too, we have "the numbers of heroic poesy," which emphasize by their harmonious dignity the ludicrousness of the matter. Triplets, usually a sign of increased elevation in Dryden, are used with similar effect:

> For ancient *Decker* prophesi'd long since,
> That in this Pile should Reign a mighty Prince,
> Born for a scourge of Wit, and flayle of Sense.[13]

The skilful manner in which Dryden mingles direct and oblique attack is particularly clear in Flecknoe's speeches, which are introduced and terminated with due heightening of style and make up more than half of the poem. In a direct lampoon the lines

> The rest to some faint meaning make pretence,
> But *Shadwell* never deviates into sense,[14]

would be severe enough. They are rendered lethal by being uttered as an encomium.

One of the characteristics of the heroic idiom which Dryden adapts to his own purpose is the dignified *descriptio* of time and place. The great event is ushered in by a formal passage:

> Now Empress Fame had publisht the renown
> Of *Shadwell's* Coronation through the Town.
> Rows'd by report of Fame, the Nations meet,
> From near *Bun-hill* and distant *Watling-street.* . . .[15]

The scene of the solemnity is described with equal pomp:

> Close to the Walls which fair *Augusta* bind,
> (The fair *Augusta* much to fears inclin'd)
> An ancient fabrick rais'd t'inform the sight,
> There stood of yore, and *Barbican* it hight.[16]

In these passages the mock-heroic application of methods of description familiar in classical literature to scenes of contemporary "low" life is a reminder of the realistic bias of Dryden's mind—a bias characteristic of much of the best Augustan poetry.[17] He is very successful in his delineation of the "low" quarters of the town, "brothel-houses," and the haunts of "the suburbian Muse." The whole background of the poem (and not least the trap-door at the end, which parodies the heavy humour of Shadwell's play *The Virtuoso*) is reminiscent of the setting of a low comedy or farce. To remember Shadwell's dramatic propensities is to relish the poetic justice of the joke.

"As Virgil in his fourth Georgic, of the Bees, perpetually raises the lowness of his subject, by the loftiness of his words," Dryden observes in his remarks on *Le Lutrin*, "and ennobles it by comparisons drawn from empires, and from monarchs . . . we see Boileau pursuing him in the same flights, and scarcely yielding to his master." [18] The mock-heroic imagery of *MacFlecknoe* is no less brilliant. The joyful business of comparing small men to giants and making pygmies of them in the process begins in the third line of the poem, where we hear that Flecknoe,

> . . . like *Augustus*, young
> Was call'd to Empire and had govern'd long.[19]

The unfortunate Shadwell is compared in turn to Arion, to "young *Ascanius* . . . *Rome's* other hope and Pillar of the State," to Hannibal, and to "*Romulus* . . . by *Tyber's Brook*." [20] The tendency to blasphemy which is never far away in Dryden, whether in satire or panegyric, becomes very marked in the account of the signs and omens which foreshadowed Shadwell's coming. Flecknoe's speech parodies John the Baptist's:

> *Heywood* and *Shirley* were but Types of thee,
> Thou last great Prophet of Tautology:
> Even I, a dunce of more renown than they,
> Was sent before but to prepare thy way:

> And coarsely clad in *Norwich* Drugget came
> To teach the Nations in thy greater name.[21]

The manner in which the mantle of Flecknoe falls on the shoulders of Shadwell recalls the case of Elijah, who left the earth in the other direction.

It is not only in mock-heroic imagery (imagery which diminishes by irony) that *MacFlecknoe* excels. Brilliant examples of direct satirical imagery may also be found, notably in the latter part of Flecknoe's second speech, which makes relatively little use of irony and is written in a style closer to that of direct satire than most other parts of the poem:

> When did his Muse from *Fletcher* scenes purloin,
> As thou whole Eth'ridg dost transfuse to thine?
> But so transfused as Oyls on Waters flow,
> His always floats above, thine sinks below.
> This is thy Province, this thy wondrous way,
> New Humours to invent for each new Play:
> This is that boasted Byas of thy mind,
> By which one way, to dullness, 'tis inclined,
> Which makes thy writings lean on one side still,
> And, in all changes, that way bends thy will.[22]
> Nor let thy mountain belly make pretence
> Of likeness; thine's a tympany [23] of sense.
> A Tun of Man in thy large Bulk is writ,
> But sure thou'rt but a Kilderkin of wit.[24]

In such a passage the satire is wholly conveyed by the images. Starting with the simple object of name-calling, the poet chooses an image: as he gives expression to it another starts up in his mind, and the new image is tossed about until a third presents itself to his attention. The result is satire of great power: satire which differs completely—one may note in passing—from anything in *Le Lutrin*.

III

One of the passages in the *Discourse concerning . . . Satire* most frequently quoted and applied to Dryden's own satiric method occurs in the section devoted to complimenting the Earl of Dorset and Middlesex.

> How easy is it to call rogue and villain, and that wittily! But how hard to make a man appear a fool, a blockhead, or a knave, without using any of these opprobrious terms! To spare the grossness of the names, and to do the thing yet more severely, is to draw a full face, and to make the nose and cheeks stand out, and yet not to employ any depth of shadowing. This is the mystery of that noble trade, which yet no master can teach to his apprentice. . . . There is . . . a vast difference betwixt the slovenly butchering of a man, and the fineness of a stroke that separates the head from the body, and leaves it standing in its place. A man may be capable, as Jack Ketch's wife said of his servant, of a plain piece of work, a bare hanging; but to make a malefactor die sweetly was only belonging to her husband.[25]

In spite of this praise of indirectness in satire, however, Dryden cannot conceal the fact that he prefers the direct Juvenal to the indirect Horace. Admitting that "the manner of Juvenal" is inferior to that of Horace, he claims that "Juvenal has excelled him in his performance. Juvenal has railed more wittily than Horace has rallied." [26] Indirectness is not the most striking characteristic of Dryden's own satire. While "raillery" is perhaps a better word to describe *MacFlecknoe* than "railing," the obliquity of the attack can easily be exaggerated. The fundamental irony is the mock-heroic conception of the whole, and the brilliant heroic idiom in which it is written. The ridicule is much more direct than that in *A Tale of a Tub* or *Jonathan Wild the Great*. Qualities in fact ridiculous are nominally praised; but they are given their true names, "dulness," "nonsense," "tautology." Dryden does not tell us that Shadwell is a great poet, as Fielding tells us that Wild is a great man. Instead, and with the greatest gusto, he hammers out his lines of magnificent abuse:

> Success let others teach, learn thou from me
> Pangs without birth, and fruitless Industry.[27]

That Dryden is at liberty to speak out in this way is largely due to the fact that the heroic idiom is continually asserting that the hero is a great man, in a manner in which no prose style would be powerful enough to do. Helped by the "ostentation" of the verse (to borrow a good term from Charles Williams), Dryden is at liberty to use direct abuse without being inartistic. This is particularly evident in the speeches. The reader enjoys hearing Shadwell being abused without feeling that he is assisting in an unmannerly brawl; and the elevation of the verse adds authority to the condemnation. This mingling of irony with direct abuse is more effective than pure irony.

In writing *MacFlecknoe* Dryden had no intention of ridiculing his own heroic style, of which the greatest example still lay before him, or the heroic poem as a genre. If "parody" is taken, as in modern usage it often is, to mean a composition which ridicules the style of a given poet or poetic kind by exaggeration (as in Swinburne's self-parodies), then *MacFlecknoe* is innocent of parodic intention; except that one or two touches—principally the conclusion, and the archaisms "whilom," "hight," and "yore"—ridicule the manner of Flecknoe, Shadwell, and bad poets in general. But if by parody is meant "a kind of writing, in which the words of an author or his thoughts are taken, and by a slight change adapted to some new purpose," [28] several parodic passages may be found. They are not intended to ridicule their originals, but merely—as in the lines about the "Mother-Strumpets," [29] which parody Cowley—to amuse the reader by the allusion, and by the contrast between the original subject of the passage and that to which it is now applied. The elements of parody in *MacFlecknoe* are simply specific instances of the mock-heroic conception of the whole poem. [30]

Appreciation of the devastating satire of *MacFlecknoe* should not be allowed to blind us to its sheer comedy. It is one of the few poems that Dryden wrote for his own satisfaction, and there is no doubt that he enjoyed himself. His delight is evident everywhere, in the brilliant imagery lavished on Shadwell—

> His goodly Fabrick fills the eye
> And seems design'd for thoughtless Majesty:
> Thoughtless as Monarch Oakes that shade the plain,
> And, spread in solemn state, supinely reign [31]

—or in the hilarious couplet of advice which Flecknoe bestows on his successor:

> Let Father *Flecknoe* fire thy mind with praise
> *And Uncle Ogleby thy envy raise.*[32]

Throughout the poem there is an element of imaginative fantasy surpassed in *The Rape of the Lock* but lacking in many parts of the *Dunciad*. Shadwell is a *creation* in a sense in which Cibber is not. *MacFlecknoe* is not only a satire: it is also a comedy. Mere scorn withers. It is the ironic sympathy in Dryden's poem, the mischievous joy in contemplation, that gives life to a creature of the comic imagination. Shadwell takes his place as a member of the same company as Sir John Falstaff himself.

NOTES

[1] *Dissertation sur Joconde* (1669).

[2] *Essays*, ii, 80.

[3] Ibid., ii, 79.

[4] This was no doubt added by the publisher of the first edition, which seems to have been pirated. See Hugh Macdonald, *John Dryden: A Bibliography* (1939), p. 30.

[5] *Essays*, ii, 107.

[6] Ibid., ii, 105.

[7] Ibid., ii, 108.

[8] Ibid. For an examination of Dryden's debt to *Le Lutrin* see A. F. B. Clark's *Boileau and the French Classical Critics in England* (1925), particularly pp. 156-8.

[9] *The First Satire of the Second Book of Horace*, ll. 25-6.

[10] (a) *MacFlecknoe*, ll. 7-10; (b) *Absalom*, ll. 31-4. All quotations in this chapter and the next are from *The Poems of John Dryden*, Oxford edition, ed. John Sargeaunt (1913).

[11] Johnson's *Lives*, i, 383.

[12] Compare the much "lower" sententious passage, 36 lines long, followed by the usual *prosecutio* ("This Hudibras by proof found true"), with which Hudibras, II, iii begins.

[13] ll. 87-9.

[14] ll. 19-20. Here and elsewhere Sargeaunt follows the early editions in reading "Sh———."

[15] ll. 94-7.

[16] ll. 64-7.

[17] This device became essential to the "Augustan Eclogue," a descriptive piece modelled on the classical eclogue which dealt with the urban scene in a highly realistic manner.

[18] *Essays*, ii, 107-8.

[19] ll. 3-4.

[20] ll. 43, 108-9, 112-13, 130-31.

[21] ll. 29-34.

²² As has often been pointed out, these lines parody a passage from the epilogue to Shadwell's *The Humorists:*

> A Humor is the Byas of the Mind,
> By which with violence 'tis one way inclin'd:
> It makes our Actions lean on one side still,
> And in all Changes that way bends the Will. (15–18.)

The parody is particularly appropriate because Ben Jonson was the focus of most of the disputes between Dryden and Shadwell.

²³ "A kind of obstructed flatulence that swells the body like a drum." Johnson.

²⁴ 183–96 ("Kilderkin" = a small barrel of wine, contrasting with "Tun").

²⁵ *Essays*, ii, 92–3.

²⁶ Ibid., 94–5.

²⁷ ll. 147–8.

²⁸ Johnson's *Dictionary*.

²⁹ ll. 72–3.

³⁰ "Parody" is only one of the critical terms which have changed their meaning since the Augustan age. To investigate the meaning of some of these words is one of the objects of this study.

³¹ ll. 25–8.

³² ll. 173–4. (My italics.)

VIVIAN DE S. PINTO

✍

John Wilmot, Earl of Rochester, and the Right Veine of Satire

I

For more than two centuries judgements of the Court poets of the reign of Charles II have been coloured by the legends which have clustered round their lives and personalities. The "Whig view of history" (shared by many who were by no means Whigs in politics) regarded them simply as the debauched and worthless companions of Charles II who wrote sophisticated love songs and bawdy lampoons. Macaulay in the second chapter of his *History of England* (1849) speaks in horrified tones of "the open profligacy of the Court and the Cavaliers" and the "outrageous profaneness and licentiousness of the Buckinghams and the Sedleys." "The Restoration Muse," writes Beljame about thirty years later, "did not . . . aim very high, it sought neither lofty ideas nor style: its ideal was a slight, delicate thought in simple and harmonious form." Leigh Hunt in his review of Keats's *Poems* of 1817 in the *Examiner* declared that "the school which existed till lately since the restoration of Charles the 2d, was rather a school of wit and ethics in verse than anything else; nor was the verse, with the exception of Dryden's, of a very high order."

Here we can see the origins of the stereotyped view of the Restoration literary scene presented by nearly all the literary historians: a frivolous, licentious Court, where a number of profligate, dilettante

From *Essays and Studies* 1953 (London: John Murray, 1953), pp. 56–70. Reprinted by permission of The English Association and the author.

courtiers write rather worthless verses, and one great poet who pan-
ders to their taste and half ruins his genius by his servility:

> Dryden in immortal strain
> Had raised the Table Round again,
> But that a ribald King and Court
> Bade him toil to make them sport;
> Demanded for their niggard pay,
> Fit for their souls, a looser lay,
> Licentious satire, song and play;
> The world defrauded of the high design
> Profaned the God-given strength and marred
> the mighty line.

Scott was no Whig but this view of the literary history of the Restoration harmonized well with the conception of the Glorious Revolution
of 1688 as the turning point in English history, when the wicked,
papistical Stuarts were expelled and the foundations of the sober
Protestant individualistic England of the Victorian age were securely
laid.

II

The work of twentieth-century scholars and critics has done much to
clear the reputation of the Restoration Court Wits. Charles Whibley's
chapter on them in *The Cambridge History of English Literature* was
a pioneer work of rehabilitation by a clear-sighted critic who refused
to allow his judgement to be warped by traditional views. More
recently an American scholar Professor J. H. Wilson in his admirable
book *The Court Wits of the Restoration* has shown that a great part of
the commonly accepted mass of anecdotes concerning these writers is
apocryphal. For instance there is no evidence for the story that the
Countess of Shrewsbury held the Duke of Buckingham's horse while
he fought his duel with her husband or the still more lurid sequel that
he slept with her in his bloodstained shirt after the duel. The commonly repeated tale about the exploits of Rochester and Buckingham,
when they are said to have set up as innkeepers on the Newmarket
Road, appears to be synthetic romance concocted by some eighteenth-
century hack writer. Finally there seems to be no real historical basis
for the allegation which has done most harm to Rochester's reputation.
John Dryden was certainly cudgelled by ruffians in Rose Alley, Covent
Garden, on a December night in 1679, but it seems very unlikely that

Rochester had any connection with this outrage, which was probably instigated by the Duchess of Portsmouth and perhaps perpetrated by her homicidal brother-in-law, the Earl of Pembroke.

III

The group of Restoration Wits (Andrew Marvell's "Merry Gang") consisted of men who were living between two worlds, one of which was dying, the other struggling into existence. One was the old world of medieval and renaissance culture with its conception of an integrated theocentric universe and on earth of a sovereign at the apex of an ordered society with a Court consisting of his trusted servants, who were representative of the accepted moral, aesthetic and religious ideals of the nation. Shakespeare and others saw that this world was in danger even in the sixteenth century:

> Take but degree away, untune that string,
> And hark what discord follows!

It was the world that Clarendon tried (and failed) to restore in 1660 after the collapse of the Puritan régime. Then there was the new world of what in the language of Spengler can be called "civilization" as opposed to "culture," the world of the great modern city, of international trade and finance, political parties and newspapers with its atomized society of "free" individuals and its Copernican universe of infinite space governed not by the laws of God but by mathematical laws which the scientists were busy discovering. In such a world the Court would cease to be the real centre of national life and become merely a fashionable club for idle irresponsible young people. Spenser in his *Mother Hubberds Tale* had already noted the beginning of the process when he contrasted the "rightfull courtier" with the "young lustie gallants" who spent their time playing "thriftless games" and ruined themselves with "courtezans and costly riotize." An anonymous ballad writer of the reign of James I contrasted the Old Courtier of the Queen with the King's New Courtier:

> A new flourishing gallant, new come to his land,
> Who kept a brace of new painted creatures to his command,
> And could take up a thousand readily upon his new bond,
> And be drunk at a new Tavern till be not able to go or stand.

The development suggested by these extracts was enormously accelerated by the Civil War and the exile of the Court. Dr. F. R.

Leavis has commented acutely on the change in the courtly background which took place after the Restoration.

"Charles II was a highly intelligent man of liberal interests, and his mob of gentlemen cultivated conversation and the Muses. But that the fine order, what was referred to above as the 'Court culture,' did not survive the period of disruption, exile and 'travels' is apparent even in the best things of Etherege, Sedley, Rochester and the rest: the finest specimens of the tenderly or cynically gallant and polite lack the positive fineness, the implicit subtlety, examined above in Carew. The cheaper things remind us forcibly that to indicate the background of Restoration poetry we must couple with the court, not as earlier the country house, but the coffee-house, and that the coffee-house is on intimate terms with the Green Room." [1]

Dr. Leavis is speaking here particularly of the lyric which was the characteristic poetic form of the old "Court culture." Many good lyrics were written in the Restoration period, but the tradition of the courtly lyric that began with Wyatt was dying with that integrated courtly culture of which it was the fine flower. The need for a new kind of English poetry was as manifest in the sixteen-seventies as it was in the seventeen-nineties and the nineteen-twenties.

IV

Two ways were open to the courtier poet in the reign of Charles II. He could accept what might be called the new orthodoxy based on the illusion of the approach of an "Augustan" age, a world of good sense and good taste combining rationalism with dignity and grace. It was the new city described by Dryden at the end of *Annus Mirabilis:*

> Methinks already from this chymic flame,
> I see a city of more precious mould;
> Rich as the town that gives the Indies name
> With silver pav'd and all divine with gold.

> .   .   .   .

> More great than human now and more august,
> Now deified she from her fires does rise:
> Her widening streets on new foundations trust,
> And, opening, into larger parts she flies.

This vision was exciting in 1666. It was to lead to the smugness of Addison, the complacency of Thomson's *Liberty* and Dr. Pangloss's "best of all possible worlds." In such a world politics, trade and science would be the serious occupations of men of sense; poetry would be an ornament and a recreation. The poets would strive to be "smooth" and "correct" and Waller had provided them with suitable models. The traditional escape from everyday banality was the golden arcadia of the pastoral tradition. This became the correct "poetical" subject (as romantic medievalism was in the Victorian age). In *Lycidas* the theme had been charged with imaginative grandeur for the last time. In the hands of court poets like Sedley and Sheffield it became dainty, graceful and suitable for the "tenderly or cynically gallant or polite." The Restoration song-writers (*pace* Dr. Leavis) still had some of the grace and charm of the old Court culture but they were the progenitors of Johnson's poets who used "descriptions copied from descriptions, imitations copied from imitations . . . traditional imagery and traditional similes" and to Crabbe's "sleepy bards";

> On Mincio's banks in Caesar's bounteous reign
> If Tityrus found the Golden Age again,
> Must sleepy bards the flattering dream prolong,
> Mechanic echoes of the Mantuan song?

There was, however, another way open to the courtier poet in the reign of Charles II; it was more difficult and less likely to gain applause. This was the way of realistic satire which was to be the most vital kind of English poetry for nearly a hundred years. Such a poetry would ignore the tradition of the "poetic" subject and would concentrate on the contradictions and the ironies of a society which professed to be "rational," "elegant" and "polite" but was actually greedy, heartless and cynical, a world in which it was only a step from Whitehall to Mother Bennet's brothel, and which fully justified the description of Defoe:

> Wealth (howsoever got) in England makes
> Lords, of mechanics! Gentlemen, of rakes!
> Antiquity and Birth are needless here.
> 'Tis Impudence and Money makes a Peer.

One of the mistresses of Louis XIV is reported to have said that beneath his magnificent exterior that monarch "puait comme une charogne." One possible function of the poet in the new world that was coming into existence at the Restoration was to make poetry out of the contrasts between the highflown professions and ornamental façade of the English aristocracy and the "stinking carcass" that lay behind them. Such satire could only be successfully written by poets who had thoroughly absorbed the culture of that aristocracy and understood its excellencies as well as its weaknesses. Such was the satire of the great Augustan poets, Dryden, Pope, Swift and Johnson. The pioneer was not, however, as all the text-books tell us, John Dryden, but the youngest and most gifted of the Restoration courtier poets, John Wilmot, Earl of Rochester, whom Andrew Marvell, no mean judge, declared to be "the best English satyrist" and to have "the right veine."

V

The most surprising quality of Rochester's genius was the rapid development of his mind. He started as a wholehearted disciple of Thomas Hobbes, that eloquent and persuasive materialist. On his death-bed, he declared that the "absurd and foolish Philosophy, which the world so much admired, propagated by Mr. Hobbs and others, had undone him, and many more, of the best parts in the Nation." [2] From the beginning Rochester's utterances have that quality of "terrifying honesty" which Mr. T. S. Eliot has ascribed to Blake. The logical outcome of Hobbes's thoroughgoing materialism and sensationalism was the complete rejection of the Petrarchan convention which had dominated courtly love poetry since the days of Wyatt. In a lyric probably written very early in his career Rochester defiantly reverses the sentiments expressed in Lovelace's famous poem:

> I could not love thee, Dear, so much,
> Loved I not honour more.

For the young disciple of Hobbes "love" (of this sort) and "honour" were simply examples of what their master called "the frequence of insignificant speech":

> How perfect Cloris, & how free
> Would these enjoyments prouve,
> But you with formall jealousie
> Are still tormenting Love.
>
> Lett us (since witt instructs us how)
> Raise pleasure to the topp,

> If Rivall bottle you'l allow
> I'le suffer rivall fopp
>
> .   .   .   .
>
> All this you freely may confess
> Yet wee'll not disagree
> For did you love your pleasures less
> You were not fitt for mee.

This hedonism leads inevitably to the naked self-worship proclaimed in his Epistle to Mulgrave, a poem probably written about 1669:

> But from a Rule I have (upon long Trial)
> T'avoid with Care all sort of Self-denial,
> Which way soe'er Desire and Fancy lead,
> (Contemning Fame) that Path I boldly tread.

This, of course, was the principle governing the lives of most of the men of Rochester's class in the reign of Charles II, but he was the only one who had the courage to proclaim it openly. One suspects that it was statements of this kind quite as much as any of his licentious exploits which injured Rochester's reputation. Like Shaw's Andrew Undershaft, he not only did wrong things, "he said them and thought them: that was what was so dreadful." The Rochester who wrote these lines was the perfect "wild gallant" of the period, portrayed by his friend Etherege in his famous play as Dorimant, the prototype of a long line of attractive rakes in English comedy from Congreve's Mirabel to Wilde's Lord Goring. He was the embodiment of the type which Mr. W. H. Auden has called the Aesthetic Hero, the man who lives entirely for pleasure only and whose life bears no relation to truth. Eleven years after he wrote the Epistle to Mulgrave, when he was lying on his death-bed at Woodstock, he had reached a position diametrically opposed to that of Dorimant. His ideal now was the Religious Hero, the completely selfless character portrayed by the Second Isaiah, whose description of the Suffering Servant of Jahweh he paraphrased in the following words:

"The meanness of his appearance and Person has made vain and foolish people disparage Him because he was not dressed in such a Fools-coat as they delight in." [3] The dying poet has now discovered that only in the contemplation of a figure embodying Absolute Truth could he find that "felicity and glory" which he mentions in one of his

letters to his wife. His position could now be summed up in the words
of Oscar Wilde reported by André Gide: "Above all, not happiness.
Pleasure! We must always want the most tragic." [4]

VI

Rochester's mind was essentially dialectical. He was always aware
of the voice of the opponent. Robert Parsons in his Funeral Sermon
reports an illuminating story which Rochester told him in the last days
of his life.

"One day at an Atheistical Meeting, at a person of Qualitie's, I
undertook to manage the Cause, and was the principal Disputant
against God and Piety, and for my performances received the applause
of the whole company; upon which my mind was terribly struck, and
I immediately reply'd thus to my self. Good God! that a Man, that
walks upright, that sees the wonderful works of God, and has the uses
of his senses and reason, should use them to the defying of his
Creator." [5] Rochester was always "replying to himself." His celebrated
"conversion" was no *volte-face*. It was the end of a dialectical process
which had been going on for years. His satiric poems are of two kinds.
Some, like his attacks on Mulgrave and Sir Car Scroope are simply
lampoons in the fashion of the day and only distinguished from the
numerous other examples of this kind of writing, the work of the
authors whom Dryden called "our common libellers," by their greater
literary force and pungency. He wrote other poems, however, which
are what Wordsworth called in the Preface to his Poems of 1815
"philosophic satire." They must be read as stages in that exploration
of reality that led from the gentlemanly dissipation of Dorimant to
the rapt contemplation of the figure of the Suffering Servant.

VII

Mr. Ian Jack in his recent study of *Augustan Satire*, in which
strangely enough Rochester is hardly mentioned, rightly stresses the
elements of "imitation" and parody (in the old sense of the word) in
this kind of writing. The Augustan satirists were the products of a
classical education, but this education instead of leaving behind it,
as it usually does in the modern world, simply some vague memories
of ancient masterpieces and a few tags, still at this time provided a
living culture. In a man of genius this culture could become creative.
Rochester was the first author who used his cultural background
creatively in the manner afterwards developed by Dryden, Pope and

Johnson.[6] Not only his brilliant adaptation of the tenth satire of the First Book of Horace, but each of his major satiric poems is both a criticism of contemporary life and also the result of a creative use of his reading. As Burnet writes: "Sometimes other mens thoughts mixed with his Composures, but that flowed rather from the Impressions they made on him when he read them, by which they came to return upon him as his own thoughts; than that he servilely copied from any." [7] Two satiric poems which perhaps mark an early stage in his exploration of contemporary realities are both "parodies" of the heroic manner and "imitations" shot through with memories of ancient and modern literature. The famous lines *Upon Nothing* are really a kind of ironic inversion of Cowley's *Hymn to Light* and at the same time the poet makes use of the conception of Nothing as an active force, found in the Latin poems of Wouwerus and Passerat quoted by Johnson in his account of Rochester in *The Lives of the Poets*. Behind the whole poem also lie still more august antecedents, the Book of Genesis, the first verses of the Fourth Gospel and the Aristotelian doctrine of Form and Matter. In the last stanzas the irony is transferred from metaphysics to contemporary society:

> *Nothing*, who dwell'st with Fools in grave Disguise,
> For whom they reverend Shapes and Forms devise,
> Lawn Sleeves, and Furs, and Gowns, when they like thee
>   look Wise.

. . . .

> The Great Man's Gratitude to his best Friend,
> King's Promises, Whore's Vows, tow'rds thee they bend,
> Flow swiftly into thee, and in thee ever end.

The emptiness that lies behind the outward shows of humanity is visualized here as a positive force with special reference to the contemporary scene. Swift's doctrine of man as a "micro-coat" is clearly foreshadowed. Pope must have studied this poem carefully for he wrote a clever "imitation" of it in his youth and the Triumph of Dullness at the end of the *Dunciad* probably owes a good deal to Rochester's Triumph of Nothing.

The Maimed Debauchee, that "masterpiece of heroic irony" as Charles Whibley called it, recalls Davenant as *Upon Nothing* recalls Cowley. The stately metre and diction of *Gondibert* are used to exhibit the old age of a gentlemanly rake who is ironically equated

to a superannuated admiral watching a naval battle. Like all Rochester's best satiric work this poem is not a statement but a vision.
We are made to see the absurdly fierce old sailor:

> From his fierce Eyes Flashes of Rage he throws,
>   As from black Clouds when Lightning breaks away,
> Transported thinks himself amidst his Foes,
>   And absent, yet enjoys the bloody Day.

The image is, as it were, superimposed on that of the old roué urging
on his young friends to the life of pleasure:

> My Pains at last some Respite shall afford,
>   When I behold the Battels you maintain:
> When Fleets of Glasses sail around the Board,
>   From whose Broad-sides Volleys of Wit shall rain.

Are we looking at a riotous banquet or a sea-fight? It is impossible to
say: the two images are fused into a single whole. Again there are
layers of allusion here. Not only Gondibert, but the sea-fights in
Dryden's *Annus Mirabilis* are suggested, and the poem is also certainly
a kind of ironic "parody" of Horace's *Vixi puellis nuper idoneus*.

VIII

An important phase of Rochester's development is to be seen in his
satiric treatment of the relations between the sexes. In the old courtly
world of "degree" and subordination, women were either regarded as
wives and daughters owing obedience to the authority of husbands
and fathers or as the idealized object of courtly love, Petrarchan
"mistresses" worshipped by adoring "servants." These traditional relationships were breaking down in the middle of the seventeenth
century and indeed Donne's *Songs and Sonets* show that the process
had begun much earlier. If, as Hobbes taught, goodness and badness
were to be equated with pleasure and pain, pleasure was obviously
to be chosen, and Rochester, following the example of his king and
his fellow courtiers took his pleasure with many women. The dialectical bent of his mind, however, made him see the matter from the
woman's standpoint and in two of his most interesting satiric poems
it is a woman who speaks. These are, I believe, the only Augustan
satires where the woman's point of view is expressed with real sympathy and understanding. Rochester saw that the relationship between
the sexes, in his own class at any rate, at that time was more in the

nature of war than of "love." In a fragment that survives in his auto-
graph in the Portland collection he puts into the mouth of a cultivated
woman an indignant protest against the condition of women in contemporary society:

> What vaine unnecessary things are men
> How well we doe without 'em, tell me then
> Whence comes that meane submissiveness wee finde
> This ill bred age has wrought on woman kinde . . .

The speaker of those lines shows the gallants of Whitehall, not as the
Strephons and Damons of the pastoral convention, but as cynical
sensualists choosing and buying their mistresses like horses at a fair:

> To the Pell Mell, Playhous nay the drawing roome
> Their Woemen Fayres, these Woemen Coursers come
> To chaffer, chuse, & ride their bargains home,
> Att the appearance of an unknown face
> Up steps the Arrogant pretending Ass
> Pulling by th' elbow his companion Huff
> Cryes looke, de God that wench is well enough . . .

In Rochester's most finished social satire, *A Letter from Artemisa in
the Town to Cloe in the Country*, again the voice of a cultivated and
intelligent woman is heard. Artemisa is made to lament the decay of
"love" between the sexes and its transformation into a commercialized
game:

> *Love,* the most gen'rous Passion of the Mind;
> The softest Refuge Innocence can find:
> The safe Director of unguided Youth:
> Fraught with kind Wishes, and secur'd by Truth:
> That Cordial-drop Heav'n in our Cup has thrown,
> To make the nauseous Draught of Life go down:
> On which one only Blessing God might raise,
> In Lands of Atheists, Subsidies of Praise:
> For none did e'er so dull and stupid prove,
> But felt a God, and bless'd his Pow'r in Love:
> This only Joy, for which poor we are made,
> Is grown, like Play, to be an arrant Trade.

It is true that Rochester is not speaking here in his own person but the
rhythm and imagery of this passage show that this is a view of sex

which he could understand and appreciate. It is Artemisa's friend the eccentric country lady who tells the story of Corinna, a picture of a Restoration prostitute etched with the vigour, the vitality and the unsentimental indignation of Hogarth:

> Now scorn'd of all, forsaken and opprest,
> She's a *Memento Mori* to the rest:
> Diseas'd, decay'd, to take up half a Crown
> Must Mortgage her long Scarf, and Manto Gown;
> Poor Creature, who unheard of, as a Fly,
> In some dark Hole must all the Winter lye: . . .

Johnson may well have had this passage in mind when he wrote the story of Misella (*Rambler,* nos. 170–72).

IX

The culminating point in Rochester's spiritual odyssey is reached in his famous *Satyr against Mankind.* It is to be noted that this poem in some form was apparently circulating as early as the spring of 1675–76 and therefore antedates all Dryden's satiric poetry. It was formerly regarded chiefly as an "imitation" of the Eighth Satire of Boileau. S. F. Crocker in his valuable study of the background of the poem [8] has shown that it owes a much greater debt to Rochester's study of Montaigne and especially of the *Apologie de Raimond de Sébond,* and that it also contains echoes of the *Maximes* of La Rochefoucauld and other French works. Nevertheless it is a profoundly original work, for Rochester, like Pope, is never so original as when he is making full use of his reading. He never wrote anything more moving than the image of the fruitless quest of mankind misled by the *ignis fatuus* of reason at the beginning of the poem. It was the passage which Goethe quoted (without acknowledgement) in his *Dichtung und Wahrheit* and which Tennyson is reported by Lecky to have been in the habit of declaiming "with almost terrible force."

> Then old Age and Experience, Hand in Hand,
> Lead him to Death, and make him understand,
> After a Search so painful, and so long,
> That all his Life he has been in the wrong.

Rochester never saw "old Age" but he lived through more "Experience" in his thirty-three years than most men in three score and ten.

These lines undoubtedly sum up his own realization that "the life of reason" as conceived by his class and generation was an illusion. They make us feel what it was like, after the intoxication of youth had passed to face the fact that you were living in the soulless "universe of death" of the new "scientific" philosophy:

> Hudled in Dirt, this reas'ning Engine lyes,
> Who was so proud, so witty, and so wise . . .

The application of the term "reas'ning Engine" to man is highly significant. It is probably an allusion to a phrase of Robert Boyle who called men "engines endowed with wills" [9] and it is a bitterly ironic commentary on the mechanistic conception of humanity which was the logical outcome of the new science.

The dialogue on reason with the "formal Band and Beard" which follows ends with a denunciation of the fashionable intellectualism of the period in terms that recall D. H. Lawrence's insistence on the claims of "blood" as opposed to those of intellect. Rochester's "right Reason" is a reason that admits the claims of the body as well as those of the mind:

> Thus whil'st against false Reas'ning I inveigh,
> I own right Reason, which I would obey;
> That Reason, which distinguishes by Sense,
> And gives us Rules of Good and Ill from thence;
> That bounds Desires with a reforming Will,
> To keep them more in Vigour, not to kill:

From Reason he passes to Man, contemporary "civilized" Man, whom he compares with the beasts:

> Be Judge your self, I'll bring it to the Test,
> Which is the basest Creature, Man, or Beast:
> Birds feed on Birds, Beasts on each other Prey;
> But Savage Man alone, does Man betray.
> Press'd by Necessity, *They* kill for Food;
> Man undoes Man, to do himself no good.
> With Teeth and Claws by Nature arm'd, *They* hunt
> Nature's Allowance, to supply their Want:
> But Man, with Smiles, Embraces, Friendships, Praise,
> Inhumanly, his Fellow's Life betrays:
> With voluntary Pains works his Distress;

Not through Necessity, but Wantonness.
For Hunger, or for Love, *They* bite or tear,
Whilst wretched Man is still in Arms for Fear:
For Fear he arms and is of Arms afraid;
From Fear to Fear successively betray'd.
Base Fear, the source whence his best Passions came,
His boasted Honour, and his dear-bought Fame.
The lust of Pow'r, to which he's such a Slave,
And for the which alone he dares be brave . . .

This passage, as Crocker has shown, owes much to Montaigne, but its application and satiric force are Rochester's own. Here he is piercing the defences of his own class, the governing class of Europe, and showing what really lies behind phrases like "honour" and "fame." Again this is a passage that communicates forward to Swift. It contains the essence of *Gulliver's Travels:* the King of Brobdingnag's denunciation of the Europeans as portrayed by Gulliver and the superiority of those wise and humane quadrupeds, the Houyhnhnms, to the filthy, cowardly Yahoos.

X

The nihilism of the *Satyr against Mankind* is slightly mitigated in a curious epilogue or "postscript" added, apparently, after the rest of the poem had been printed, possibly as a rejoinder to the "Answer" ascribed to "the Reverend Mr. Griffith," which appeared in the summer of 1679 shortly after the publication of the broadside containing the first printed version of Rochester's poem. In this epilogue Rochester agrees to "recant" his "Paradox" if he can find one truly good man:

a meek humble Man of modest Sense,
Who preaching Peace does practise Continence;
Whose pious Life's a Proof he does believe
Mysterious Truths which no Man can conceive.

These rather uninspired lines seem to show Rochester trying to force himself to believe that a merely ethical hero could now satisfy him. He found "felicity and glory," however, not in an abstract ideal of this kind, but in the very different vision that came to him like a thunderbolt when he was listening to Robert Parsons reading the Second Isaiah's description of the Suffering Servant on 19th June, 1680. Parsons in his Funeral Sermon tells us that Rochester's "vow and purpose" in his last sickness was to produce "an Idea of Divine Poetry, under the Gospel, useful to the teaching of virtue . . . as his profane Verses have been to destroy it." He also tells that in the nine weeks that elapsed between his "conversion" and his death "he was so much master of his reason, and had so clear an understanding (saving thirty hours, about the middle of it when he was delirious) that he never dictated or spoke more composed in his life." [10] It is clear from these passages that Rochester dictated something (unfortunately Parsons gives no details) in the last weeks of his life and also that he planned to write "Divine Poetry." Two poems first published in Thorncome's edition of 1685 may well have been dictated by him on his death-bed. They are called *Consideratus Considerandus* and *Plain Dealings Downfall,* and both seem to be connected with the vision of the Suffering Servant. Both present images of virtue as despised and rejected like the Man of Sorrows in the Second Isaiah. *Plain Dealings Downfall* has a terseness and homely realism that recall the manner of George Herbert:

> Long time Plain Dealing in the Hauty Town,
> Wand'ring about, though in a thread-bare Gown,
> At last unanimously was cry'd down.
>
> When almost starv'd she to the Country fled
> In hopes though meanly, she shou'd there be fed,
> And tumble nightly on a Pea-straw Bed.
>
> But Knav'ry knowing her intent, took post,
> And Rumour'd her approach through every Coast,
> Vowing his Ruin that shou'd be her host.
>
> Frighted at this, each *Rustick* shut his door,
> Bid her begone, and trouble him no more,
> For he that entertain'd her must be poor.
>
> At this grief seiz'd her, grief too great to tell,
> When weeping, sighing, fainting, down she fell,
> Whil's Knavery Laughing, Rung her passing Bell.

In this powerful little poem, as in the concluding lines of *The Vanity of Human Wishes,* we seem to see the transition from satire to religious poetry. The emphasis is not so much on "the Hauty Town" (as it was in the story of Corinna) or upon the almost medieval image of "knavery," but upon the sorrow of the betrayed country girl, who becomes a tragic figure putting a mean and heartless world to shame. Rochester was not the greatest of the Augustan satirists, but he was the boldest spiritual adventurer among them. Strange as the collocation of the two names may seem to many readers, he seems to have reached at the end of his life a position not unlike that of the poet who was to write *The Ruined Cottage* and *Peter Bell* a little more than a hundred years after his death.

NOTES

1. *Revaluation*, p. 34 [above, p. 48].
2. Robert Parsons, *A Sermon. Preached at the Funeral of the Rt. Honourable John Earl of Rochester* (Oxford, 1680), p. 26.
3. Gilbert Burnet, *Some Passages of the Life and Death of the Right Honourable John Earl of Rochester* (London, 1680), p. 142.
4. André Gide, *Oscar Wilde* (London, 1951), p. 28.
5. Robert Parsons, op. cit., p. 23.
6. Dryden's earliest satire, *MacFlecknoe*, was probably written in 1678. Rochester's chief satiric poems seem to have been in circulation about 1675–76 though it is possible that some of them were written at an earlier date.
7. Gilbert Burnet, op. cit., p. 14.
8. *West Virginia University Studies* III, *Philological Papers*, Vol. 2, May 1937.
9. Quoted by E. A. Burtt in *The Metaphysical Foundations of Modern Science*, p. 176.
10. Robert Parsons, op. cit., pp. 7, 33.